SHIN YOSHIDA

This is the final volume. The curtain is finally falling on
Yuya and his friends' story. But you can look forward to
finding out what sort of future lies in store for them—and to
seeing more of Miyoshi's outstanding art!

D0126846

NAOHITO MIYOSHI

To those of you who came to the midsummer JVC venues,
either in Tokyo or Osaka, the letters and encouragement
I received from you were an incredible source of energy.
They're the greatest reward this job has ever given me!

MASAHIRO HIKOKUBO

Did you enjoy Yuya and company's Action Duels?
I'm looking forward to the day when we meet again.
I'm grateful to you for reading all the way to the end!
Many thanks!!

7

YU-GI-OH! ARC-V

SHONEN JUMP MANGA EDITION

ORIGINAL CONCEPT BY
Kazuki Takahashi

PRODUCTION SUPPORT: **STUDIO DICE**

STORY BY
Shin Yoshida

ART BY
Naohito Miyoshi

DUEL COORDINATOR
Masahiro Hikokubo

TRANSLATION + ENGLISH ADAPTATION
Sarah Neufeld and John Werry, HC Language Solutions, Inc.

TOUCH-UP ART + LETTERING **John Hunt**

DESIGNER **Stacie Yamaki**

SHONEN JUMP EDITOR **Mike Montesa**

GRAPHIC NOVEL EDITOR **Karla Clark**

YU-GI-OH! ARC-V © 2014 by Kazuki Takahashi, Shin Yoshida, Naohito Miyoshi, Masahiro Hikokubo/SHUEISHA Inc.
Based on Animation TV series YU-GI-OH! ARC-V
© 1996 Kazuki Takahashi
© 2014 NAS • TV TOKYO

Printed in the U.S.A.

Published by VIZ Media, LLC
P.O. Box 77010
San Francisco, CA 94107

10 9 8 7 6 5 4 3 2 1

First printing, June 2020

VIZ MEDIA
viz.com

SHONEN JUMP
shonenjump.com

Arc of Destiny!!

ORIGINAL CONCEPT BY **Kazuki Takahashi**
PRODUCTION SUPPORT: **STUDIO DICE**
STORY BY **Shin Yoshida**
ART BY **Naohito Miyoshi**
DUEL COORDINATOR **Masahiro Hikokubo**

CHARACTERS

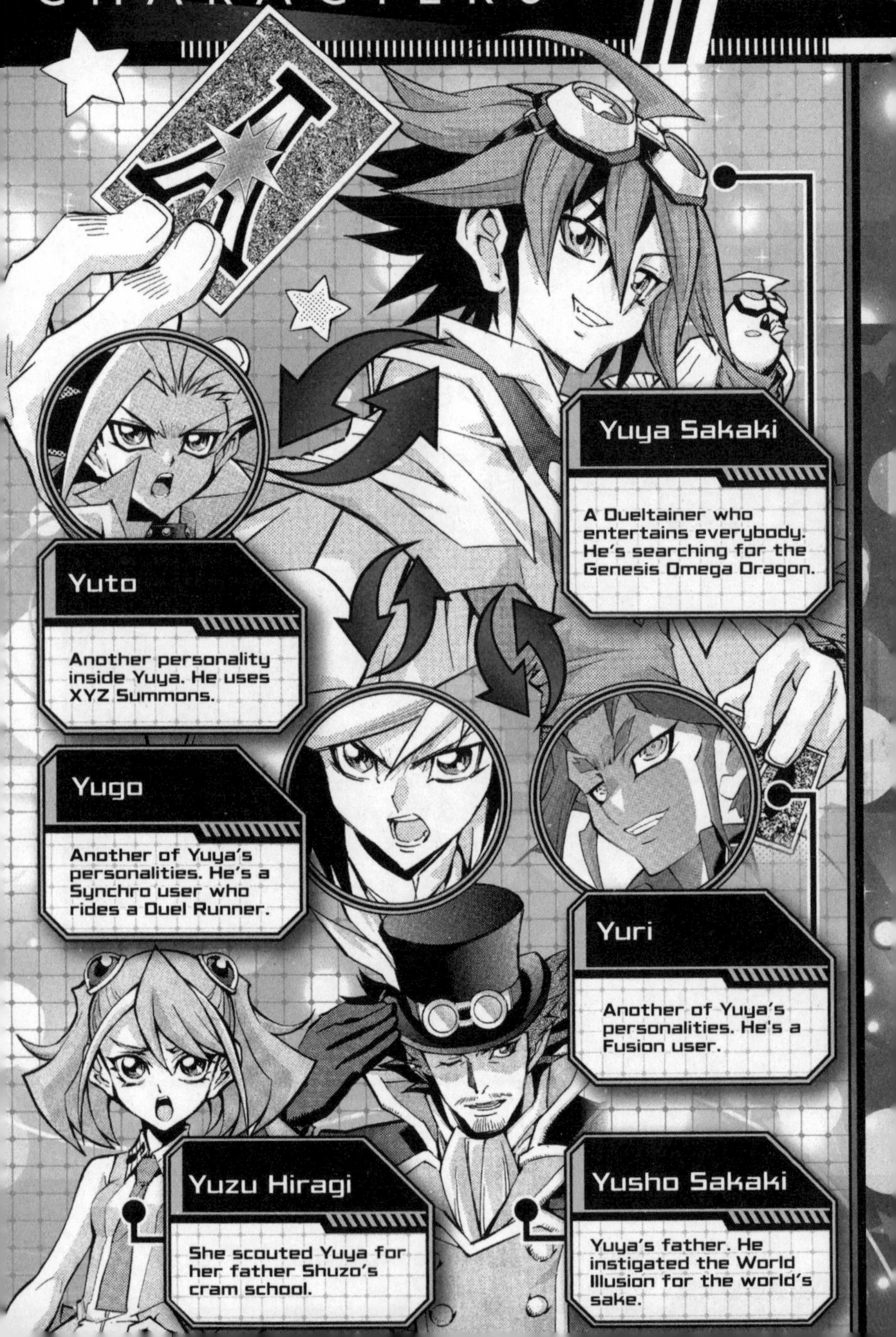

Yuya Sakaki

A Dueltainer who entertains everybody. He's searching for the Genesis Omega Dragon.

Yuto

Another personality inside Yuya. He uses XYZ Summons.

Yugo

Another of Yuya's personalities. He's a Synchro user who rides a Duel Runner.

Yuri

Another of Yuya's personalities. He's a Fusion user.

Yuzu Hiragi

She scouted Yuya for her father Shuzo's cram school.

Yusho Sakaki

Yuya's father. He instigated the World Illusion for the world's sake.

YU-GI-OH! ARC-V

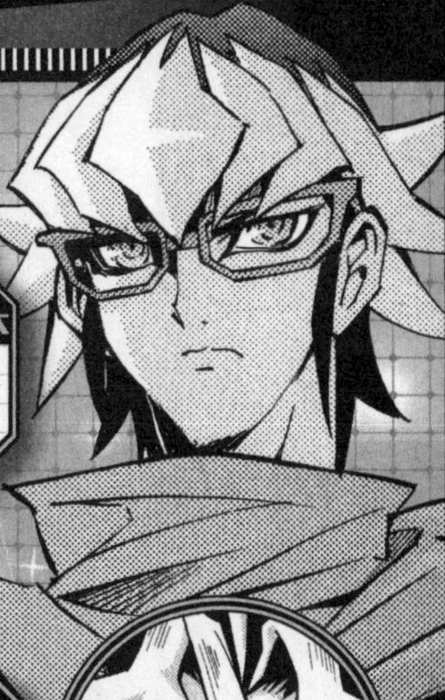

Reiji Akaba

President of the Leo Corporation. He's using his company to hunt Yuya.

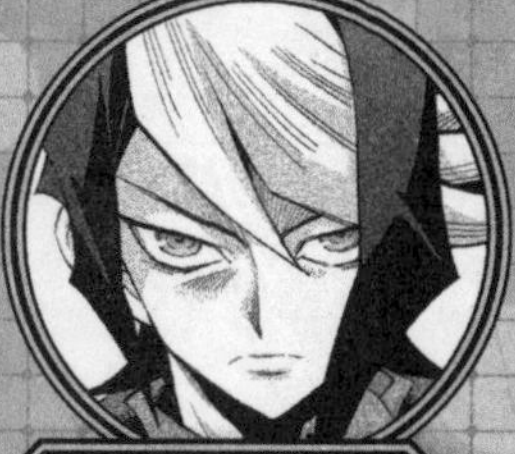

Shun Kurosaki

The Leo Corporation's second assassin. He challenged Yuya to a no-holds-barred Duel!

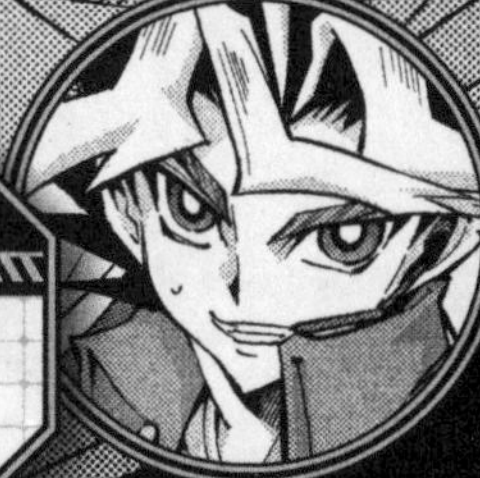

Sora Shiunin

After his Duel with Yuya, he regained memories he had intentionally lost. He is actually part of Eve's group.

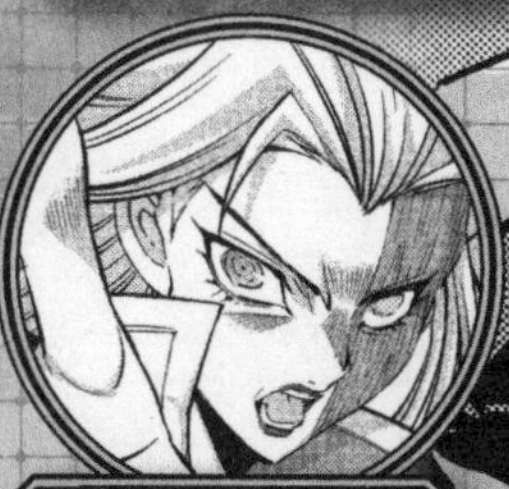

Eve

In search of Adam, who disappeared beyond the horizon of space-time, she pursues Yuya and the others.

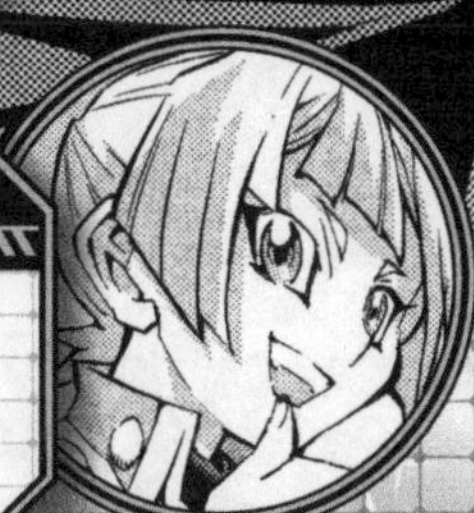

Shingo Sawatari

The first Leo Corporation Duelist to face off against Yuya.

STORY

Solid Vision with mass has plunged the world into the era of Action Duels. Yuya Sakaki, a Dueltainer, has come to this time from the future in search of the Genesis Omega Dragon [G.O.D.]. Reiji Akaba, who is pursuing Yuya and G.O.D., has also arrived in this time shortly before Yuya. Having become the president of Leo Corporation, he sends his company's Duelists–Sawatari, Kurosaki and Sora–after Yuya. Finally, Yuya and Akaba finally face off in person. However, a masked man named Ren interrupts their Duel. This plunges them into a three-way battle with Eve's group for control of G.O.D. Having found and infiltrated the group's main base, Yuya finally gets a chance to Duel Eve. However, before they can finish their battle, G.O.D. awakens. Does Yuya still have a shot at victory?!

7 Arc of Destiny!!

SCALE 38	Our Pride!!	7
SCALE 39	Across Time and Space!!	39
SCALE 40	The Adam Factors!!	71
SCALE 41	Reiji's Power!!	103
SCALE 42	Two G.O.D.s!!	135
SCALE 43	Head-to-Head Cards!!	167
SCALE 44	Action Battle!!	199
SCALE 45	Arc of Destiny!!	231

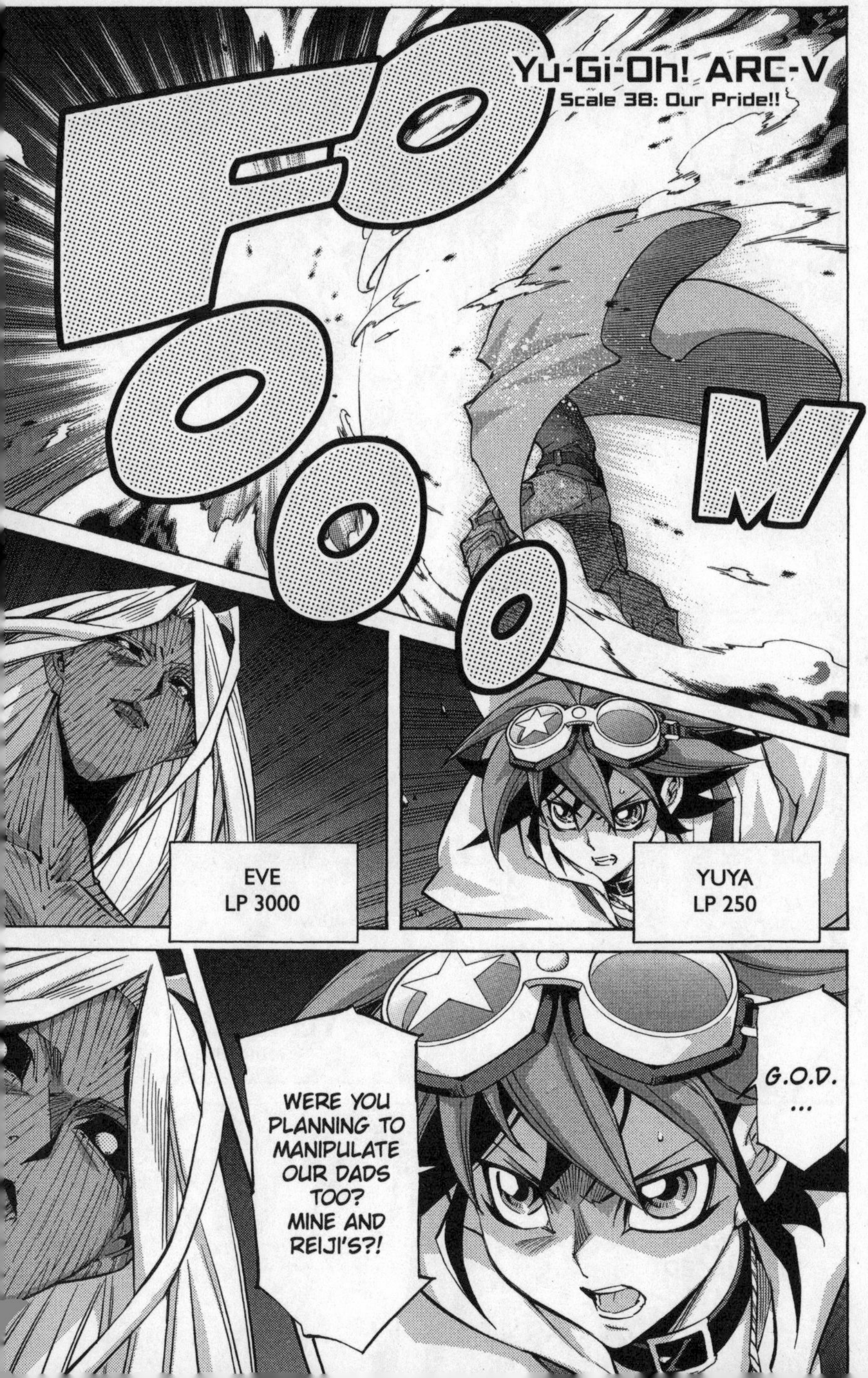
Yu-Gi-Oh! ARC-V
Scale 38: Our Pride!!
FOOOOM
YUYA LP 250
EVE LP 3000
G.O.D. ...
WERE YOU PLANNING TO MANIPULATE OUR DADS TOO? MINE AND REIJI'S?!

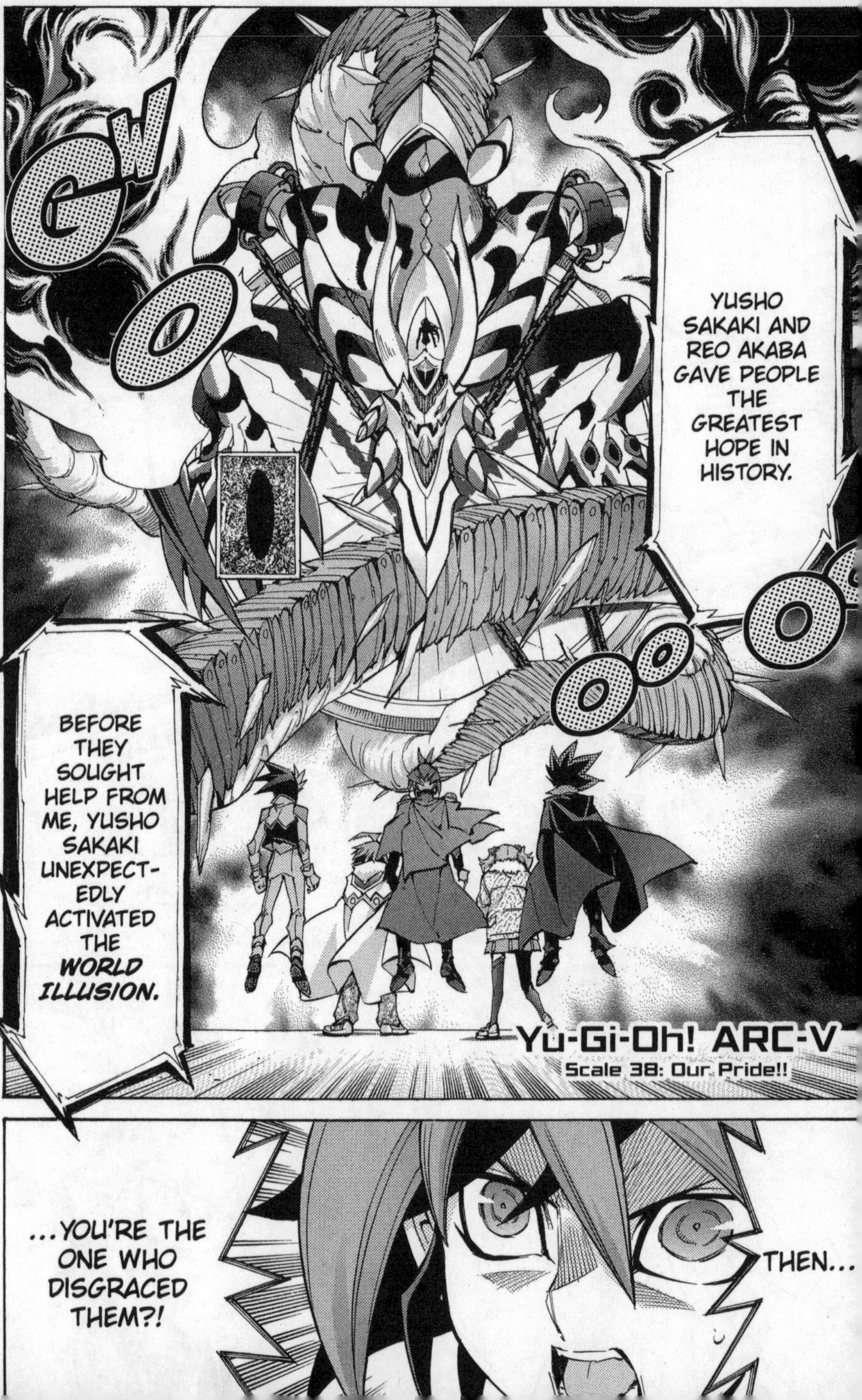
GWOOOOOOO
YUSHO SAKAKI AND REO AKABA GAVE PEOPLE THE GREATEST HOPE IN HISTORY.
BEFORE THEY SOUGHT HELP FROM ME, YUSHO SAKAKI UNEXPECTEDLY ACTIVATED THE *WORLD ILLUSION*.
Yu-Gi-Oh! ARC-V
Scale 38: Our Pride!!
THEN...
...YOU'RE THE ONE WHO DISGRACED THEM?!

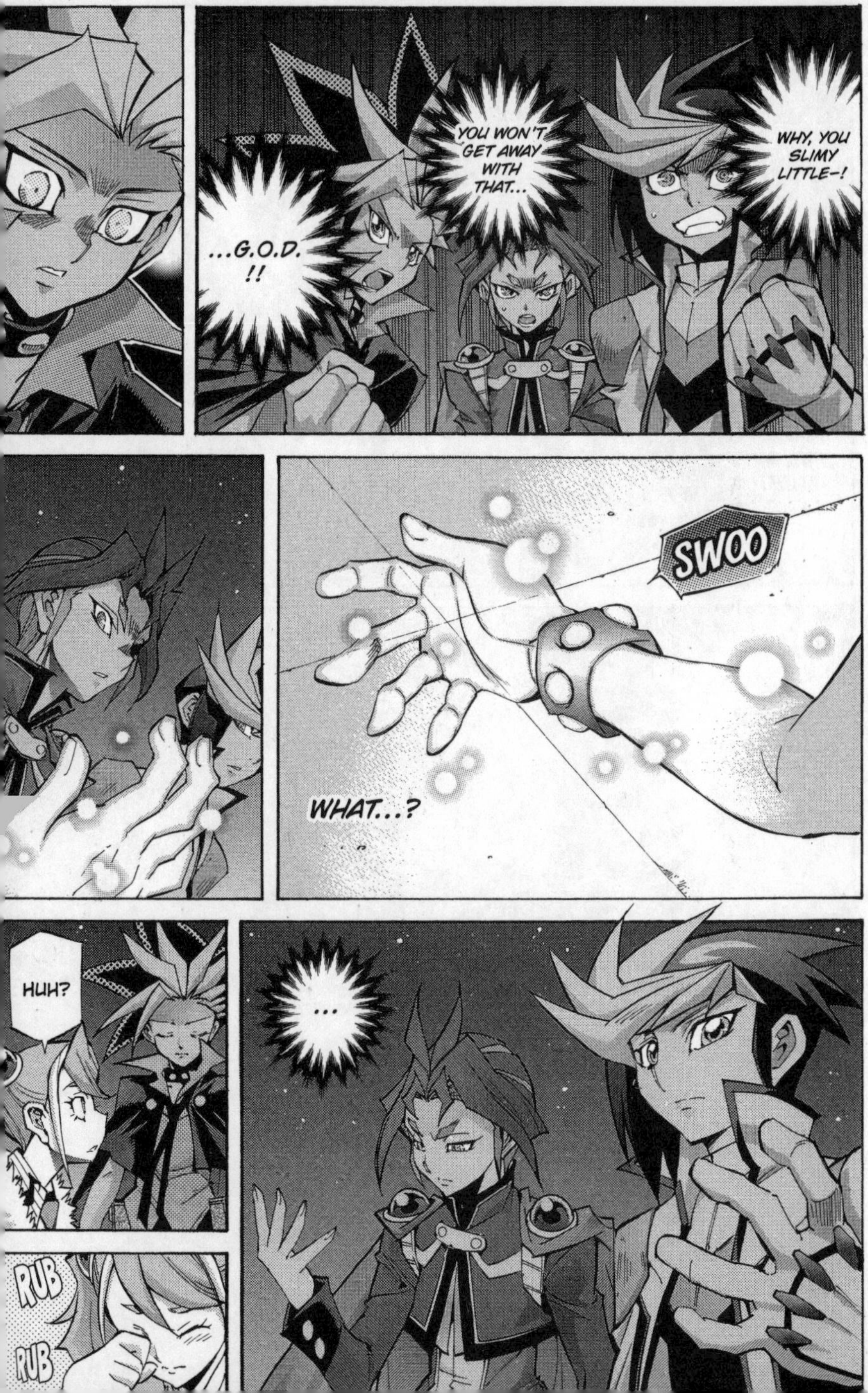
WHY, YOU SLIMY LITTLE-!
YOU WON'T GET AWAY WITH THAT...
...G.O.D. !!
SWOO
WHAT...?
...
HUH?
RUB
RUB

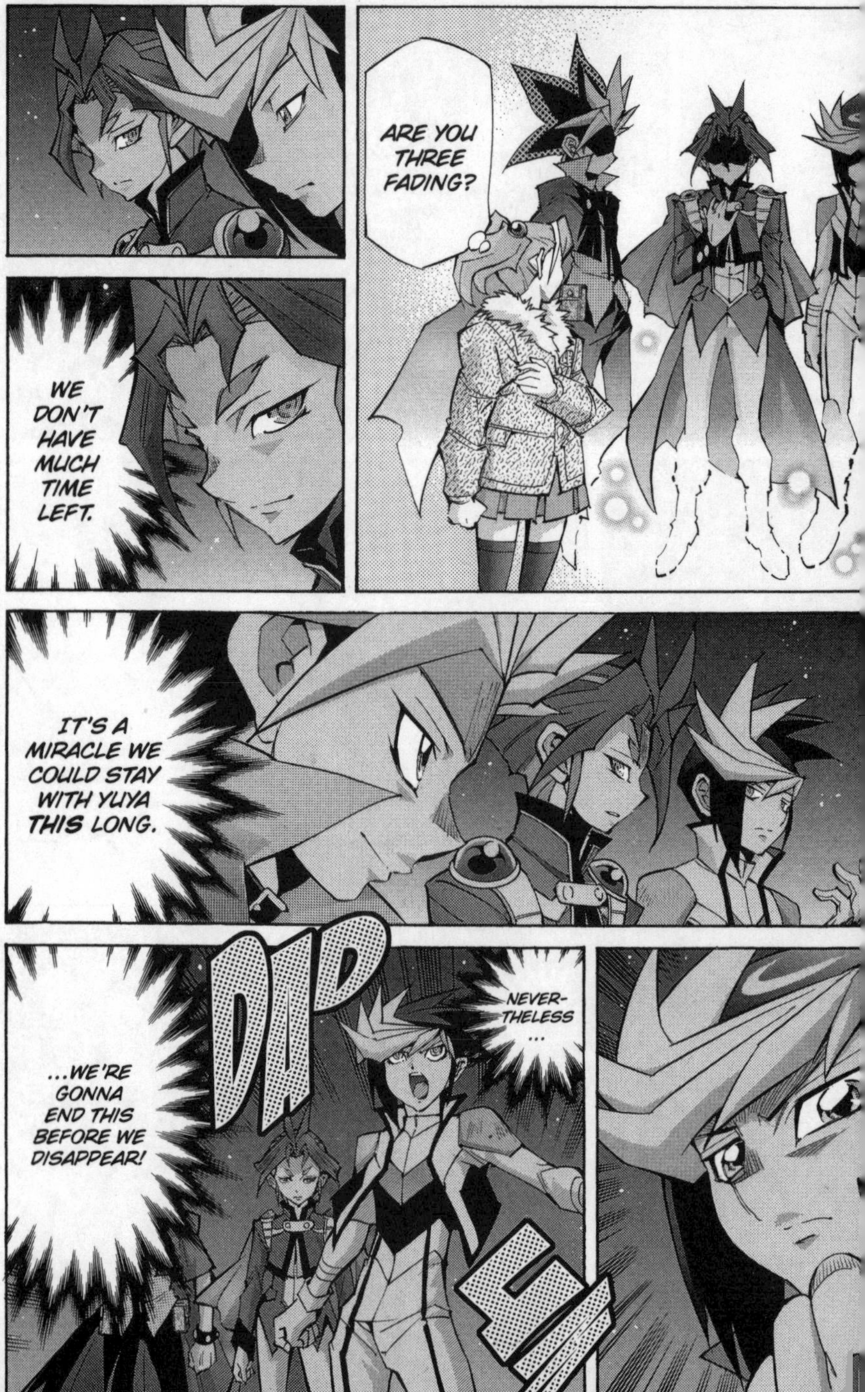
ARE YOU THREE FADING?
WE DON'T HAVE MUCH TIME LEFT.
IT'S A MIRACLE WE COULD STAY WITH YUYA THIS LONG.
NEVER-THELESS...
DAP
...WE'RE GONNA END THIS BEFORE WE DISAPPEAR!

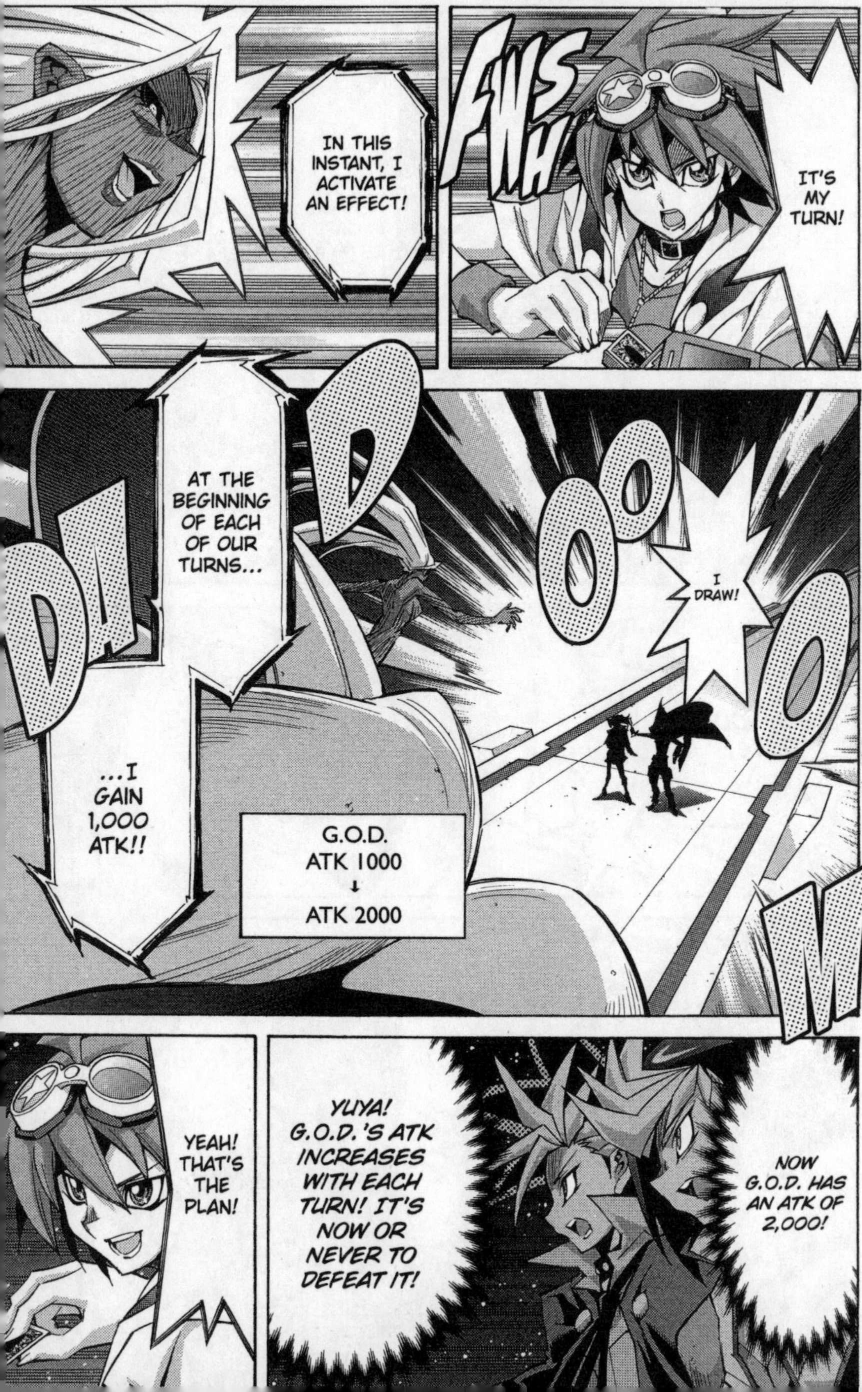
IT'S MY TURN!
IN THIS INSTANT, I ACTIVATE AN EFFECT!
I DRAW!
AT THE BEGINNING OF EACH OF OUR TURNS...
...I GAIN 1,000 ATK!!
G.O.D. ATK 1000 ↓ ATK 2000
NOW G.O.D. HAS AN ATK OF 2,000!
YUYA! G.O.D.'S ATK INCREASES WITH EACH TURN! IT'S NOW OR NEVER TO DEFEAT IT!
YEAH! THAT'S THE PLAN!

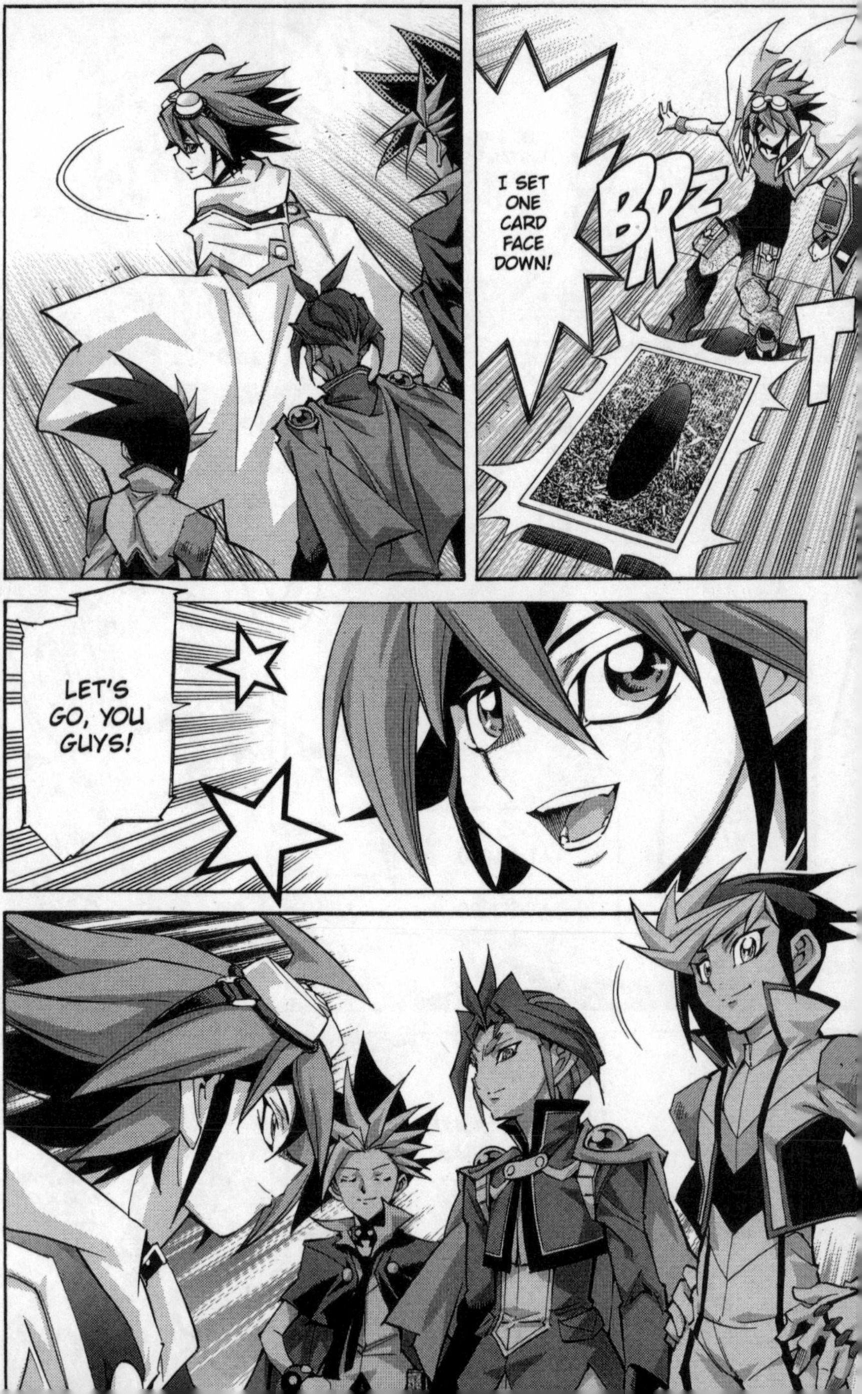
I SET ONE CARD FACE DOWN!
BRZZT
LET'S GO, YOU GUYS!

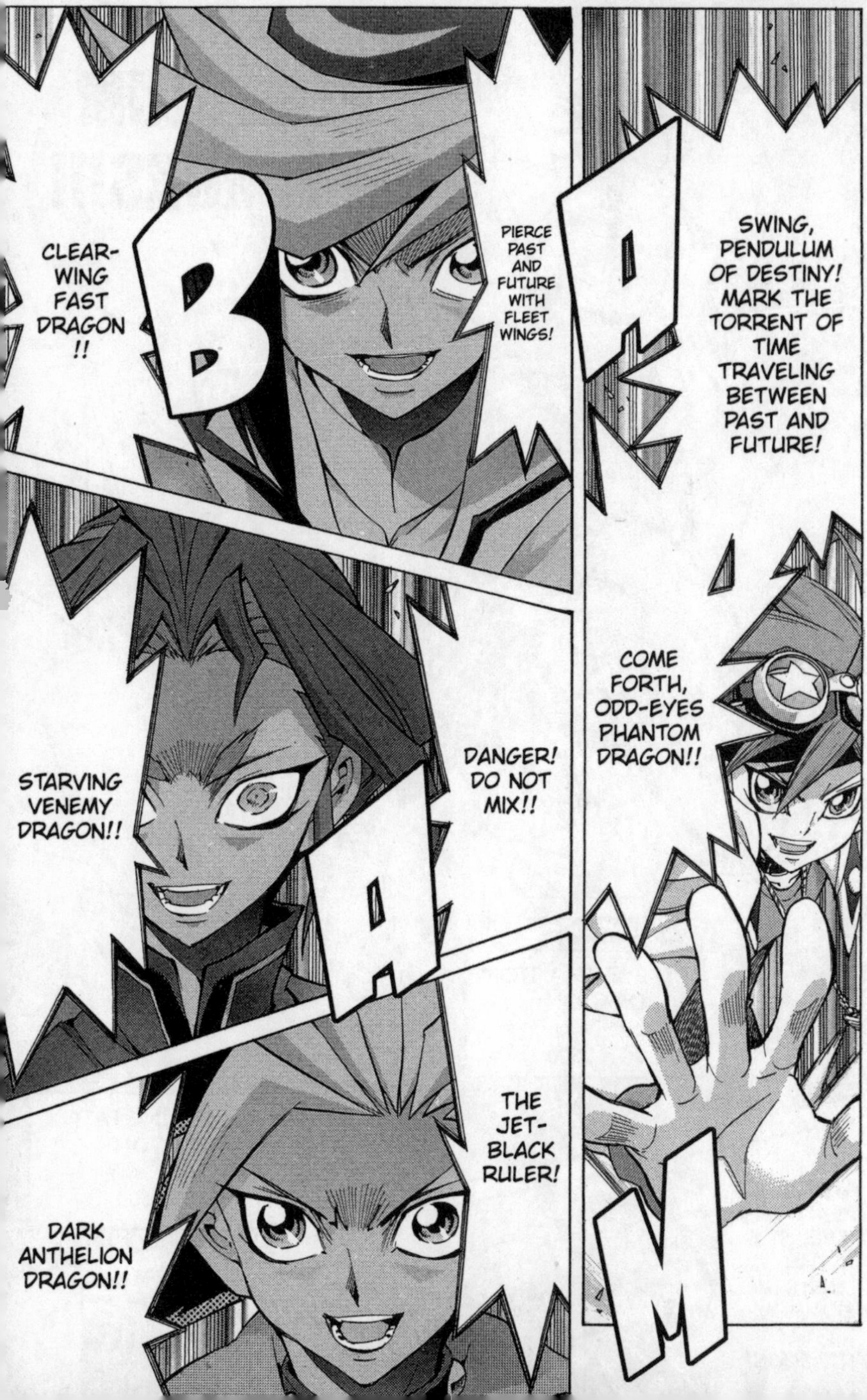
SWING, PENDULUM OF DESTINY! MARK THE TORRENT OF TIME TRAVELING BETWEEN PAST AND FUTURE!
COME FORTH, ODD-EYES PHANTOM DRAGON!!
PIERCE PAST AND FUTURE WITH FLEET WINGS!
CLEAR-WING FAST DRAGON!!
DANGER! DO NOT MIX!!
STARVING VENEMY DRAGON!!
THE JET-BLACK RULER!
DARK ANTHELION DRAGON!!
BAAM

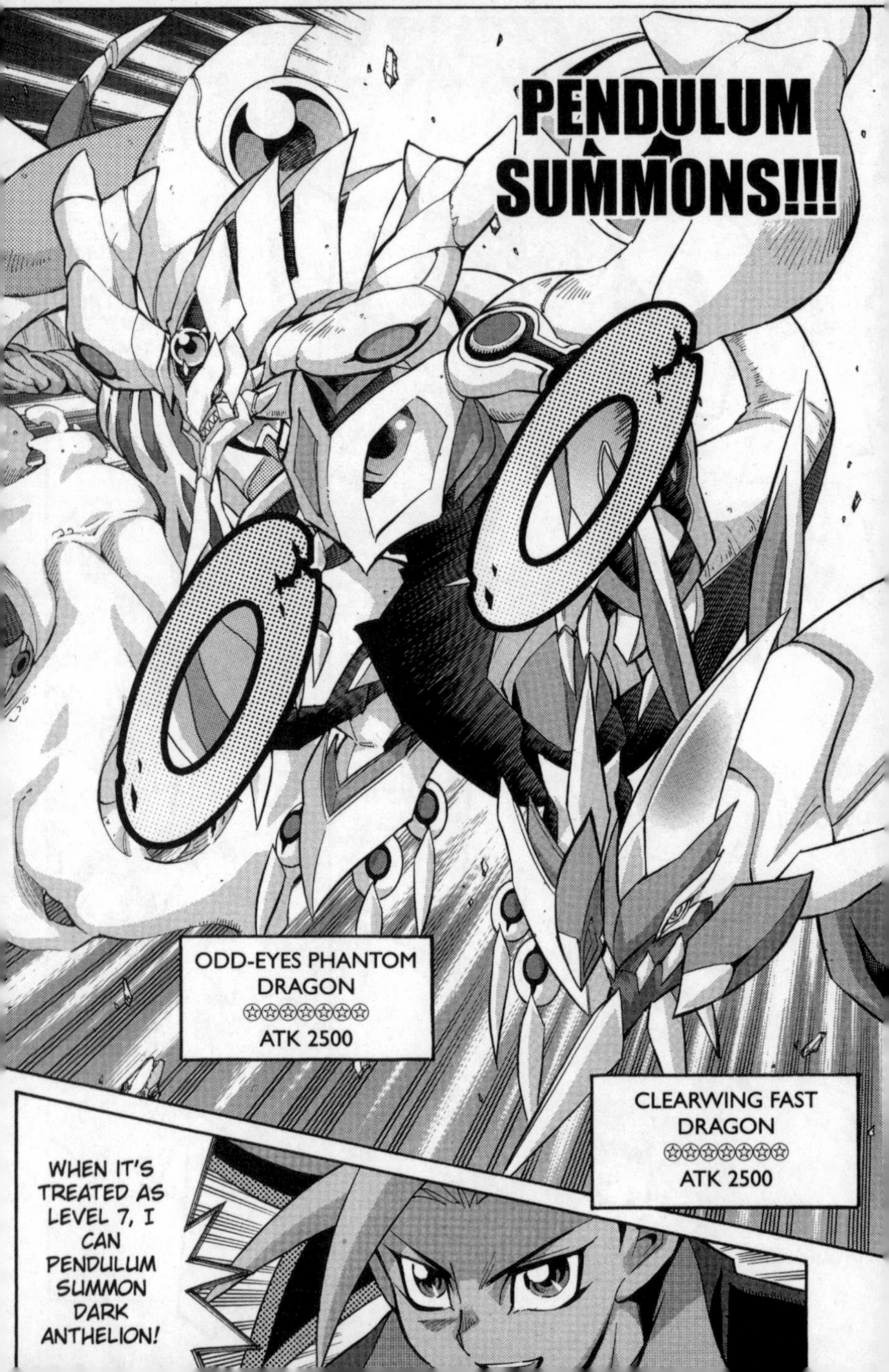
PENDULUM SUMMONS!!!
ODD-EYES PHANTOM DRAGON
☆☆☆☆☆☆☆
ATK 2500
CLEARWING FAST DRAGON
☆☆☆☆☆☆☆
ATK 2500
WHEN IT'S TREATED AS LEVEL 7, I CAN PENDULUM SUMMON DARK ANTHELION!

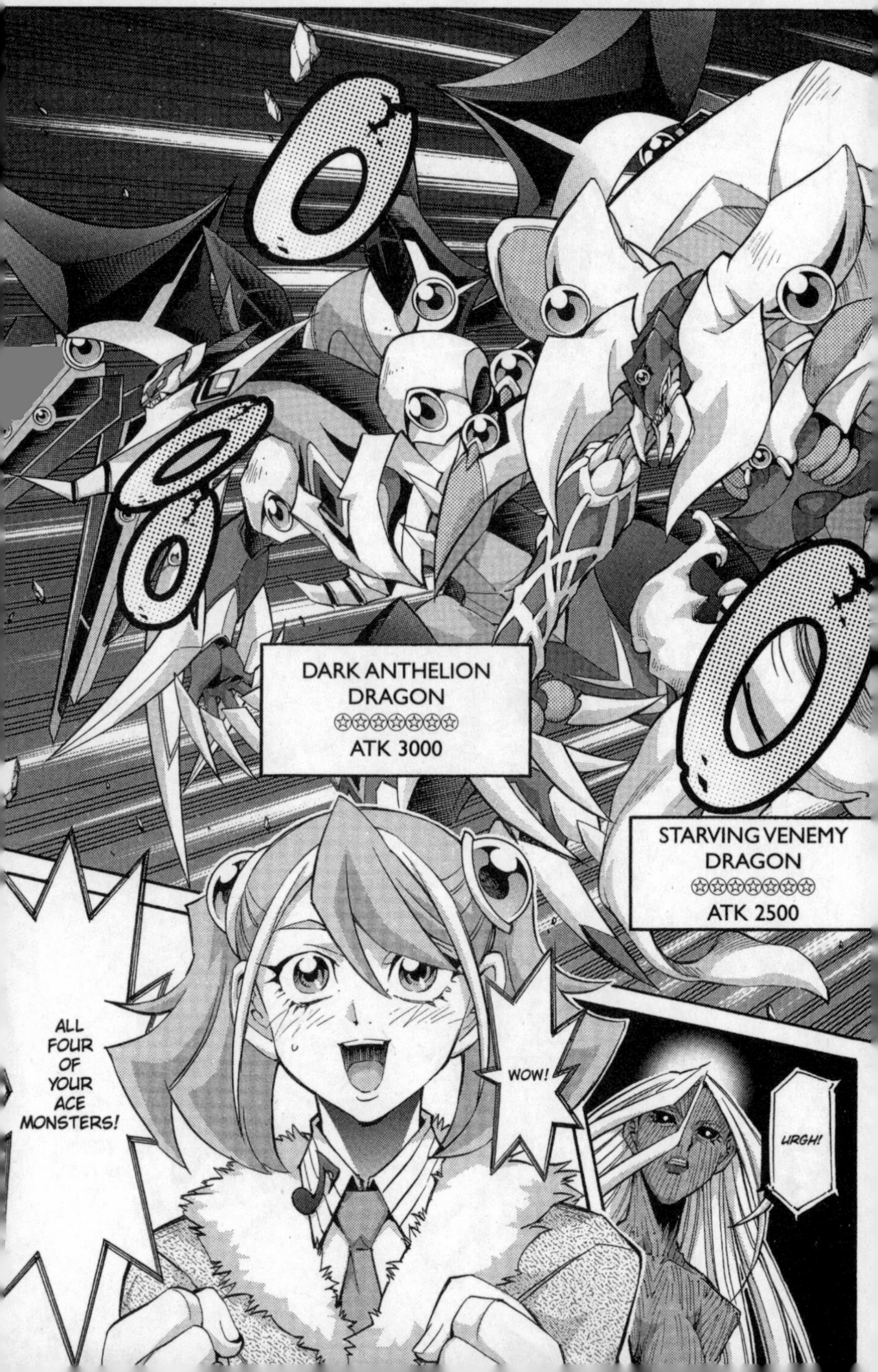

DARK ANTHELION DRAGON
ATK 3000
STARVING VENEMY DRAGON
ATK 2500
URGH!
WOW!
ALL FOUR OF YOUR ACE MONSTERS!

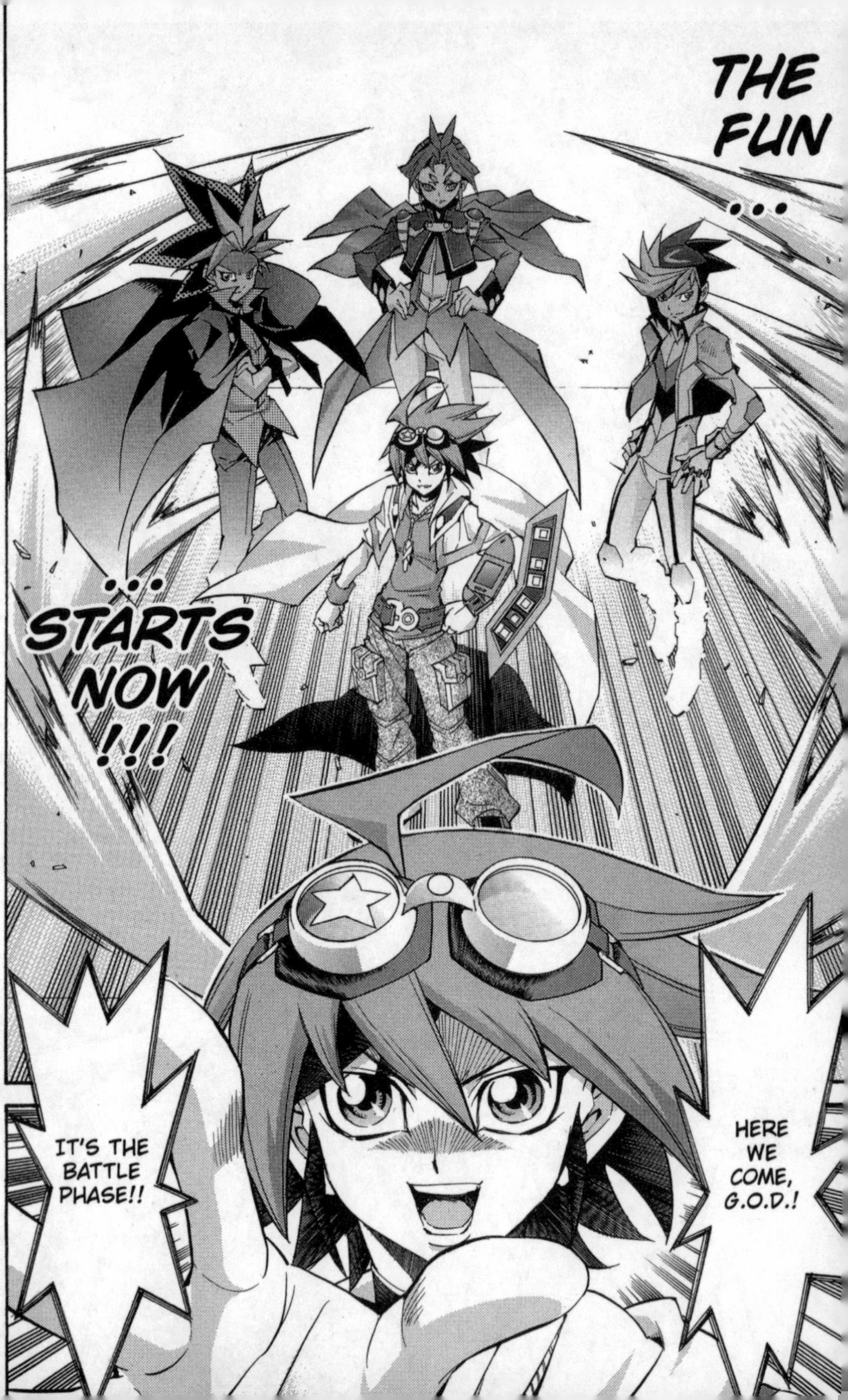
THE FUN ...
... STARTS NOW !!!
HERE WE COME, G.O.D.!
IT'S THE BATTLE PHASE!!

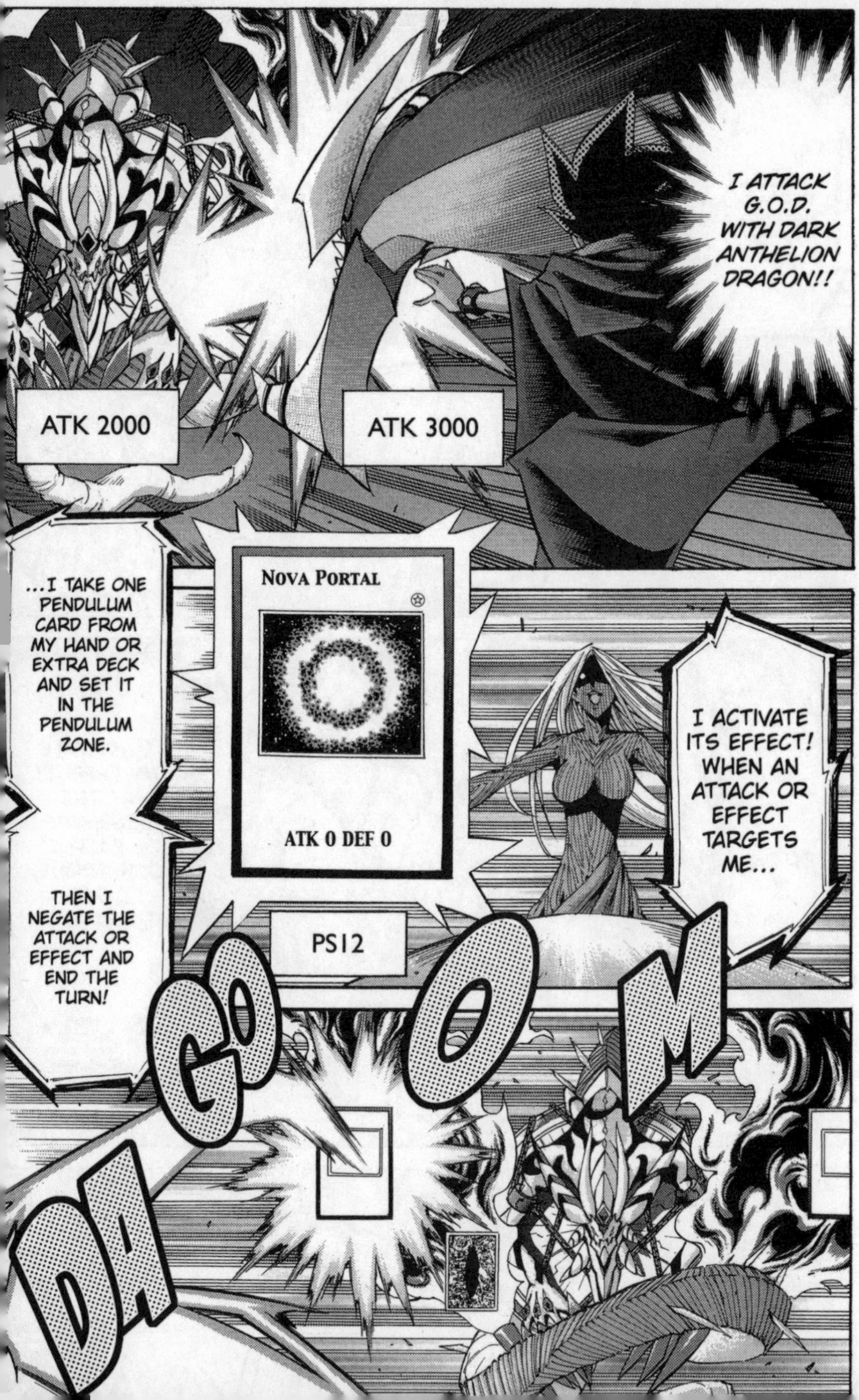
I ATTACK G.O.D. WITH DARK ANTHELION DRAGON!!
ATK 3000
ATK 2000
I ACTIVATE ITS EFFECT! WHEN AN ATTACK OR EFFECT TARGETS ME...
NOVA PORTAL
ATK 0 DEF 0
PS12
...I TAKE ONE PENDULUM CARD FROM MY HAND OR EXTRA DECK AND SET IT IN THE PENDULUM ZONE.
THEN I NEGATE THE ATTACK OR EFFECT AND END THE TURN!
DAGOOM

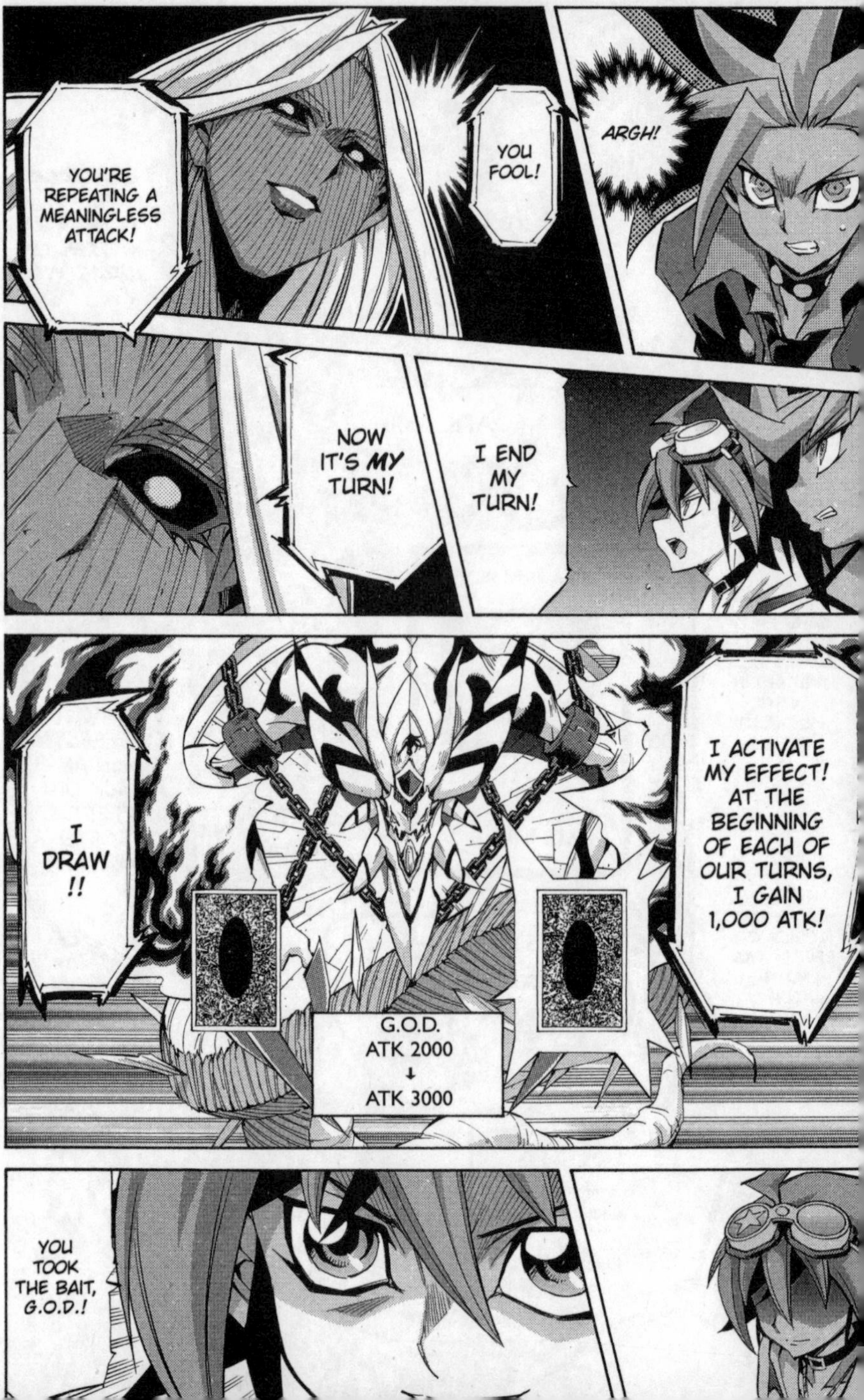
ARGH!
YOU FOOL!
YOU'RE REPEATING A MEANINGLESS ATTACK!
I END MY TURN!
NOW IT'S *MY* TURN!
I ACTIVATE MY EFFECT! AT THE BEGINNING OF EACH OF OUR TURNS, I GAIN 1,000 ATK!
I DRAW !!
G.O.D. ATK 2000 ↓ ATK 3000
YOU TOOK THE BAIT, G.O.D.!

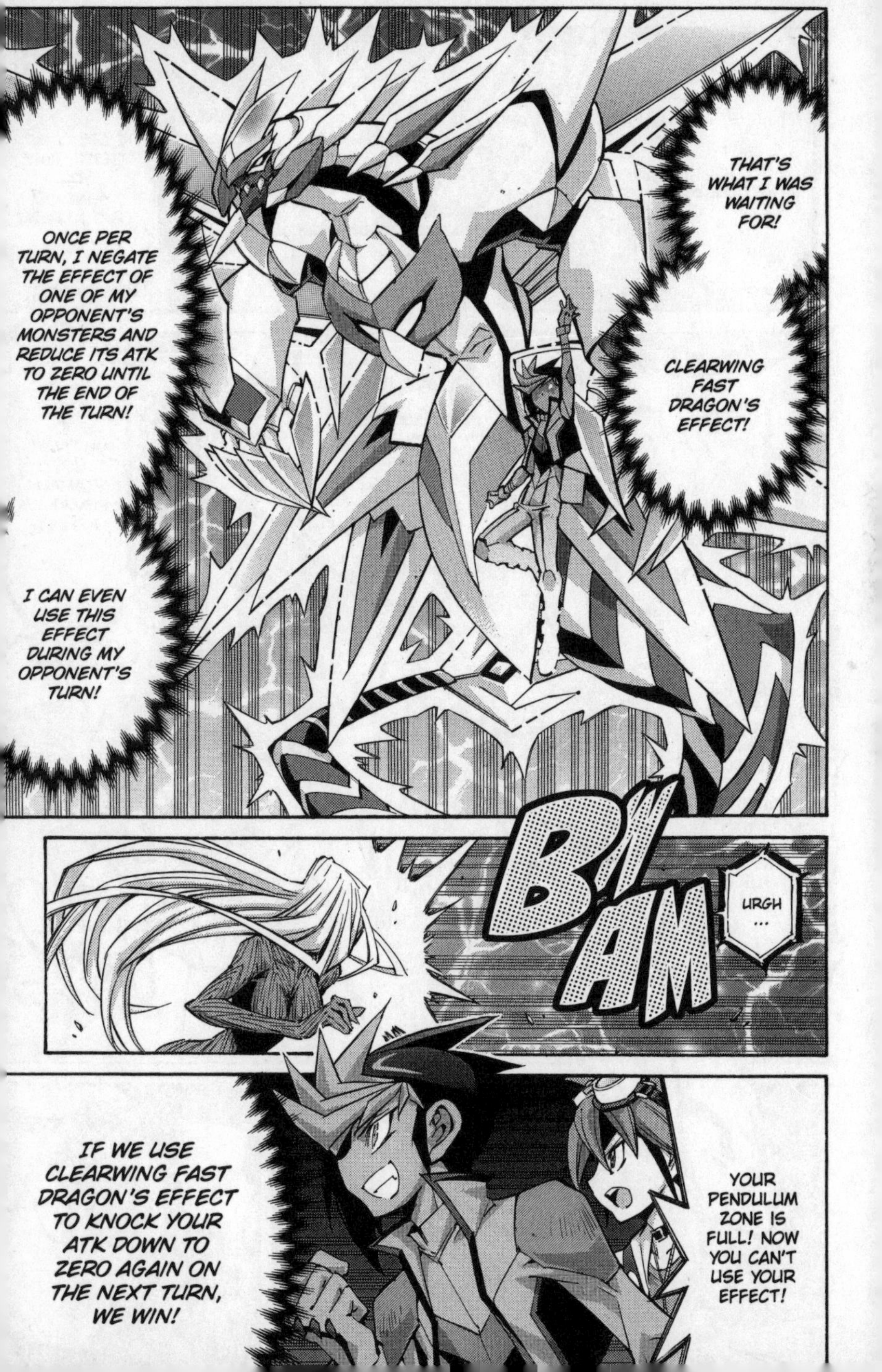
THAT'S WHAT I WAS WAITING FOR!
CLEARWING FAST DRAGON'S EFFECT!
ONCE PER TURN, I NEGATE THE EFFECT OF ONE OF MY OPPONENT'S MONSTERS AND REDUCE ITS ATK TO ZERO UNTIL THE END OF THE TURN!
I CAN EVEN USE THIS EFFECT DURING MY OPPONENT'S TURN!
URGH...
BAM
YOUR PENDULUM ZONE IS FULL! NOW YOU CAN'T USE YOUR EFFECT!
IF WE USE CLEARWING FAST DRAGON'S EFFECT TO KNOCK YOUR ATK DOWN TO ZERO AGAIN ON THE NEXT TURN, WE WIN!

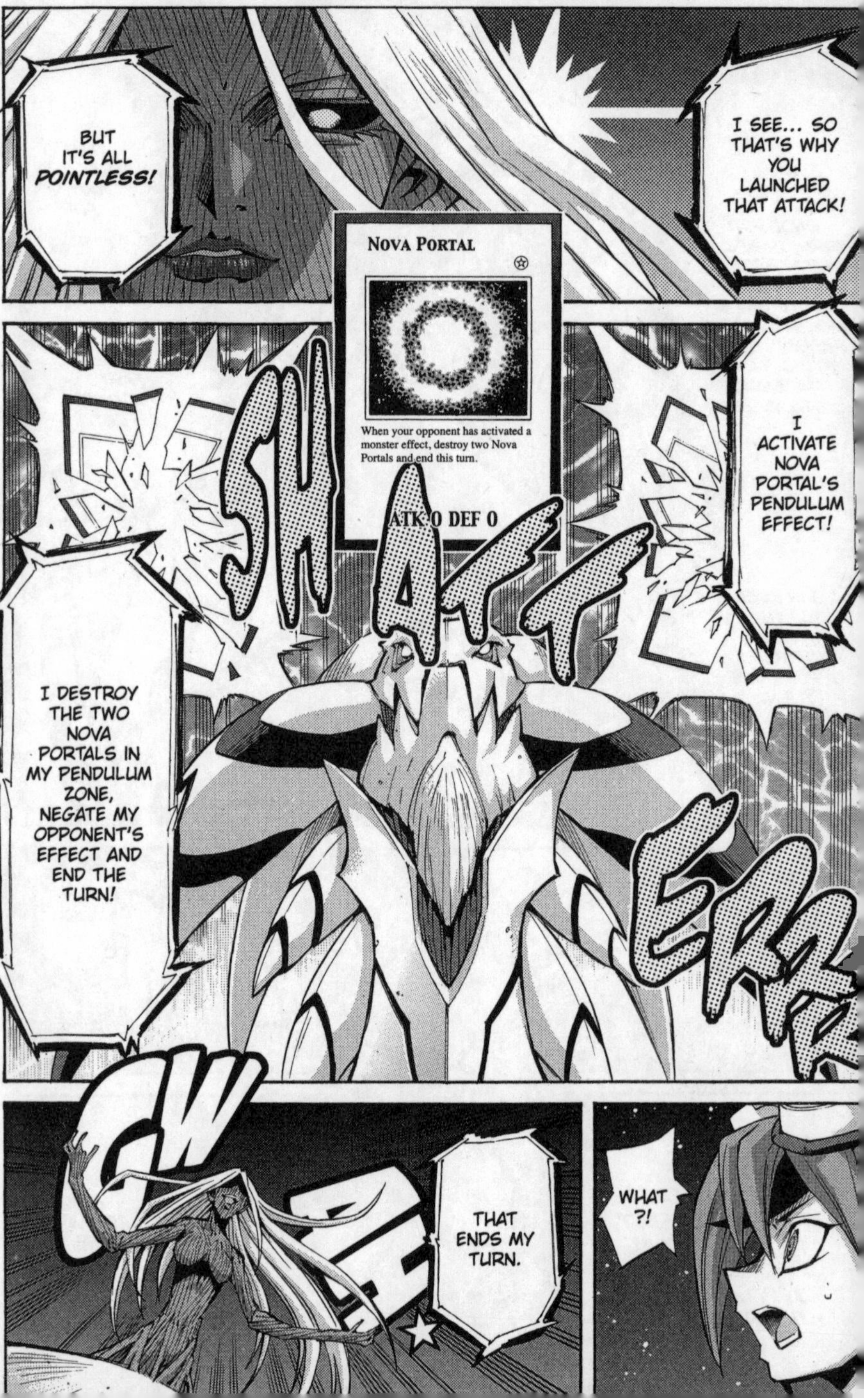
I SEE... SO THAT'S WHY YOU LAUNCHED THAT ATTACK!
BUT IT'S ALL *POINTLESS!*
NOVA PORTAL
When your opponent has activated a monster effect, destroy two Nova Portals and end this turn.
ATK 0 DEF 0
I ACTIVATE NOVA PORTAL'S PENDULUM EFFECT!
SHATT
ERR
I DESTROY THE TWO NOVA PORTALS IN MY PENDULUM ZONE, NEGATE MY OPPONENT'S EFFECT AND END THE TURN!
WHAT?!
THAT ENDS MY TURN.
CW

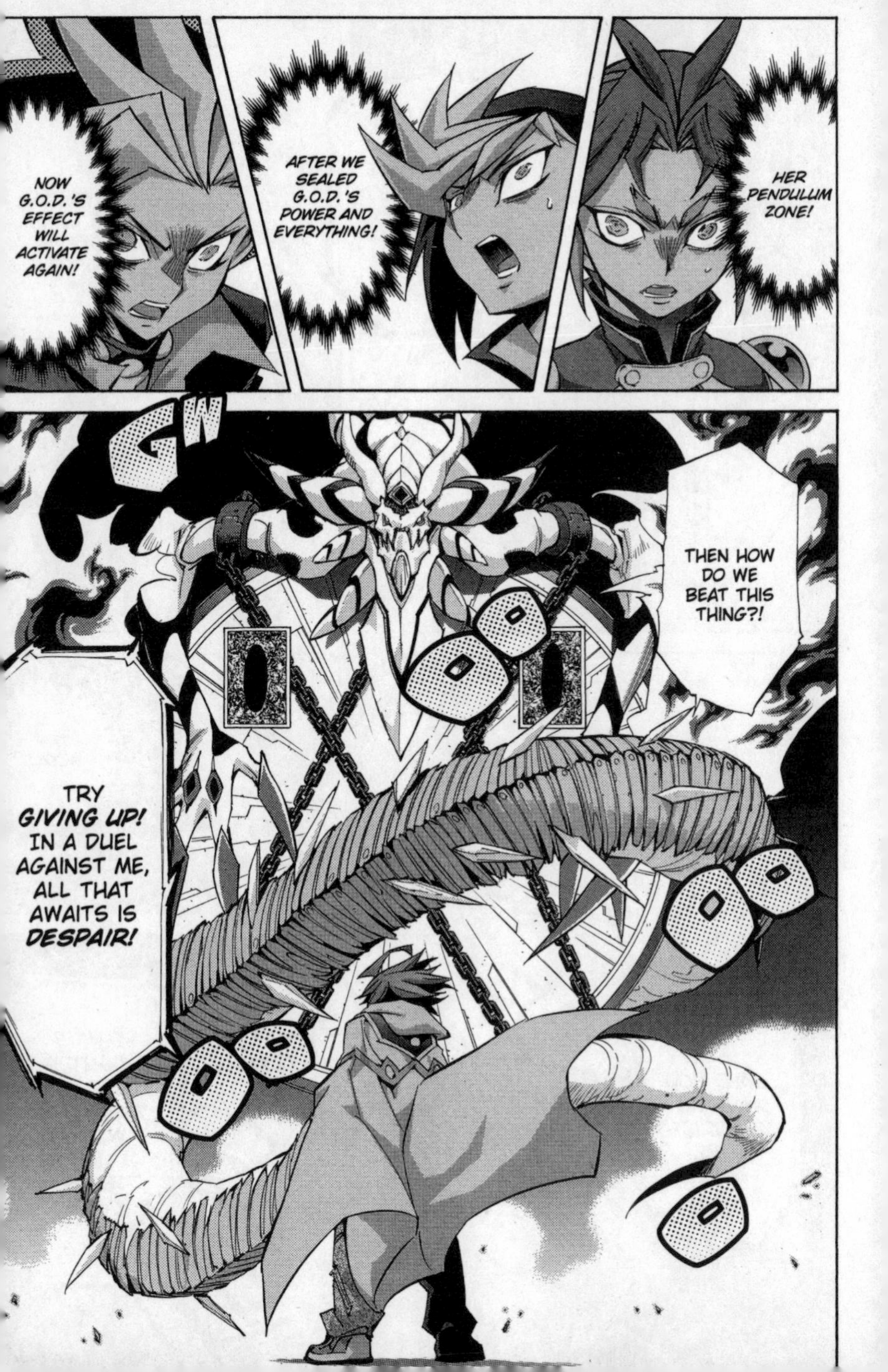
HER PENDULUM ZONE!
AFTER WE SEALED G.O.D.'S POWER AND EVERYTHING!
NOW G.O.D.'S EFFECT WILL ACTIVATE AGAIN!
THEN HOW DO WE BEAT THIS THING?!
GN
TRY GIVING UP! IN A DUEL AGAINST ME, ALL THAT AWAITS IS DESPAIR!

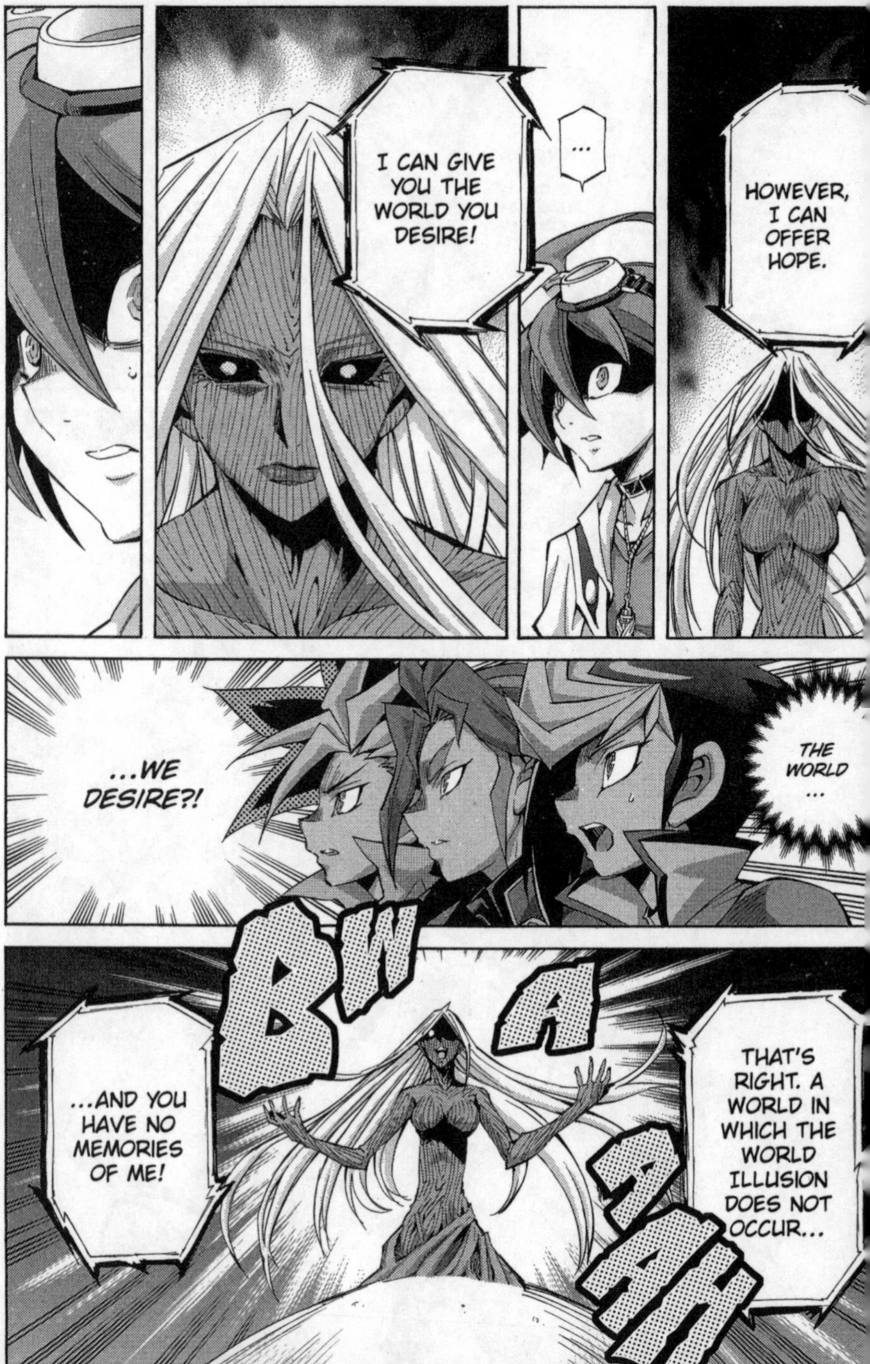
HOWEVER, I CAN OFFER HOPE.
...
I CAN GIVE YOU THE WORLD YOU DESIRE!
THE WORLD ...
...WE DESIRE?!
THAT'S RIGHT. A WORLD IN WHICH THE WORLD ILLUSION DOES NOT OCCUR...
BWAAAH
...AND YOU HAVE NO MEMORIES OF ME!

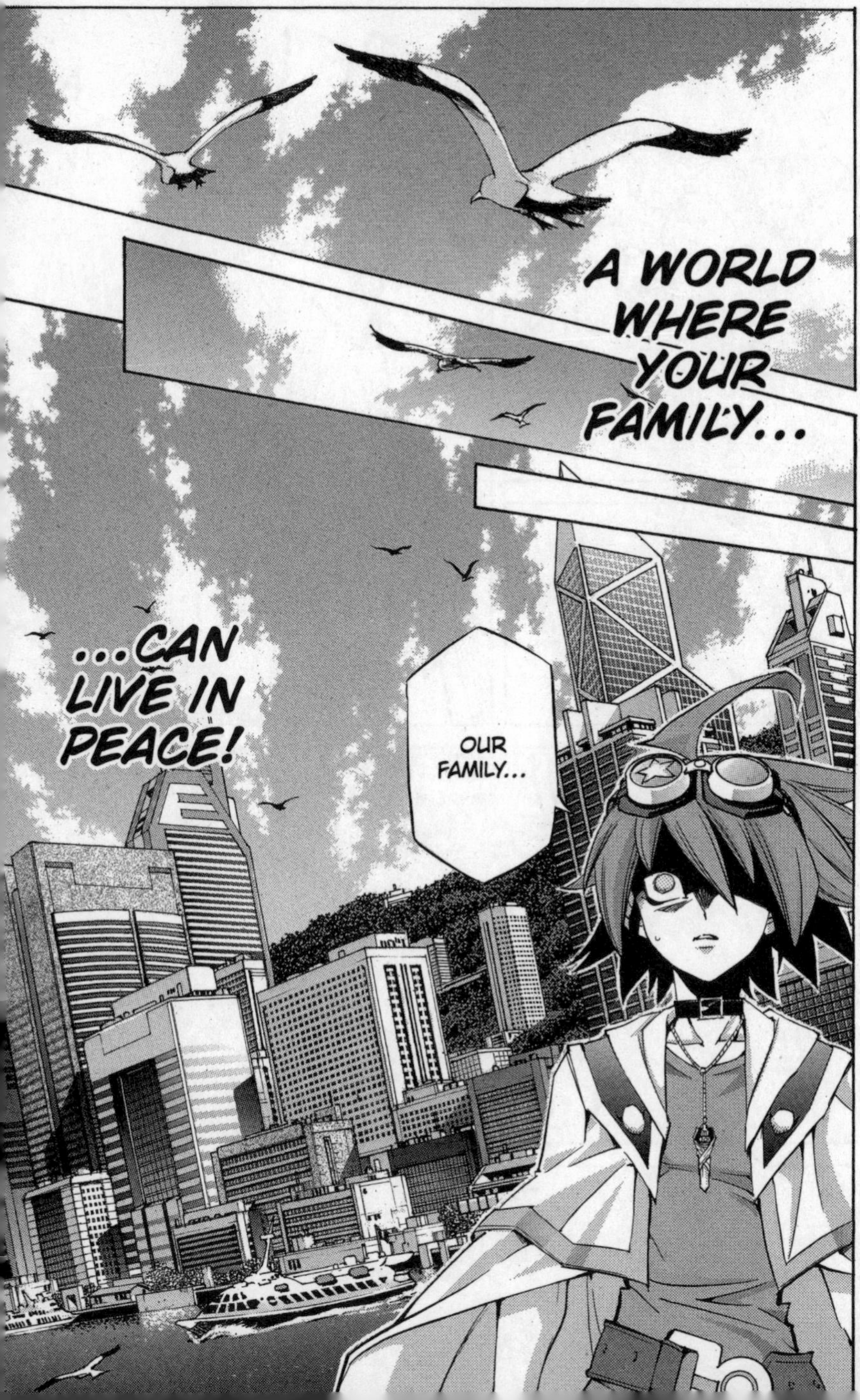
A WORLD WHERE YOUR FAMILY...
...CAN LIVE IN PEACE!
OUR FAMILY...

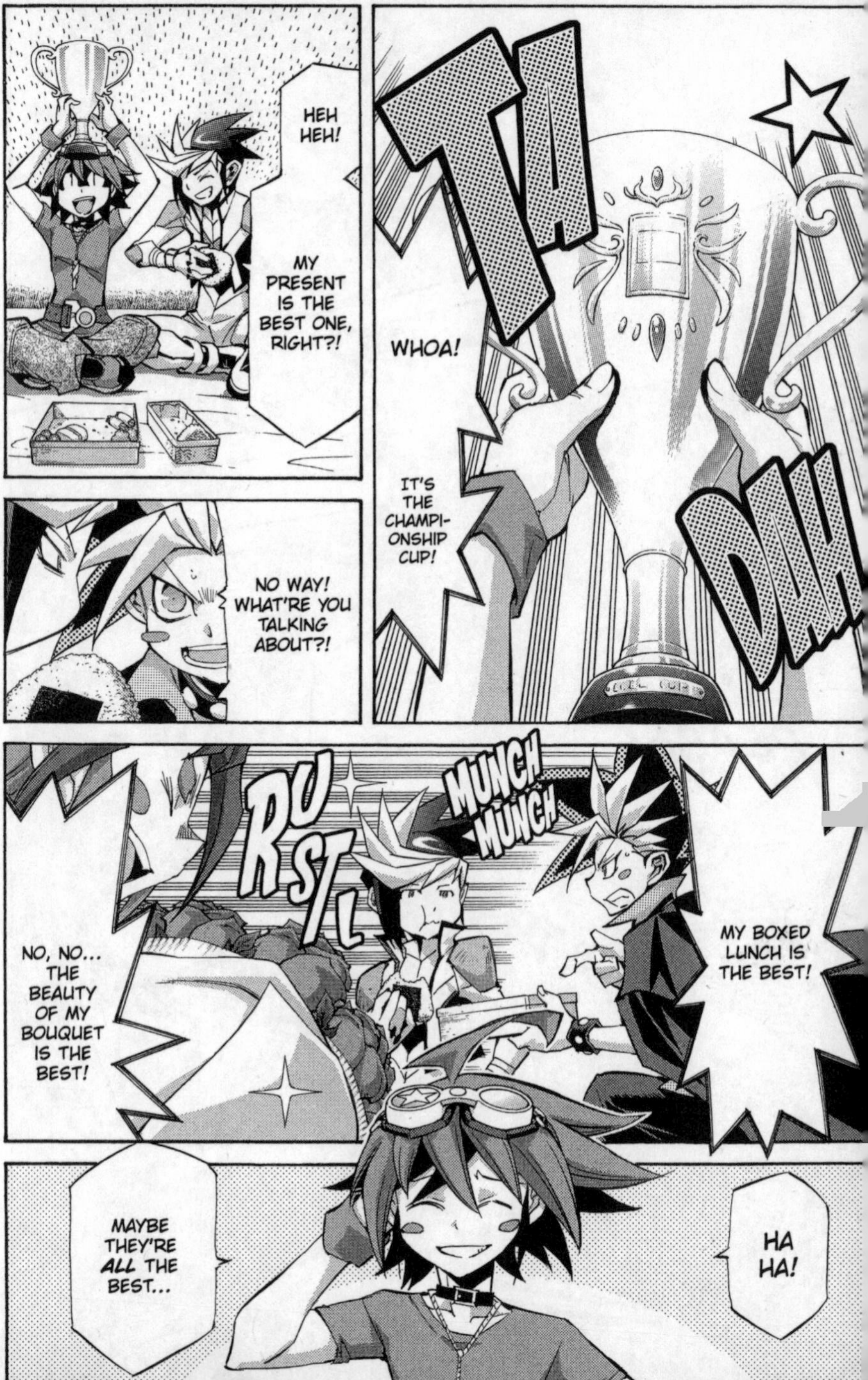
TA
DAH
WHOA!
IT'S THE CHAMPIONSHIP CUP!
HEH HEH!
MY PRESENT IS THE BEST ONE, RIGHT?!
NO WAY! WHAT'RE YOU TALKING ABOUT?!
MY BOXED LUNCH IS THE BEST!
MUNCH MUNCH
RUSTL
NO, NO... THE BEAUTY OF MY BOUQUET IS THE BEST!
HA HA!
MAYBE THEY'RE *ALL* THE BEST...

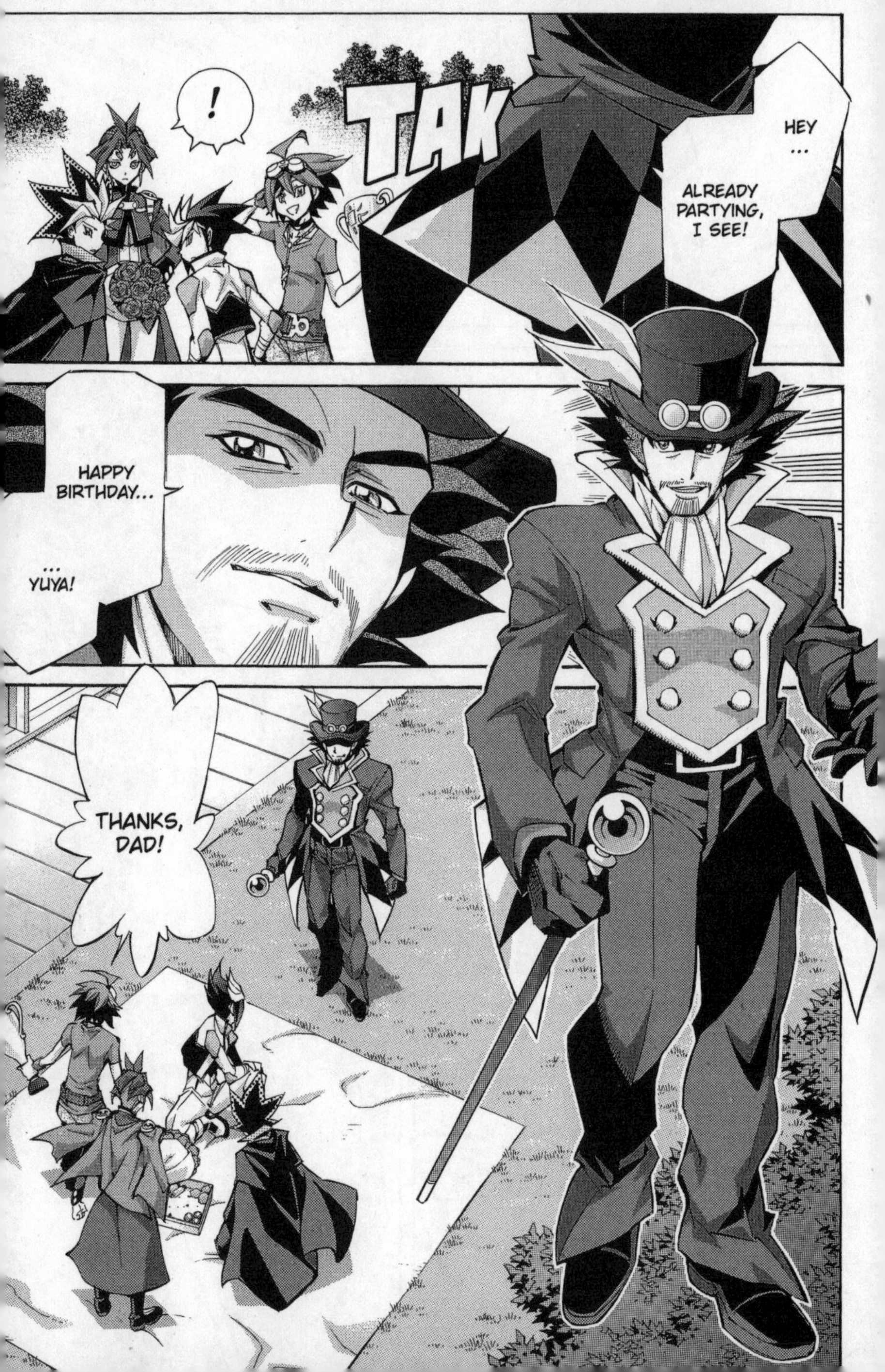
HEY ...
ALREADY PARTYING, I SEE!
TAK
!
HAPPY BIRTHDAY...
... YUYA!
THANKS, DAD!

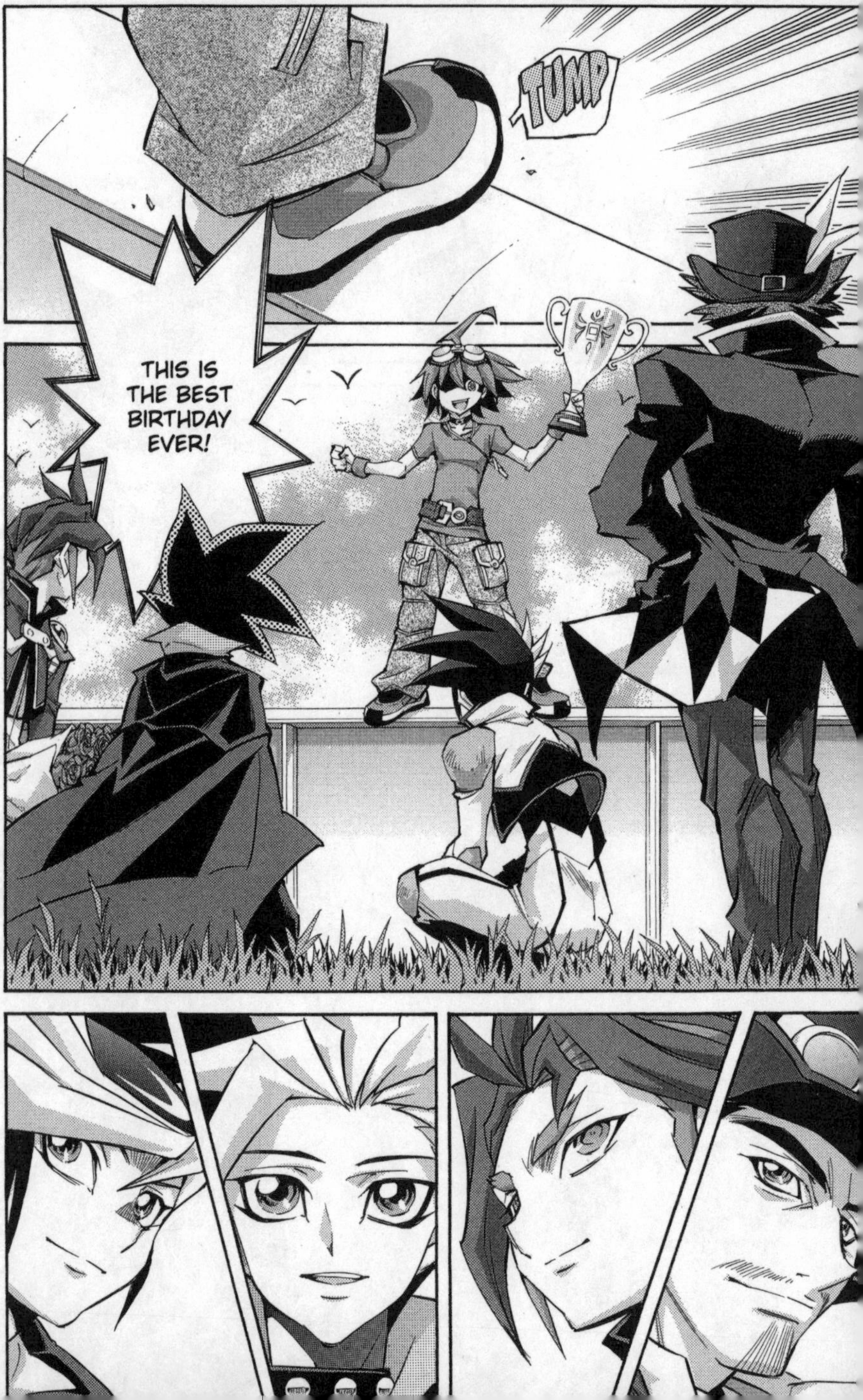
TUMP
THIS IS THE BEST BIRTHDAY EVER!

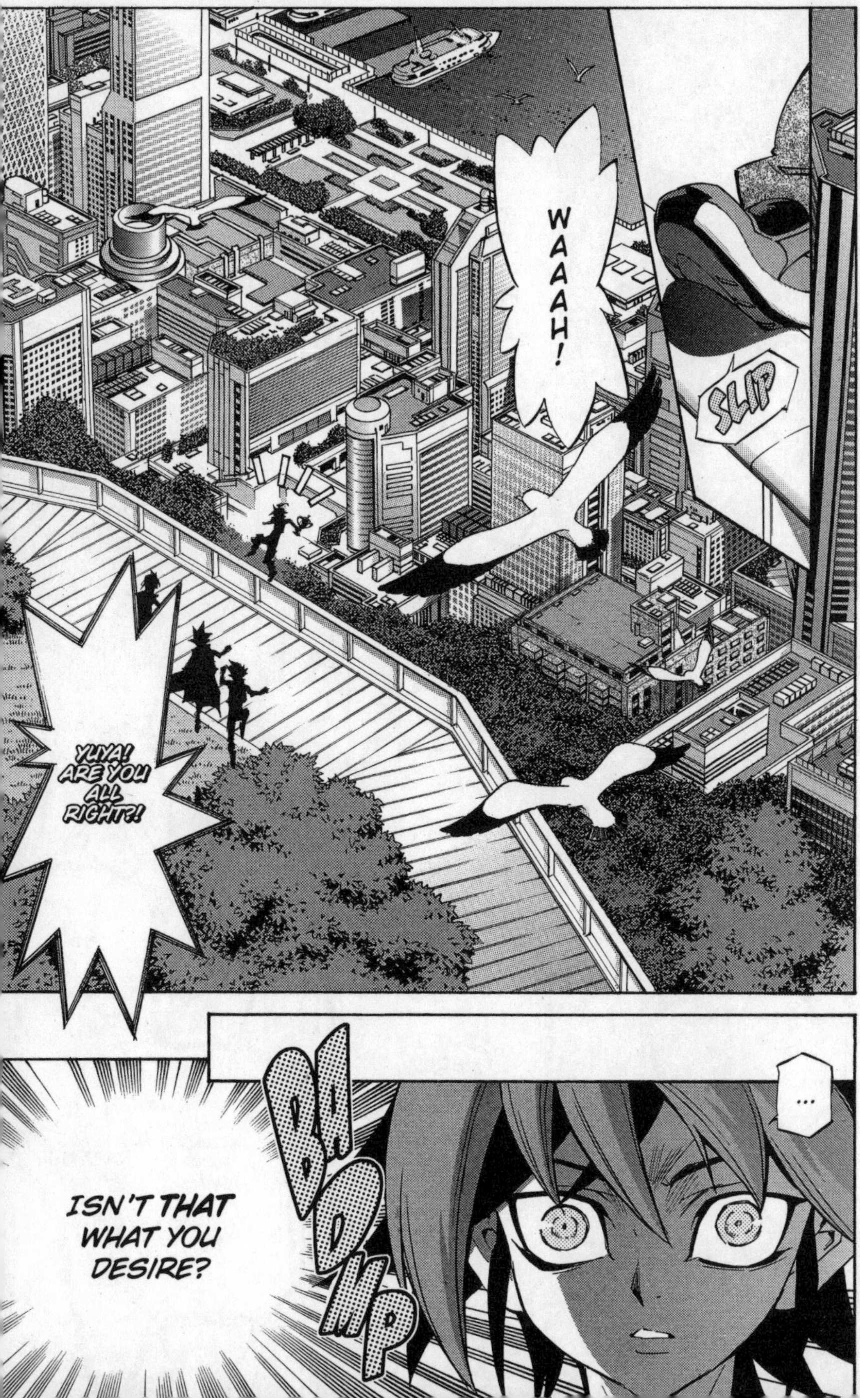
SLIP
WAAAAH!
YUYA! ARE YOU ALL RIGHT?!
...
BADUMP
ISN'T THAT WHAT YOU DESIRE?

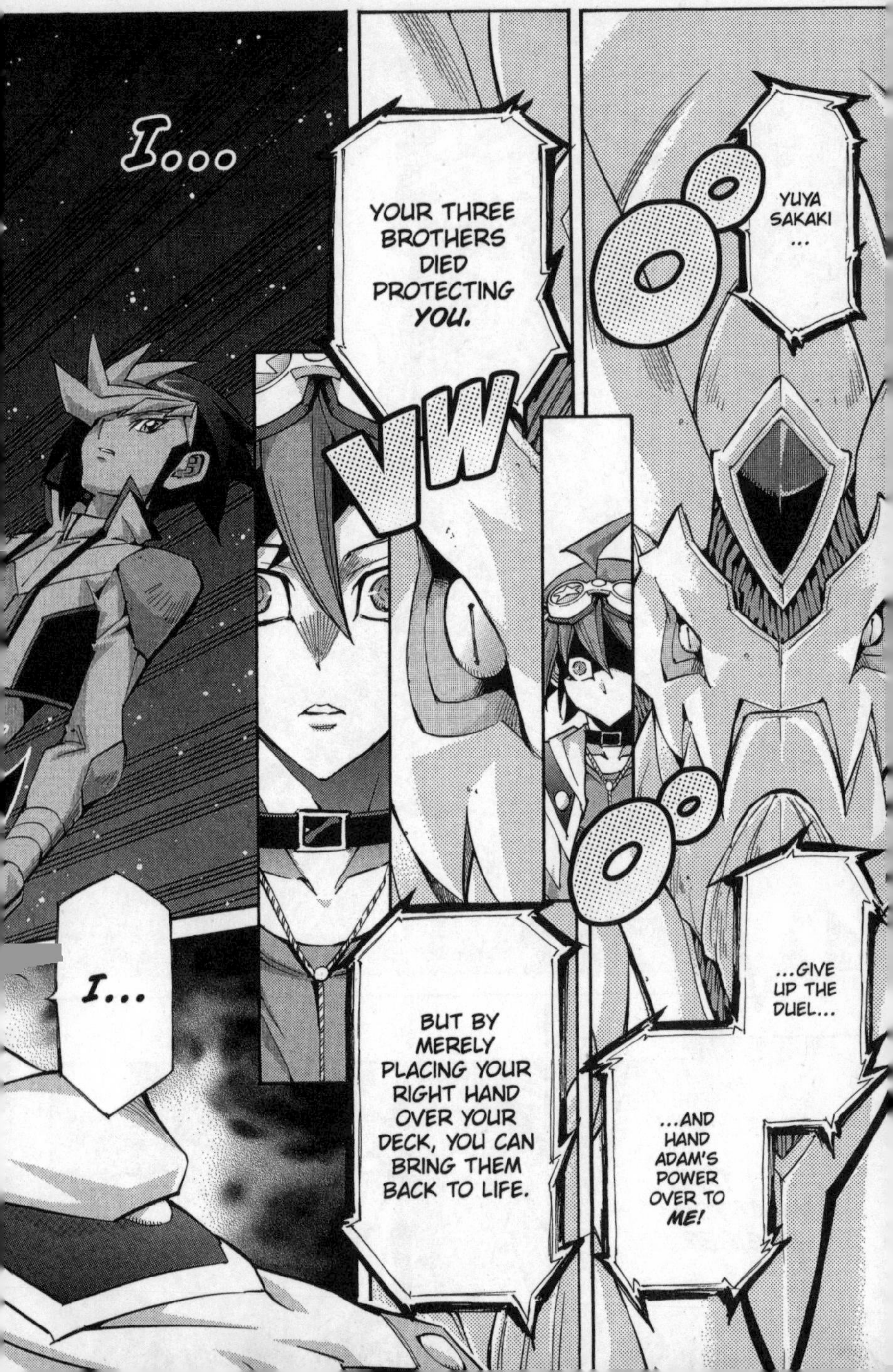
YUYA SAKAKI ...
OOO
OOO
...GIVE UP THE DUEL...
...AND HAND ADAM'S POWER OVER TO ME!
YOUR THREE BROTHERS DIED PROTECTING YOU.
VW
BUT BY MERELY PLACING YOUR RIGHT HAND OVER YOUR DECK, YOU CAN BRING THEM BACK TO LIFE.
Iooo
I...

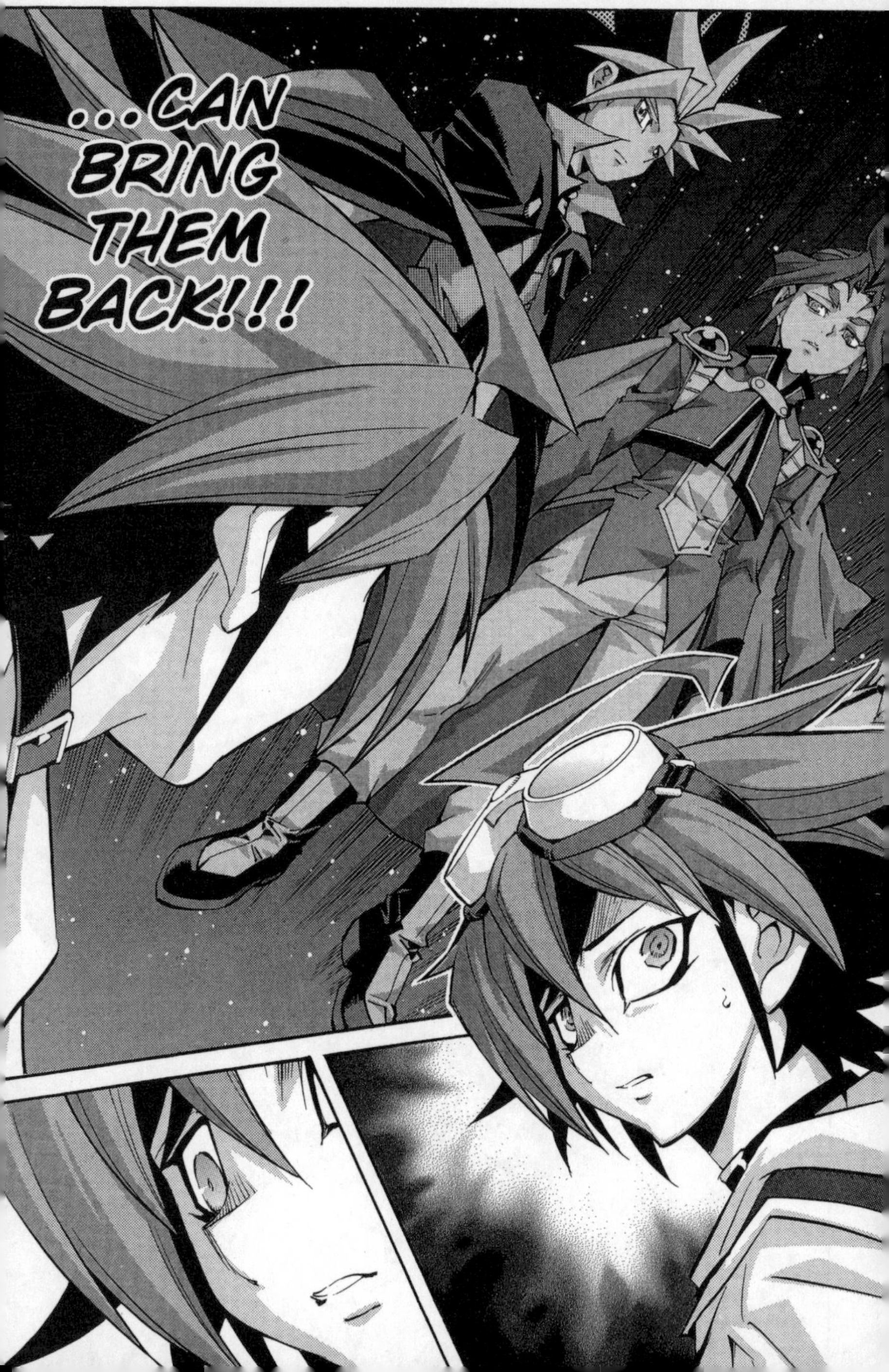
...CAN BRING THEM BACK!!!

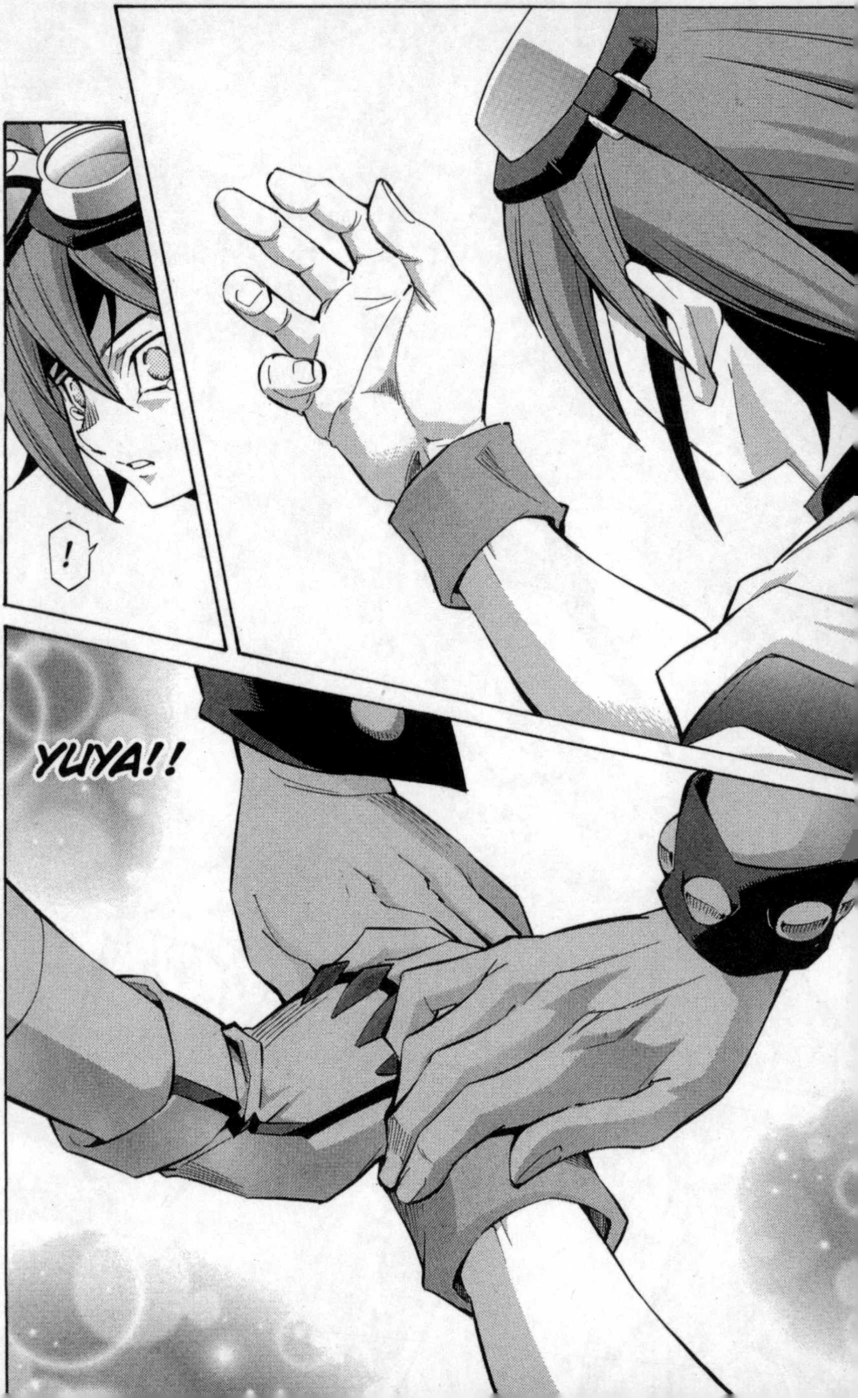
!
YUYA!!

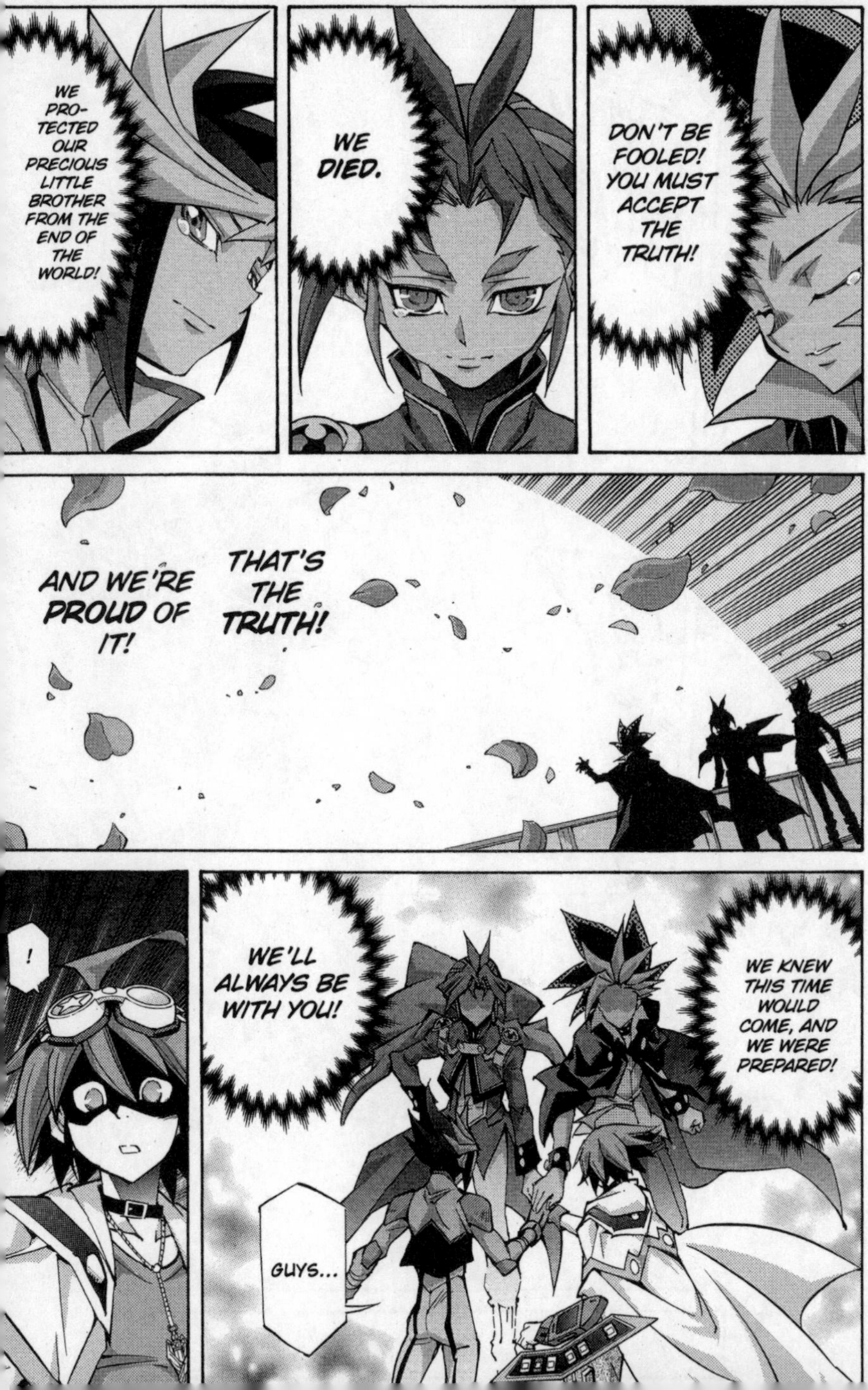
DON'T BE FOOLED! YOU MUST ACCEPT THE TRUTH!
WE DIED.
WE PROTECTED OUR PRECIOUS LITTLE BROTHER FROM THE END OF THE WORLD!
THAT'S THE TRUTH!
AND WE'RE PROUD OF IT!
WE KNEW THIS TIME WOULD COME, AND WE WERE PREPARED!
WE'LL ALWAYS BE WITH YOU!
GUYS...
!

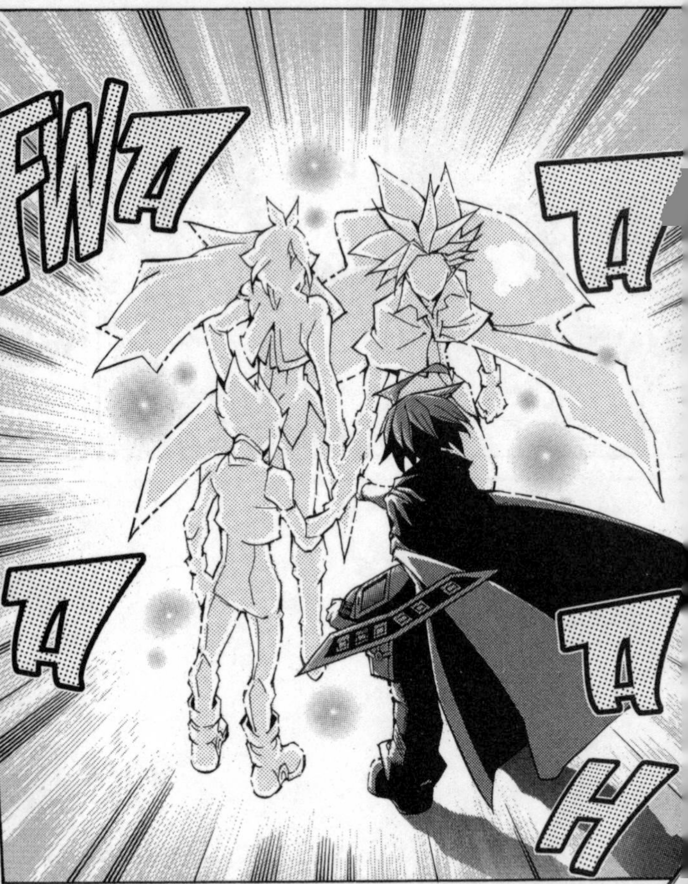
FWA
TATATAH
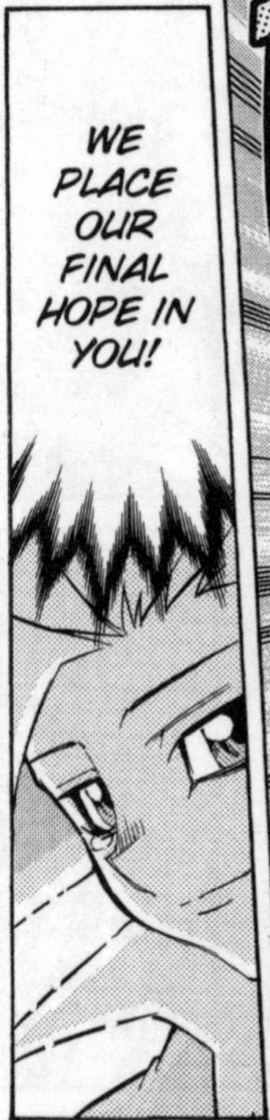
WE PLACE OUR FINAL HOPE IN YOU!
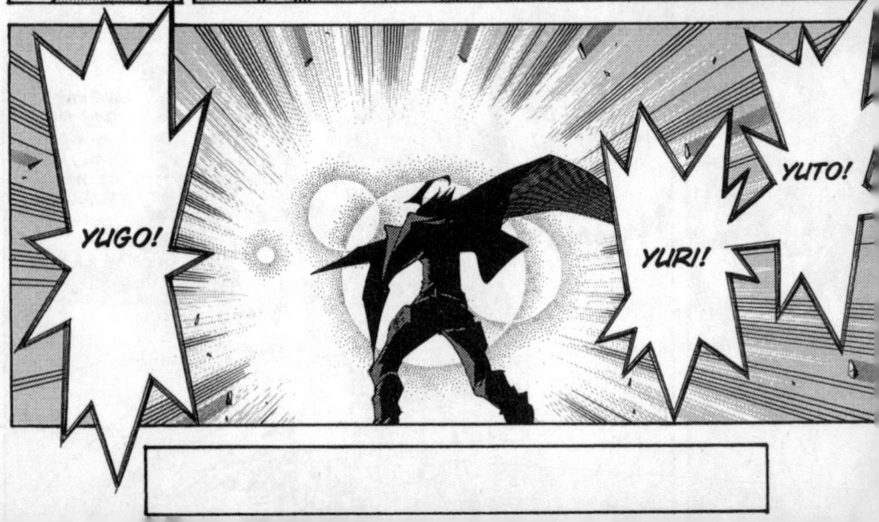
YUTO!
YURI!
YUGO!

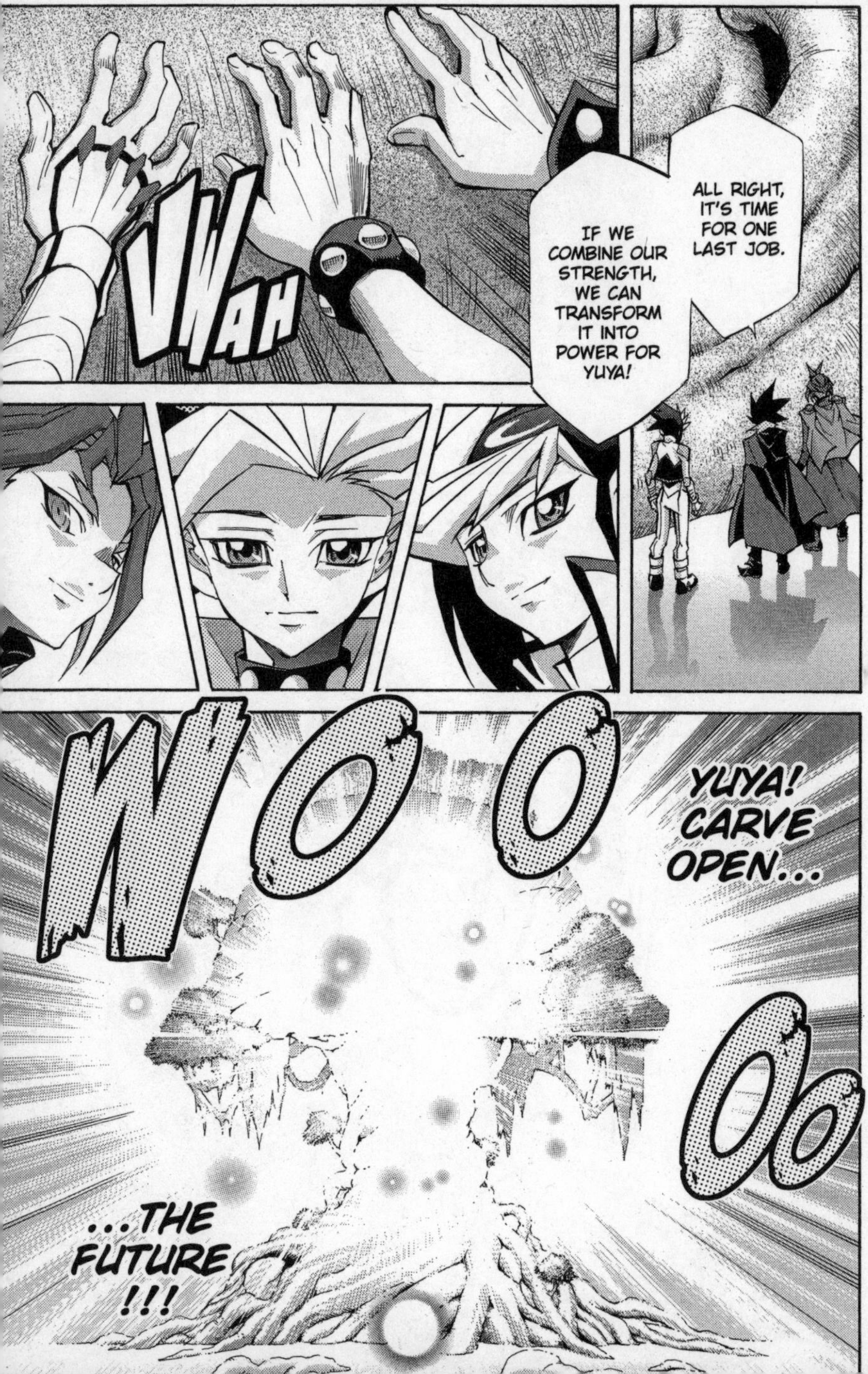
ALL RIGHT, IT'S TIME FOR ONE LAST JOB.
IF WE COMBINE OUR STRENGTH, WE CAN TRANSFORM IT INTO POWER FOR YUYA!
VWAH
WOOOO
YUYA! CARVE OPEN...
...THE FUTURE!!!

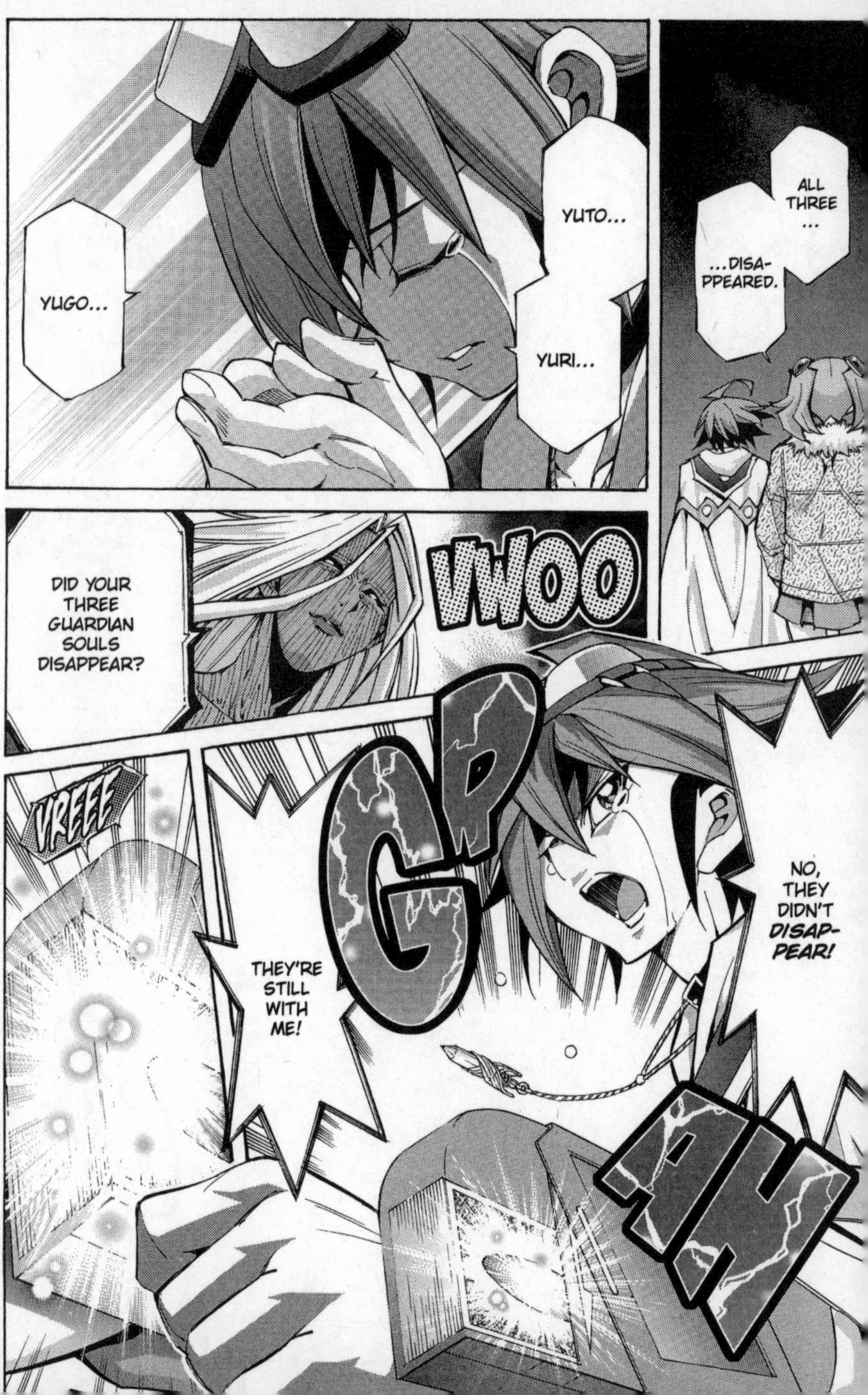
ALL THREE ...
...DISAPPEARED.
YUTO...
YURI...
YUGO...
VWOO
DID YOUR THREE GUARDIAN SOULS DISAPPEAR?
GP
NO, THEY DIDN'T DISAPPEAR!
THEY'RE STILL WITH ME!
VREEE
AH

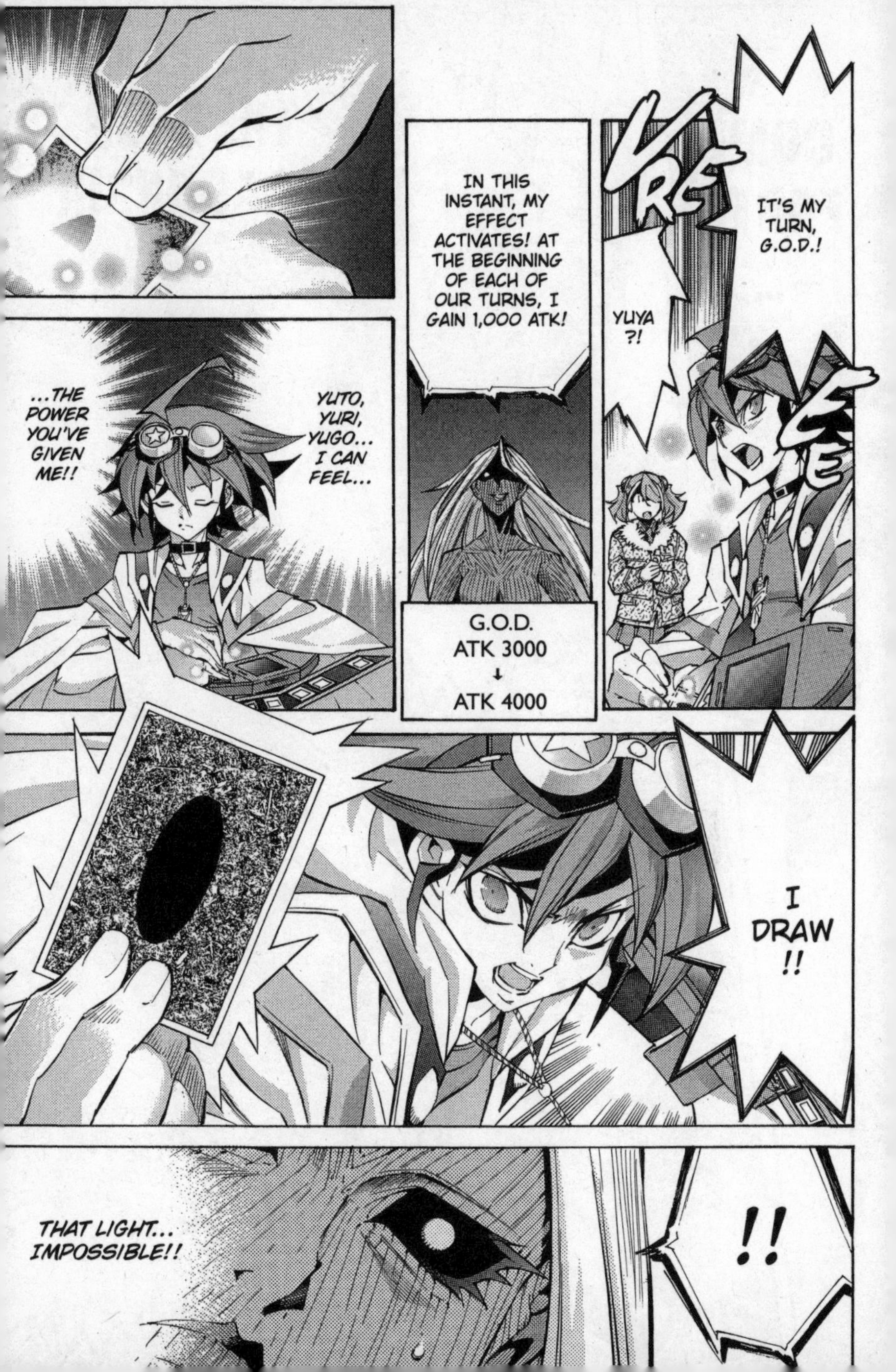
VREEE
IT'S MY TURN, G.O.D.!
YUYA ?!
IN THIS INSTANT, MY EFFECT ACTIVATES! AT THE BEGINNING OF EACH OF OUR TURNS, I GAIN 1,000 ATK!
G.O.D.
ATK 3000
↓
ATK 4000
YUTO, YURI, YUGO... I CAN FEEL...
...THE POWER YOU'VE GIVEN ME!!
I DRAW !!
!!
THAT LIGHT... IMPOSSIBLE!!

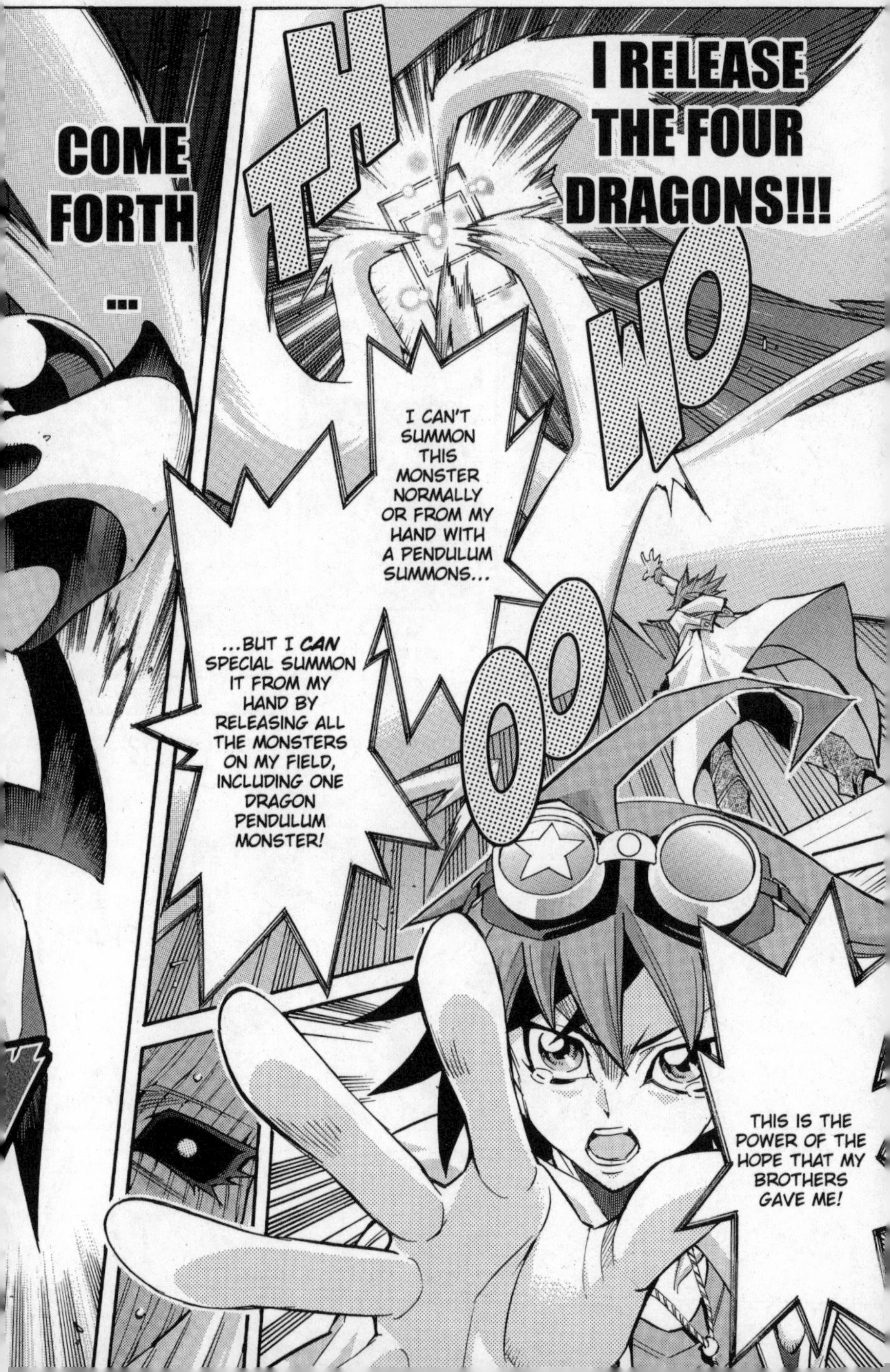
I RELEASE THE FOUR DRAGONS!!!
TH
WO
I CAN'T SUMMON THIS MONSTER NORMALLY OR FROM MY HAND WITH A PENDULUM SUMMONS...
OOO
...BUT I *CAN* SPECIAL SUMMON IT FROM MY HAND BY RELEASING ALL THE MONSTERS ON MY FIELD, INCLUDING ONE DRAGON PENDULUM MONSTER!
THIS IS THE POWER OF THE HOPE THAT MY BROTHERS GAVE ME!
COME FORTH
...

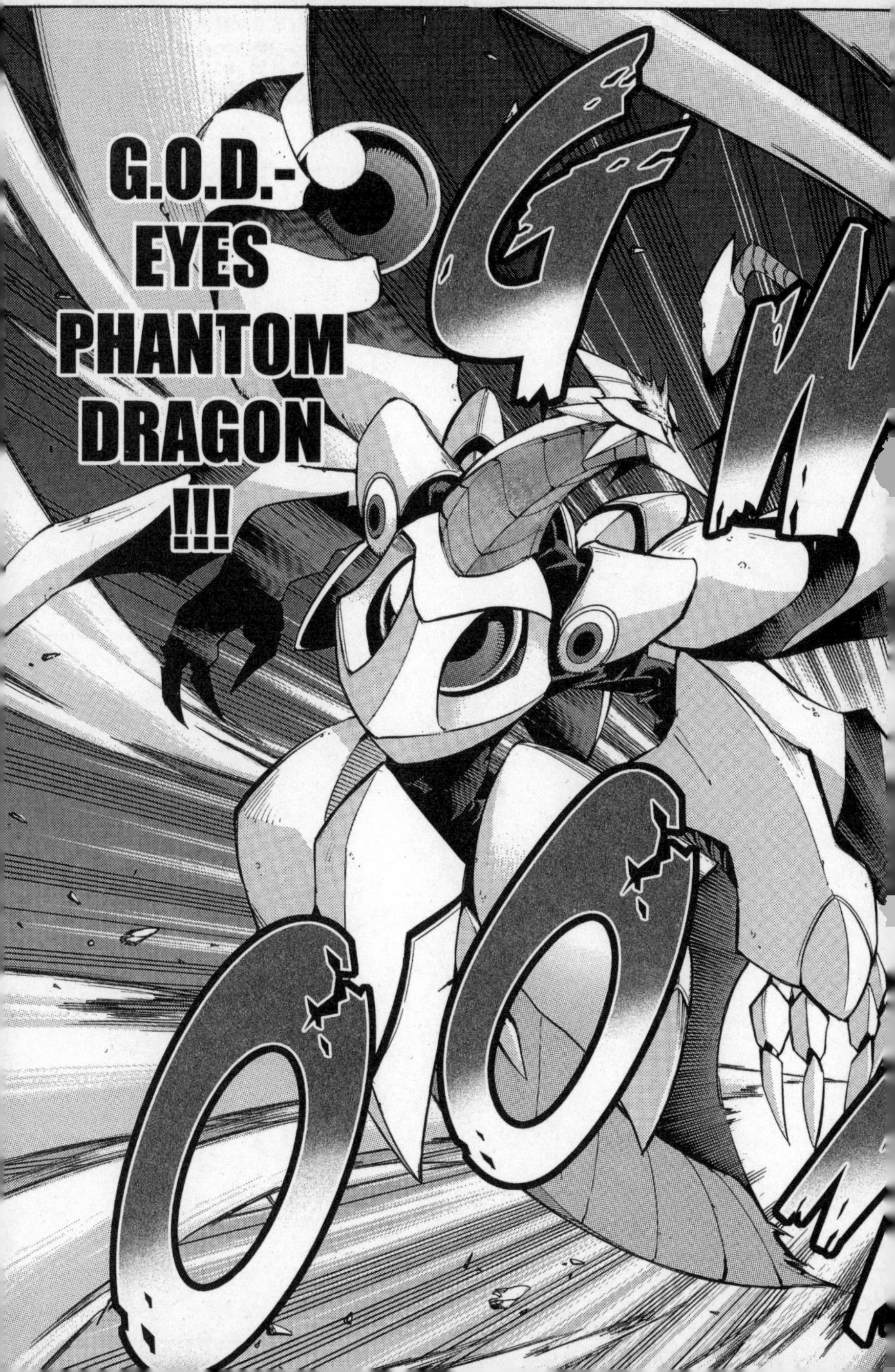
G.O.D.-EYES PHANTOM DRAGON !!!

G.O.D.-EYES PHANTOM DRAGON

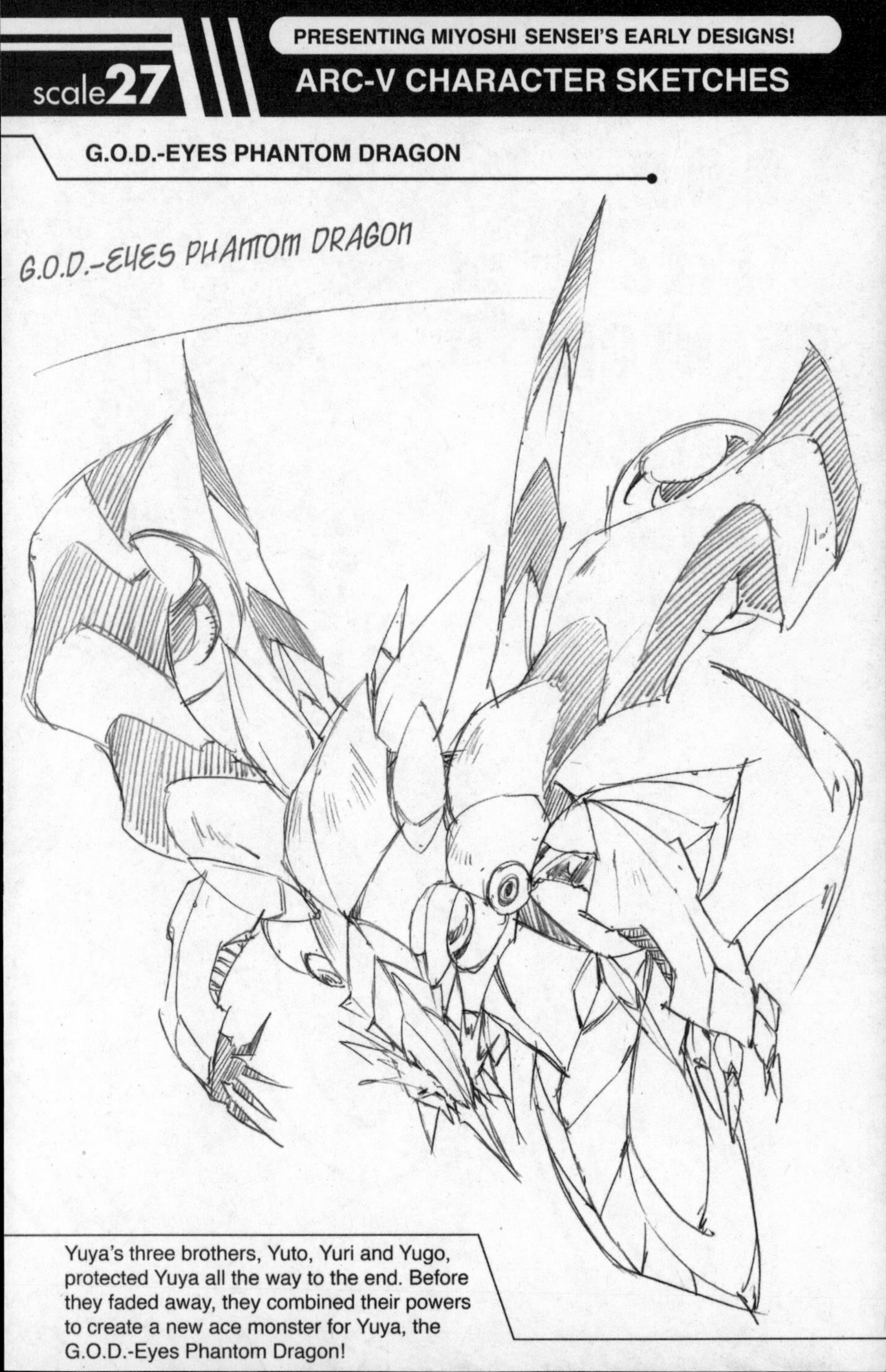
G.O.D.-EYES PHANTOM DRAGON

Yuya's three brothers, Yuto, Yuri and Yugo, protected Yuya all the way to the end. Before they faded away, they combined their powers to create a new ace monster for Yuya, the G.O.D.-Eyes Phantom Dragon!

Yu-Gi-Oh! ARC-V
Scale 39: Across Time and Space!!

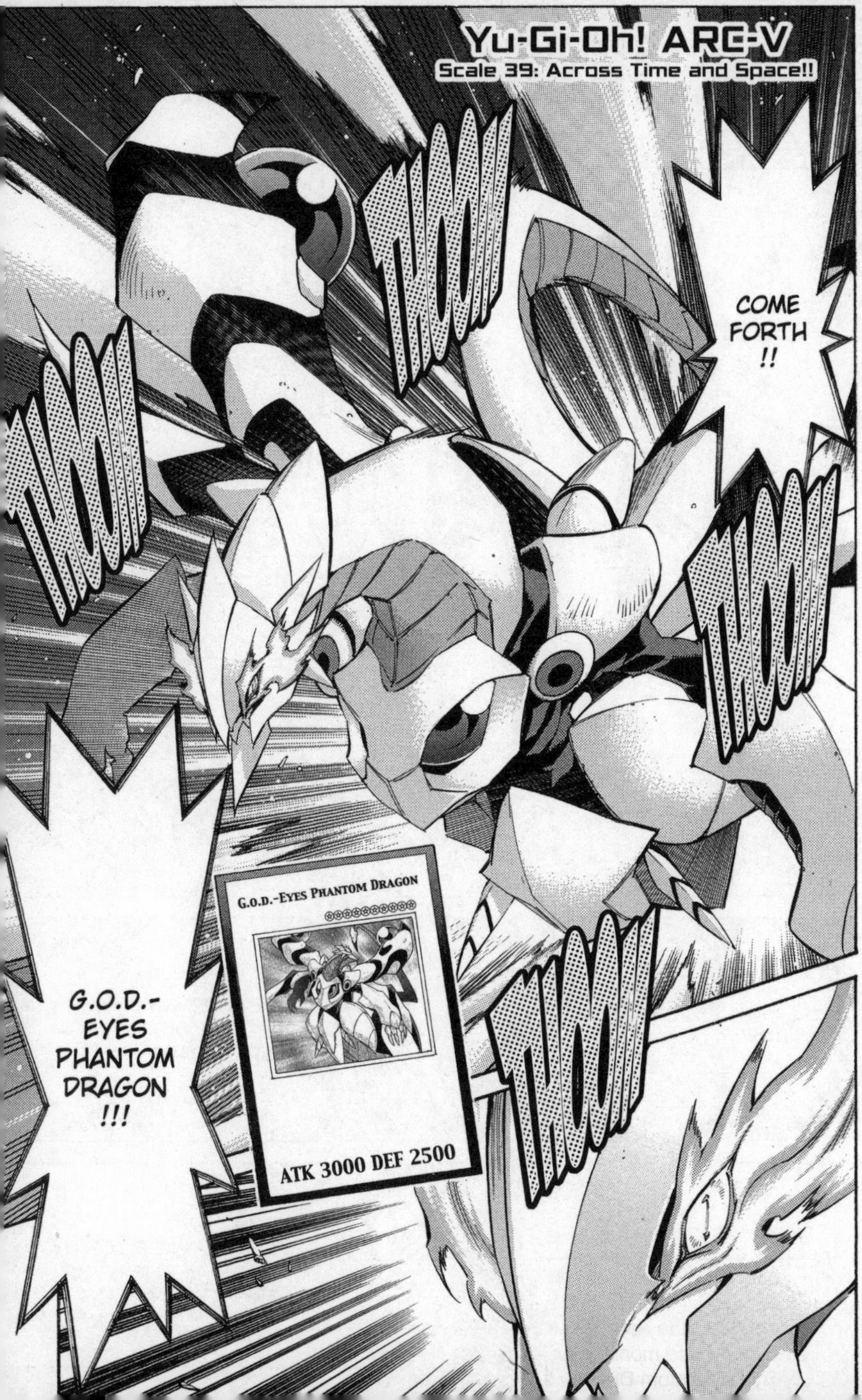
THOOM
COME FORTH!!
THOOM
THOOM
THOOM
THOOM
G.O.D.-EYES PHANTOM DRAGON
ATK 3000 DEF 2500
G.O.D.-EYES PHANTOM DRAGON!!!

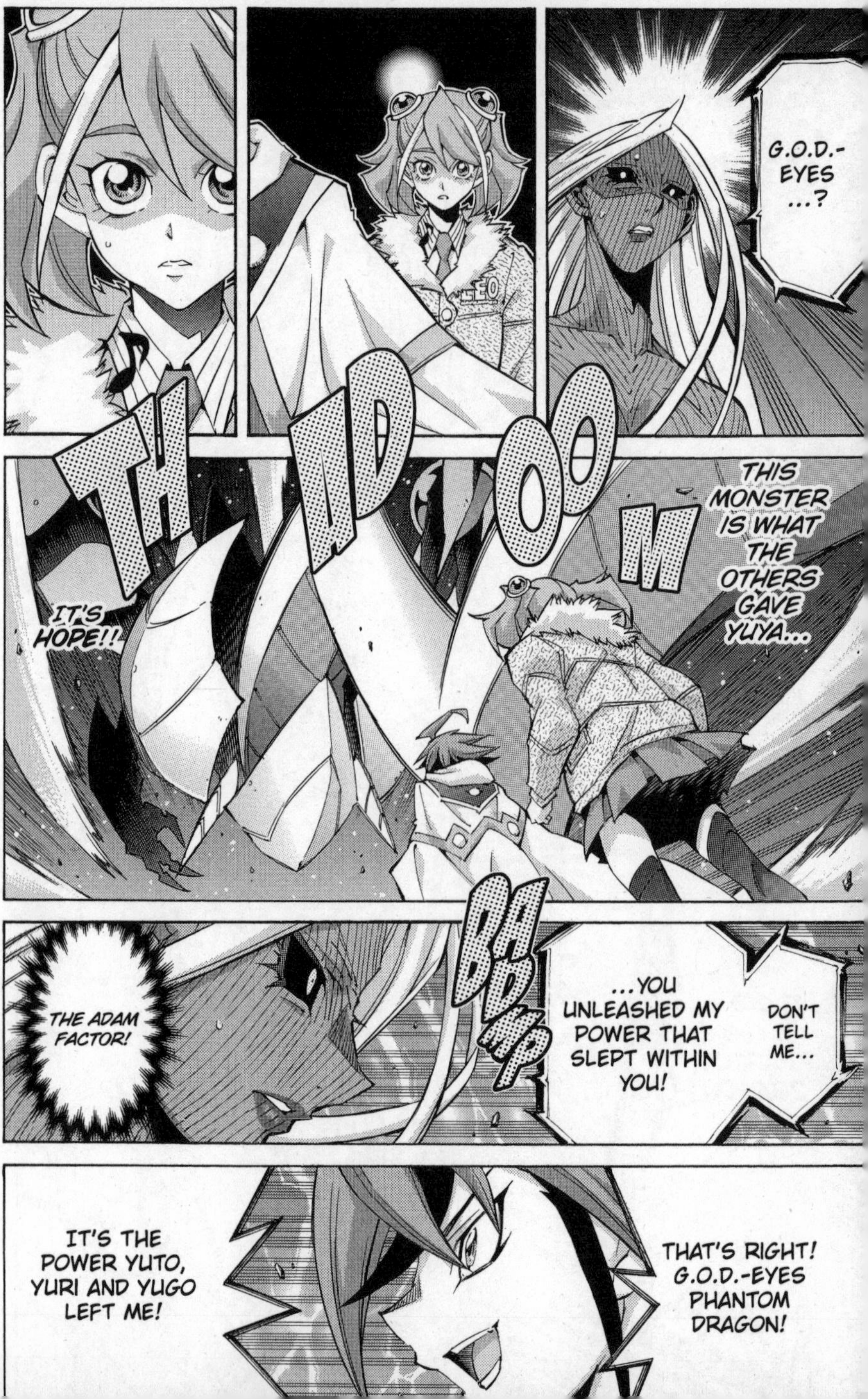
G.O.D.-EYES ...?
THIS MONSTER IS WHAT THE OTHERS GAVE YUYA...
THADOOM
IT'S HOPE!!
DON'T TELL ME...
...YOU UNLEASHED MY POWER THAT SLEPT WITHIN YOU!
BADUMP
THE ADAM FACTOR!
THAT'S RIGHT! G.O.D.-EYES PHANTOM DRAGON!
IT'S THE POWER YUTO, YURI AND YUGO LEFT ME!

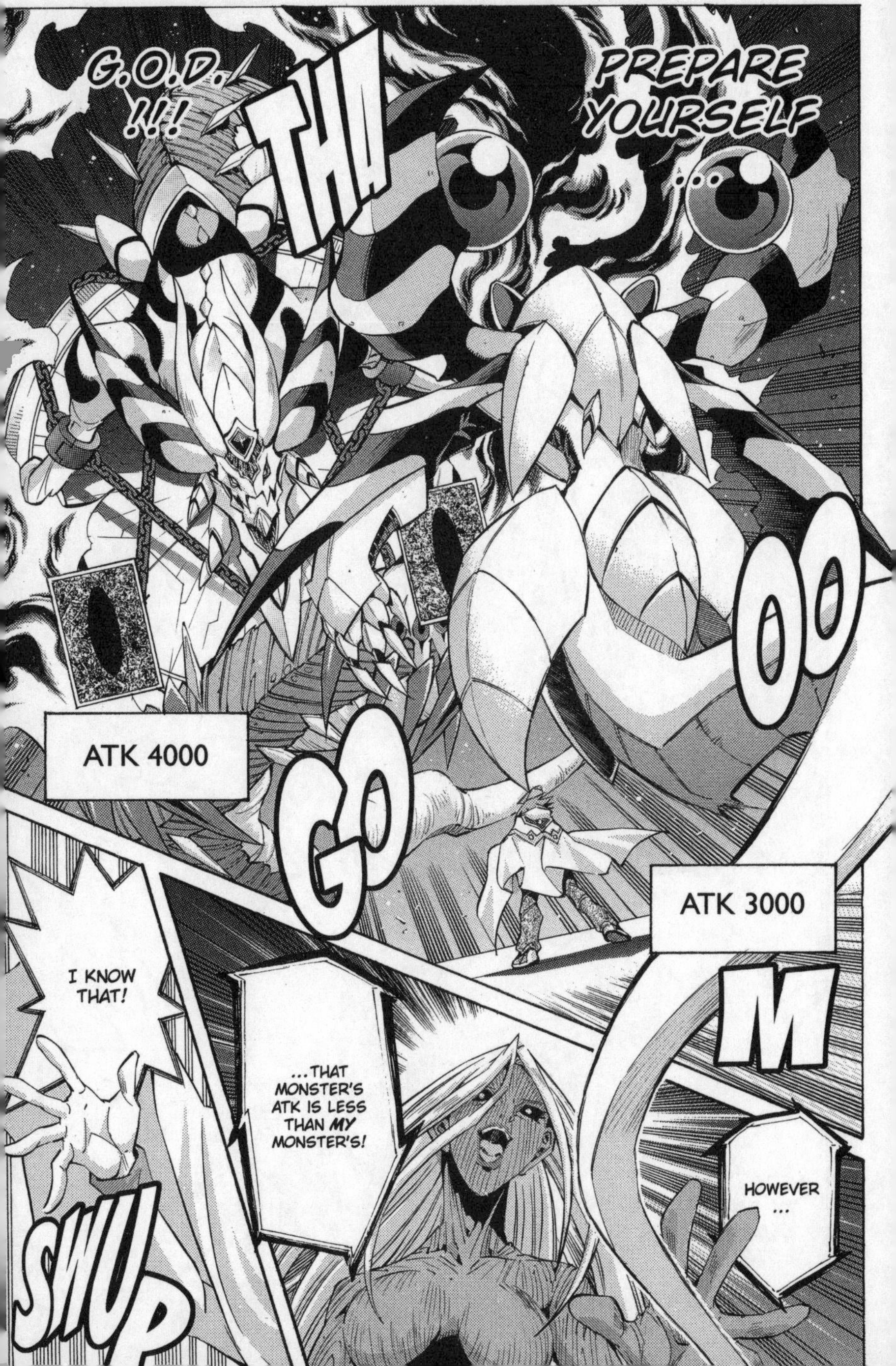
PREPARE YOURSELF
...
THA
G.O.D. !!!
OO
GO
ATK 3000
ATK 4000
M
HOWEVER ...
...THAT MONSTER'S ATK IS LESS THAN *MY* MONSTER'S!
I KNOW THAT!
SWUP

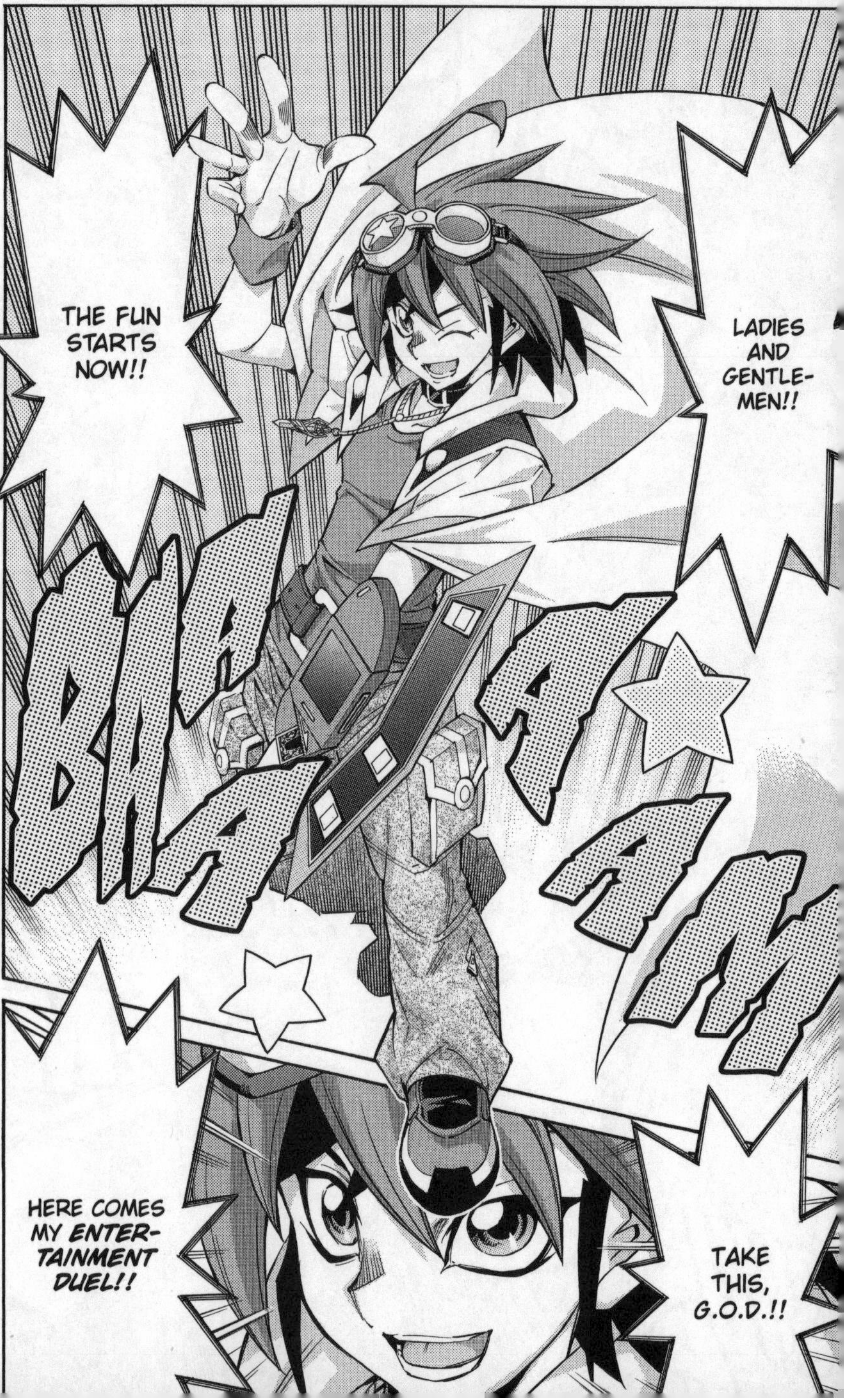
LADIES AND GENTLEMEN!!
THE FUN STARTS NOW!!
TAKE THIS, G.O.D.!!
HERE COMES MY *ENTERTAINMENT DUEL*!!

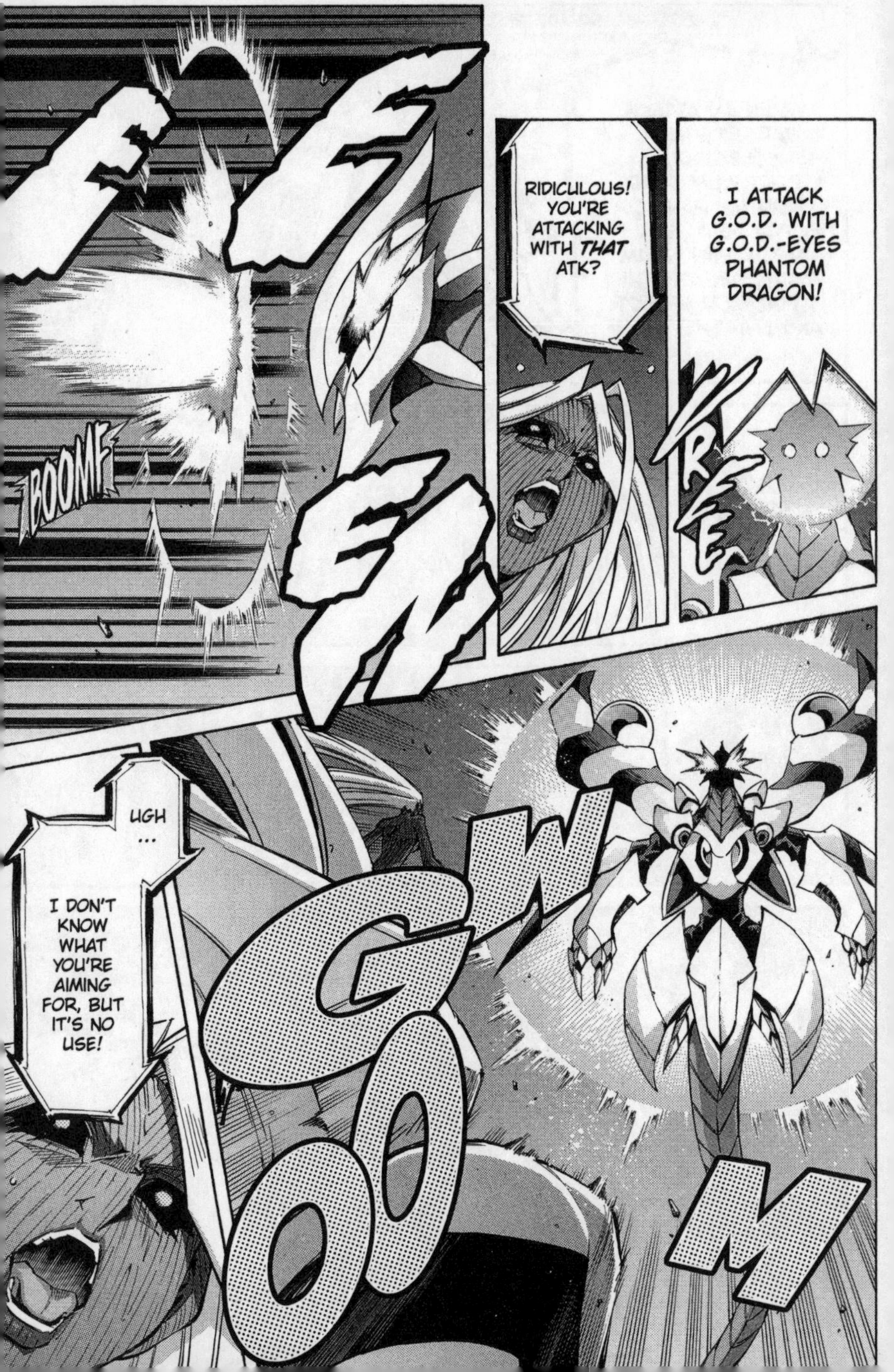
I ATTACK G.O.D. WITH G.O.D.-EYES PHANTOM DRAGON!
RIDICULOUS! YOU'RE ATTACKING WITH *THAT* ATK?
BOOMF
UGH ...
I DON'T KNOW WHAT YOU'RE AIMING FOR, BUT IT'S NO USE!
GWOOM

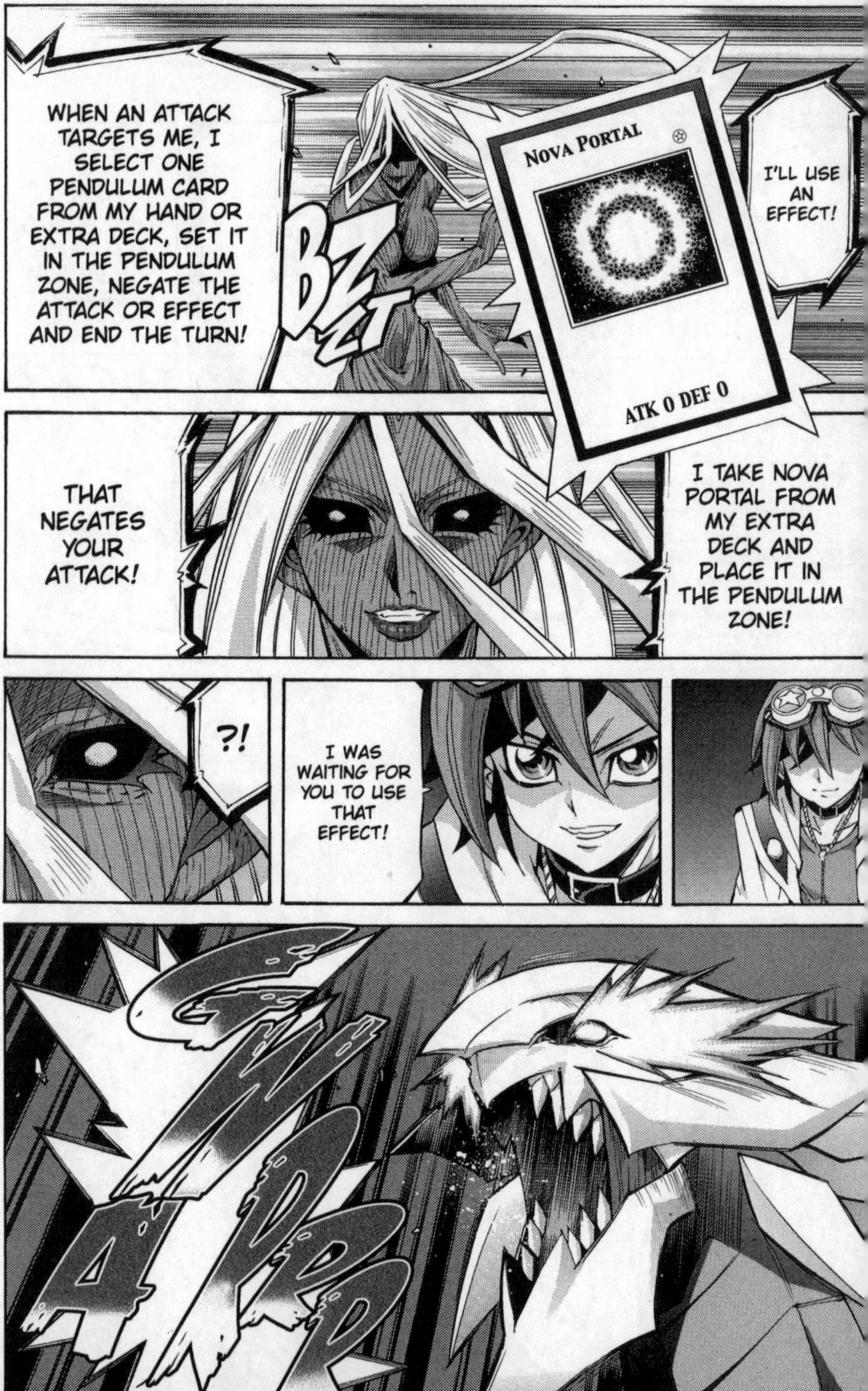
I'LL USE AN EFFECT!
NOVA PORTAL
ATK 0 DEF 0
WHEN AN ATTACK TARGETS ME, I SELECT ONE PENDULUM CARD FROM MY HAND OR EXTRA DECK, SET IT IN THE PENDULUM ZONE, NEGATE THE ATTACK OR EFFECT AND END THE TURN!
I TAKE NOVA PORTAL FROM MY EXTRA DECK AND PLACE IT IN THE PENDULUM ZONE!
THAT NEGATES YOUR ATTACK!
I WAS WAITING FOR YOU TO USE THAT EFFECT!
?!

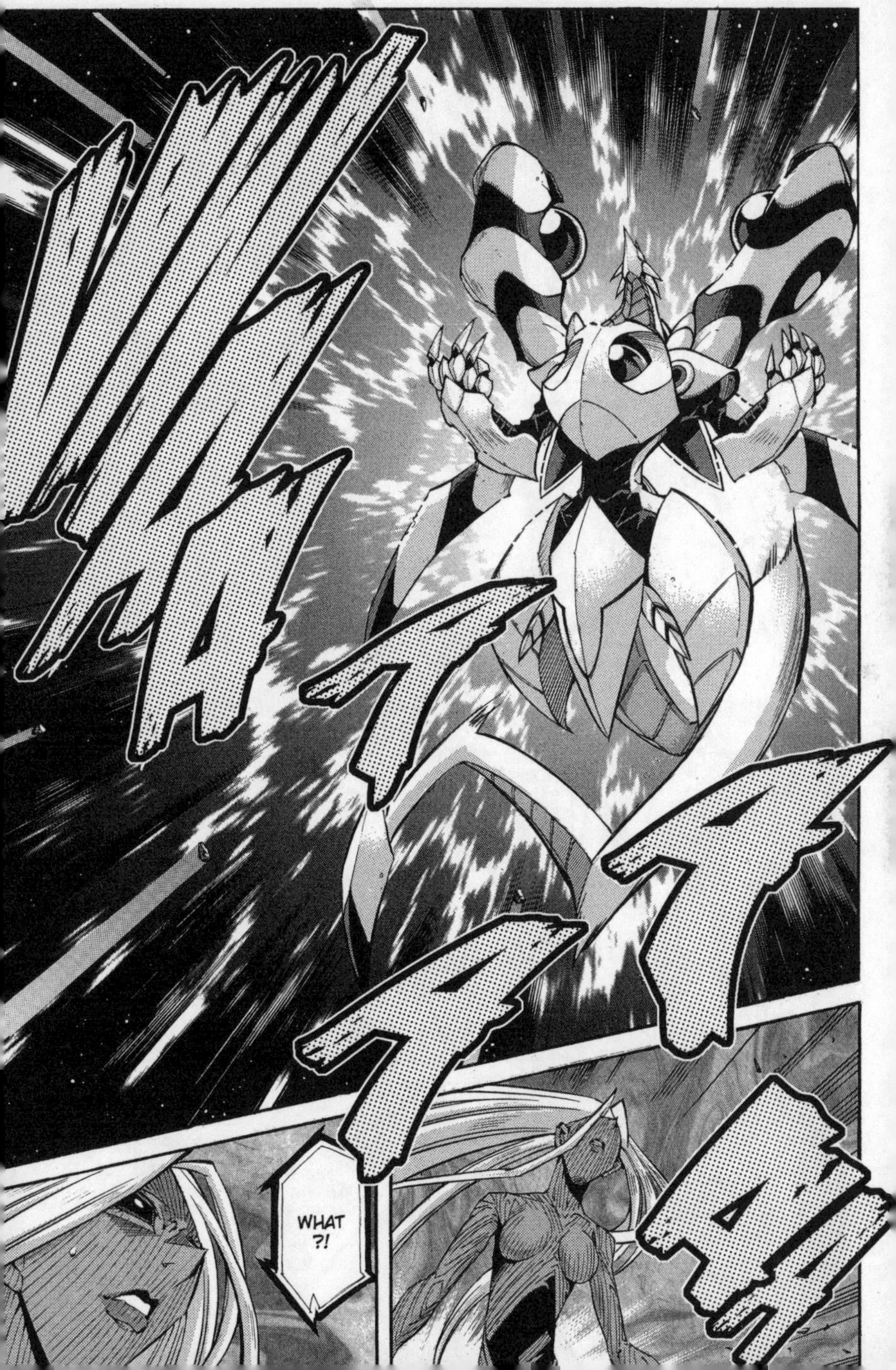
WHAT ?!

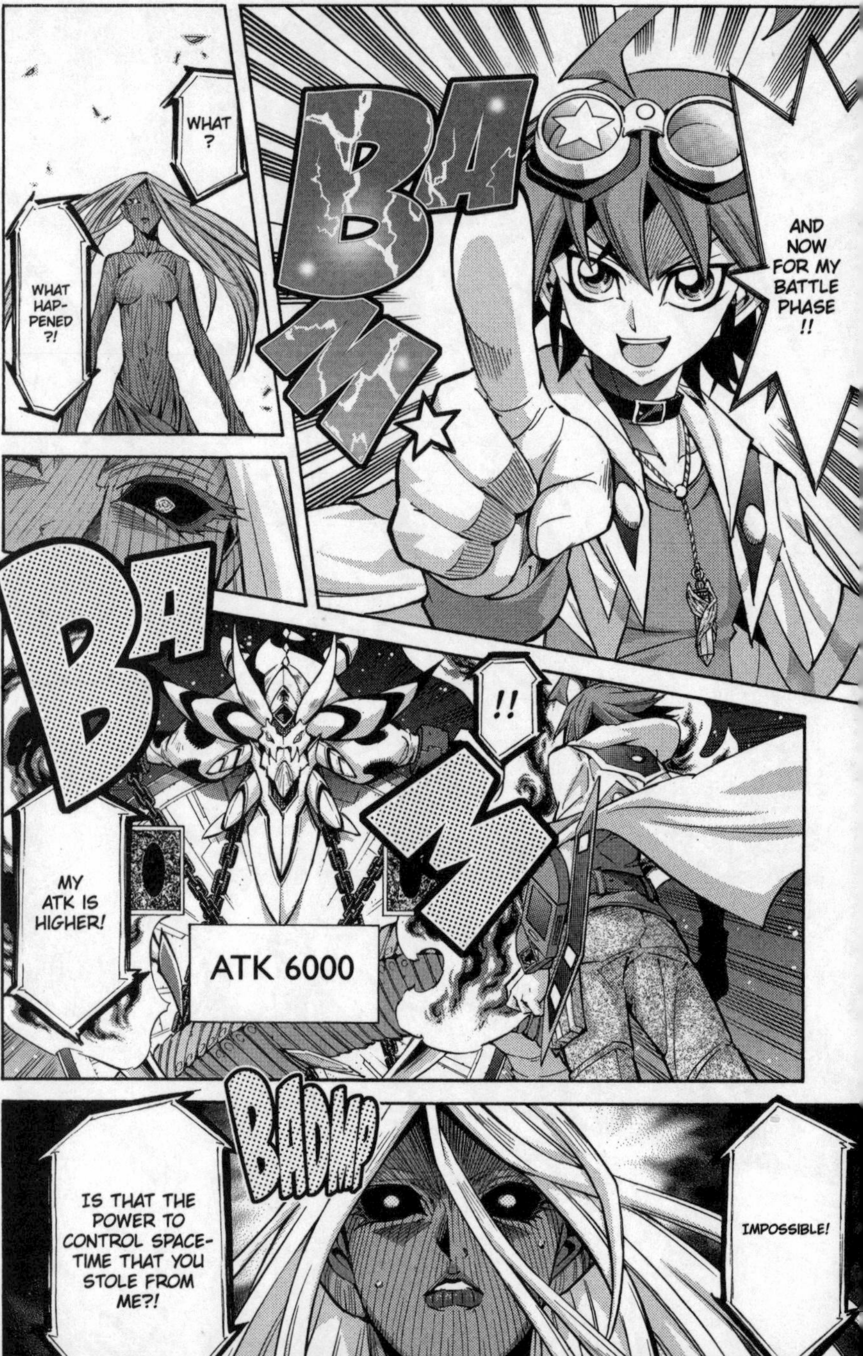
AND NOW FOR MY BATTLE PHASE!!
BAM
WHAT?
WHAT HAPPENED?!
!!
BAM
MY ATK IS HIGHER!
ATK 6000
IMPOSSIBLE!
BADMP
IS THAT THE POWER TO CONTROL SPACE-TIME THAT YOU STOLE FROM ME?!

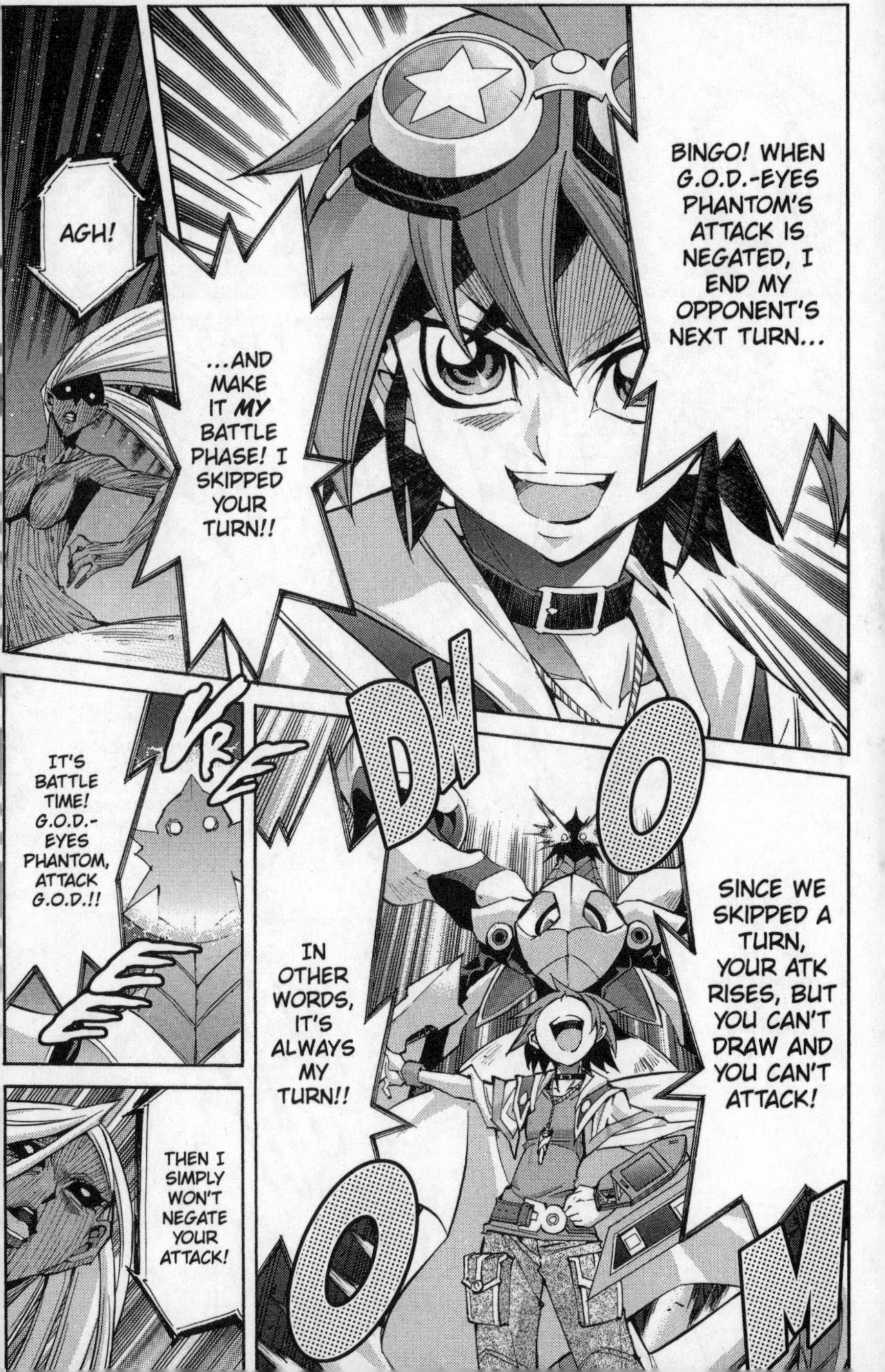

BINGO! WHEN G.O.D.-EYES PHANTOM'S ATTACK IS NEGATED, I END MY OPPONENT'S NEXT TURN...
...AND MAKE IT *MY* BATTLE PHASE! I SKIPPED YOUR TURN!!
AGH!
DWOOM
SINCE WE SKIPPED A TURN, YOUR ATK RISES, BUT YOU CAN'T DRAW AND YOU CAN'T ATTACK!
IN OTHER WORDS, IT'S ALWAYS MY TURN!!
IT'S BATTLE TIME! G.O.D.-EYES PHANTOM, ATTACK G.O.D.!!
THEN I SIMPLY WON'T NEGATE YOUR ATTACK!

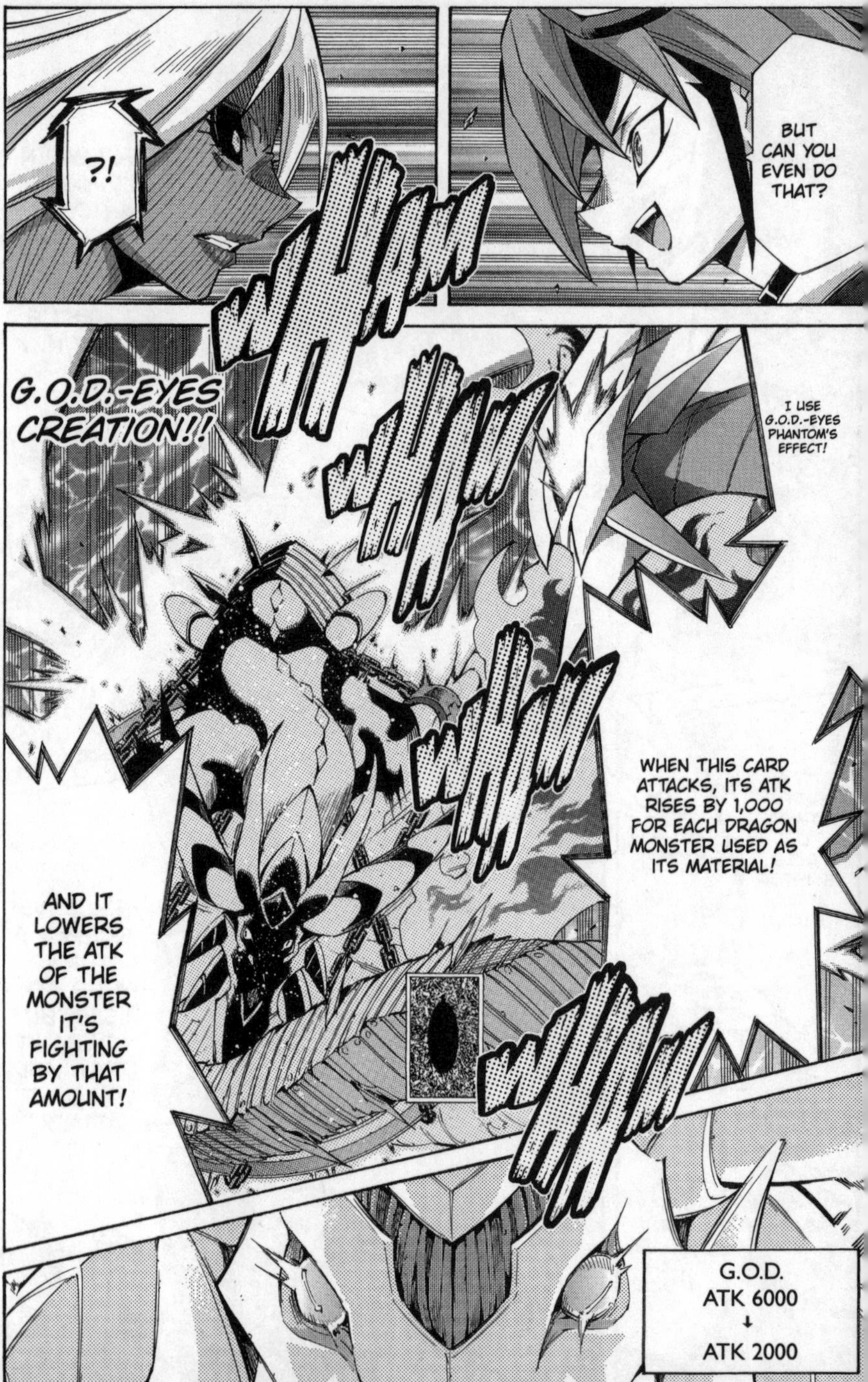
BUT CAN YOU EVEN DO THAT?
?!
I USE G.O.D.-EYES PHANTOM'S EFFECT!
G.O.D.-EYES CREATION!!
WHEN THIS CARD ATTACKS, ITS ATK RISES BY 1,000 FOR EACH DRAGON MONSTER USED AS ITS MATERIAL!
AND IT LOWERS THE ATK OF THE MONSTER IT'S FIGHTING BY THAT AMOUNT!
G.O.D.
ATK 6000
↓
ATK 2000

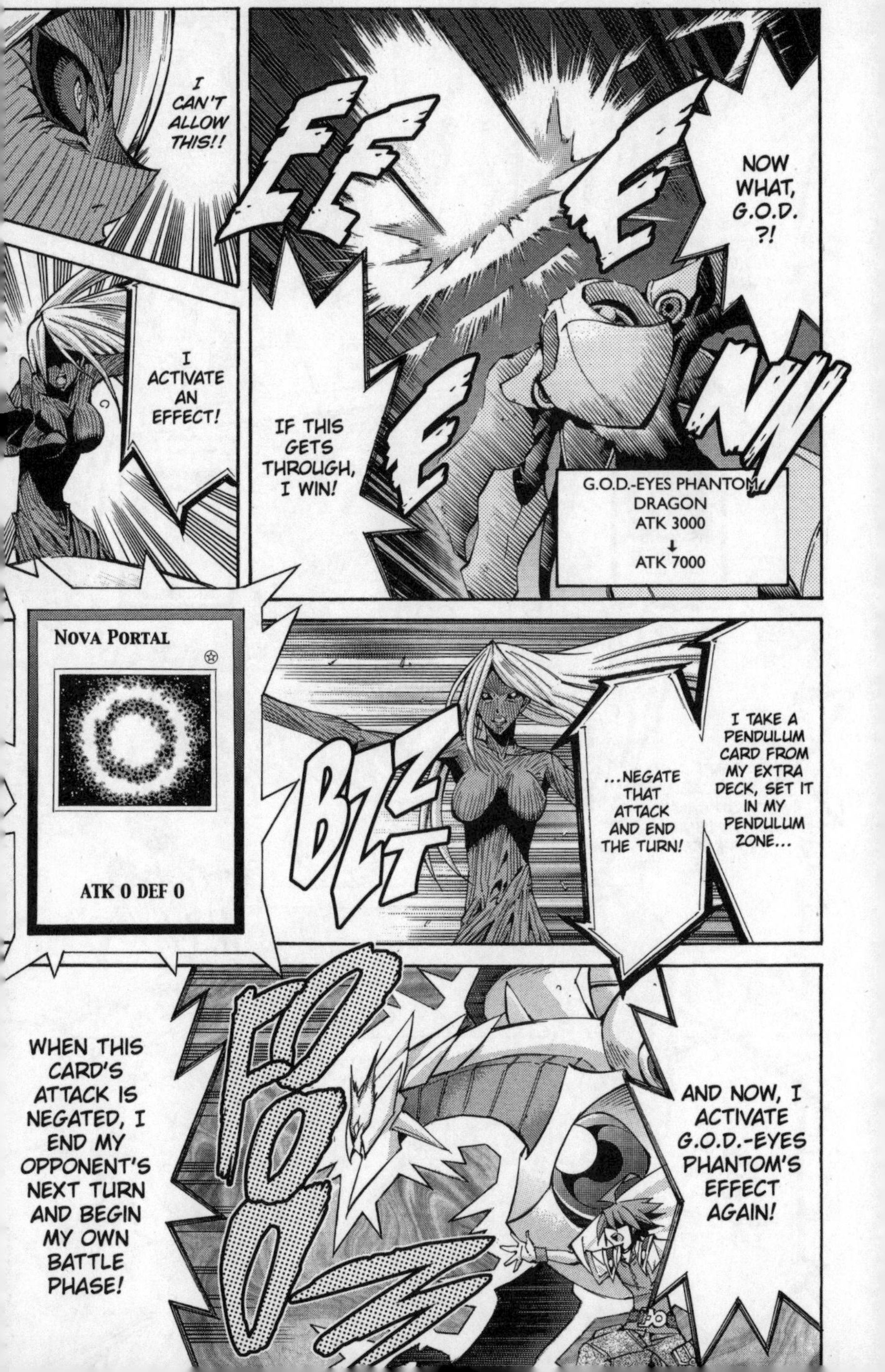
NOW WHAT, G.O.D. ?!
IF THIS GETS THROUGH, I WIN!
G.O.D.-EYES PHANTOM DRAGON ATK 3000 ↓ ATK 7000
I CAN'T ALLOW THIS!!
I ACTIVATE AN EFFECT!
I TAKE A PENDULUM CARD FROM MY EXTRA DECK, SET IT IN MY PENDULUM ZONE...
...NEGATE THAT ATTACK AND END THE TURN!
BZZT
NOVA PORTAL
ATK 0 DEF 0
AND NOW, I ACTIVATE G.O.D.-EYES PHANTOM'S EFFECT AGAIN!
WHEN THIS CARD'S ATTACK IS NEGATED, I END MY OPPONENT'S NEXT TURN AND BEGIN MY OWN BATTLE PHASE!

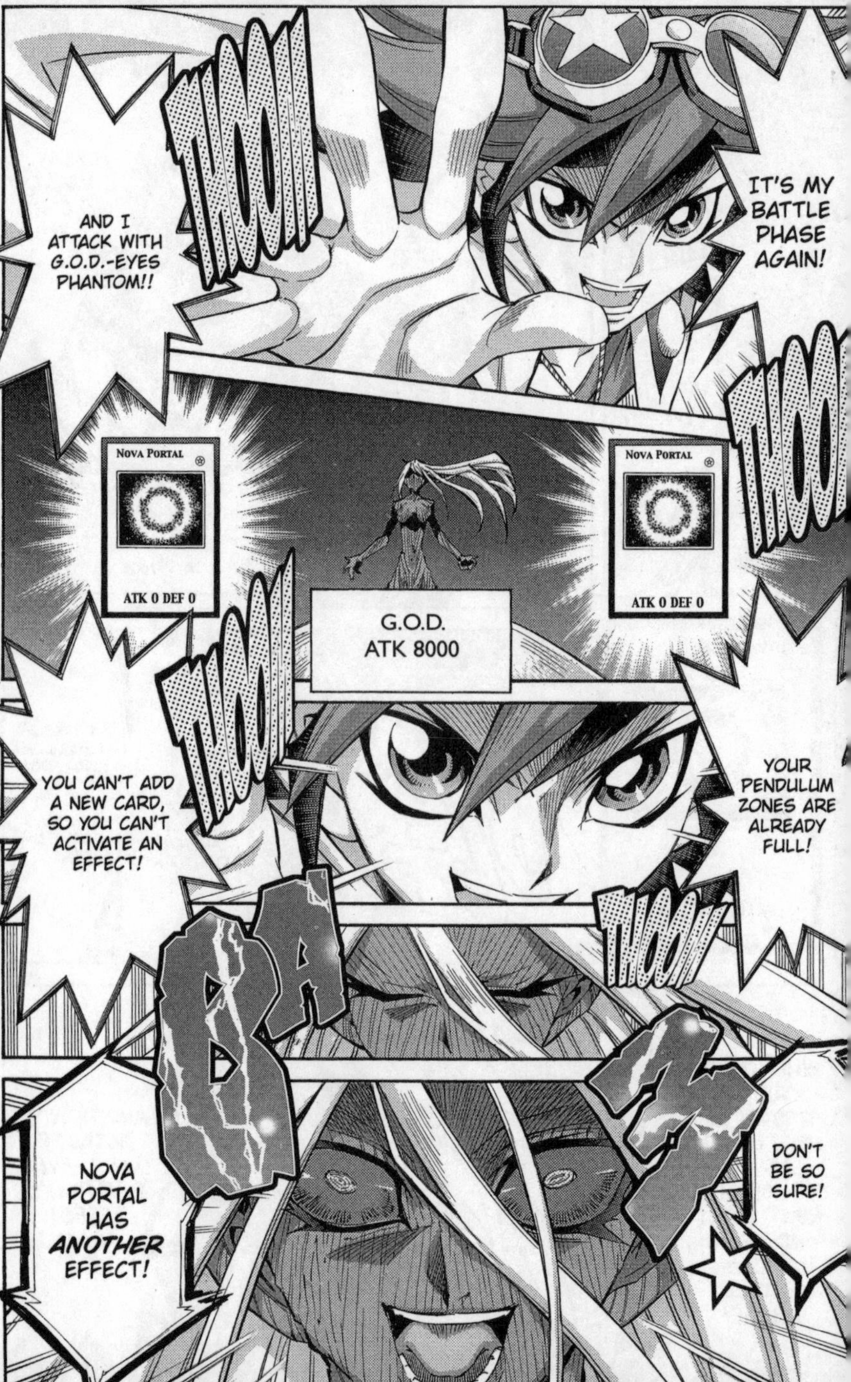
THOOM
IT'S MY BATTLE PHASE AGAIN!
AND I ATTACK WITH G.O.D.-EYES PHANTOM!!
THOOM
Nova Portal
ATK 0 DEF 0
Nova Portal
ATK 0 DEF 0
G.O.D.
ATK 8000
THOOM
YOUR PENDULUM ZONES ARE ALREADY FULL!
YOU CAN'T ADD A NEW CARD, SO YOU CAN'T ACTIVATE AN EFFECT!
THOOM
GA
DON'T BE SO SURE!
NOVA PORTAL HAS *ANOTHER* EFFECT!

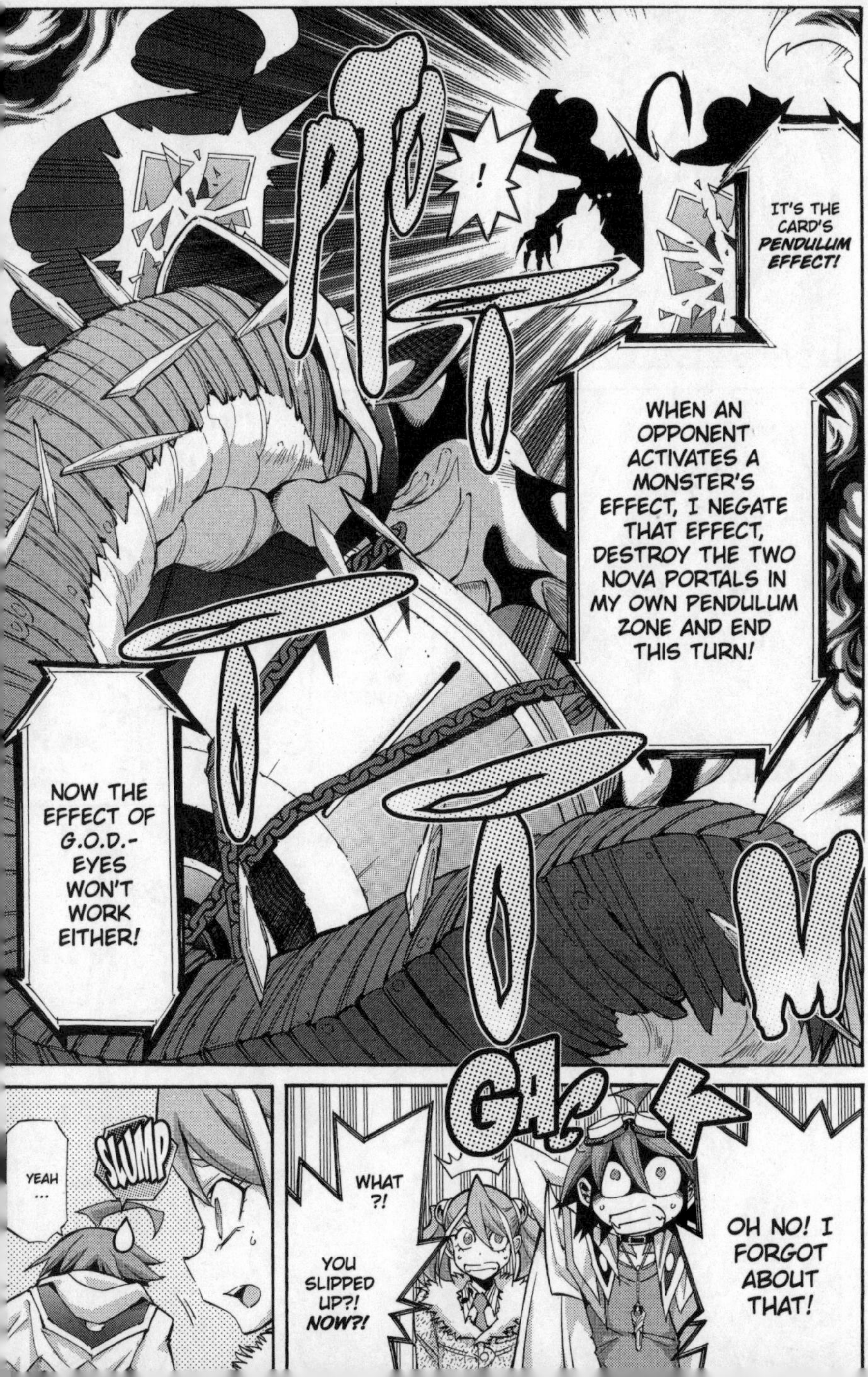
IT'S THE CARD'S *PENDULUM EFFECT!*
WHEN AN OPPONENT ACTIVATES A MONSTER'S EFFECT, I NEGATE THAT EFFECT, DESTROY THE TWO NOVA PORTALS IN MY OWN PENDULUM ZONE AND END THIS TURN!
NOW THE EFFECT OF G.O.D.-EYES WON'T WORK EITHER!
GACK
OH NO! I FORGOT ABOUT THAT!
WHAT?!
YOU SLIPPED UP?! *NOW?!*
SLUMP
YEAH...

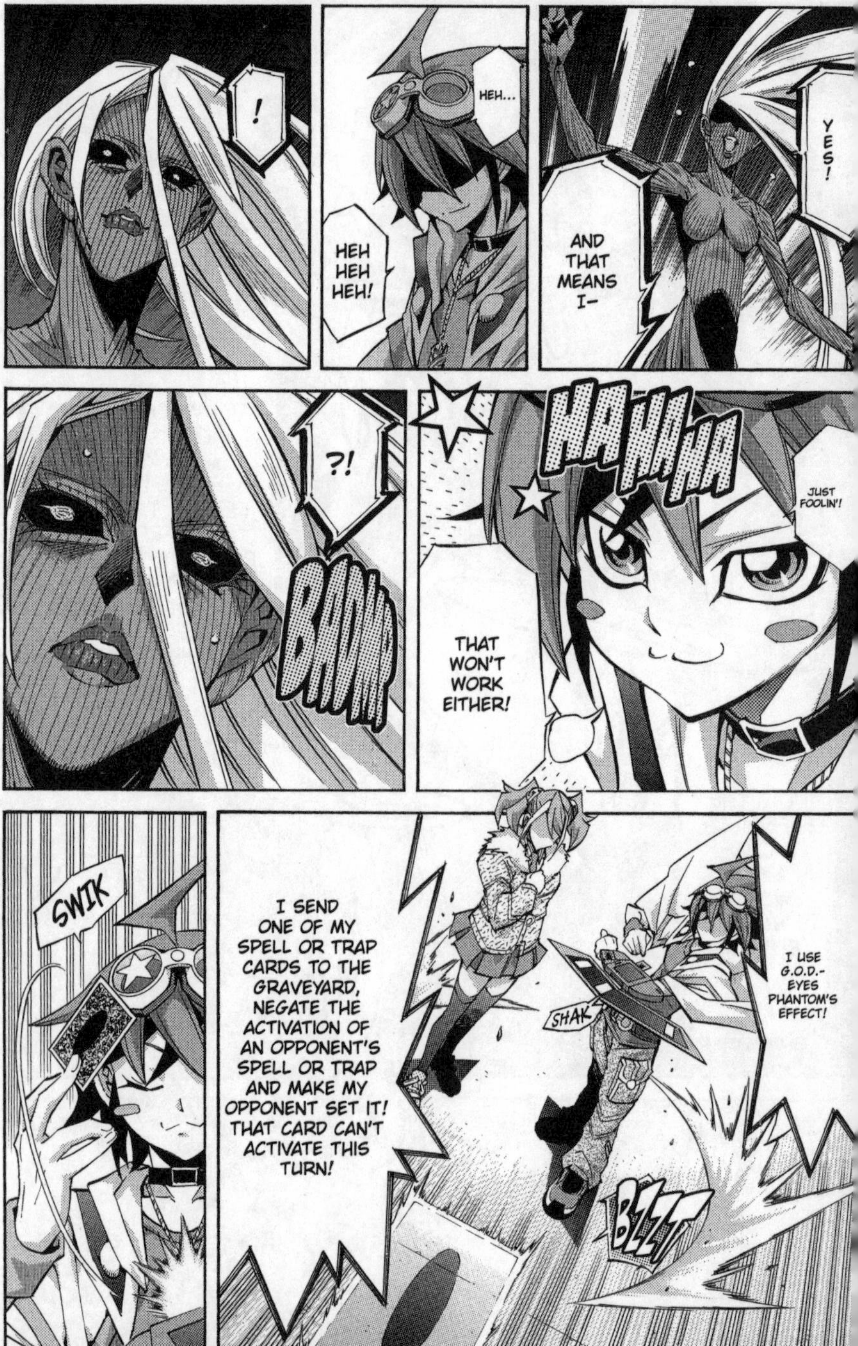
YES!
AND THAT MEANS I–
HEH...
HEH HEH HEH!
!
HAHAHA
JUST FOOLIN'!
THAT WON'T WORK EITHER!
?!
I USE G.O.D.-EYES PHANTOM'S EFFECT!
SHAK
I SEND ONE OF MY SPELL OR TRAP CARDS TO THE GRAVEYARD, NEGATE THE ACTIVATION OF AN OPPONENT'S SPELL OR TRAP AND MAKE MY OPPONENT SET IT! THAT CARD CAN'T ACTIVATE THIS TURN!
BZZT
SWIK

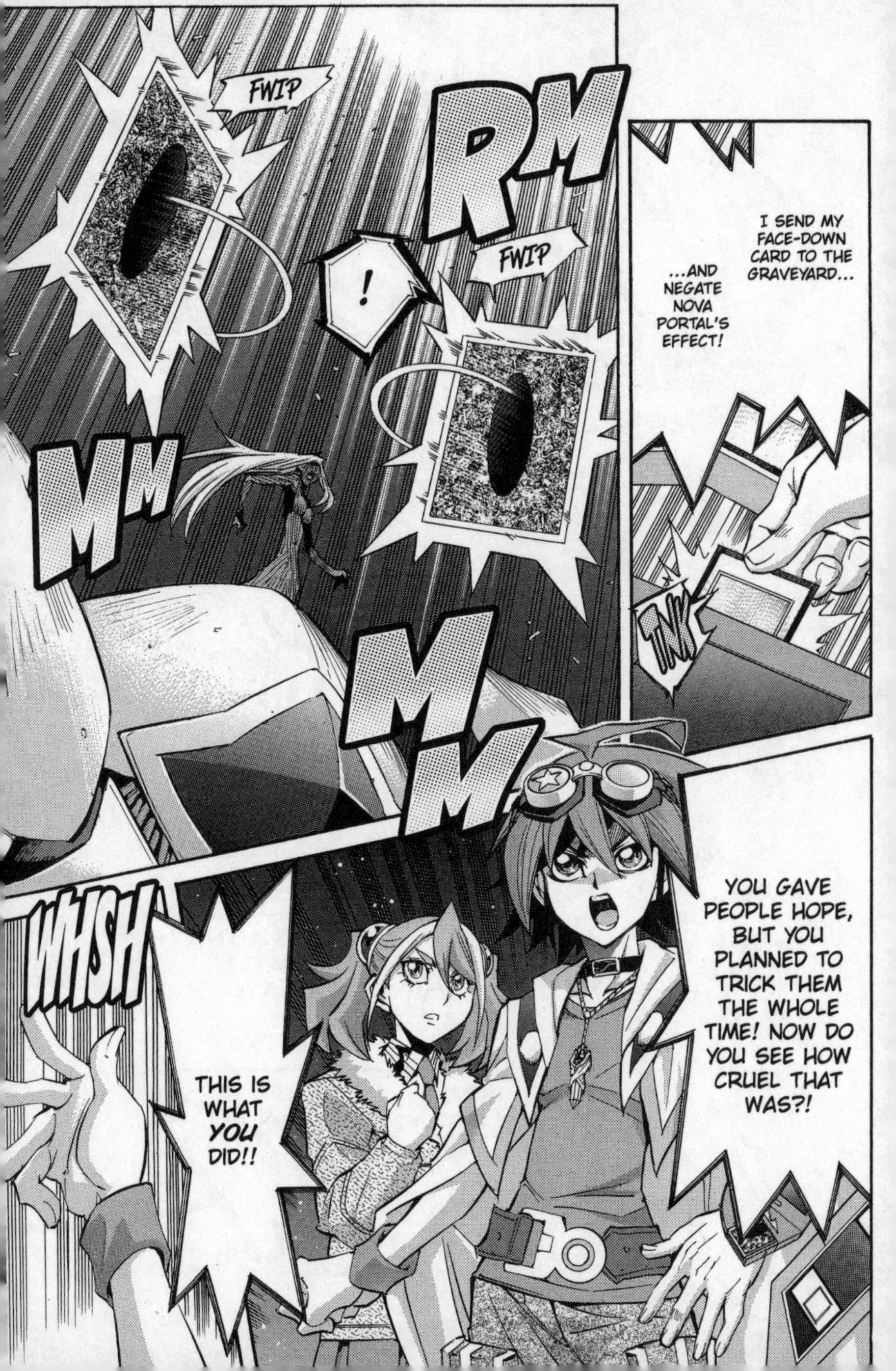
I SEND MY FACE-DOWN CARD TO THE GRAVEYARD...
...AND NEGATE NOVA PORTAL'S EFFECT!
TNK
RM
FWIP
FWIP
!
MM
MM
YOU GAVE PEOPLE HOPE, BUT YOU PLANNED TO TRICK THEM THE WHOLE TIME! NOW DO YOU SEE HOW CRUEL THAT WAS?!
THIS IS WHAT YOU DID!!
WHSH

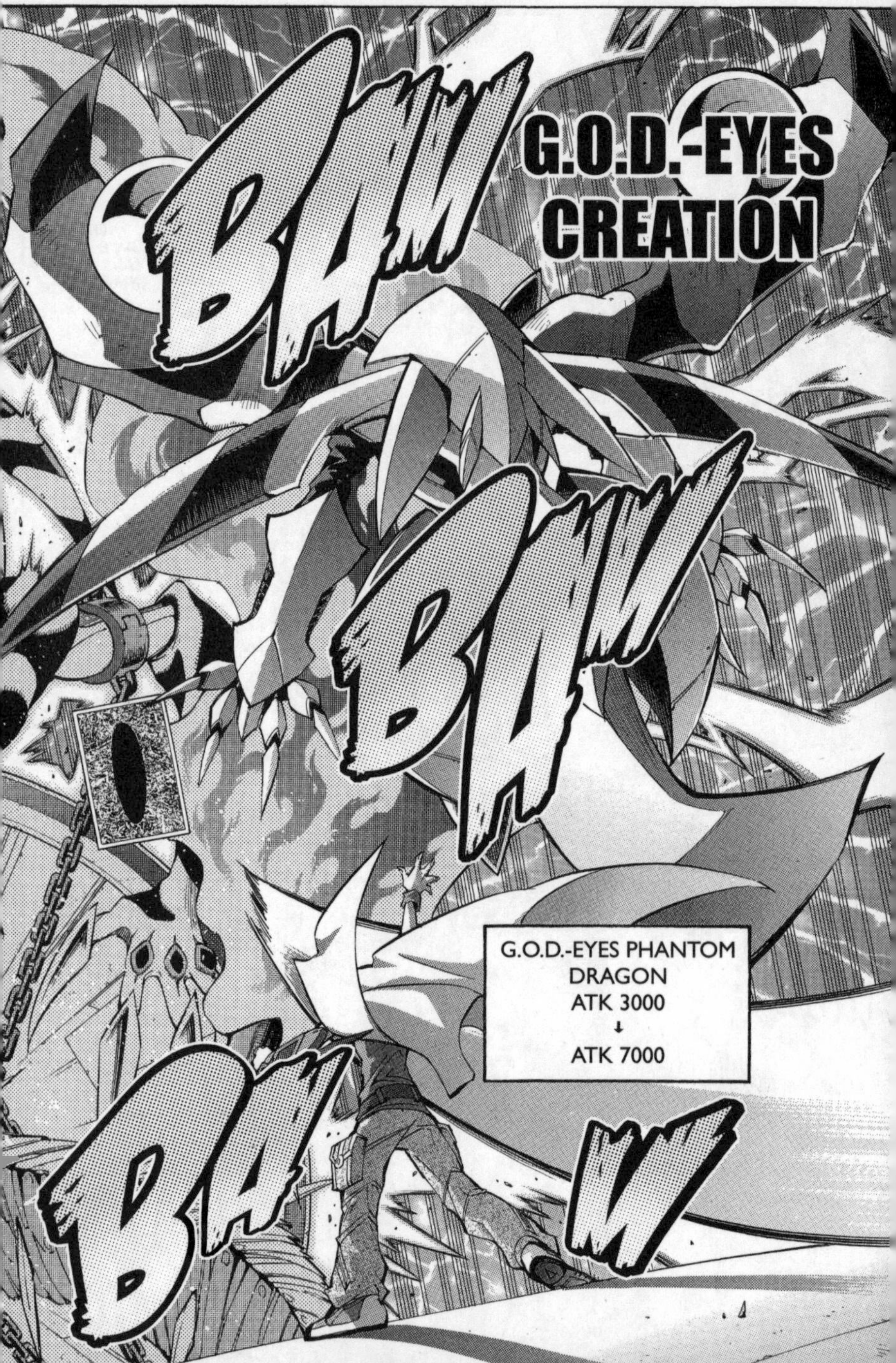
G.O.D.-EYES CREATION
BAM
BAM
G.O.D.-EYES PHANTOM DRAGON ATK 3000 ↓ ATK 7000
BAM

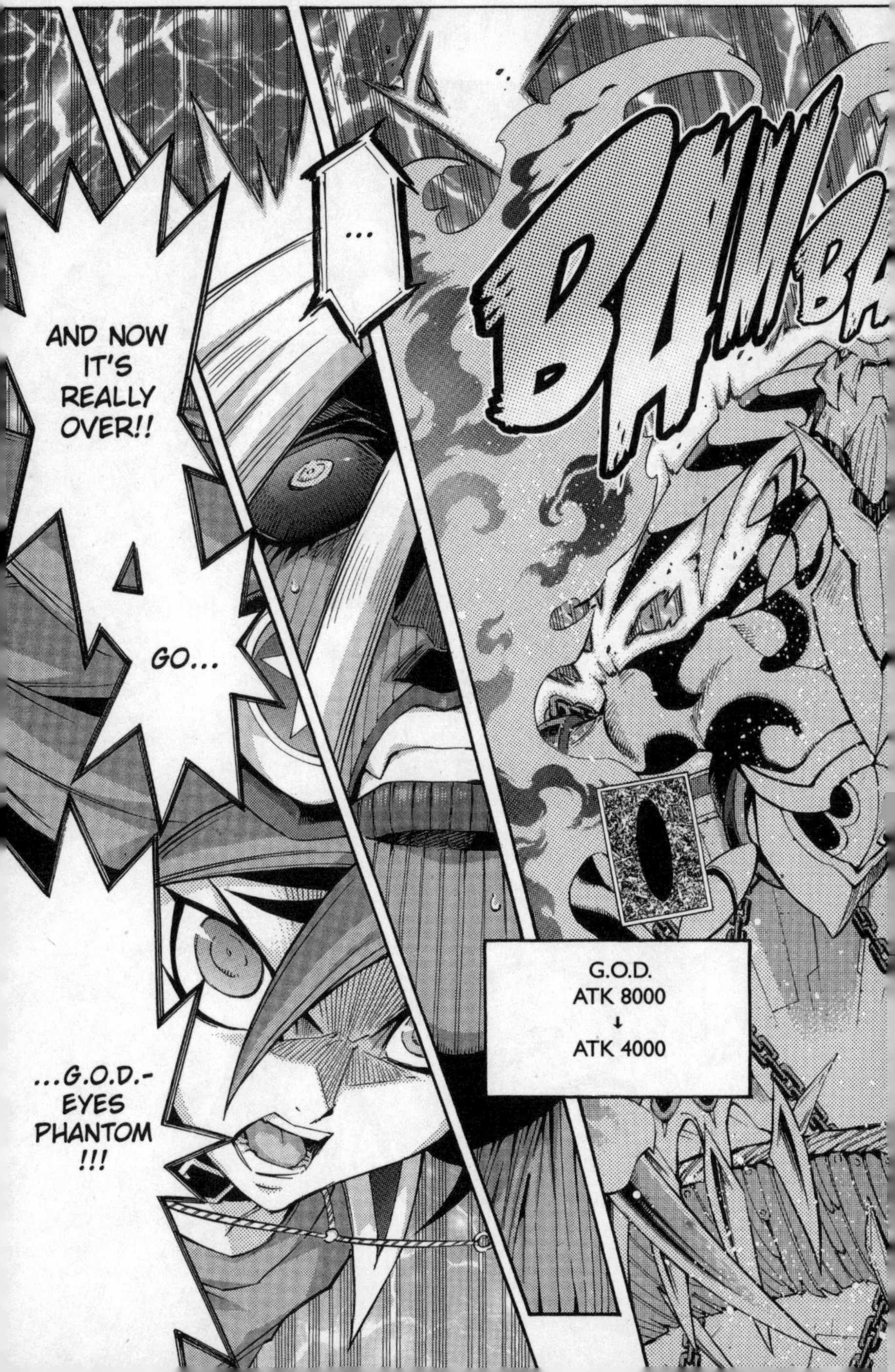

BAM BA
G.O.D. ATK 8000 ↓ ATK 4000
...
AND NOW IT'S REALLY OVER!!
GO...
...G.O.D.-EYES PHANTOM!!!

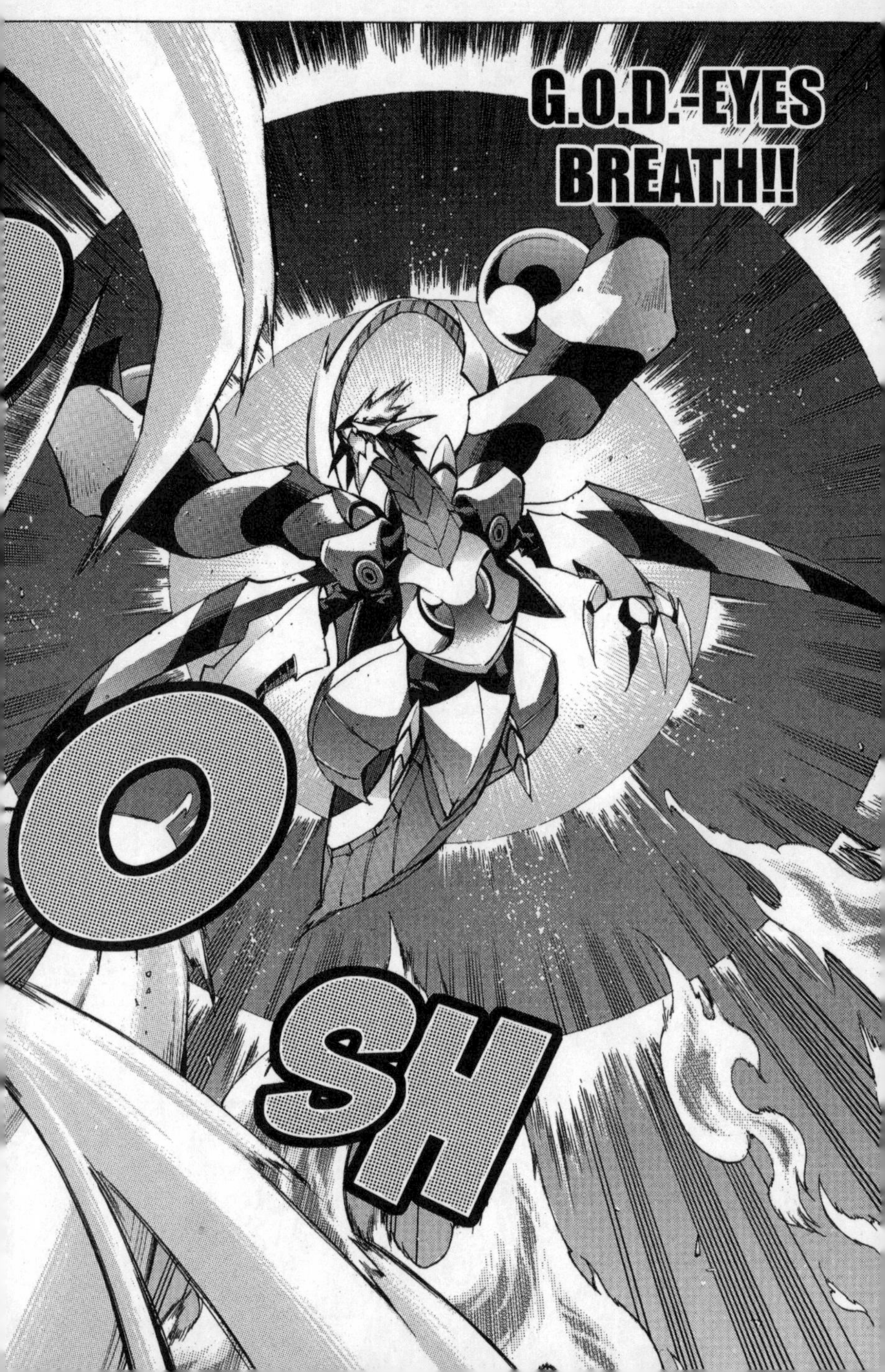
G.O.D.-EYES BREATH!!
OSH

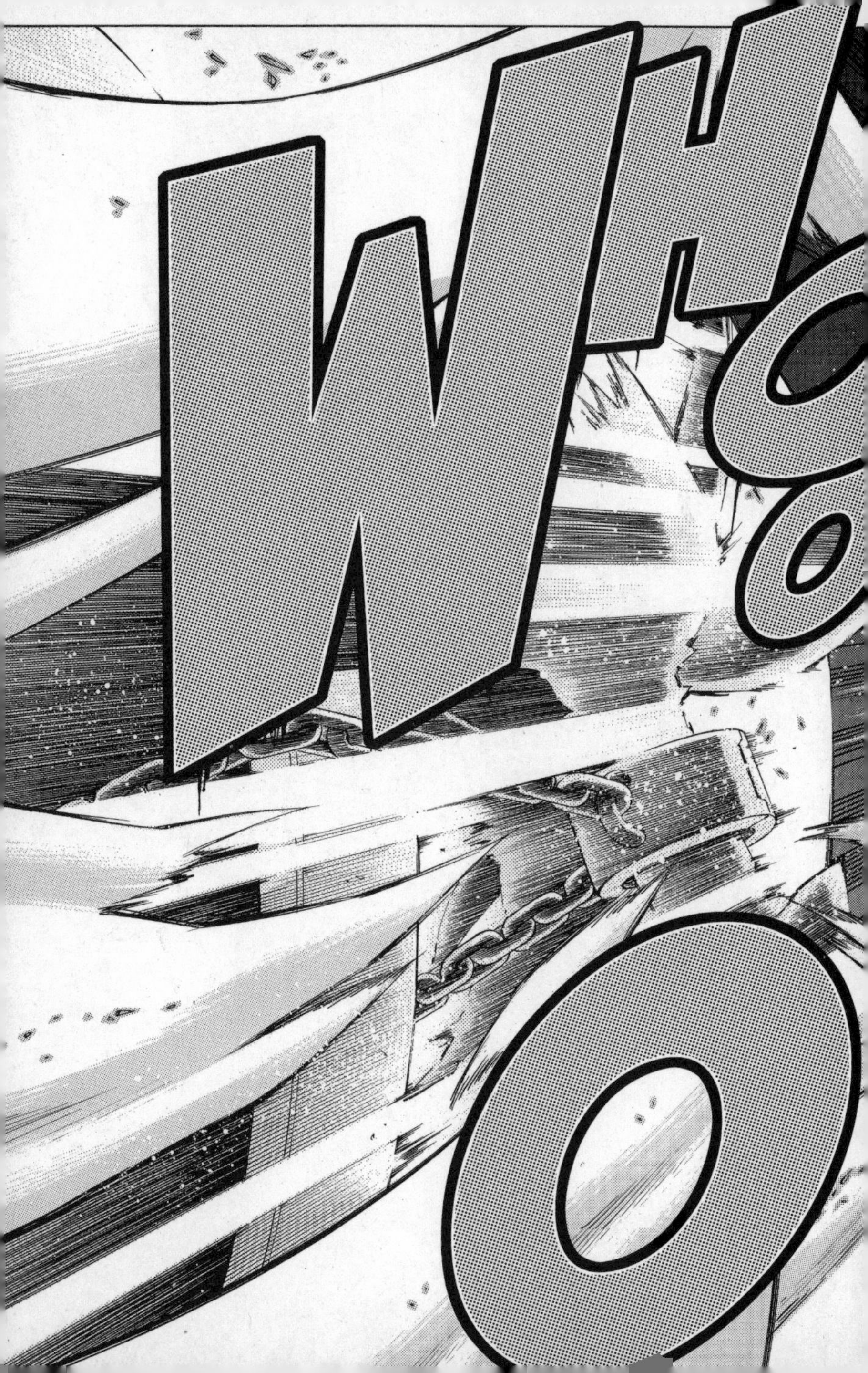
WHOO

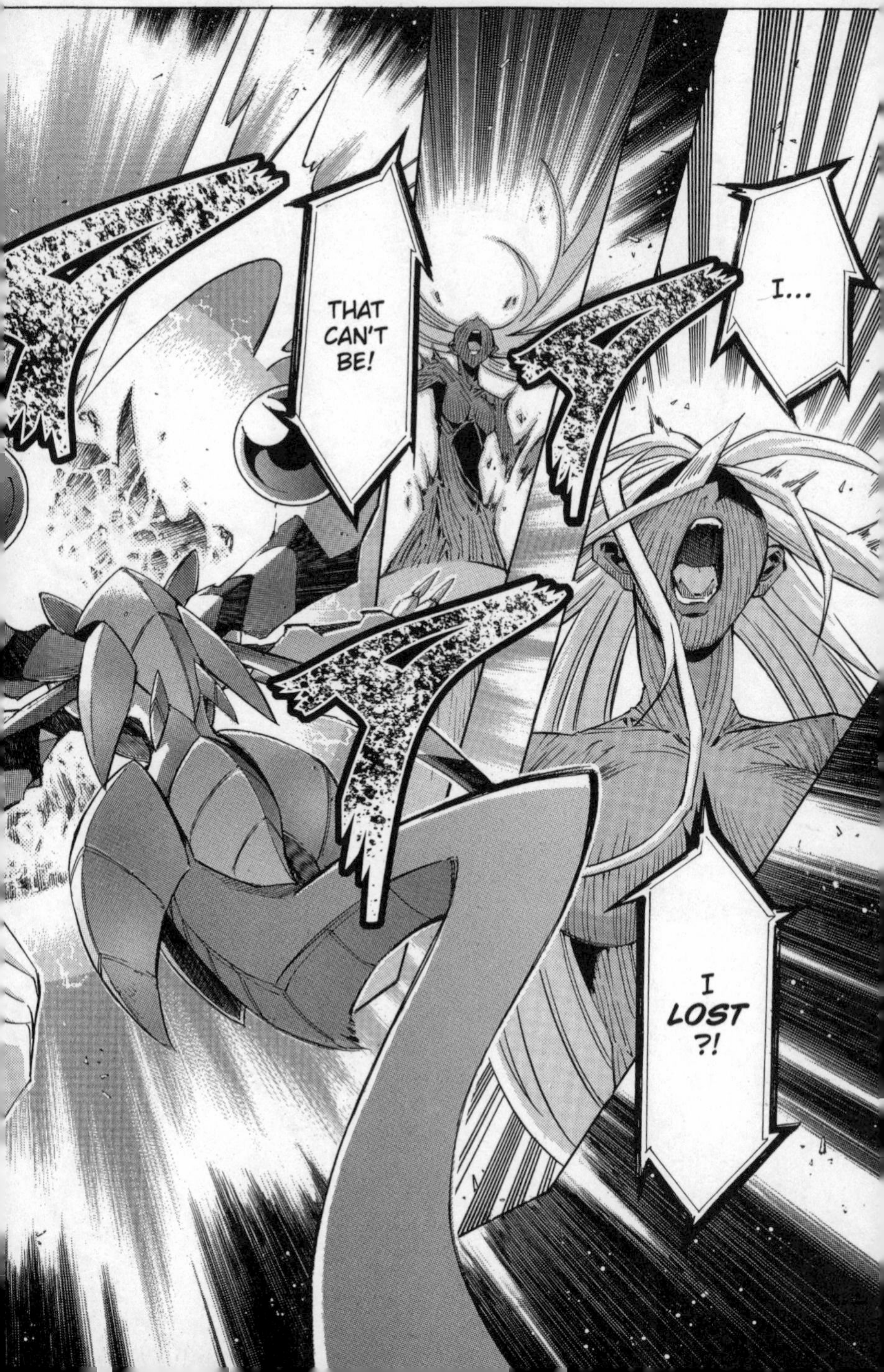
I...
THAT CAN'T BE!
I LOST?!

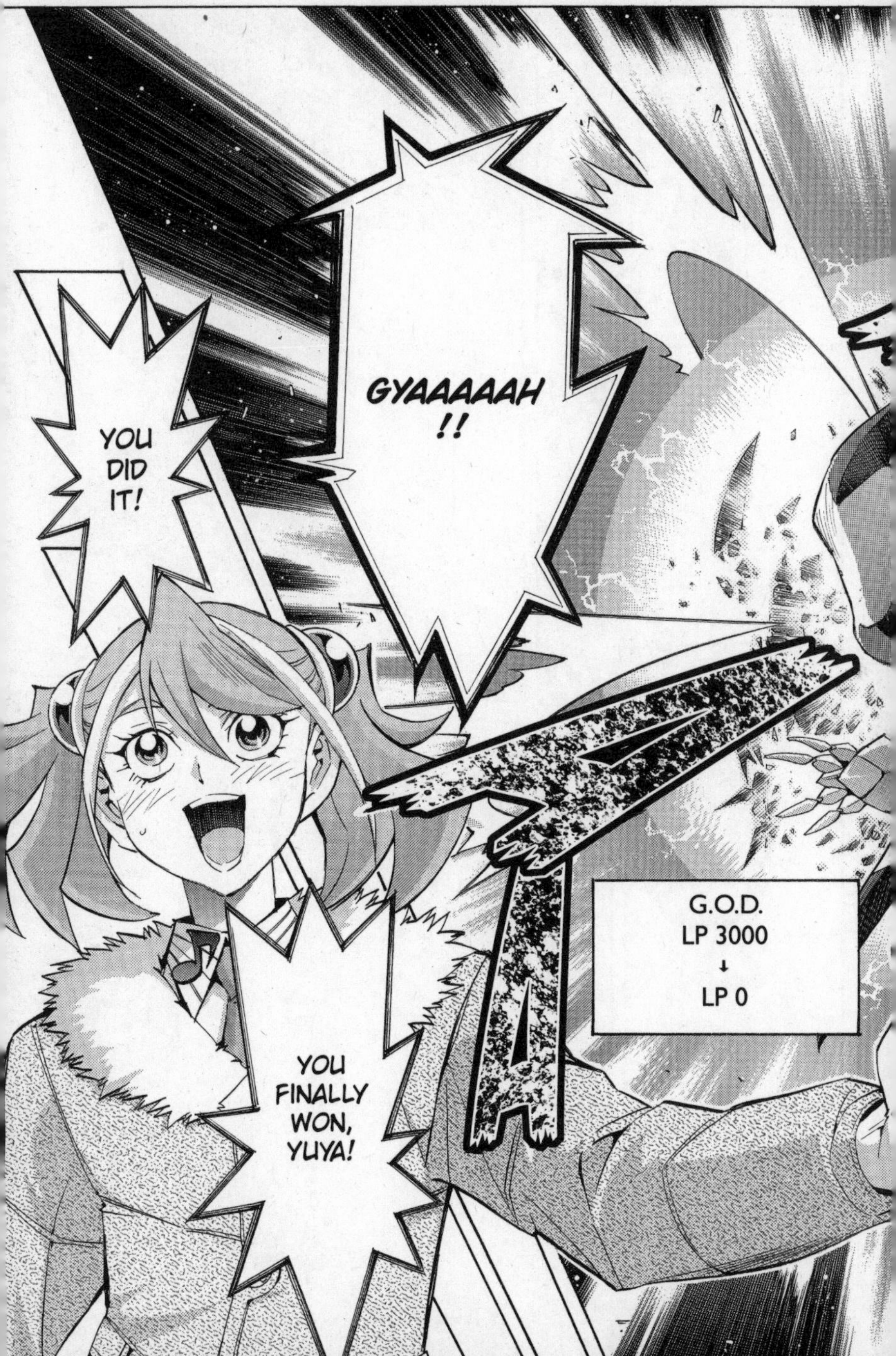
GYAAAAAH!!
YOU DID IT!
G.O.D. LP 3000 ↓ LP 0
YOU FINALLY WON, YUYA!

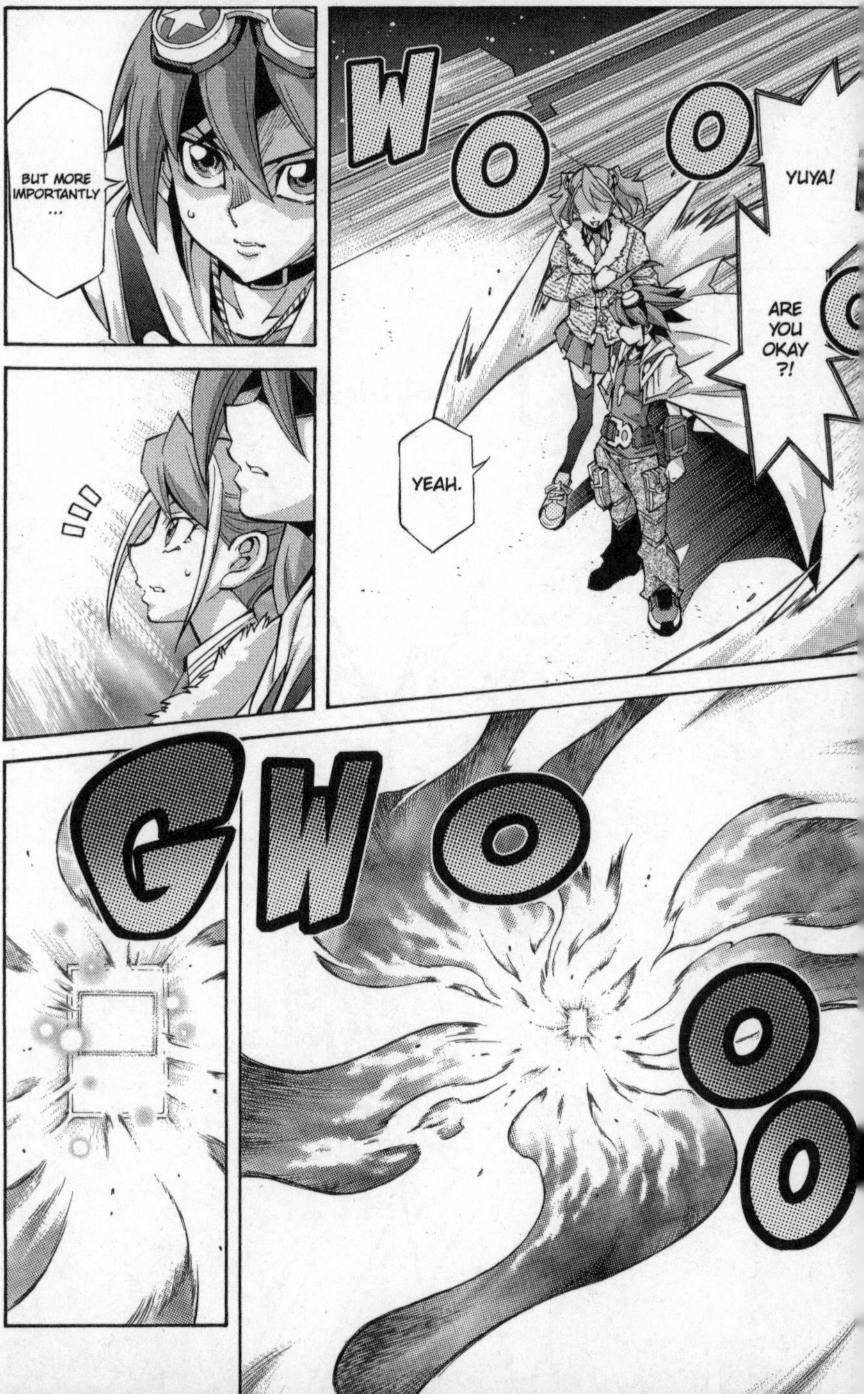
WOOO
YUYA!
ARE YOU OKAY ?!
YEAH.
BUT MORE IMPORTANTLY ...
GWOOOO

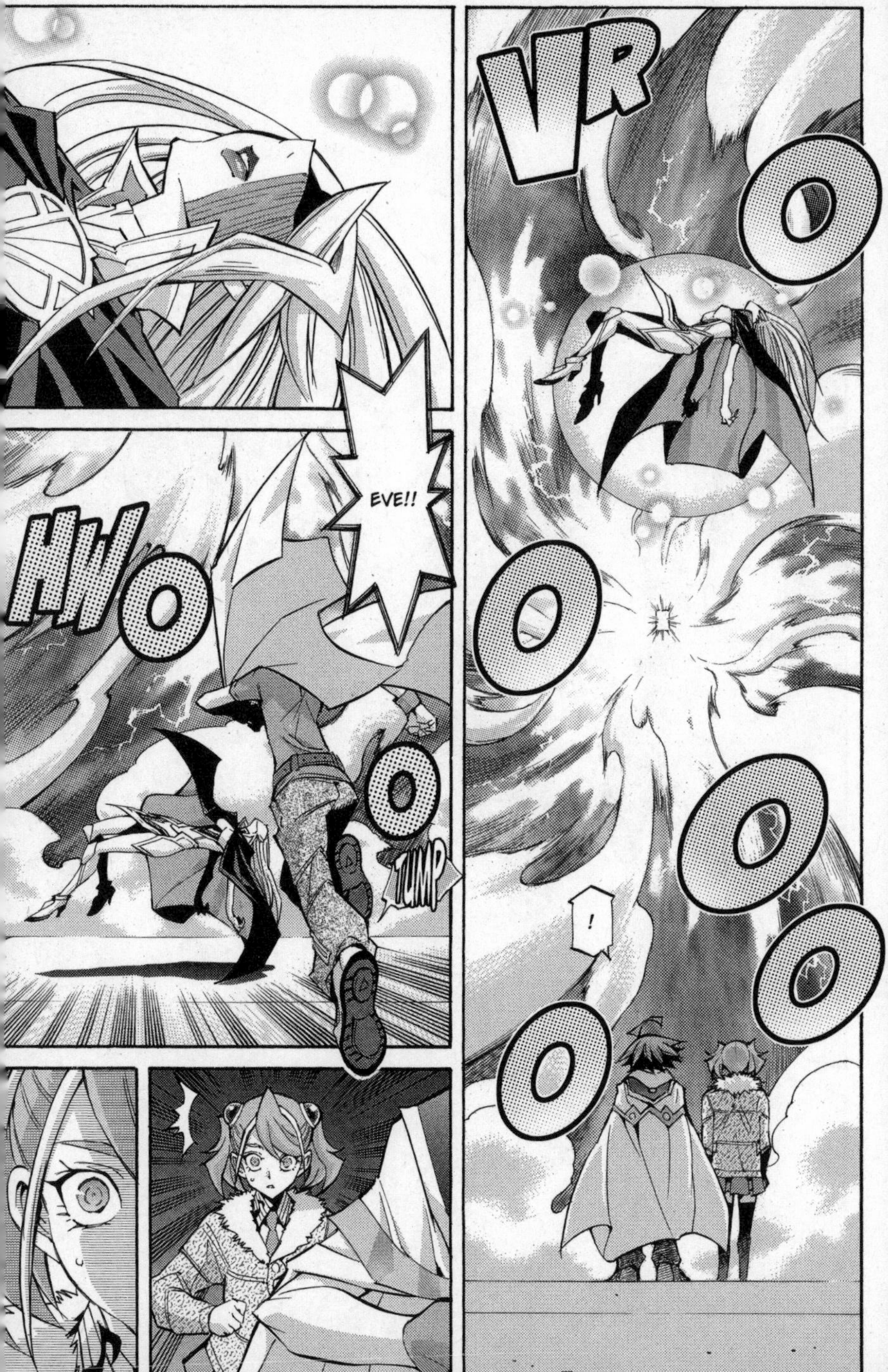
VROOOOO
!
EVE!!
HWOO
TUMP

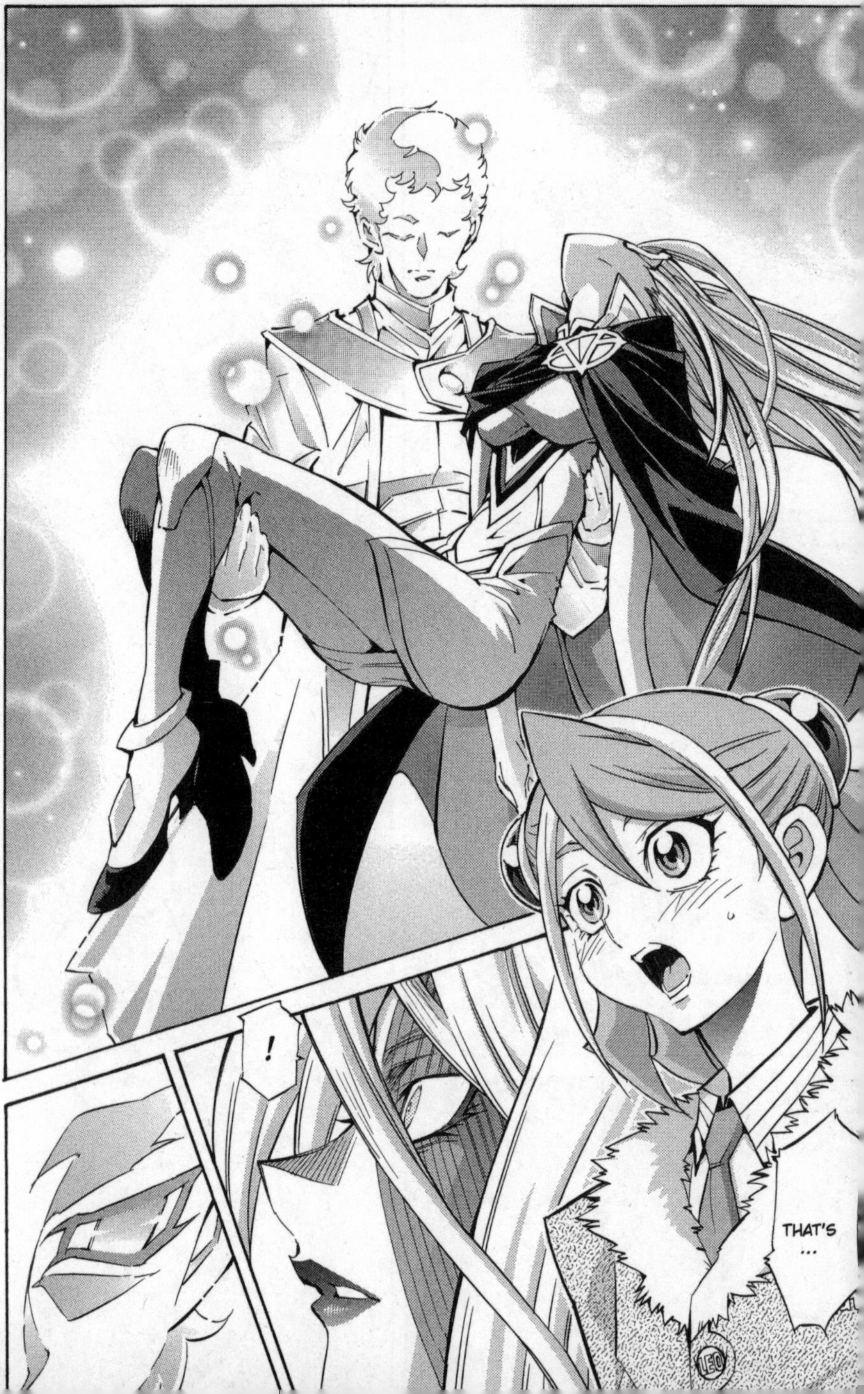
THAT'S ...
!

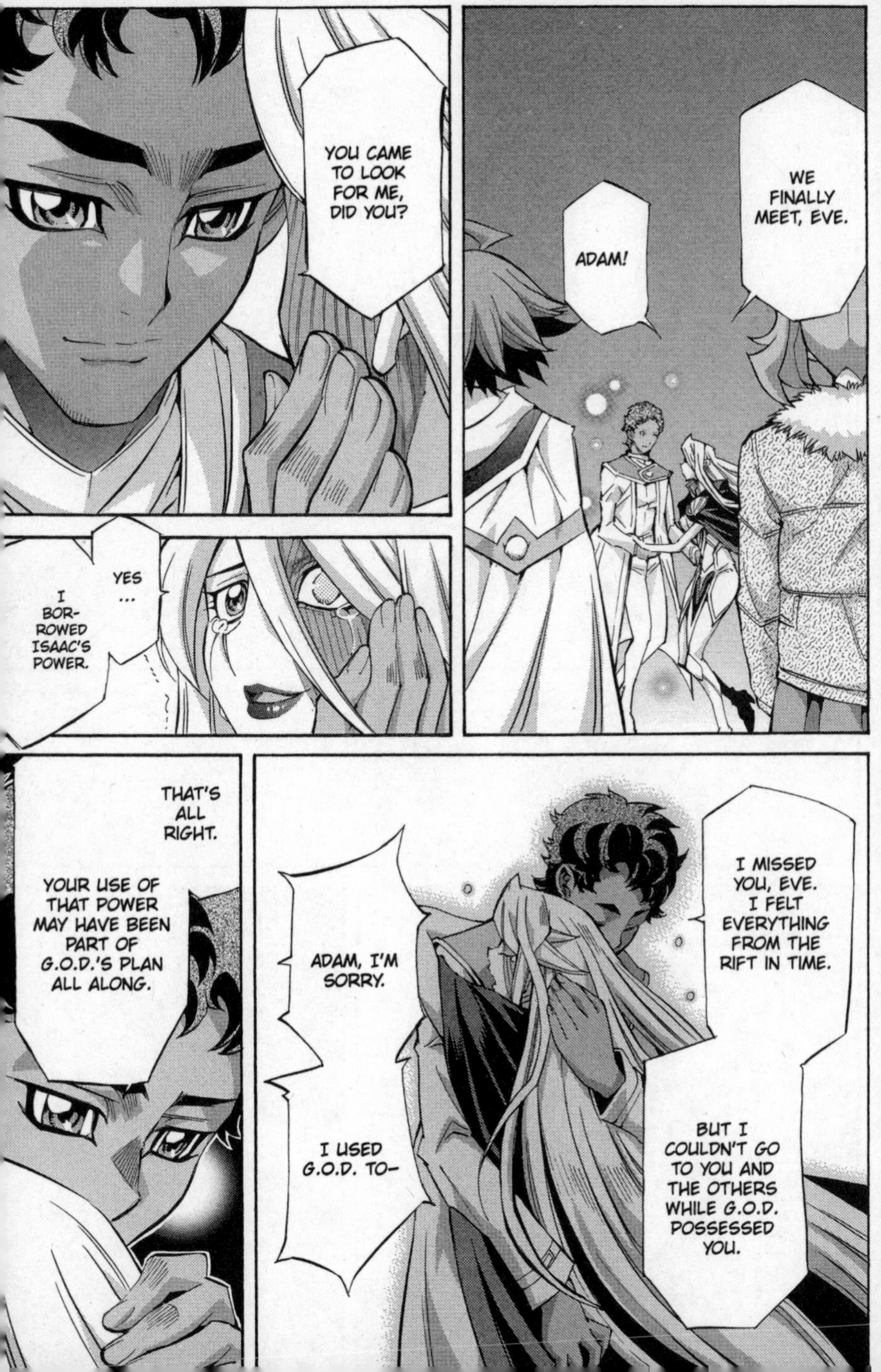
WE FINALLY MEET, EVE.
ADAM!
YOU CAME TO LOOK FOR ME, DID YOU?
YES... I BORROWED ISAAC'S POWER.
I MISSED YOU, EVE. I FELT EVERYTHING FROM THE RIFT IN TIME.
BUT I COULDN'T GO TO YOU AND THE OTHERS WHILE G.O.D. POSSESSED YOU.
ADAM, I'M SORRY.
I USED G.O.D. TO–
THAT'S ALL RIGHT.
YOUR USE OF THAT POWER MAY HAVE BEEN PART OF G.O.D.'S PLAN ALL ALONG.

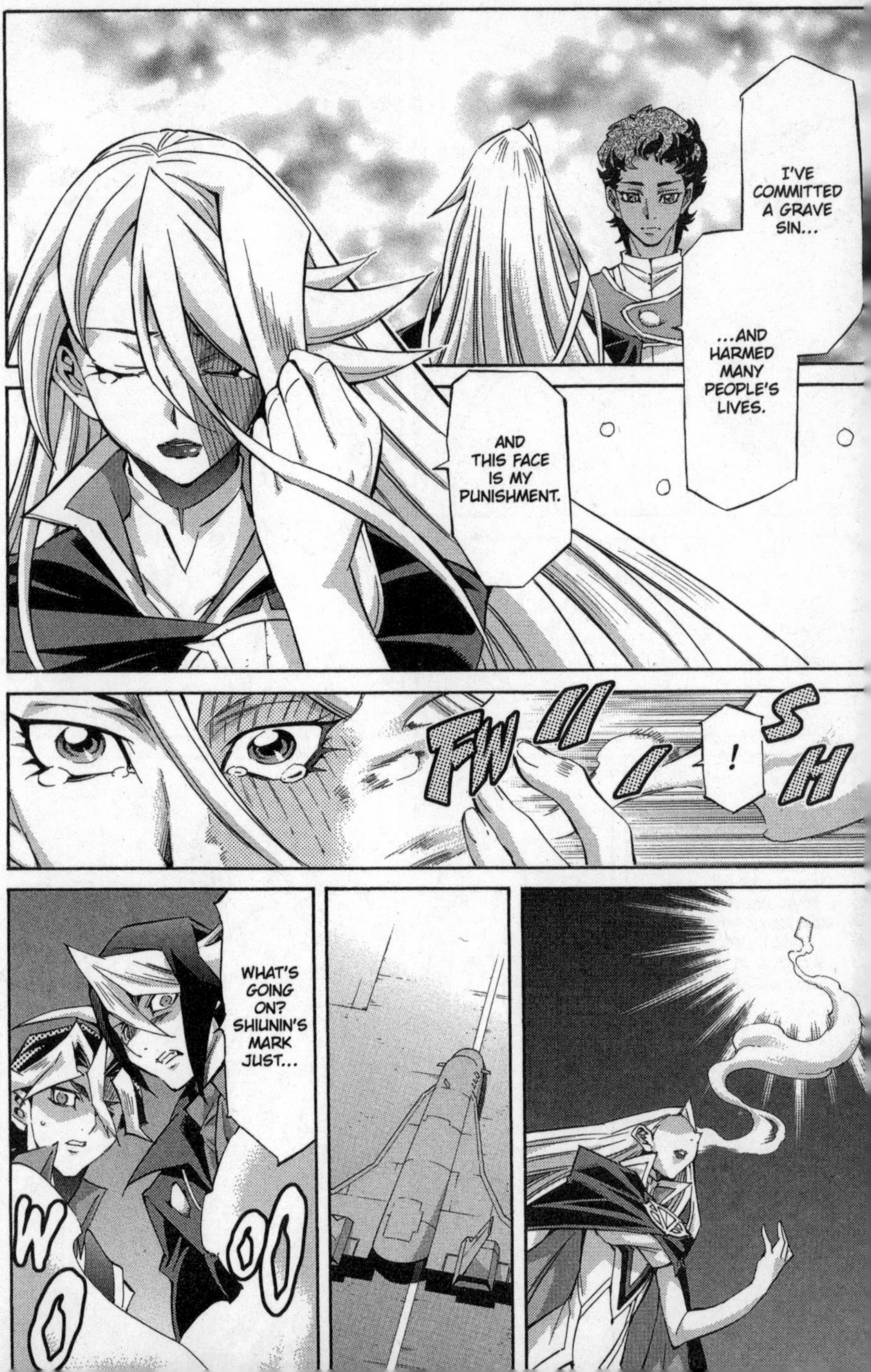
I'VE COMMITTED A GRAVE SIN...
...AND HARMED MANY PEOPLE'S LIVES.
AND THIS FACE IS MY PUNISHMENT.
!
FWIISH
WHAT'S GOING ON? SHIUNIN'S MARK JUST...
WOOO

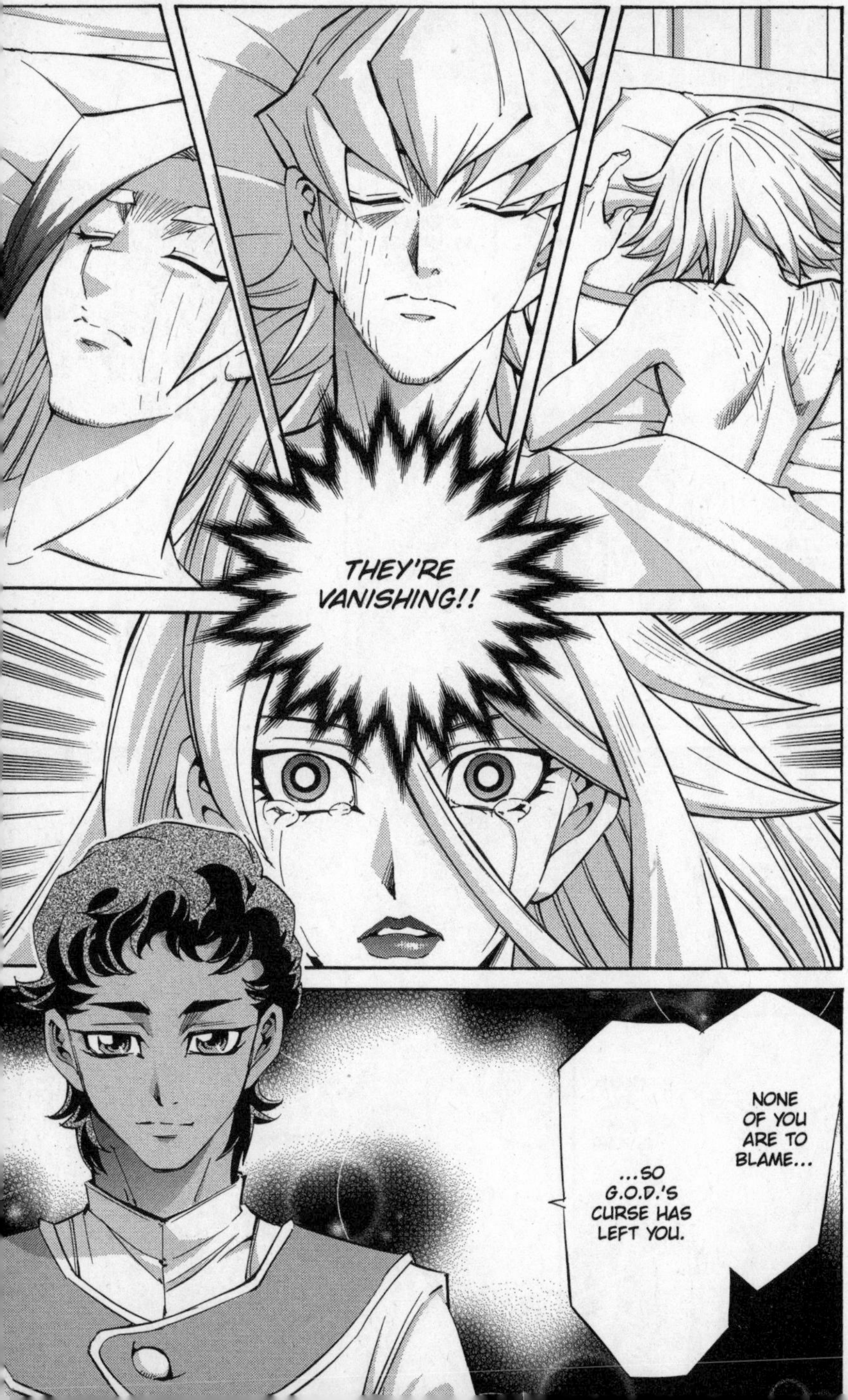
THEY'RE VANISHING!!
NONE OF YOU ARE TO BLAME...
...SO G.O.D.'S CURSE HAS LEFT YOU.

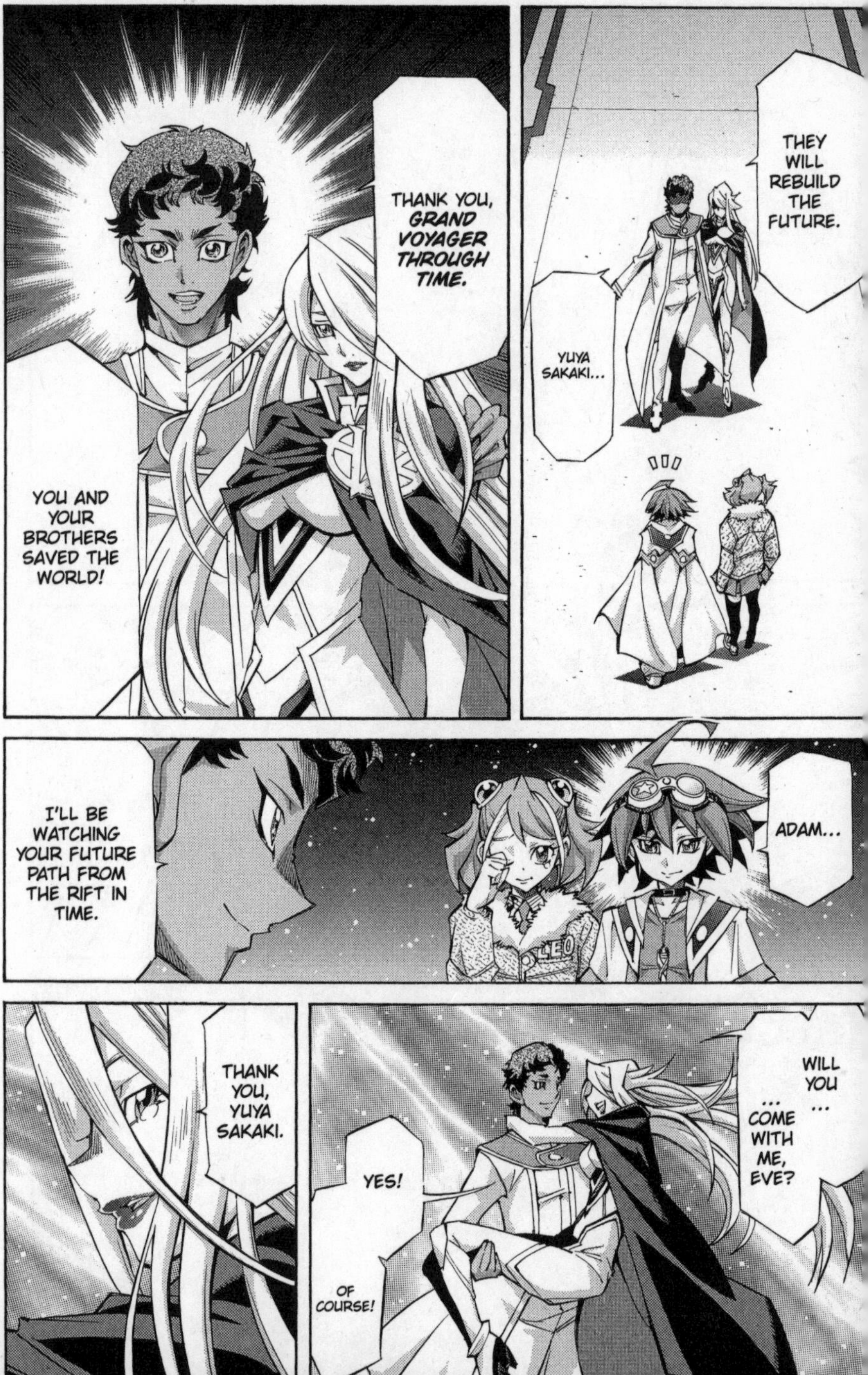
THEY WILL REBUILD THE FUTURE.
YUYA SAKAKI...
THANK YOU, GRAND VOYAGER THROUGH TIME.
YOU AND YOUR BROTHERS SAVED THE WORLD!
ADAM...
I'LL BE WATCHING YOUR FUTURE PATH FROM THE RIFT IN TIME.
WILL YOU ... COME WITH ME, EVE?
YES!
OF COURSE!
THANK YOU, YUYA SAKAKI.

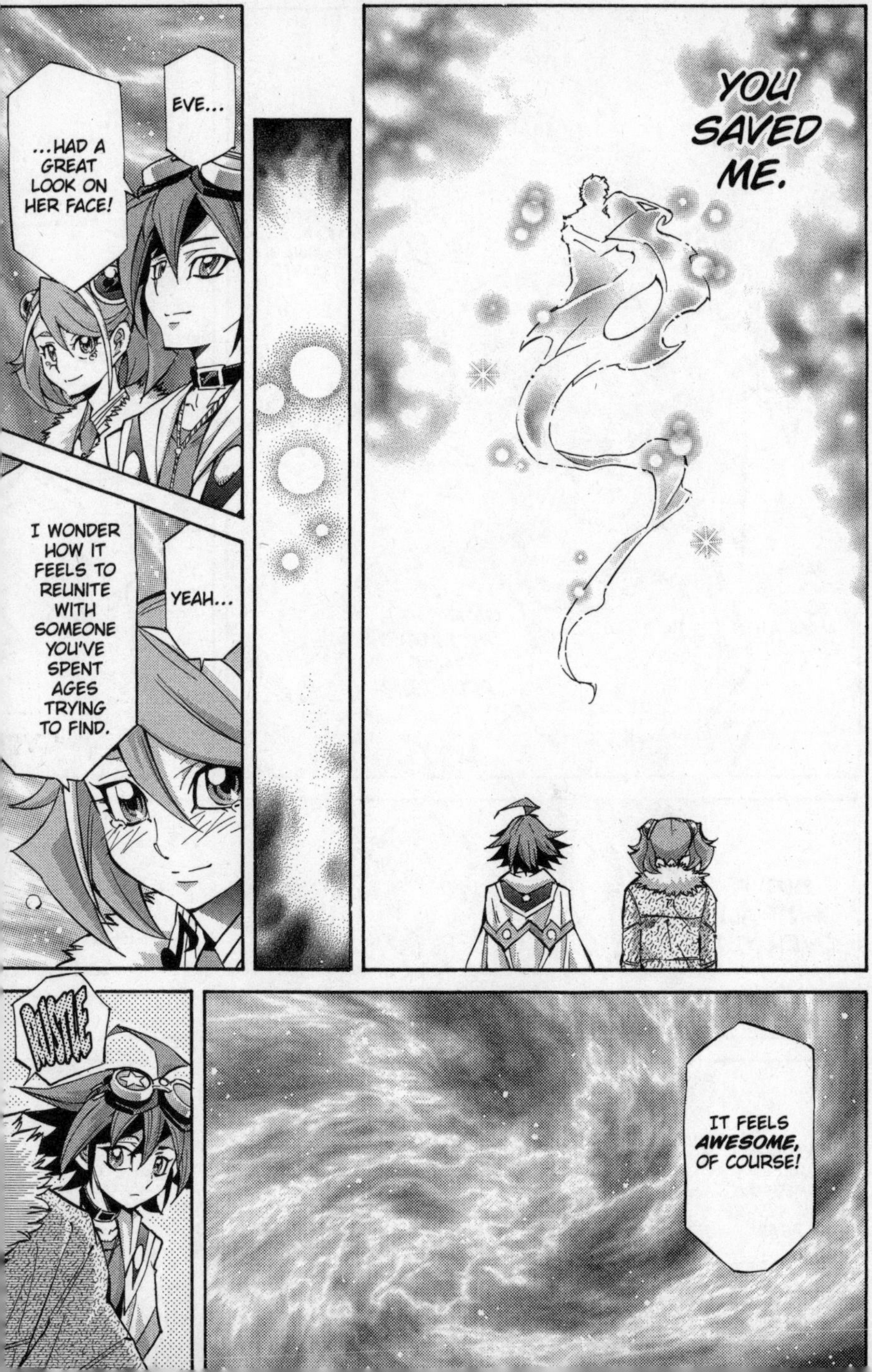
YOU SAVED ME.
EVE...
...HAD A GREAT LOOK ON HER FACE!
YEAH...
I WONDER HOW IT FEELS TO REUNITE WITH SOMEONE YOU'VE SPENT AGES TRYING TO FIND.
IT FEELS **AWESOME,** OF COURSE!
RUSTLE

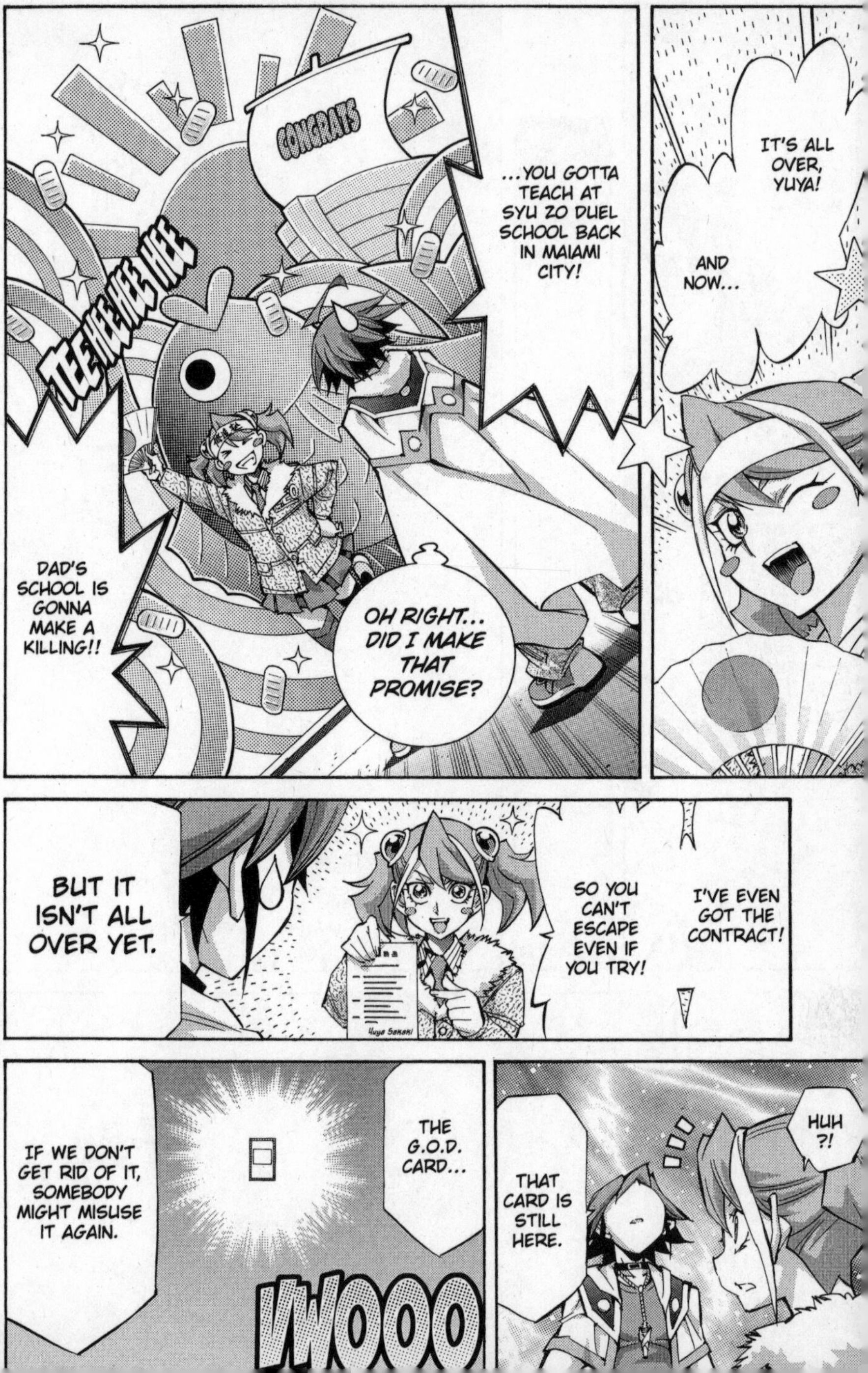
IT'S ALL OVER, YUYA!
AND NOW...
...YOU GOTTA TEACH AT SYU ZO DUEL SCHOOL BACK IN MAIAMI CITY!
CONGRATS
TEE HEE HEE HEE
OH RIGHT... DID I MAKE THAT PROMISE?
DAD'S SCHOOL IS GONNA MAKE A KILLING!!
I'VE EVEN GOT THE CONTRACT!
SO YOU CAN'T ESCAPE EVEN IF YOU TRY!
Yuya Sakaki
BUT IT ISN'T ALL OVER YET.
HUH ?!
THAT CARD IS STILL HERE.
THE G.O.D. CARD...
IF WE DON'T GET RID OF IT, SOMEBODY MIGHT MISUSE IT AGAIN.
VWOOO

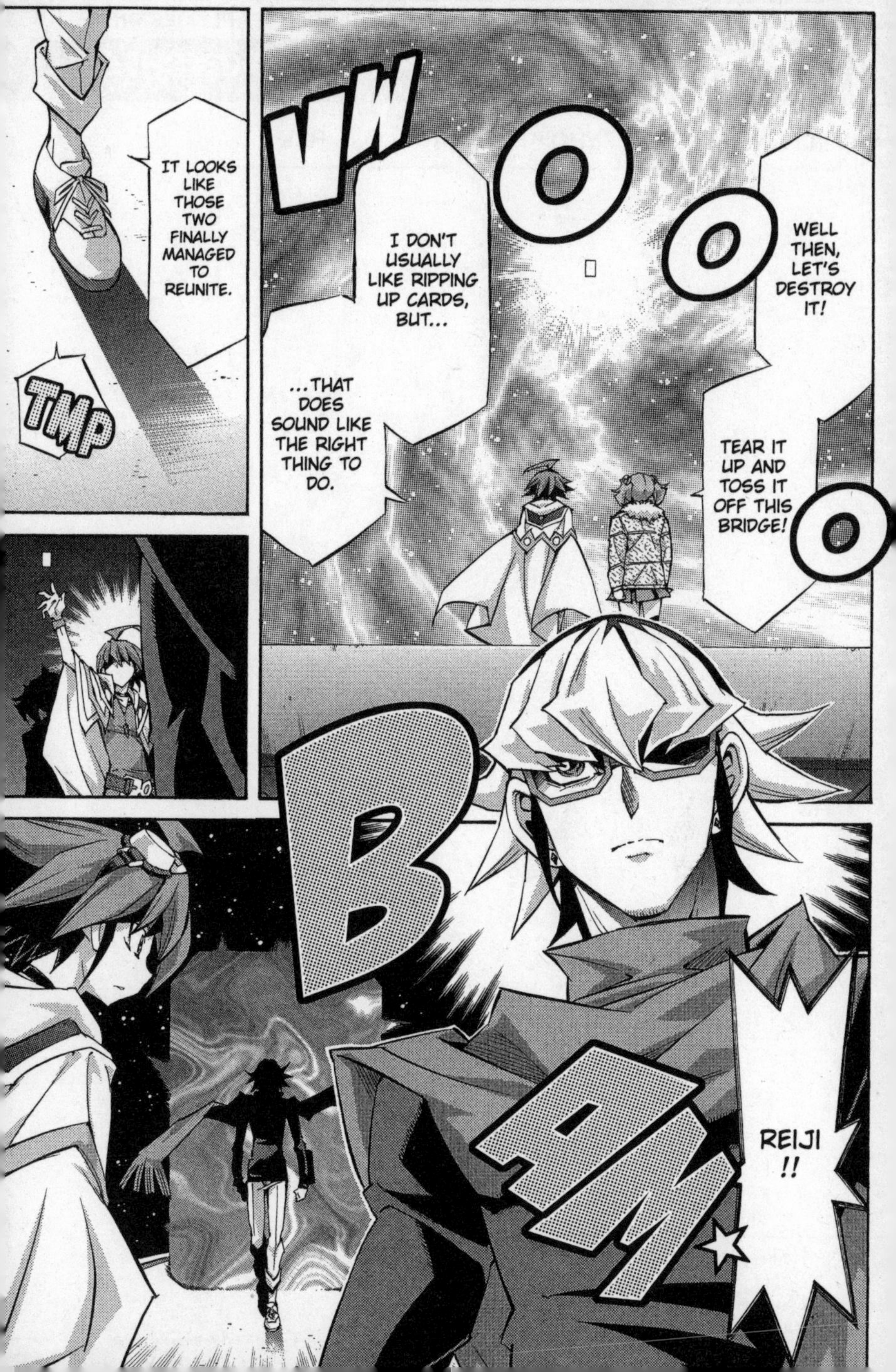
WELL THEN, LET'S DESTROY IT!
TEAR IT UP AND TOSS IT OFF THIS BRIDGE!
VWOOOO
I DON'T USUALLY LIKE RIPPING UP CARDS, BUT...
...THAT DOES SOUND LIKE THE RIGHT THING TO DO.
IT LOOKS LIKE THOSE TWO FINALLY MANAGED TO REUNITE.
TMP
REIJI!!
BAM

scale 28 ARC-V CHARACTER SKETCHES

DIVINE GO-D/D/D ZERO KING ZERO G.O.D. REIJI

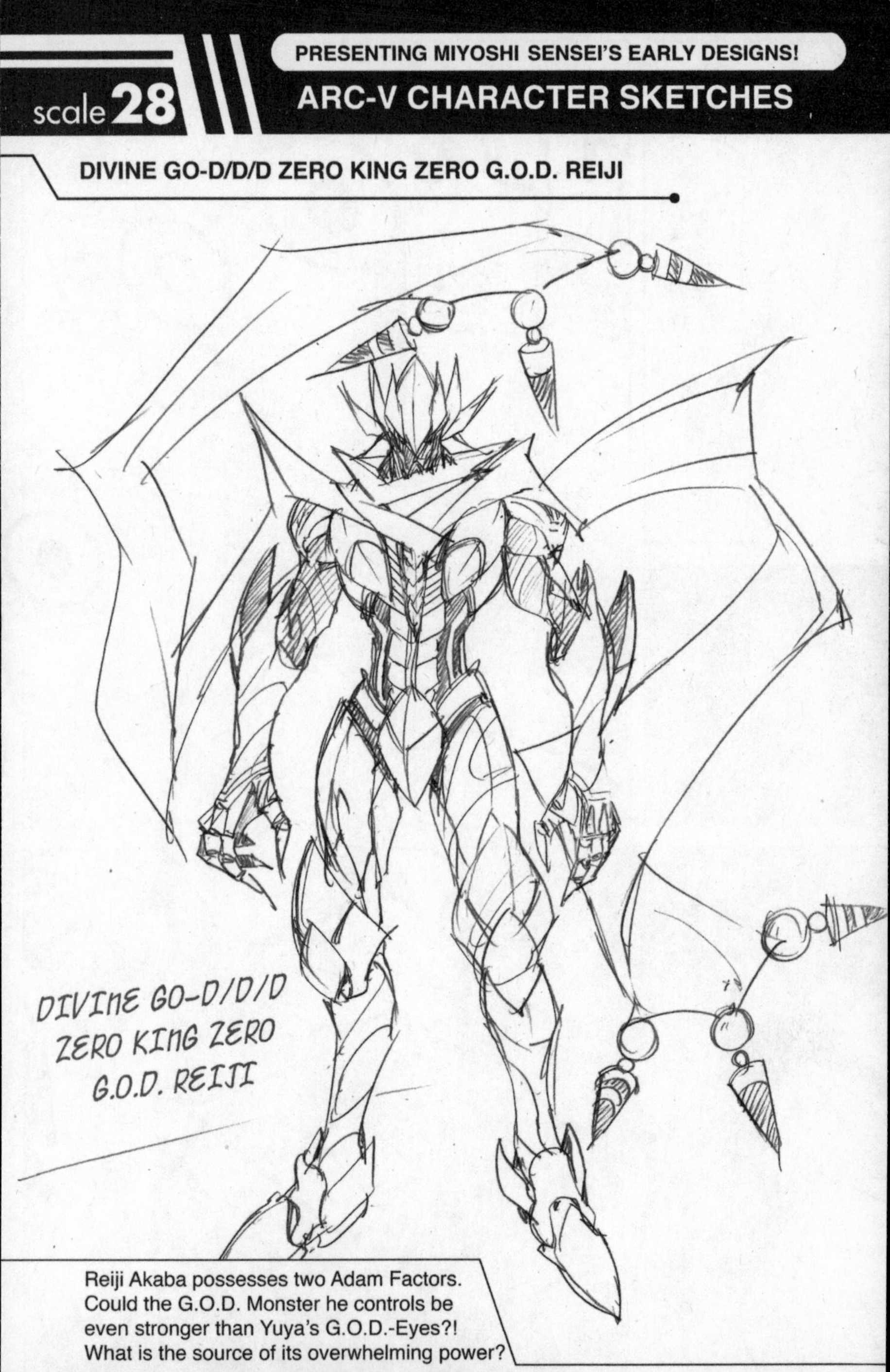
DIVINE GO-D/D/D
ZERO KING ZERO
G.O.D. REIJI

Reiji Akaba possesses two Adam Factors. Could the G.O.D. Monster he controls be even stronger than Yuya's G.O.D.-Eyes?! What is the source of its overwhelming power?

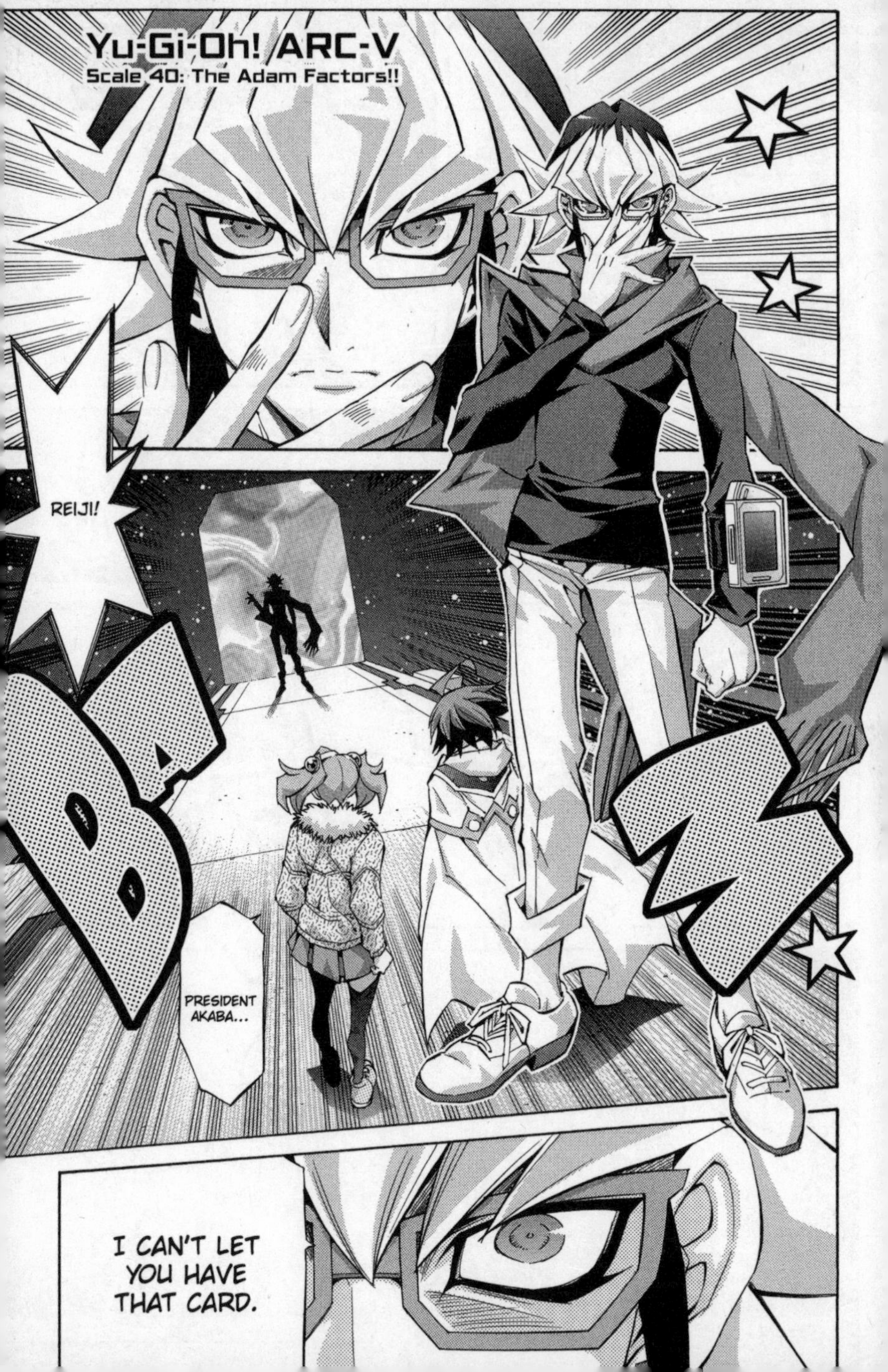
Yu-Gi-Oh! ARC-V
Scale 40: The Adam Factors!!
REIJI!
PRESIDENT AKABA...
I CAN'T LET YOU HAVE THAT CARD.

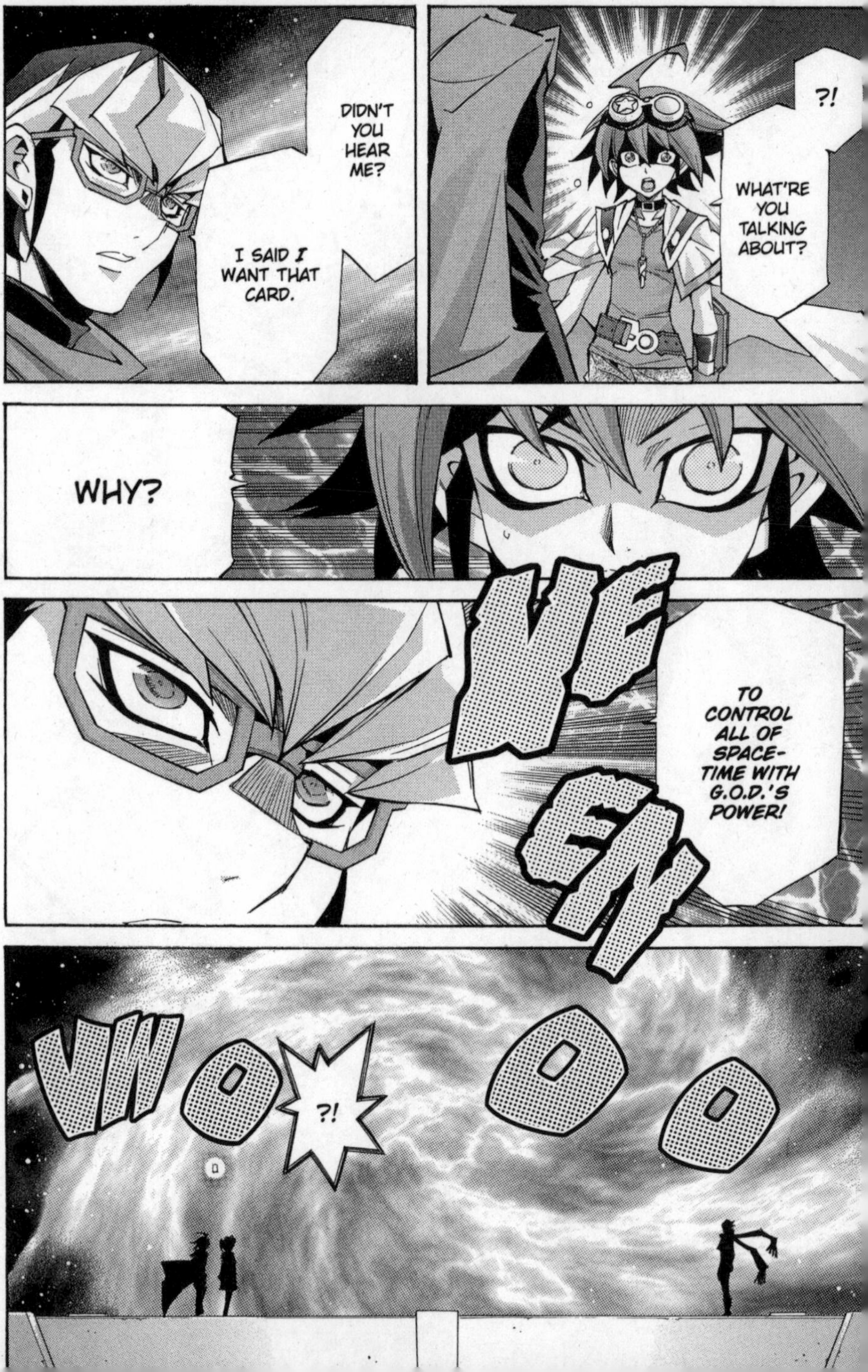
?!
WHAT'RE YOU TALKING ABOUT?
DIDN'T YOU HEAR ME?
I SAID I WANT THAT CARD.
WHY?
TO CONTROL ALL OF SPACE-TIME WITH G.O.D.'S POWER!
VEEN
VWOOO
?!

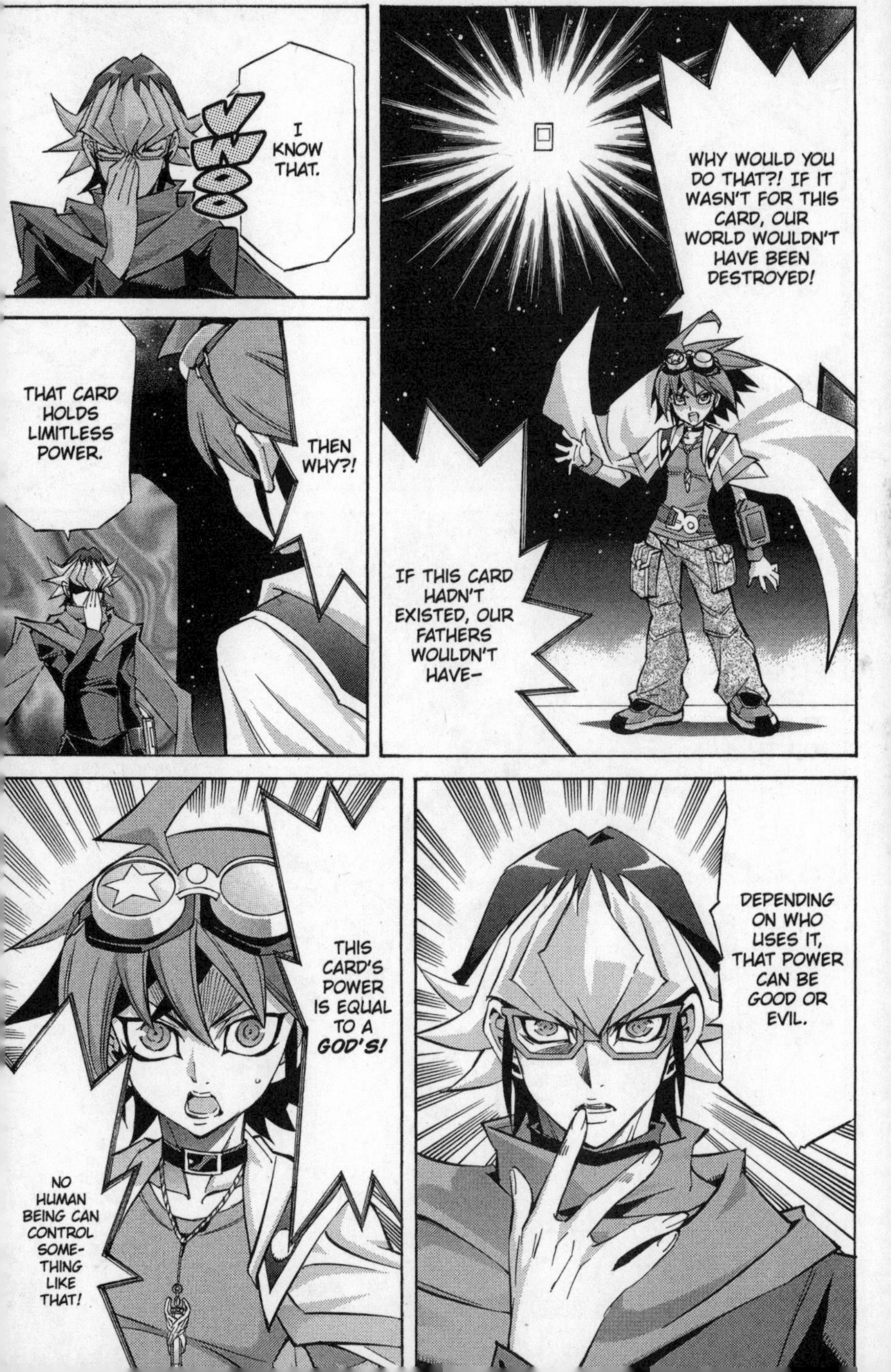
WHY WOULD YOU DO THAT?! IF IT WASN'T FOR THIS CARD, OUR WORLD WOULDN'T HAVE BEEN DESTROYED!
IF THIS CARD HADN'T EXISTED, OUR FATHERS WOULDN'T HAVE-
I KNOW THAT.
VWOO
THAT CARD HOLDS LIMITLESS POWER.
THEN WHY?!
DEPENDING ON WHO USES IT, THAT POWER CAN BE GOOD OR EVIL.
THIS CARD'S POWER IS EQUAL TO A *GOD'S!*
NO HUMAN BEING CAN CONTROL SOME-THING LIKE THAT!

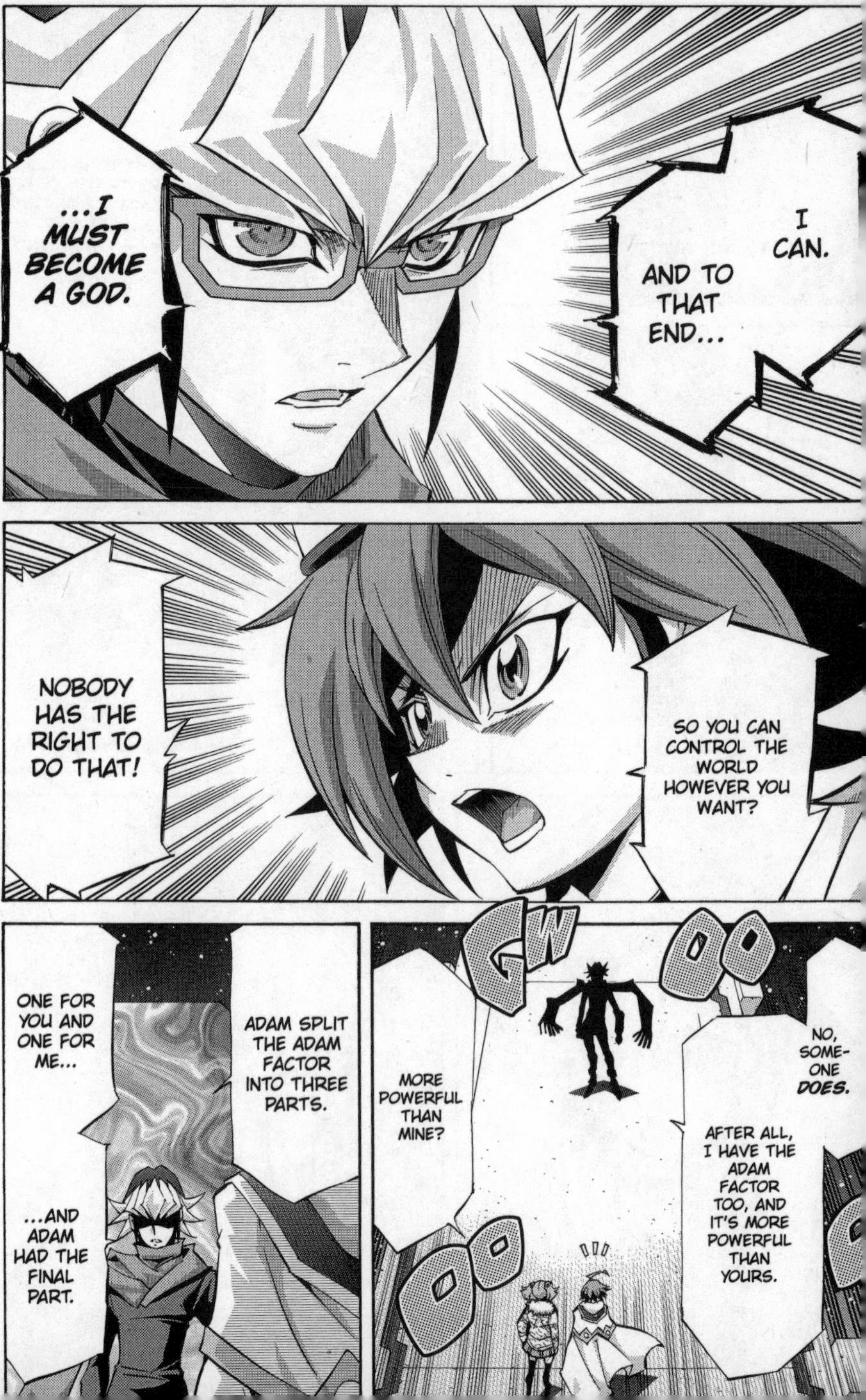
I CAN.
AND TO THAT END...
...I MUST BECOME A GOD.
SO YOU CAN CONTROL THE WORLD HOWEVER YOU WANT?
NOBODY HAS THE RIGHT TO DO THAT!
GW
OO
NO, SOME-ONE *DOES.*
AFTER ALL, I HAVE THE ADAM FACTOR TOO, AND IT'S MORE POWERFUL THAN YOURS.
MORE POWERFUL THAN MINE?
OO
ADAM SPLIT THE ADAM FACTOR INTO THREE PARTS.
ONE FOR YOU AND ONE FOR ME...
...AND ADAM HAD THE FINAL PART.

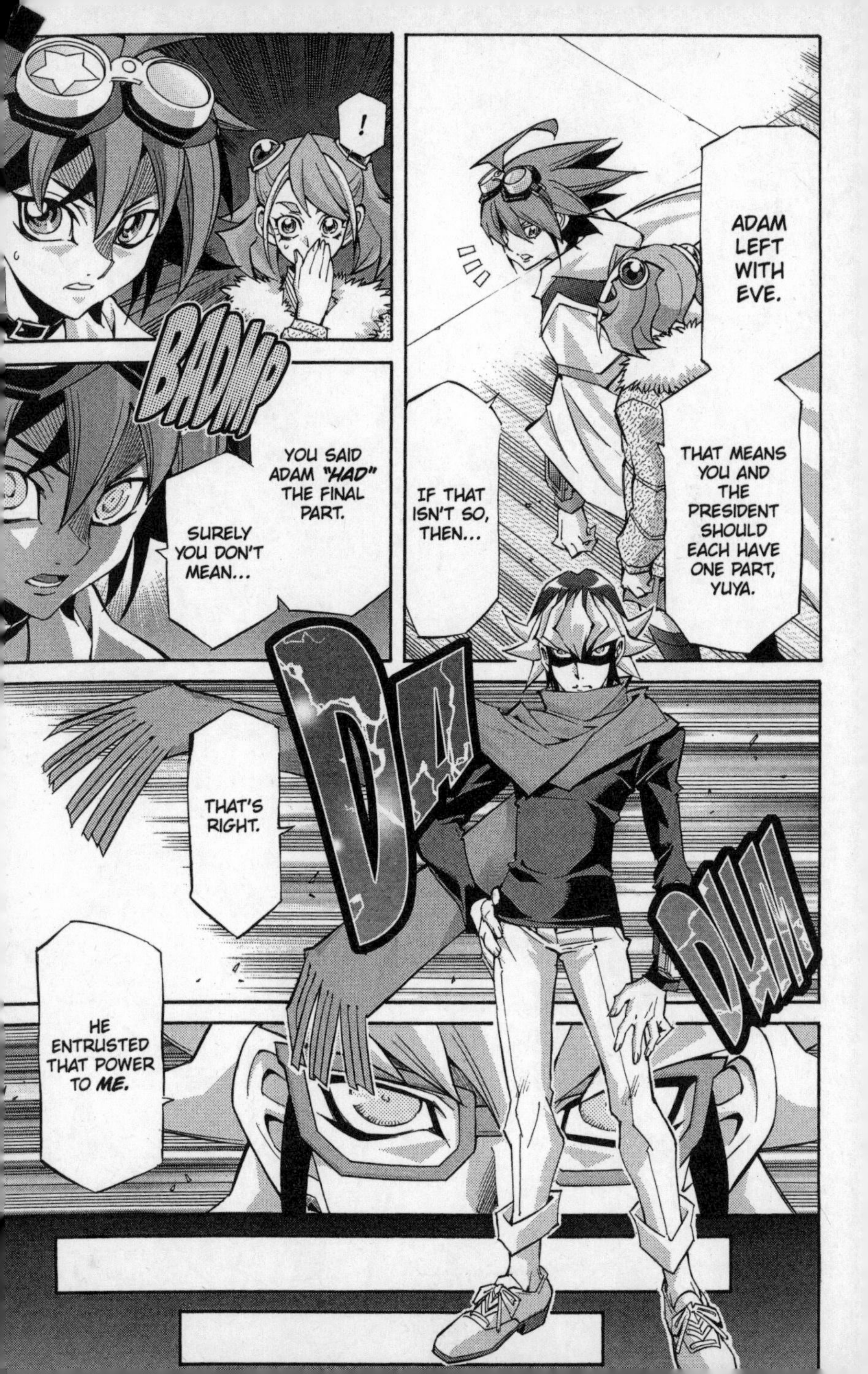
ADAM LEFT WITH EVE.
THAT MEANS YOU AND THE PRESIDENT SHOULD EACH HAVE ONE PART, YUYA.
IF THAT ISN'T SO, THEN...
!
BADOMP
YOU SAID ADAM "HAD" THE FINAL PART.
SURELY YOU DON'T MEAN...
THAT'S RIGHT.
DA
DUM
HE ENTRUSTED THAT POWER TO ME.

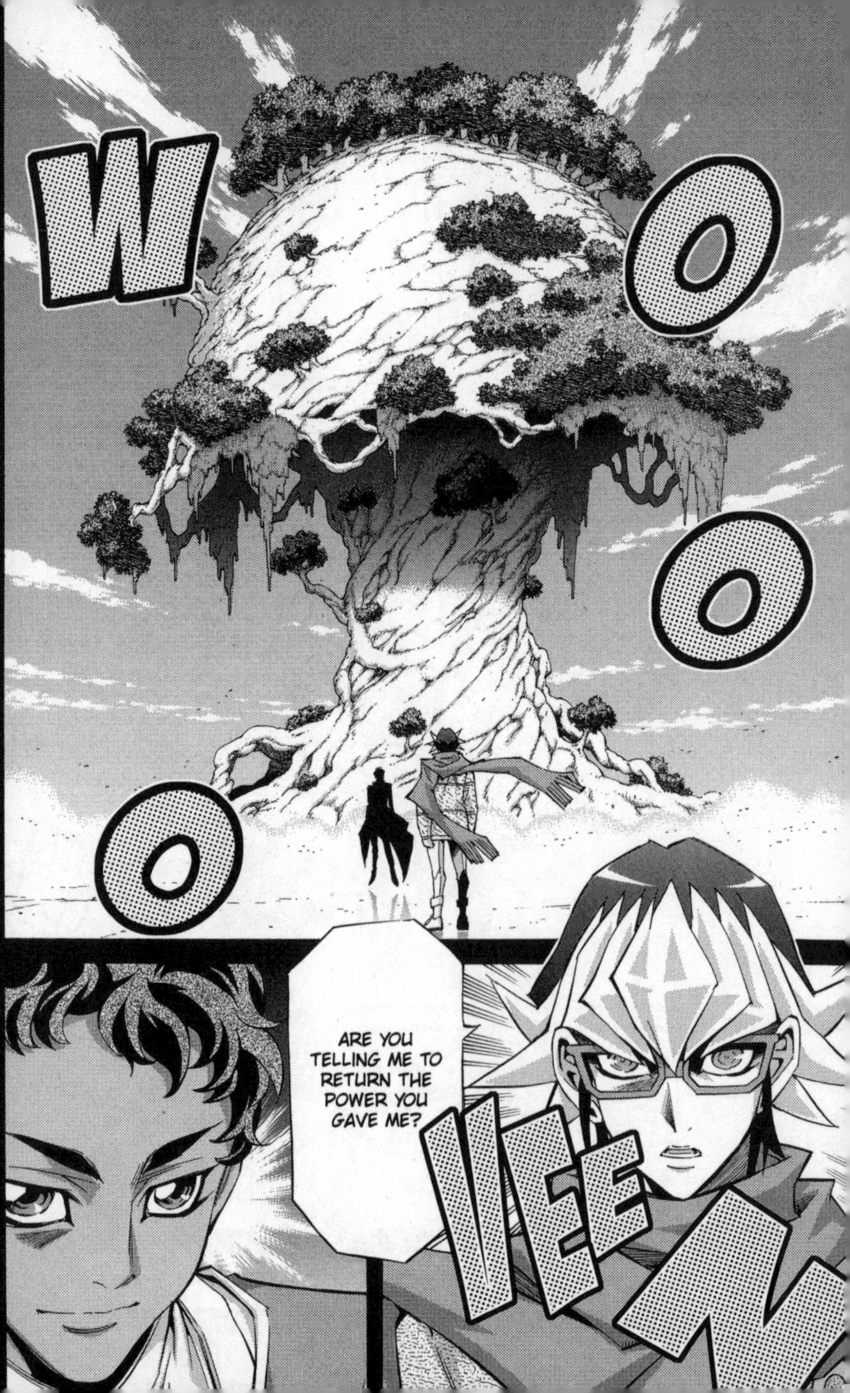
WOOO
ARE YOU TELLING ME TO RETURN THE POWER YOU GAVE ME?
VEEN

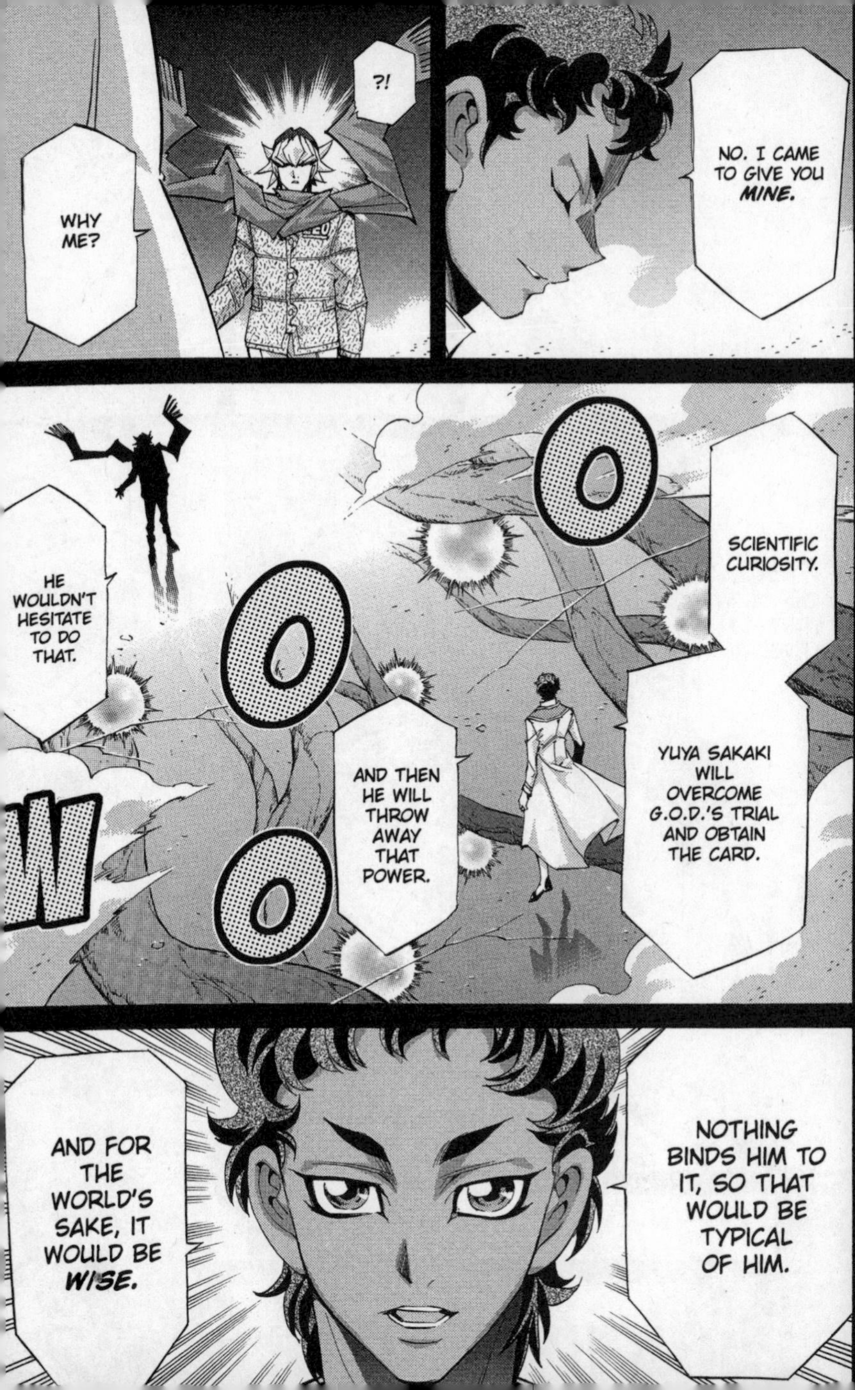
NO. I CAME TO GIVE YOU MINE.
?!
WHY ME?
SCIENTIFIC CURIOSITY.
OOOW
YUYA SAKAKI WILL OVERCOME G.O.D.'S TRIAL AND OBTAIN THE CARD.
AND THEN HE WILL THROW AWAY THAT POWER.
HE WOULDN'T HESITATE TO DO THAT.
NOTHING BINDS HIM TO IT, SO THAT WOULD BE TYPICAL OF HIM.
AND FOR THE WORLD'S SAKE, IT WOULD BE WISE.

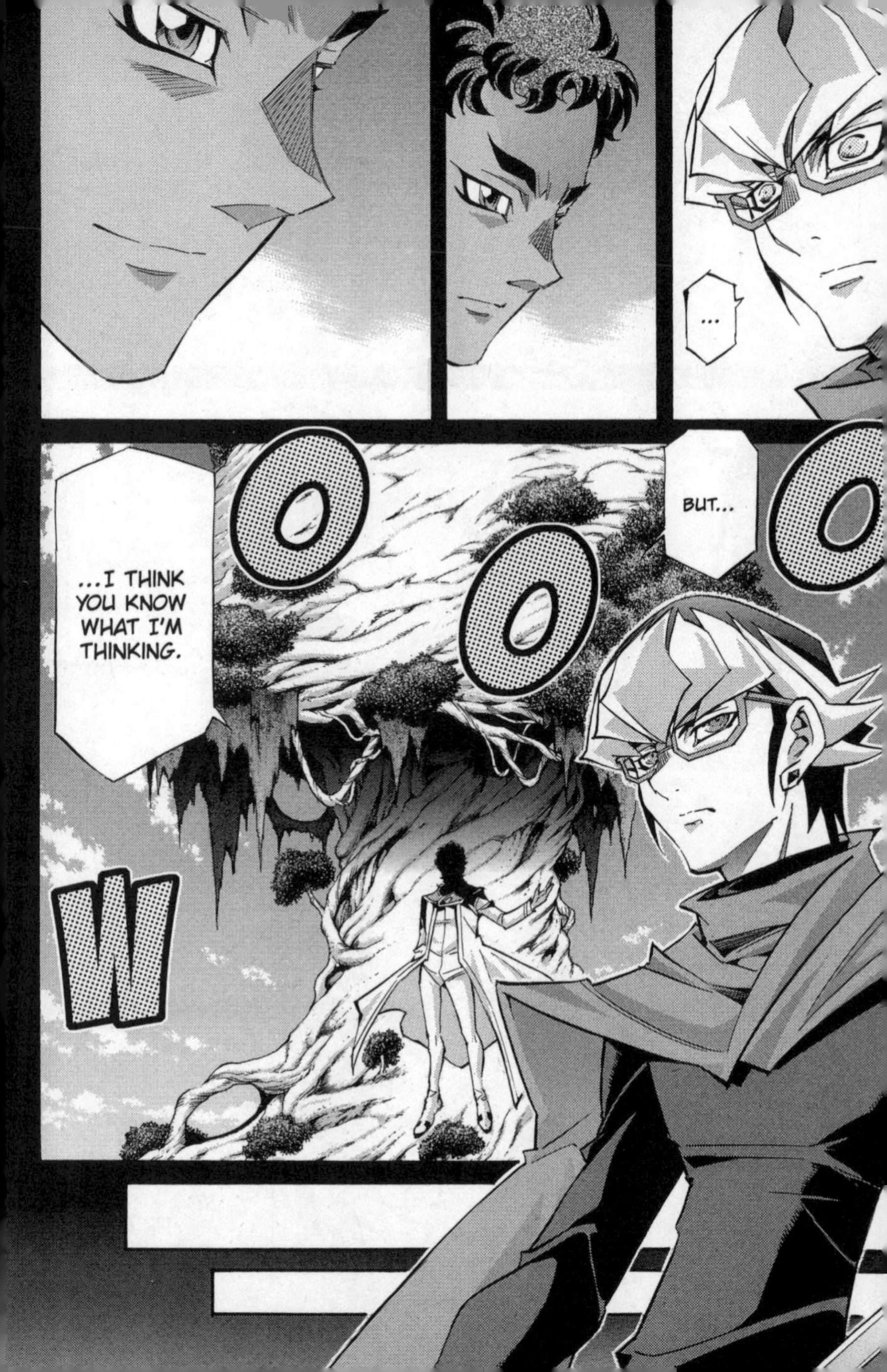
...
BUT...
...I THINK YOU KNOW WHAT I'M THINKING.
WOOO

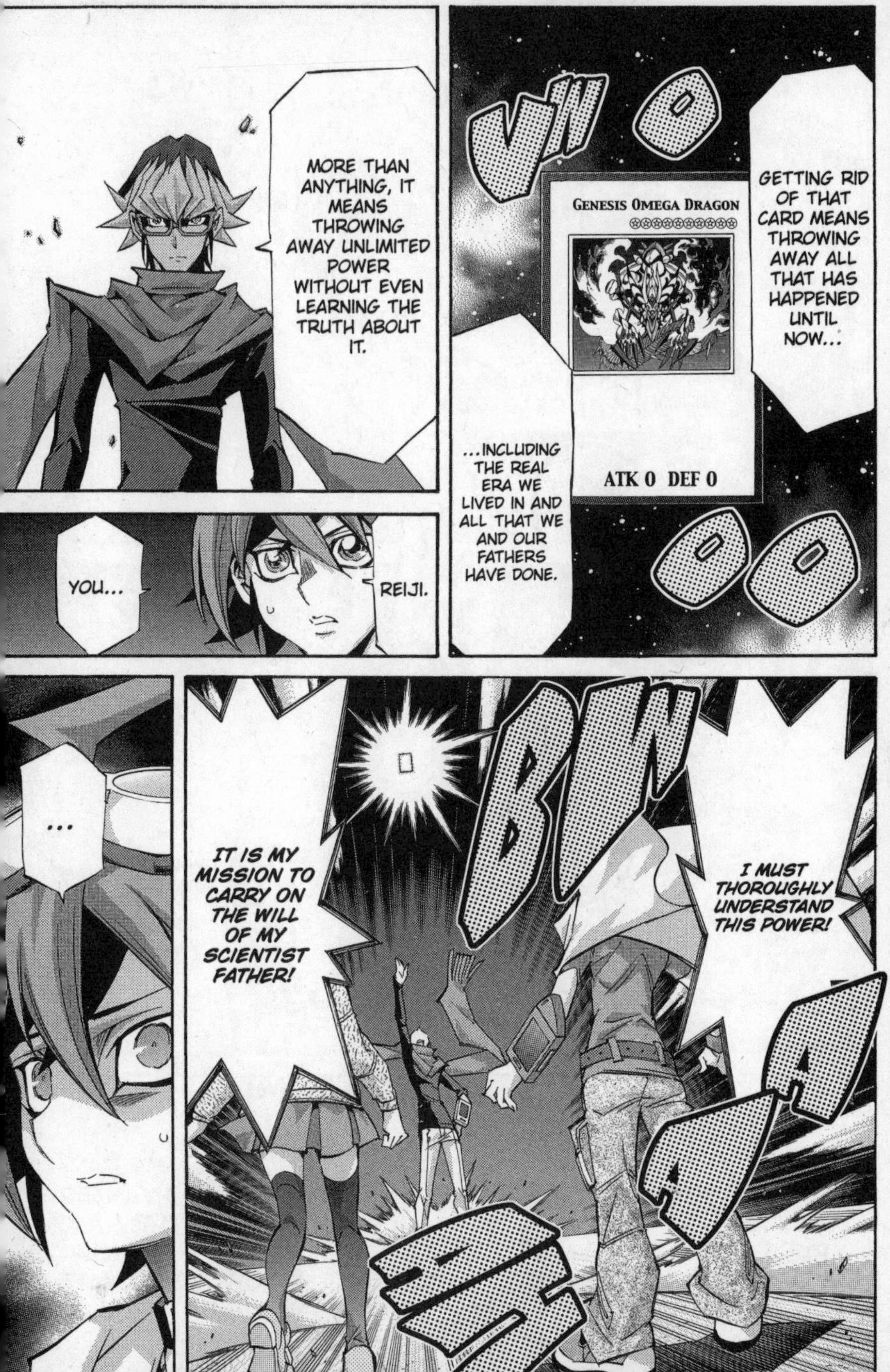

GETTING RID OF THAT CARD MEANS THROWING AWAY ALL THAT HAS HAPPENED UNTIL NOW...
VWN
GENESIS OMEGA DRAGON
ATK 0 DEF 0
...INCLUDING THE REAL ERA WE LIVED IN AND ALL THAT WE AND OUR FATHERS HAVE DONE.
MORE THAN ANYTHING, IT MEANS THROWING AWAY UNLIMITED POWER WITHOUT EVEN LEARNING THE TRUTH ABOUT IT.
REIJI.
YOU...
I MUST THOROUGHLY UNDERSTAND THIS POWER!
BWAA
IT IS MY MISSION TO CARRY ON THE WILL OF MY SCIENTIST FATHER!
...

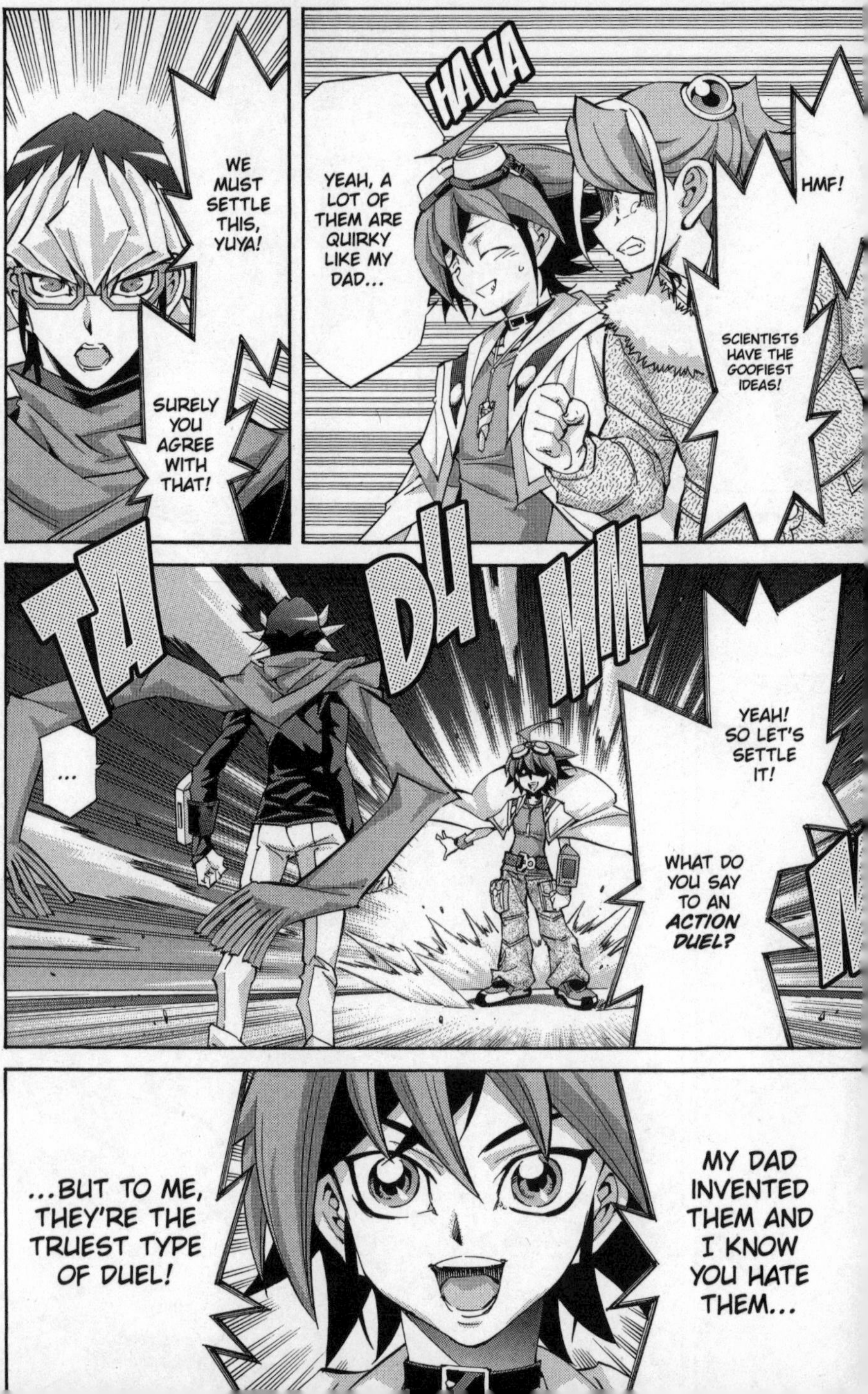
HMF!
SCIENTISTS HAVE THE GOOFIEST IDEAS!
YEAH, A LOT OF THEM ARE QUIRKY LIKE MY DAD...
HA HA
WE MUST SETTLE THIS, YUYA!
SURELY YOU AGREE WITH THAT!
TA DUMM
YEAH! SO LET'S SETTLE IT!
WHAT DO YOU SAY TO AN *ACTION DUEL?*
...
MY DAD INVENTED THEM AND I KNOW YOU HATE THEM...
...BUT TO ME, THEY'RE THE TRUEST TYPE OF DUEL!

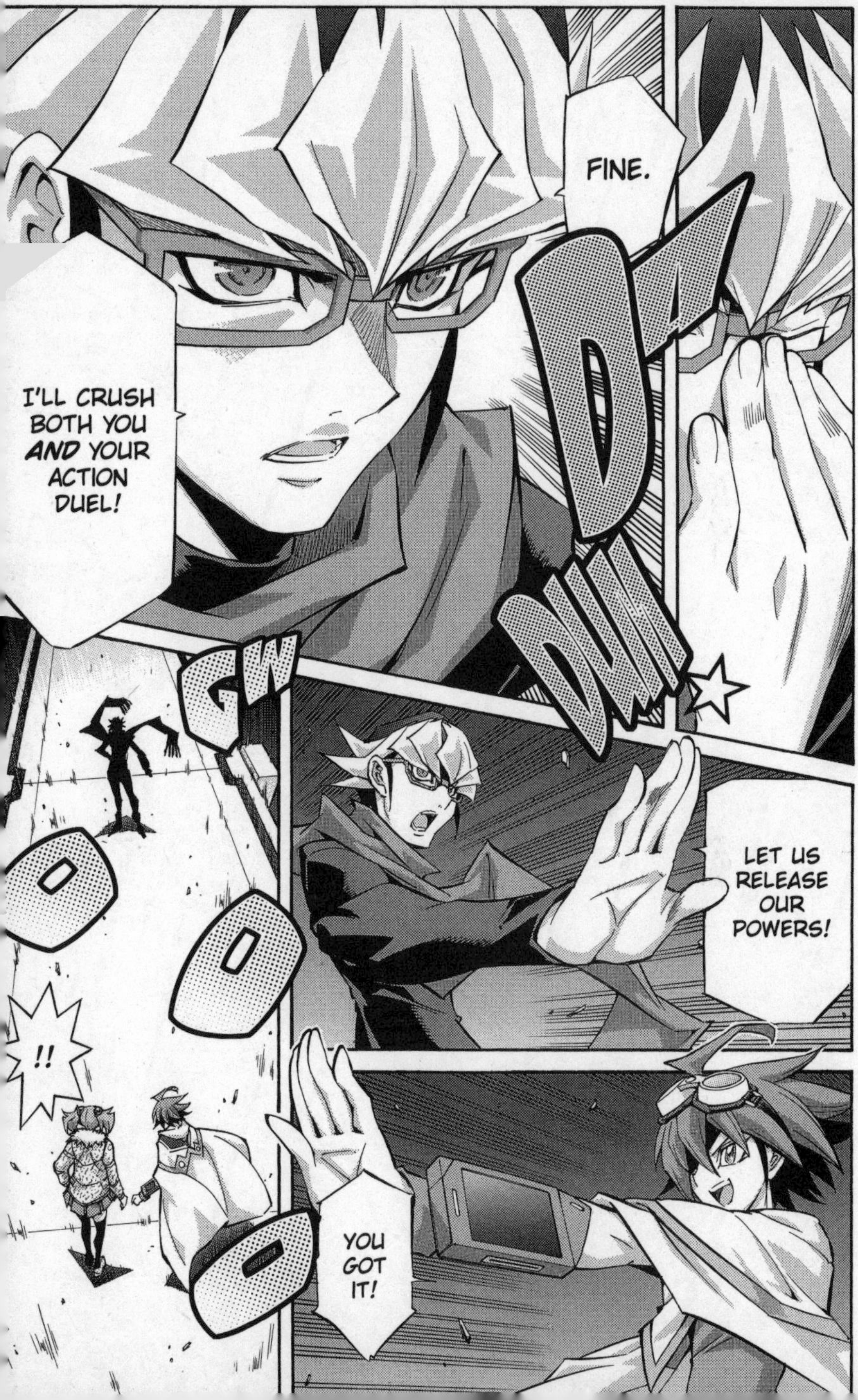
FINE.
I'LL CRUSH BOTH YOU *AND* YOUR ACTION DUEL!
DA-DUM!
LET US RELEASE OUR POWERS!
GWOOO
!!
YOU GOT IT!

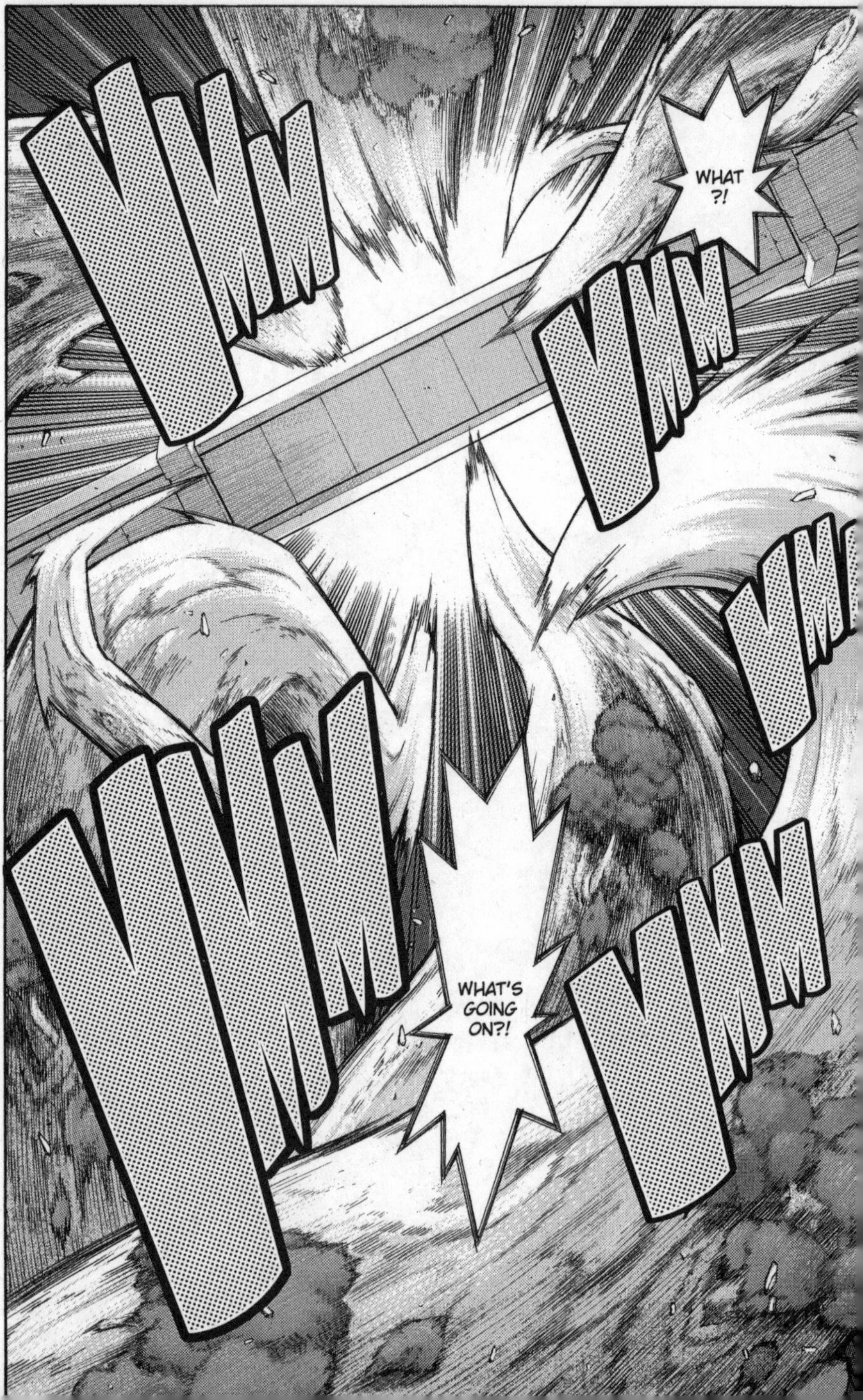
WHAT ?!
WHAT'S GOING ON?!

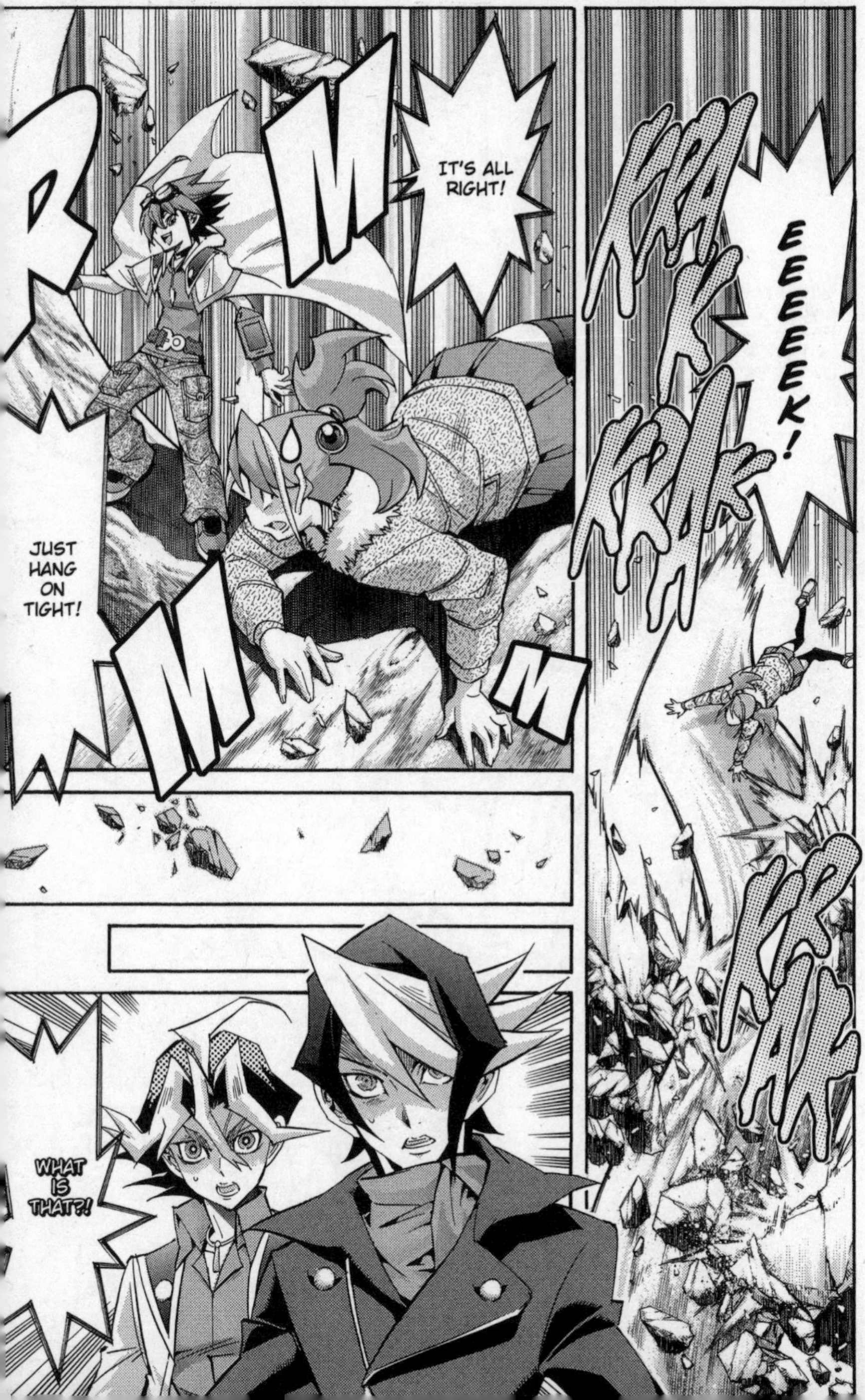
KRAK KRAK
EEEEEEK!
KRAK
RMMM
IT'S ALL RIGHT!
JUST HANG ON TIGHT!
WHAT IS THAT?!

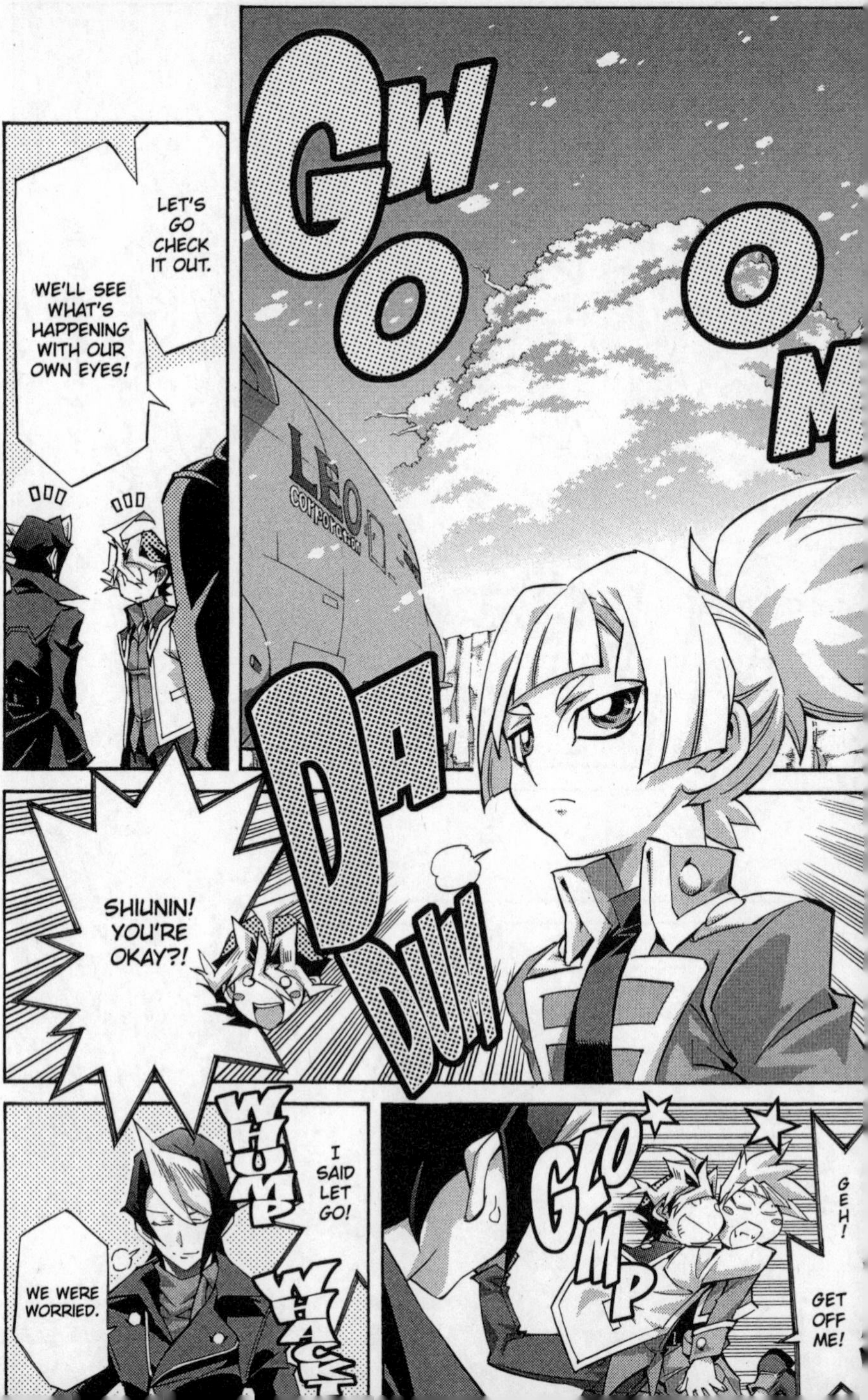
GWOOOM
LEO CORPORATION
DADUM
LET'S GO CHECK IT OUT.
WE'LL SEE WHAT'S HAPPENING WITH OUR OWN EYES!
SHIUNIN! YOU'RE OKAY?!
GEH!
GLOMP
GET OFF ME!
WHUMP
I SAID LET GO!
WHACK
WE WERE WORRIED.

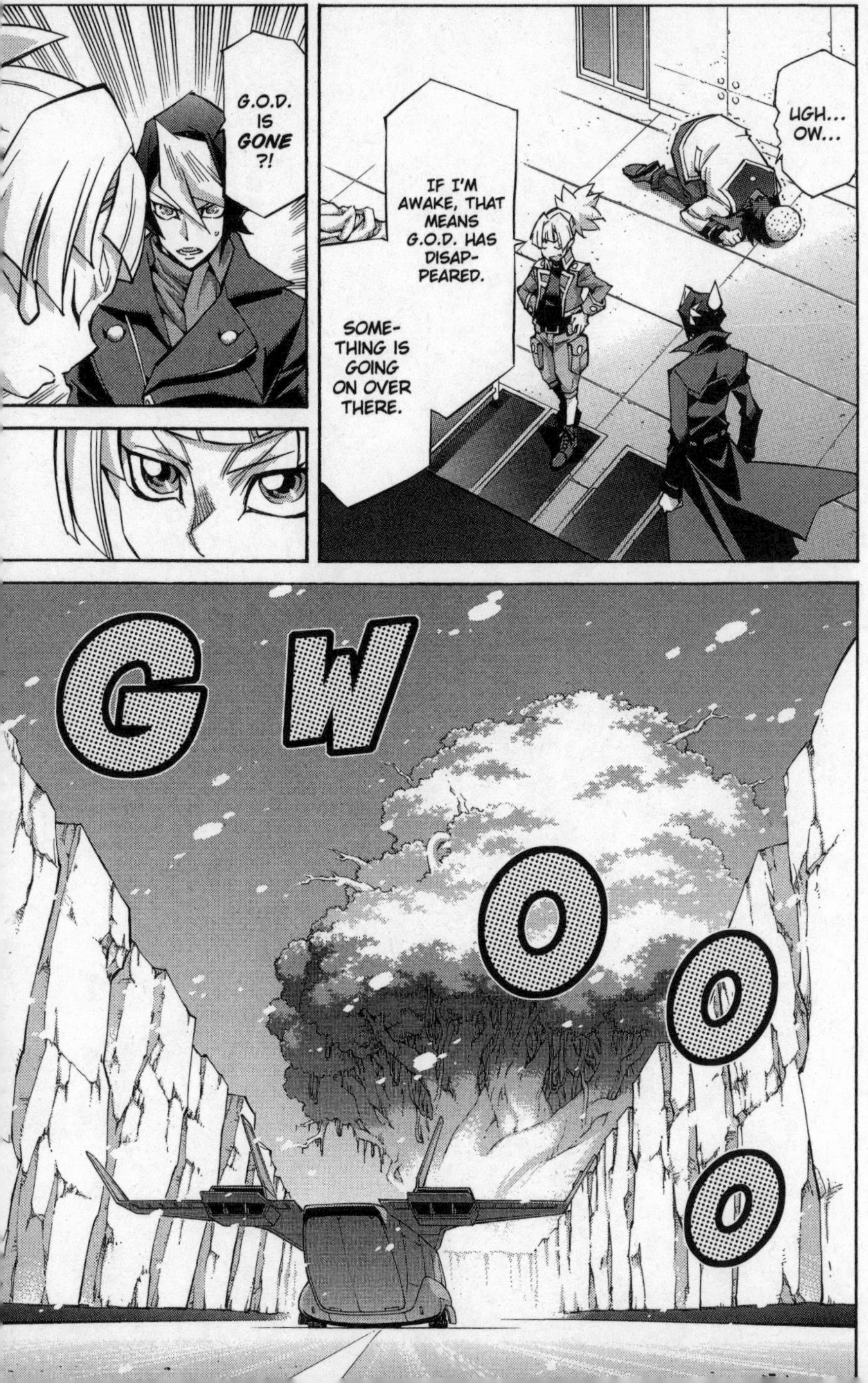
UGH... OW...
IF I'M AWAKE, THAT MEANS G.O.D. HAS DISAPPEARED.
SOMETHING IS GOING ON OVER THERE.
G.O.D. IS GONE?!
GWOOOO

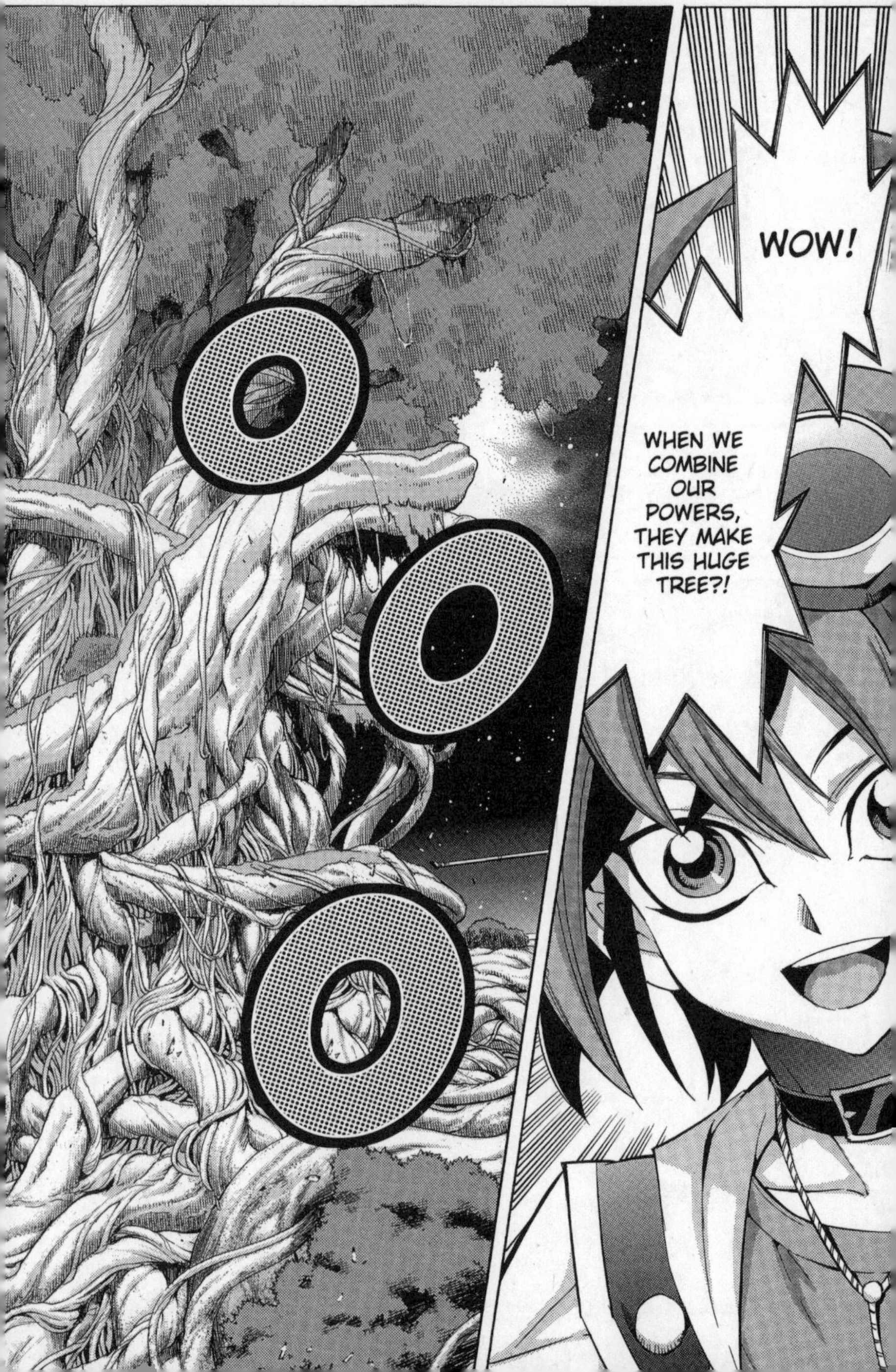
WOW!
WHEN WE COMBINE OUR POWERS, THEY MAKE THIS HUGE TREE?!
OOO

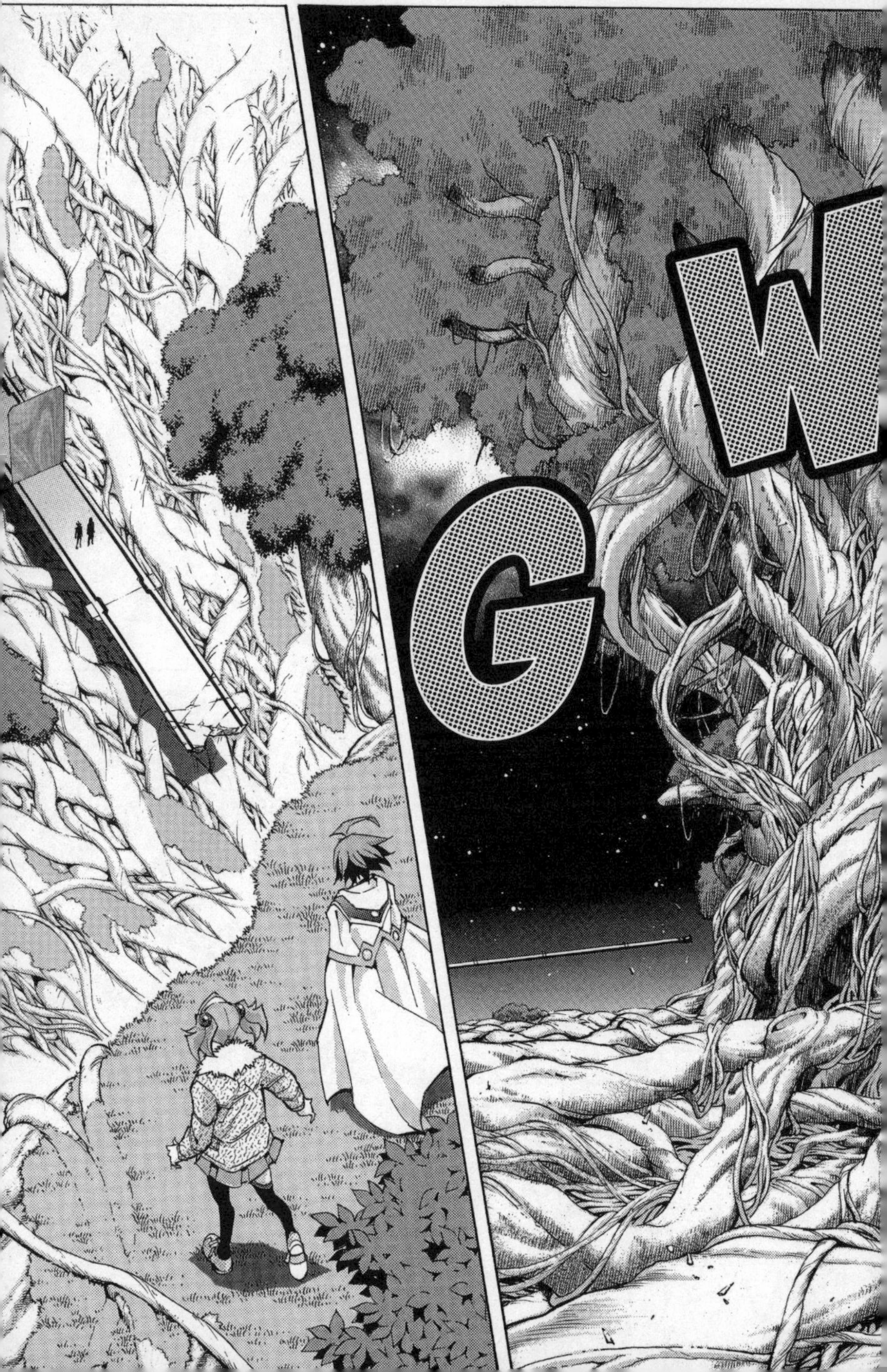
GW

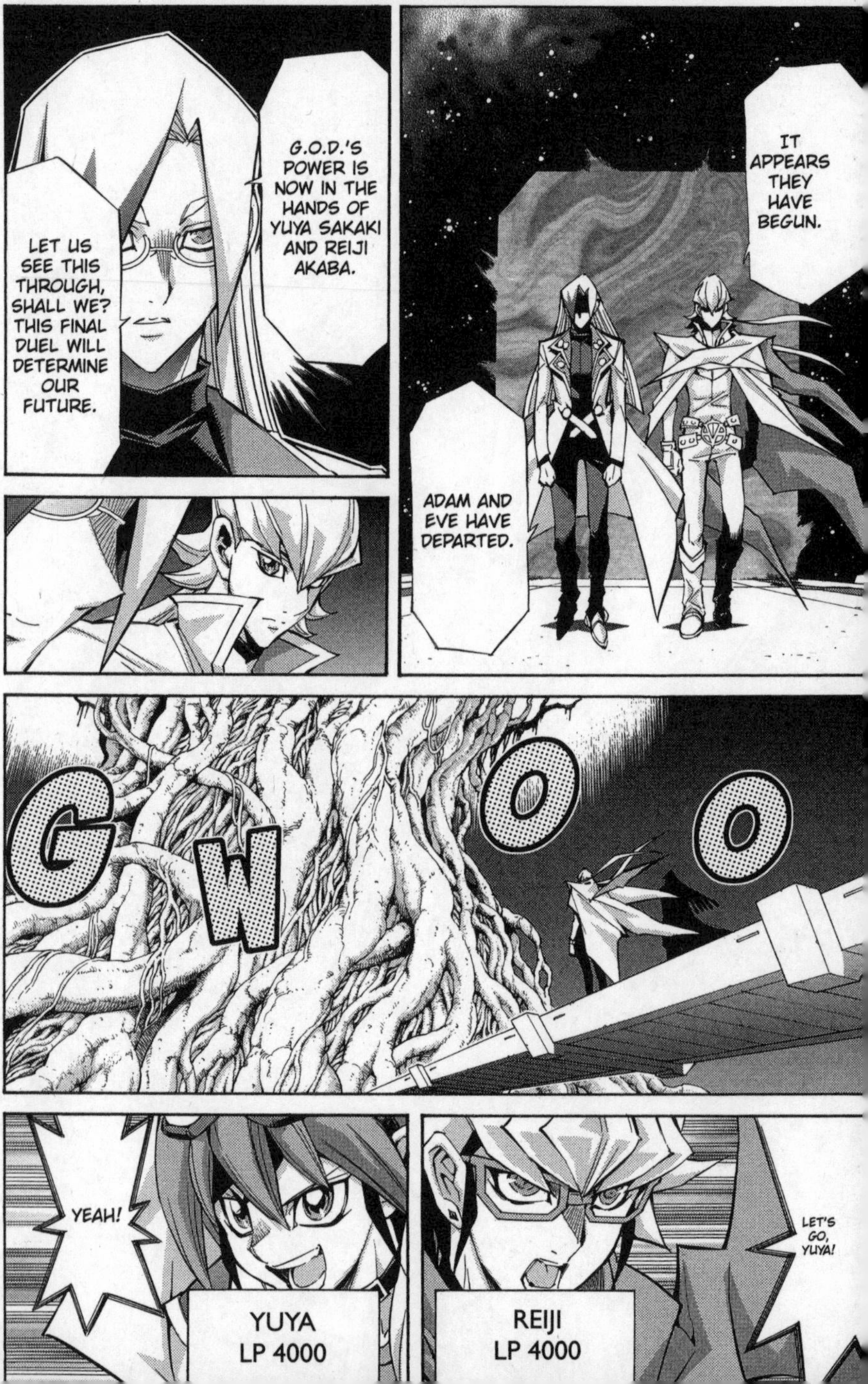
IT APPEARS THEY HAVE BEGUN.
ADAM AND EVE HAVE DEPARTED.
G.O.D.'S POWER IS NOW IN THE HANDS OF YUYA SAKAKI AND REIJI AKABA.
LET US SEE THIS THROUGH, SHALL WE? THIS FINAL DUEL WILL DETERMINE OUR FUTURE.
GWOOO
LET'S GO, YUYA!
REIJI
LP 4000
YEAH!
YUYA
LP 4000

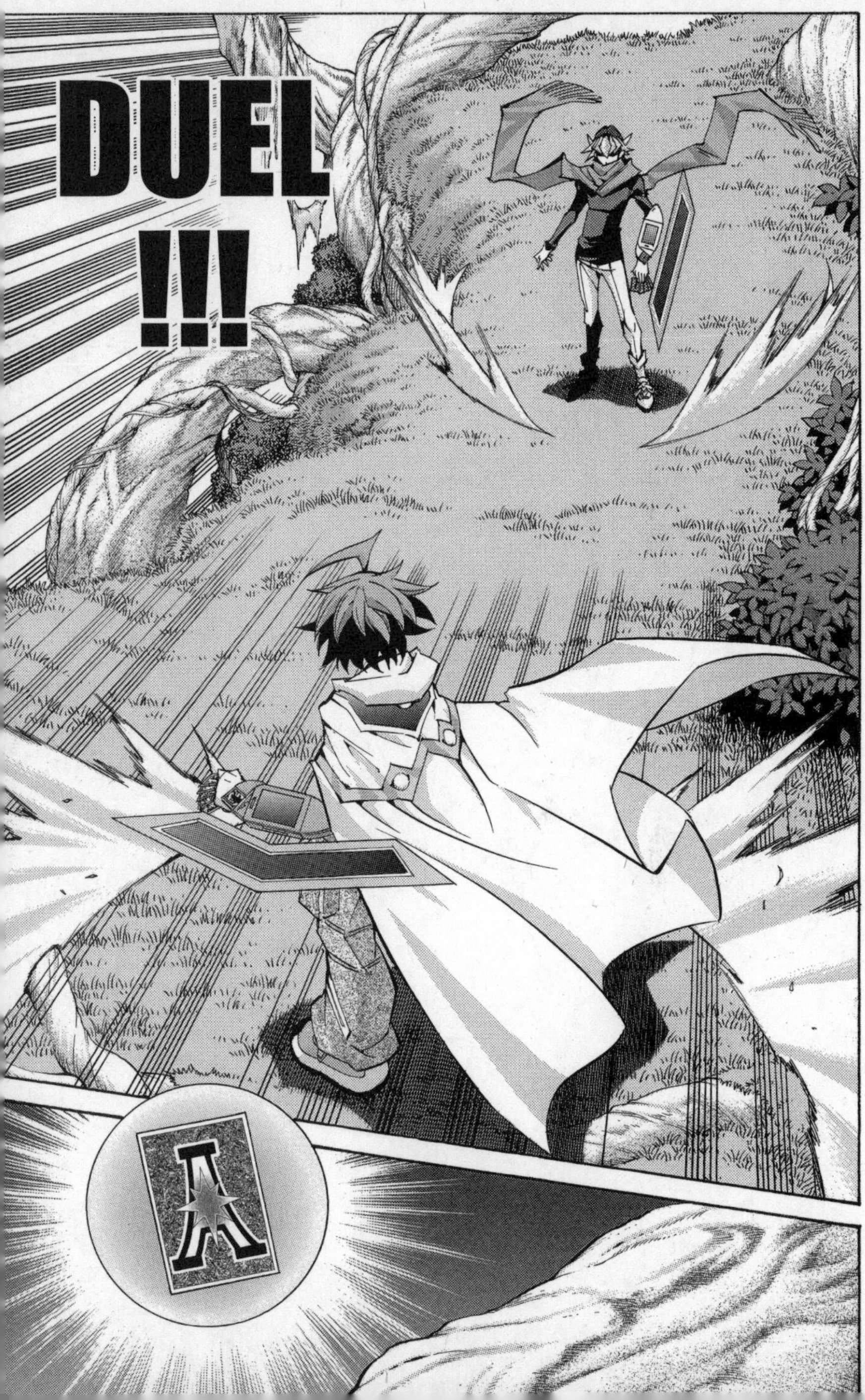
DUEL !!!

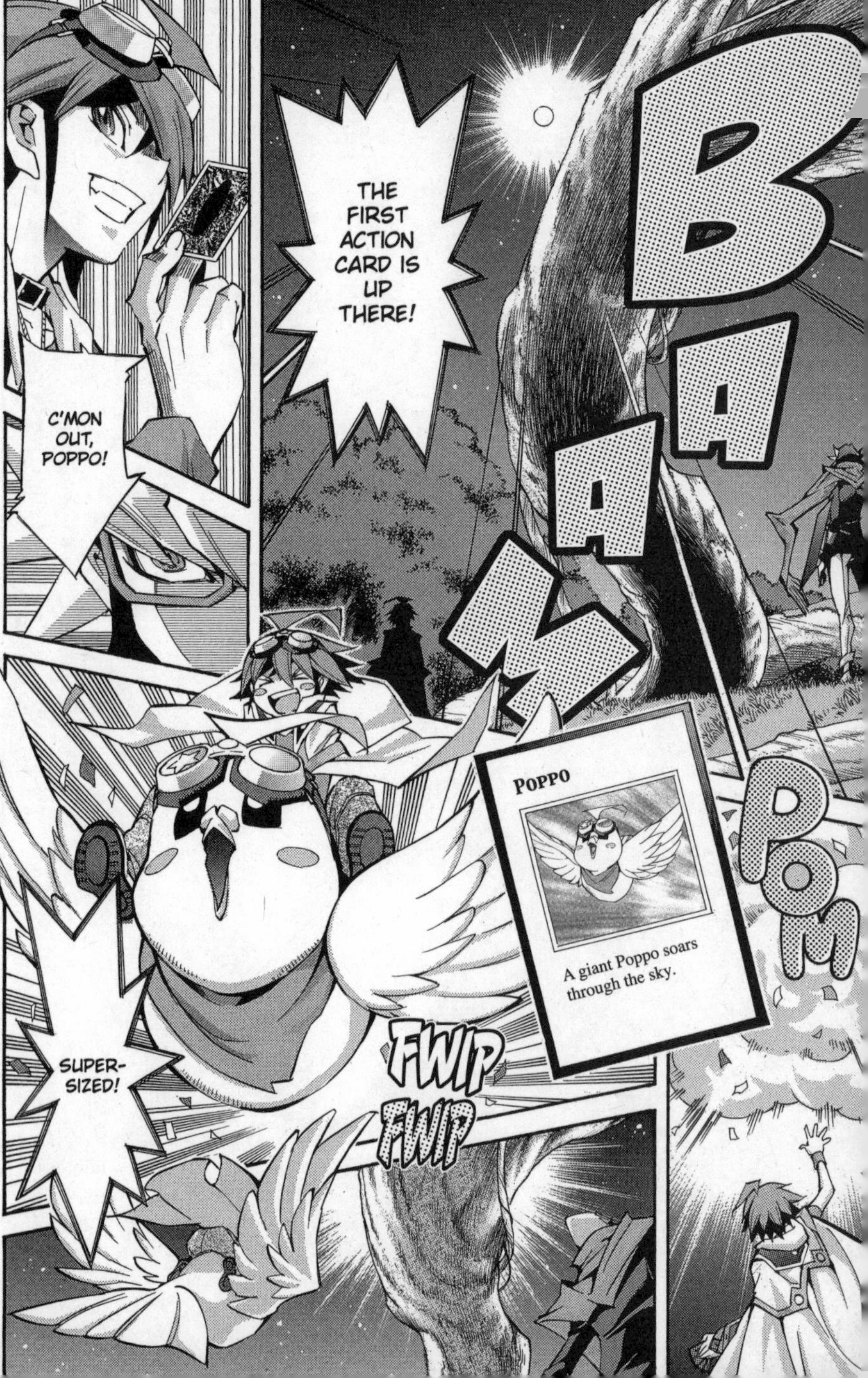
BAAAM
THE FIRST ACTION CARD IS UP THERE!
C'MON OUT, POPPO!
POPPO
A giant Poppo soars through the sky.
POM
FWIP FWIP
SUPER-SIZED!

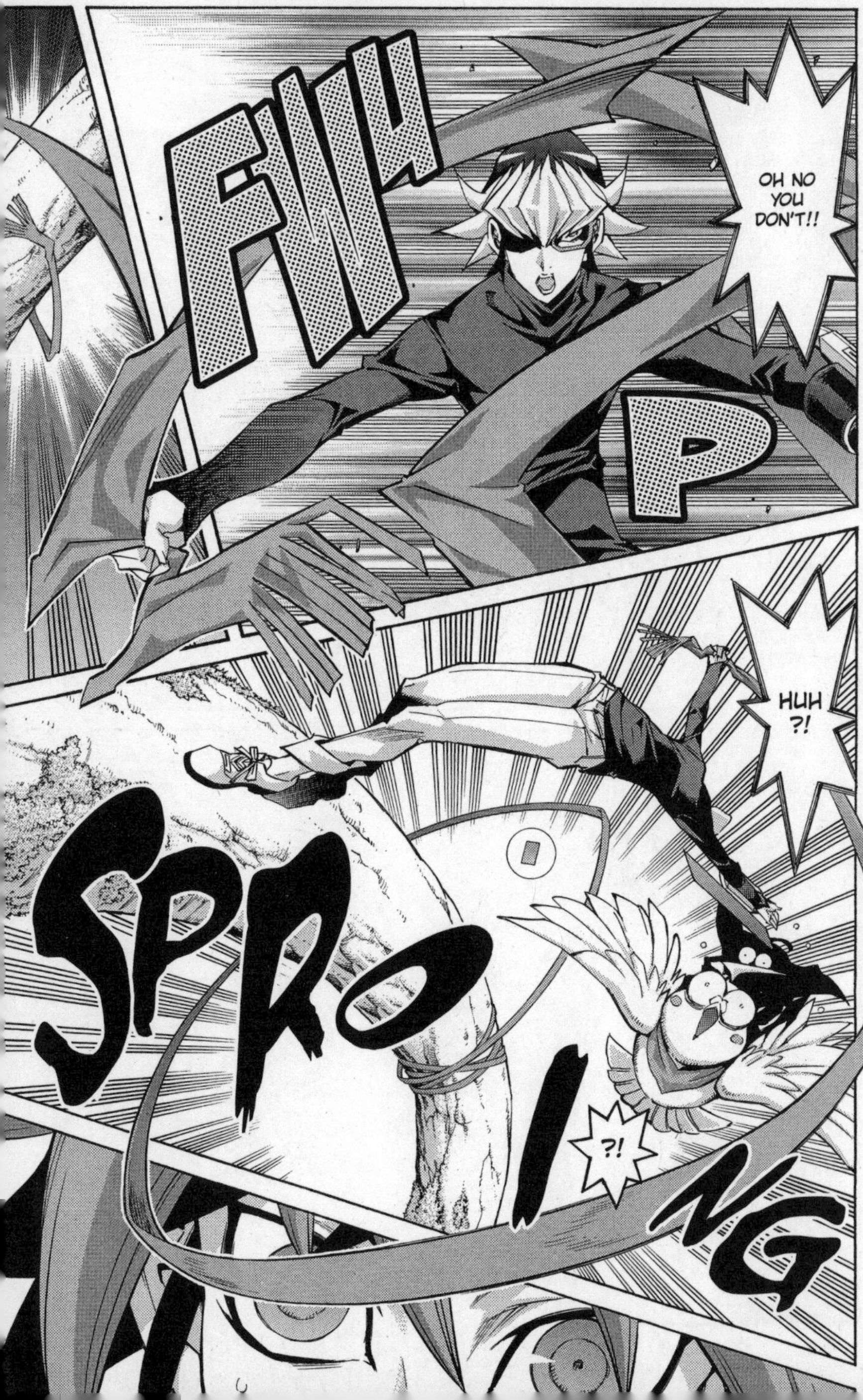
OH NO YOU DON'T!!
FWIP
HUH ?!
?!
SPROING

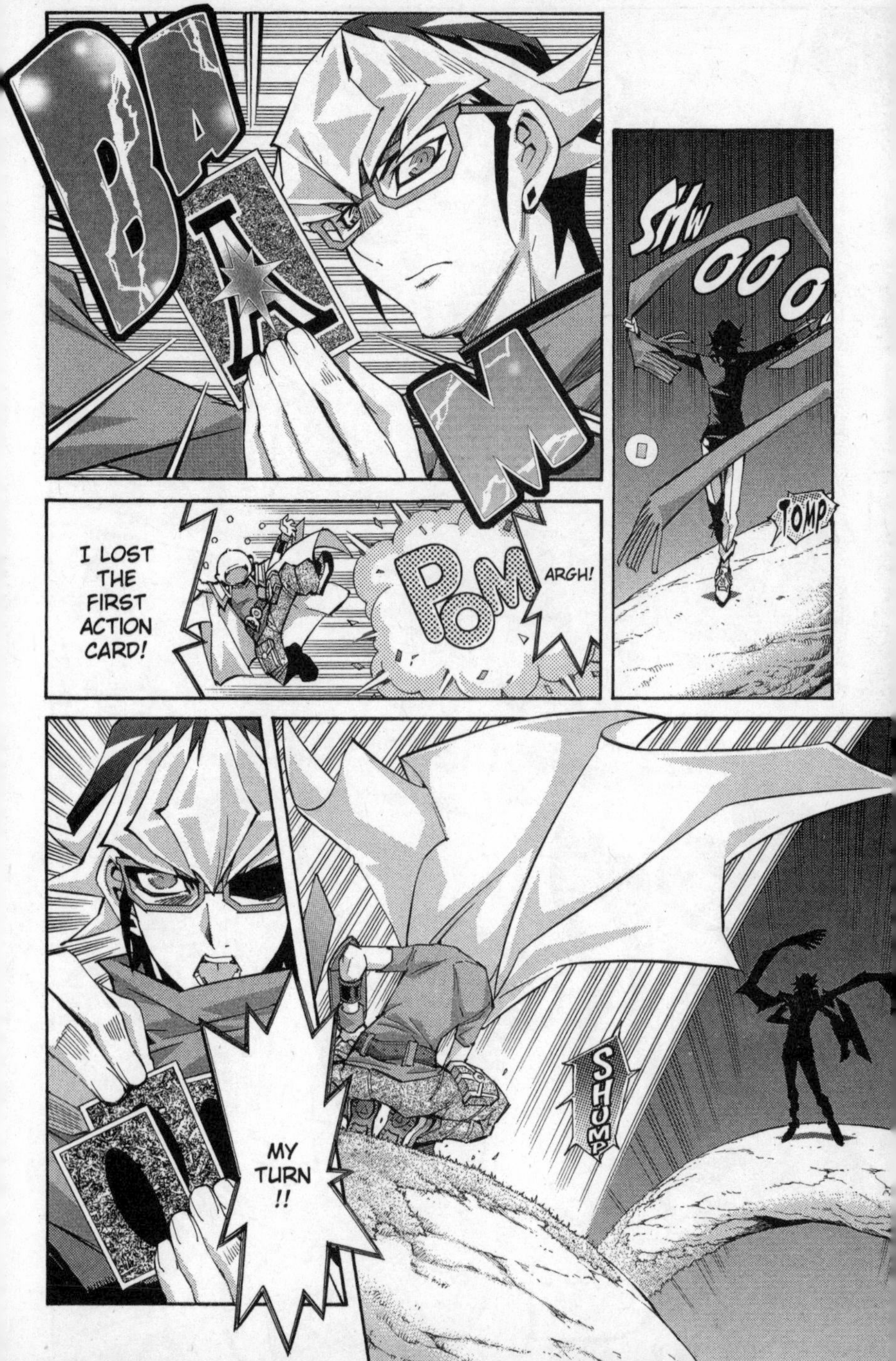
SHWOOOO
TOMP
BADAM
ARGH!
POM
I LOST THE FIRST ACTION CARD!
SHUMP
MY TURN!!

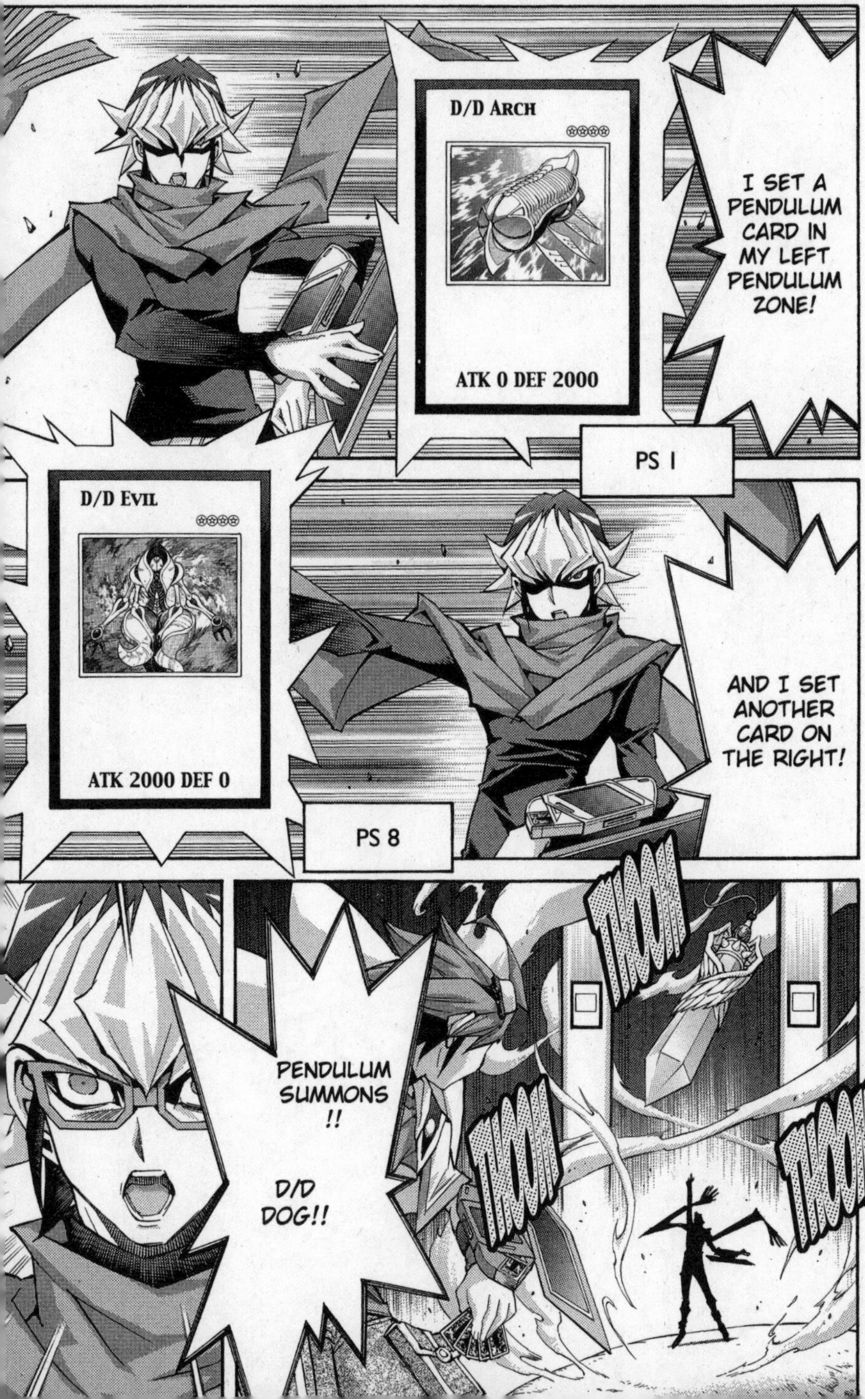
I SET A PENDULUM CARD IN MY LEFT PENDULUM ZONE!
D/D ARCH
ATK 0 DEF 2000
PS 1
AND I SET ANOTHER CARD ON THE RIGHT!
D/D EVIL
ATK 2000 DEF 0
PS 8
THOOM
THOOM
THOOM
PENDULUM SUMMONS!!
D/D DOG!!

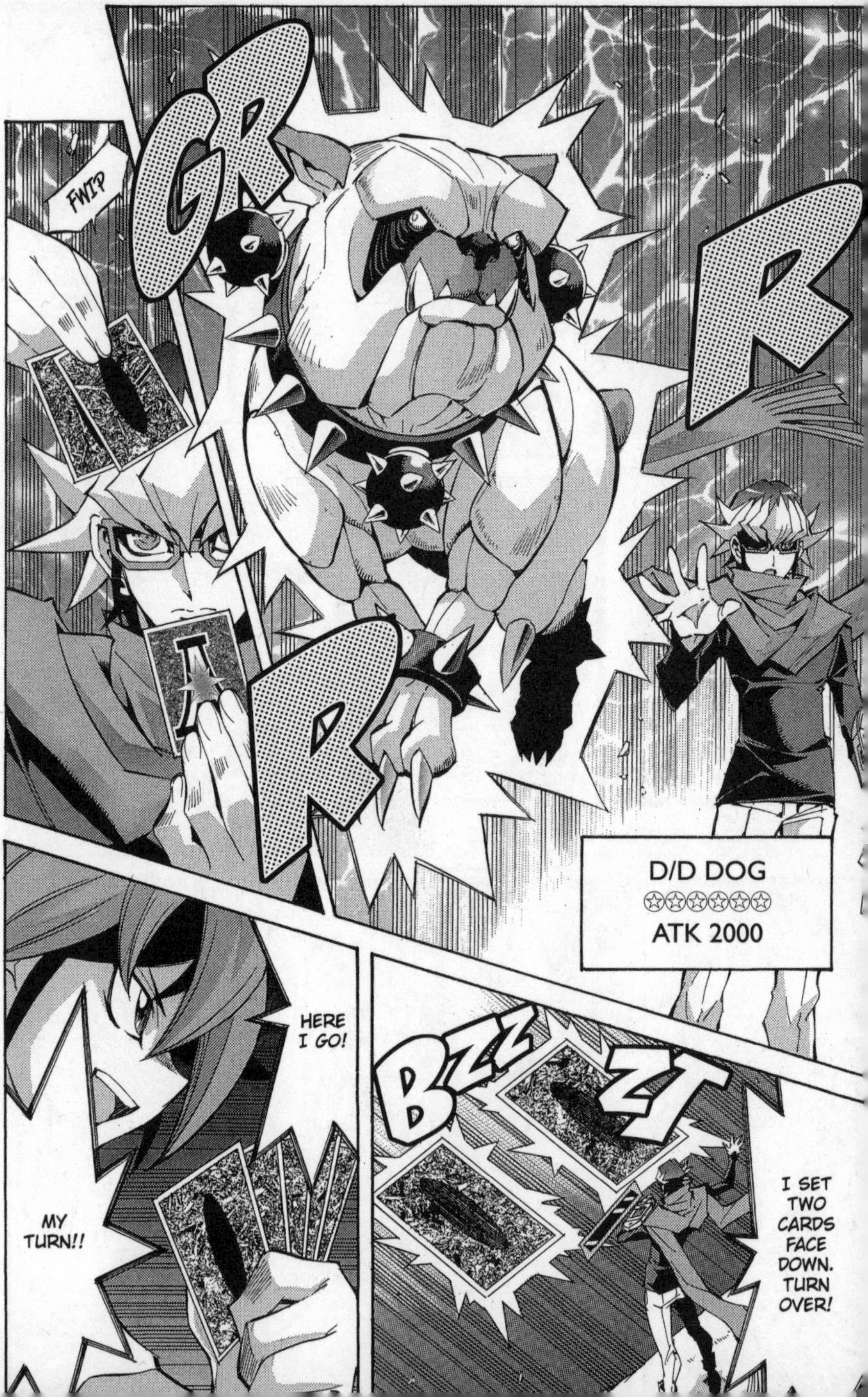
GRRR
FWIP
D/D DOG
☆☆☆☆☆☆
ATK 2000
BZZZT
I SET TWO CARDS FACE DOWN. TURN OVER!
HERE I GO!
MY TURN!!

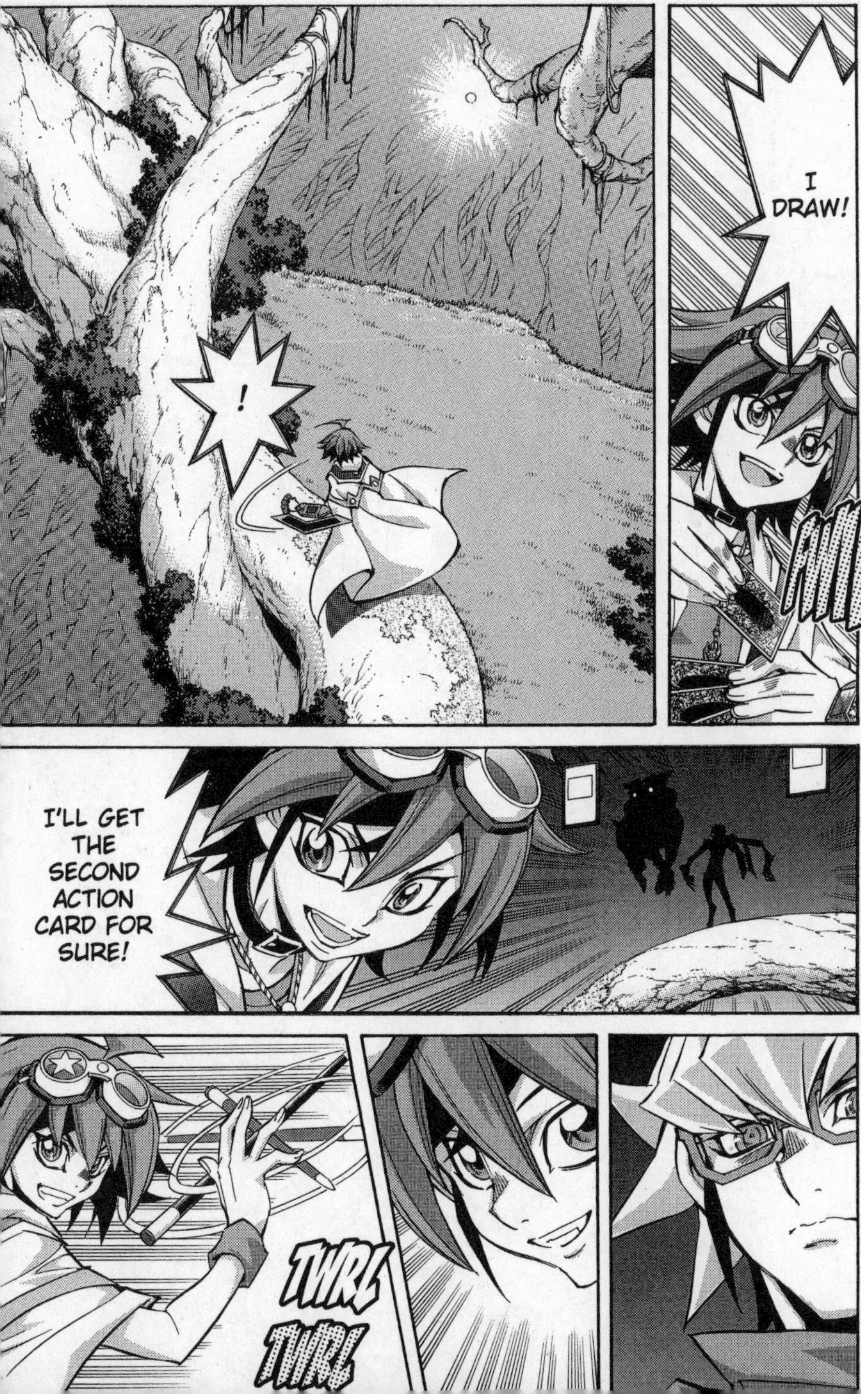
I DRAW!
AWIP
!
I'LL GET THE SECOND ACTION CARD FOR SURE!
TWIRL
TWIRL

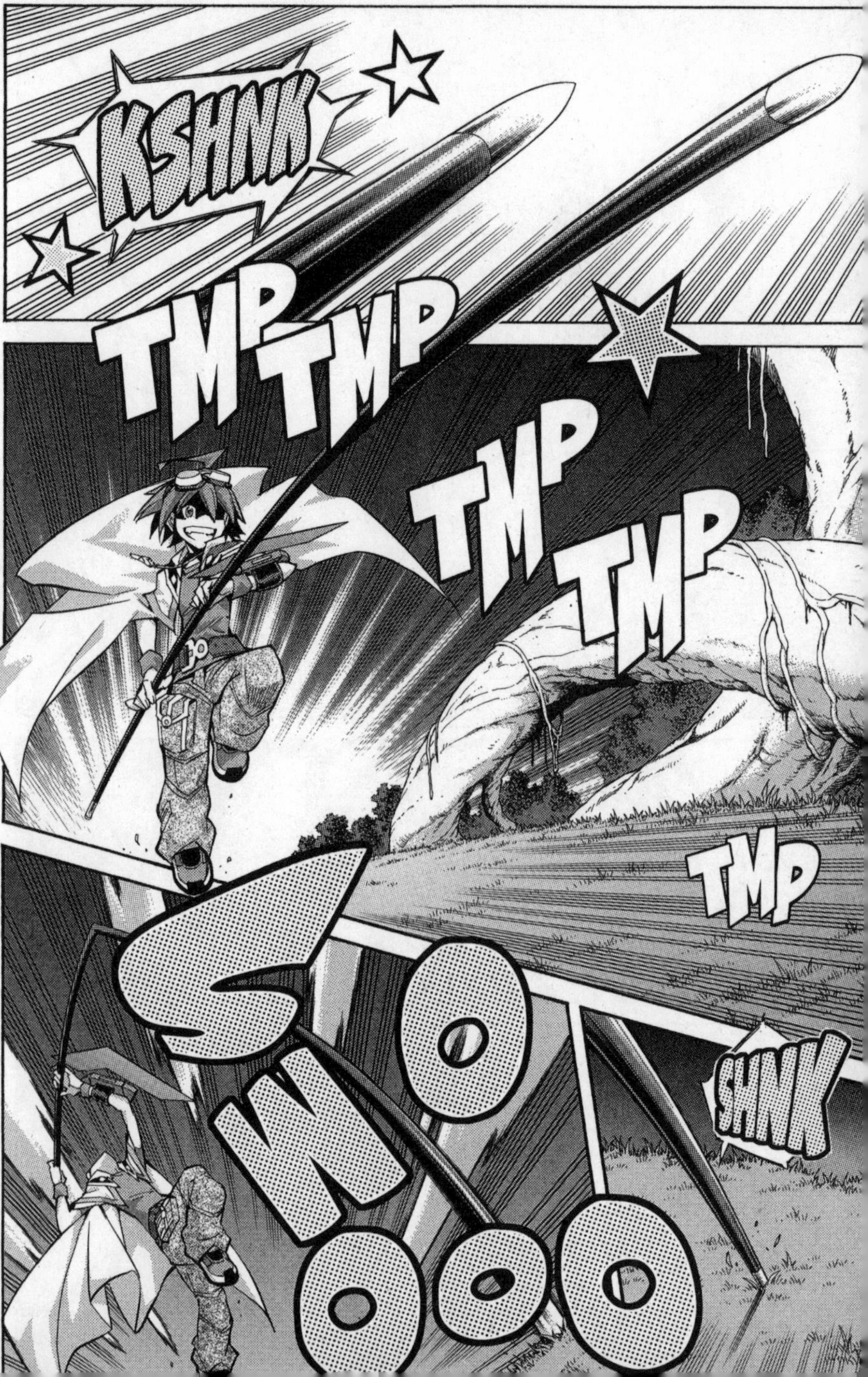
KSHNK
TMP TMP
TMP
TMP
TMP
SHNK
SWOOOO

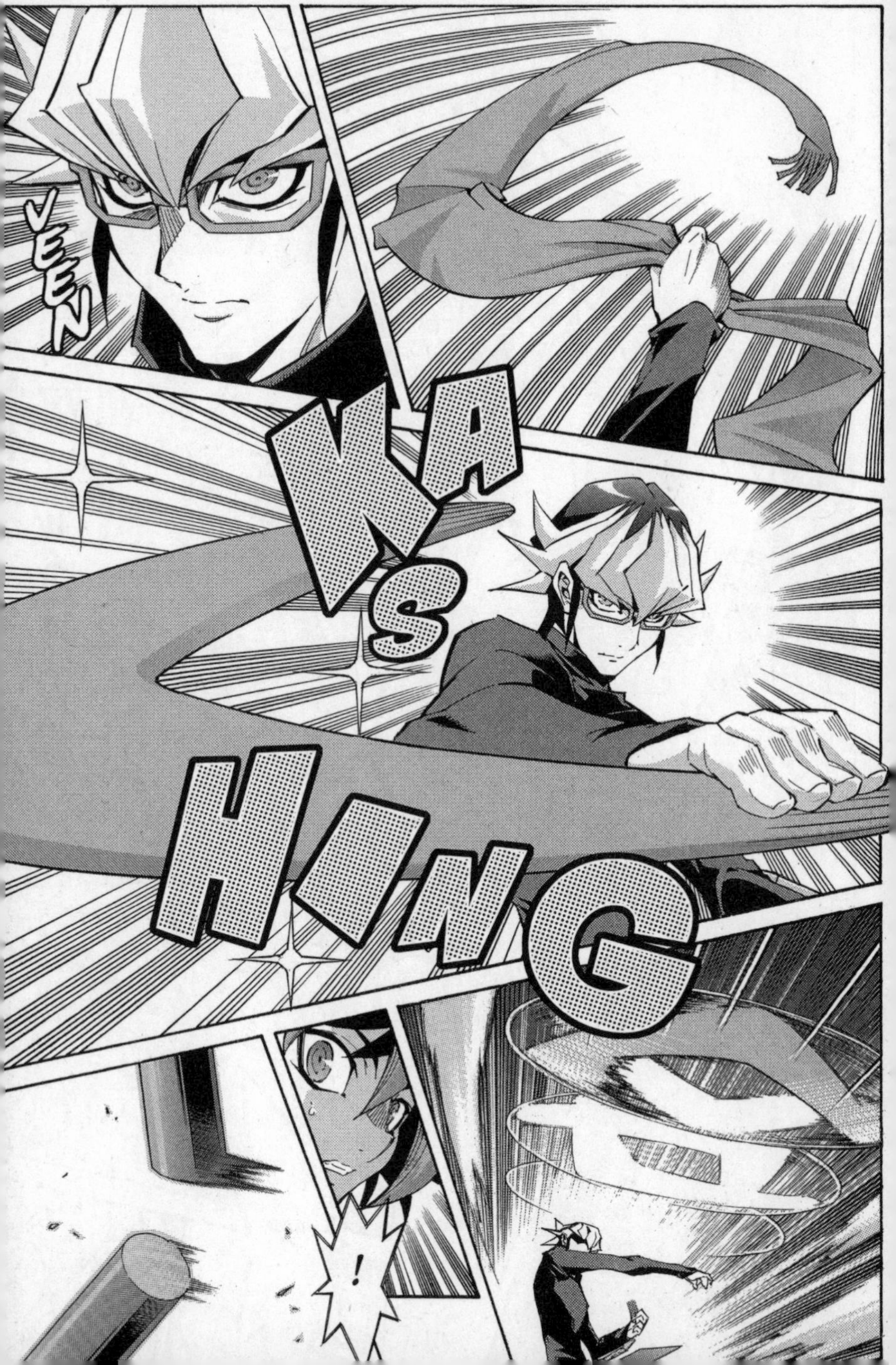
VEEN
WASHING
!

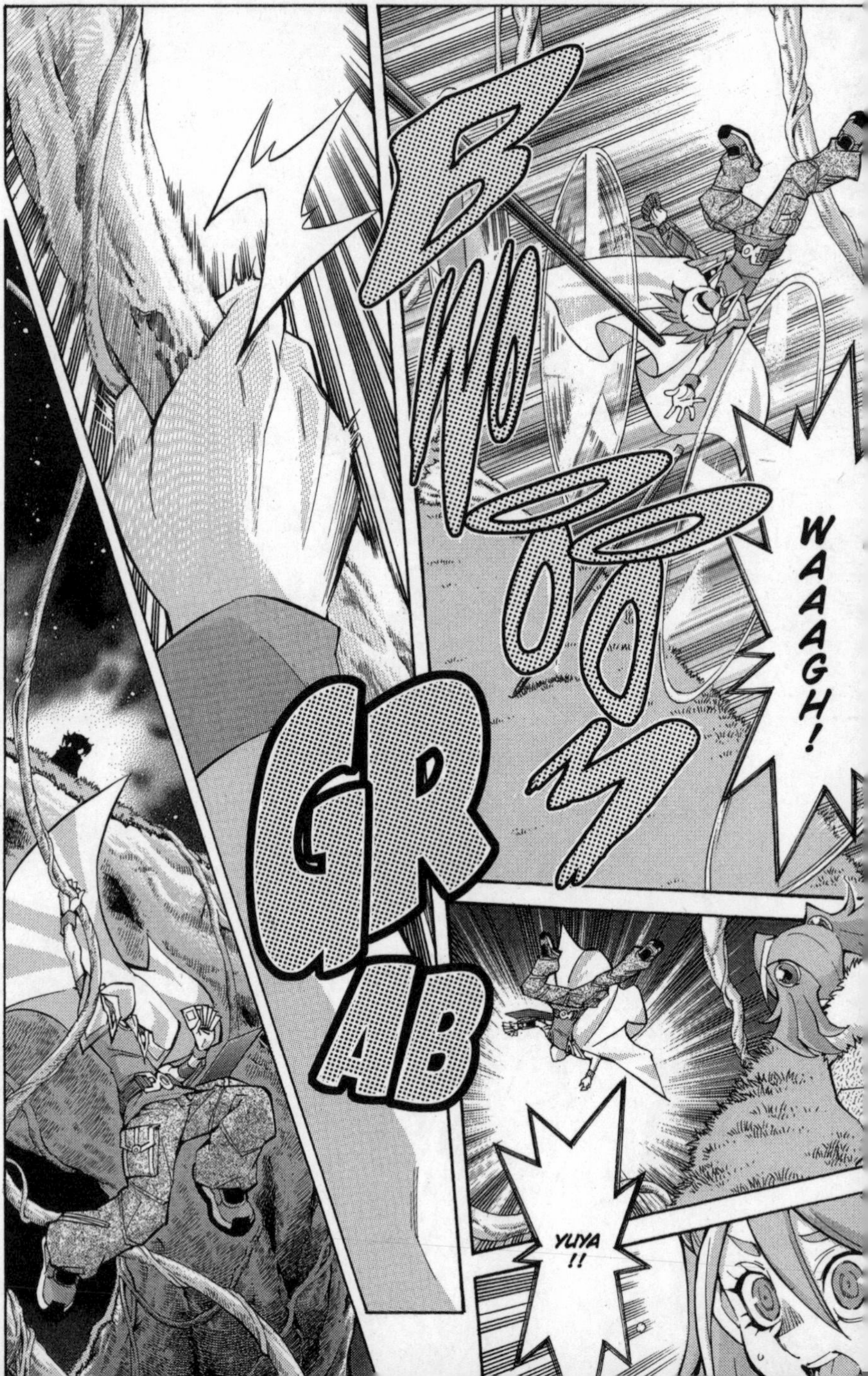
WAAAAGH!
BWOOOM
YUYA!!
GRAB

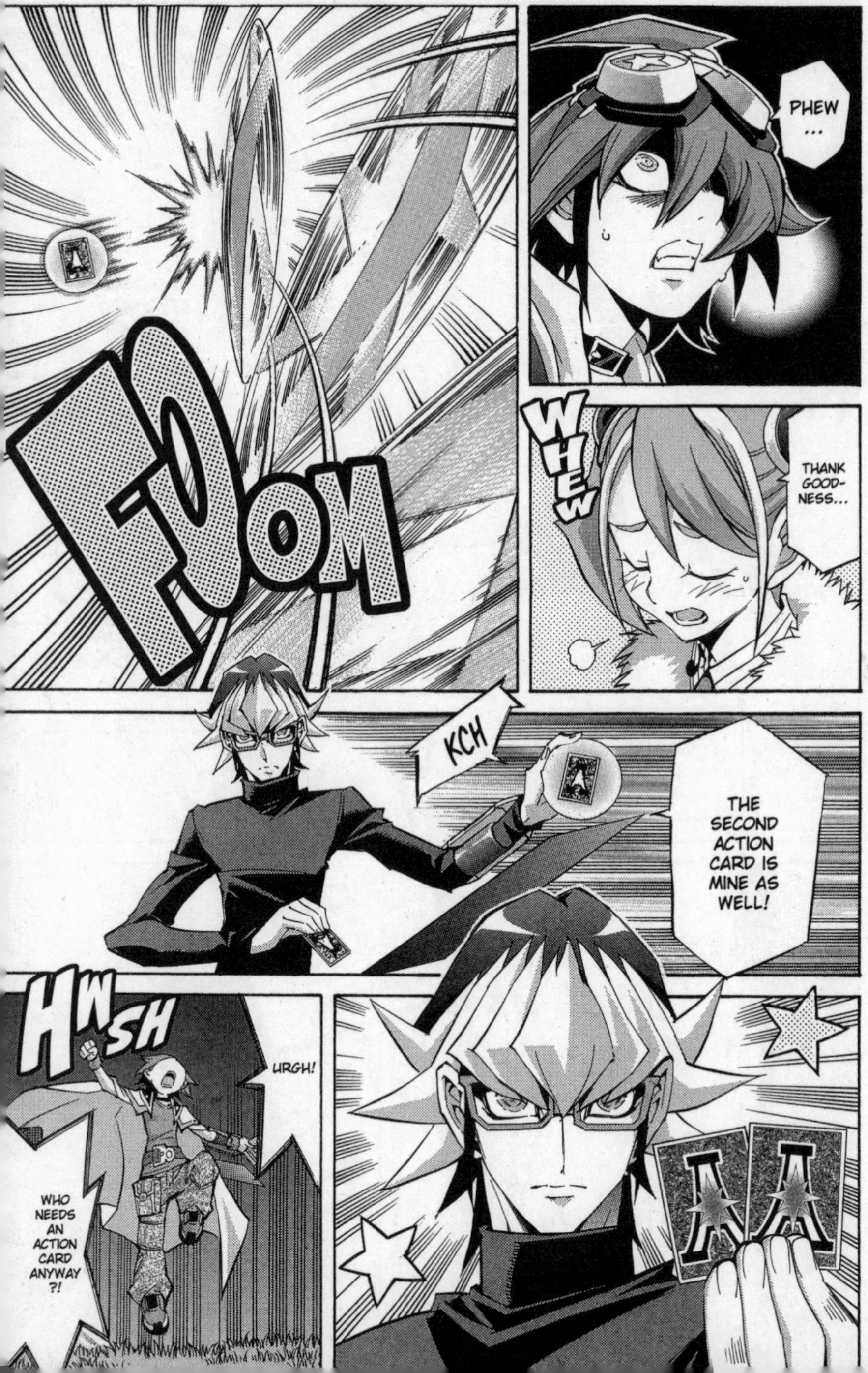
PHEW ...
WHEW
THANK GOODNESS...
FOOM
THE SECOND ACTION CARD IS MINE AS WELL!
KCH
HWSH
URGH!
WHO NEEDS AN ACTION CARD ANYWAY ?!

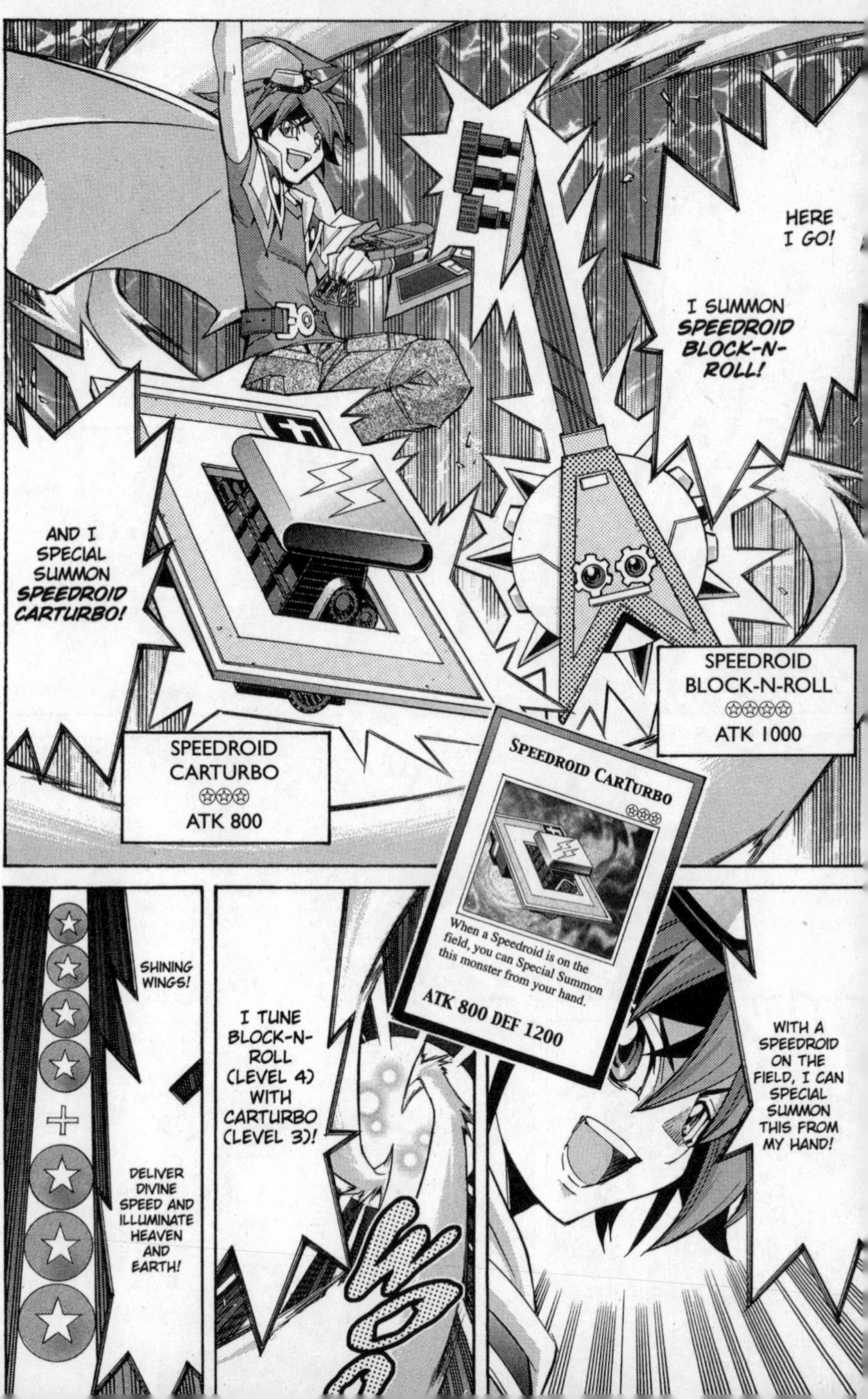
HERE I GO!
I SUMMON SPEEDROID BLOCK-N-ROLL!
SPEEDROID BLOCK-N-ROLL ATK 1000
AND I SPECIAL SUMMON SPEEDROID CARTURBO!
SPEEDROID CARTURBO ATK 800
Speedroid CarTurbo
When a Speedroid is on the field, you can Special Summon this monster from your hand.
ATK 800 DEF 1200
WITH A SPEEDROID ON THE FIELD, I CAN SPECIAL SUMMON THIS FROM MY HAND!
I TUNE BLOCK-N-ROLL (LEVEL 4) WITH CARTURBO (LEVEL 3)!
SHINING WINGS!
DELIVER DIVINE SPEED AND ILLUMINATE HEAVEN AND EARTH!

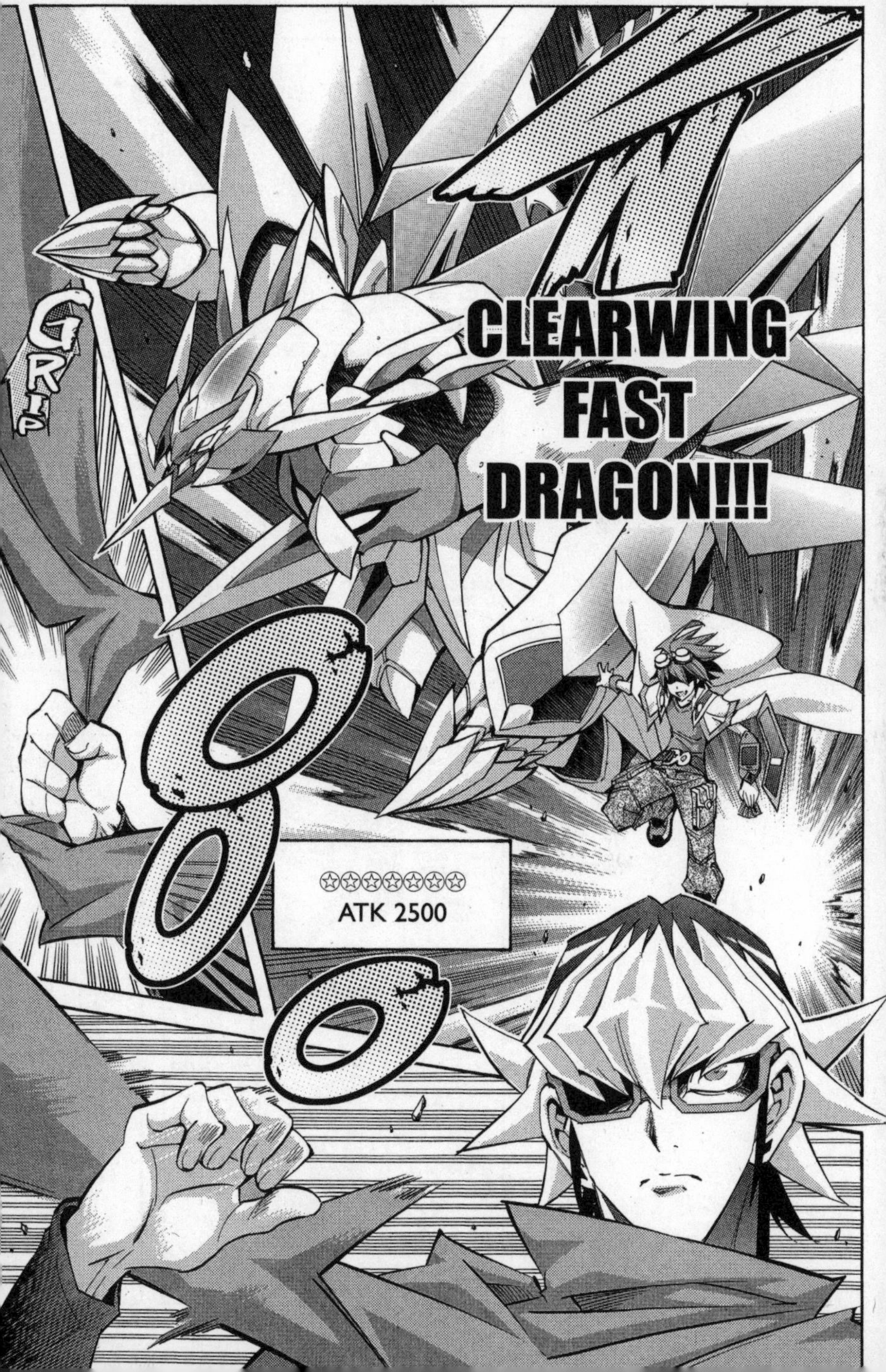
CLEARWING FAST DRAGON!!!
GRIP
ATK 2500

The Guys Behind ARC-V!

SHIN YOSHIDA

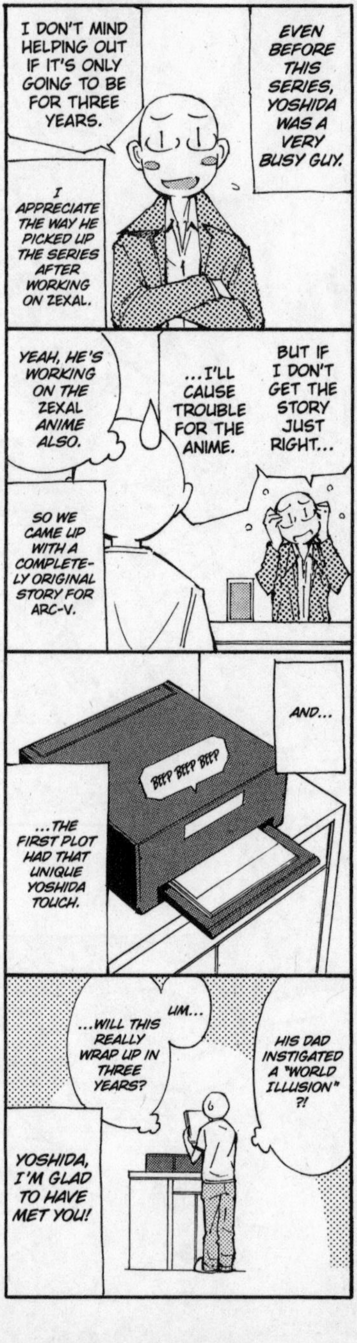
EVEN BEFORE THIS SERIES, YOSHIDA WAS A VERY BUSY GUY.
I DON'T MIND HELPING OUT IF IT'S ONLY GOING TO BE FOR THREE YEARS.
I APPRECIATE THE WAY HE PICKED UP THE SERIES AFTER WORKING ON ZEXAL.
BUT IF I DON'T GET THE STORY JUST RIGHT...
...I'LL CAUSE TROUBLE FOR THE ANIME.
YEAH, HE'S WORKING ON THE ZEXAL ANIME ALSO.
SO WE CAME UP WITH A COMPLETE-LY ORIGINAL STORY FOR ARC-V.
AND...
BEEP BEEP BEEP
...THE FIRST PLOT HAD THAT UNIQUE YOSHIDA TOUCH.
HIS DAD INSTIGATED A "WORLD ILLUSION"?!
UM...
...WILL THIS REALLY WRAP UP IN THREE YEARS?
YOSHIDA, I'M GLAD TO HAVE MET YOU!

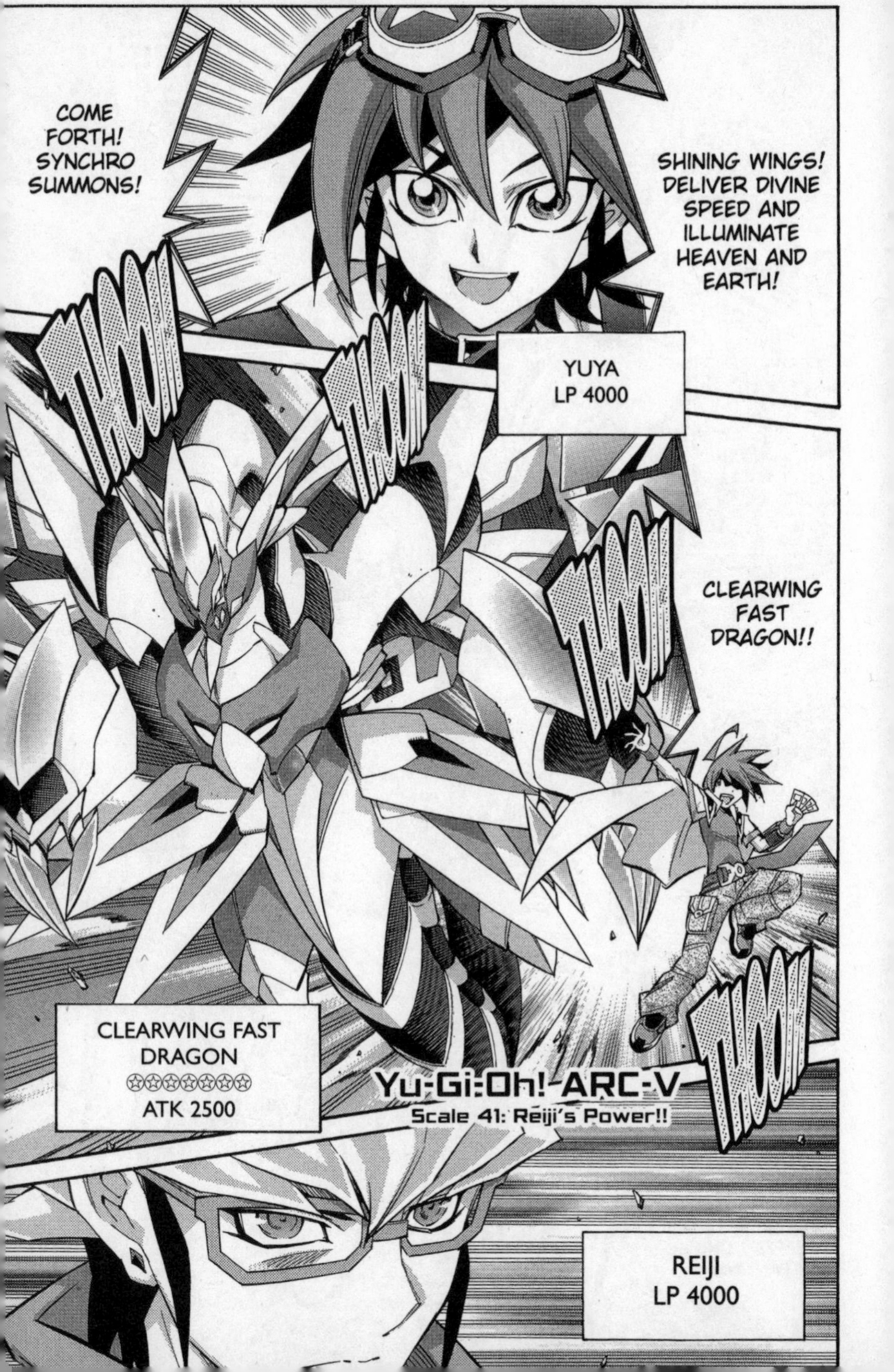

SHINING WINGS! DELIVER DIVINE SPEED AND ILLUMINATE HEAVEN AND EARTH!
COME FORTH! SYNCHRO SUMMONS!
YUYA
LP 4000
THOOM
THOOM
CLEARWING FAST DRAGON!!
THOOM
THOOM
CLEARWING FAST DRAGON
☆☆☆☆☆☆☆☆
ATK 2500
Yu-Gi-Oh! ARC-V
Scale 41: Reiji's Power!!
REIJI
LP 4000

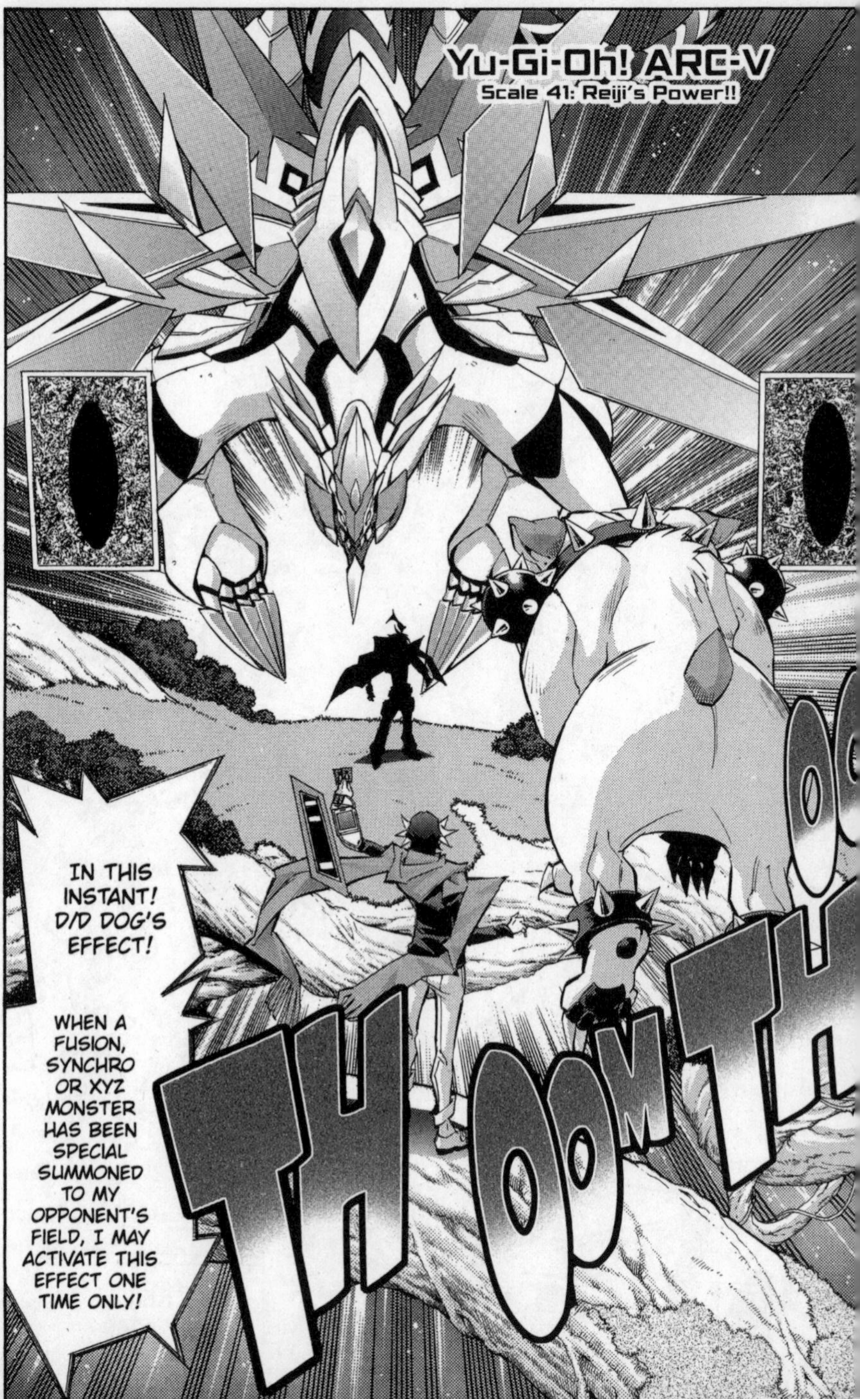
Yu-Gi-Oh! ARC-V
Scale 41: Reiji's Power!!
IN THIS INSTANT! D/D DOG'S EFFECT!
WHEN A FUSION, SYNCHRO OR XYZ MONSTER HAS BEEN SPECIAL SUMMONED TO MY OPPONENT'S FIELD, I MAY ACTIVATE THIS EFFECT ONE TIME ONLY!
THOOM THOOM

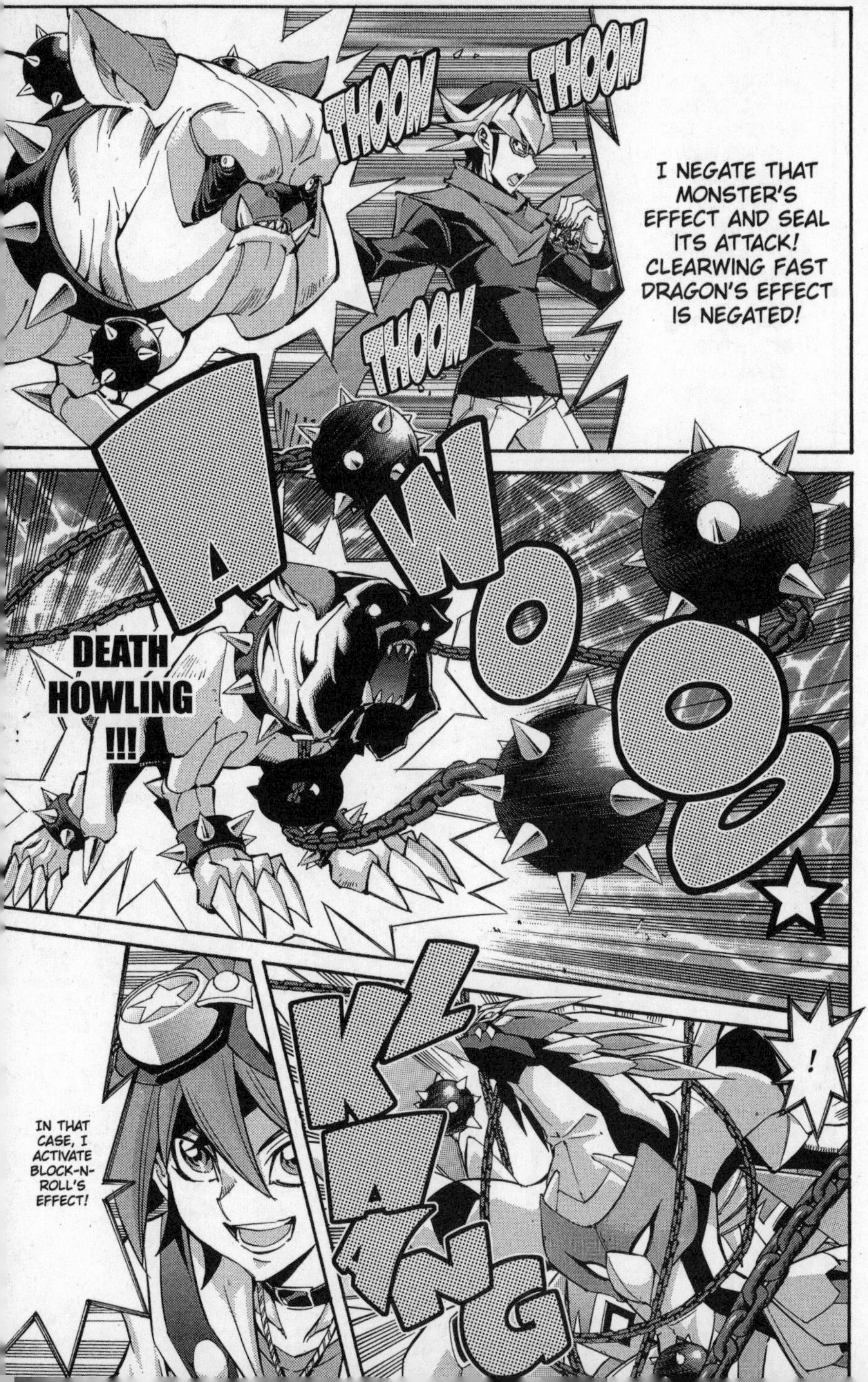
THOOM
THOOM
I NEGATE THAT MONSTER'S EFFECT AND SEAL ITS ATTACK! CLEARWING FAST DRAGON'S EFFECT IS NEGATED!
THOOM
AWOOO
DEATH HOWLING!!!
!
KLANG
IN THAT CASE, I ACTIVATE BLOCK-N-ROLL'S EFFECT!

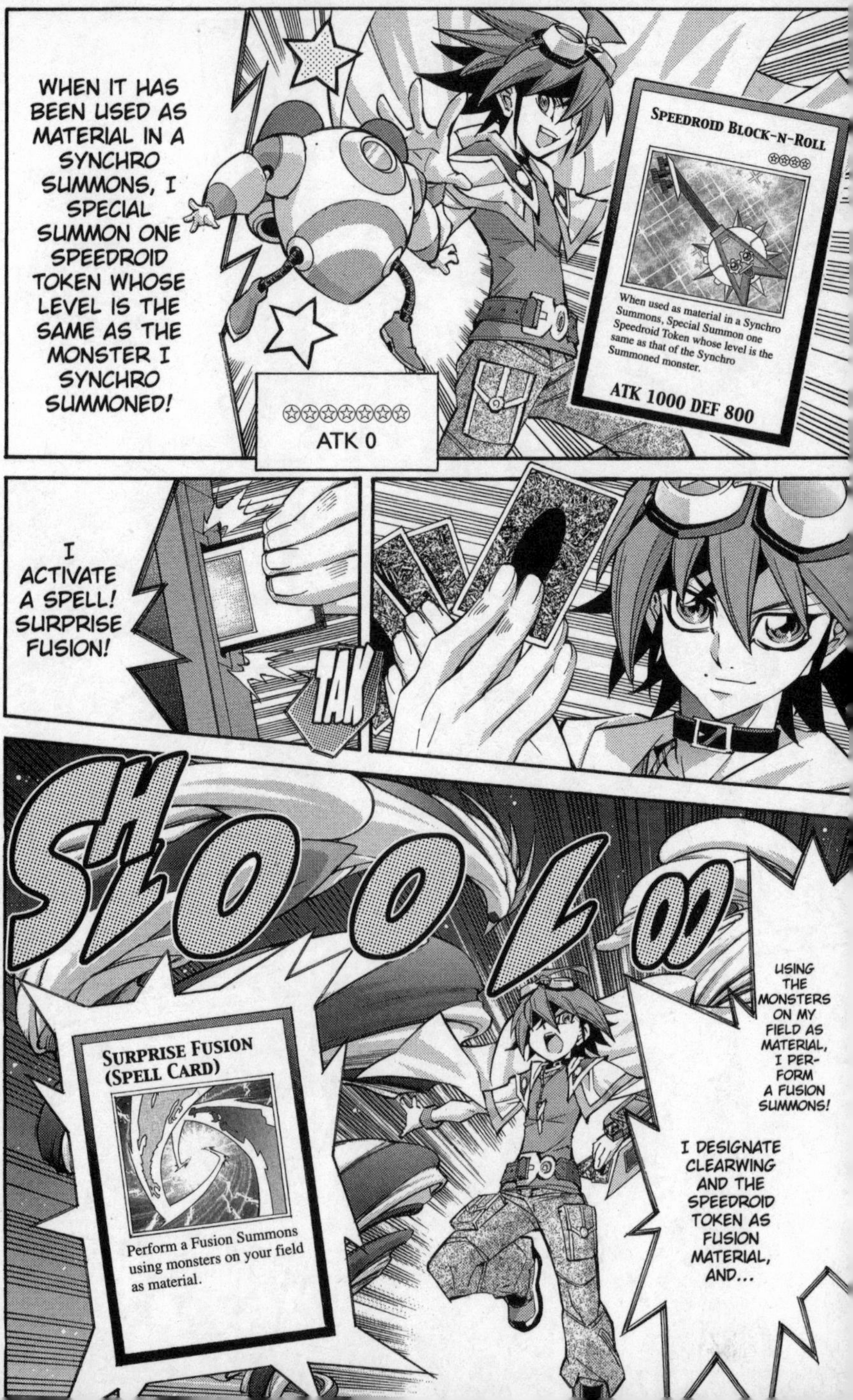
SPEEDROID BLOCK-N-ROLL
When used as material in a Synchro Summons, Special Summon one Speedroid Token whose level is the same as that of the Synchro Summoned monster.
ATK 1000 DEF 800
WHEN IT HAS BEEN USED AS MATERIAL IN A SYNCHRO SUMMONS, I SPECIAL SUMMON ONE SPEEDROID TOKEN WHOSE LEVEL IS THE SAME AS THE MONSTER I SYNCHRO SUMMONED!
ATK 0
I ACTIVATE A SPELL! SURPRISE FUSION!
TAK
SHLOOOLOO
USING THE MONSTERS ON MY FIELD AS MATERIAL, I PER-FORM A FUSION SUMMONS!
I DESIGNATE CLEARWING AND THE SPEEDROID TOKEN AS FUSION MATERIAL, AND...
SURPRISE FUSION (SPELL CARD)
Perform a Fusion Summons using monsters on your field as material.

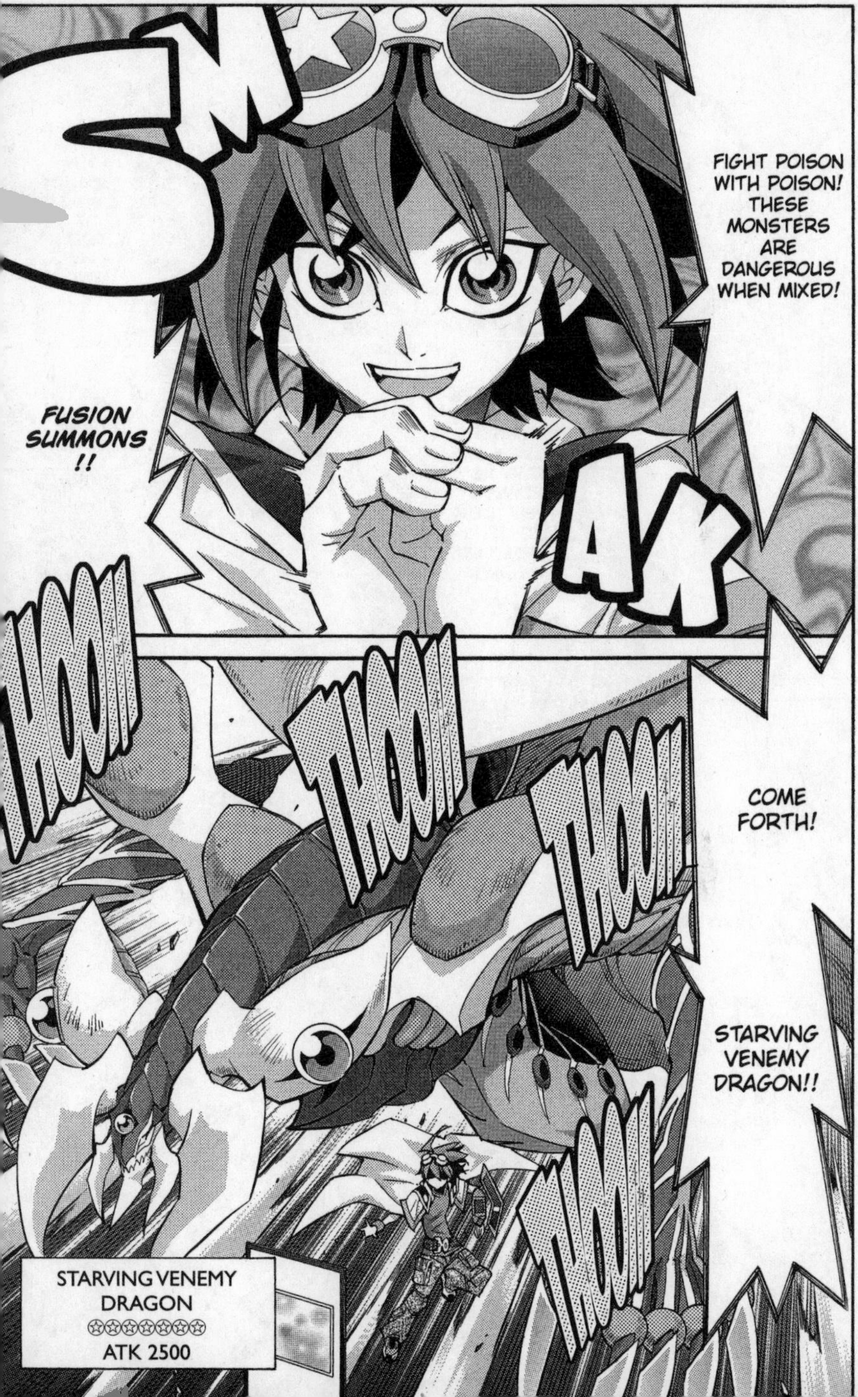
FIGHT POISON WITH POISON! THESE MONSTERS ARE DANGEROUS WHEN MIXED!
FUSION SUMMONS !!
COME FORTH!
STARVING VENEMY DRAGON!!
THOOM
THOOM
THOOM
HOOM
STARVING VENEMY DRAGON
ATK 2500

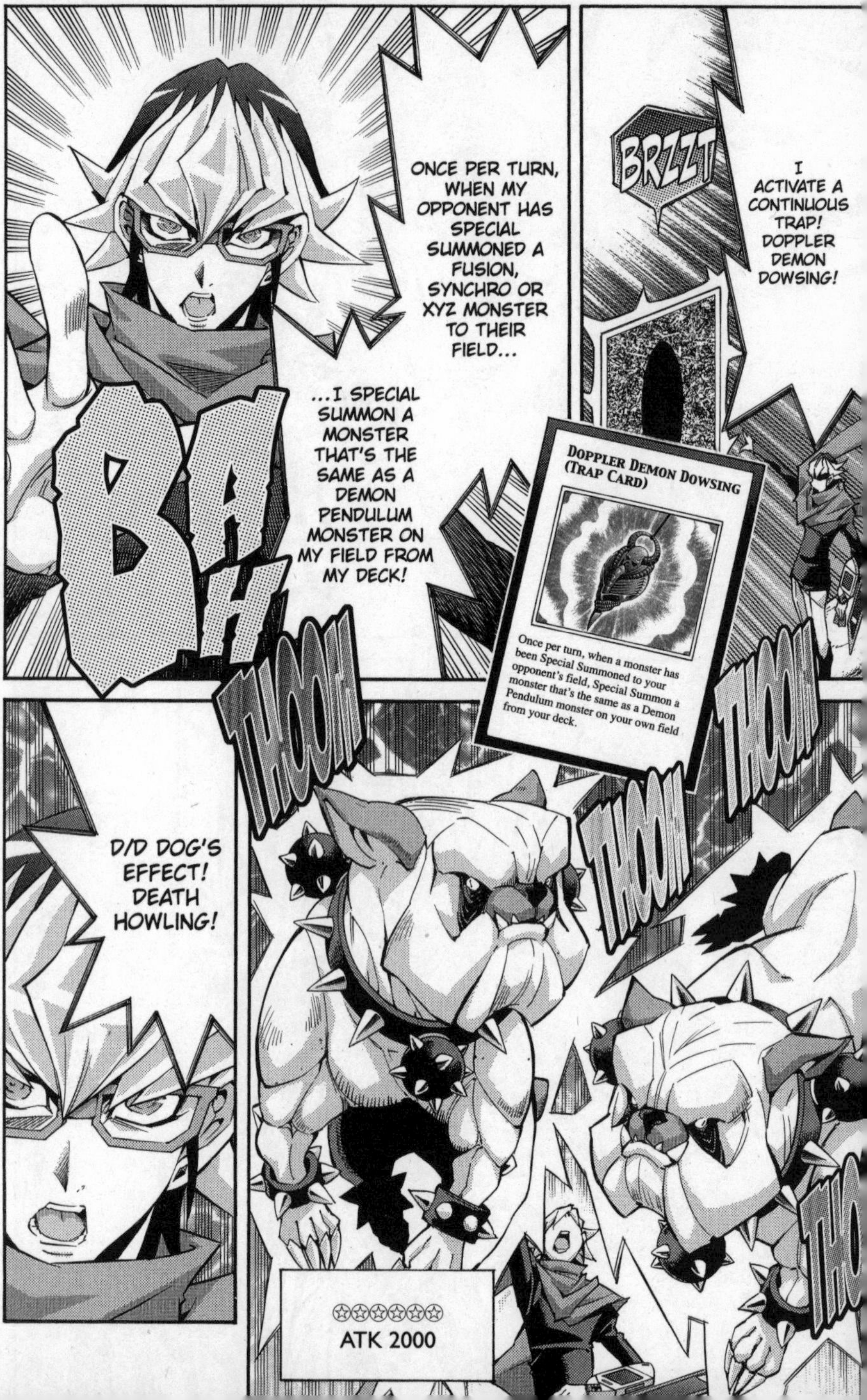
BRZZT
I ACTIVATE A CONTINUOUS TRAP! DOPPLER DEMON DOWSING!
DOPPLER DEMON DOWSING (TRAP CARD)
Once per turn, when a monster has been Special Summoned to your opponent's field, Special Summon a monster that's the same as a Demon Pendulum monster on your own field from your deck.
ONCE PER TURN, WHEN MY OPPONENT HAS SPECIAL SUMMONED A FUSION, SYNCHRO OR XYZ MONSTER TO THEIR FIELD...
...I SPECIAL SUMMON A MONSTER THAT'S THE SAME AS A DEMON PENDULUM MONSTER ON MY FIELD FROM MY DECK!
BAH
THOOM
THOOM
THOOM
THOOM
ATK 2000
D/D DOG'S EFFECT! DEATH HOWLING!

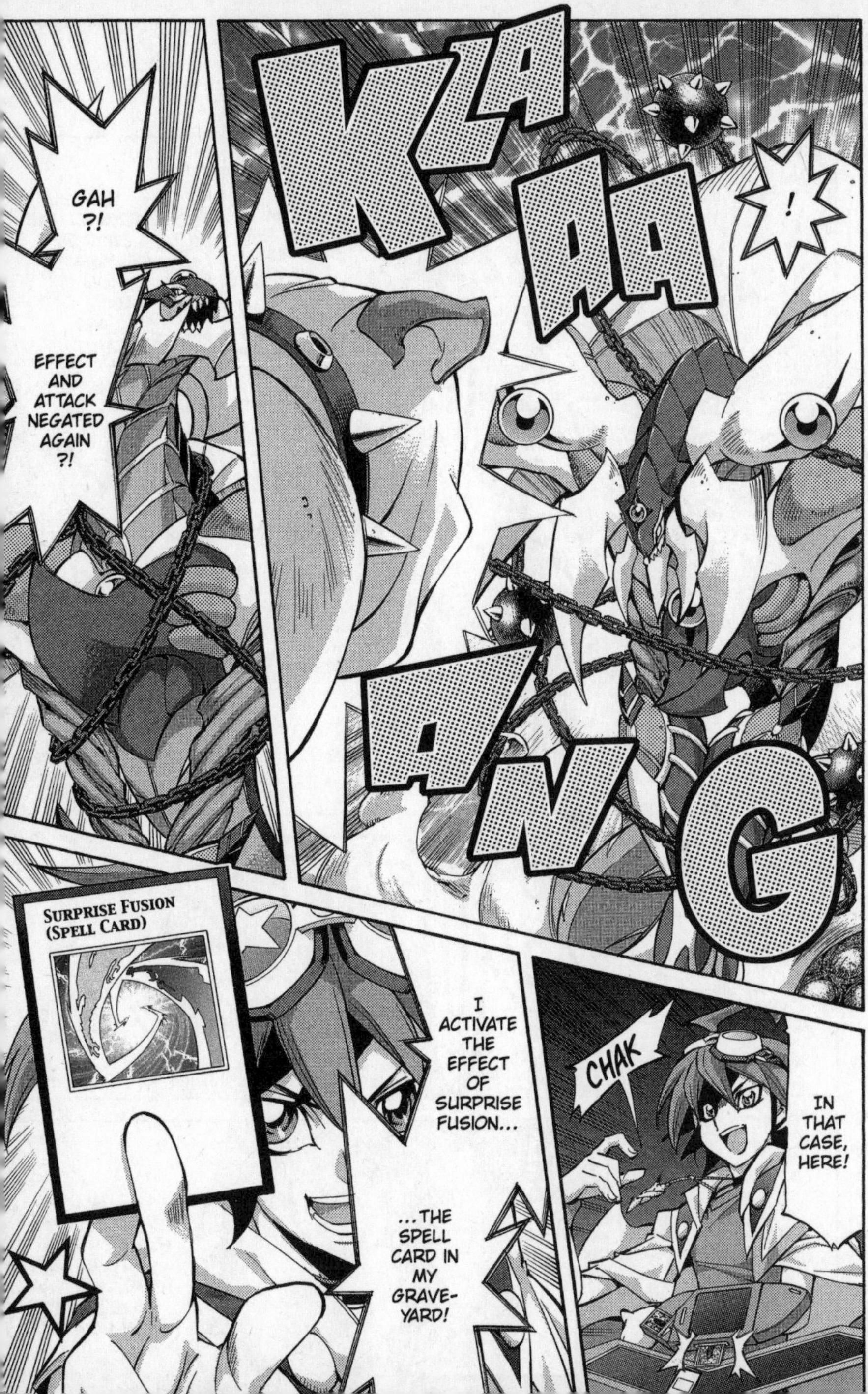
K'ZAAANG
!
GAH ?!
EFFECT AND ATTACK NEGATED AGAIN ?!
CHAK
IN THAT CASE, HERE!
I ACTIVATE THE EFFECT OF SURPRISE FUSION...
...THE SPELL CARD IN MY GRAVEYARD!
SURPRISE FUSION (SPELL CARD)

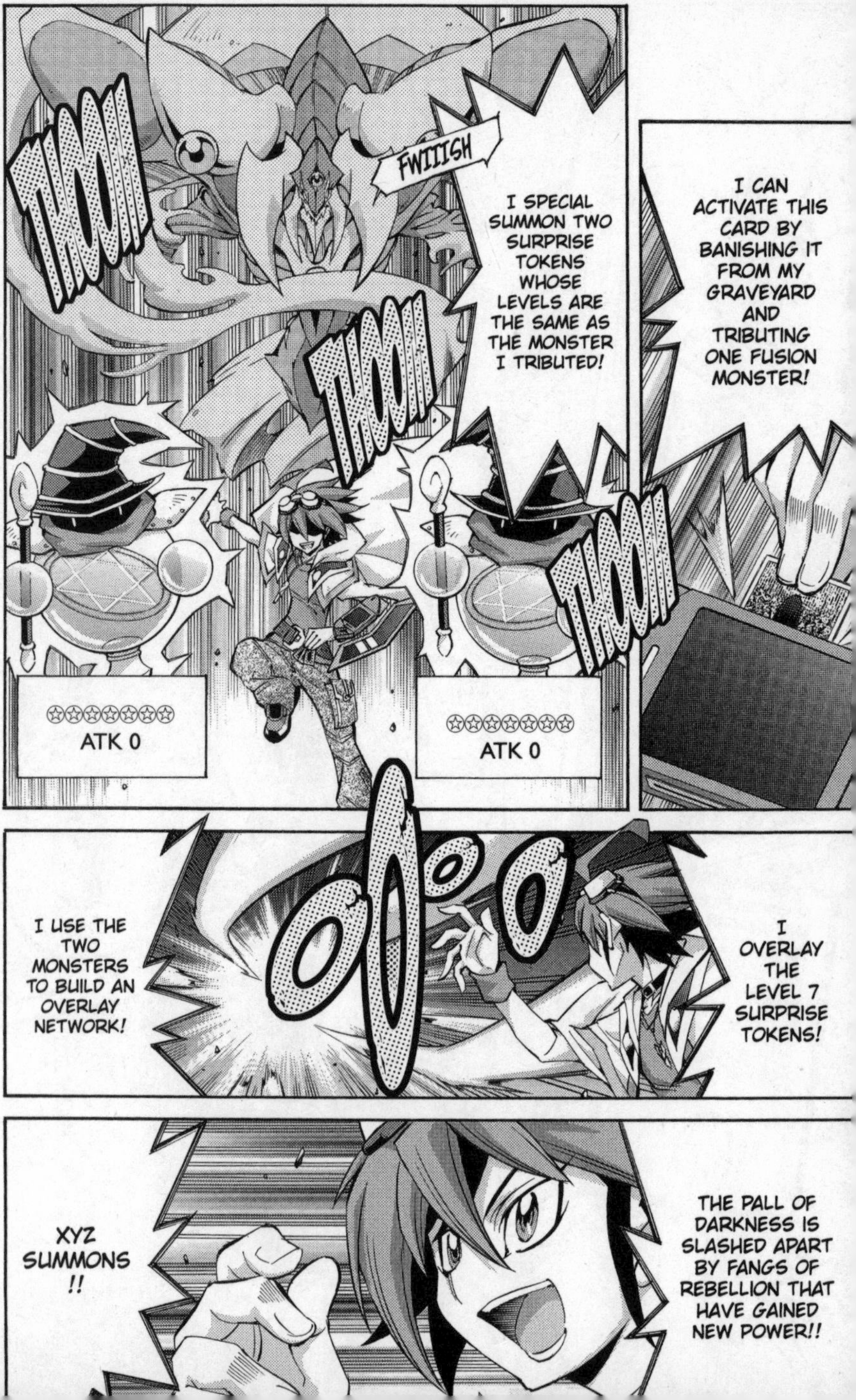
I CAN ACTIVATE THIS CARD BY BANISHING IT FROM MY GRAVEYARD AND TRIBUTING ONE FUSION MONSTER!
THOOM
FWIIISH
I SPECIAL SUMMON TWO SURPRISE TOKENS WHOSE LEVELS ARE THE SAME AS THE MONSTER I TRIBUTED!
THOOM
THOOM
☆☆☆☆☆☆☆ ATK 0
☆☆☆☆☆☆☆ ATK 0
I OVERLAY THE LEVEL 7 SURPRISE TOKENS!
I USE THE TWO MONSTERS TO BUILD AN OVERLAY NETWORK!
THE PALL OF DARKNESS IS SLASHED APART BY FANGS OF REBELLION THAT HAVE GAINED NEW POWER!!
XYZ SUMMONS !!

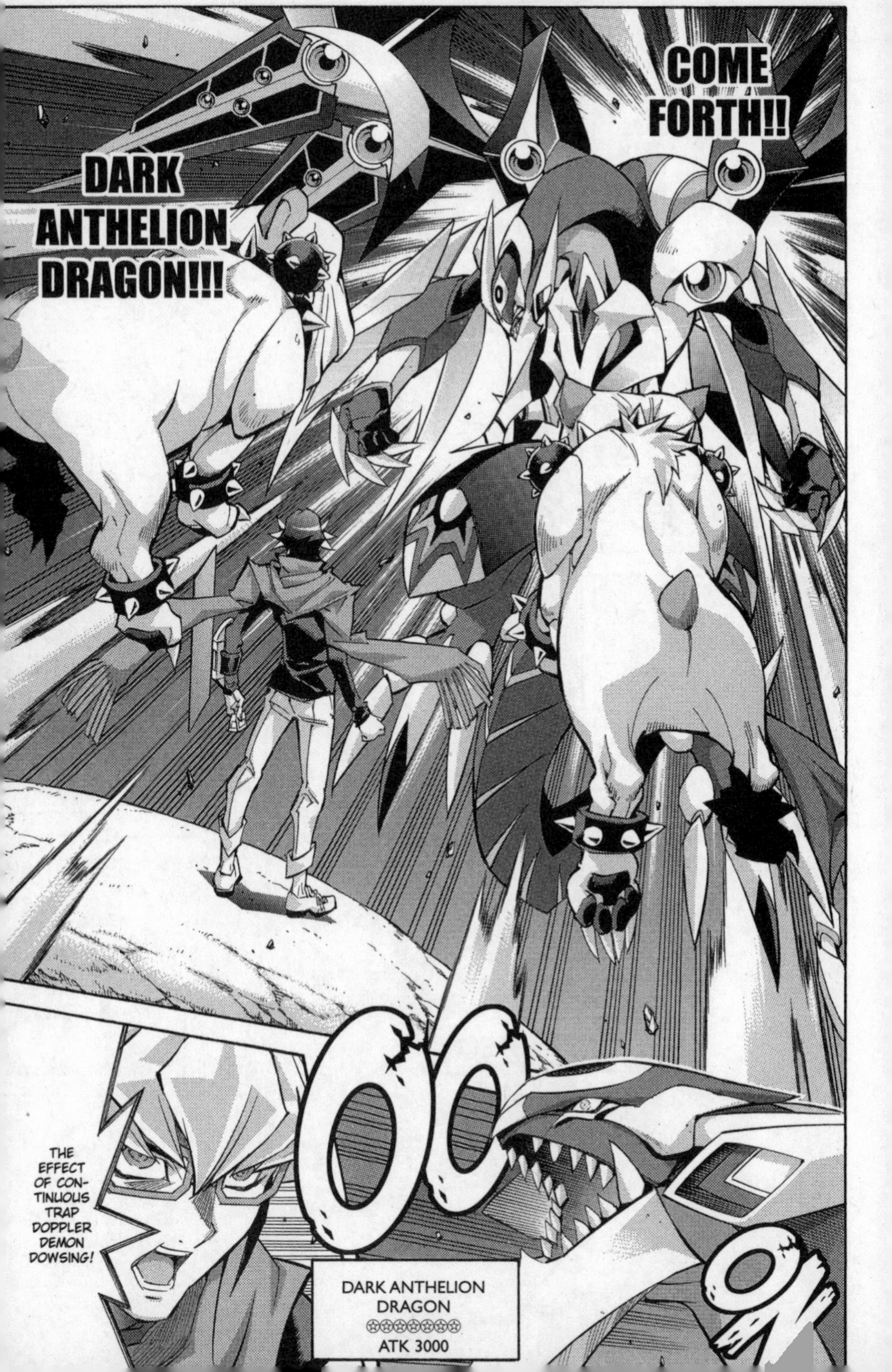
COME FORTH!!
DARK ANTHELION DRAGON!!!
DARK ANTHELION DRAGON
✪✪✪✪✪✪✪
ATK 3000
THE EFFECT OF CON-TINUOUS TRAP DOPPLER DEMON DOWSING!

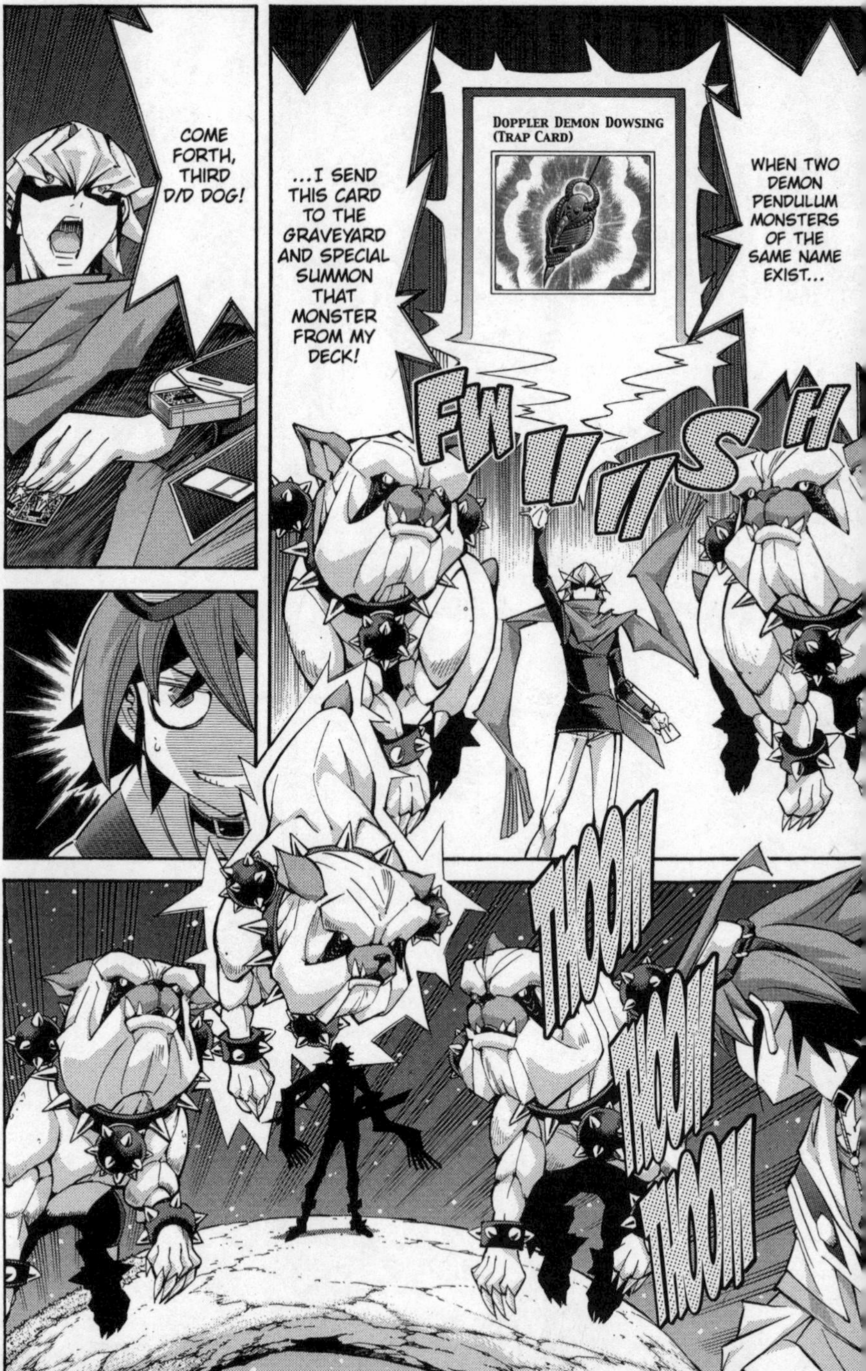
WHEN TWO DEMON PENDULUM MONSTERS OF THE SAME NAME EXIST...
DOPPLER DEMON DOWSING
(TRAP CARD)
...I SEND THIS CARD TO THE GRAVEYARD AND SPECIAL SUMMON THAT MONSTER FROM MY DECK!
FWIISH
COME FORTH, THIRD D/D DOG!
THOOM
THOOM
THOOM
THOOM

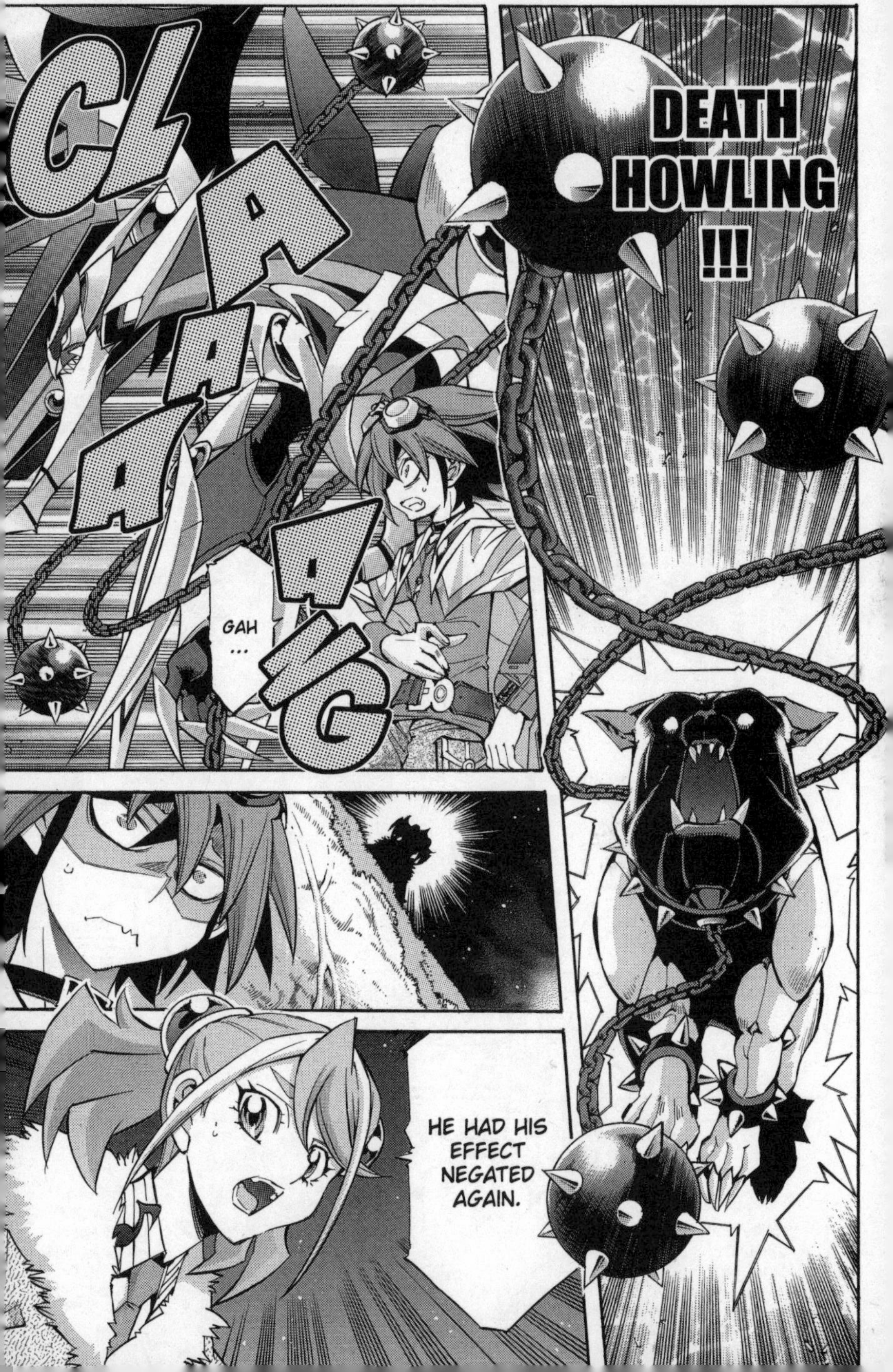
DEATH HOWLING!!!
CLAAAANG
GAH...
HE HAD HIS EFFECT NEGATED AGAIN.

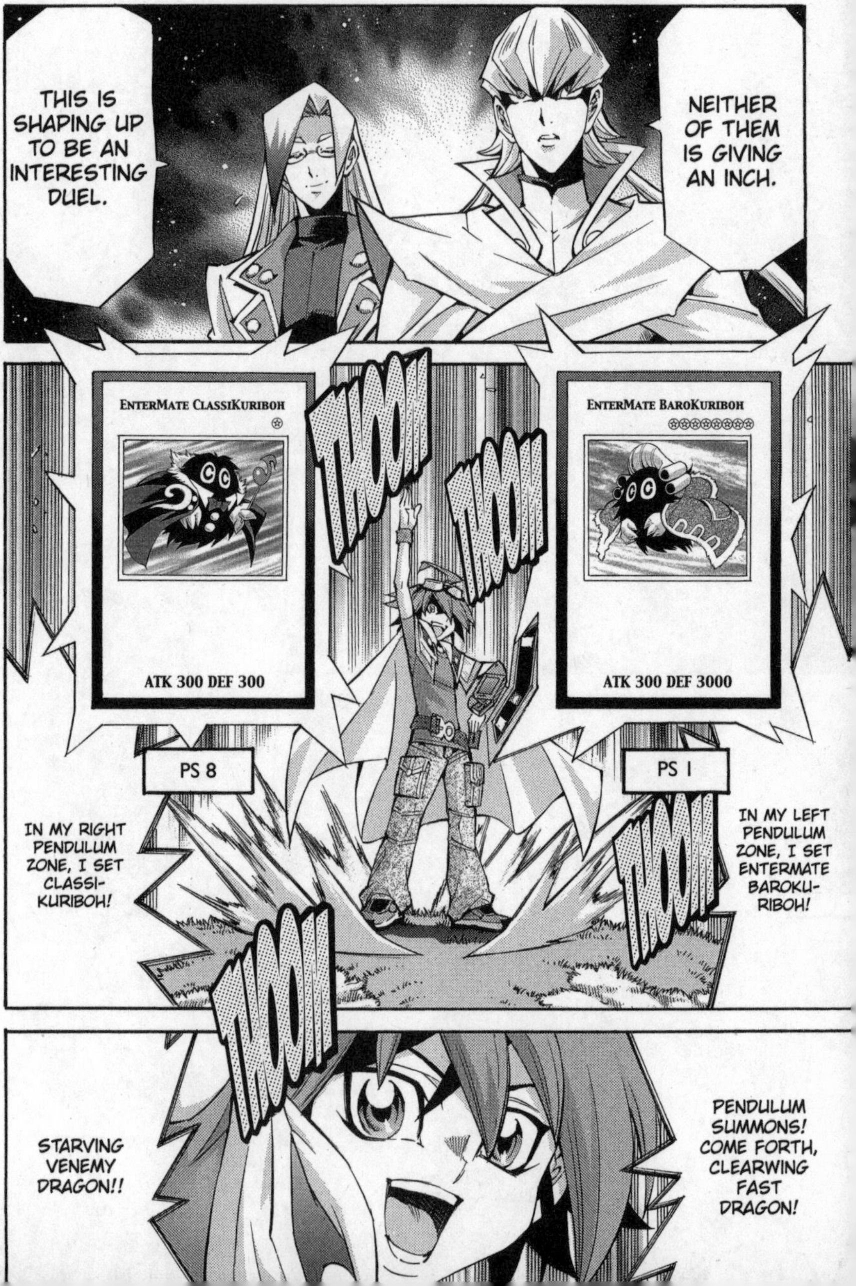

NEITHER OF THEM IS GIVING AN INCH.
THIS IS SHAPING UP TO BE AN INTERESTING DUEL.
EnterMate BaroKuriboh
ATK 300 DEF 3000
THOOM
THOOM
EnterMate ClassiKuriboh
ATK 300 DEF 300
PS 1
IN MY LEFT PENDULUM ZONE, I SET ENTERMATE BAROKURIBOH!
THOOM
PS 8
IN MY RIGHT PENDULUM ZONE, I SET CLASSI-KURIBOH!
THOOM
PENDULUM SUMMONS! COME FORTH, CLEARWING FAST DRAGON!
STARVING VENEMY DRAGON!!

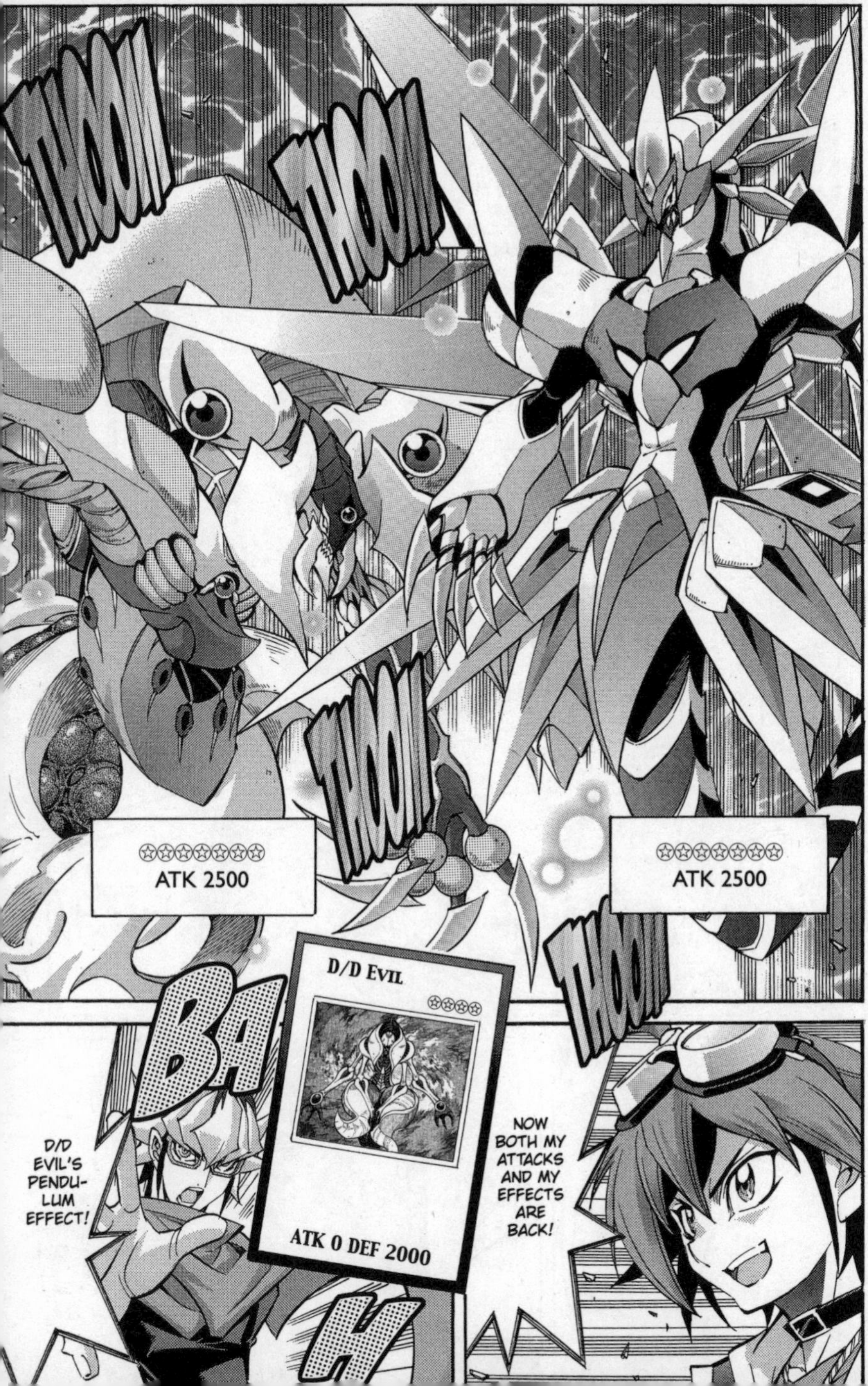
THOOM
THOOM
ATK 2500
THOOM
ATK 2500
THOOM
NOW BOTH MY ATTACKS AND MY EFFECTS ARE BACK!
D/D EVIL
ATK 0 DEF 2000
BAH
D/D EVIL'S PENDULUM EFFECT!

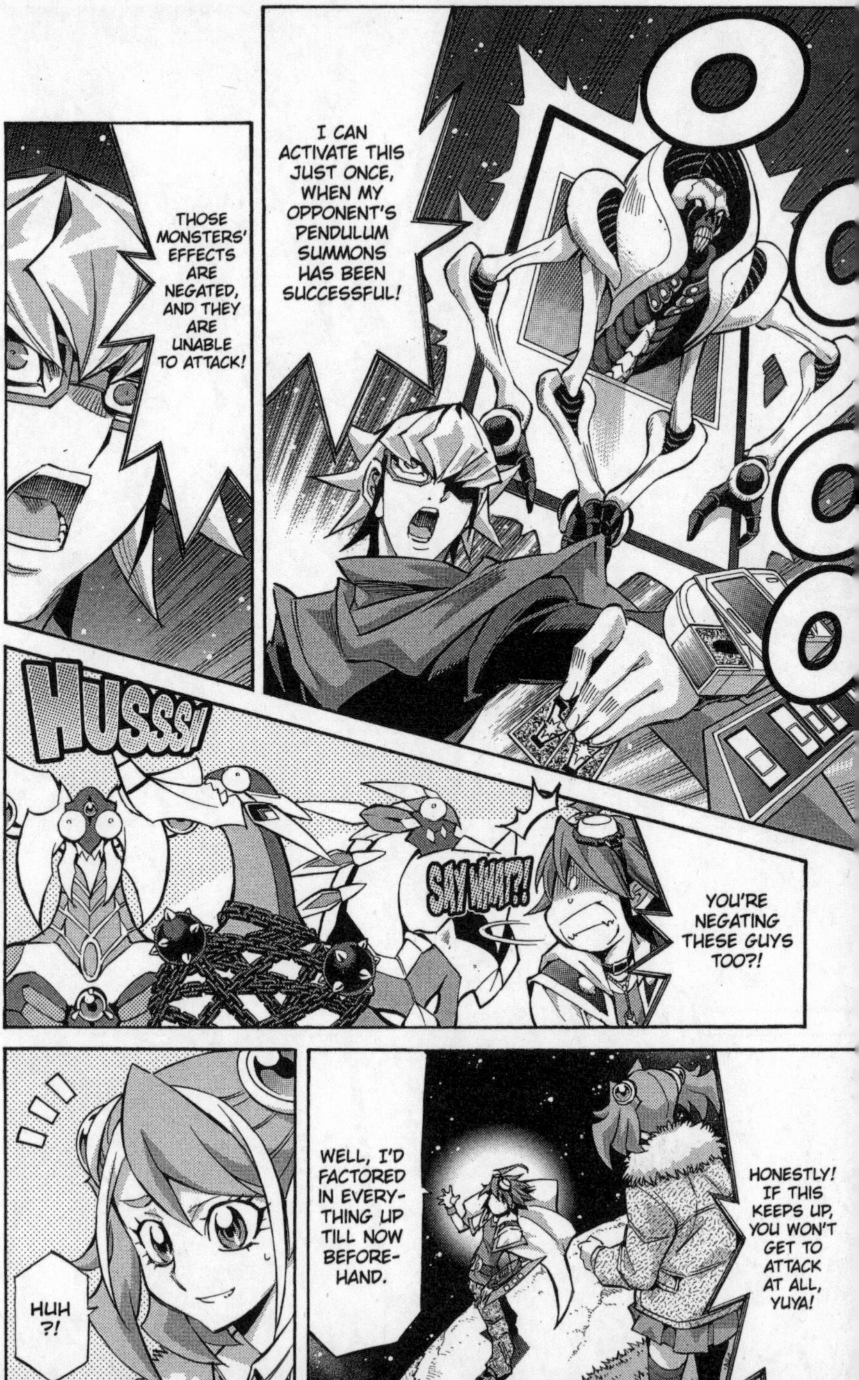
I CAN ACTIVATE THIS JUST ONCE, WHEN MY OPPONENT'S PENDULUM SUMMONS HAS BEEN SUCCESSFUL!
THOSE MONSTERS' EFFECTS ARE NEGATED, AND THEY ARE UNABLE TO ATTACK!
YOU'RE NEGATING THESE GUYS TOO?!
SAY WHAT?!
HUSSS!
HONESTLY! IF THIS KEEPS UP, YOU WON'T GET TO ATTACK AT ALL, YUYA!
WELL, I'D FACTORED IN EVERY-THING UP TILL NOW BEFORE-HAND.
HUH ?!

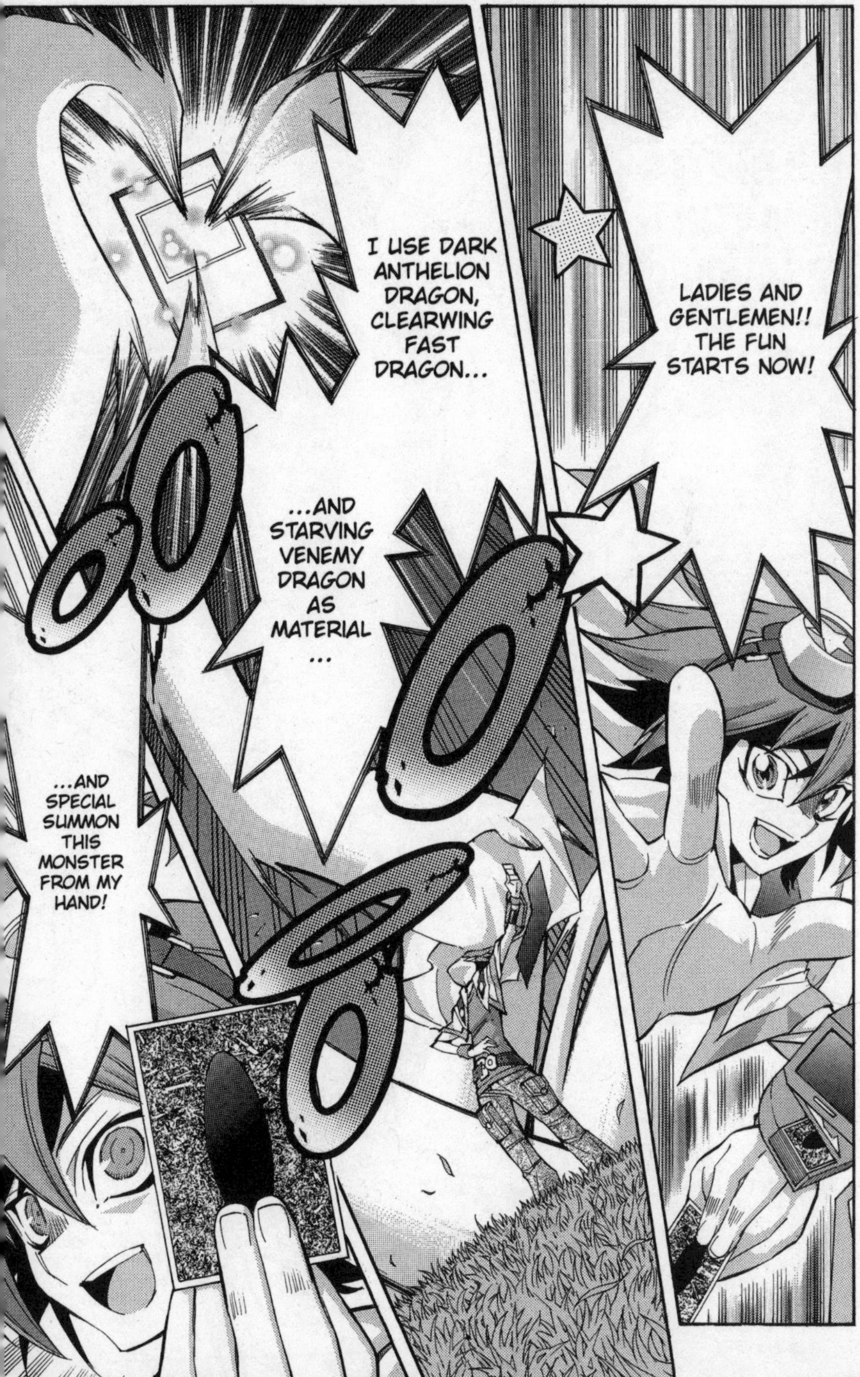
LADIES AND GENTLEMEN!! THE FUN STARTS NOW!
I USE DARK ANTHELION DRAGON, CLEARWING FAST DRAGON...
...AND STARVING VENEMY DRAGON AS MATERIAL...
...AND SPECIAL SUMMON THIS MONSTER FROM MY HAND!

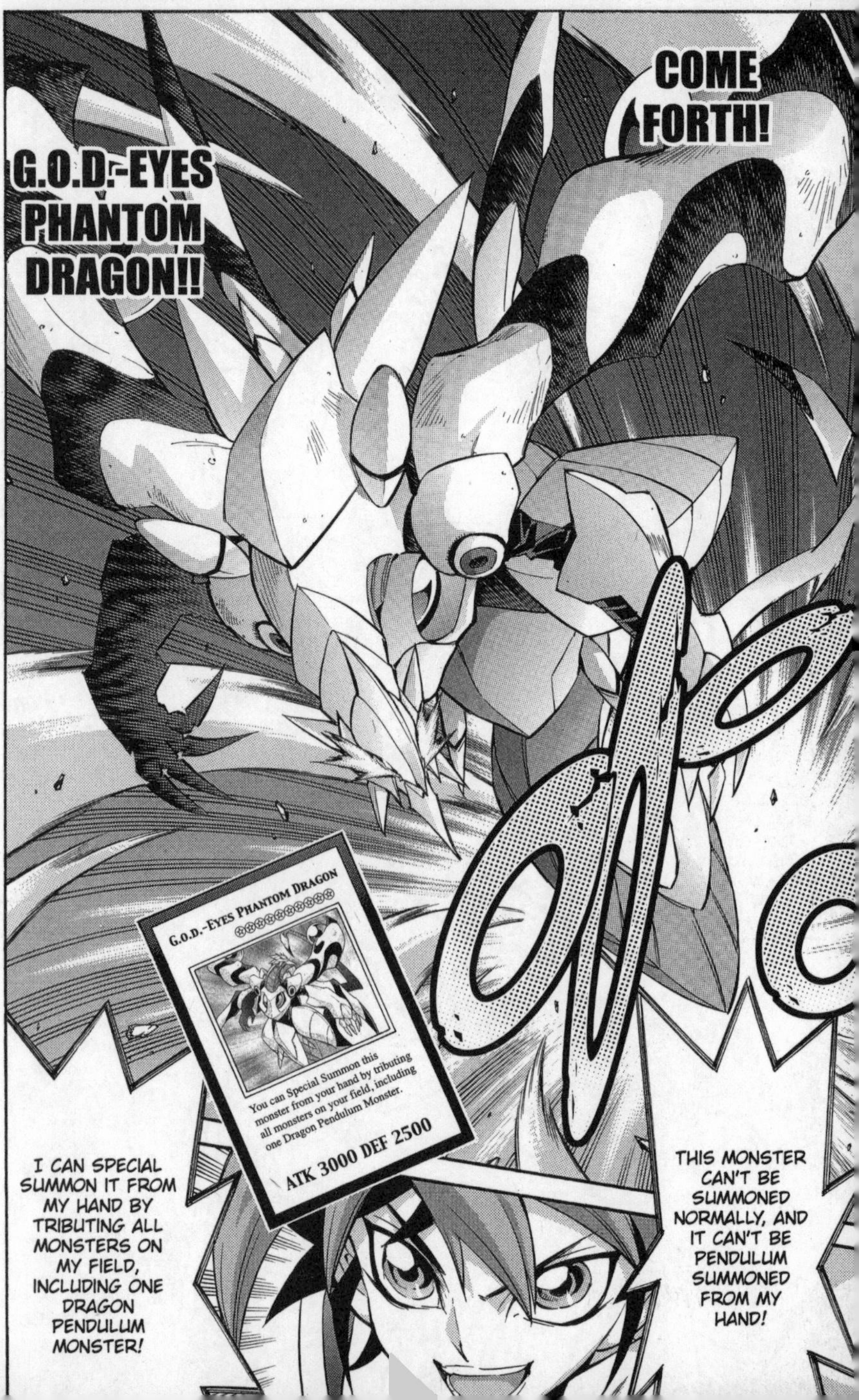
COME FORTH!
G.O.D.-EYES PHANTOM DRAGON!!
G.O.D.-EYES PHANTOM DRAGON
You can Special Summon this monster from your hand by tributing all monsters on your field, including one Dragon Pendulum Monster.
ATK 3000 DEF 2500
THIS MONSTER CAN'T BE SUMMONED NORMALLY, AND IT CAN'T BE PENDULUM SUMMONED FROM MY HAND!
I CAN SPECIAL SUMMON IT FROM MY HAND BY TRIBUTING ALL MONSTERS ON MY FIELD, INCLUDING ONE DRAGON PENDULUM MONSTER!

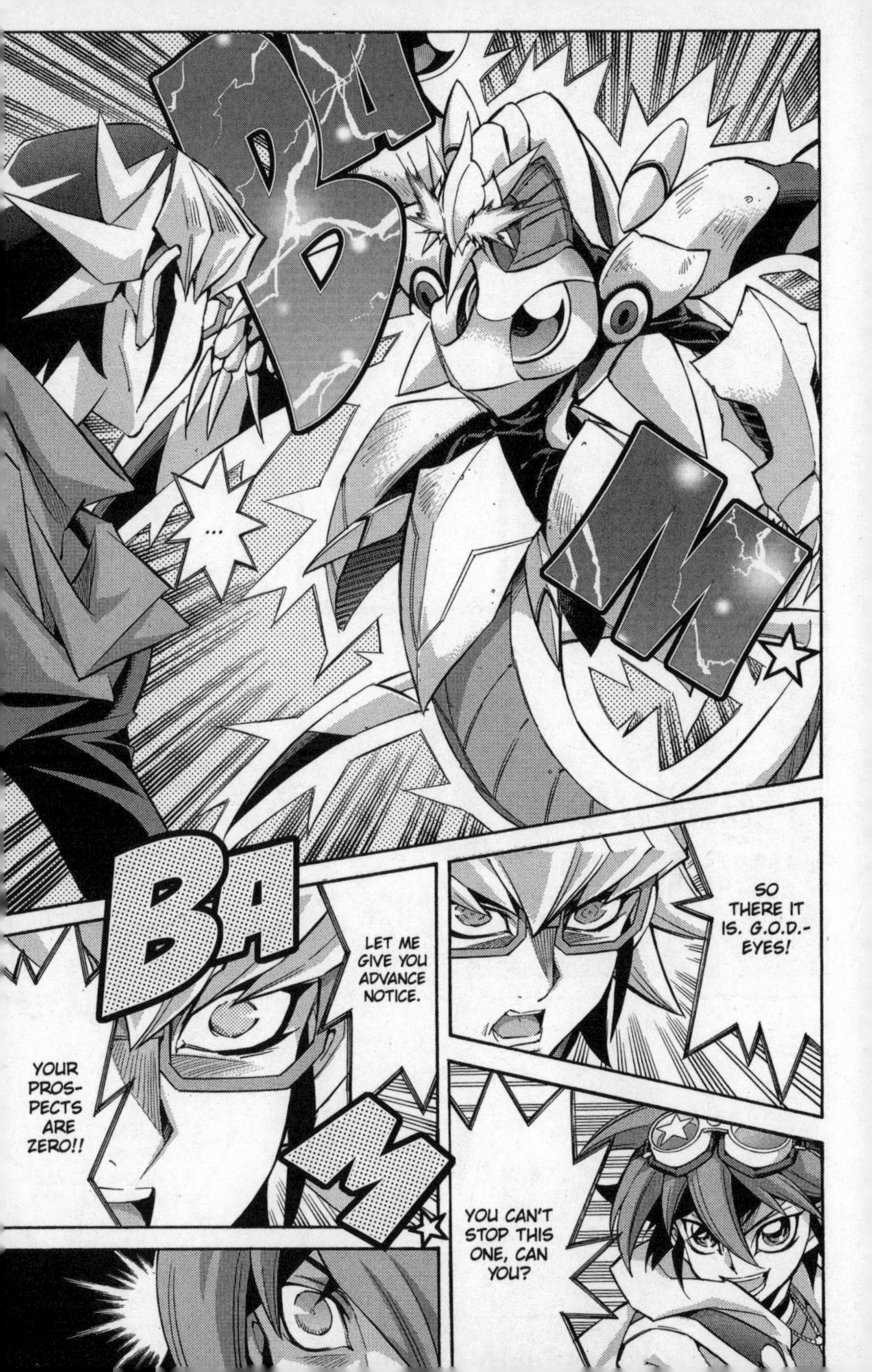
...
SO THERE IT IS. G.O.D.-EYES!
YOU CAN'T STOP THIS ONE, CAN YOU?
LET ME GIVE YOU ADVANCE NOTICE.
YOUR PROS-PECTS ARE ZERO!!
BAM

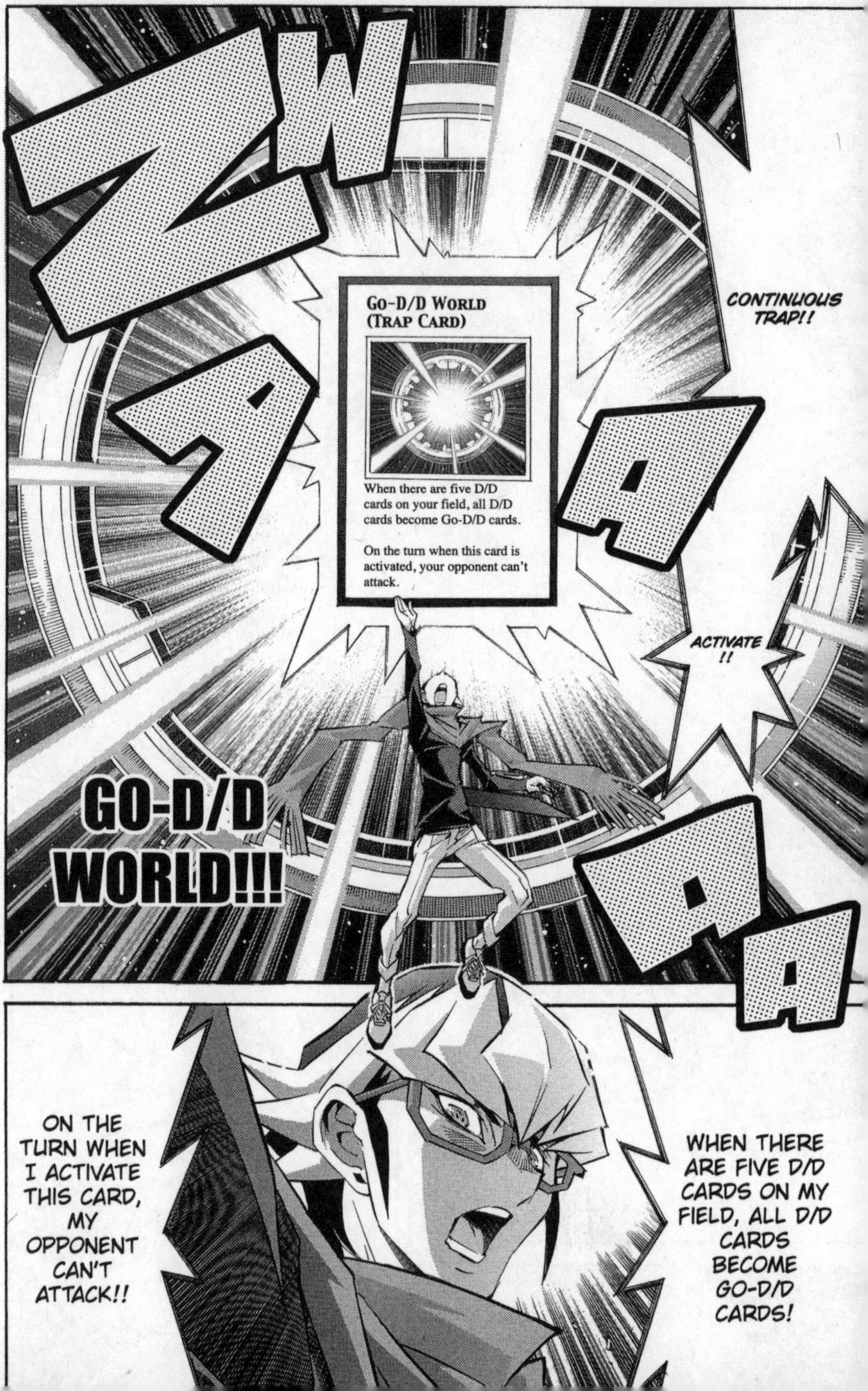
CONTINUOUS TRAP!!
ZWAAAA
GO-D/D WORLD (TRAP CARD)
When there are five D/D cards on your field, all D/D cards become Go-D/D cards.
On the turn when this card is activated, your opponent can't attack.
ACTIVATE!!
GO-D/D WORLD!!!
WHEN THERE ARE FIVE D/D CARDS ON MY FIELD, ALL D/D CARDS BECOME GO-D/D CARDS!
ON THE TURN WHEN I ACTIVATE THIS CARD, MY OPPONENT CAN'T ATTACK!!

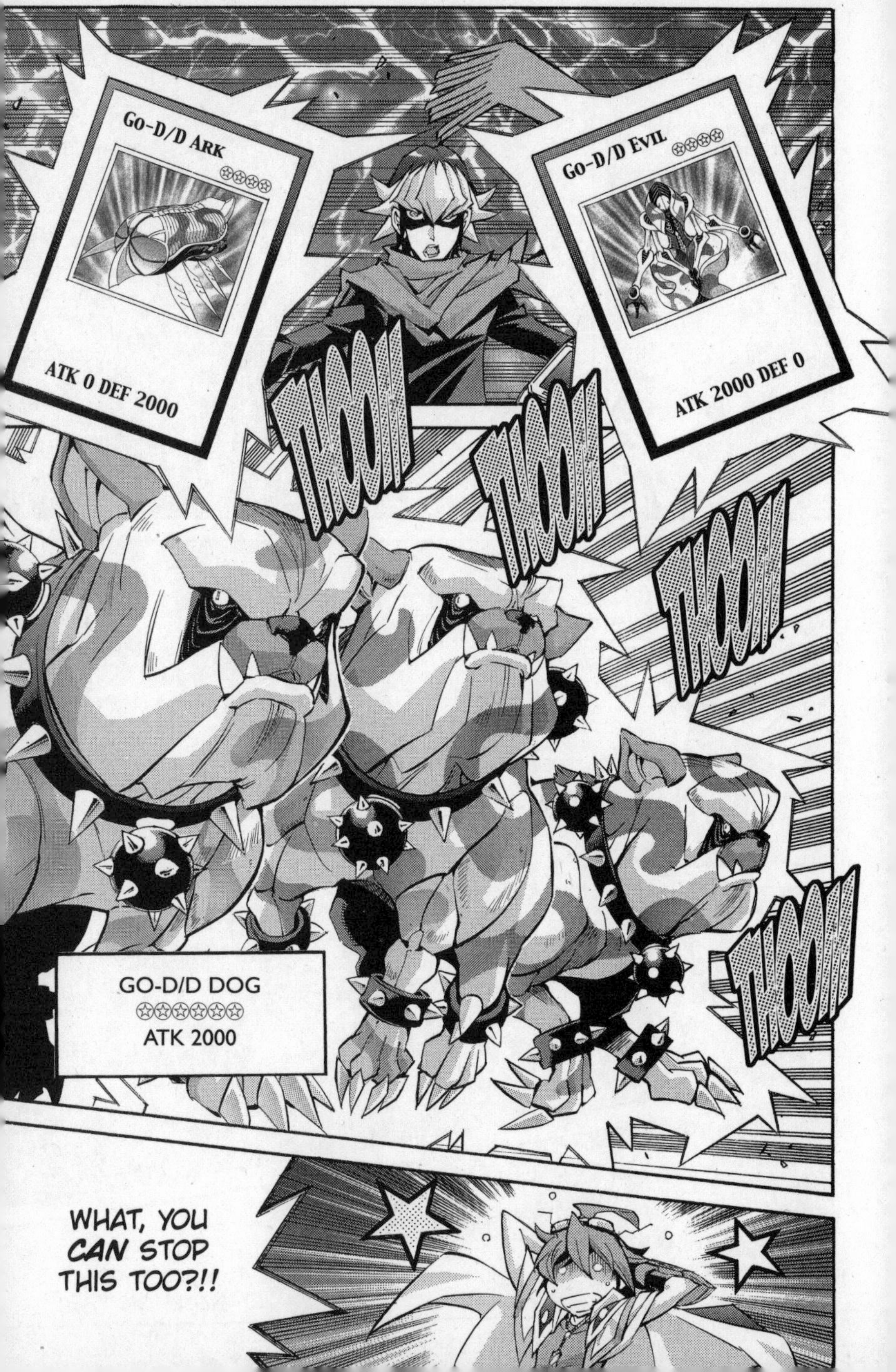

Go-D/D Evil
ATK 2000 DEF 0
Go-D/D Ark
ATK 0 DEF 2000
THOOM
THOOM
THOOM
THOOM
GO-D/D DOG
ATK 2000
WHAT, YOU *CAN* STOP THIS TOO?!!

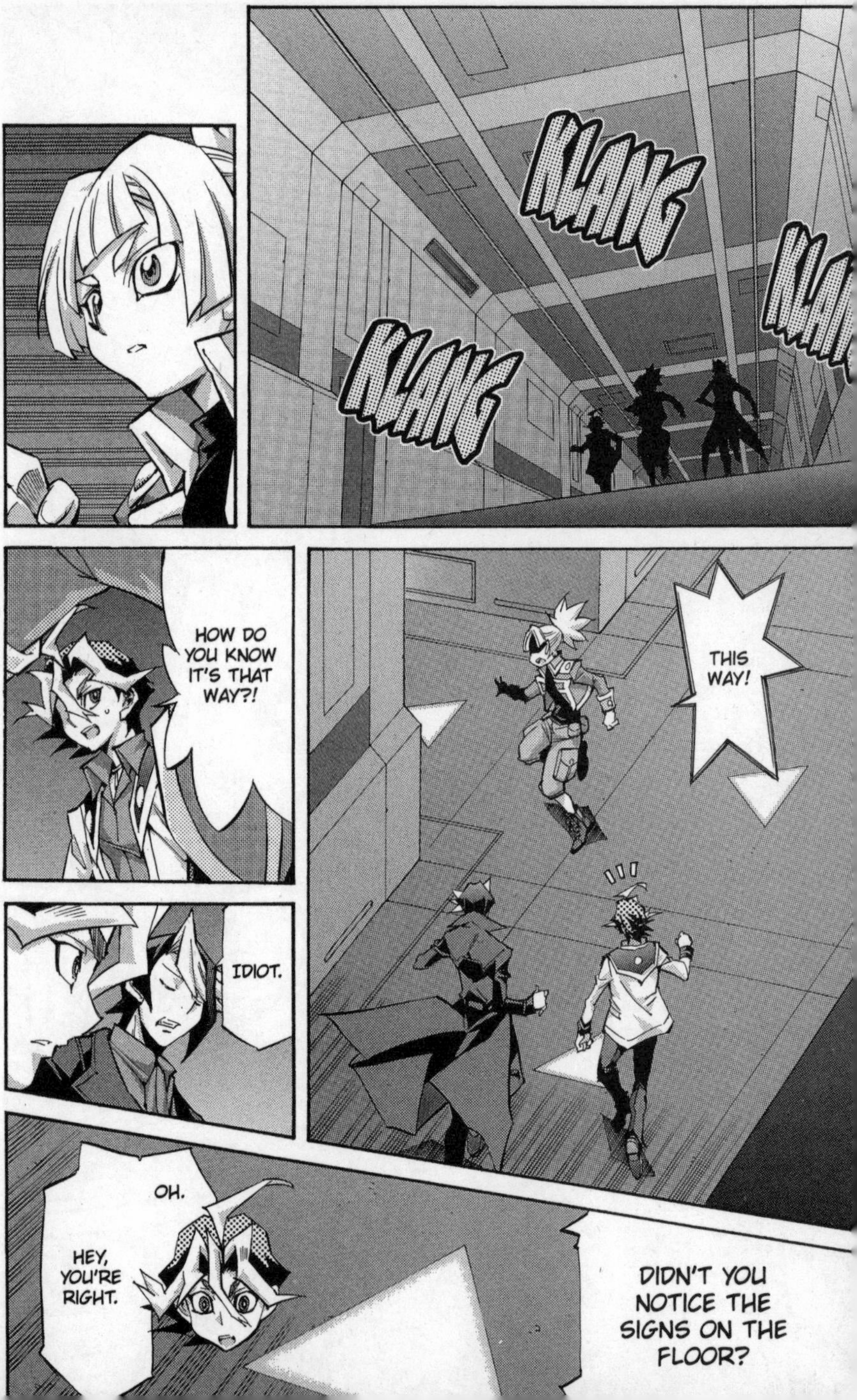
KLANG
KLANG
THIS WAY!
HOW DO YOU KNOW IT'S THAT WAY?!
IDIOT.
DIDN'T YOU NOTICE THE SIGNS ON THE FLOOR?
OH.
HEY, YOU'RE RIGHT.

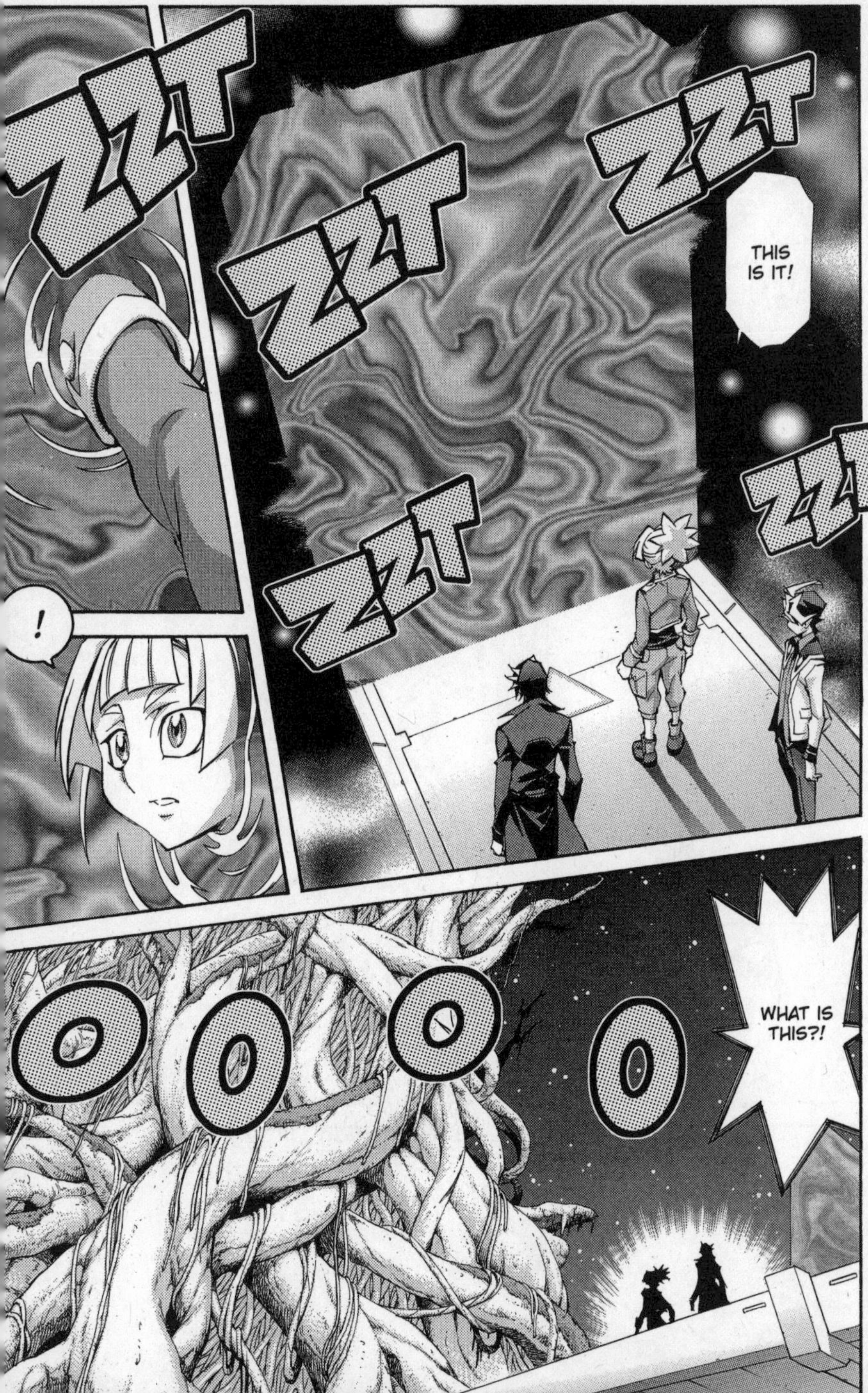
ZZT
THIS IS IT!
ZZT
ZZT
ZZT
ZZT
!
WHAT IS THIS?!
OOOO

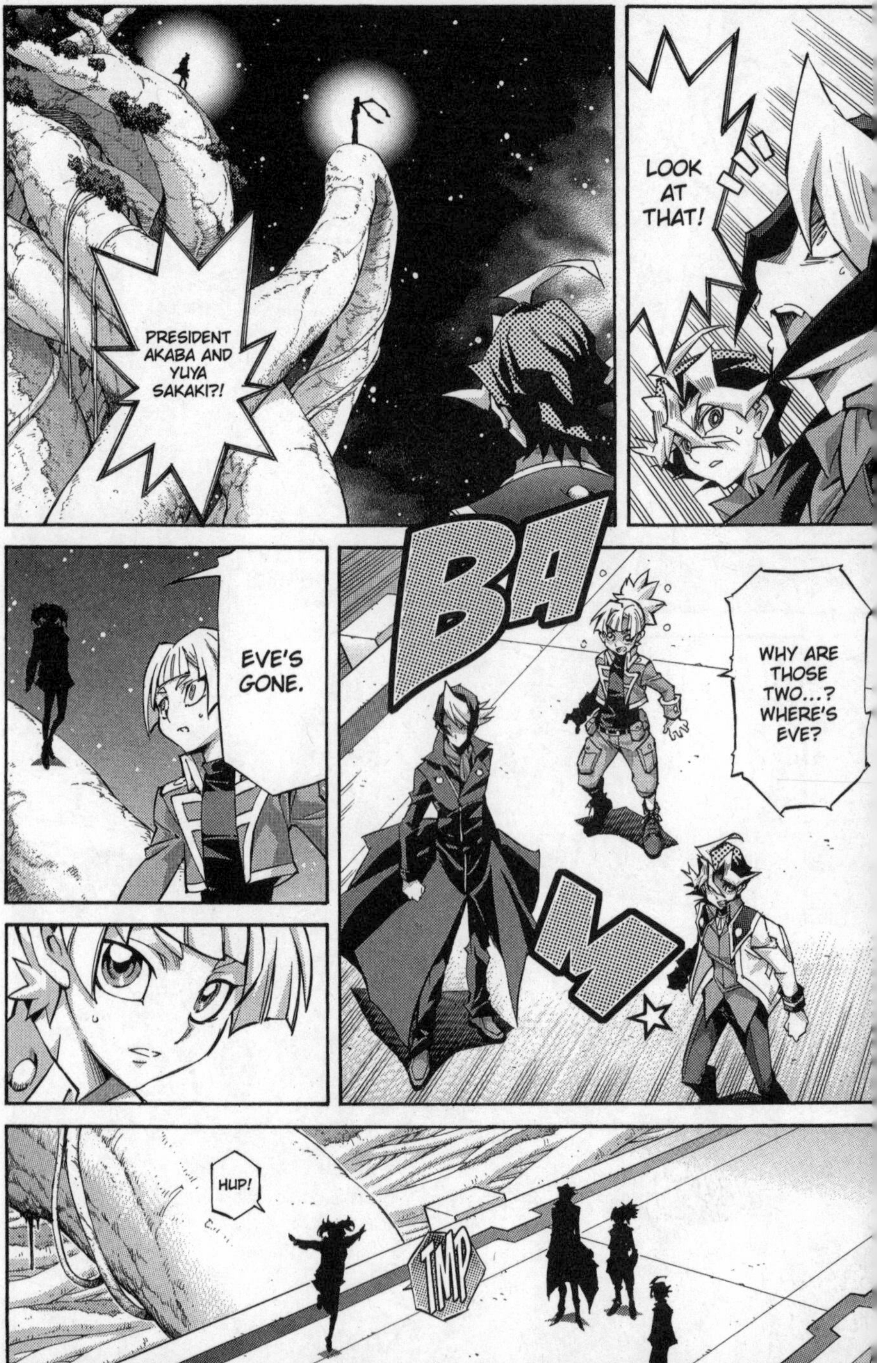
LOOK AT THAT!
PRESIDENT AKABA AND YUYA SAKAKI?!
WHY ARE THOSE TWO...? WHERE'S EVE?
BAM
EVE'S GONE.
HUP!
TMP

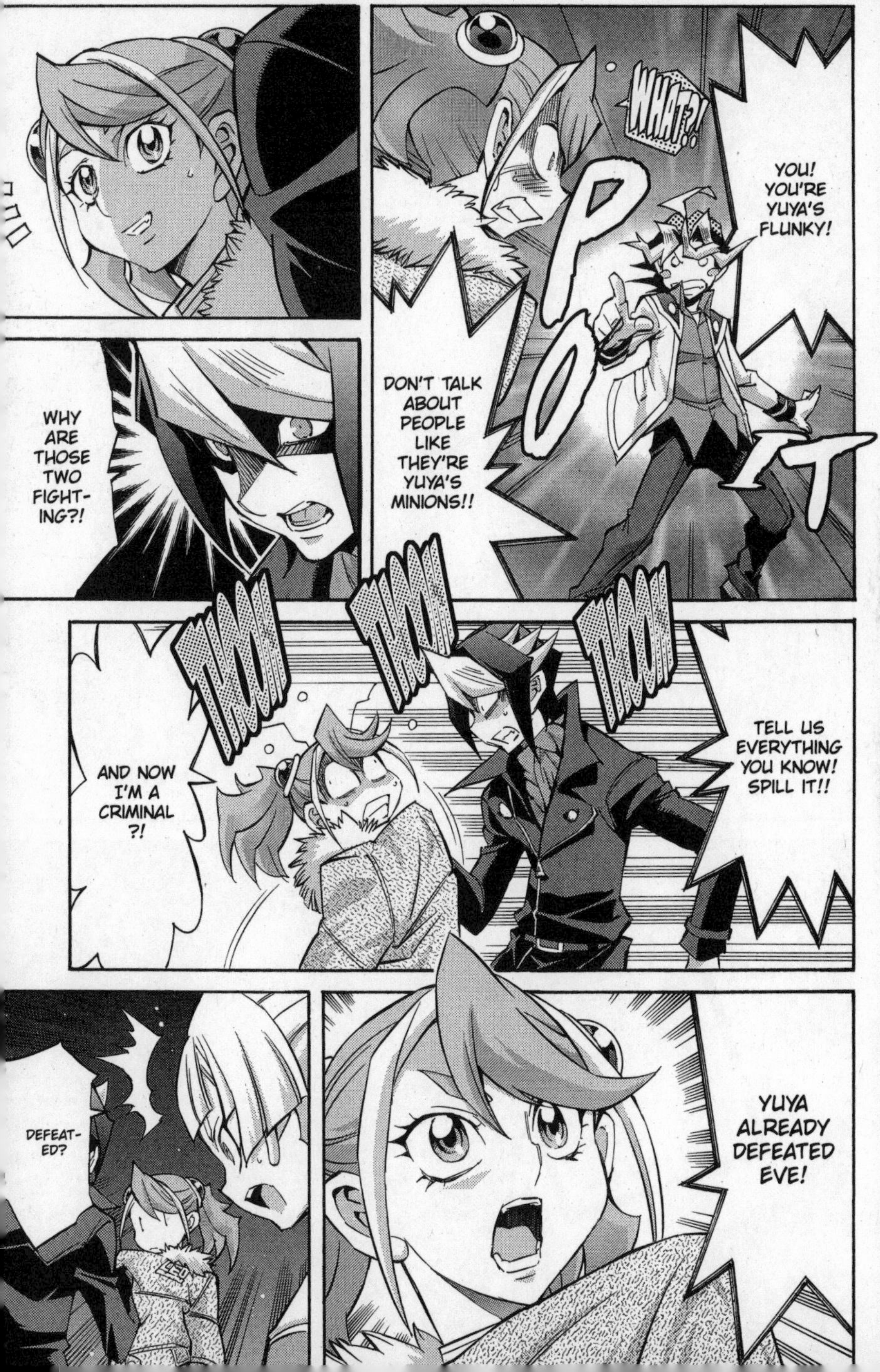
WHAT?!
YOU! YOU'RE YUYA'S FLUNKY!
DON'T TALK ABOUT PEOPLE LIKE THEY'RE YUYA'S MINIONS!!
WHY ARE THOSE TWO FIGHT-ING?!
TELL US EVERYTHING YOU KNOW! SPILL IT!!
AND NOW I'M A CRIMINAL ?!
YUYA ALREADY DEFEATED EVE!
DEFEAT-ED?

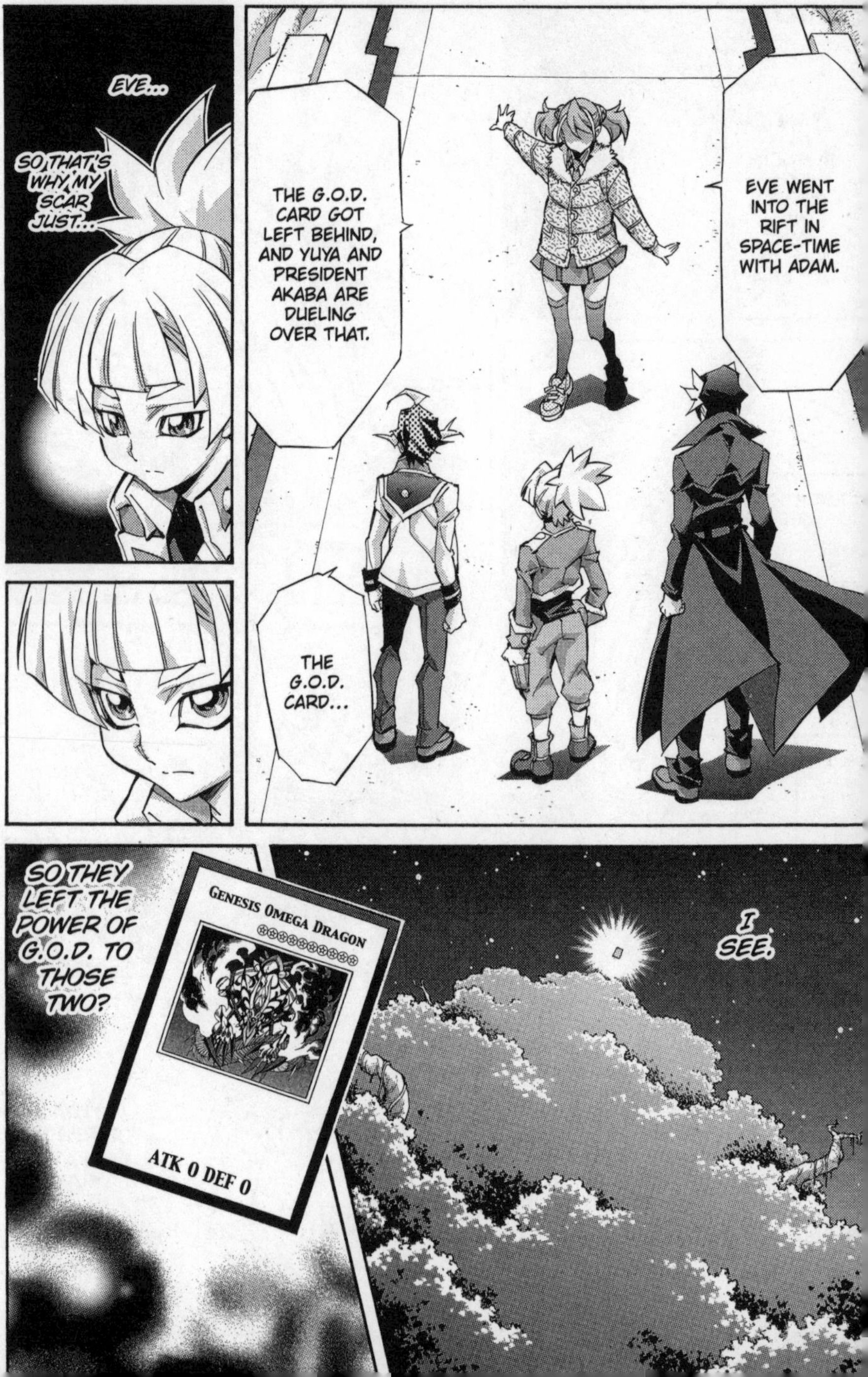
EVE WENT INTO THE RIFT IN SPACE-TIME WITH ADAM.
THE G.O.D. CARD GOT LEFT BEHIND, AND YUYA AND PRESIDENT AKABA ARE DUELING OVER THAT.
THE G.O.D. CARD...
EVE...
SO THAT'S WHY MY SCAR JUST...
I SEE.
GENESIS OMEGA DRAGON
ATK 0 DEF 0
SO THEY LEFT THE POWER OF G.O.D. TO THOSE TWO?

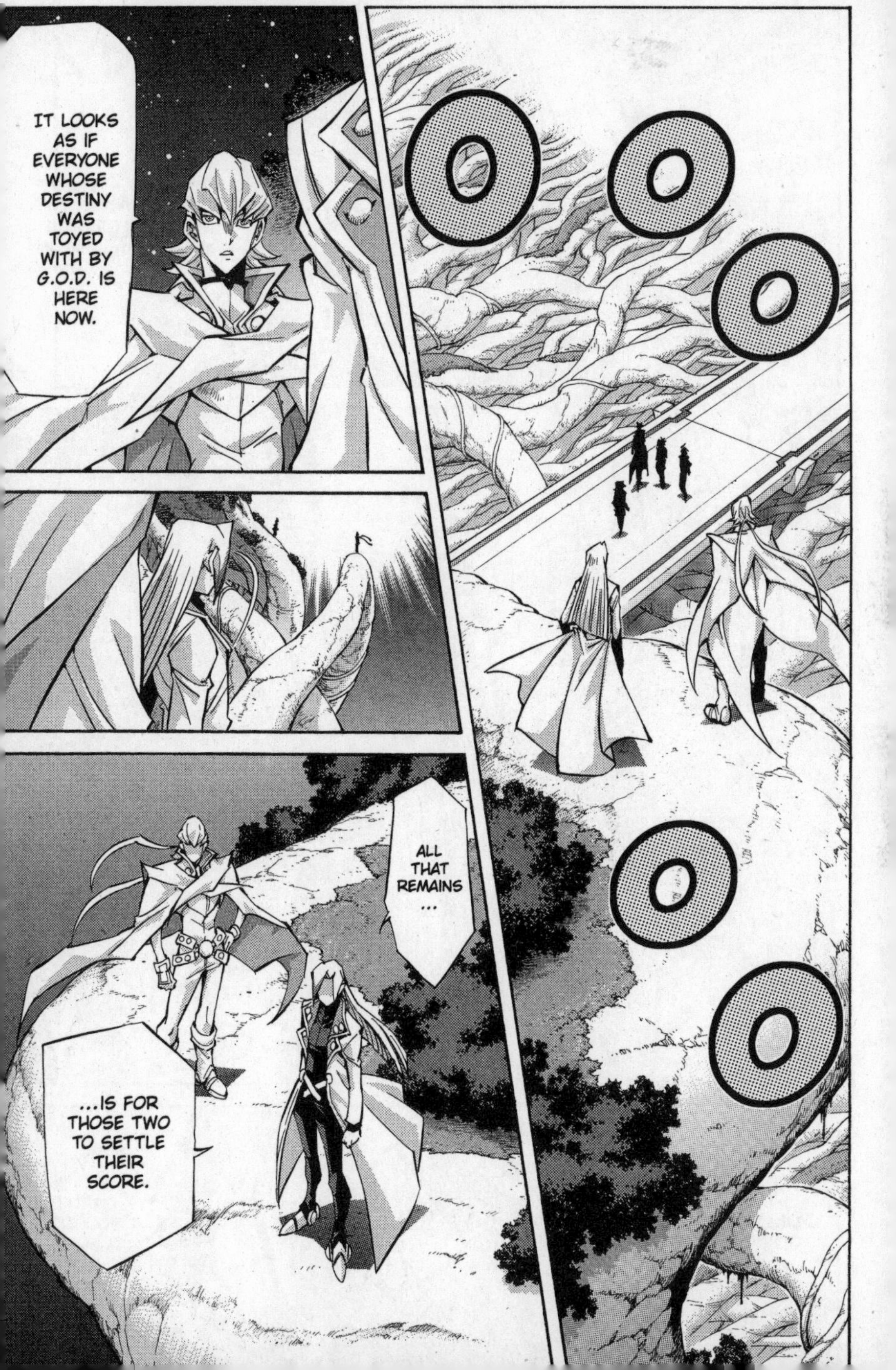
IT LOOKS AS IF EVERYONE WHOSE DESTINY WAS TOYED WITH BY G.O.D. IS HERE NOW.
ALL THAT REMAINS...
...IS FOR THOSE TWO TO SETTLE THEIR SCORE.

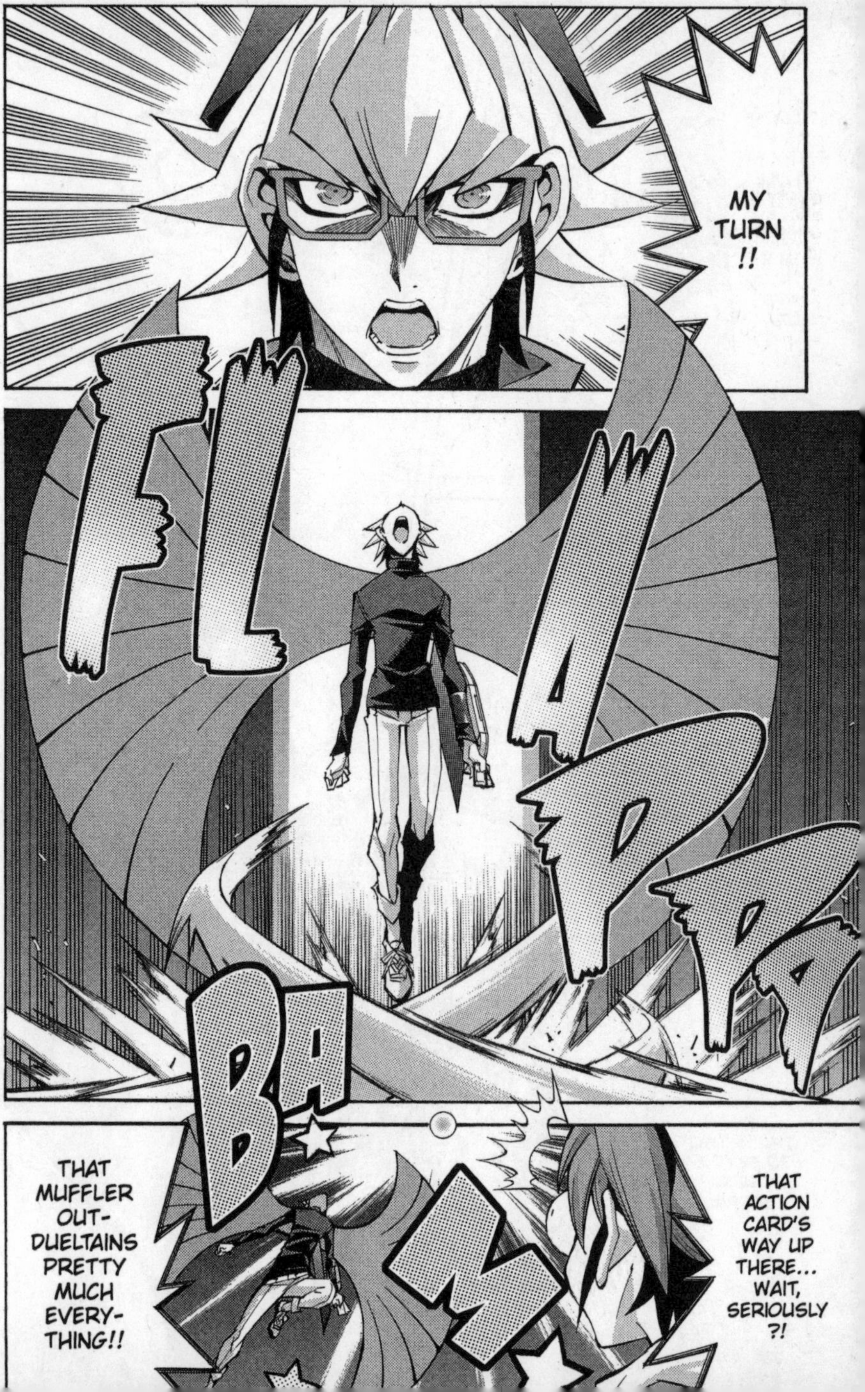
MY TURN !!
FLAPPA
BAM
THAT ACTION CARD'S WAY UP THERE... WAIT, SERIOUSLY ?!
THAT MUFFLER OUT-DUELTAINS PRETTY MUCH EVERY-THING!!

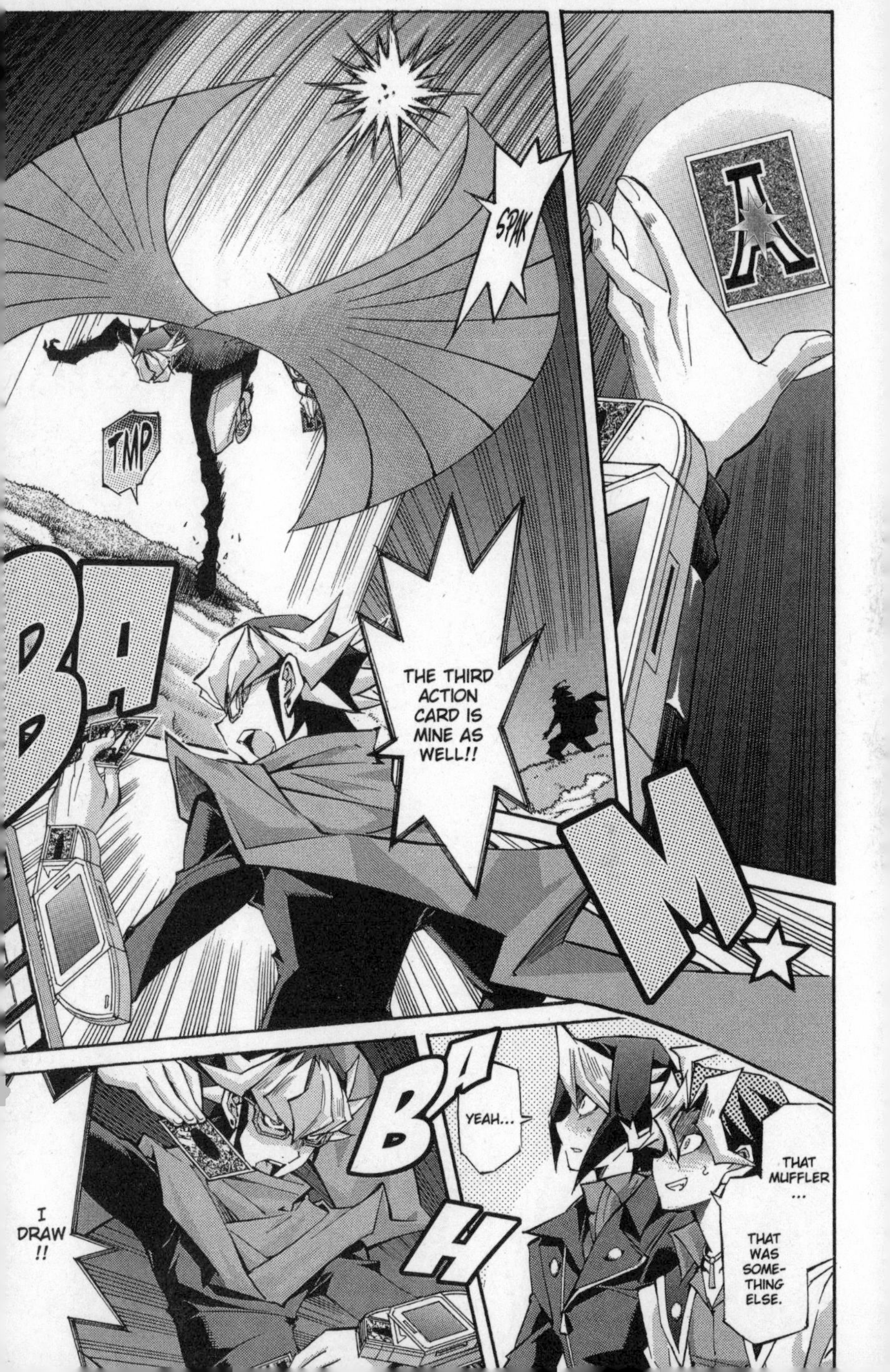
SPAK
TMP
THE THIRD ACTION CARD IS MINE AS WELL!!
BAM
THAT MUFFLER ...
THAT WAS SOMETHING ELSE.
YEAH...
BAH
I DRAW!!

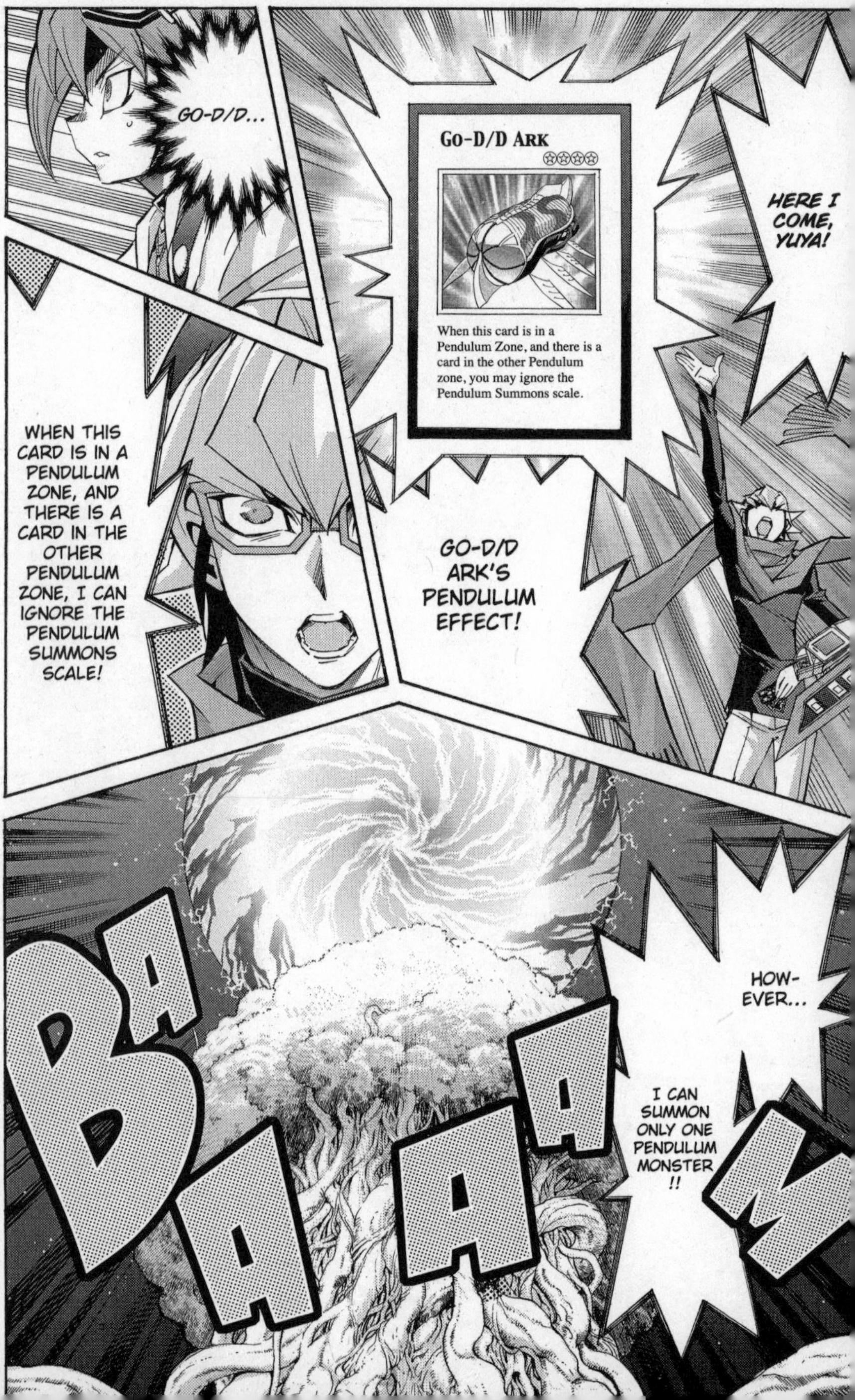
HERE I COME, YUYA!
GO-D/D ARK'S PENDULUM EFFECT!
Go-D/D Ark
When this card is in a Pendulum Zone, and there is a card in the other Pendulum zone, you may ignore the Pendulum Summons scale.
GO-D/D...
WHEN THIS CARD IS IN A PENDULUM ZONE, AND THERE IS A CARD IN THE OTHER PENDULUM ZONE, I CAN IGNORE THE PENDULUM SUMMONS SCALE!
HOW-EVER...
I CAN SUMMON ONLY ONE PENDULUM MONSTER!!
BAAAAM

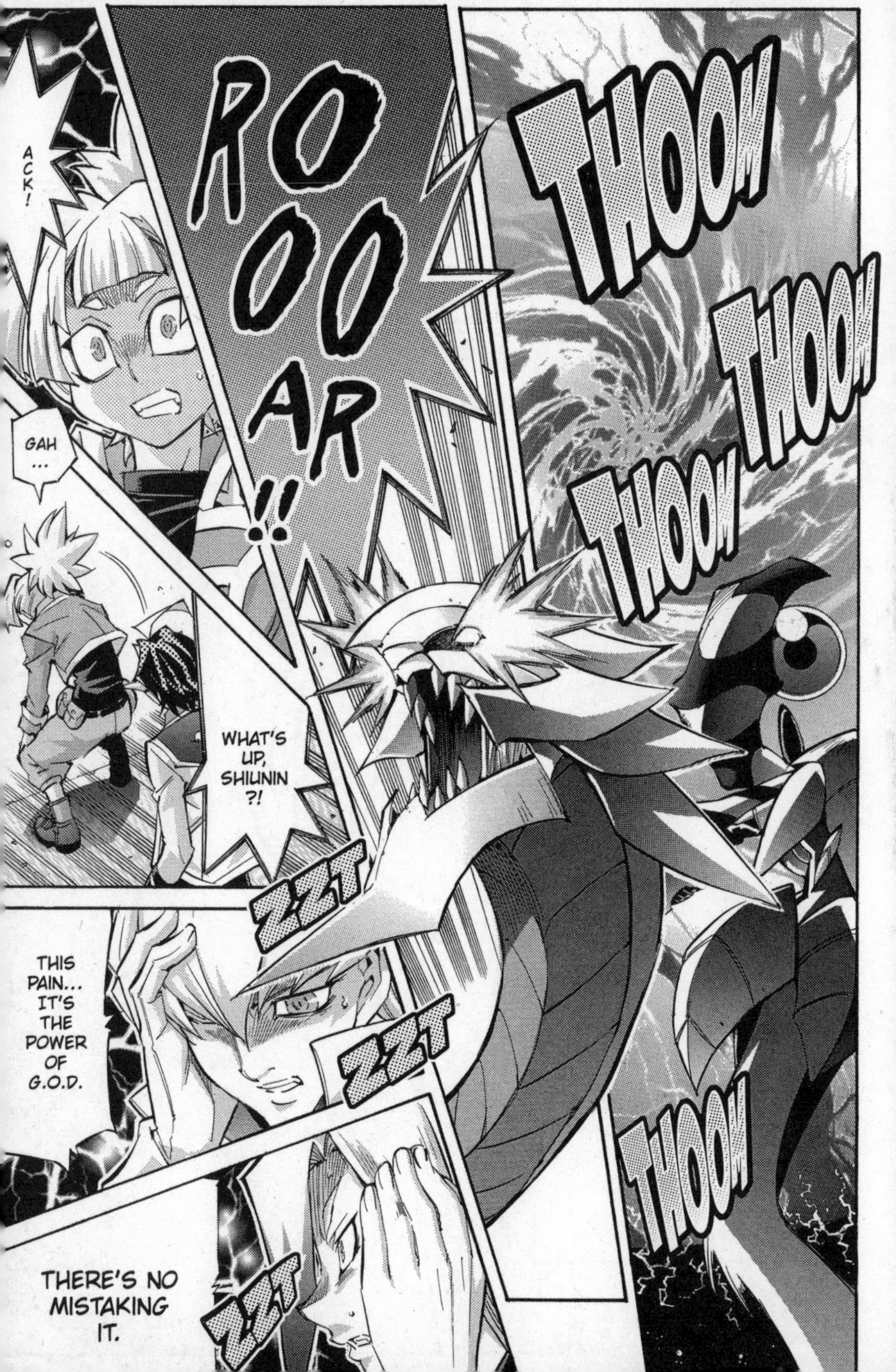
THOOM
THOOM THOOM
ROOOAR!!
ACK!
GAH...
WHAT'S UP, SHIUNIN?!
ZZT
THIS PAIN... IT'S THE POWER OF G.O.D.
ZZT
THOOM
ZZT
THERE'S NO MISTAKING IT.

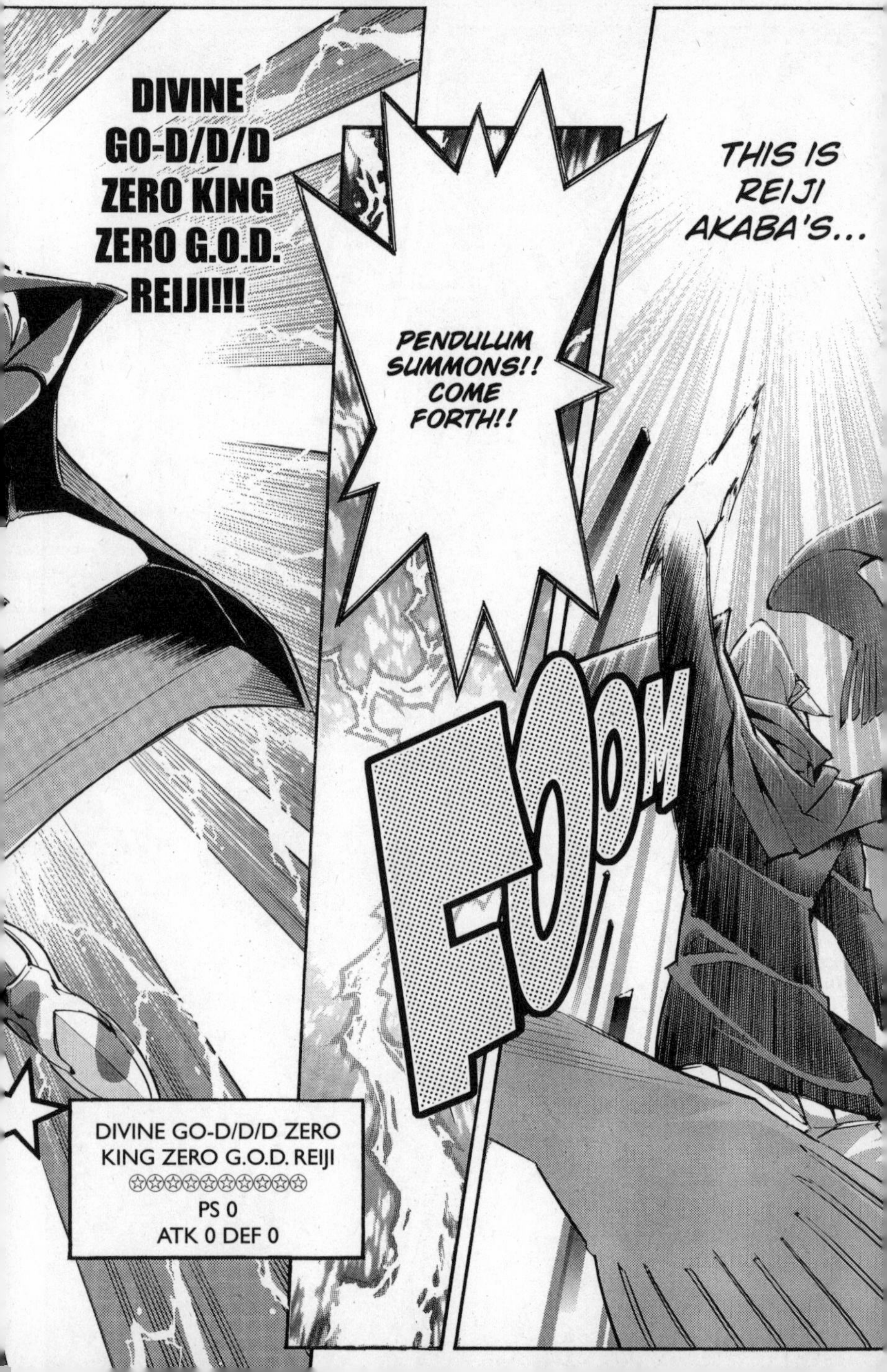
THIS IS REIJI AKABA'S...
PENDULUM SUMMONS!! COME FORTH!!
FOOM
DIVINE GO-D/D/D ZERO KING ZERO G.O.D. REIJI!!!
DIVINE GO-D/D/D ZERO KING ZERO G.O.D. REIJI
PS 0
ATK 0 DEF 0

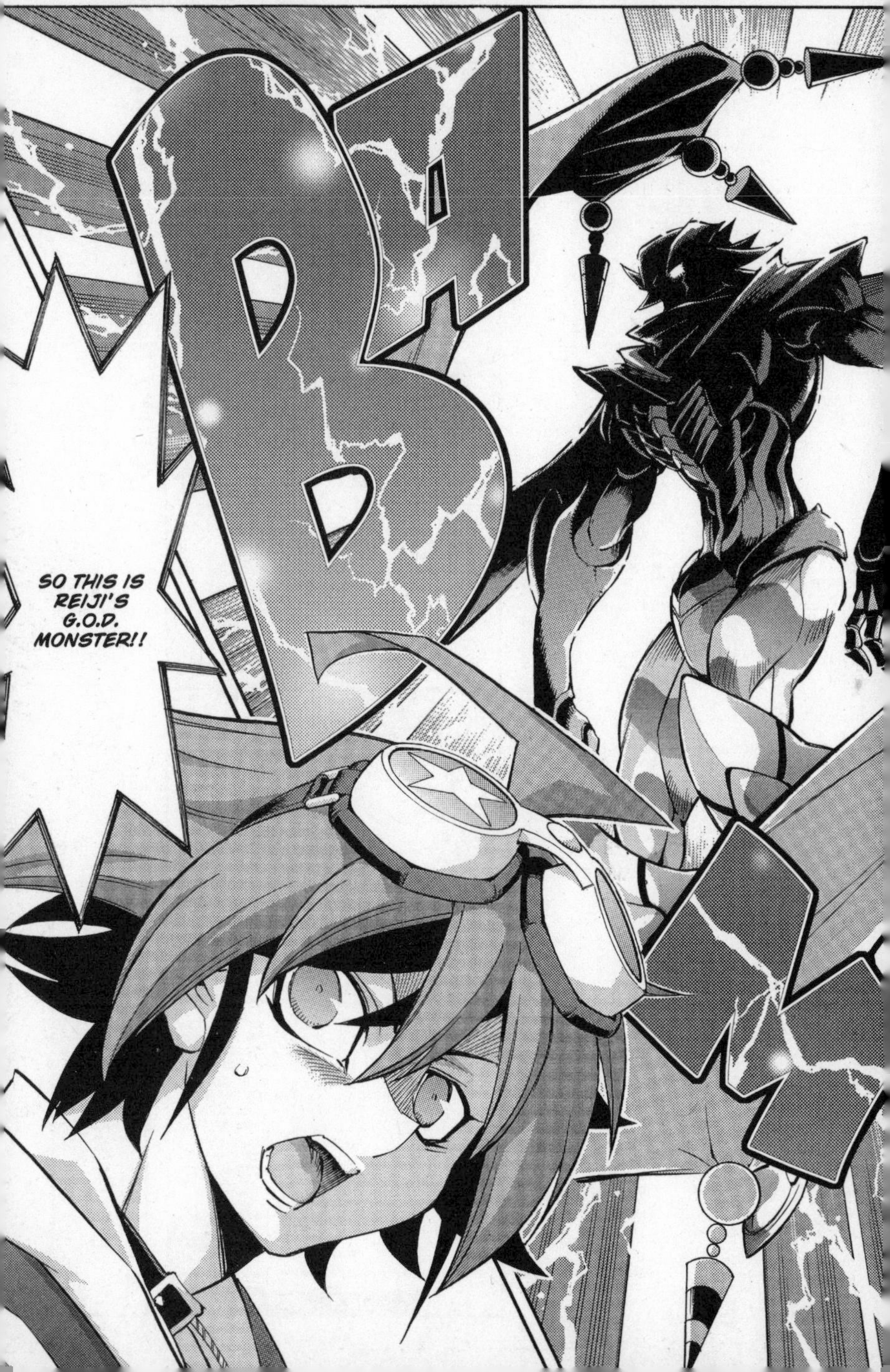
BA
SO THIS IS REIJI'S G.O.D. MONSTER!!

The Guys Behind ARC-V!

MASAHIRO HIKOKUBO

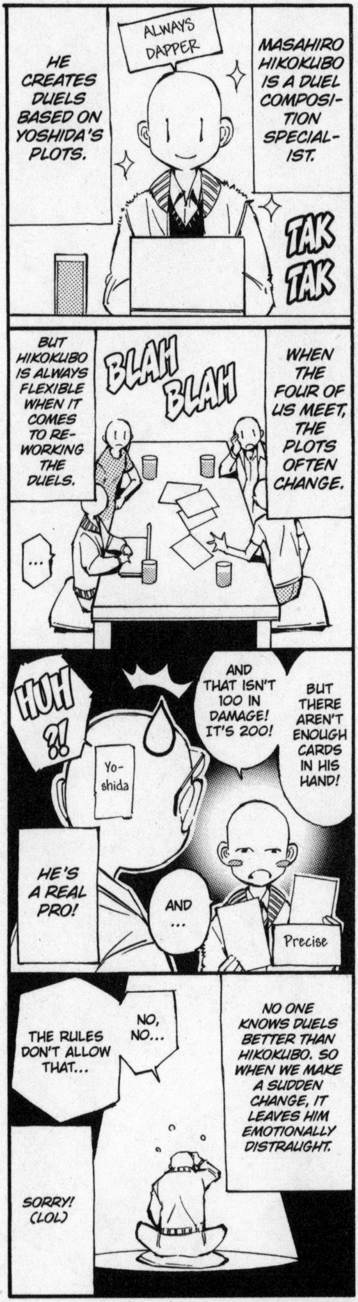

MASAHIRO HIKOKUBO IS A DUEL COMPOSITION SPECIALIST.
ALWAYS DAPPER
HE CREATES DUELS BASED ON YOSHIDA'S PLOTS.
TAK TAK
WHEN THE FOUR OF US MEET, THE PLOTS OFTEN CHANGE.
BLAH BLAH
BUT HIKOKUBO IS ALWAYS FLEXIBLE WHEN IT COMES TO RE-WORKING THE DUELS.
...
BUT THERE AREN'T ENOUGH CARDS IN HIS HAND!
AND THAT ISN'T 100 IN DAMAGE! IT'S 200!
HUH?!
Yo-shida
AND ...
Precise
HE'S A REAL PRO!
NO ONE KNOWS DUELS BETTER THAN HIKOKUBO. SO WHEN WE MAKE A SUDDEN CHANGE, IT LEAVES HIM EMOTIONALLY DISTRAUGHT.
NO, NO...
THE RULES DON'T ALLOW THAT...
SORRY! (LOL)

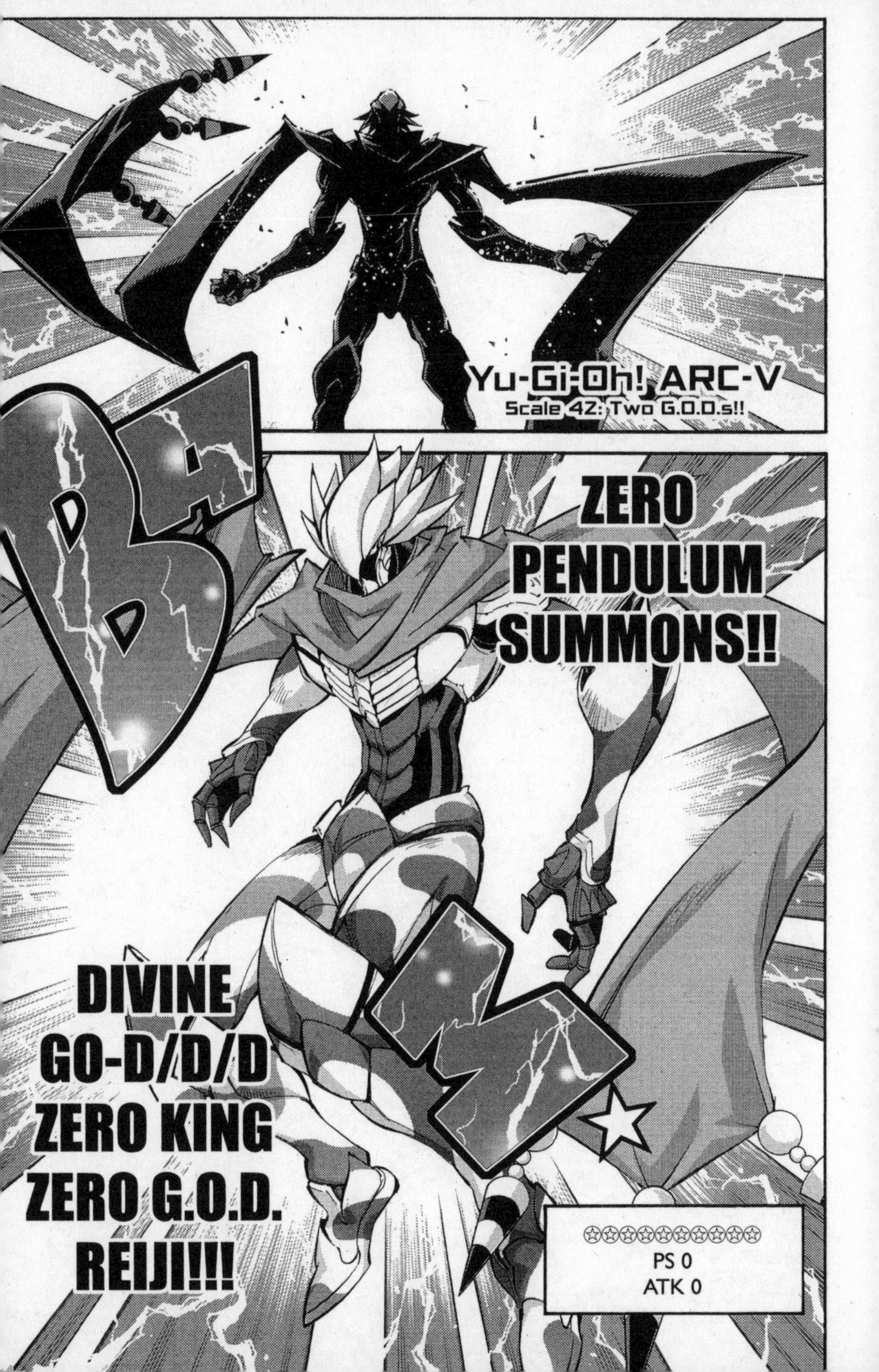
Yu-Gi-Oh! ARC-V
Scale 42: Two G.O.D.s!!
ZERO PENDULUM SUMMONS!!
BAM☆
DIVINE GO-D/D/D ZERO KING ZERO G.O.D. REIJI!!!
PS 0
ATK 0

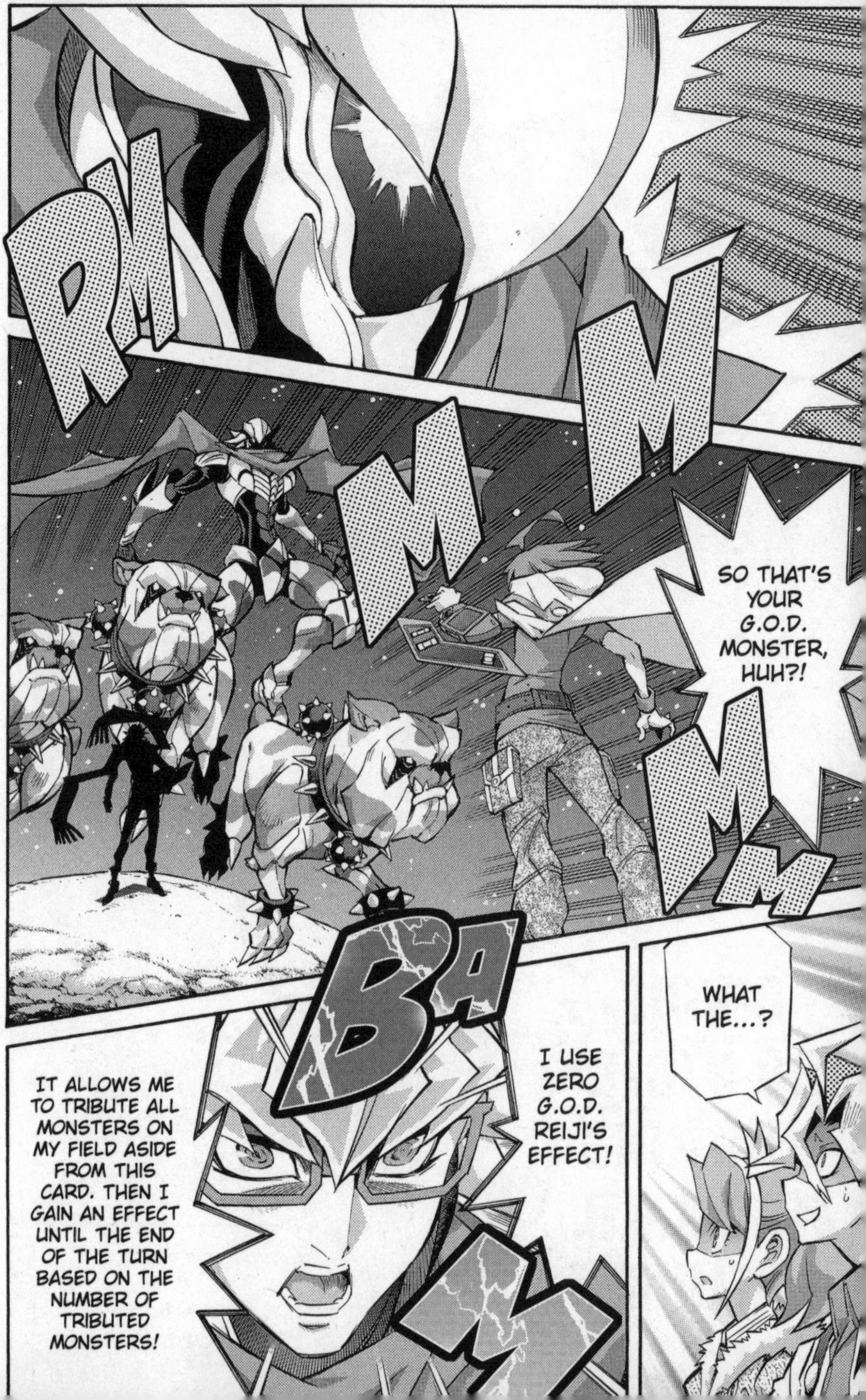
RMMMMM
SO THAT'S YOUR G.O.D. MONSTER, HUH?!
WHAT THE...?
BAM
I USE ZERO G.O.D. REIJI'S EFFECT!
IT ALLOWS ME TO TRIBUTE ALL MONSTERS ON MY FIELD ASIDE FROM THIS CARD. THEN I GAIN AN EFFECT UNTIL THE END OF THE TURN BASED ON THE NUMBER OF TRIBUTED MONSTERS!

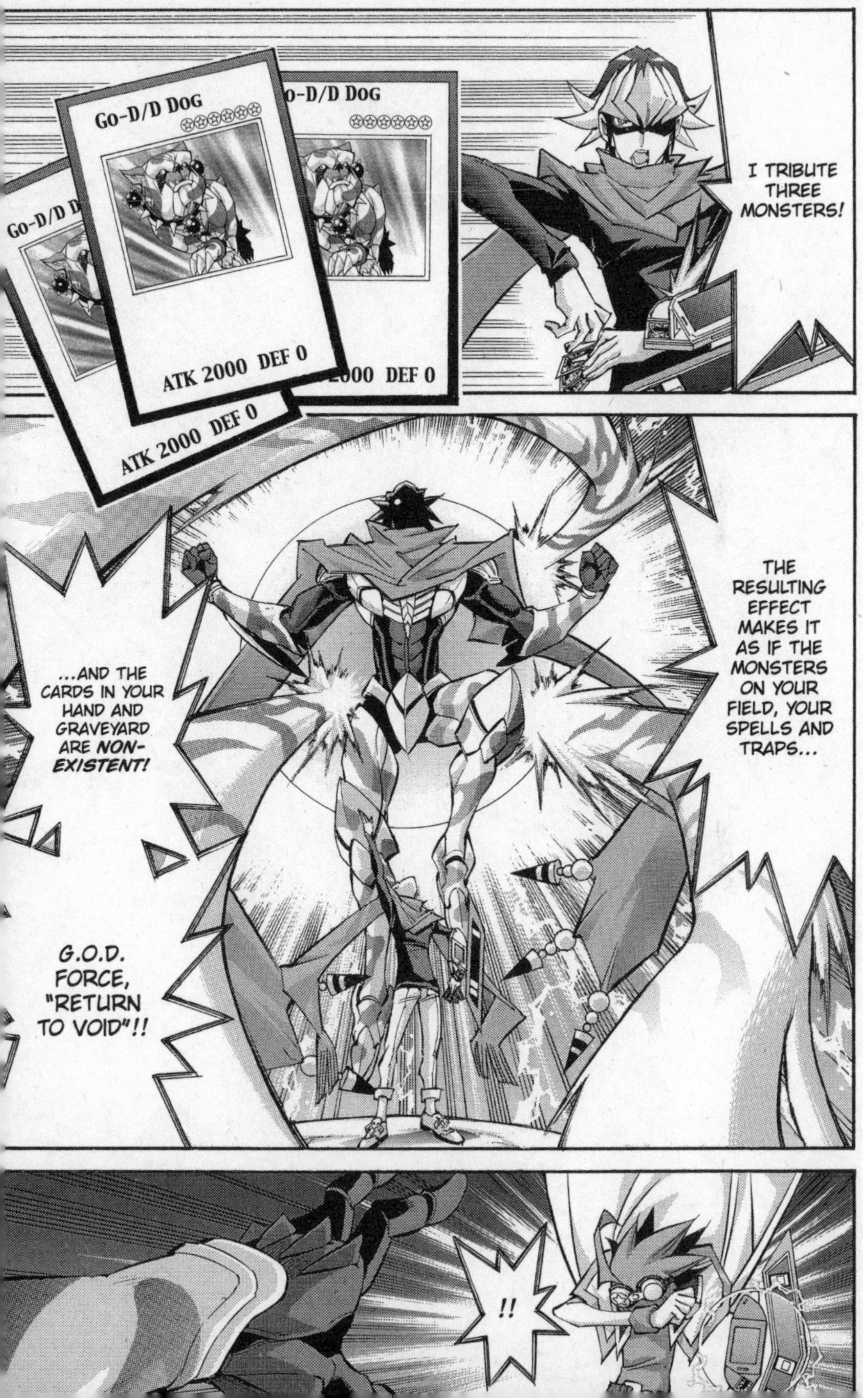
I TRIBUTE THREE MONSTERS!
Go-D/D Dog
ATK 2000 DEF 0
Go-D/D Dog
ATK 2000 DEF 0
Go-D/D Dog
ATK 2000 DEF 0
THE RESULTING EFFECT MAKES IT AS IF THE MONSTERS ON YOUR FIELD, YOUR SPELLS AND TRAPS...
...AND THE CARDS IN YOUR HAND AND GRAVEYARD ARE *NON-EXISTENT!*
G.O.D. FORCE, "RETURN TO VOID"!!
!!

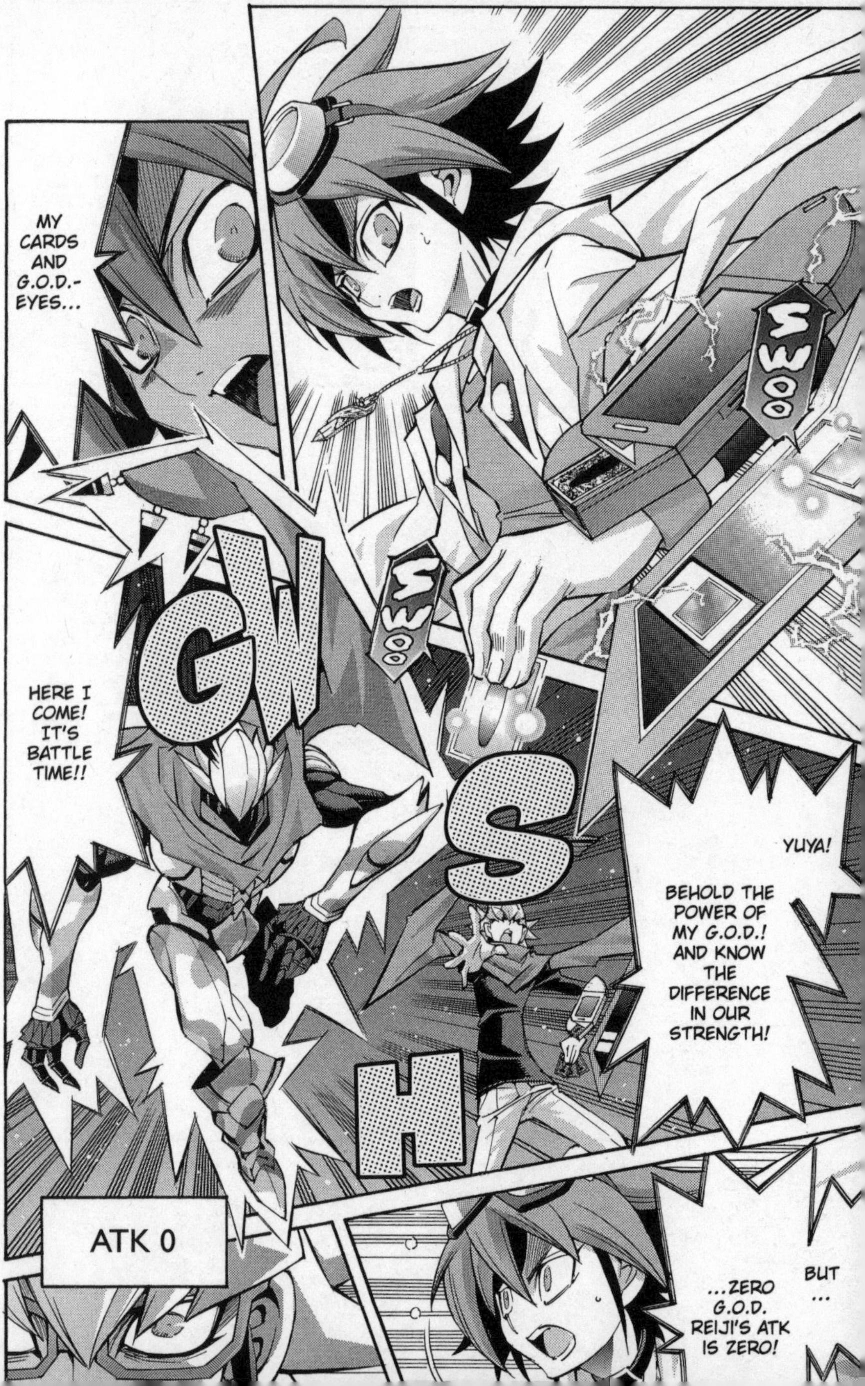
SWOO
SWOO
MY CARDS AND G.O.D.-EYES...
GWSH
HERE I COME! IT'S BATTLE TIME!!
YUYA!
BEHOLD THE POWER OF MY G.O.D.! AND KNOW THE DIFFERENCE IN OUR STRENGTH!
BUT...
...ZERO G.O.D. REIJI'S ATK IS ZERO!
ATK 0

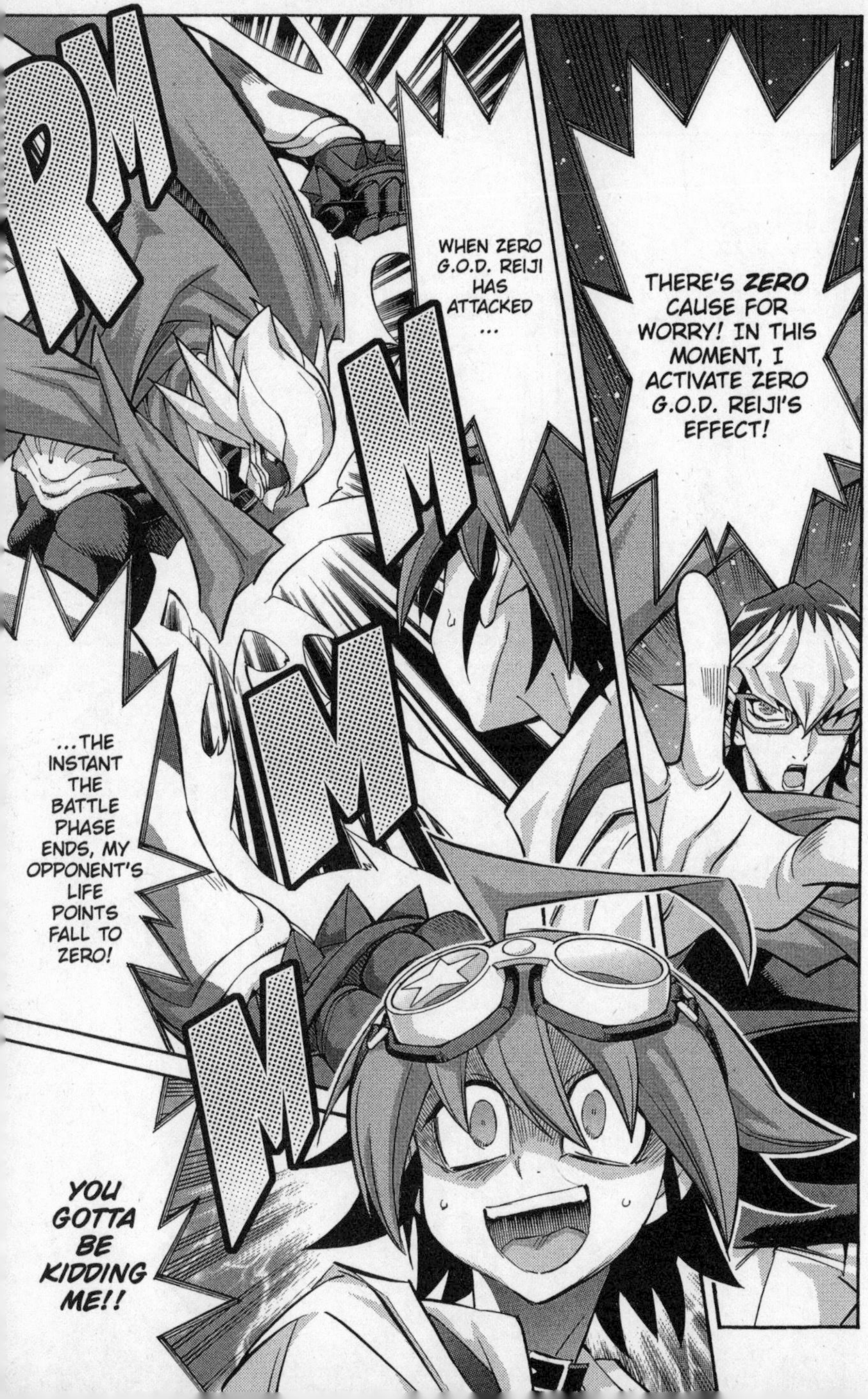
THERE'S **ZERO** CAUSE FOR WORRY! IN THIS MOMENT, I ACTIVATE ZERO G.O.D. REIJI'S EFFECT!
WHEN ZERO G.O.D. REIJI HAS ATTACKED ...
RMMMM
...THE INSTANT THE BATTLE PHASE ENDS, MY OPPONENT'S LIFE POINTS FALL TO ZERO!
YOU GOTTA BE KIDDING ME!!

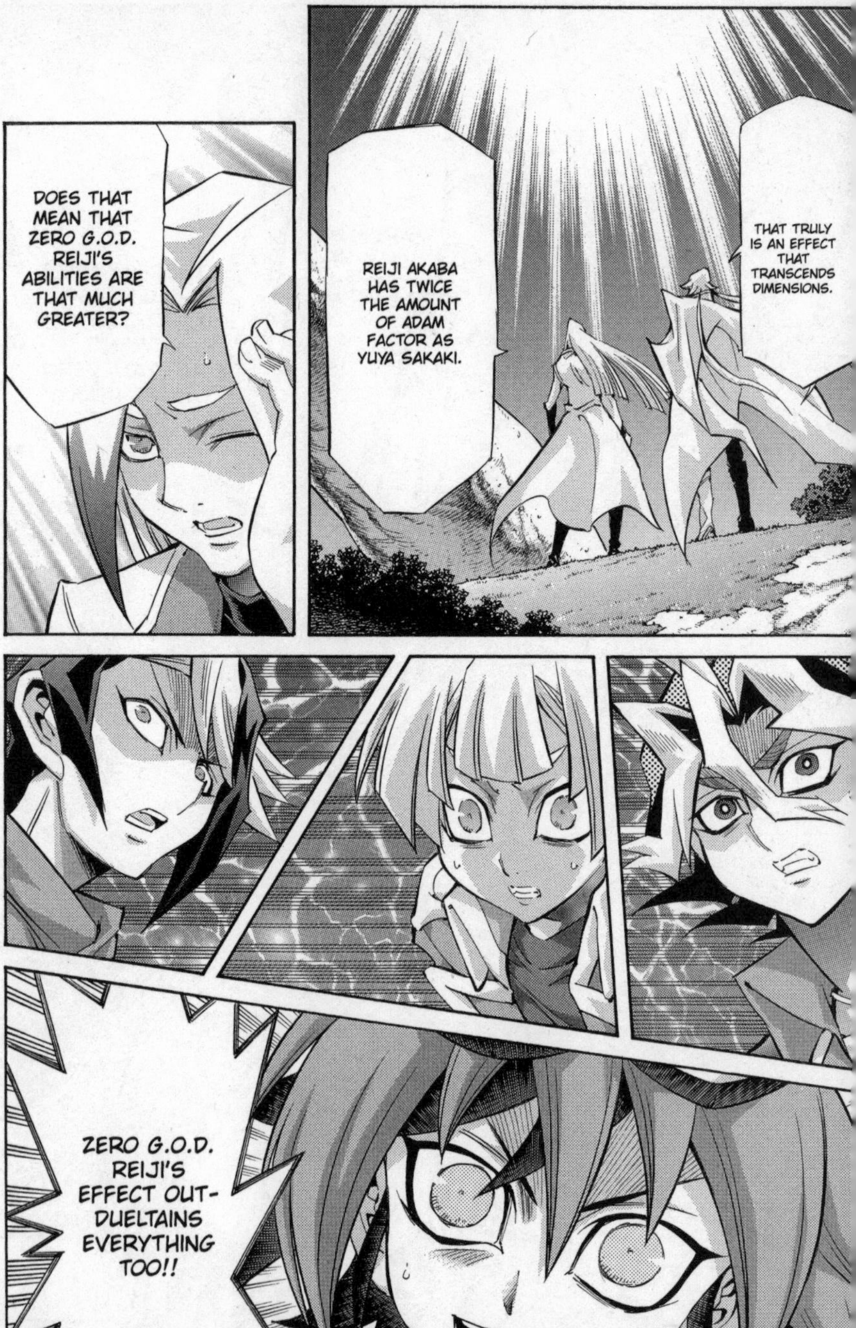
THAT TRULY IS AN EFFECT THAT TRANSCENDS DIMENSIONS.
REIJI AKABA HAS TWICE THE AMOUNT OF ADAM FACTOR AS YUYA SAKAKI.
DOES THAT MEAN THAT ZERO G.O.D. REIJI'S ABILITIES ARE THAT MUCH GREATER?
ZERO G.O.D. REIJI'S EFFECT OUT-DUELTAINS EVERYTHING TOO!!

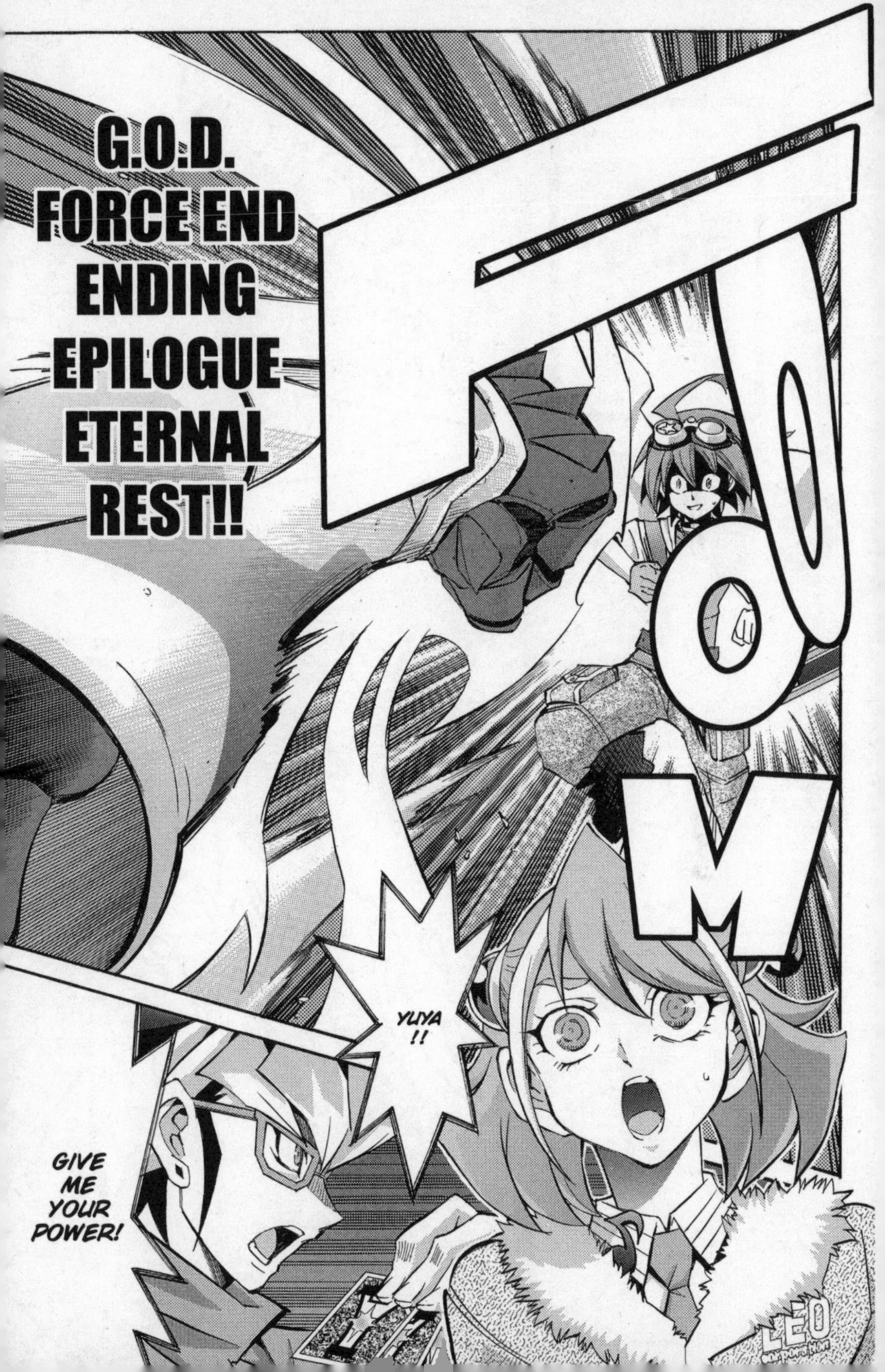
FOOM
G.O.D. FORCE END ENDING EPILOGUE ETERNAL REST!!
YUYA!!
GIVE ME YOUR POWER!

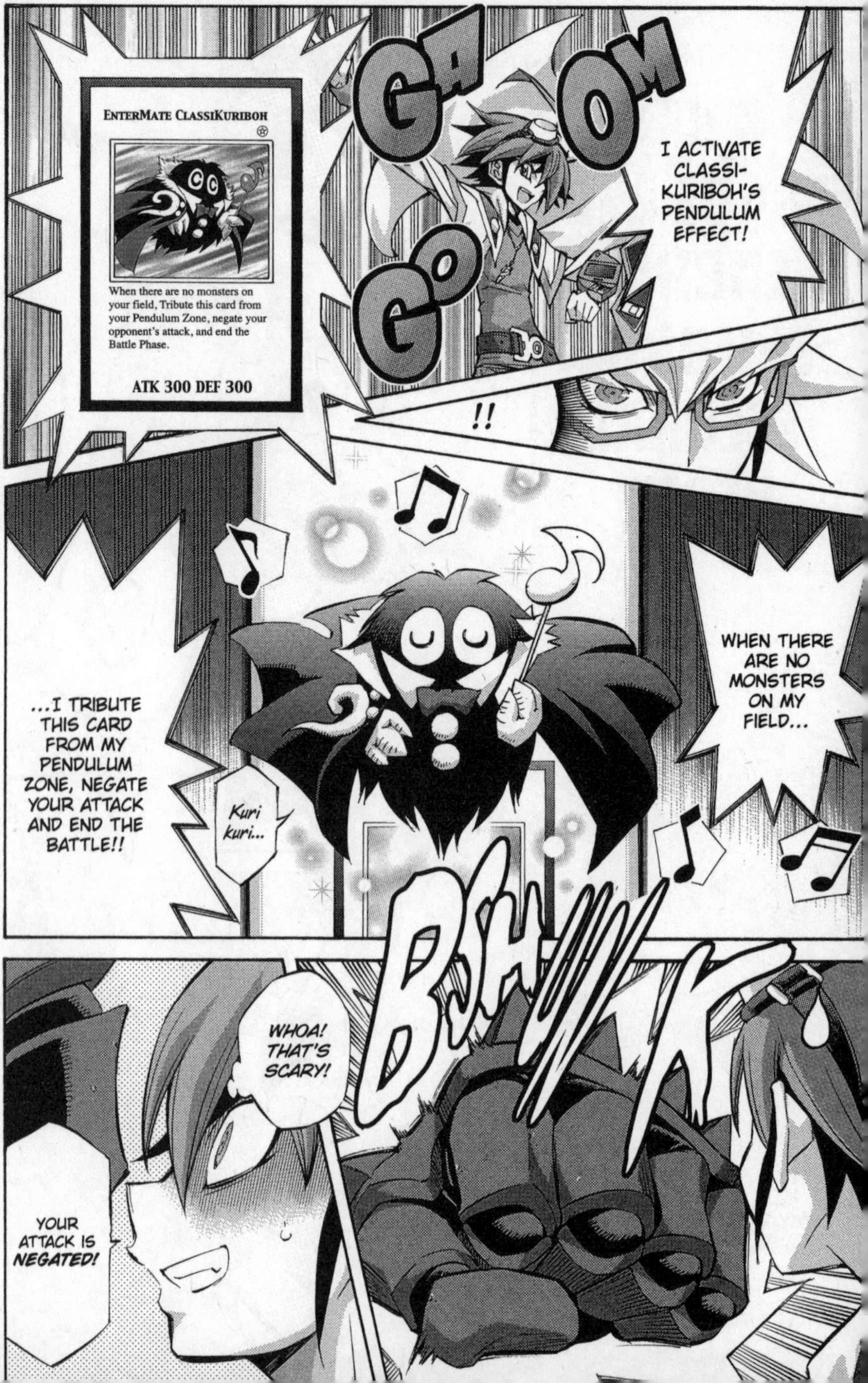
I ACTIVATE CLASSI-KURIBOH'S PENDULUM EFFECT!
ENTERMATE CLASSIKURIBOH
When there are no monsters on your field, Tribute this card from your Pendulum Zone, negate your opponent's attack, and end the Battle Phase.
ATK 300 DEF 300
!!
WHEN THERE ARE NO MONSTERS ON MY FIELD...
Kuri kuri...
...I TRIBUTE THIS CARD FROM MY PENDULUM ZONE, NEGATE YOUR ATTACK AND END THE BATTLE!!
WHOA! THAT'S SCARY!
YOUR ATTACK IS *NEGATED!*

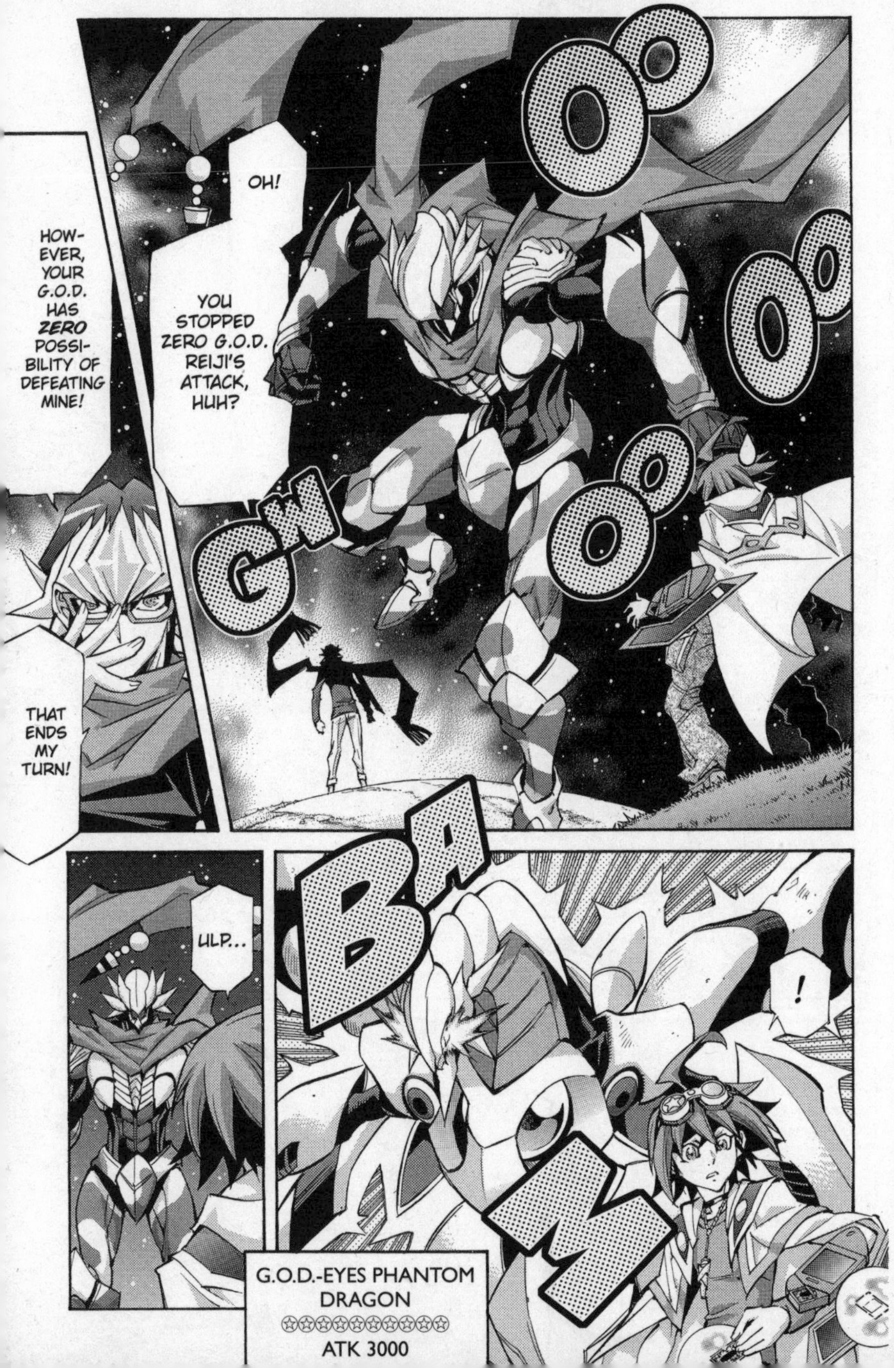

OH!
YOU STOPPED ZERO G.O.D. REIJI'S ATTACK, HUH?
GWOOOOOOOO
HOW-EVER, YOUR G.O.D. HAS **ZERO** POSSI-BILITY OF DEFEATING MINE!
THAT ENDS MY TURN!
BAM
!
G.O.D.-EYES PHANTOM DRAGON
ATK 3000
ULP...

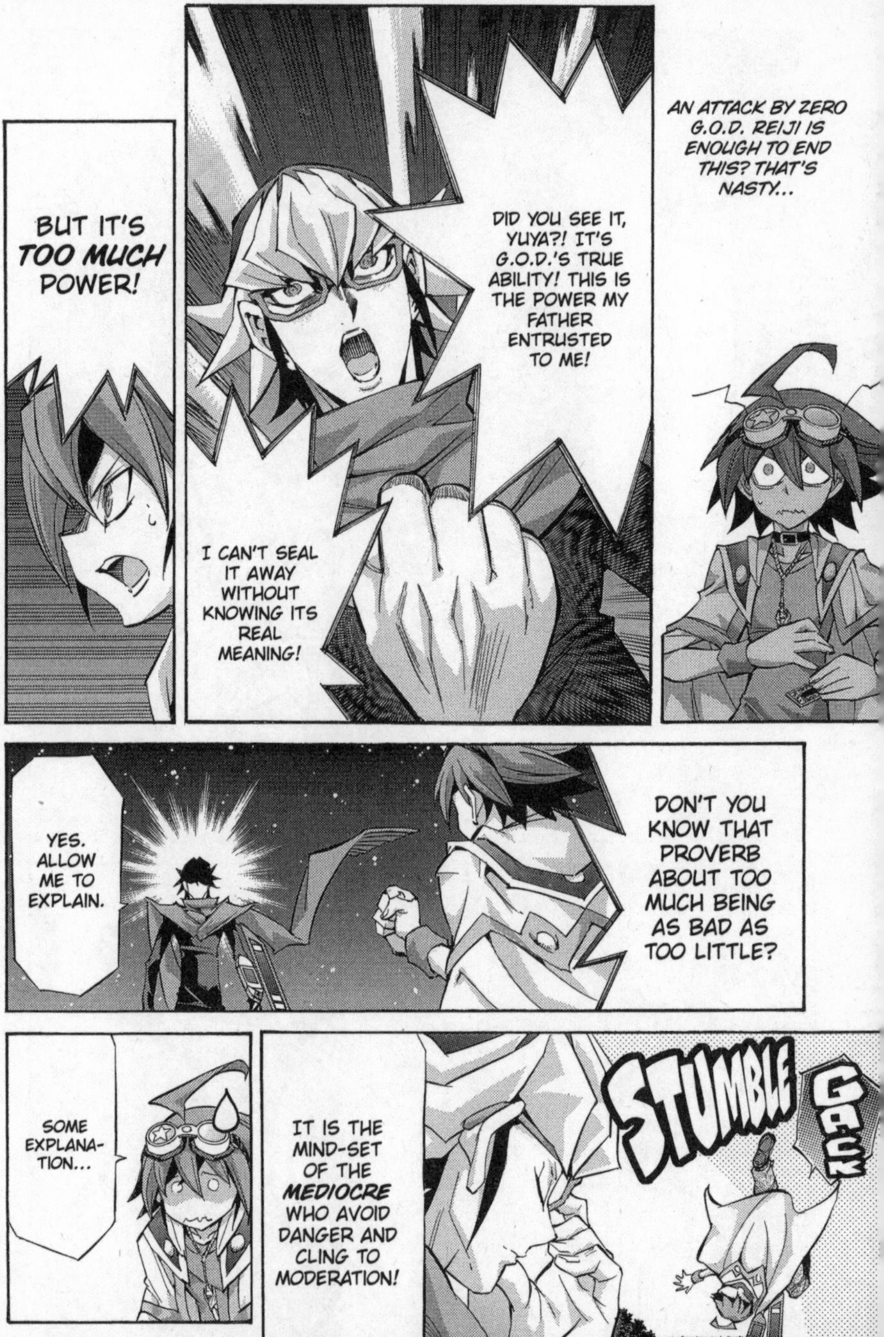
AN ATTACK BY ZERO G.O.D. REIJI IS ENOUGH TO END THIS? THAT'S NASTY...
DID YOU SEE IT, YUYA?! IT'S G.O.D.'S TRUE ABILITY! THIS IS THE POWER MY FATHER ENTRUSTED TO ME!
I CAN'T SEAL IT AWAY WITHOUT KNOWING ITS REAL MEANING!
BUT IT'S *TOO MUCH* POWER!
DON'T YOU KNOW THAT PROVERB ABOUT TOO MUCH BEING AS BAD AS TOO LITTLE?
YES. ALLOW ME TO EXPLAIN.
STUMBLE
GACK
IT IS THE MIND-SET OF THE *MEDIOCRE* WHO AVOID DANGER AND CLING TO MODERATION!
SOME EXPLANATION...

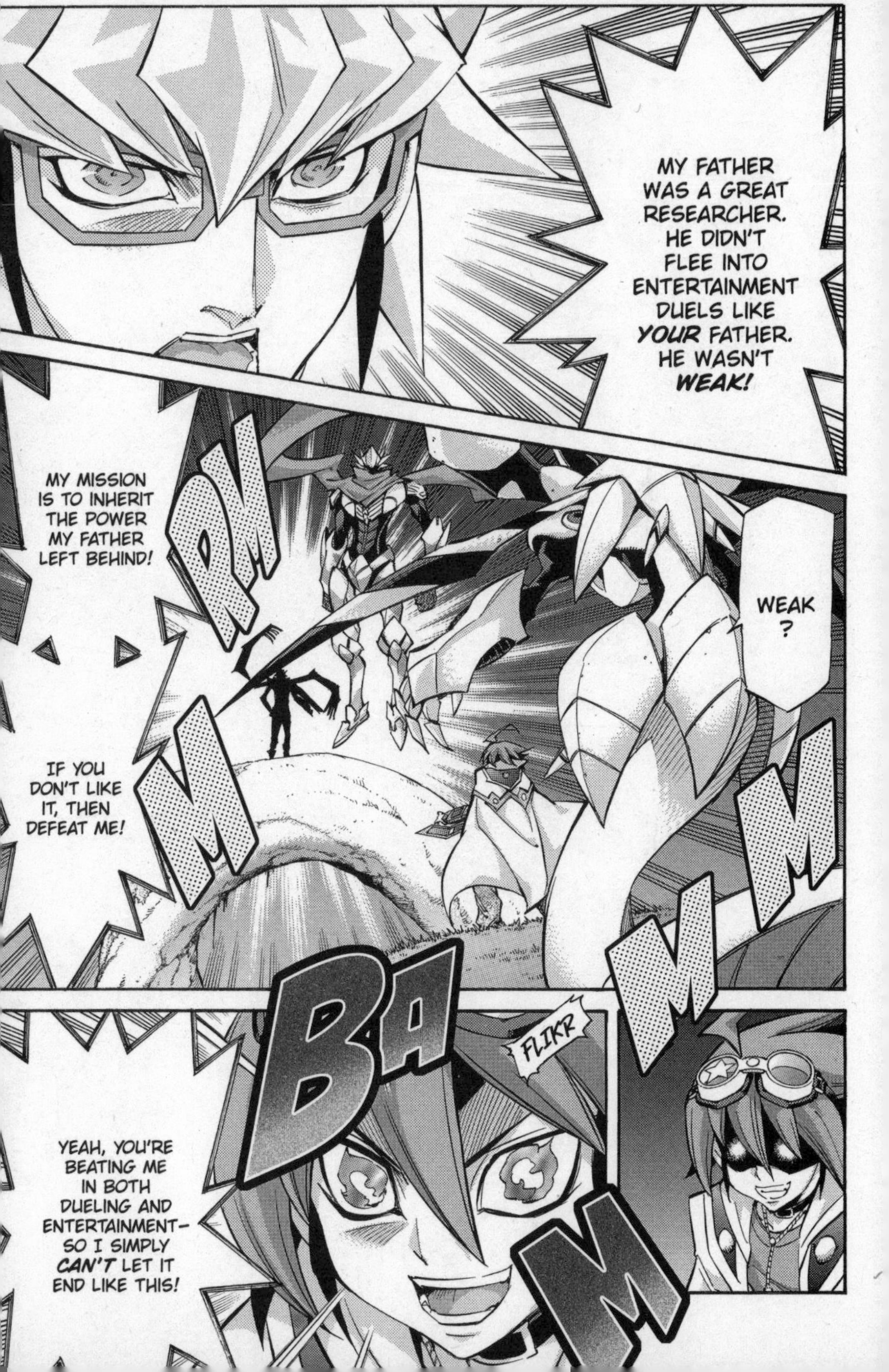
MY FATHER WAS A GREAT RESEARCHER. HE DIDN'T FLEE INTO ENTERTAINMENT DUELS LIKE ***YOUR*** FATHER. HE WASN'T ***WEAK!***
WEAK?
MY MISSION IS TO INHERIT THE POWER MY FATHER LEFT BEHIND!
RM
M
M
M
IF YOU DON'T LIKE IT, THEN DEFEAT ME!
BA
M
FLIKR
YEAH, YOU'RE BEATING ME IN BOTH DUELING AND ENTERTAINMENT—SO I SIMPLY ***CAN'T*** LET IT END LIKE THIS!

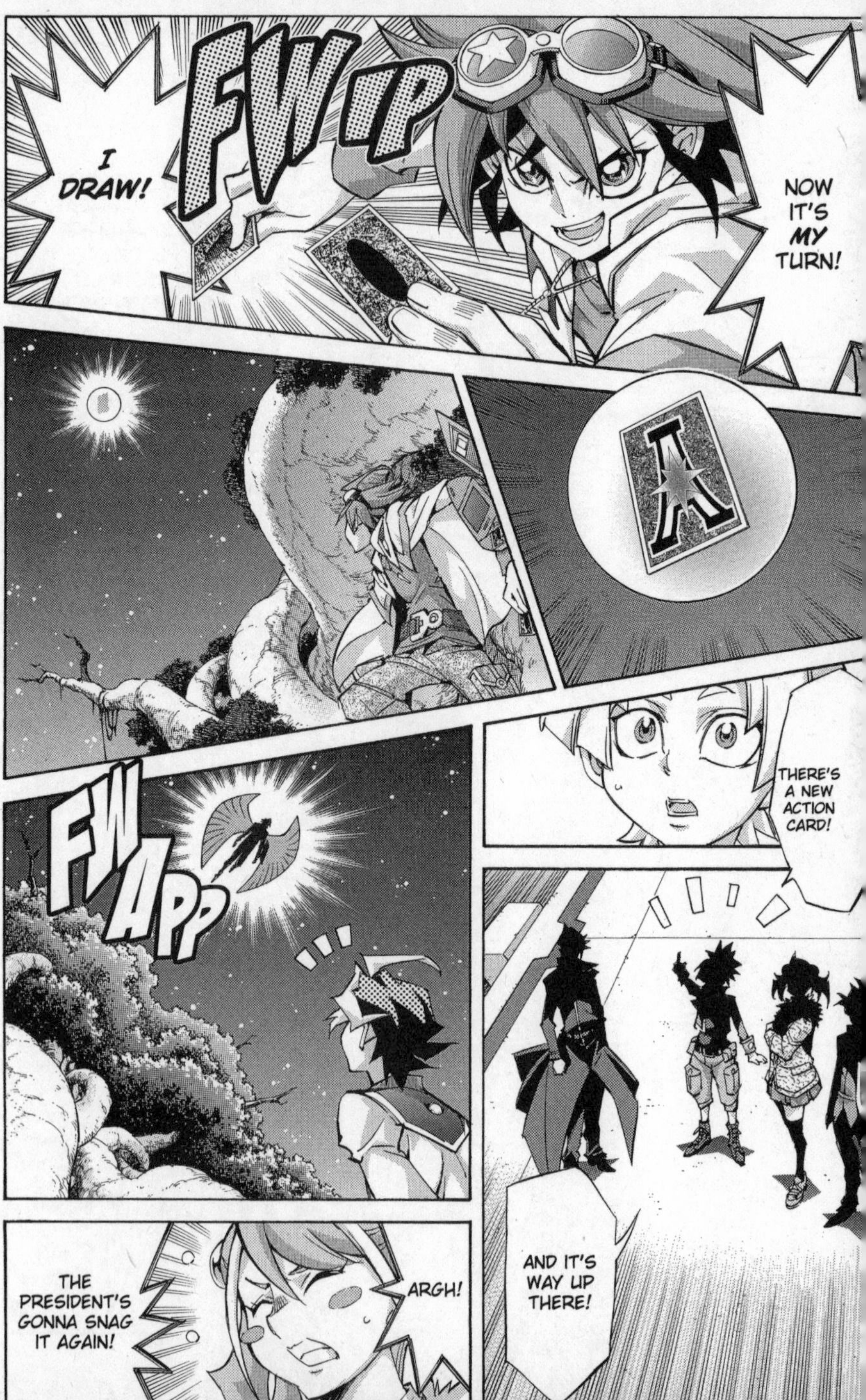
NOW IT'S MY TURN!
FWIP
I DRAW!
THERE'S A NEW ACTION CARD!
AND IT'S WAY UP THERE!
FWAPP
...
ARGH!
THE PRESIDENT'S GONNA SNAG IT AGAIN!

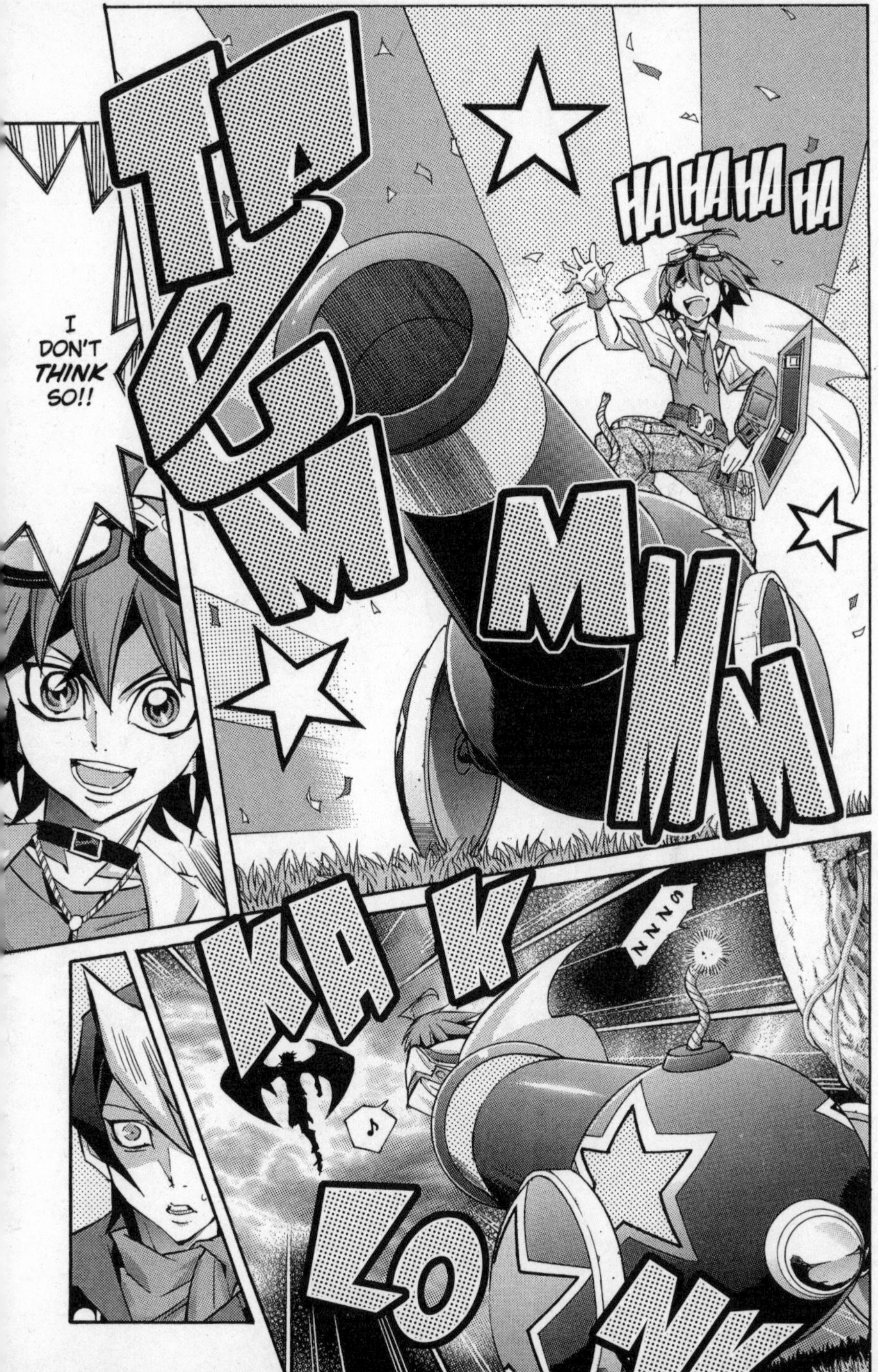
HA HA HA HA
TADUMMMMM
I DON'T THINK SO!!
GNNN
♪
KA K
LONK

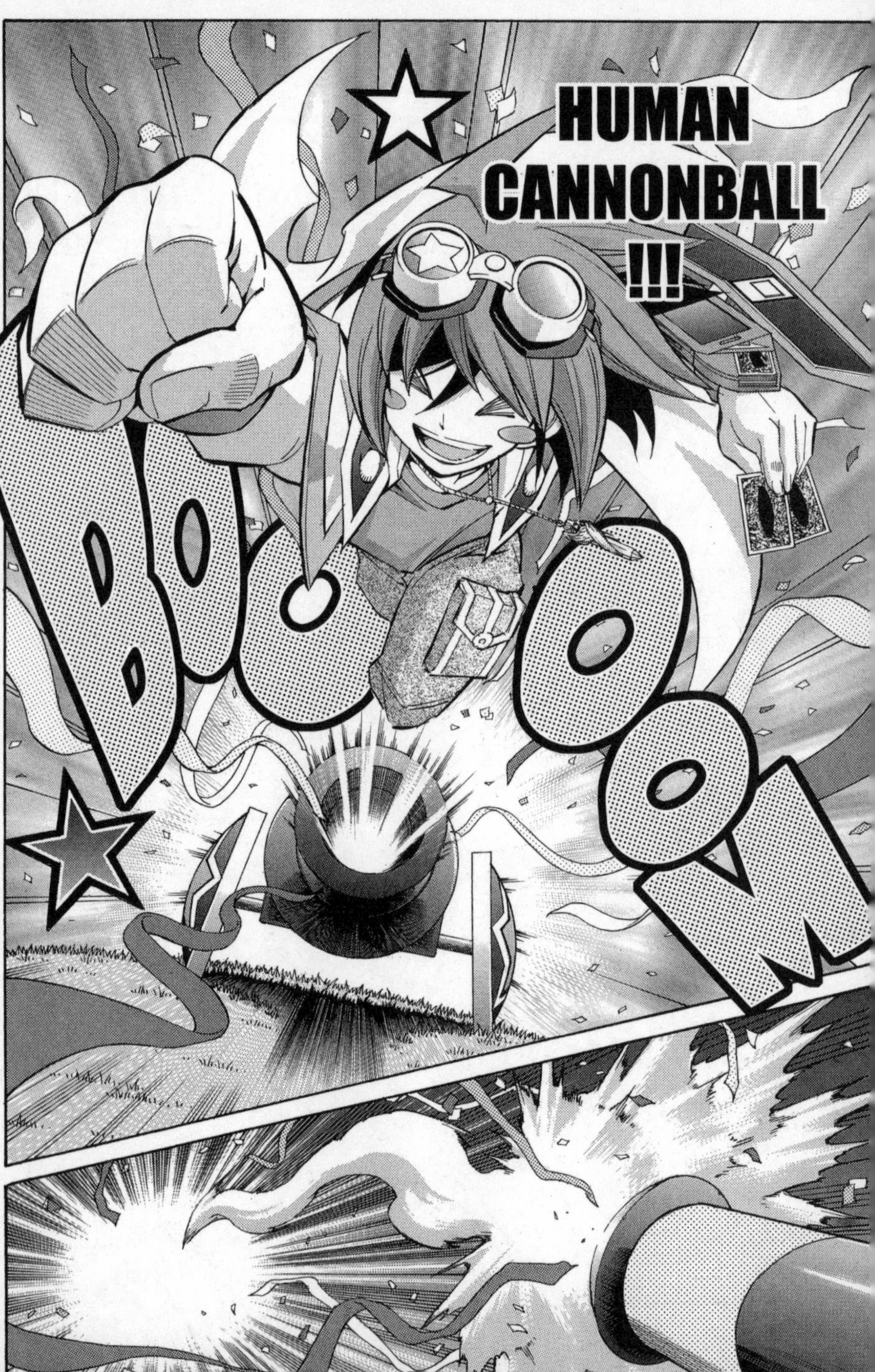
HUMAN CANNONBALL !!!
BOOOOM

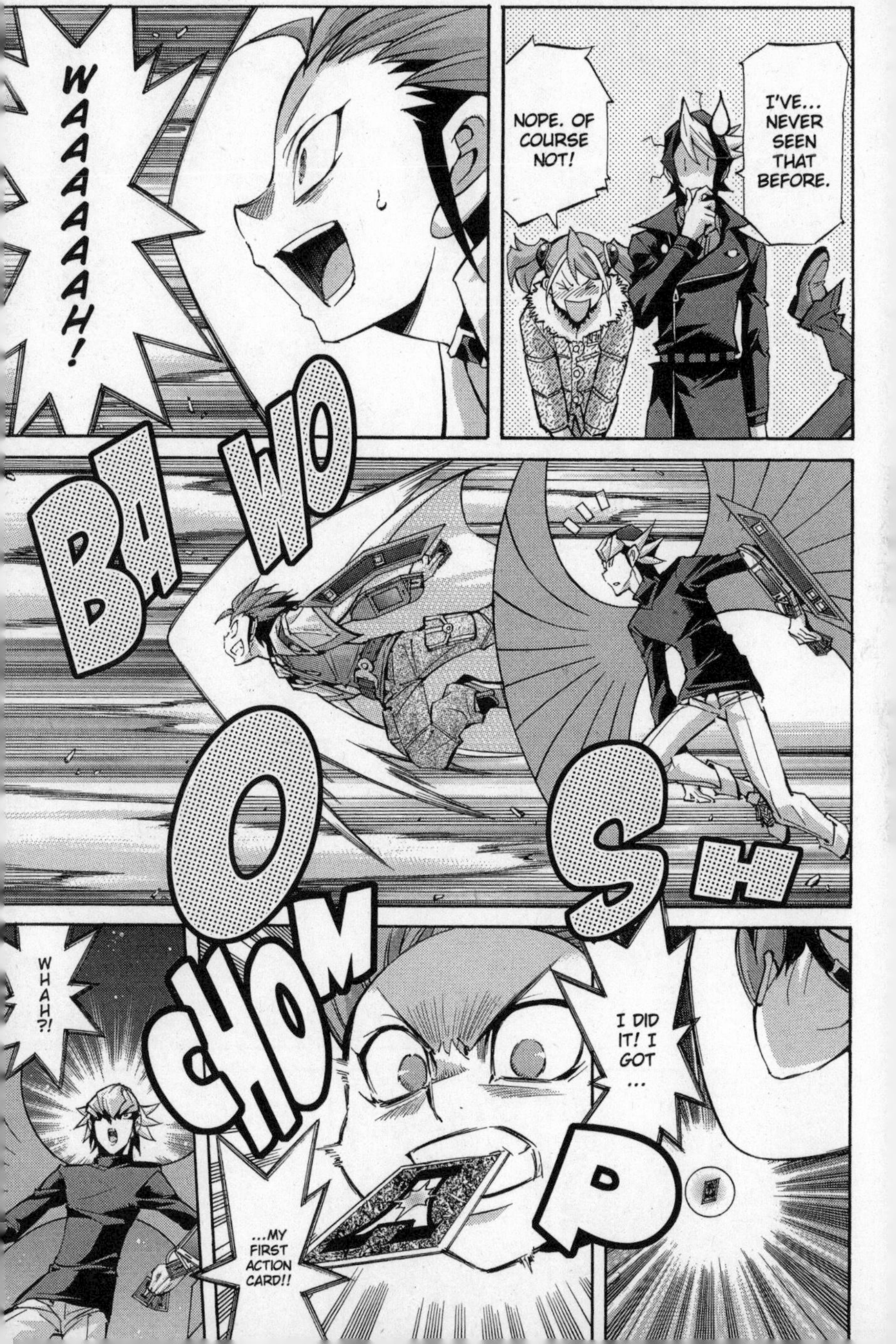
I'VE... NEVER SEEN THAT BEFORE.
NOPE. OF COURSE NOT!
WAAAAAAAAH!
...
BAWOOSH
I DID IT! I GOT ...
...MY FIRST ACTION CARD!!
CHOMP
WHAH?!

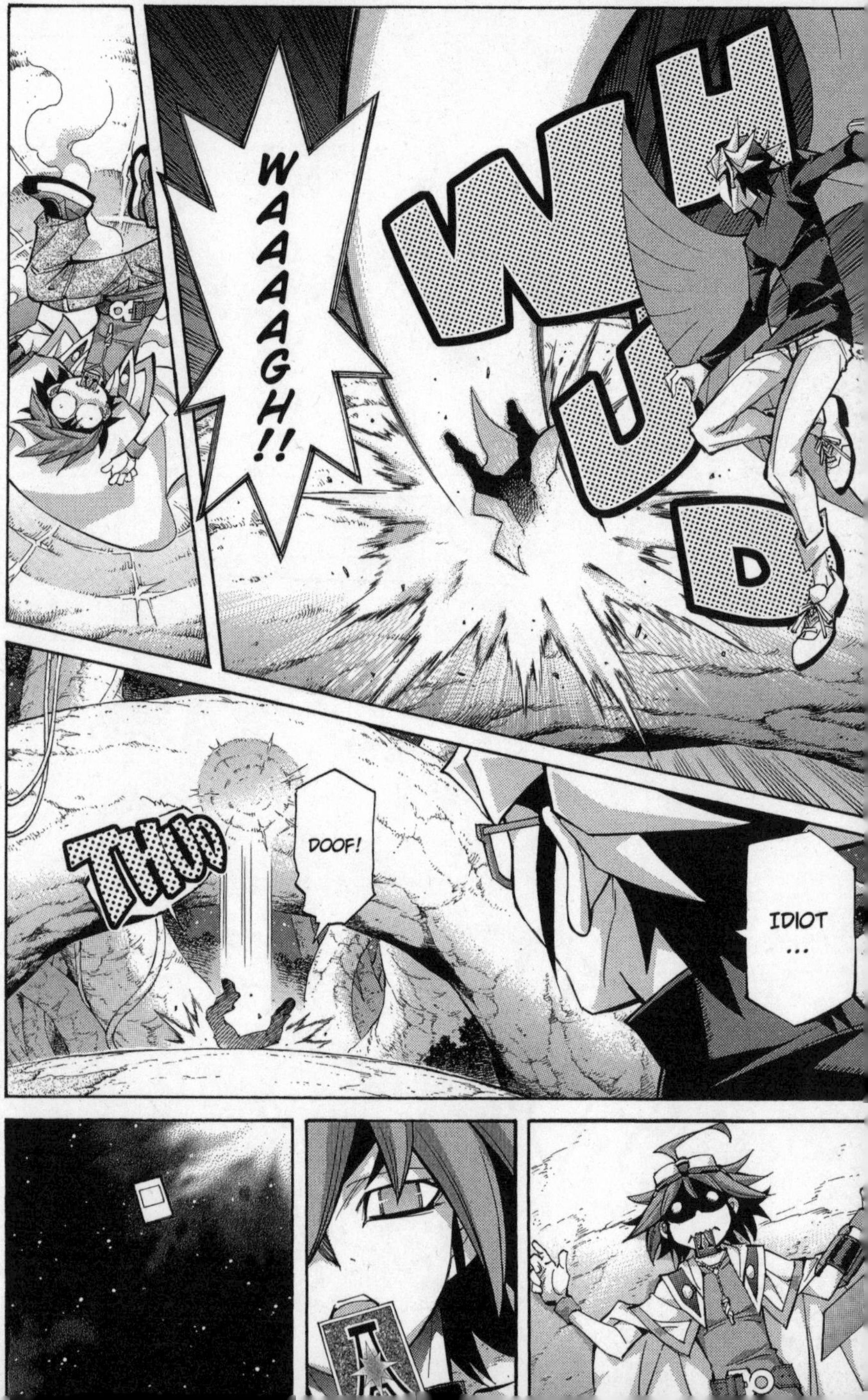
WHUD
WAAAAGH!!
IDIOT...
DOOF!
THUD

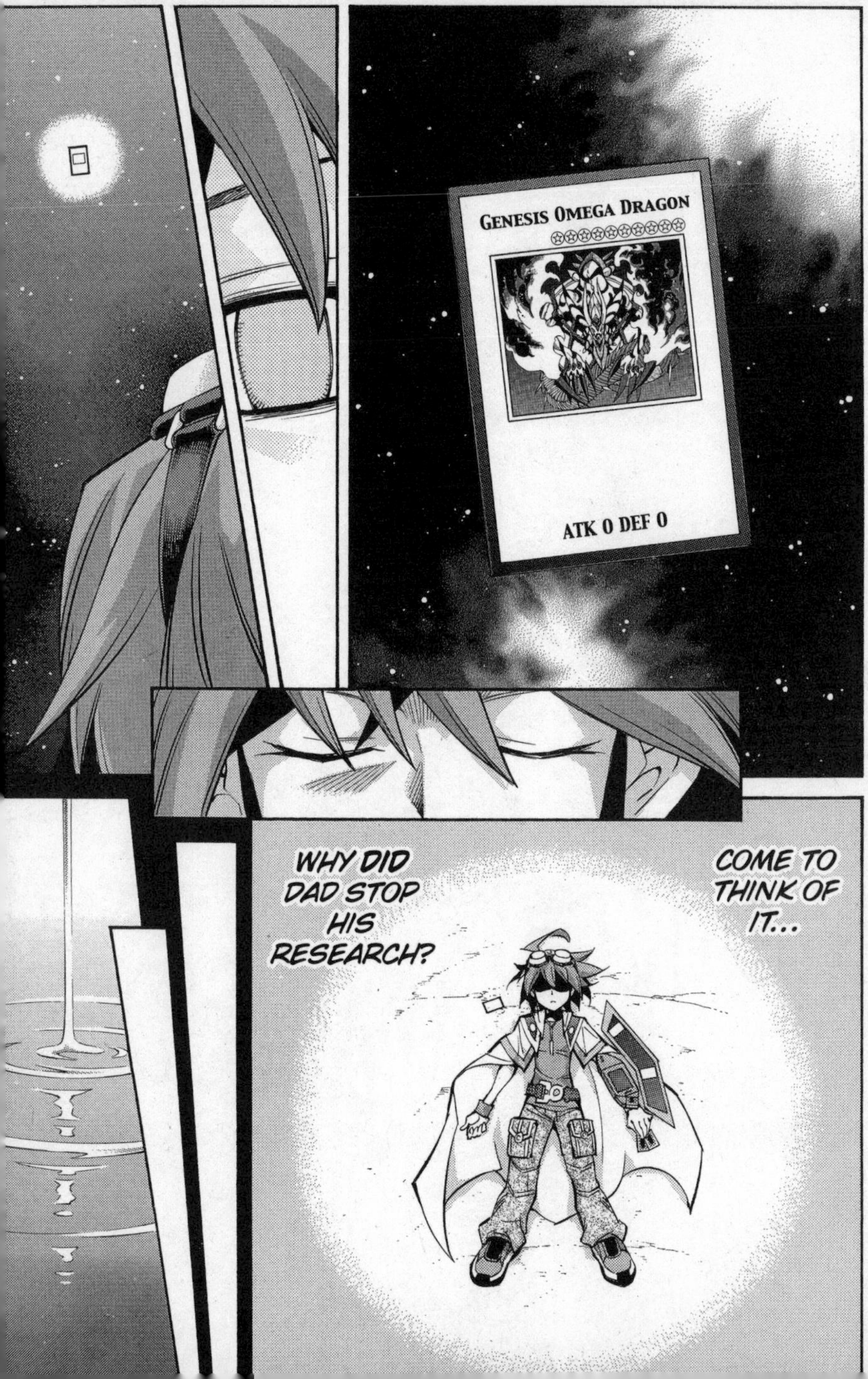
GENESIS OMEGA DRAGON
ATK 0 DEF 0
COME TO THINK OF IT...
WHY DID DAD STOP HIS RESEARCH?

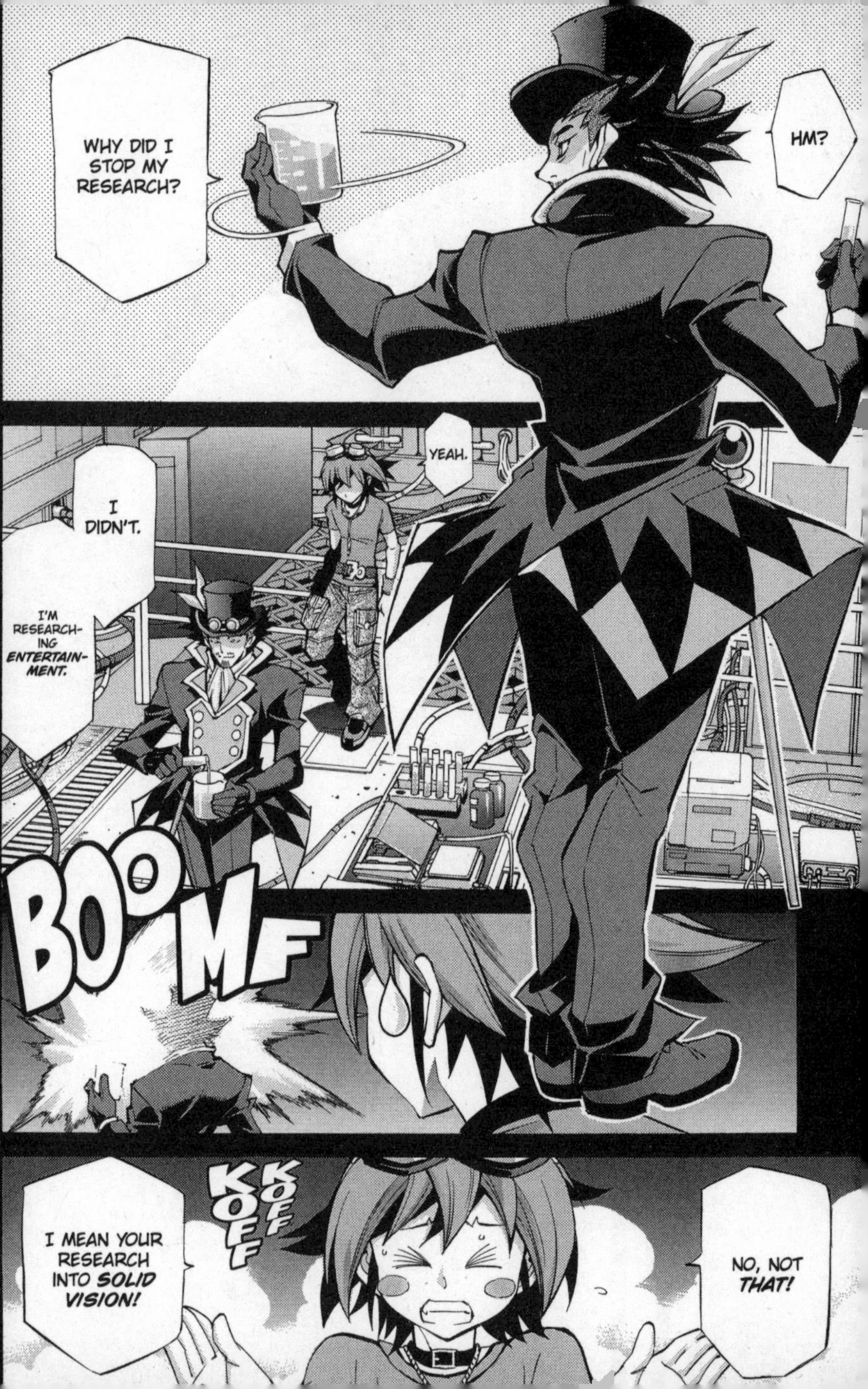
HM?
WHY DID I STOP MY RESEARCH?
YEAH.
I DIDN'T.
I'M RESEARCHING ENTERTAINMENT.
BOOMF
NO, NOT THAT!
KOFF KOFF
I MEAN YOUR RESEARCH INTO SOLID VISION!

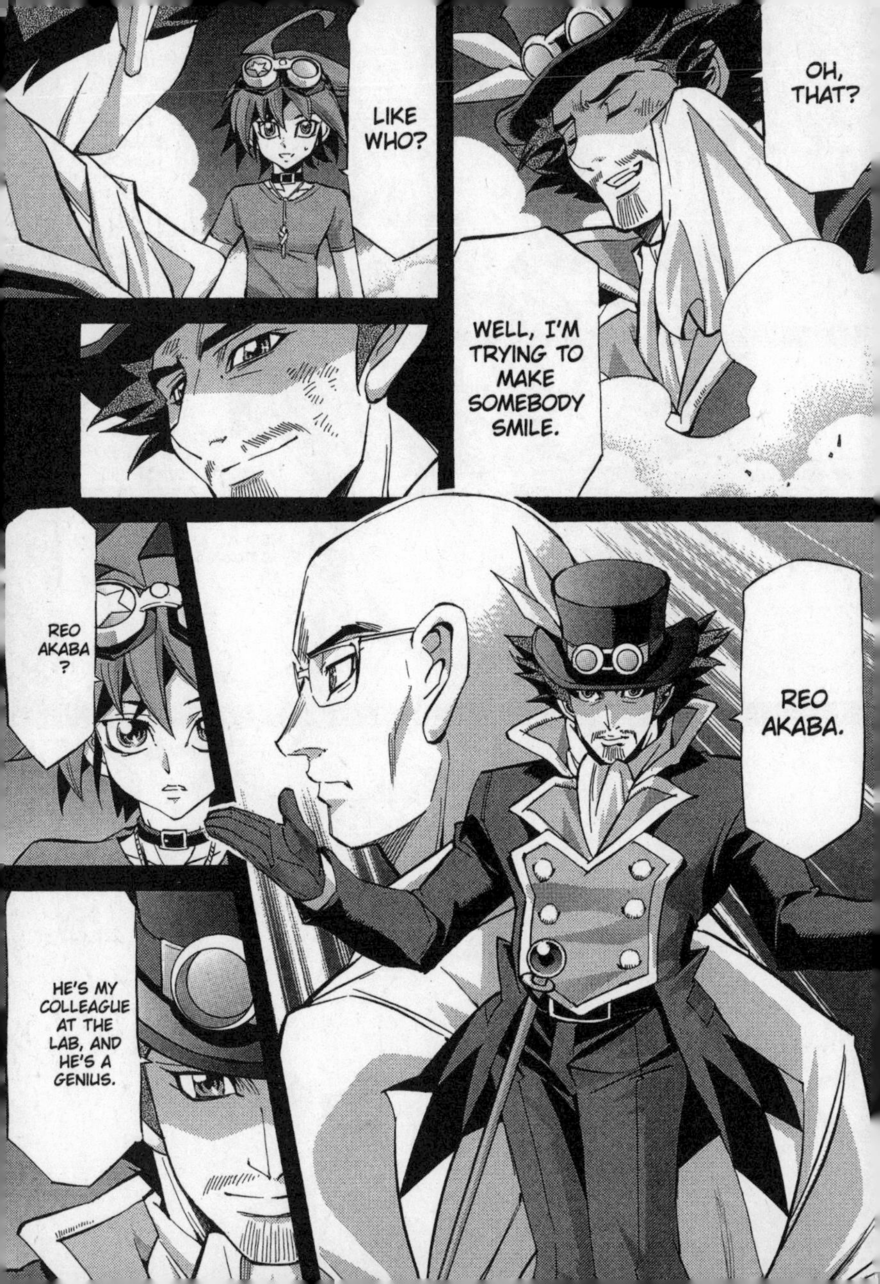
OH, THAT?
WELL, I'M TRYING TO MAKE SOMEBODY SMILE.
LIKE WHO?
REO AKABA.
REO AKABA?
HE'S MY COLLEAGUE AT THE LAB, AND HE'S A GENIUS.

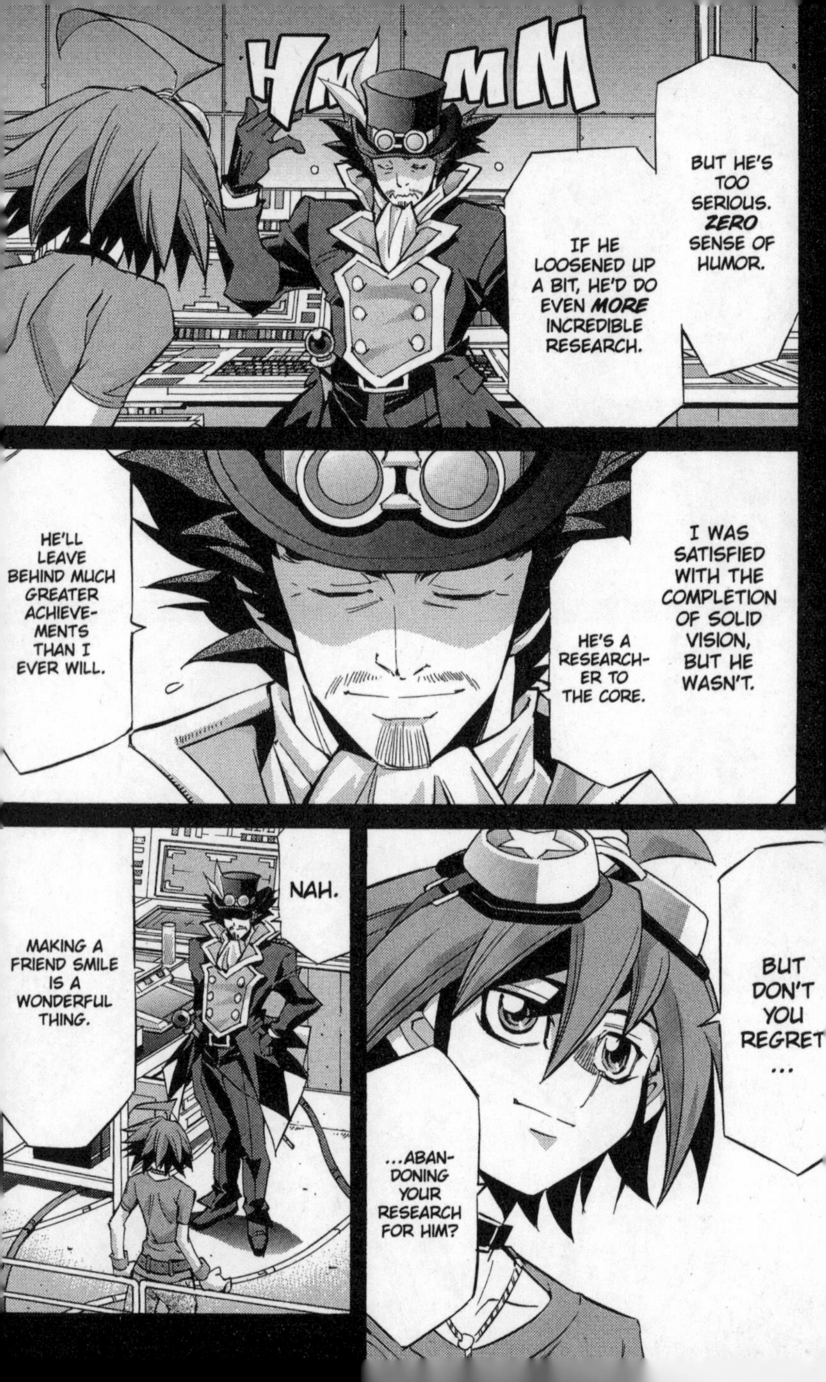

HMMM
BUT HE'S TOO SERIOUS. ***ZERO*** SENSE OF HUMOR.
IF HE LOOSENED UP A BIT, HE'D DO EVEN ***MORE*** INCREDIBLE RESEARCH.
I WAS SATISFIED WITH THE COMPLETION OF SOLID VISION, BUT HE WASN'T.
HE'S A RESEARCHER TO THE CORE.
HE'LL LEAVE BEHIND MUCH GREATER ACHIEVEMENTS THAN I EVER WILL.
BUT DON'T YOU REGRET...
...ABANDONING YOUR RESEARCH FOR HIM?
NAH.
MAKING A FRIEND SMILE IS A WONDERFUL THING.

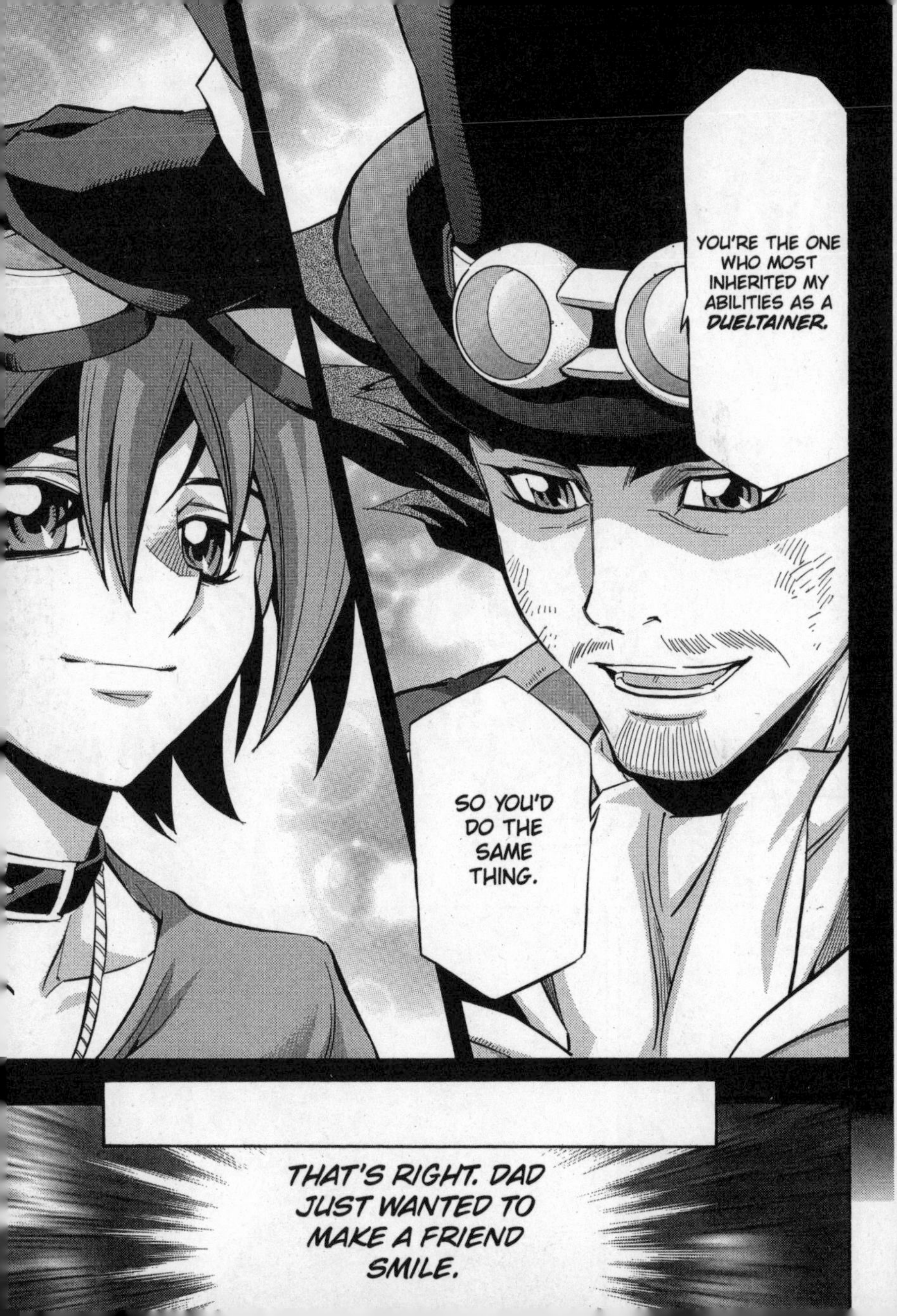
YOU'RE THE ONE WHO MOST INHERITED MY ABILITIES AS A *DUELTAINER.*
SO YOU'D DO THE SAME THING.
THAT'S RIGHT. DAD JUST WANTED TO MAKE A FRIEND SMILE.

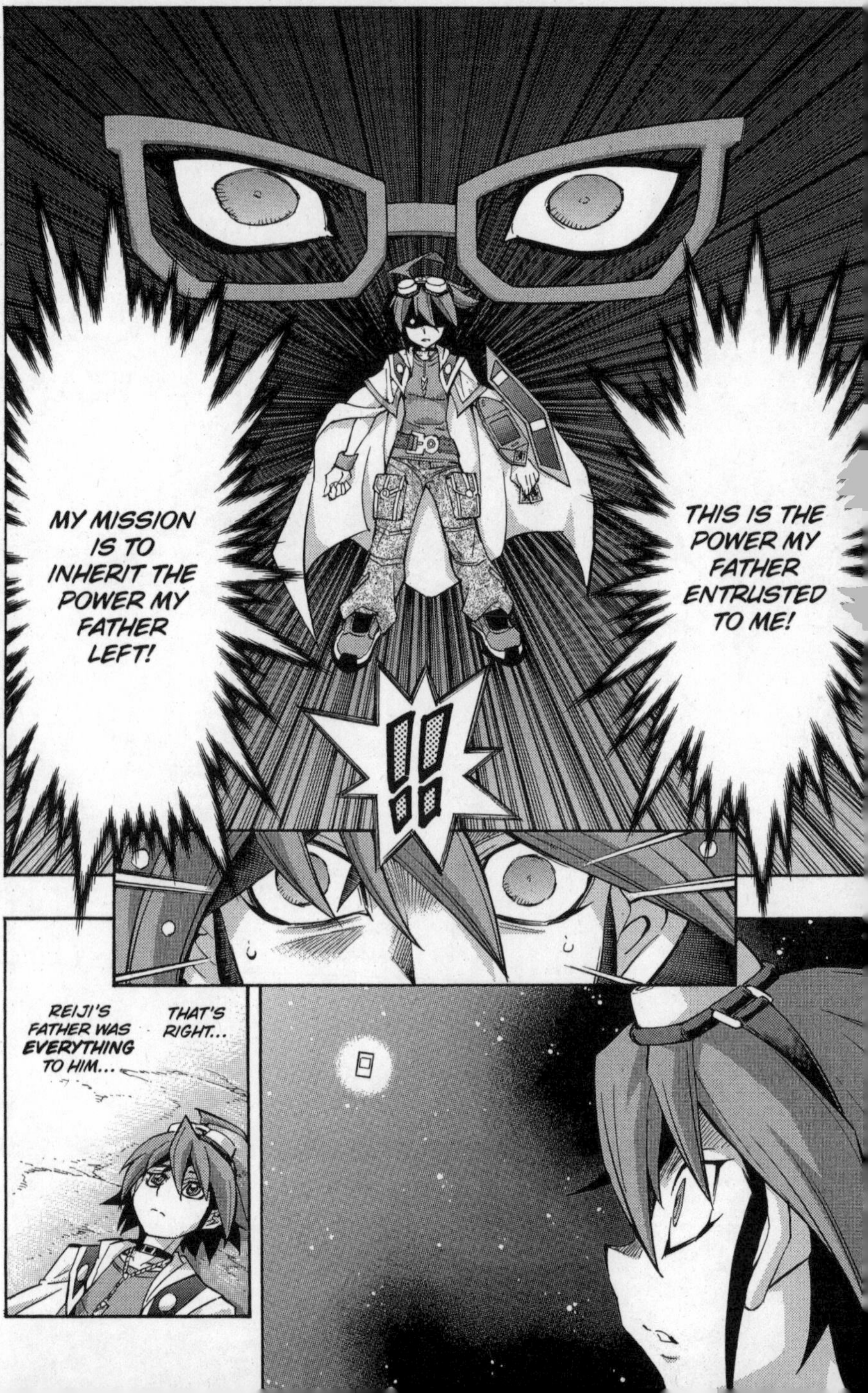
THIS IS THE POWER MY FATHER ENTRUSTED TO ME!
MY MISSION IS TO INHERIT THE POWER MY FATHER LEFT!
!!
THAT'S RIGHT...
REIJI'S FATHER WAS EVERYTHING TO HIM...

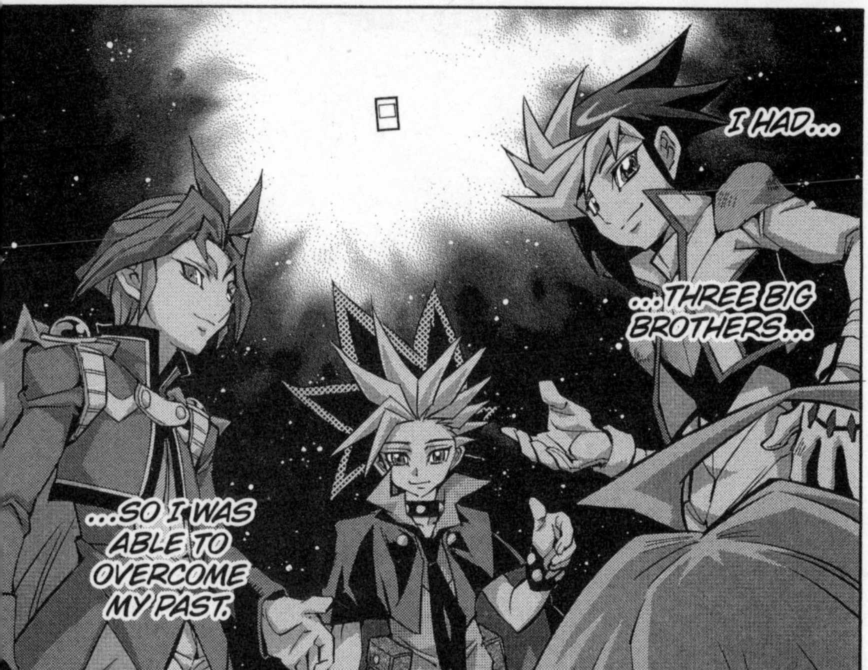
I HAD...
...THREE BIG BROTHERS...
...SO I WAS ABLE TO OVERCOME MY PAST.
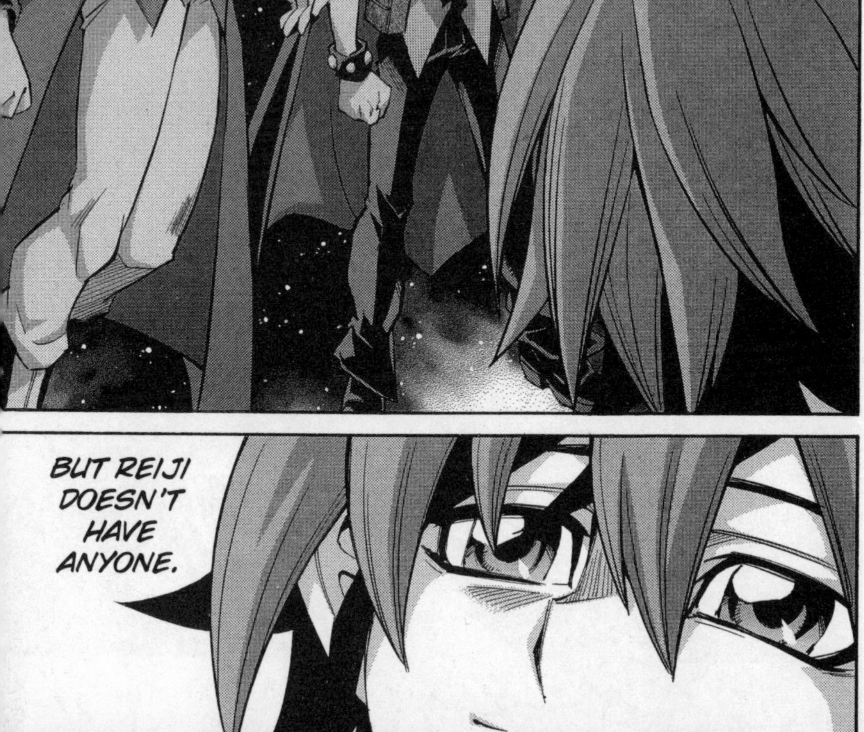
BUT REIJI DOESN'T HAVE ANYONE.

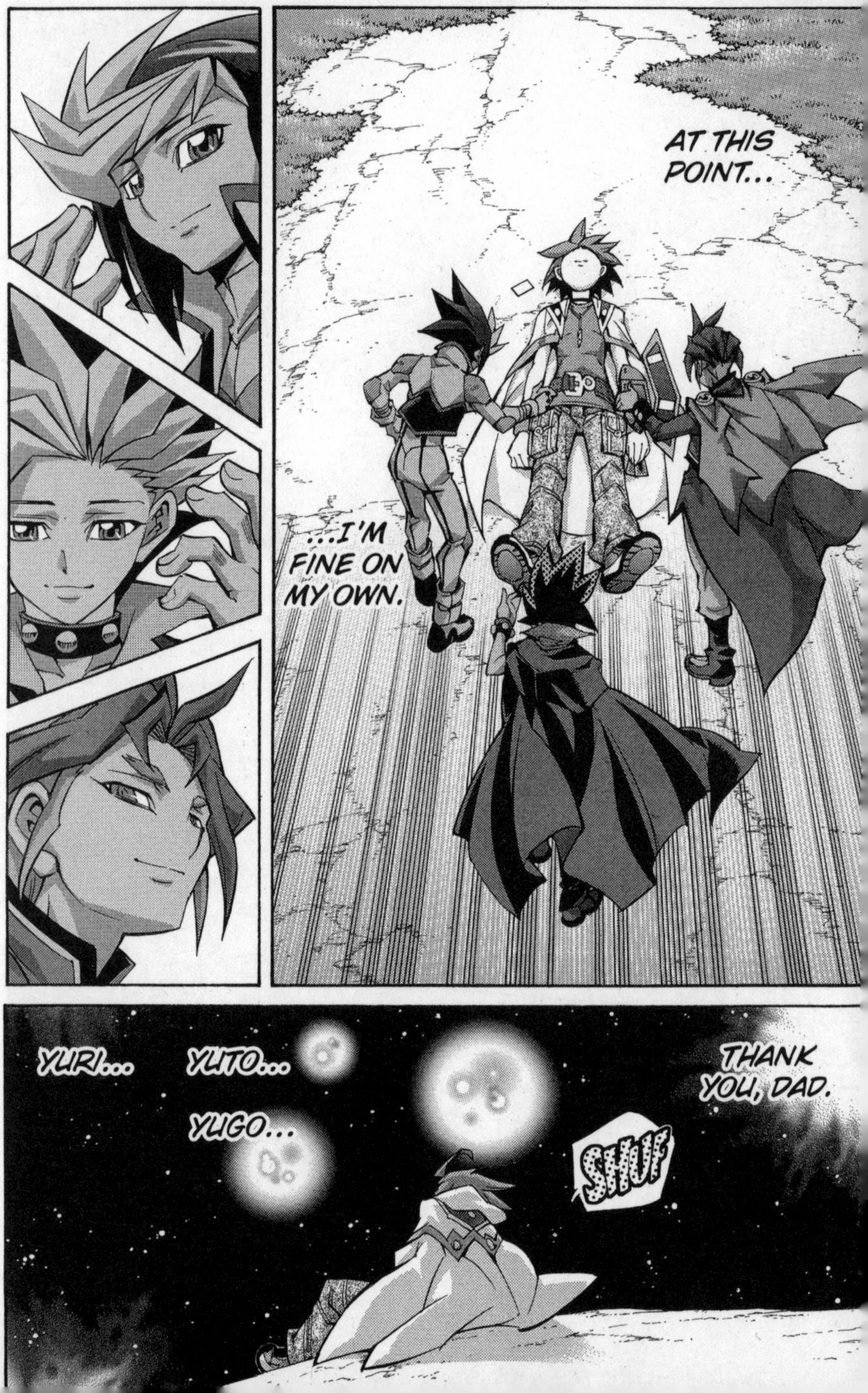
AT THIS POINT...
...I'M FINE ON MY OWN.
THANK YOU, DAD.
YUTO...
YURI...
YUGO...
SHUF

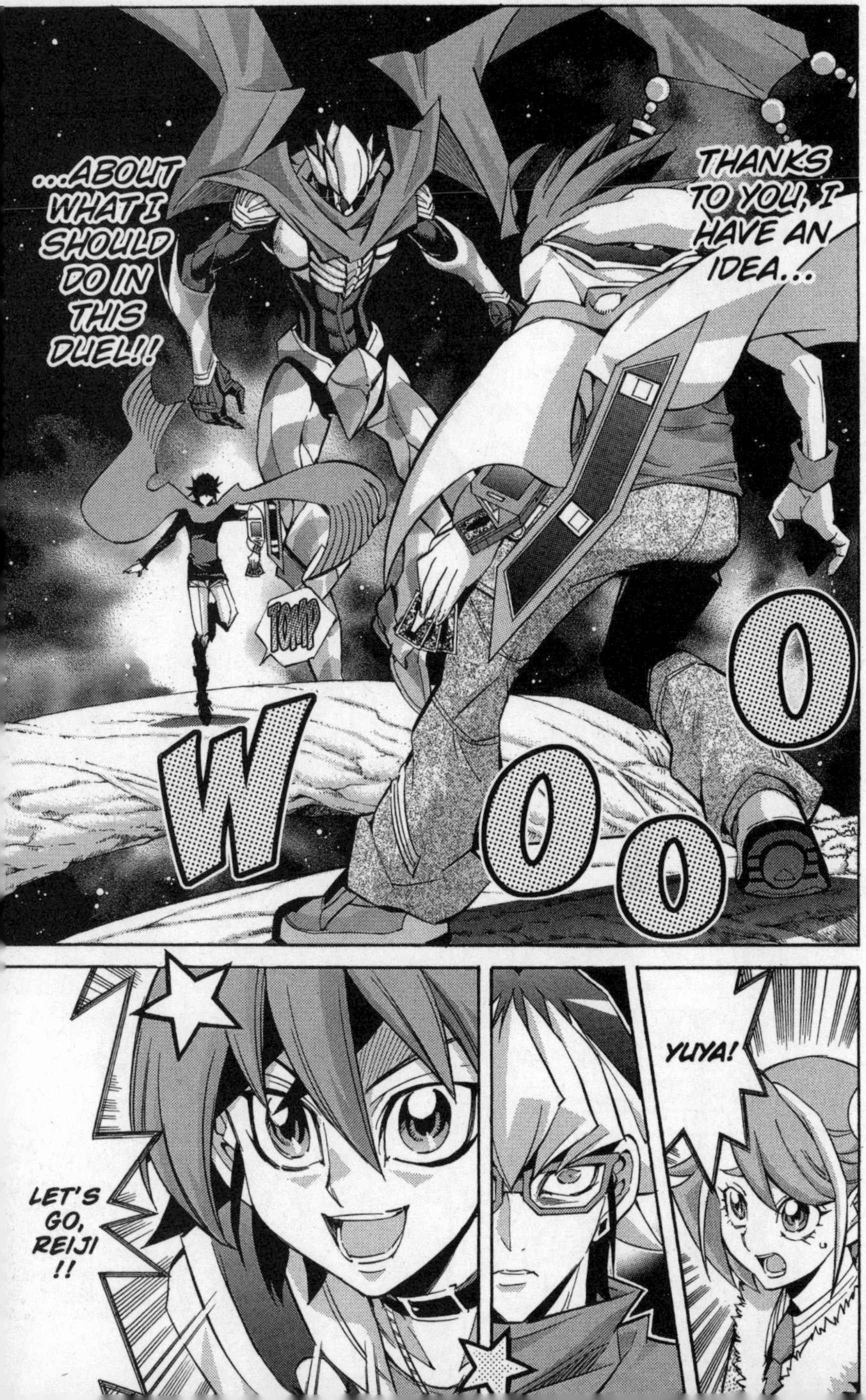

THANKS TO YOU, I HAVE AN IDEA...
...ABOUT WHAT I SHOULD DO IN THIS DUEL!!
TOMP
WOOOO
YUYA!
LET'S GO, REIJI!!

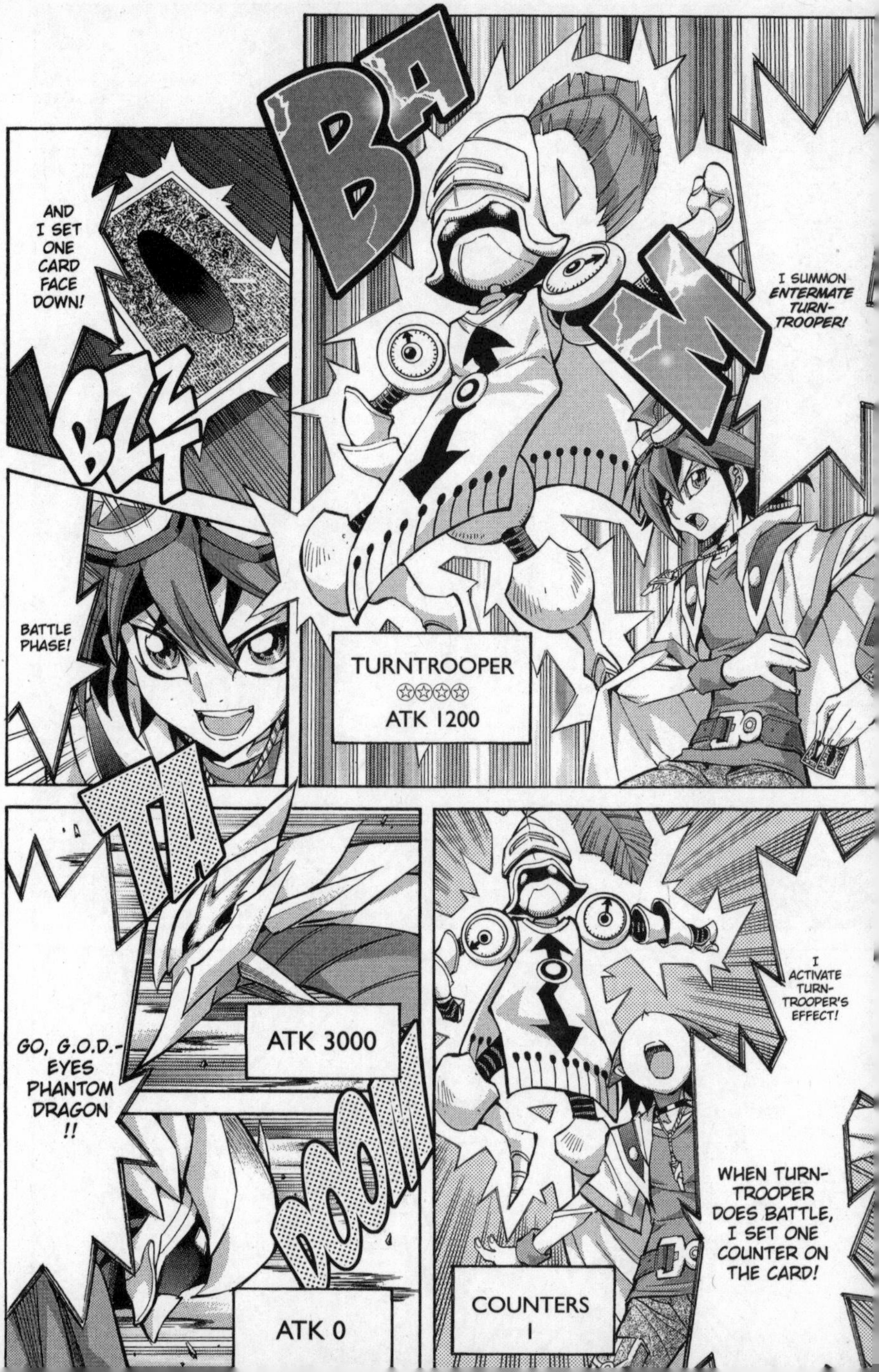
I SUMMON ENTERMATE TURN-TROOPER!
TURNTROOPER ☆☆☆☆ ATK 1200
AND I SET ONE CARD FACE DOWN!
BZZT
BATTLE PHASE!
TA
I ACTIVATE TURN-TROOPER'S EFFECT!
WHEN TURN-TROOPER DOES BATTLE, I SET ONE COUNTER ON THE CARD!
COUNTERS 1
GO, G.O.D.-EYES PHANTOM DRAGON!!
ATK 3000
BOOOM
ATK 0

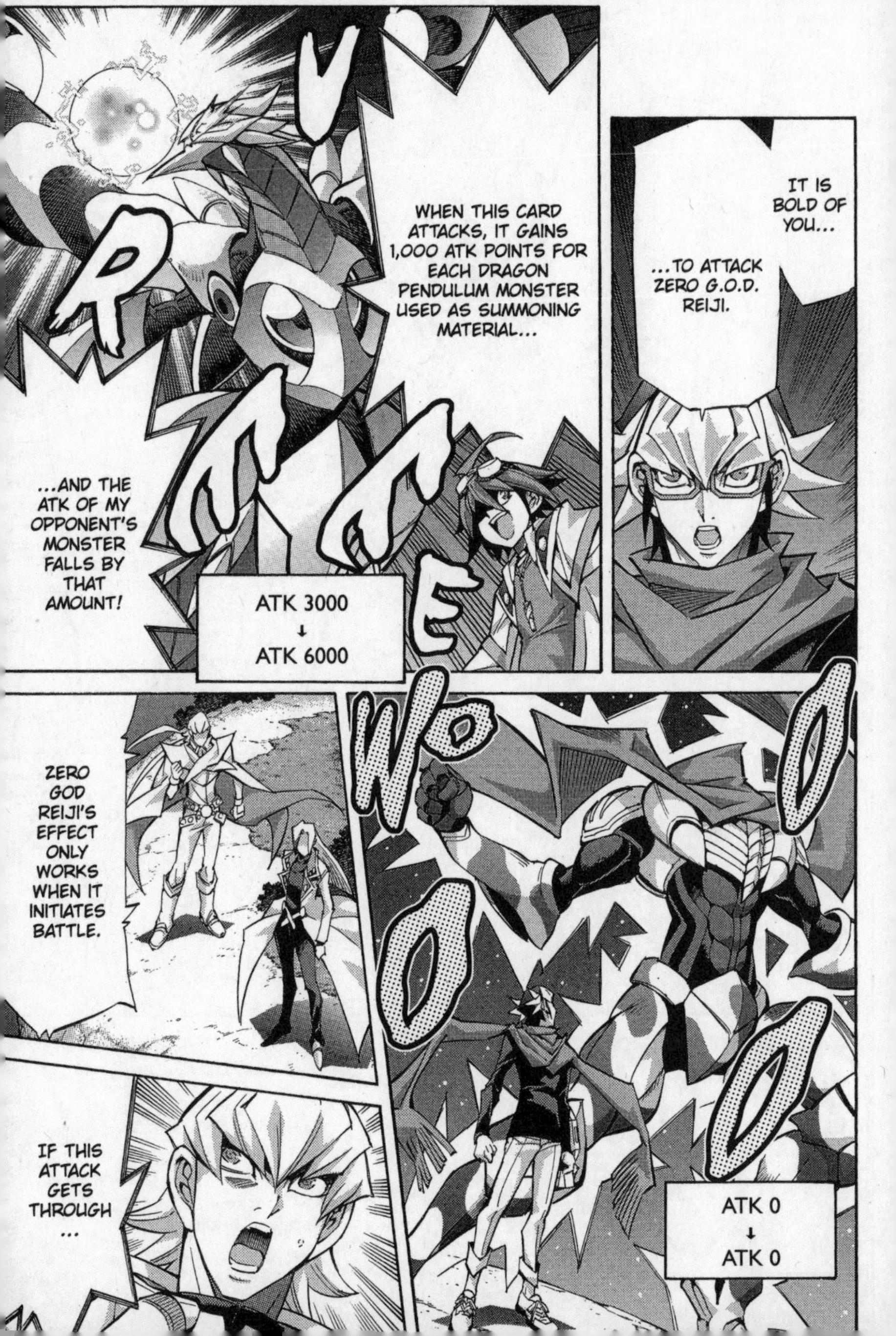
IT IS BOLD OF YOU...
...TO ATTACK ZERO G.O.D. REIJI.
WHEN THIS CARD ATTACKS, IT GAINS 1,000 ATK POINTS FOR EACH DRAGON PENDULUM MONSTER USED AS SUMMONING MATERIAL...
...AND THE ATK OF MY OPPONENT'S MONSTER FALLS BY THAT AMOUNT!
ATK 3000 ↓ ATK 6000
ATK 0 ↓ ATK 0
ZERO GOD REIJI'S EFFECT ONLY WORKS WHEN IT INITIATES BATTLE.
IF THIS ATTACK GETS THROUGH...

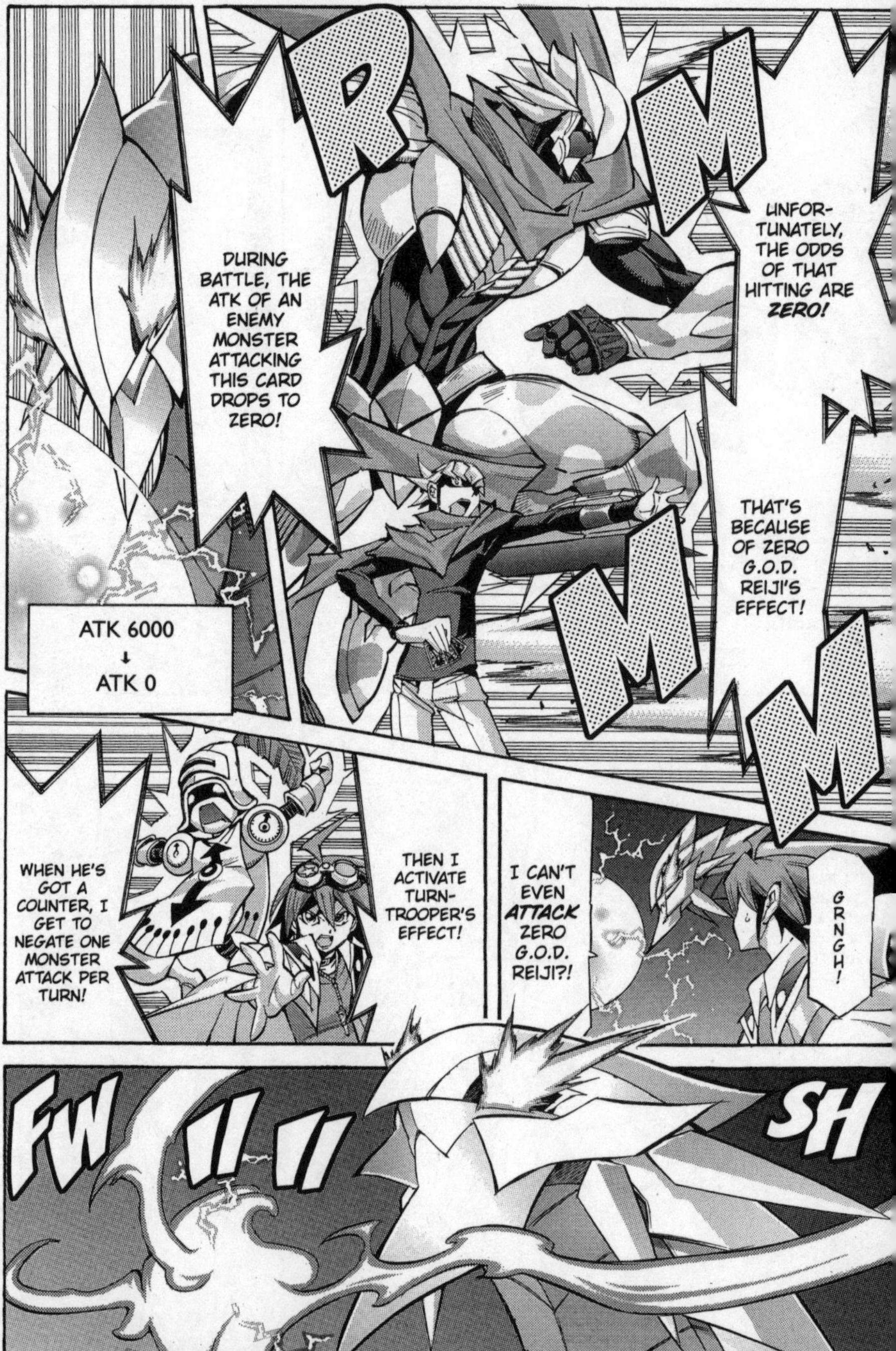
UNFORTUNATELY, THE ODDS OF THAT HITTING ARE **ZERO!**
THAT'S BECAUSE OF ZERO G.O.D. REIJI'S EFFECT!
DURING BATTLE, THE ATK OF AN ENEMY MONSTER ATTACKING THIS CARD DROPS TO ZERO!
ATK 6000 ↓ ATK 0
GRNGH!
I CAN'T EVEN ***ATTACK*** ZERO G.O.D. REIJI?!
THEN I ACTIVATE TURN-TROOPER'S EFFECT!
WHEN HE'S GOT A COUNTER, I GET TO NEGATE ONE MONSTER ATTACK PER TURN!
FWIIIISH

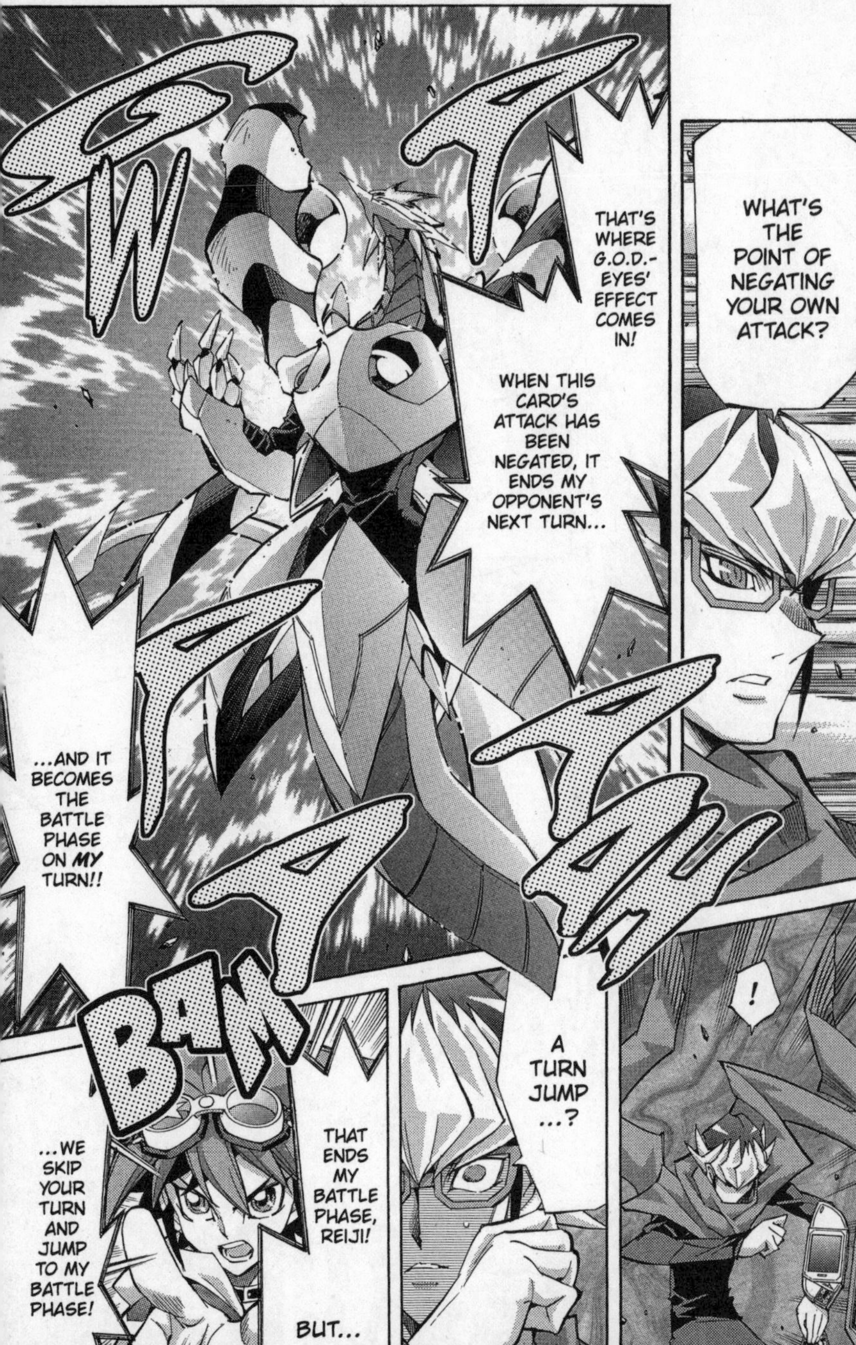
WHAT'S THE POINT OF NEGATING YOUR OWN ATTACK?
THAT'S WHERE G.O.D.-EYES' EFFECT COMES IN!
WHEN THIS CARD'S ATTACK HAS BEEN NEGATED, IT ENDS MY OPPONENT'S NEXT TURN...
...AND IT BECOMES THE BATTLE PHASE ON *MY* TURN!!
BAM
!
A TURN JUMP ...?
THAT ENDS MY BATTLE PHASE, REIJI!
BUT...
...WE SKIP YOUR TURN AND JUMP TO MY BATTLE PHASE!

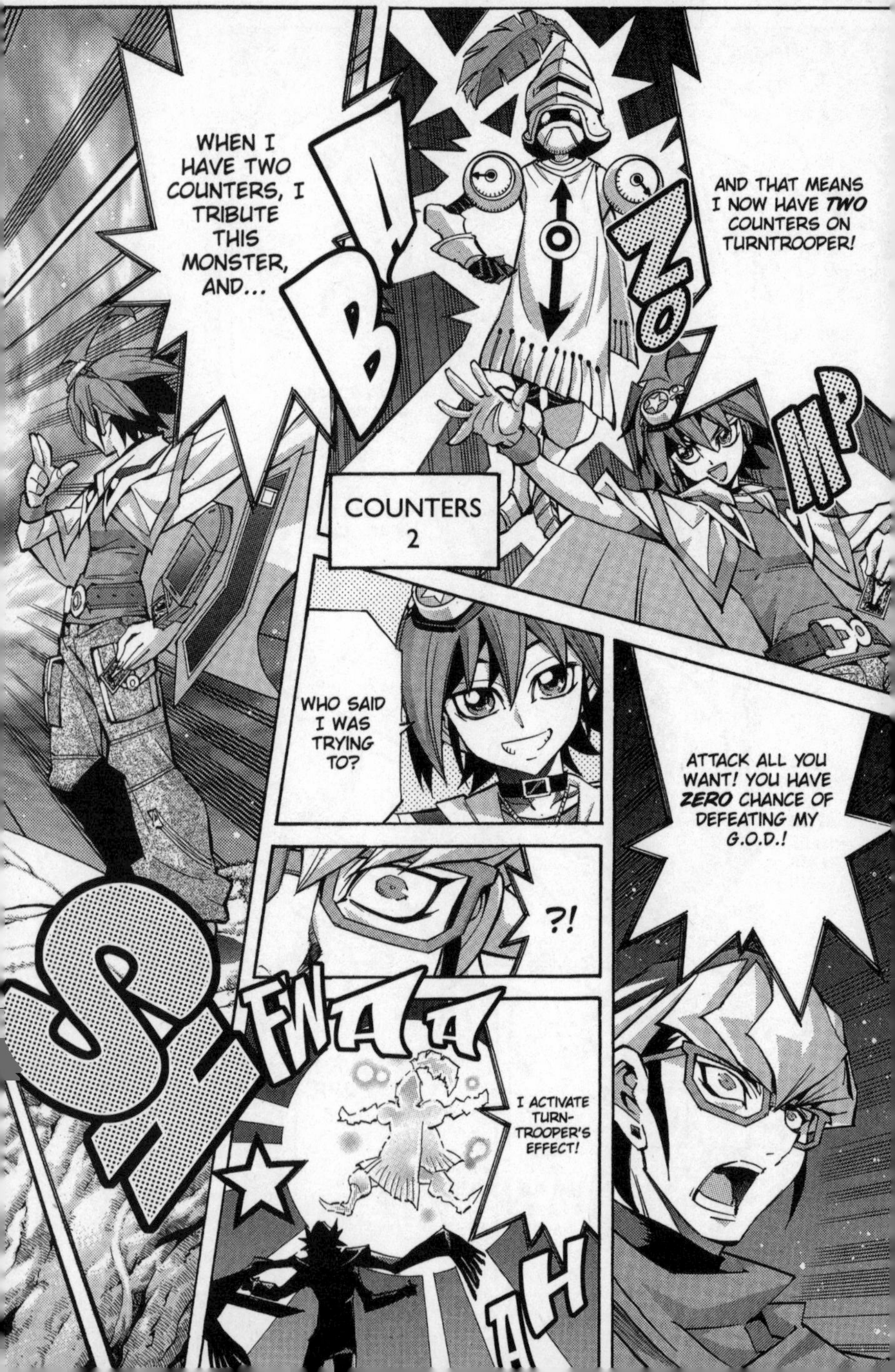
AND THAT MEANS I NOW HAVE *TWO* COUNTERS ON TURNTROOPER!
COUNTERS 2
ATTACK ALL YOU WANT! YOU HAVE *ZERO* CHANCE OF DEFEATING MY G.O.D.!
WHO SAID I WAS TRYING TO?
?!
I ACTIVATE TURN-TROOPER'S EFFECT!
WHEN I HAVE TWO COUNTERS, I TRIBUTE THIS MONSTER, AND...

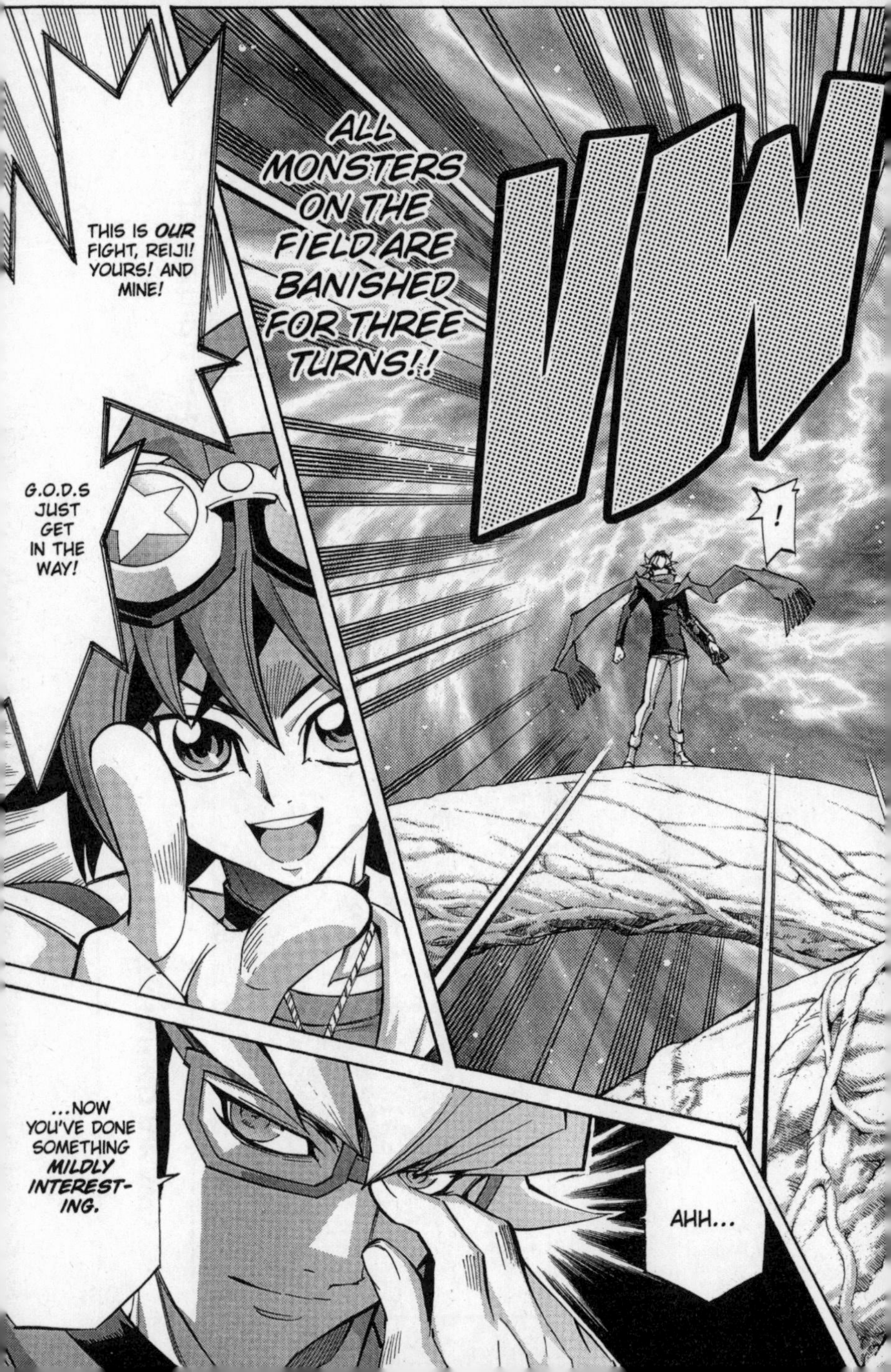
ALL MONSTERS ON THE FIELD ARE BANISHED FOR THREE TURNS!!
!
THIS IS *OUR* FIGHT, REIJI! YOURS! AND MINE!
G.O.D.S JUST GET IN THE WAY!
AHH...
...NOW YOU'VE DONE SOMETHING *MILDLY INTERESTING.*

The Guys Behind ARC-V!

TAKAHIKO AIKAWA

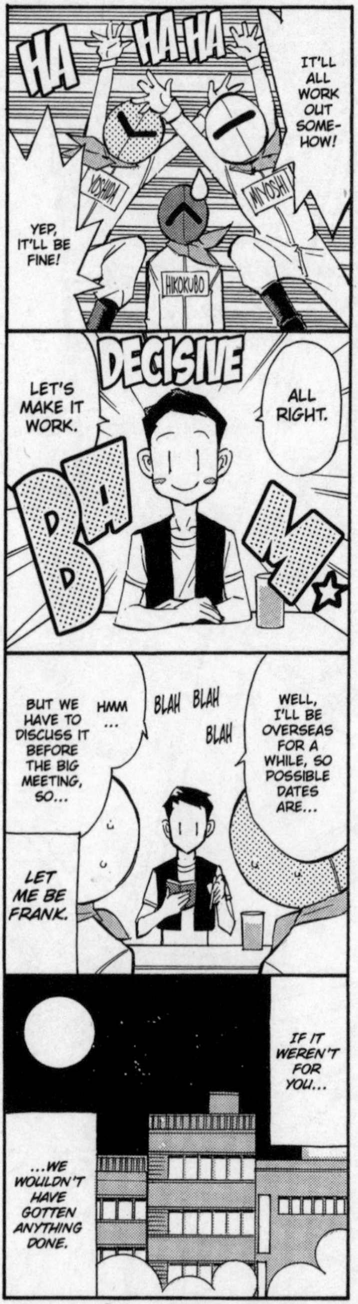
HA-HA
HA
IT'LL ALL WORK OUT SOME-HOW!
MIYOSHI
YOSHIDA
HIKOKUBO
YEP, IT'LL BE FINE!
DECISIVE
ALL RIGHT.
LET'S MAKE IT WORK.
BAM☆
WELL, I'LL BE OVERSEAS FOR A WHILE, SO POSSIBLE DATES ARE...
BLAH BLAH BLAH
HMM...
BUT WE HAVE TO DISCUSS IT BEFORE THE BIG MEETING, SO...
LET ME BE FRANK.
IF IT WEREN'T FOR YOU...
...WE WOULDN'T HAVE GOTTEN ANYTHING DONE.

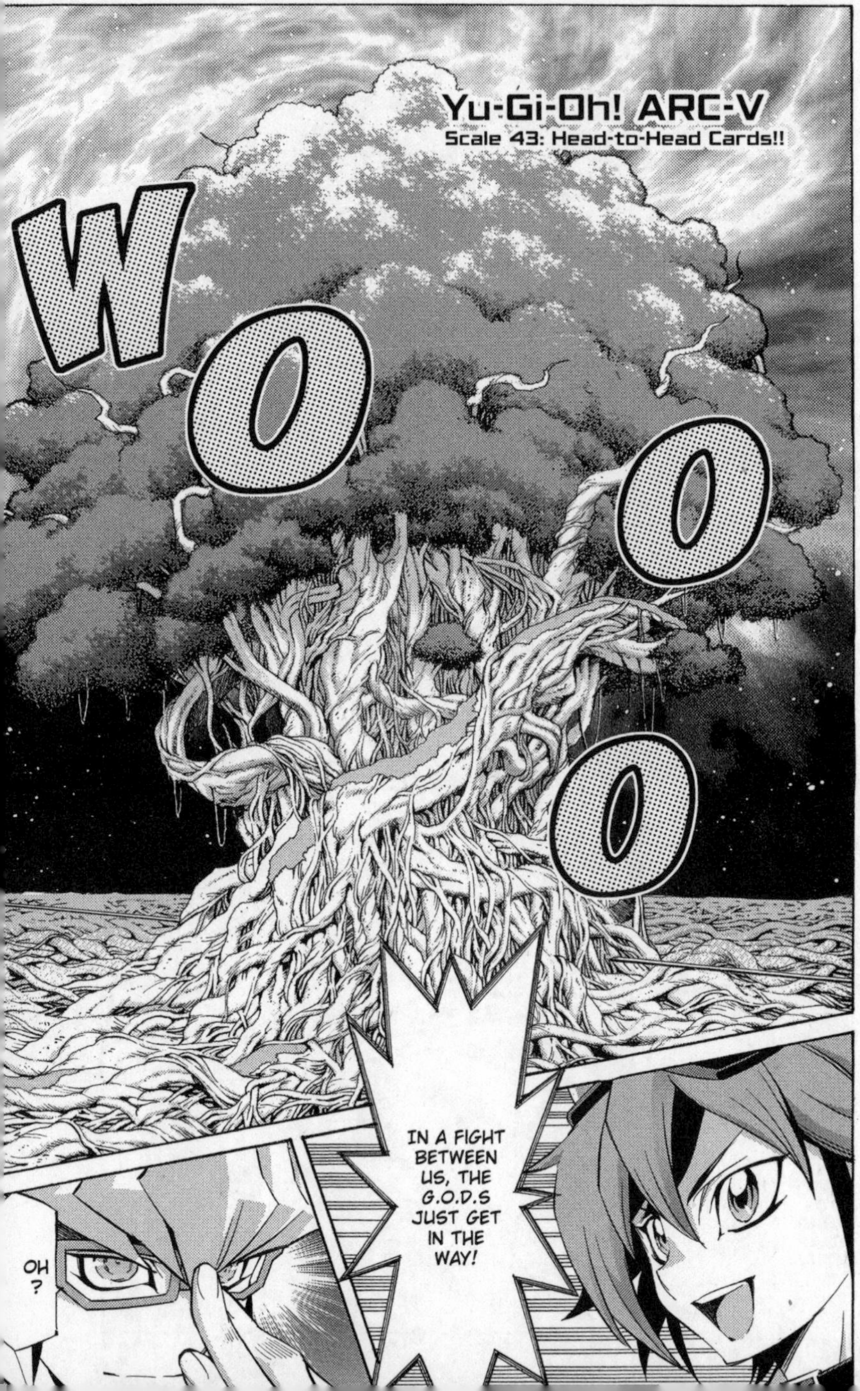
Yu-Gi-Oh! ARC-V
Scale 43: Head-to-Head Cards!!
WOOOO
IN A FIGHT BETWEEN US, THE G.O.D.S JUST GET IN THE WAY!
OH?

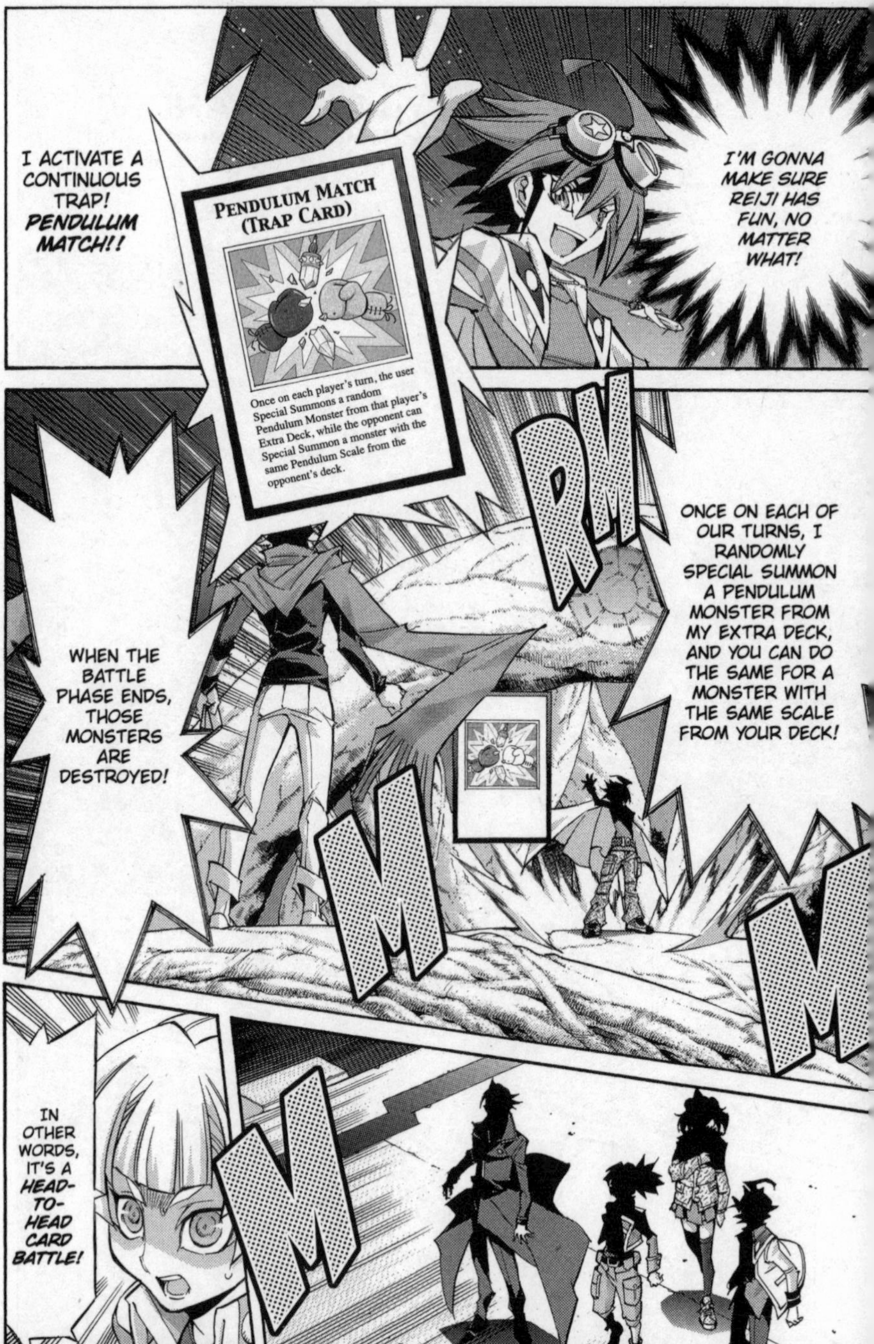
I'M GONNA MAKE SURE REIJI HAS FUN, NO MATTER WHAT!
I ACTIVATE A CONTINUOUS TRAP! PENDULUM MATCH!!
PENDULUM MATCH (TRAP CARD)
Once on each player's turn, the user Special Summons a random Pendulum Monster from that player's Extra Deck, while the opponent can Special Summon a monster with the same Pendulum Scale from the opponent's deck.
RM
ONCE ON EACH OF OUR TURNS, I RANDOMLY SPECIAL SUMMON A PENDULUM MONSTER FROM MY EXTRA DECK, AND YOU CAN DO THE SAME FOR A MONSTER WITH THE SAME SCALE FROM YOUR DECK!
WHEN THE BATTLE PHASE ENDS, THOSE MONSTERS ARE DESTROYED!
M
M
M
IN OTHER WORDS, IT'S A HEAD-TO-HEAD CARD BATTLE!

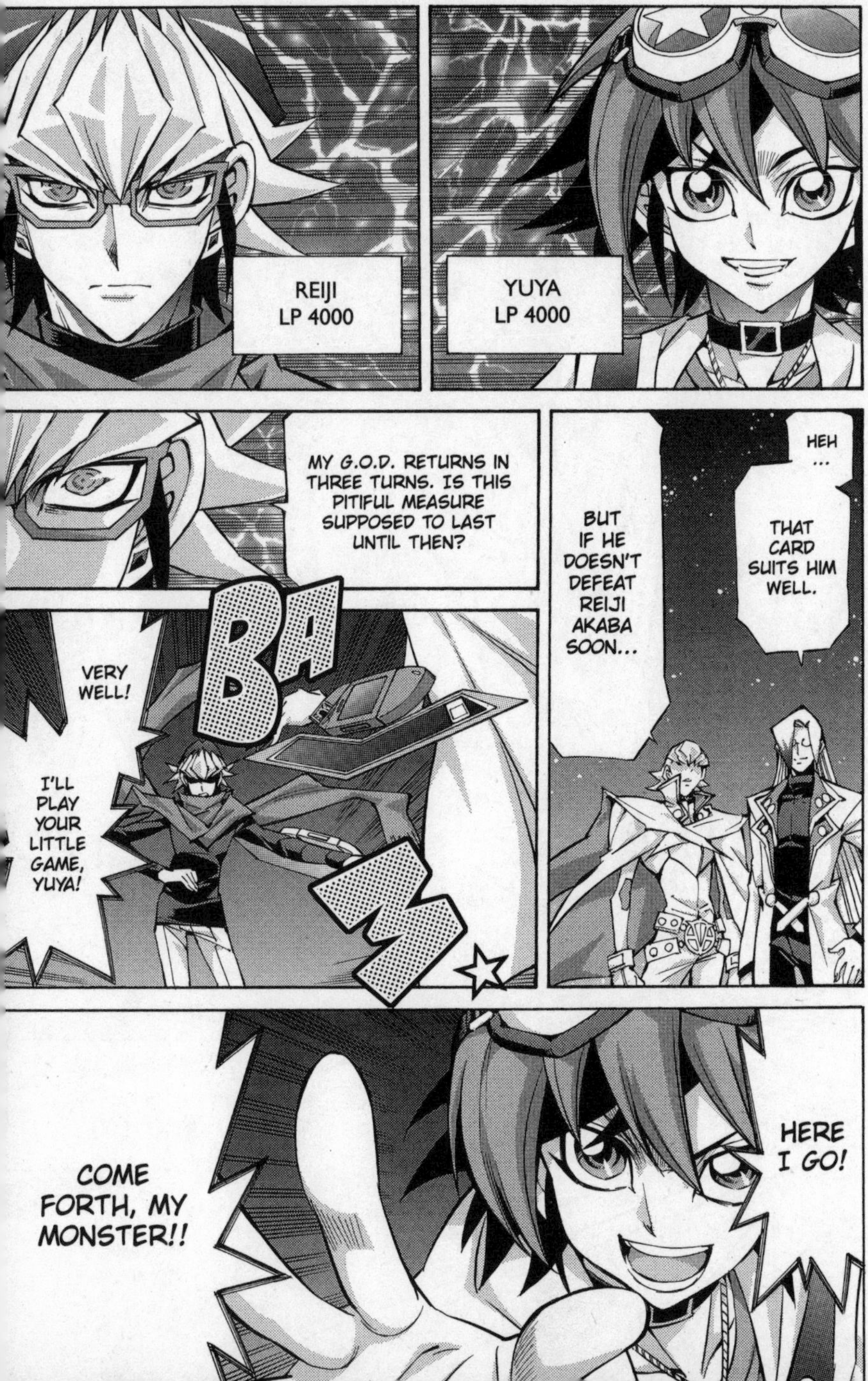
YUYA
LP 4000
REIJI
LP 4000
HEH ...
THAT CARD SUITS HIM WELL.
BUT IF HE DOESN'T DEFEAT REIJI AKABA SOON...
MY G.O.D. RETURNS IN THREE TURNS. IS THIS PITIFUL MEASURE SUPPOSED TO LAST UNTIL THEN?
BAM
VERY WELL!
I'LL PLAY YOUR LITTLE GAME, YUYA!
HERE I GO!
COME FORTH, MY MONSTER!!

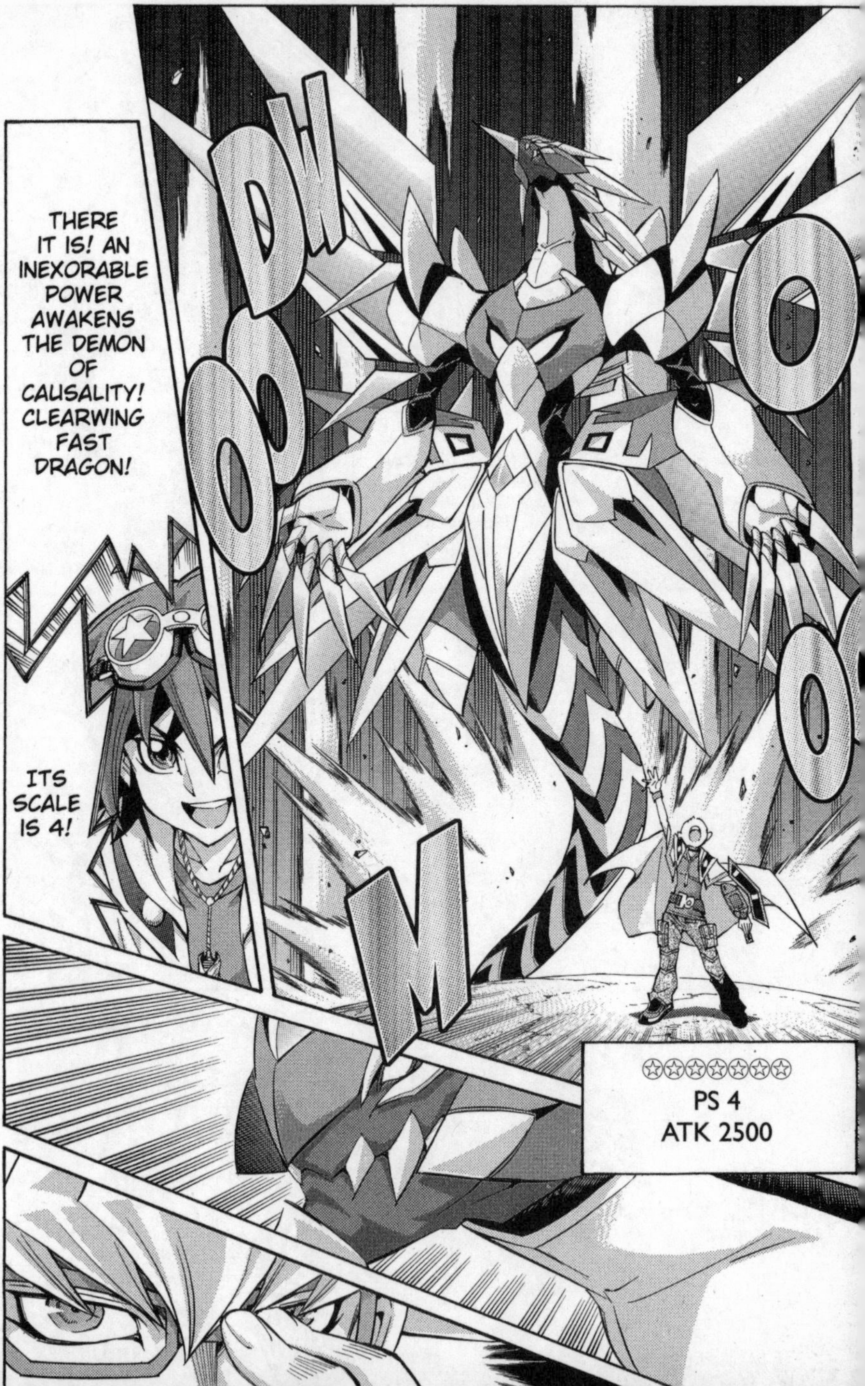
DOOOOM
THERE IT IS! AN INEXORABLE POWER AWAKENS THE DEMON OF CAUSALITY! CLEARWING FAST DRAGON!
ITS SCALE IS 4!
PS 4
ATK 2500

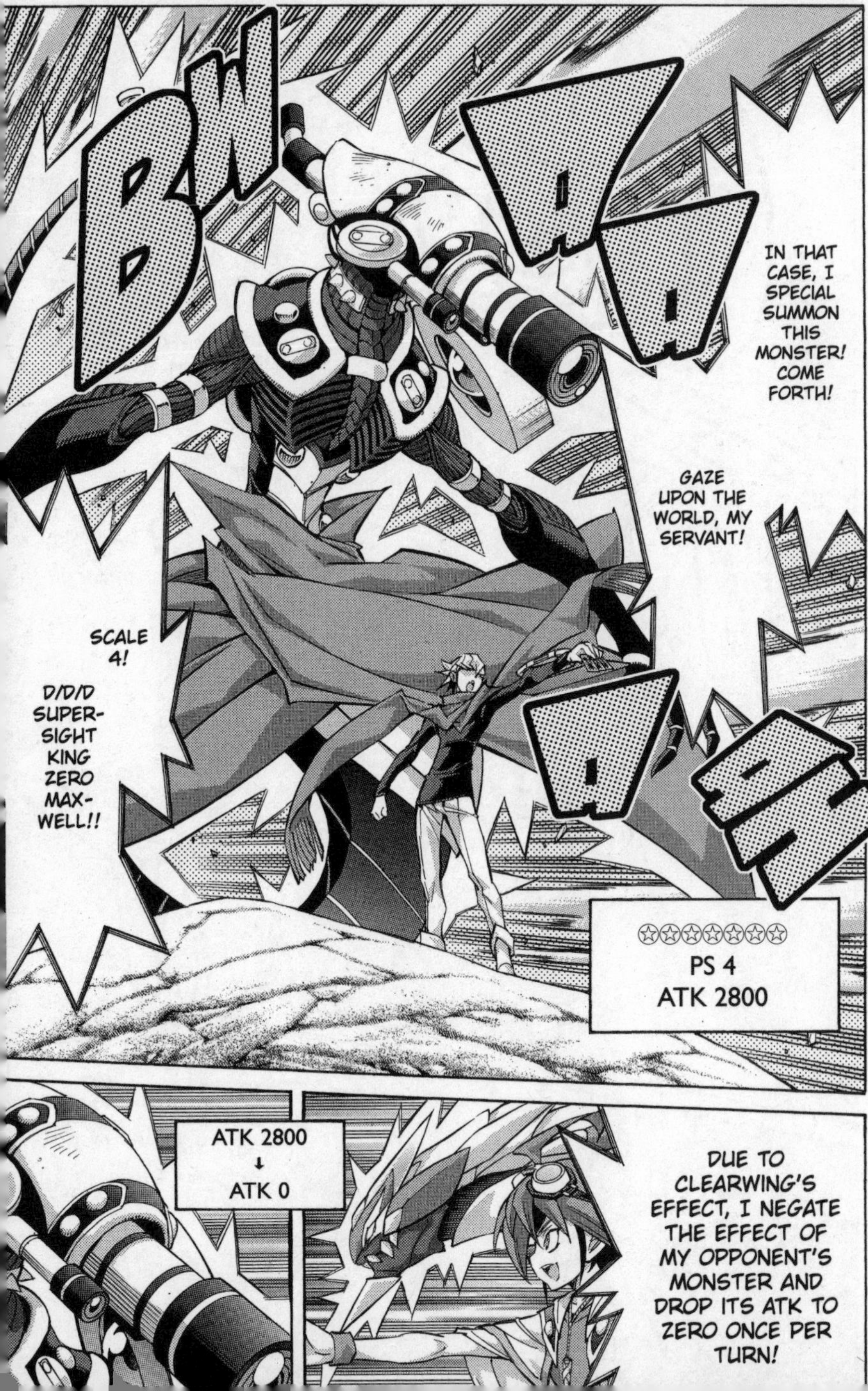
IN THAT CASE, I SPECIAL SUMMON THIS MONSTER! COME FORTH!
GAZE UPON THE WORLD, MY SERVANT!
SCALE 4!
D/D/D SUPER-SIGHT KING ZERO MAX-WELL!!
☆☆☆☆☆☆☆☆
PS 4
ATK 2800
DUE TO CLEARWING'S EFFECT, I NEGATE THE EFFECT OF MY OPPONENT'S MONSTER AND DROP ITS ATK TO ZERO ONCE PER TURN!
ATK 2800
↓
ATK 0

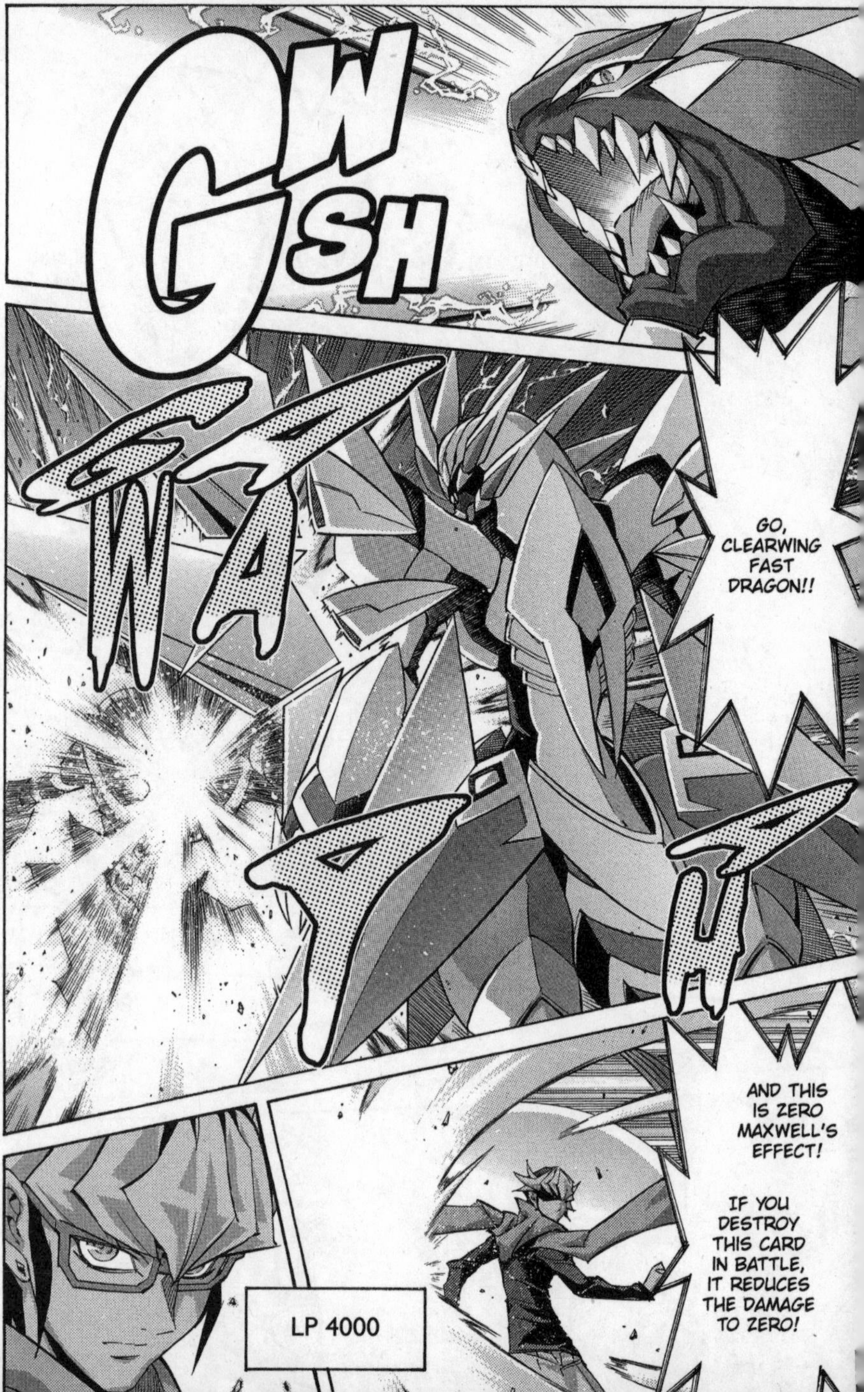
GO, CLEARWING FAST DRAGON!!
AND THIS IS ZERO MAXWELL'S EFFECT!
IF YOU DESTROY THIS CARD IN BATTLE, IT REDUCES THE DAMAGE TO ZERO!
LP 4000

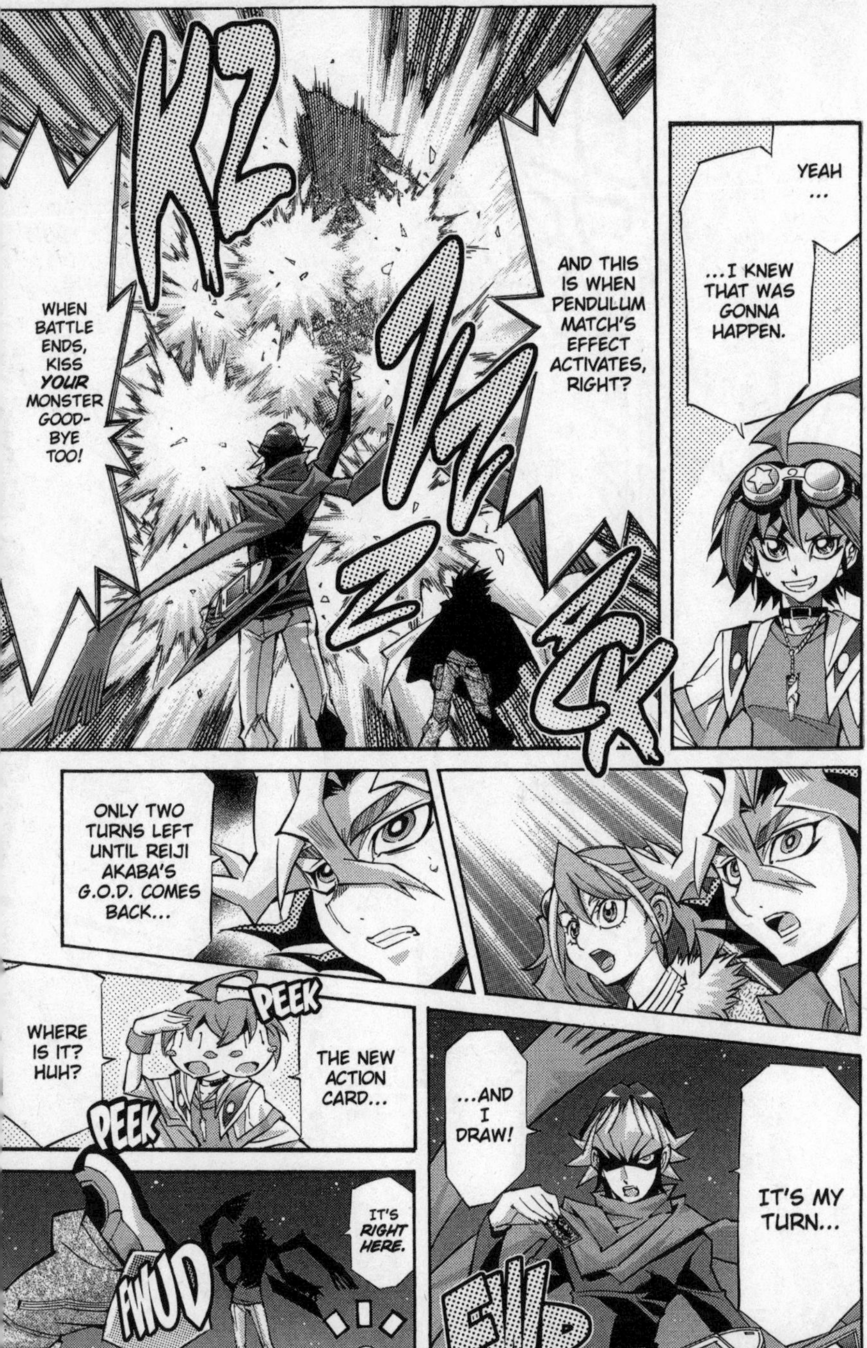

YEAH...
...I KNEW THAT WAS GONNA HAPPEN.
AND THIS IS WHEN PENDULUM MATCH'S EFFECT ACTIVATES, RIGHT?
WHEN BATTLE ENDS, KISS *YOUR* MONSTER GOOD-BYE TOO!
ONLY TWO TURNS LEFT UNTIL REIJI AKABA'S G.O.D. COMES BACK...
IT'S MY TURN...
...AND I DRAW!
FWIP
THE NEW ACTION CARD...
PEEK
WHERE IS IT? HUH?
PEEK
IT'S *RIGHT HERE.*
FWUD
...!

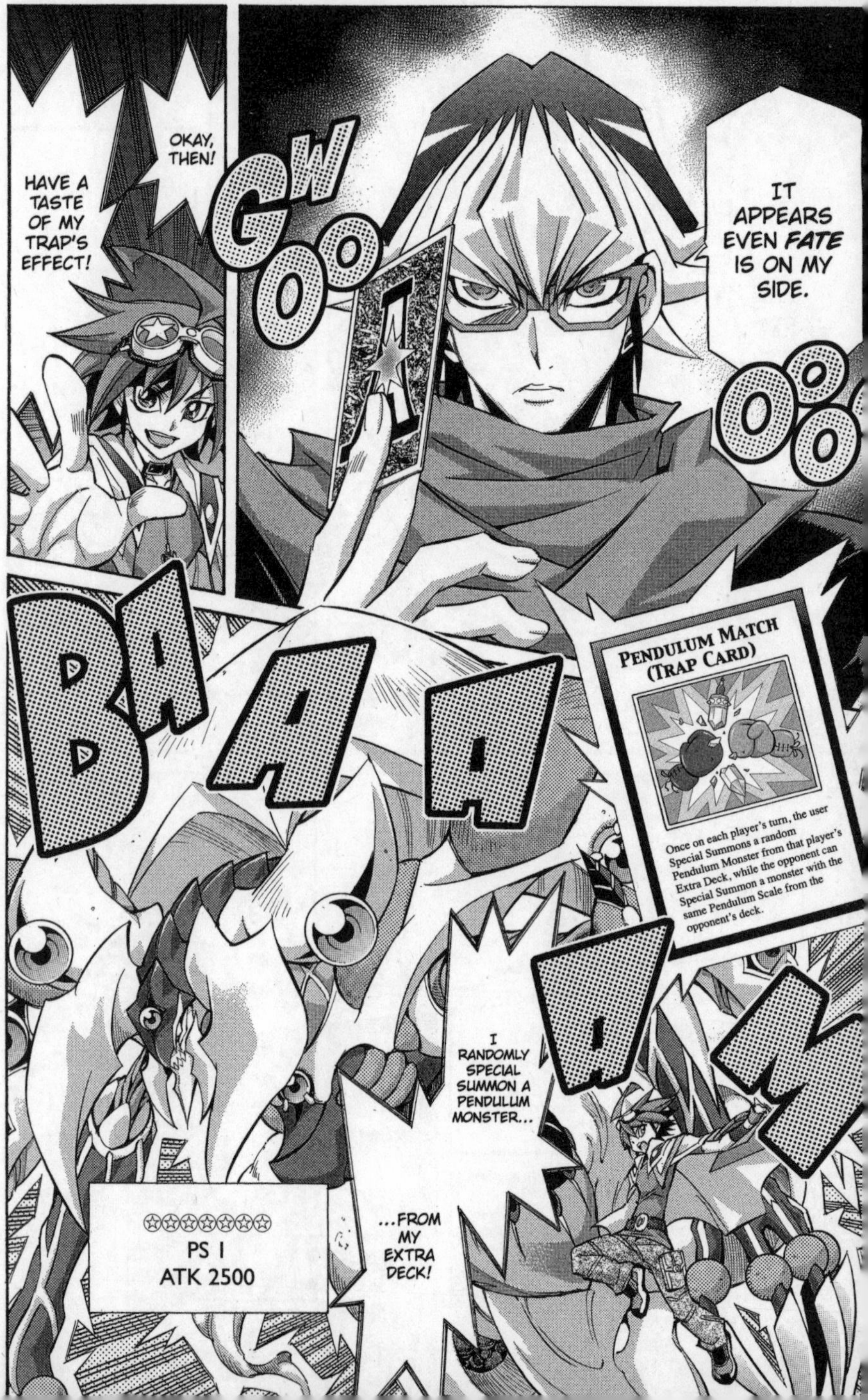
GWOOO
IT APPEARS EVEN FATE IS ON MY SIDE.
OOO
OKAY, THEN!
HAVE A TASTE OF MY TRAP'S EFFECT!
BAAAM
PENDULUM MATCH (TRAP CARD)
Once on each player's turn, the user Special Summons a random Pendulum Monster from that player's Extra Deck, while the opponent can Special Summon a monster with the same Pendulum Scale from the opponent's deck.
I RANDOMLY SPECIAL SUMMON A PENDULUM MONSTER...
...FROM MY EXTRA DECK!
☆☆☆☆☆☆☆☆
PS 1
ATK 2500

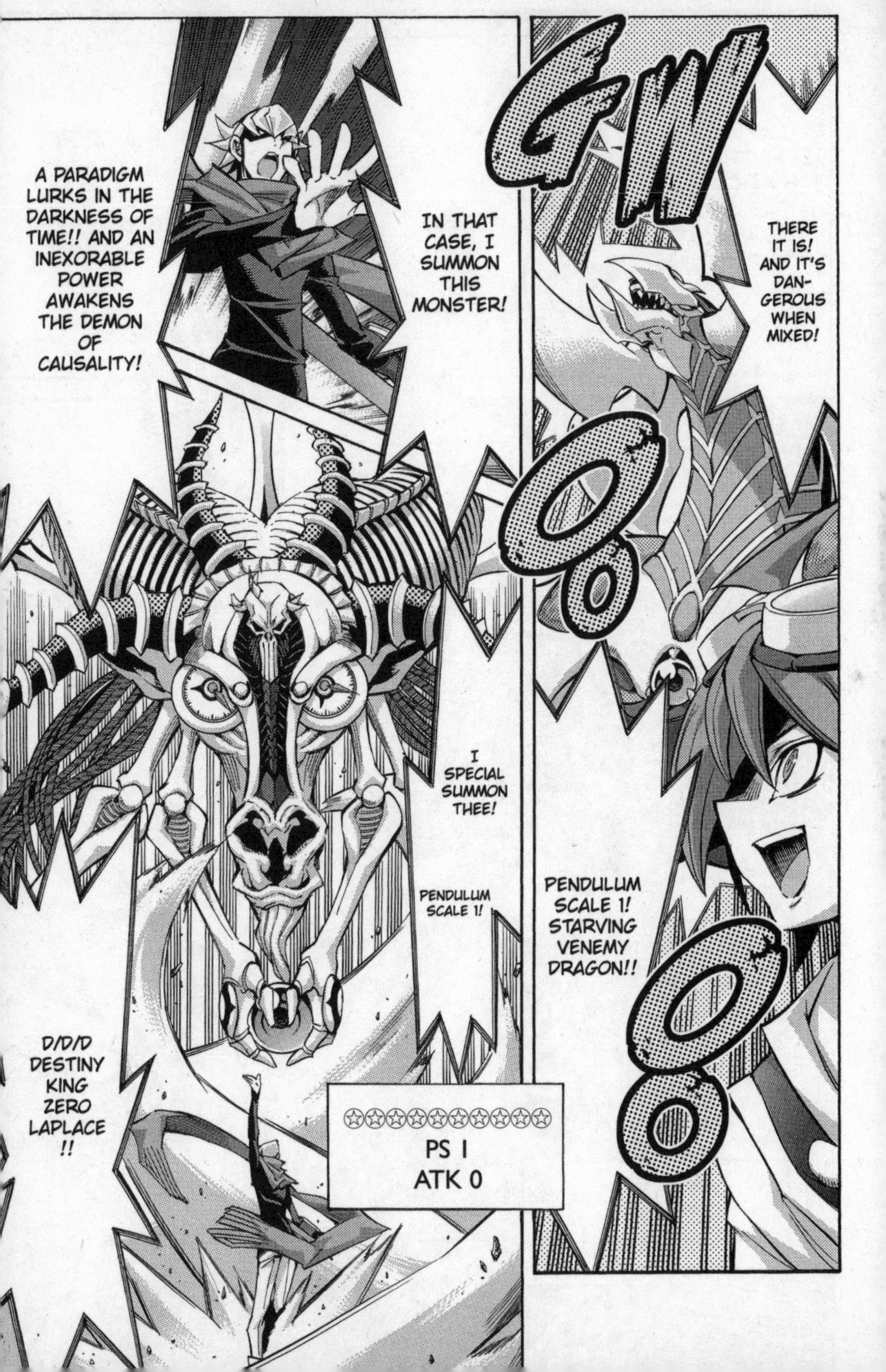
GW
THERE IT IS! AND IT'S DANGEROUS WHEN MIXED!
OO
OO
PENDULUM SCALE 1! STARVING VENEMY DRAGON!!
IN THAT CASE, I SUMMON THIS MONSTER!
A PARADIGM LURKS IN THE DARKNESS OF TIME!! AND AN INEXORABLE POWER AWAKENS THE DEMON OF CAUSALITY!
I SPECIAL SUMMON THEE!
PENDULUM SCALE 1!
PS 1
ATK 0
D/D/D DESTINY KING ZERO LAPLACE!!

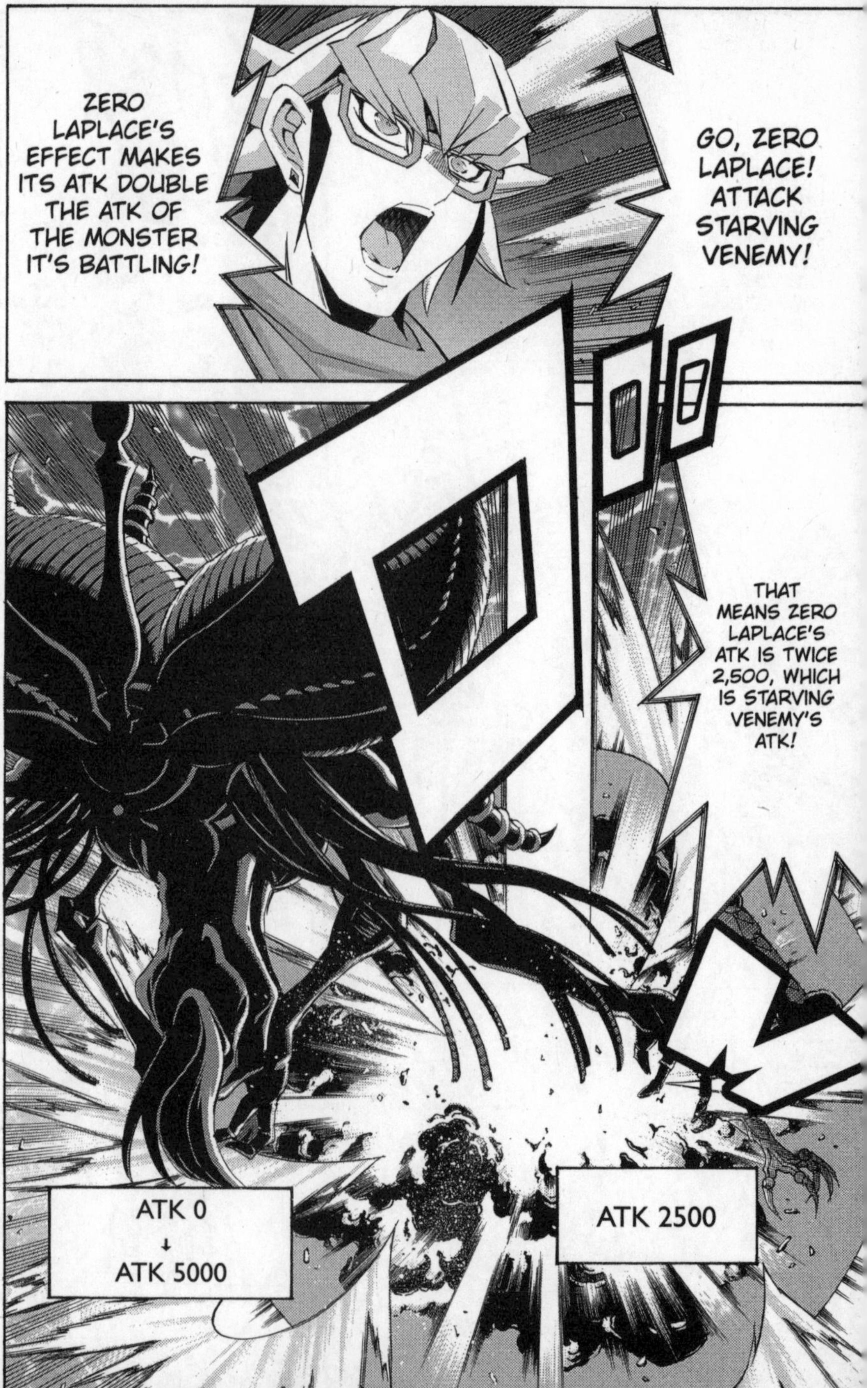
GO, ZERO LAPLACE! ATTACK STARVING VENEMY!
ZERO LAPLACE'S EFFECT MAKES ITS ATK DOUBLE THE ATK OF THE MONSTER IT'S BATTLING!
THAT MEANS ZERO LAPLACE'S ATK IS TWICE 2,500, WHICH IS STARVING VENEMY'S ATK!
ATK 2500
ATK 0
↓
ATK 5000

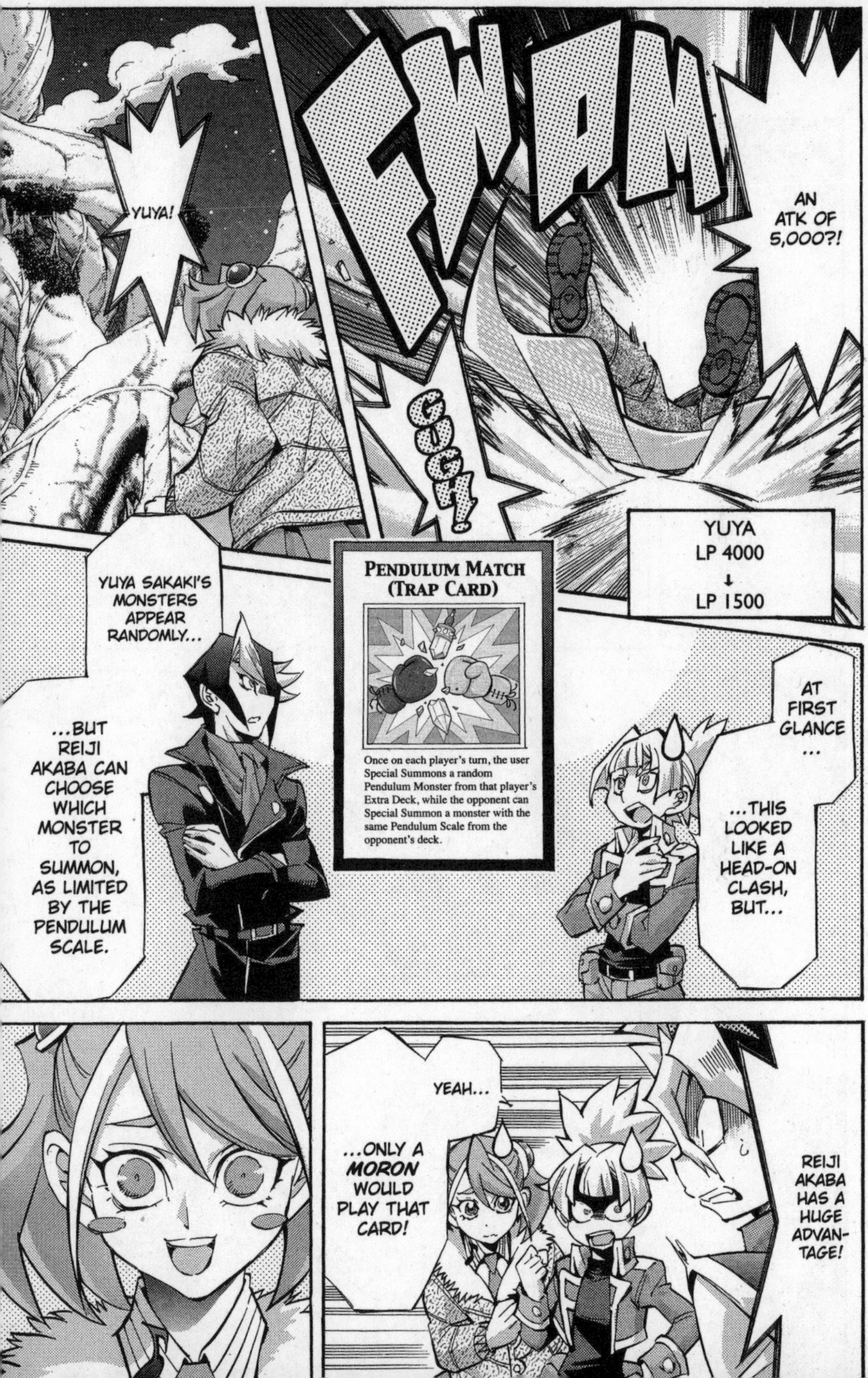
FWAM
AN ATK OF 5,000?!
GUGH!
YUYA
LP 4000
↓
LP 1500
YUYA!
AT FIRST GLANCE...
...THIS LOOKED LIKE A HEAD-ON CLASH, BUT...
PENDULUM MATCH (TRAP CARD)
Once on each player's turn, the user Special Summons a random Pendulum Monster from that player's Extra Deck, while the opponent can Special Summon a monster with the same Pendulum Scale from the opponent's deck.
YUYA SAKAKI'S MONSTERS APPEAR RANDOMLY...
...BUT REIJI AKABA CAN CHOOSE WHICH MONSTER TO SUMMON, AS LIMITED BY THE PENDULUM SCALE.
REIJI AKABA HAS A HUGE ADVANTAGE!
YEAH...
...ONLY A MORON WOULD PLAY THAT CARD!

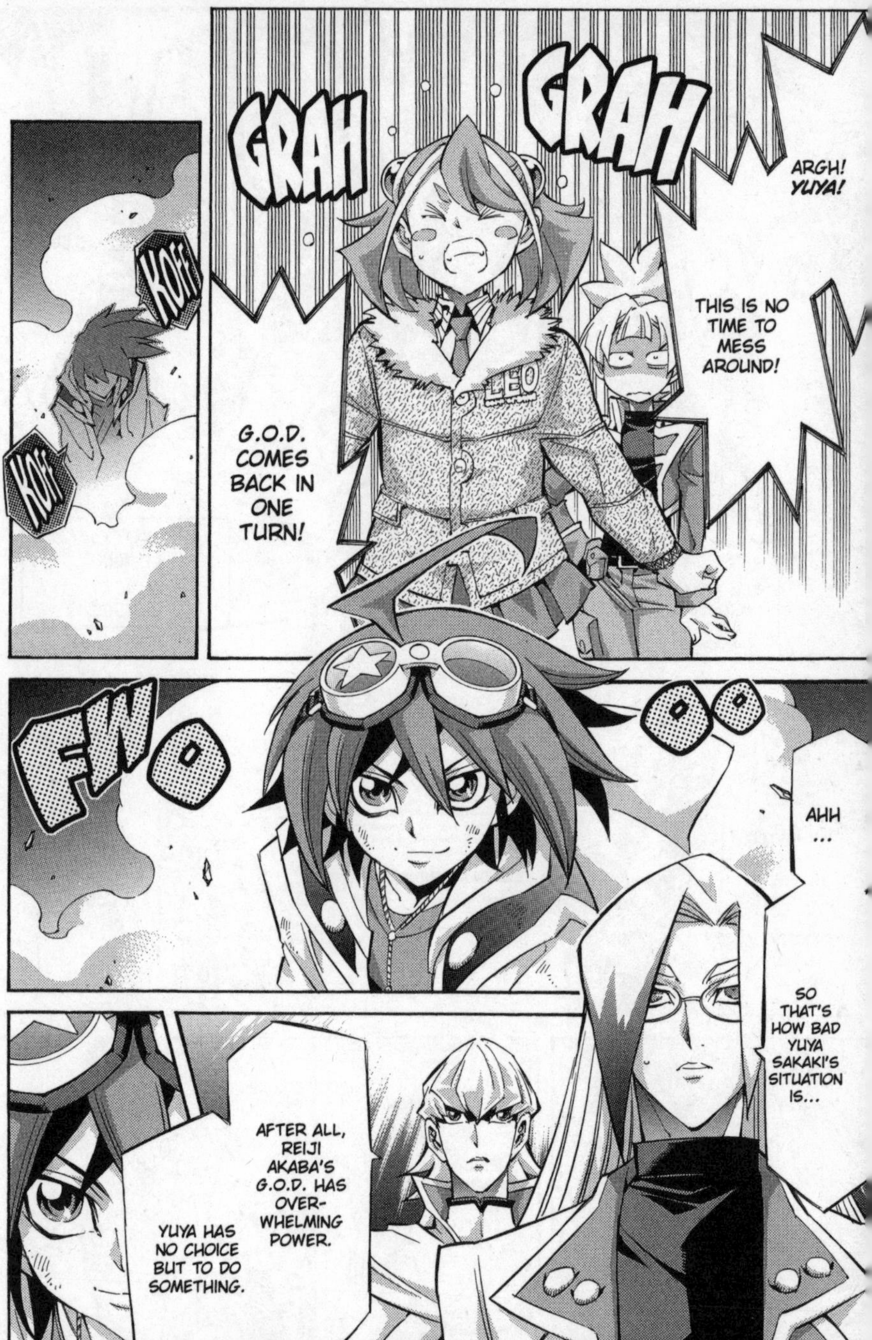
GRAH GRAH
ARGH! YUYA!
THIS IS NO TIME TO MESS AROUND!
G.O.D. COMES BACK IN ONE TURN!
LEO
KOFF
KOFF
FWOOOO
AHH ...
SO THAT'S HOW BAD YUYA SAKAKI'S SITUATION IS...
AFTER ALL, REIJI AKABA'S G.O.D. HAS OVER-WHELMING POWER.
YUYA HAS NO CHOICE BUT TO DO SOMETHING.

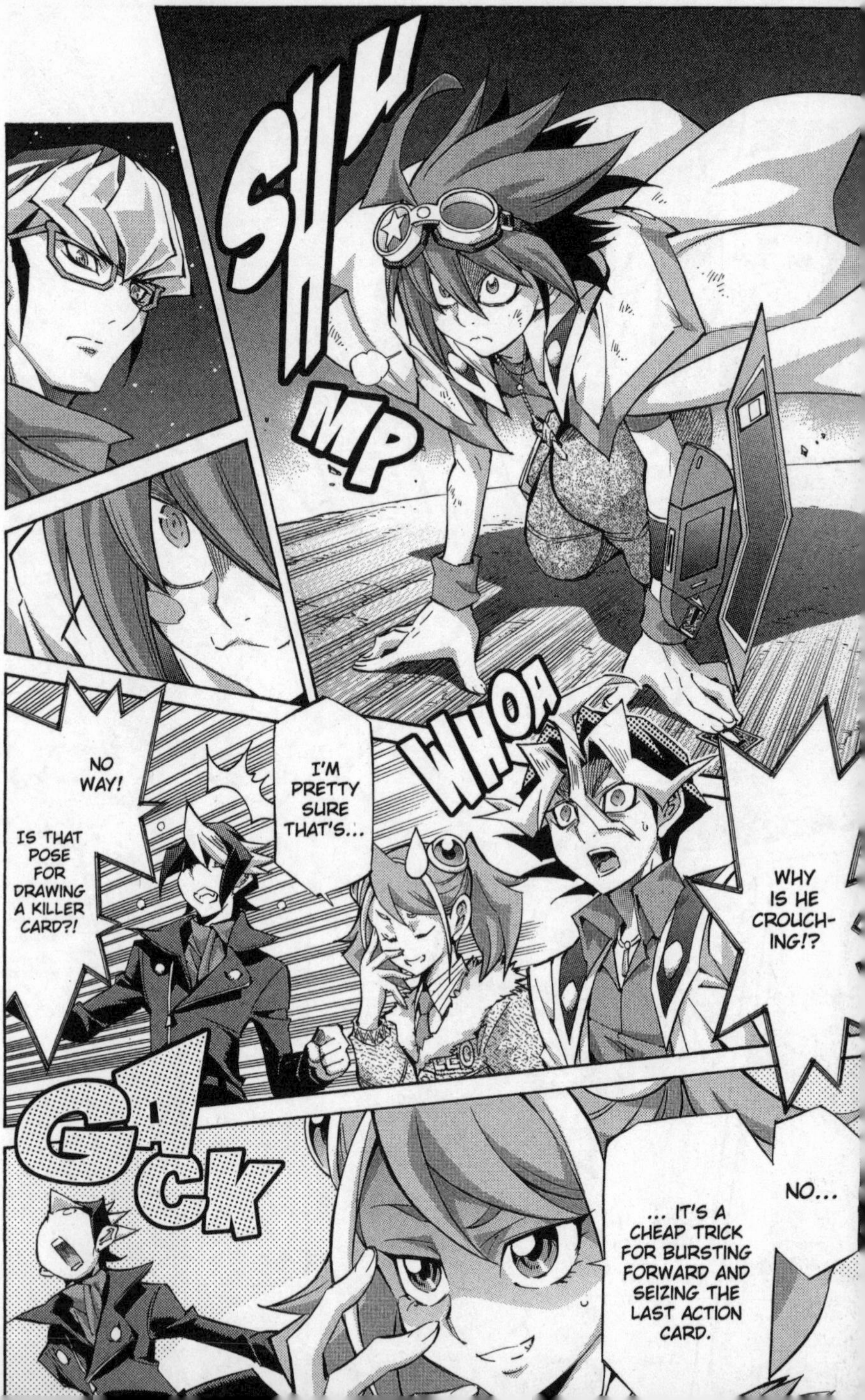
SHH
MP
WHOA
WHY IS HE CROUCHING!?
I'M PRETTY SURE THAT'S...
NO WAY!
IS THAT POSE FOR DRAWING A KILLER CARD?!
NO...
... IT'S A CHEAP TRICK FOR BURSTING FORWARD AND SEIZING THE LAST ACTION CARD.
GACK

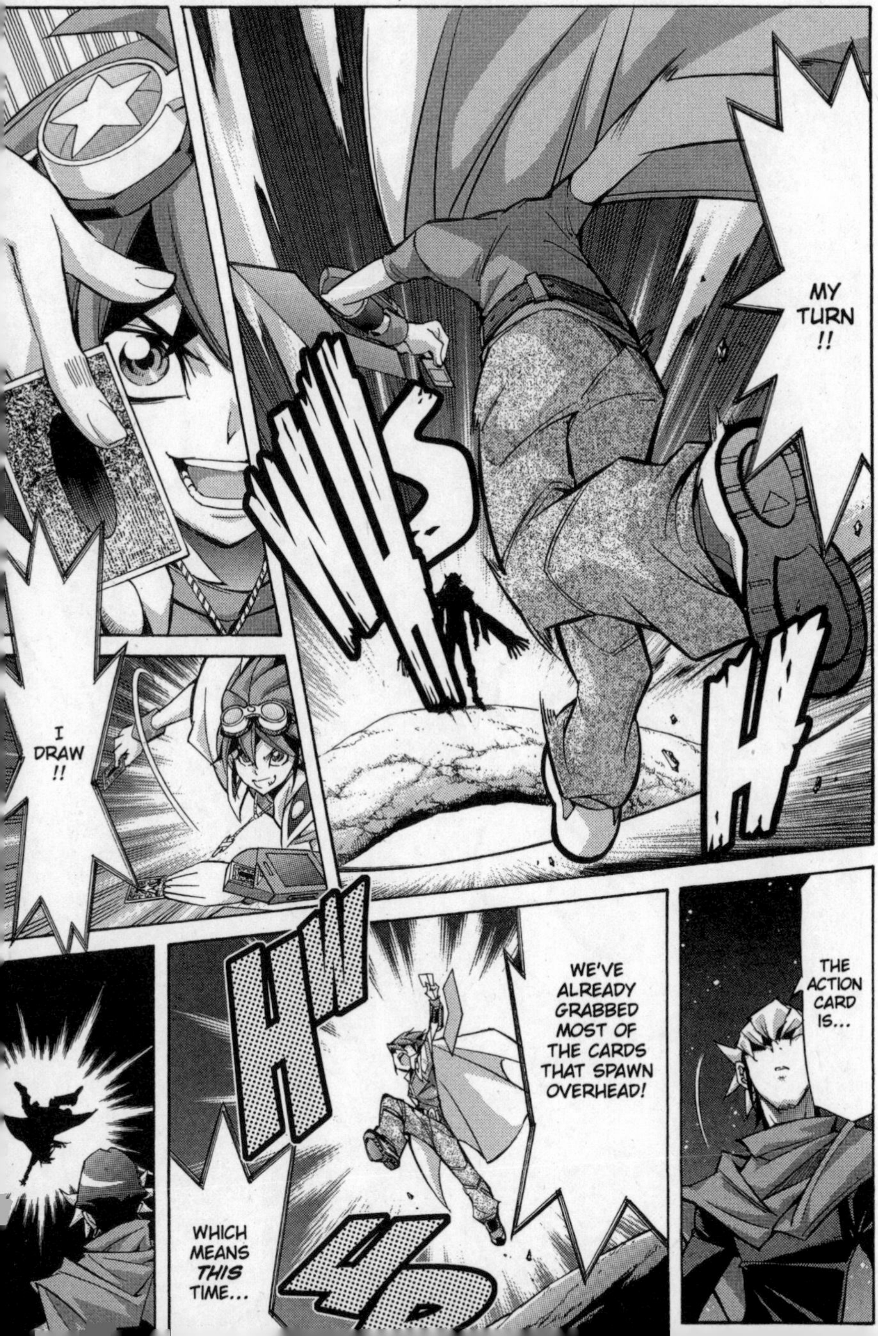
MY TURN !!
I DRAW !!
THE ACTION CARD IS...
WE'VE ALREADY GRABBED MOST OF THE CARDS THAT SPAWN OVERHEAD!
WHICH MEANS *THIS* TIME...

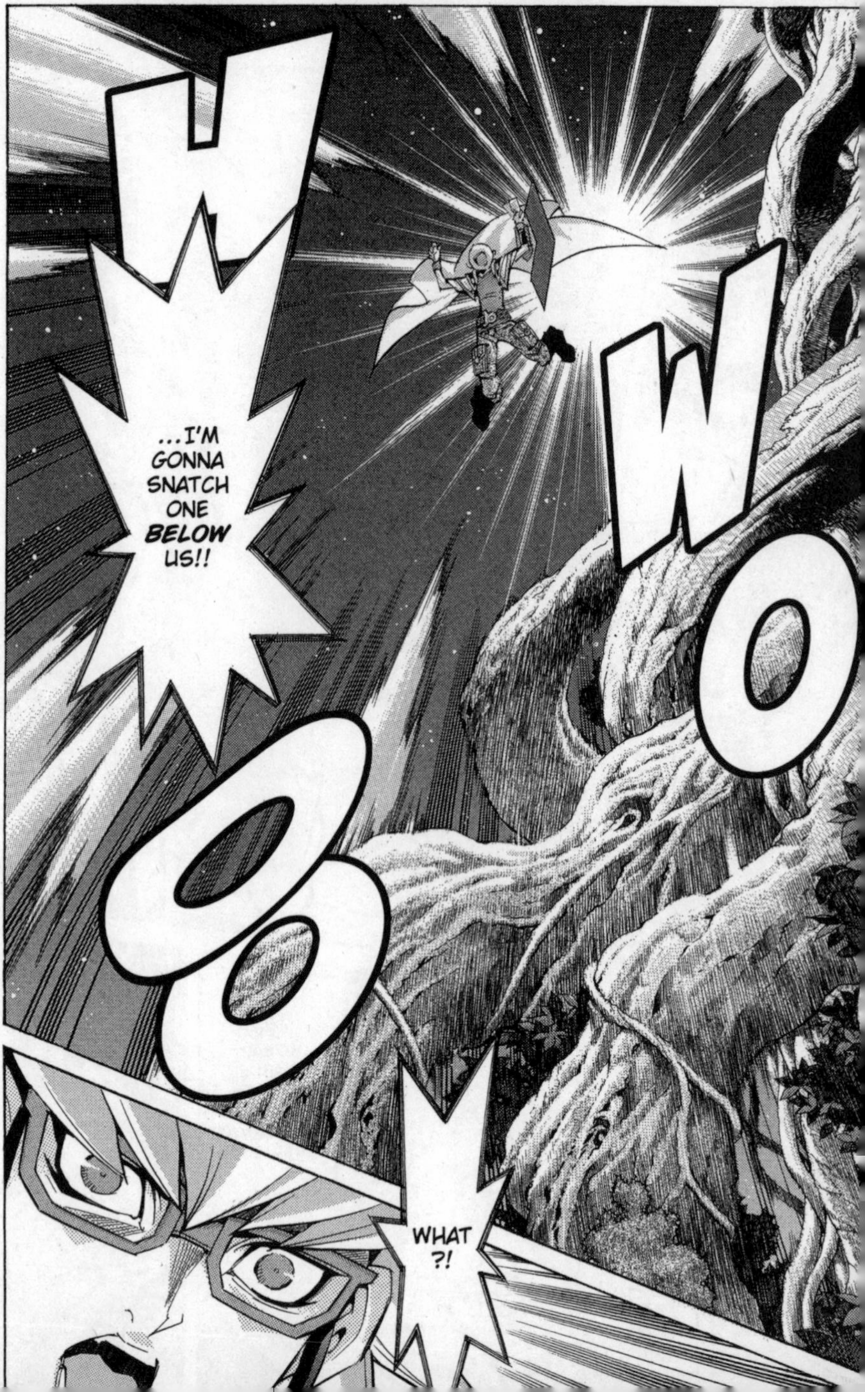
...I'M GONNA SNATCH ONE **BELOW** US!!
WHAT?!

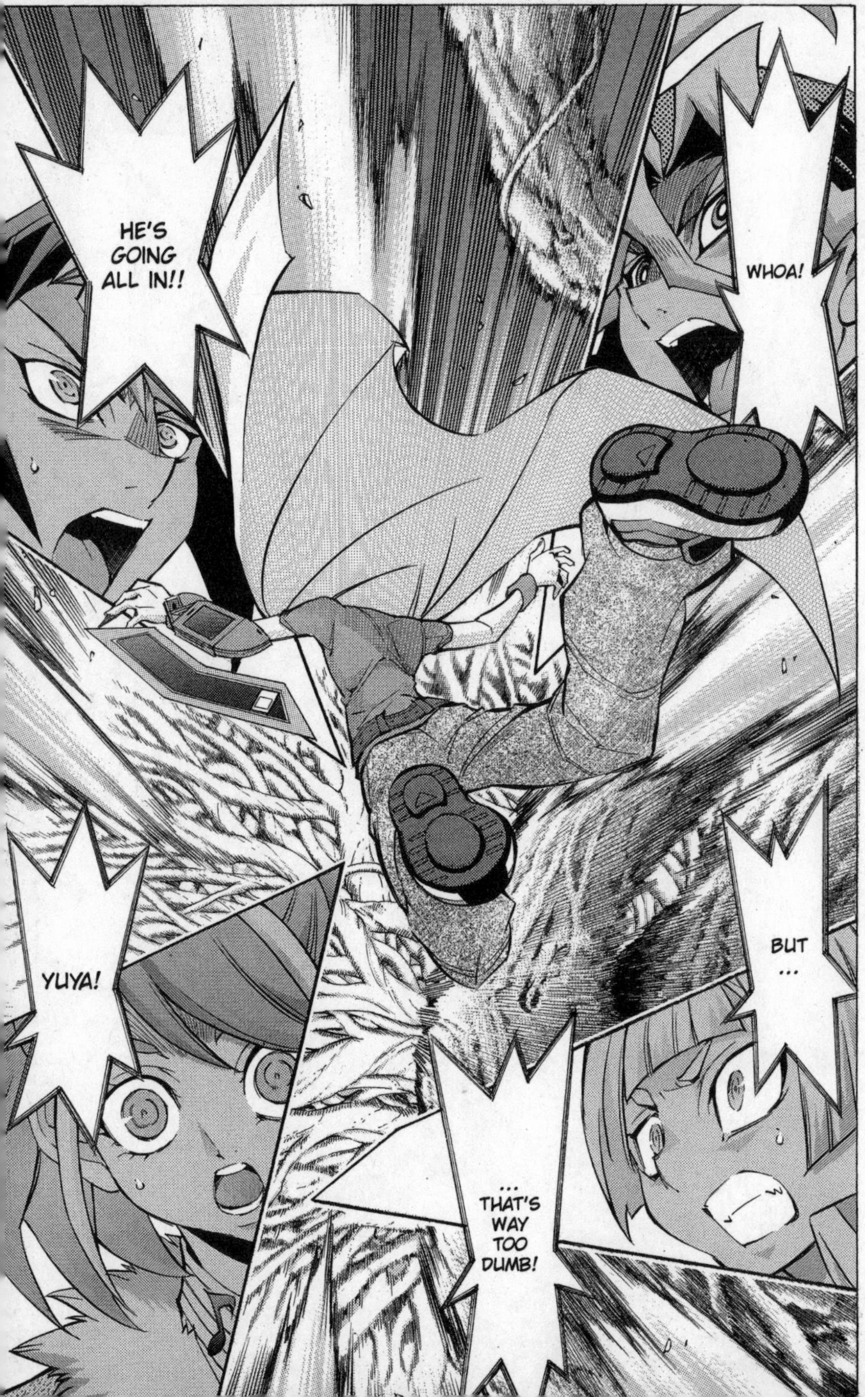
WHOA!
HE'S GOING ALL IN!!
BUT ...
... THAT'S WAY TOO DUMB!
YUYA!

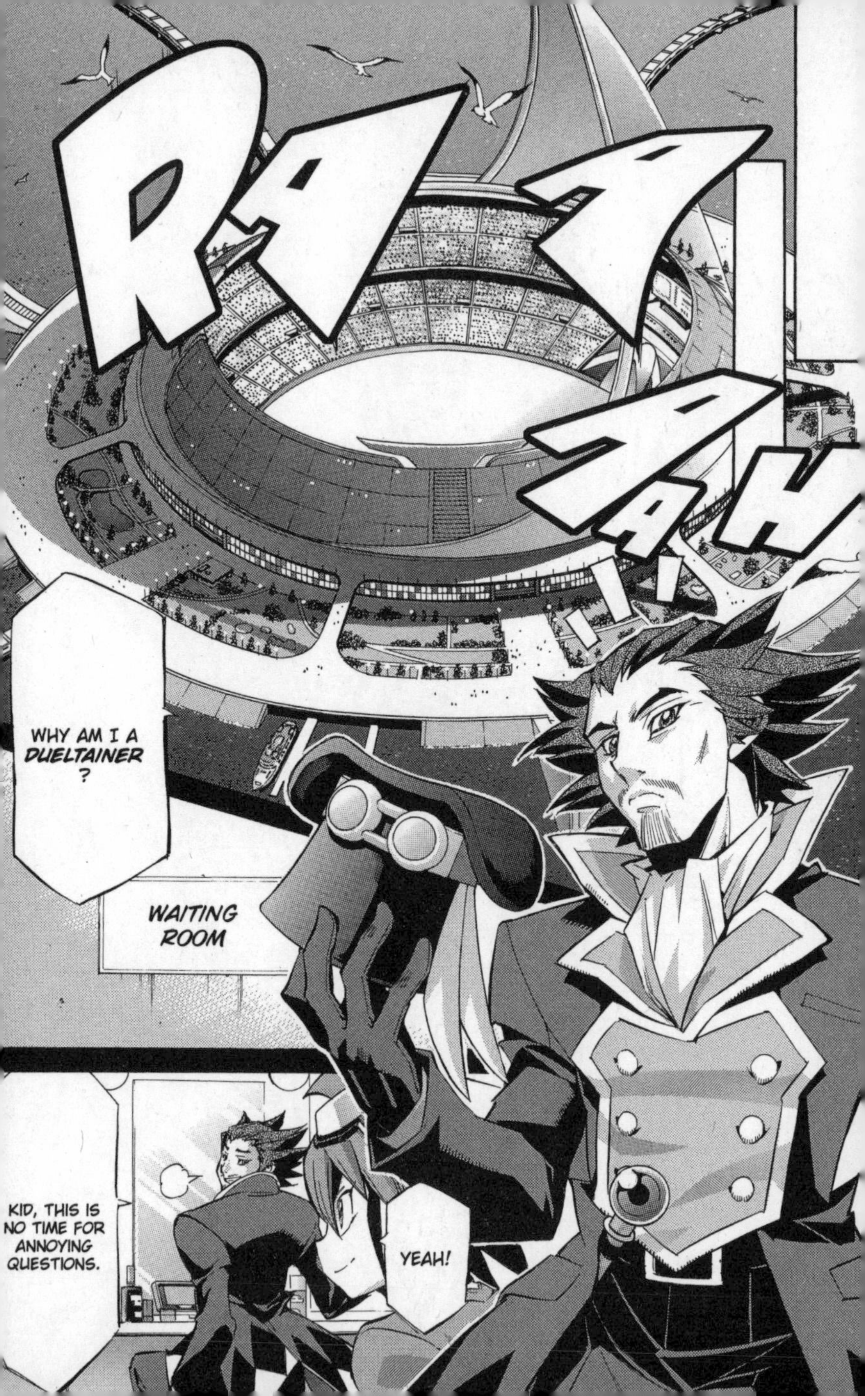
RAAAAH!!
WHY AM I A DUELTAINER?
WAITING ROOM
YEAH!
KID, THIS IS NO TIME FOR ANNOYING QUESTIONS.

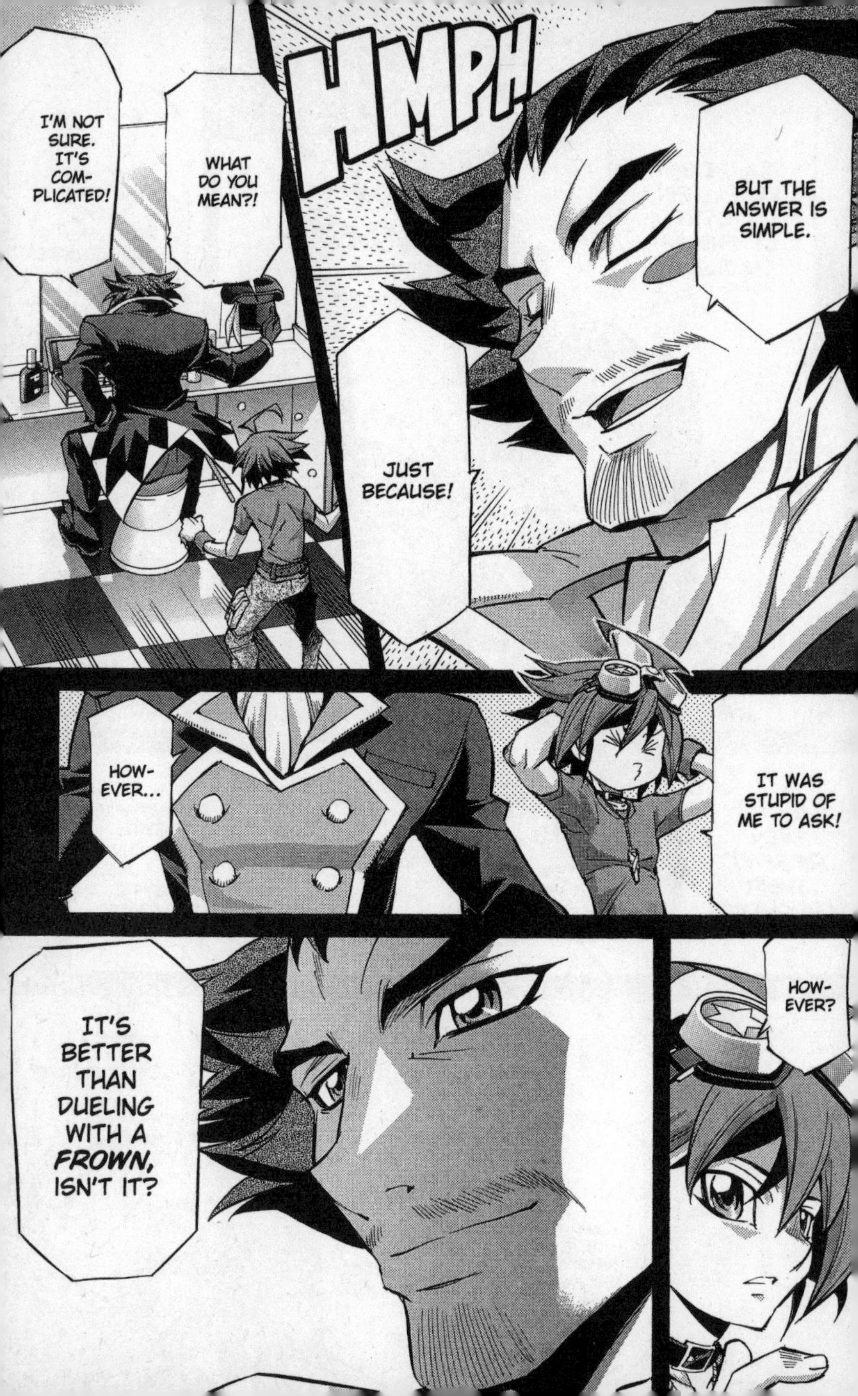
HMPH
BUT THE ANSWER IS SIMPLE.
JUST BECAUSE!
WHAT DO YOU MEAN?!
I'M NOT SURE. IT'S COM-PLICATED!
IT WAS STUPID OF ME TO ASK!
HOW-EVER...
HOW-EVER?
IT'S BETTER THAN DUELING WITH A *FROWN,* ISN'T IT?

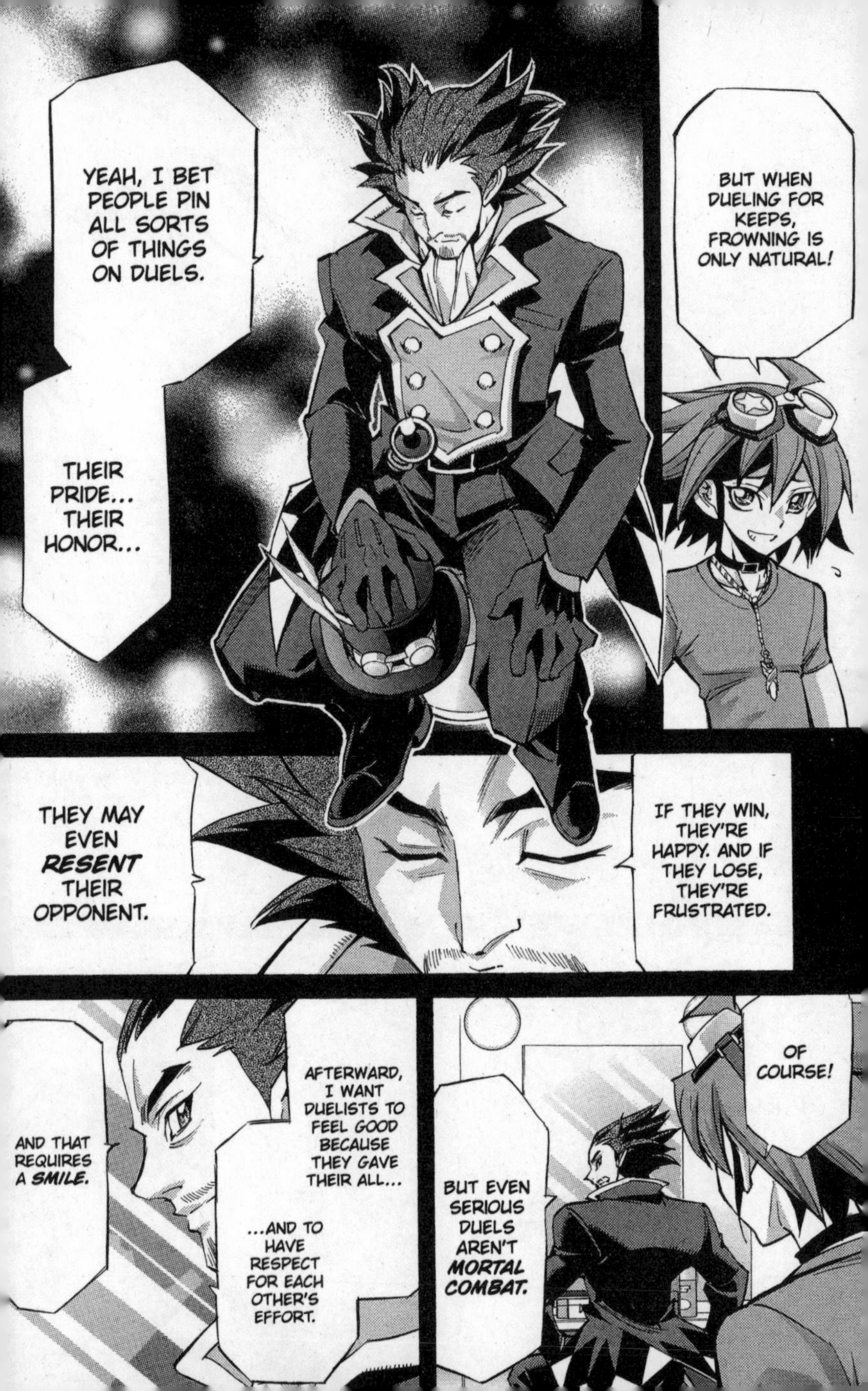
BUT WHEN DUELING FOR KEEPS, FROWNING IS ONLY NATURAL!
YEAH, I BET PEOPLE PIN ALL SORTS OF THINGS ON DUELS.
THEIR PRIDE... THEIR HONOR...
IF THEY WIN, THEY'RE HAPPY. AND IF THEY LOSE, THEY'RE FRUSTRATED.
THEY MAY EVEN ***RESENT*** THEIR OPPONENT.
OF COURSE!
BUT EVEN SERIOUS DUELS AREN'T ***MORTAL COMBAT.***
AFTERWARD, I WANT DUELISTS TO FEEL GOOD BECAUSE THEY GAVE THEIR ALL...
...AND TO HAVE RESPECT FOR EACH OTHER'S EFFORT.
AND THAT REQUIRES A ***SMILE.***

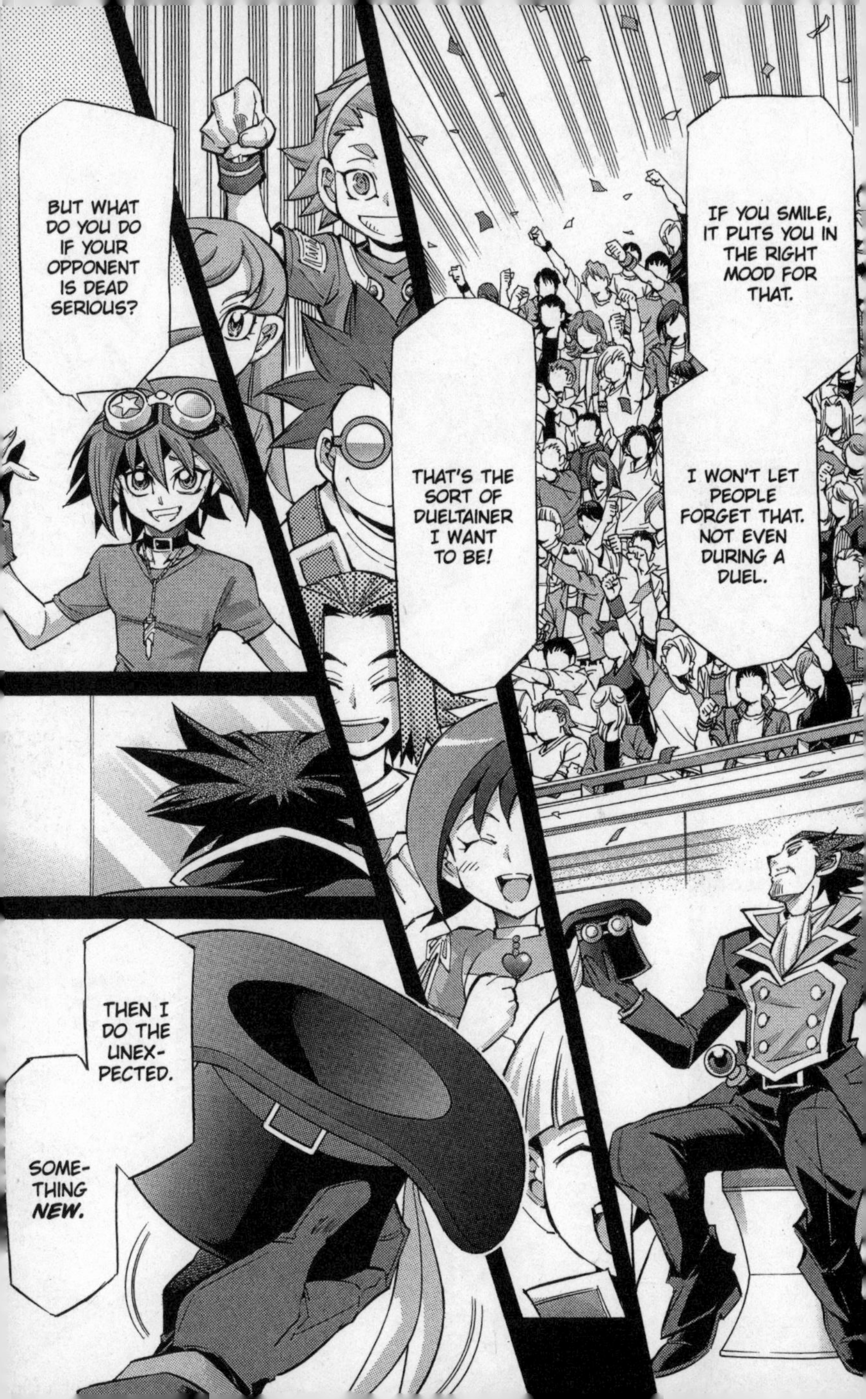
IF YOU SMILE, IT PUTS YOU IN THE RIGHT MOOD FOR THAT.
I WON'T LET PEOPLE FORGET THAT. NOT EVEN DURING A DUEL.
THAT'S THE SORT OF DUELTAINER I WANT TO BE!
BUT WHAT DO YOU DO IF YOUR OPPONENT IS DEAD SERIOUS?
THEN I DO THE UNEXPECTED.
SOME-THING *NEW*.

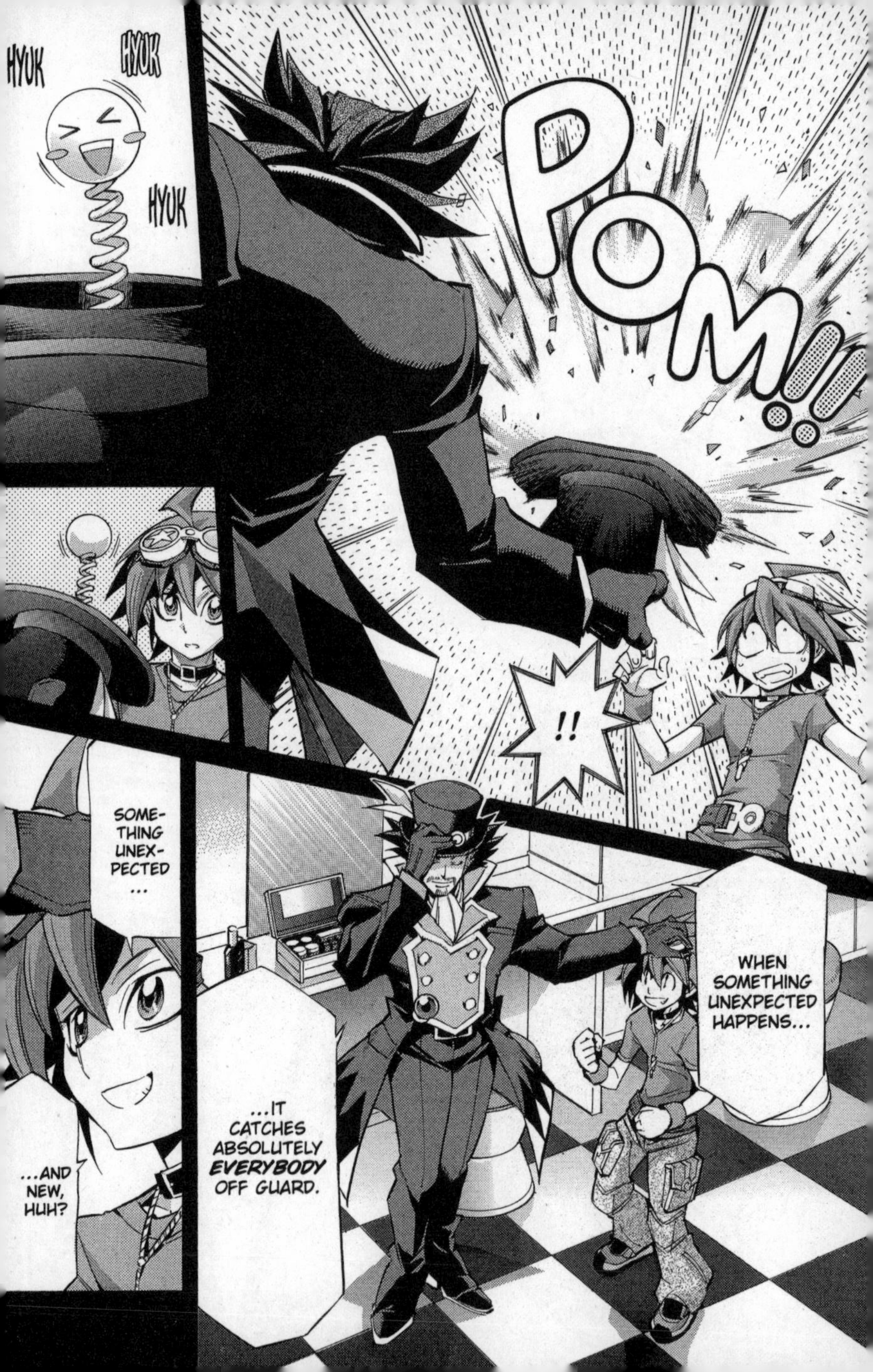
POM!!!
!!
HYUK
HYUK
HYUK
WHEN SOMETHING UNEXPECTED HAPPENS...
...IT CATCHES ABSOLUTELY *EVERYBODY* OFF GUARD.
SOME-THING UNEX-PECTED...
...AND NEW, HUH?

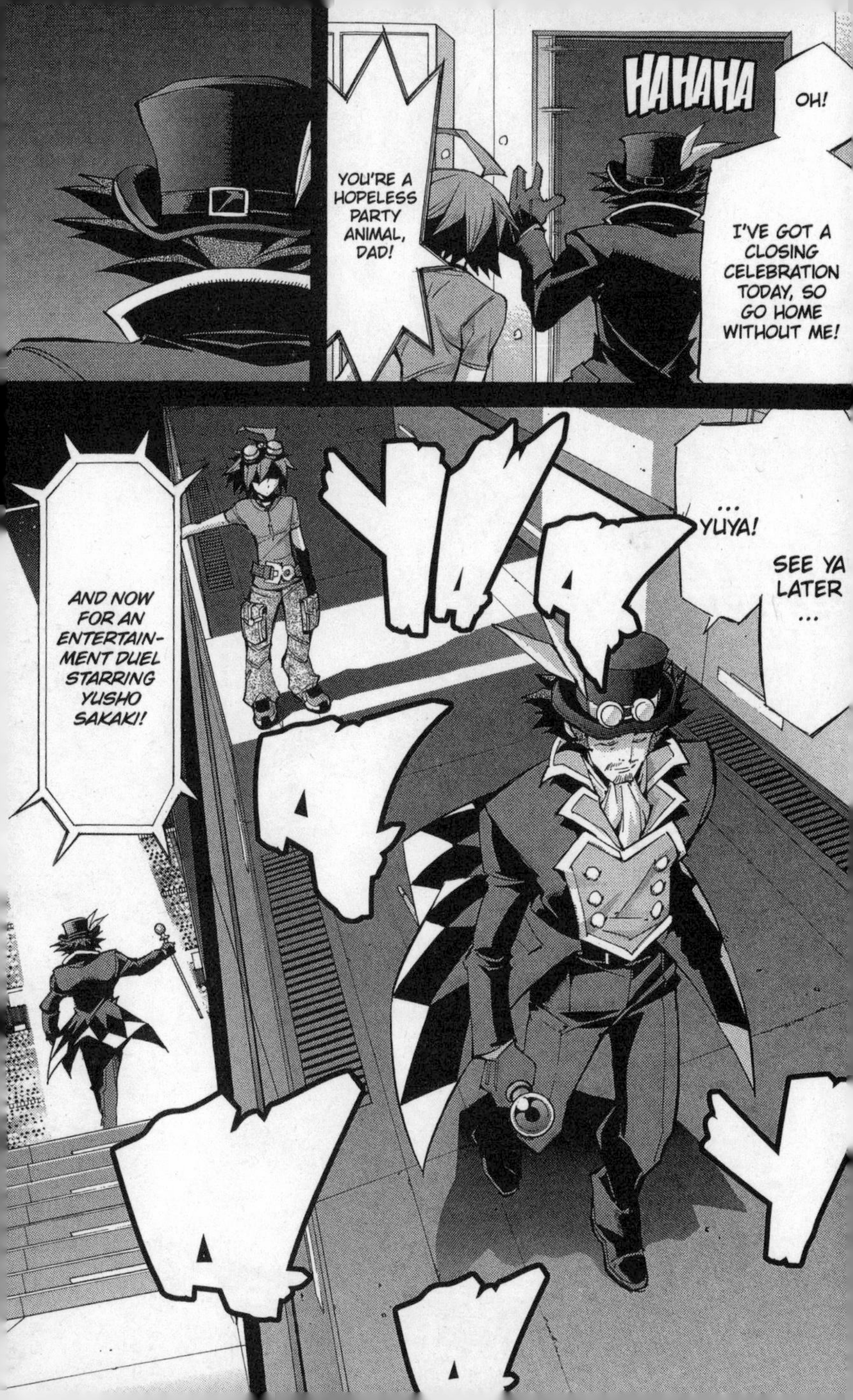
HAHAHA
OH!
I'VE GOT A CLOSING CELEBRATION TODAY, SO GO HOME WITHOUT ME!
YOU'RE A HOPELESS PARTY ANIMAL, DAD!
... YUYA!
SEE YA LATER ...
YAA
AND NOW FOR AN ENTERTAINMENT DUEL STARRING YUSHO SAKAKI!

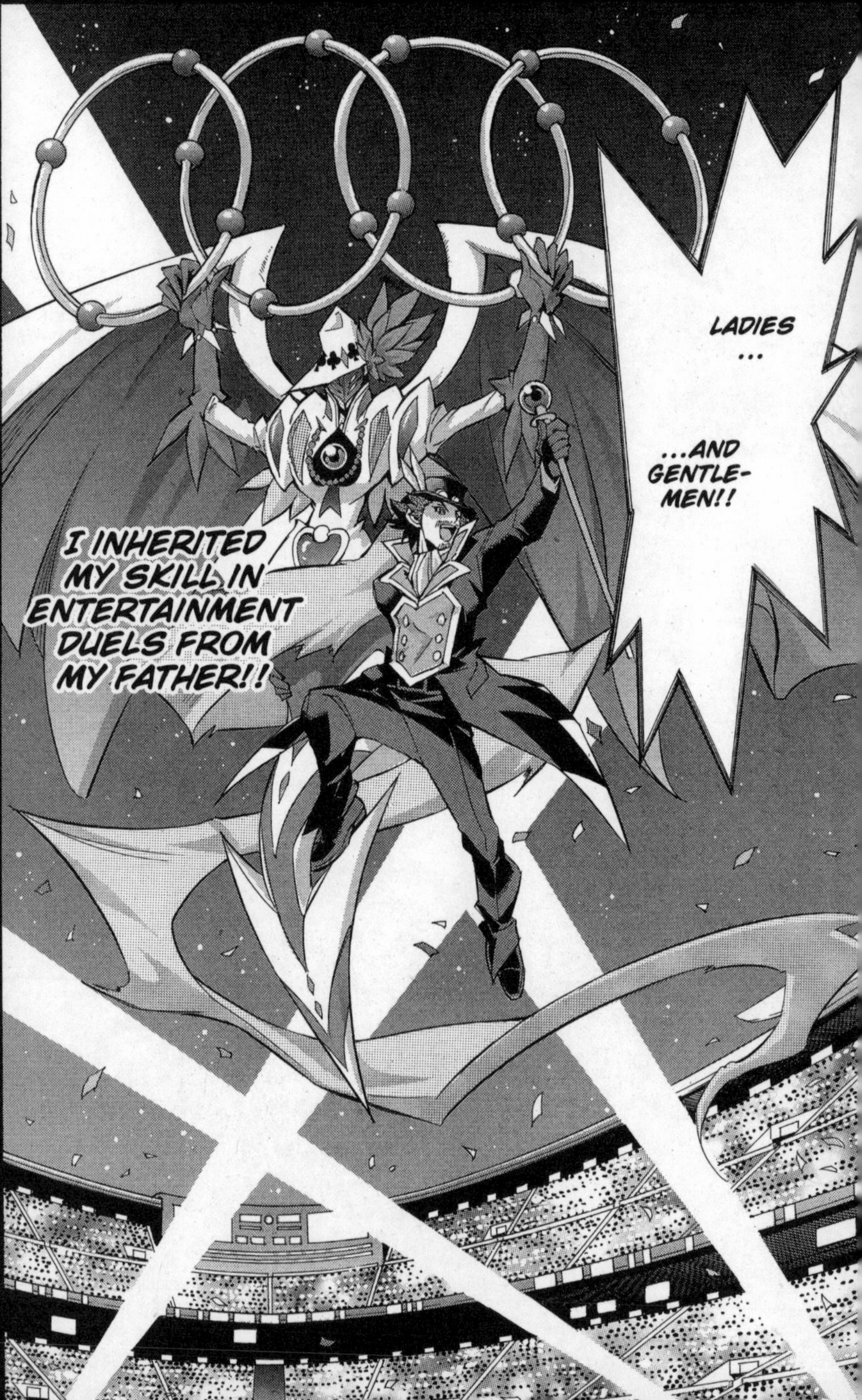
LADIES ...
...AND GENTLE-MEN!!
I INHERITED MY SKILL IN ENTERTAINMENT DUELS FROM MY FATHER!!

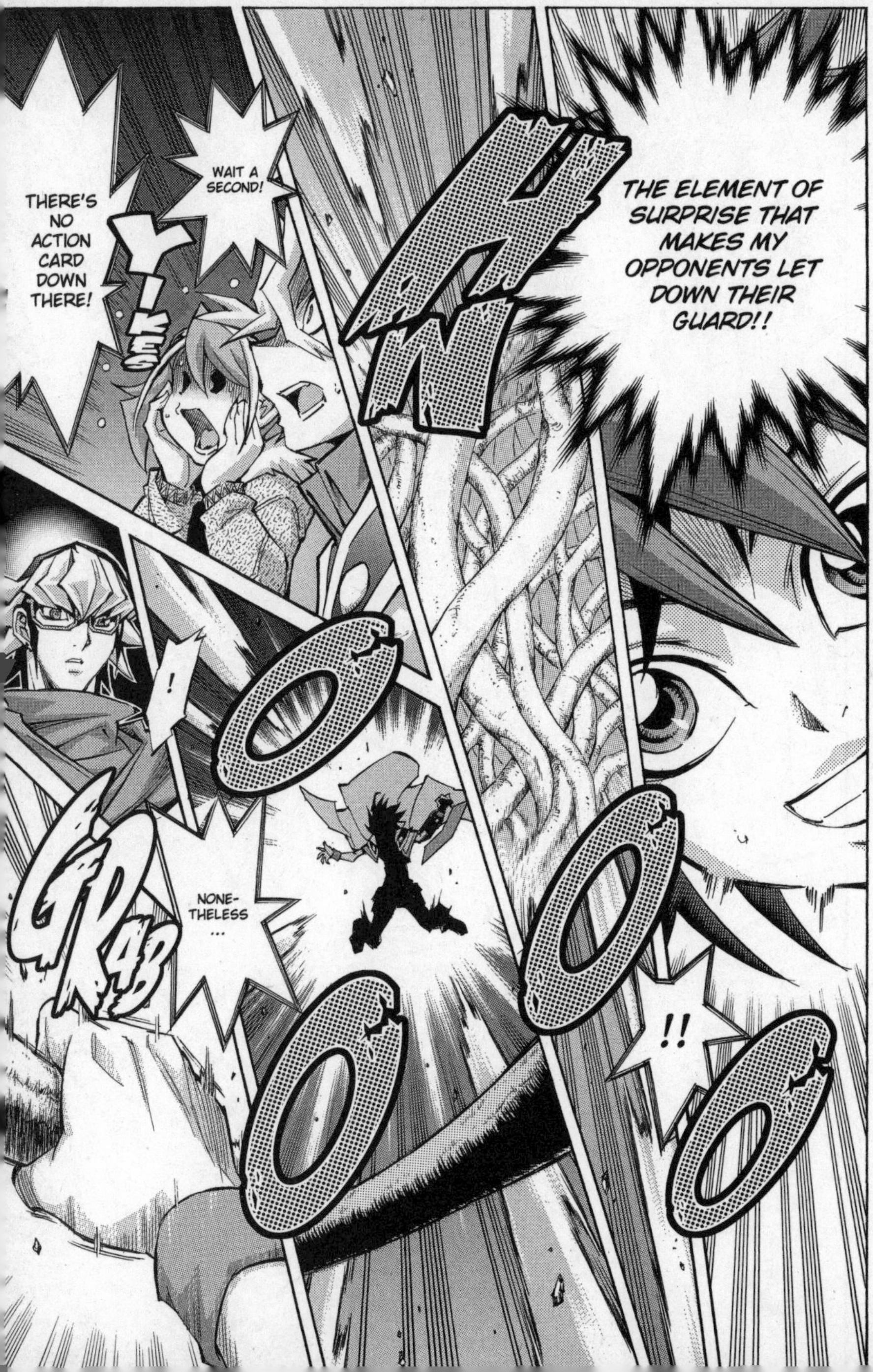

THE ELEMENT OF SURPRISE THAT MAKES MY OPPONENTS LET DOWN THEIR GUARD!!
!!
WAIT A SECOND!
THERE'S NO ACTION CARD DOWN THERE!
YIKES
!
NONE-THELESS...
GRAB

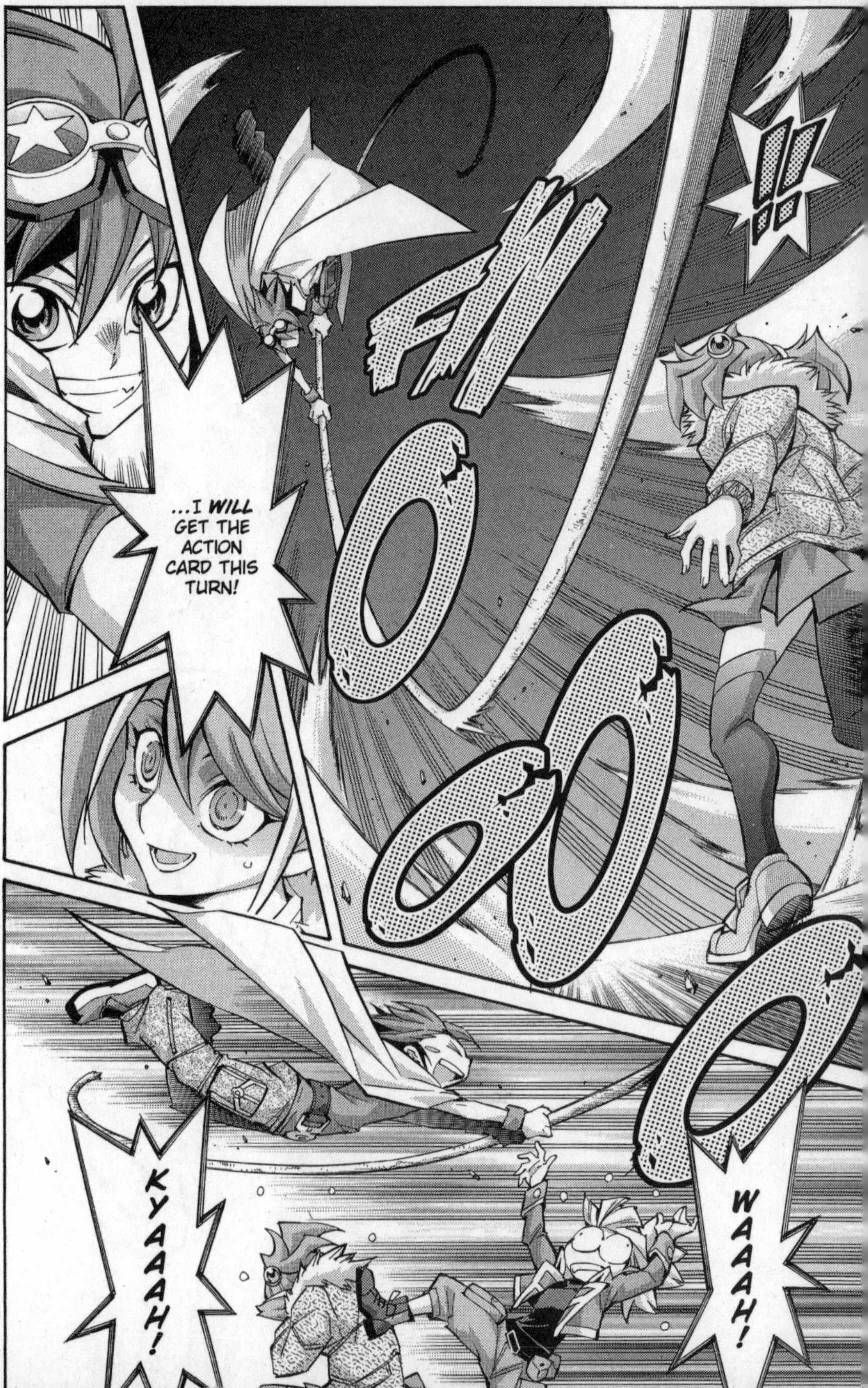
!!
FWOOOO
...I WILL GET THE ACTION CARD THIS TURN!
WAAAAH!
KYAAAH!

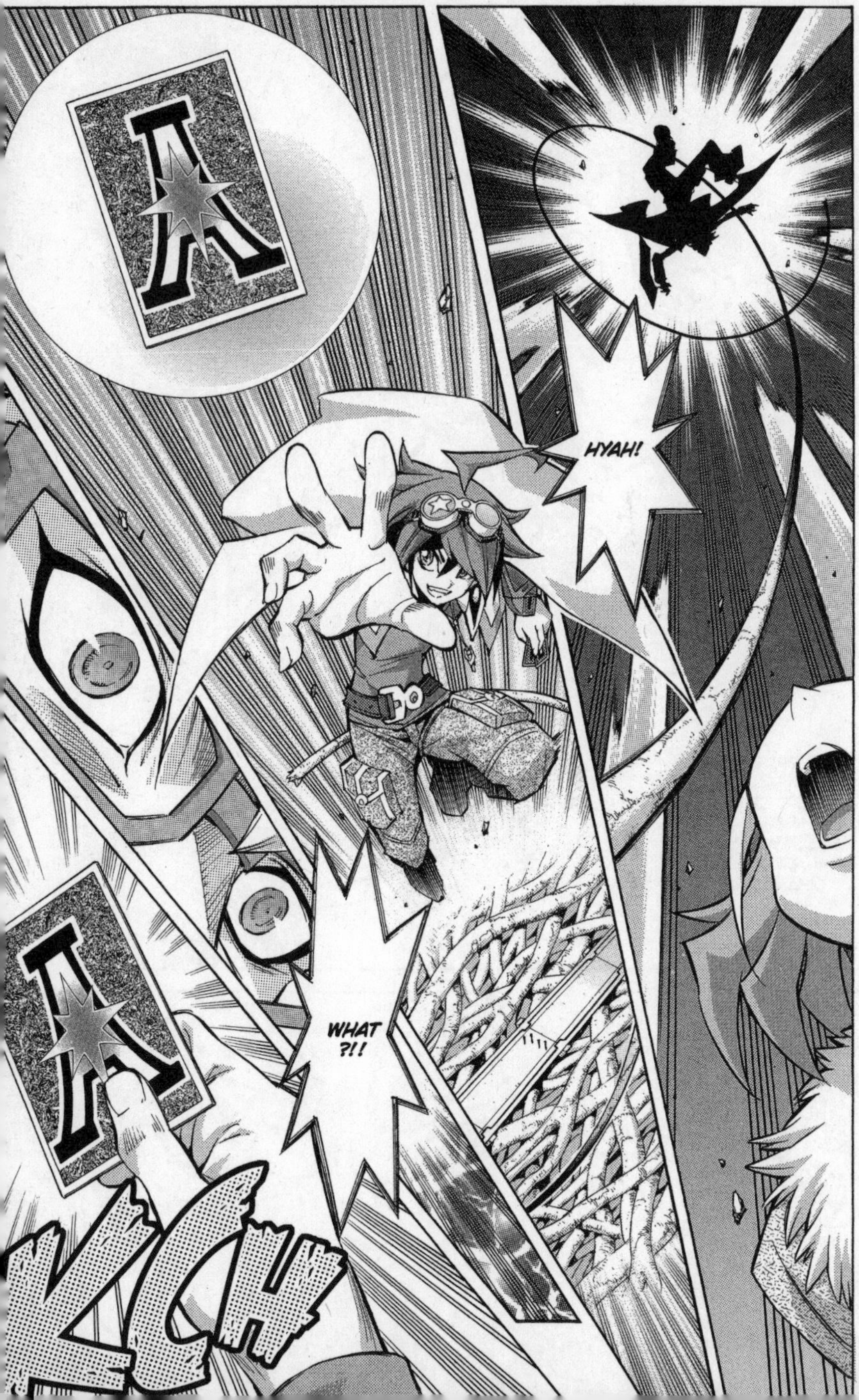
HYAH!
WHAT ?!!
KCH

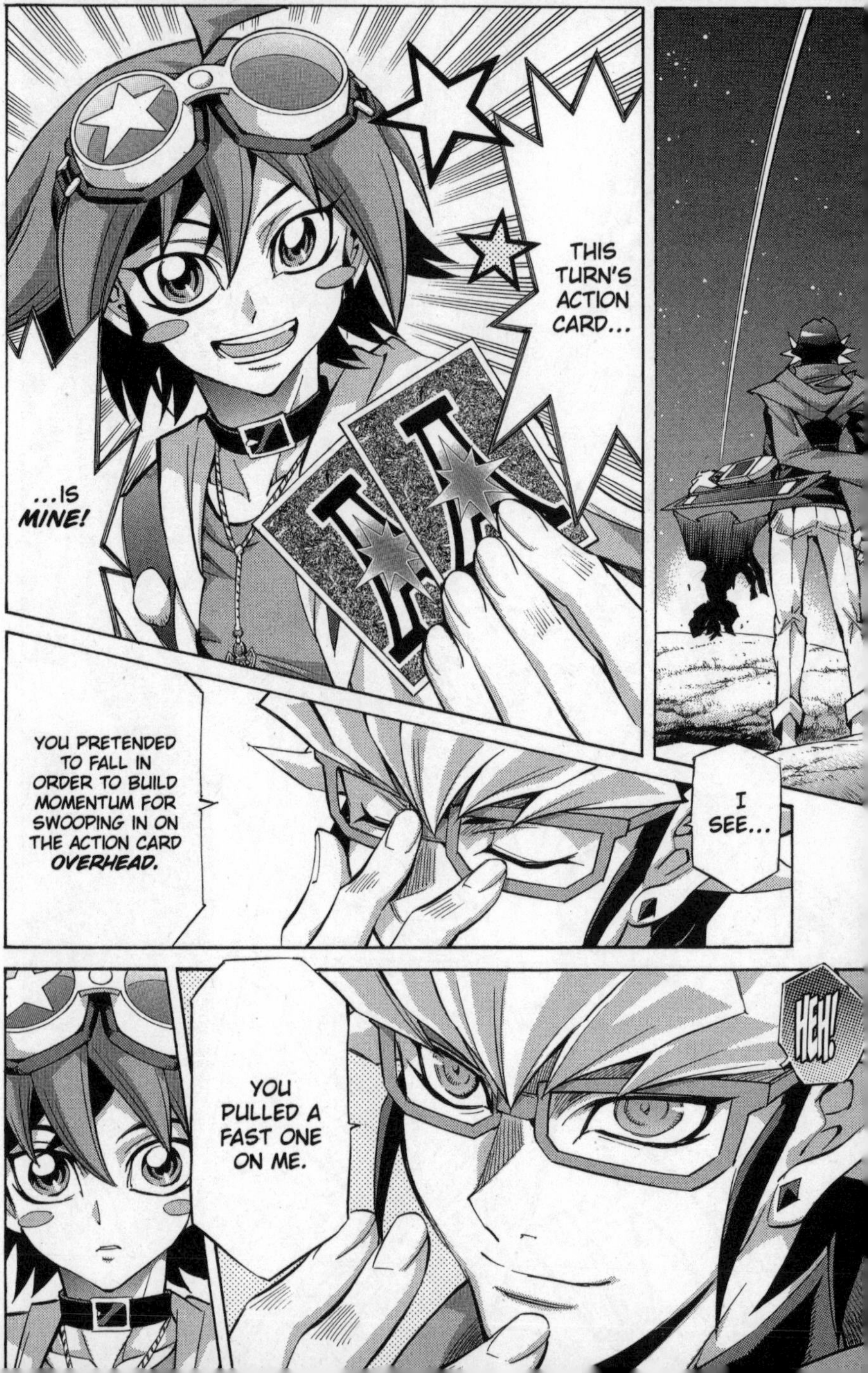
THIS TURN'S ACTION CARD...
...IS *MINE!*
I SEE...
YOU PRETENDED TO FALL IN ORDER TO BUILD MOMENTUM FOR SWOOPING IN ON THE ACTION CARD *OVERHEAD.*
HEH!
YOU PULLED A FAST ONE ON ME.

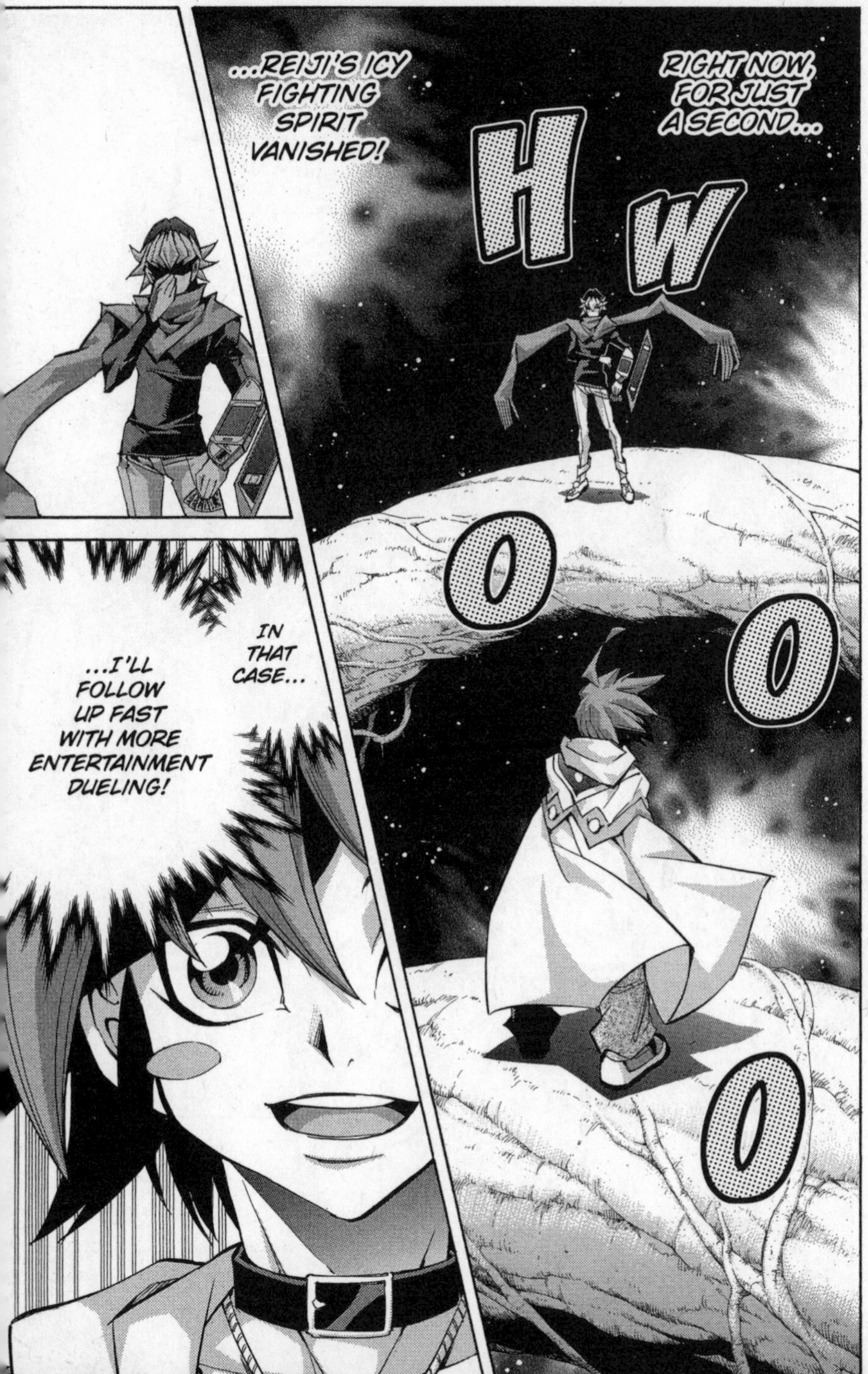
RIGHT NOW, FOR JUST A SECOND...
...REIJI'S ICY FIGHTING SPIRIT VANISHED!
HWOOO
IN THAT CASE...
...I'LL FOLLOW UP FAST WITH MORE ENTERTAINMENT DUELING!

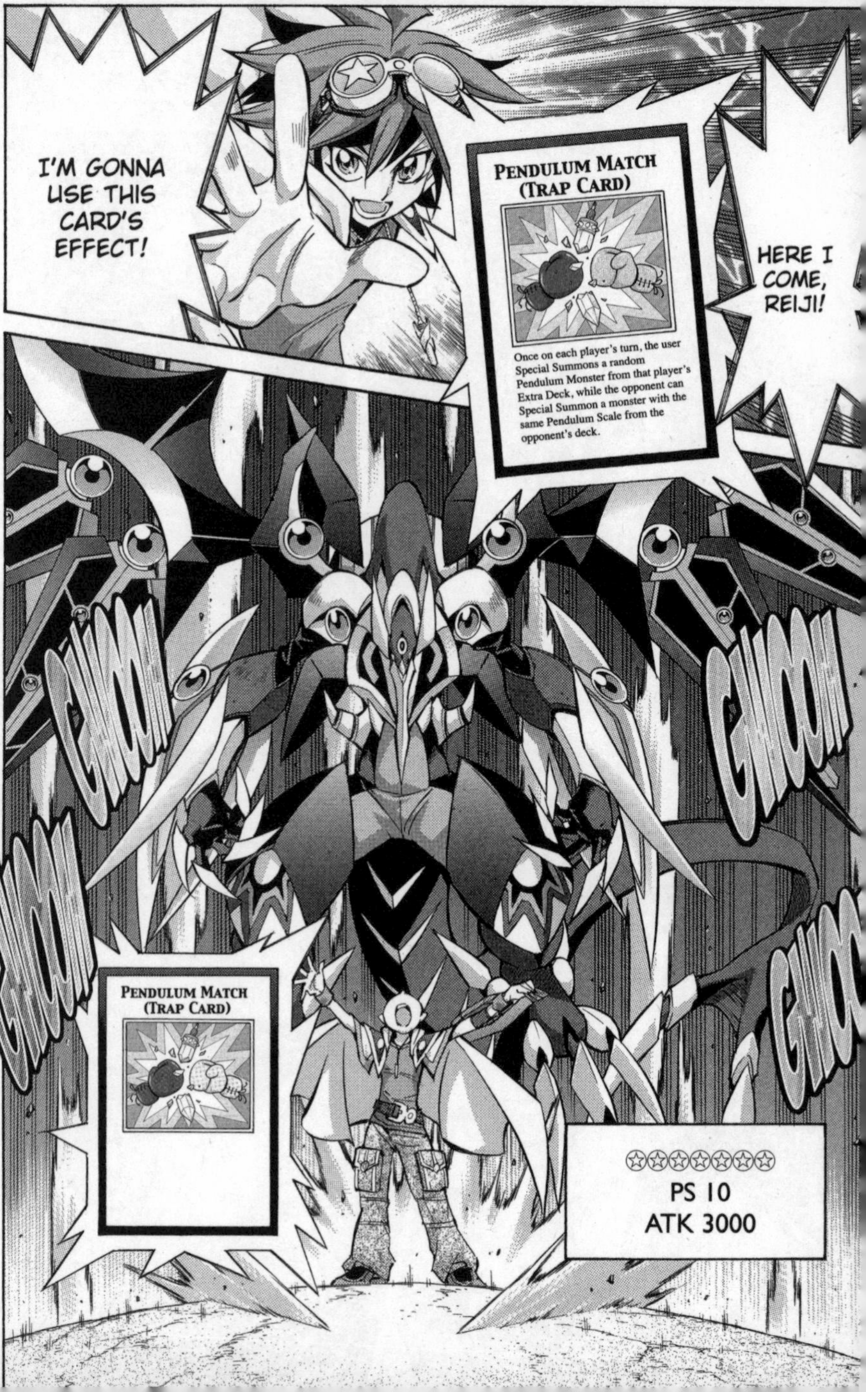
HERE I COME, REIJI!
PENDULUM MATCH (TRAP CARD)
Once on each player's turn, the user Special Summons a random Pendulum Monster from that player's Extra Deck, while the opponent can Special Summon a monster with the same Pendulum Scale from the opponent's deck.
I'M GONNA USE THIS CARD'S EFFECT!
☆☆☆☆☆☆☆☆☆☆
PS 10
ATK 3000
PENDULUM MATCH (TRAP CARD)

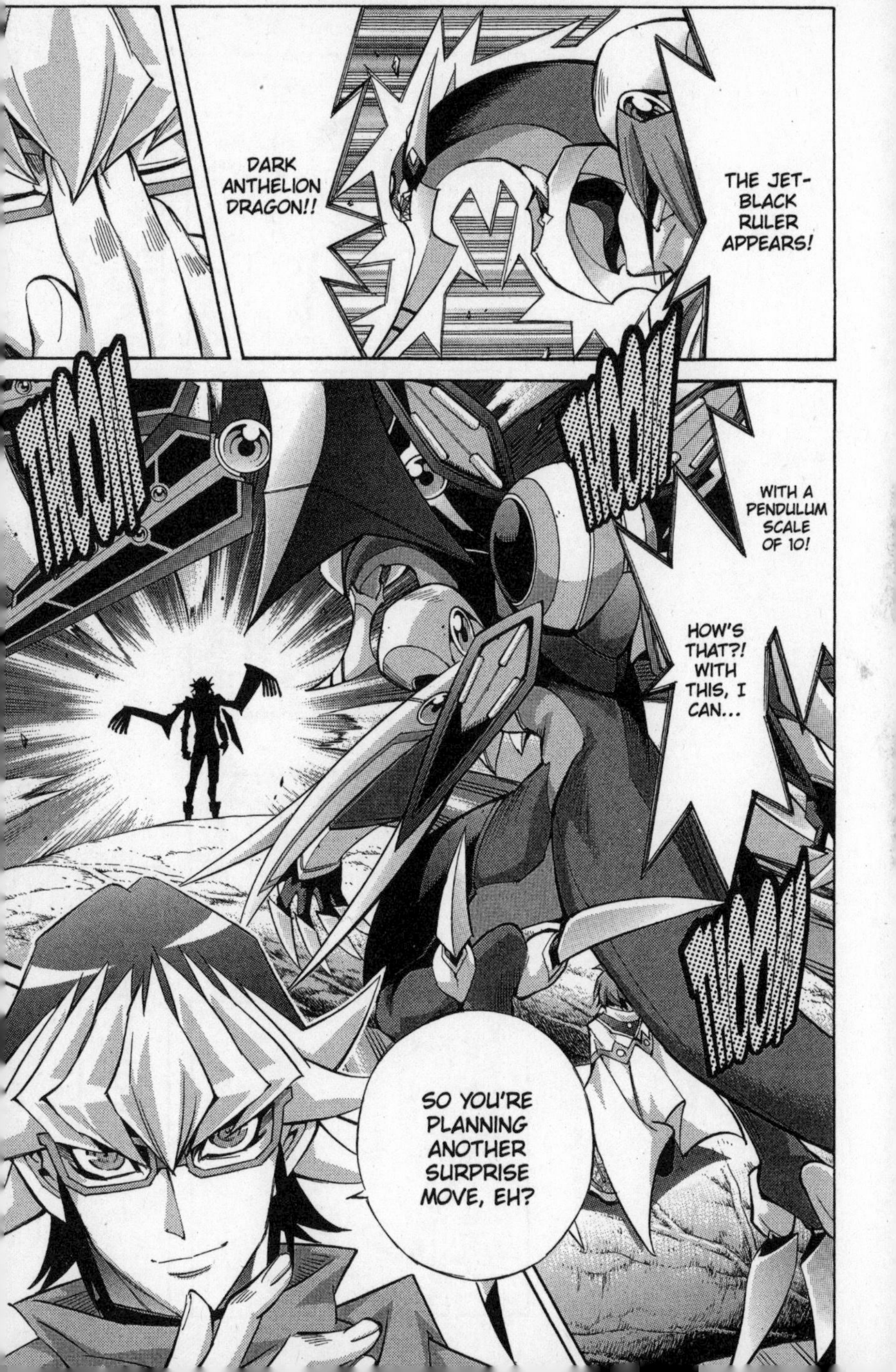
THE JET-BLACK RULER APPEARS!
DARK ANTHELION DRAGON!!
THOOM
THOOM
WITH A PENDULUM SCALE OF 10!
HOW'S THAT?! WITH THIS, I CAN...
THOOM
SO YOU'RE PLANNING ANOTHER SURPRISE MOVE, EH?

The Guys Behind ARC-V!

NAOHITO MIYOSHI

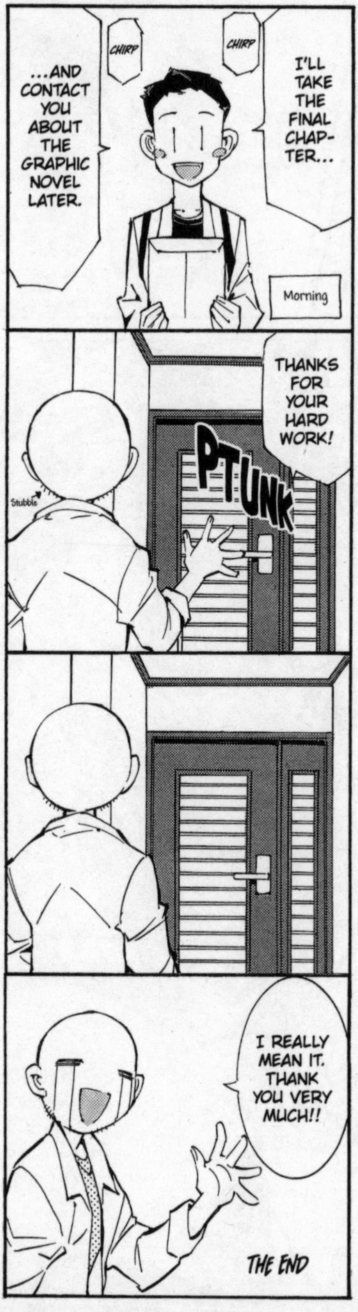
CHIRP
I'LL TAKE THE FINAL CHAPTER...
CHIRP
...AND CONTACT YOU ABOUT THE GRAPHIC NOVEL LATER.
Morning
THANKS FOR YOUR HARD WORK!
PTUNK
Stubble
I REALLY MEAN IT. THANK YOU VERY MUCH!!
THE END

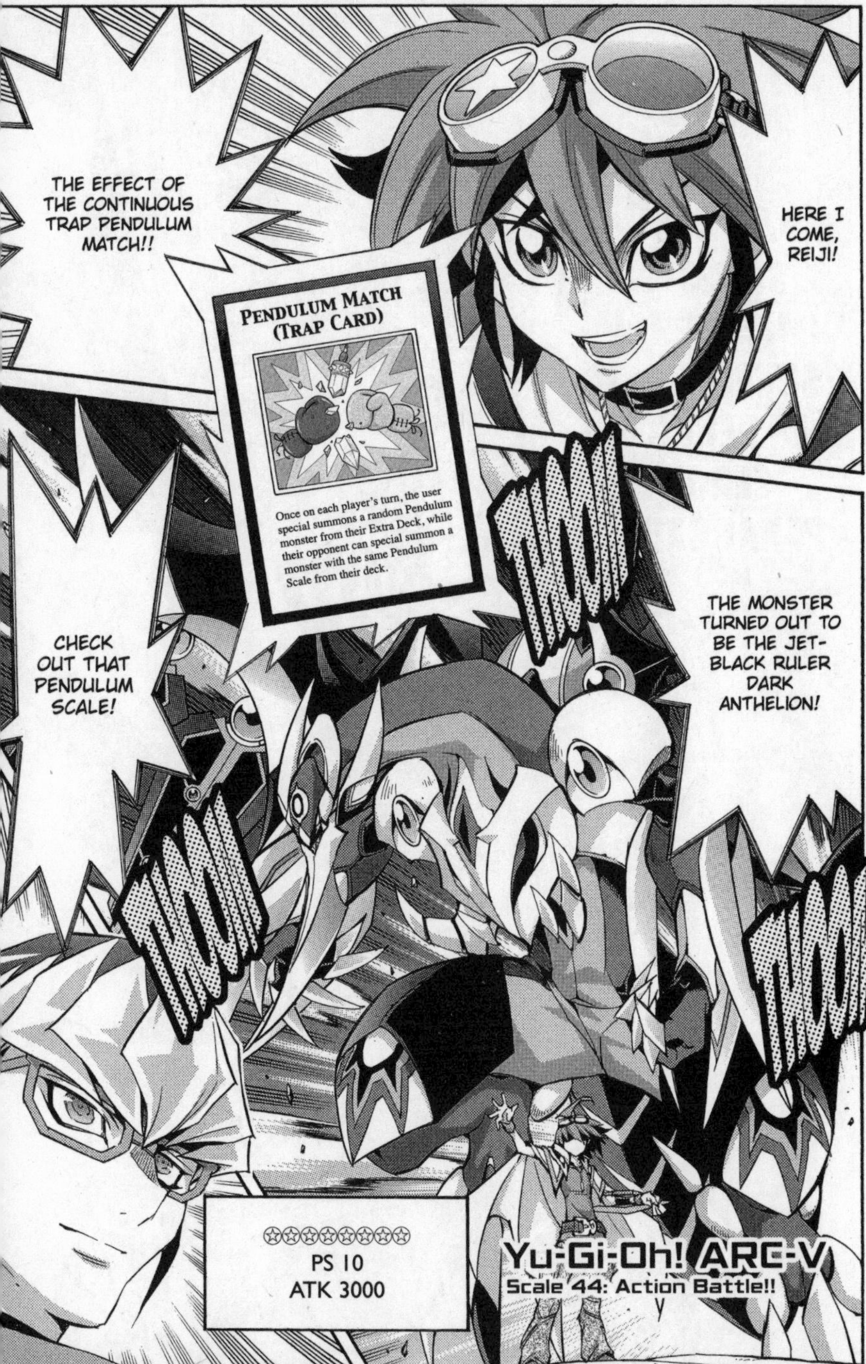
HERE I COME, REIJI!
THE EFFECT OF THE CONTINUOUS TRAP PENDULUM MATCH!!
PENDULUM MATCH (TRAP CARD)
Once on each player's turn, the user special summons a random Pendulum monster from their Extra Deck, while their opponent can special summon a monster with the same Pendulum Scale from their deck.
THOOM!!
THE MONSTER TURNED OUT TO BE THE JET-BLACK RULER DARK ANTHELION!
CHECK OUT THAT PENDULUM SCALE!
THOOM!!
THOOM!!
PS 10
ATK 3000
Yu-Gi-Oh! ARC-V
Scale 44: Action Battle!!

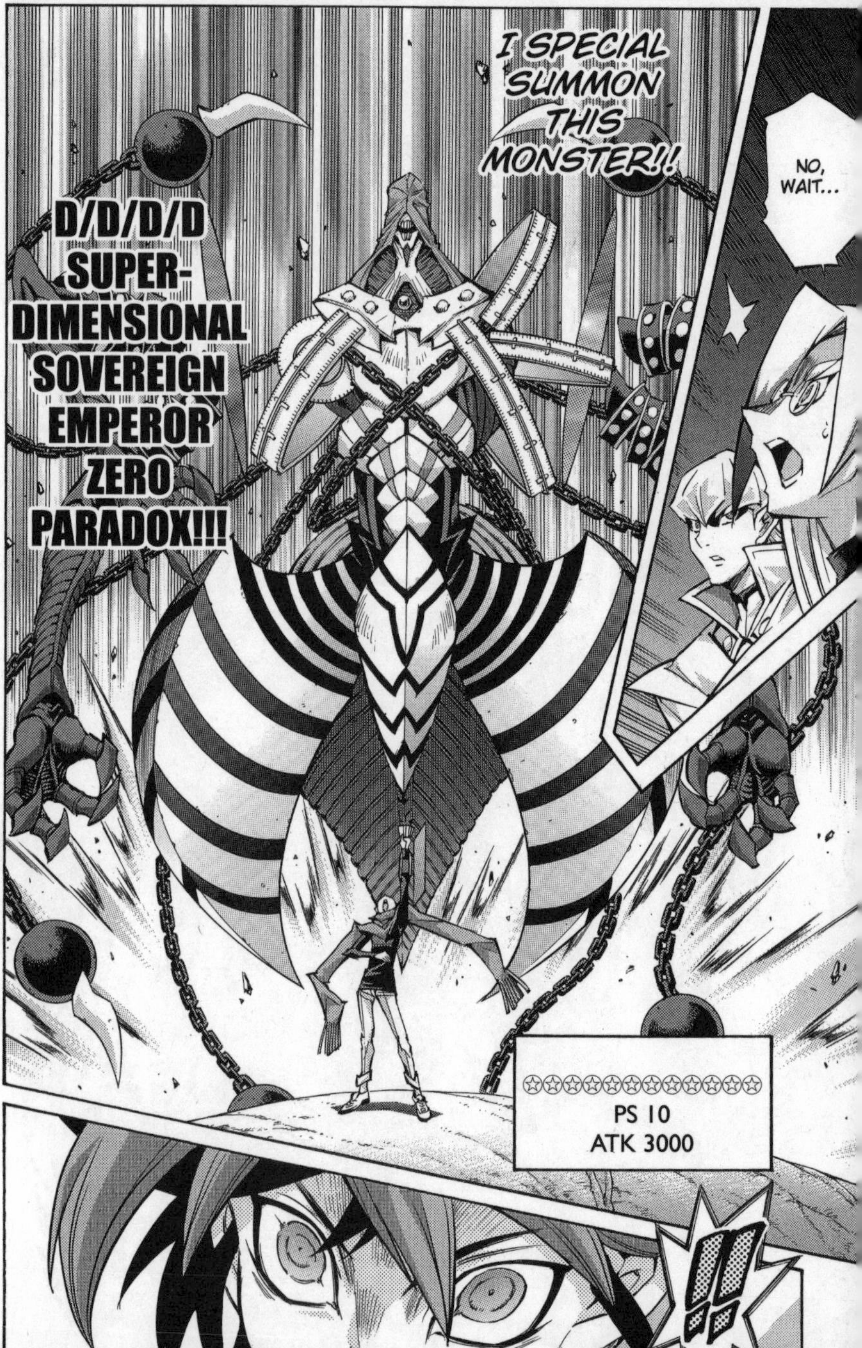
NO, WAIT...
I SPECIAL SUMMON THIS MONSTER!!
D/D/D/D SUPER-DIMENSIONAL SOVEREIGN EMPEROR ZERO PARADOX!!!
PS 10
ATK 3000
!!

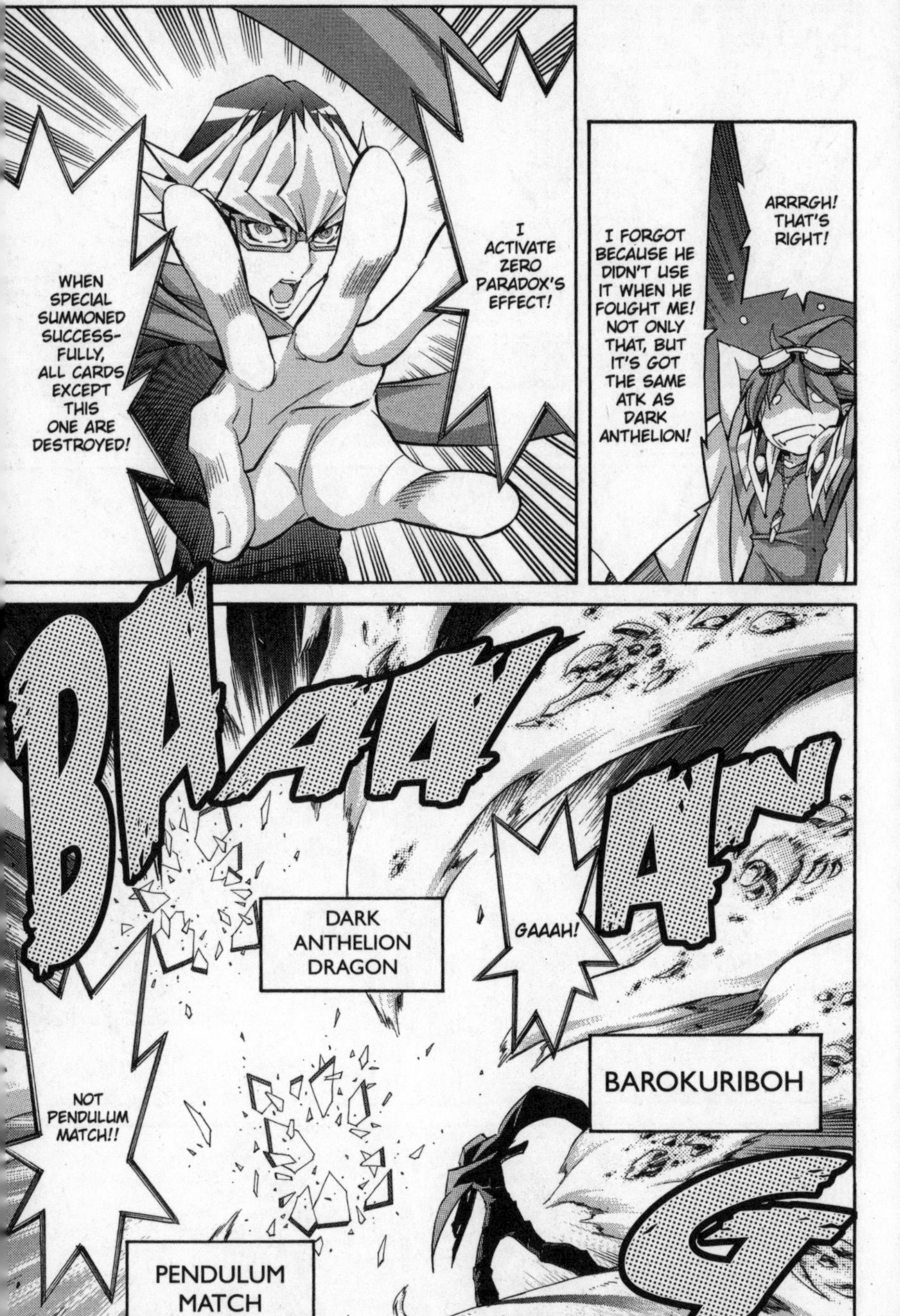
ARRRGH! THAT'S RIGHT!
I FORGOT BECAUSE HE DIDN'T USE IT WHEN HE FOUGHT ME! NOT ONLY THAT, BUT IT'S GOT THE SAME ATK AS DARK ANTHELION!
I ACTIVATE ZERO PARADOX'S EFFECT!
WHEN SPECIAL SUMMONED SUCCESS-FULLY, ALL CARDS EXCEPT THIS ONE ARE DESTROYED!
BAROKURIBOH
GAAAH!
DARK ANTHELION DRAGON
NOT PENDULUM MATCH!!
PENDULUM MATCH

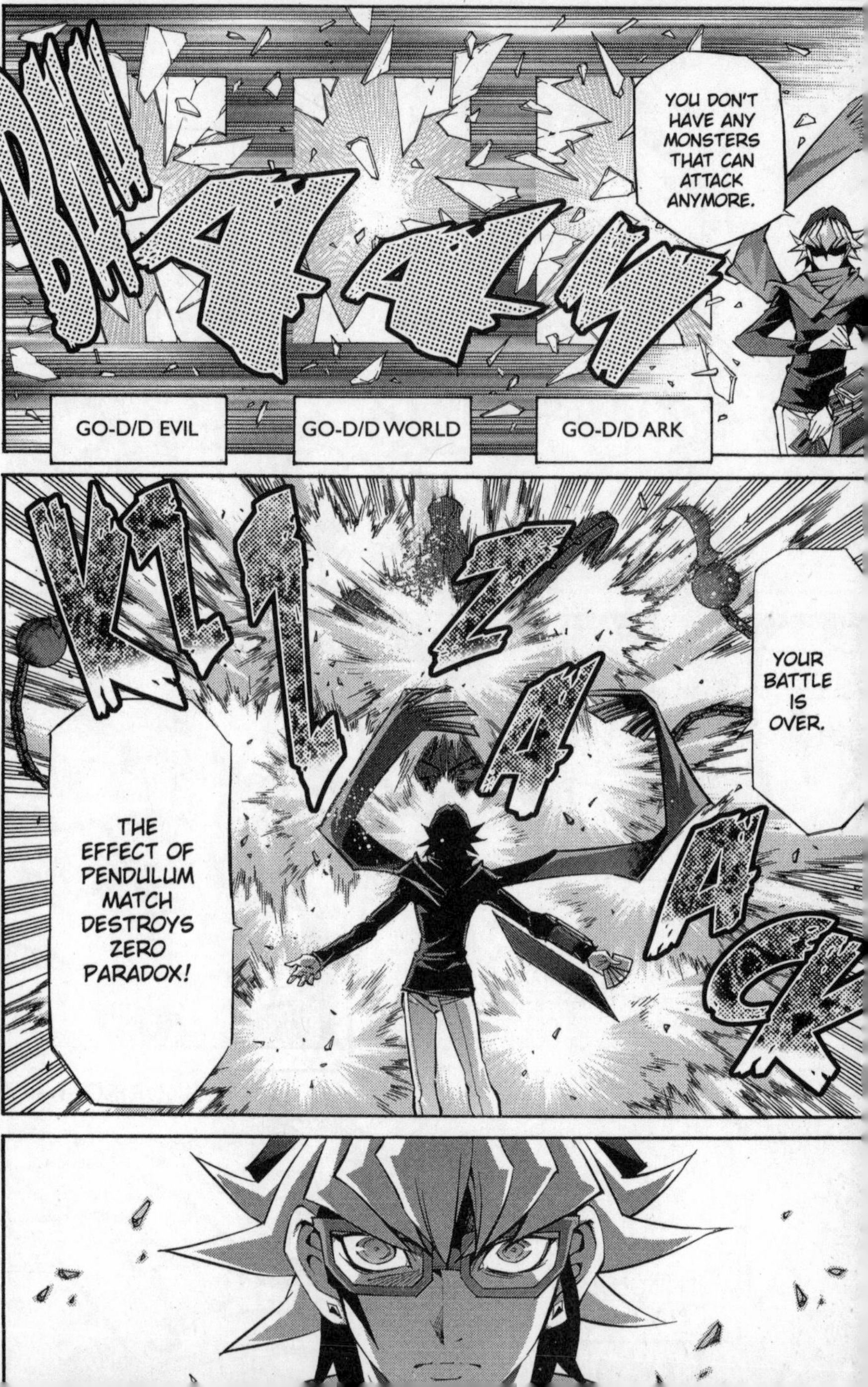
YOU DON'T HAVE ANY MONSTERS THAT CAN ATTACK ANYMORE.
GO-D/D ARK
GO-D/D WORLD
GO-D/D EVIL
YOUR BATTLE IS OVER.
THE EFFECT OF PENDULUM MATCH DESTROYS ZERO PARADOX!

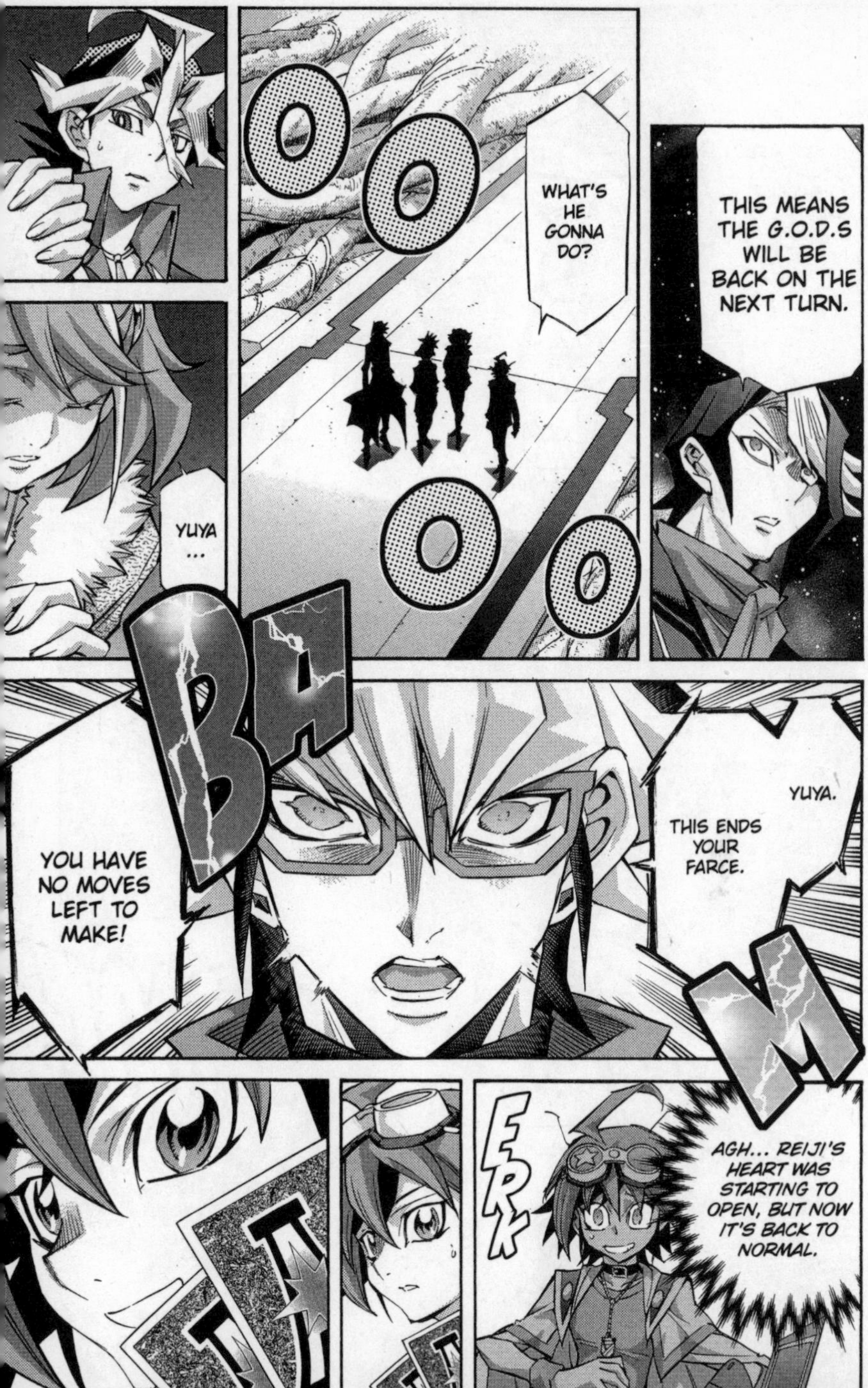
THIS MEANS THE G.O.D.S WILL BE BACK ON THE NEXT TURN.
OOOO
WHAT'S HE GONNA DO?
YUYA...
YUYA.
THIS ENDS YOUR FARCE.
YOU HAVE NO MOVES LEFT TO MAKE!
BAM
AGH... REIJI'S HEART WAS STARTING TO OPEN, BUT NOW IT'S BACK TO NORMAL.
ERK

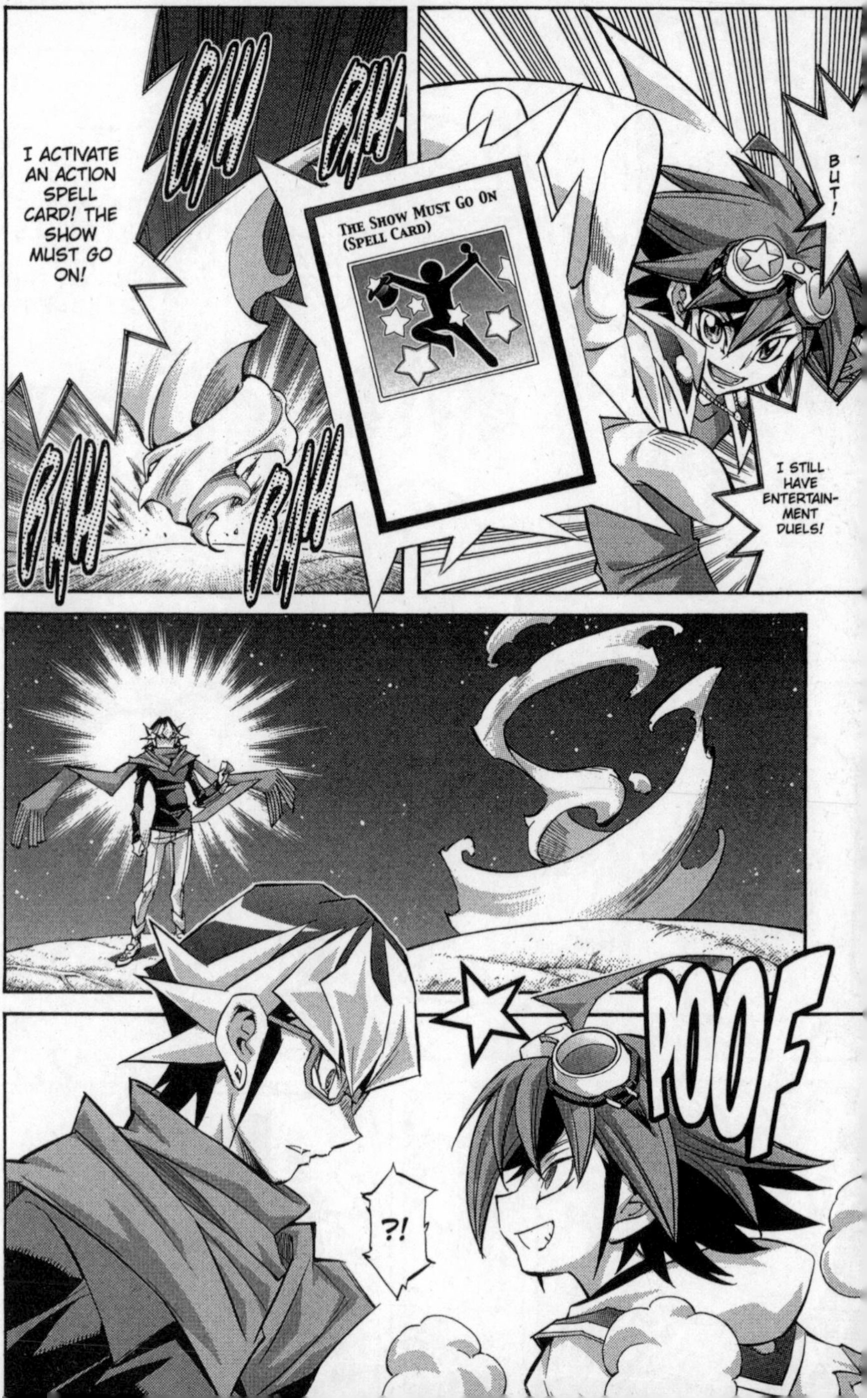
BUT!
I STILL HAVE ENTERTAINMENT DUELS!
I ACTIVATE AN ACTION SPELL CARD! THE SHOW MUST GO ON!
THE SHOW MUST GO ON
(SPELL CARD)
BAM
BAM
BAM
BAM
POOF
?!

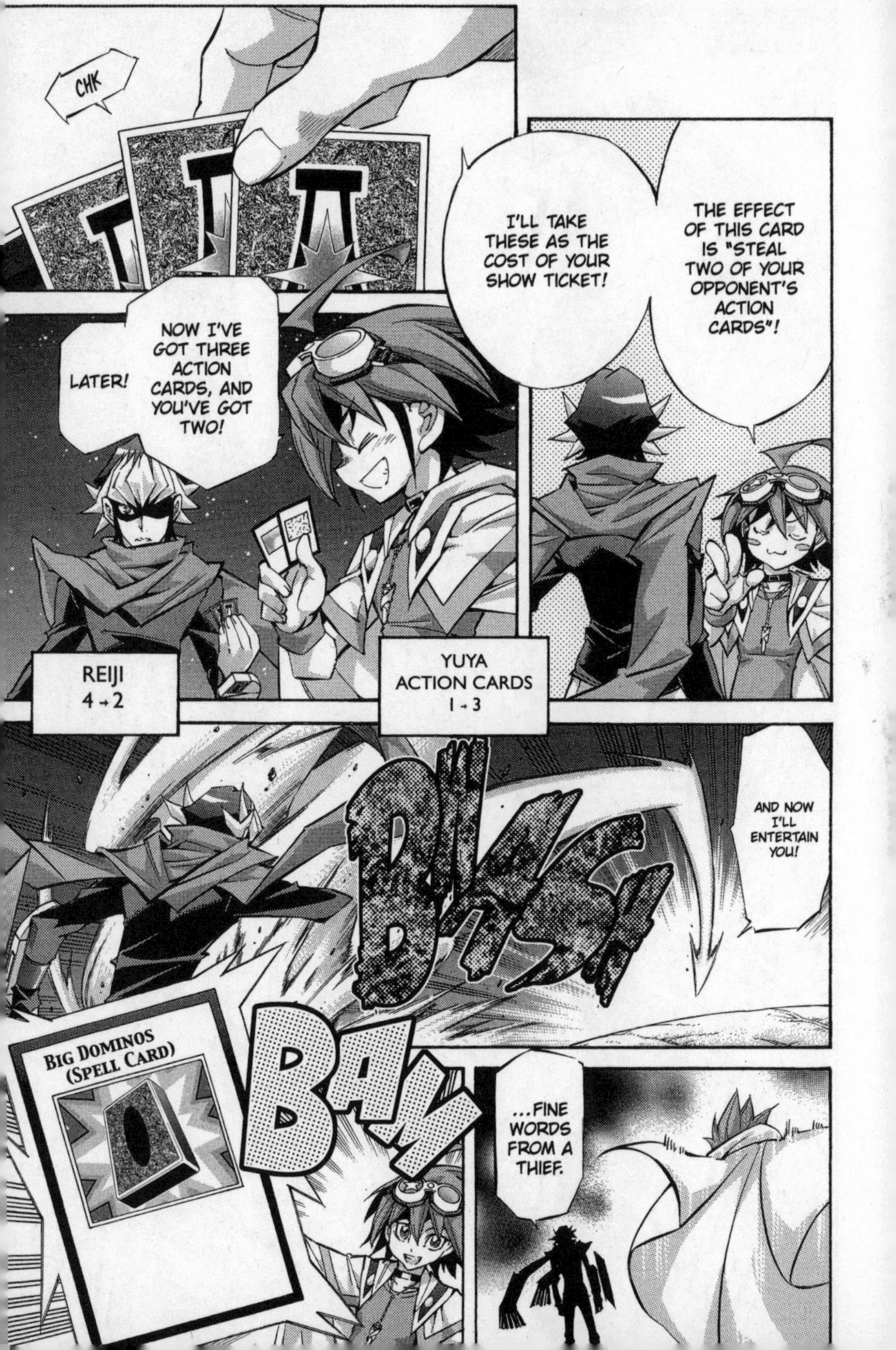
THE EFFECT OF THIS CARD IS "STEAL TWO OF YOUR OPPONENT'S ACTION CARDS"!
I'LL TAKE THESE AS THE COST OF YOUR SHOW TICKET!
CHK
NOW I'VE GOT THREE ACTION CARDS, AND YOU'VE GOT TWO!
LATER!
YUYA ACTION CARDS 1 → 3
REIJI 4 → 2
AND NOW I'LL ENTERTAIN YOU!
BASH
...FINE WORDS FROM A THIEF.
BAM
BIG DOMINOS (SPELL CARD)

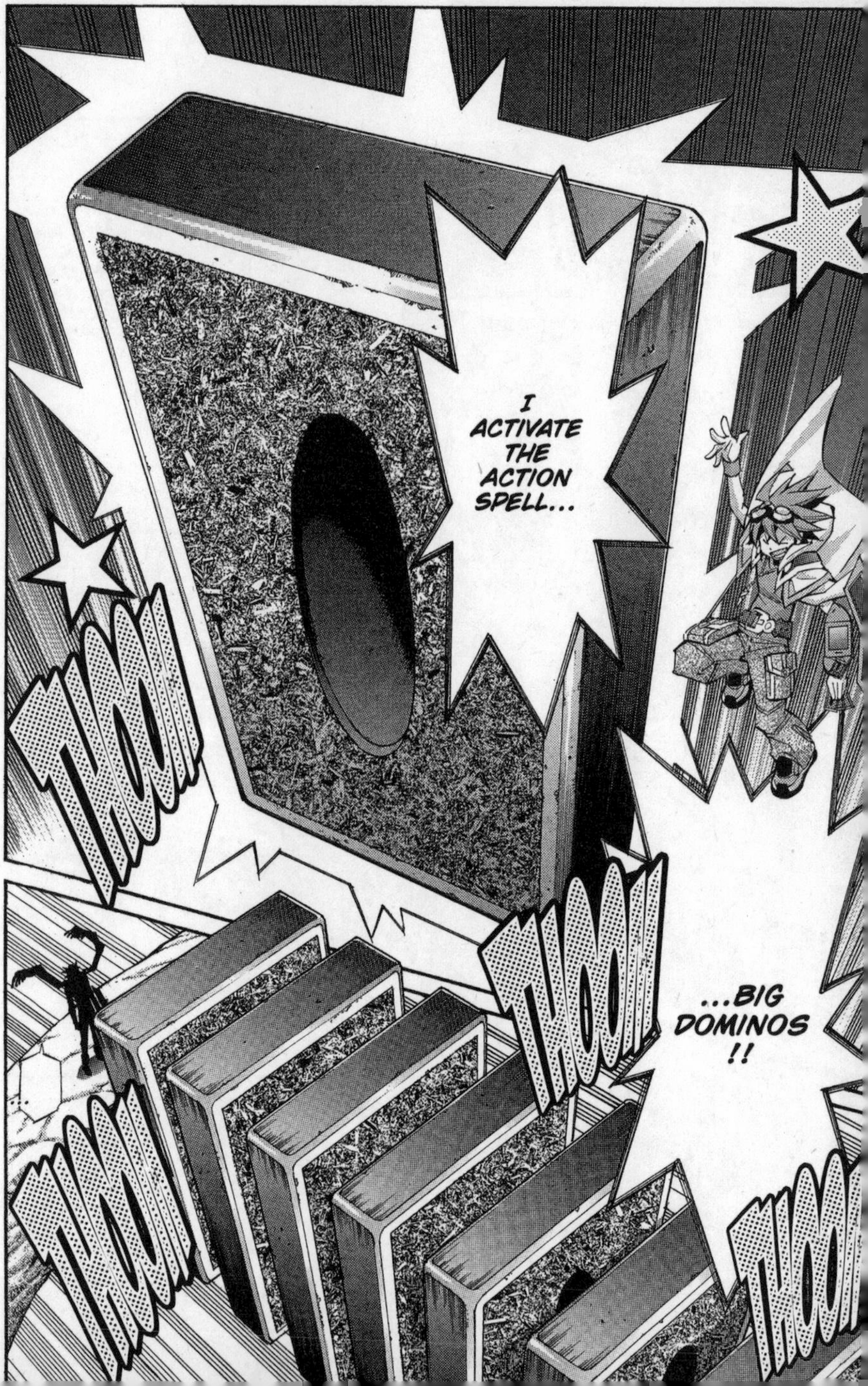
I ACTIVATE THE ACTION SPELL...
THOOM
THOOM
...BIG DOMINOS !!
THOOM
THOOM

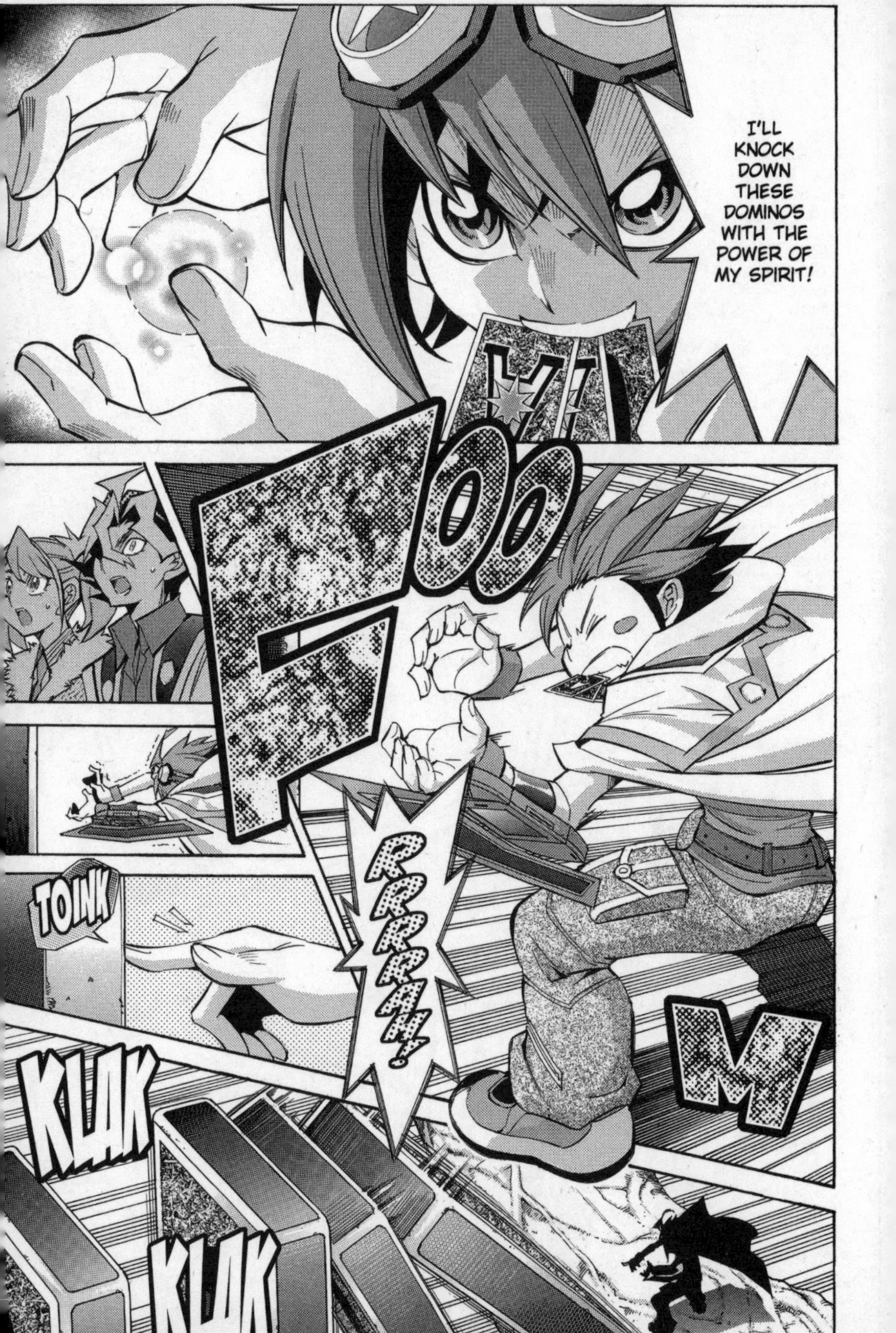
I'LL KNOCK DOWN THESE DOMINOS WITH THE POWER OF MY SPIRIT!
FOOOM
TOINK
KLAK
KLAK

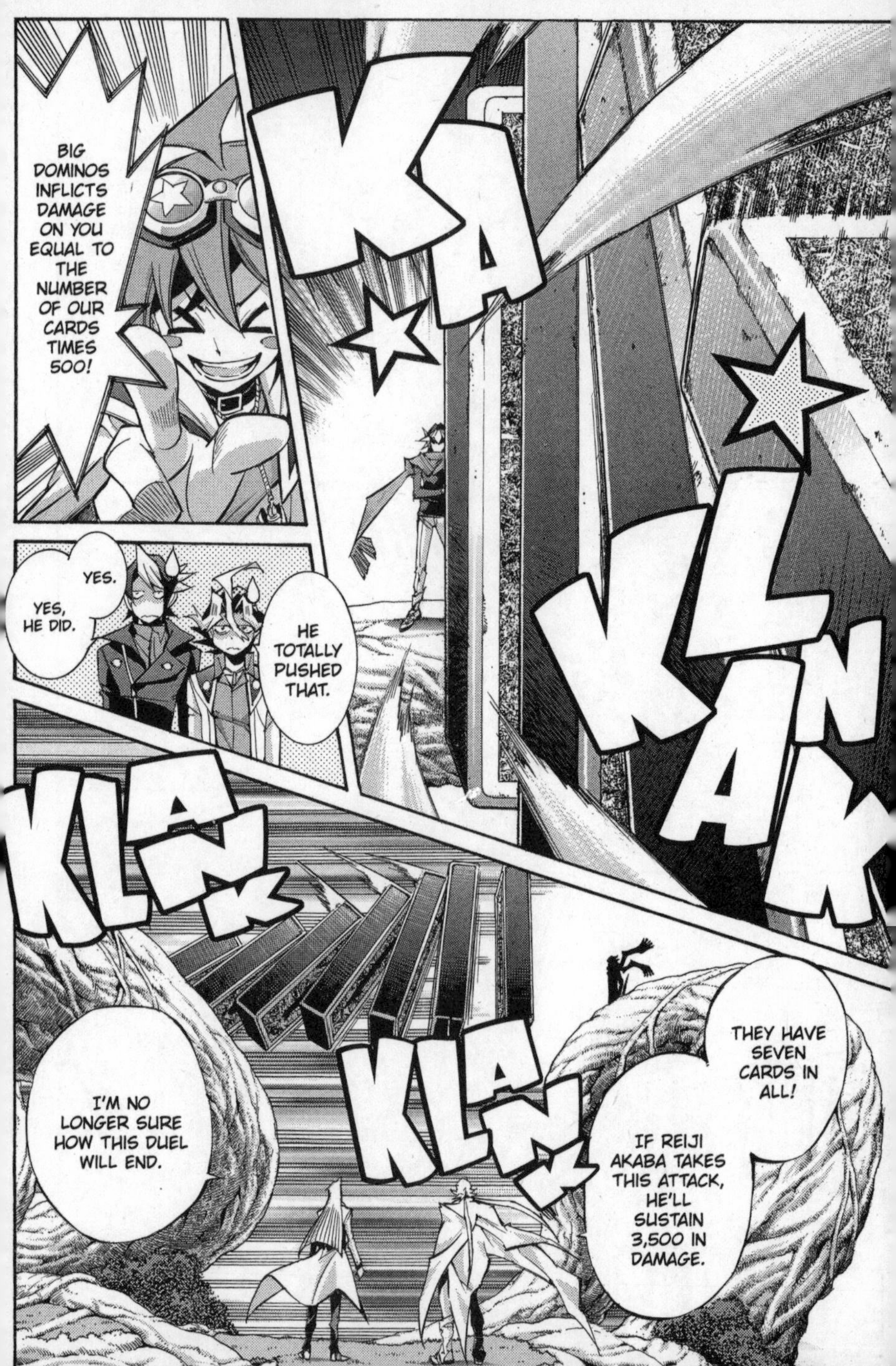
KA
KLANK
BIG DOMINOS INFLICTS DAMAGE ON YOU EQUAL TO THE NUMBER OF OUR CARDS TIMES 500!
HE TOTALLY PUSHED THAT.
YES.
YES, HE DID.
THEY HAVE SEVEN CARDS IN ALL!
IF REIJI AKABA TAKES THIS ATTACK, HE'LL SUSTAIN 3,500 IN DAMAGE.
KLANK
KLANK
I'M NO LONGER SURE HOW THIS DUEL WILL END.

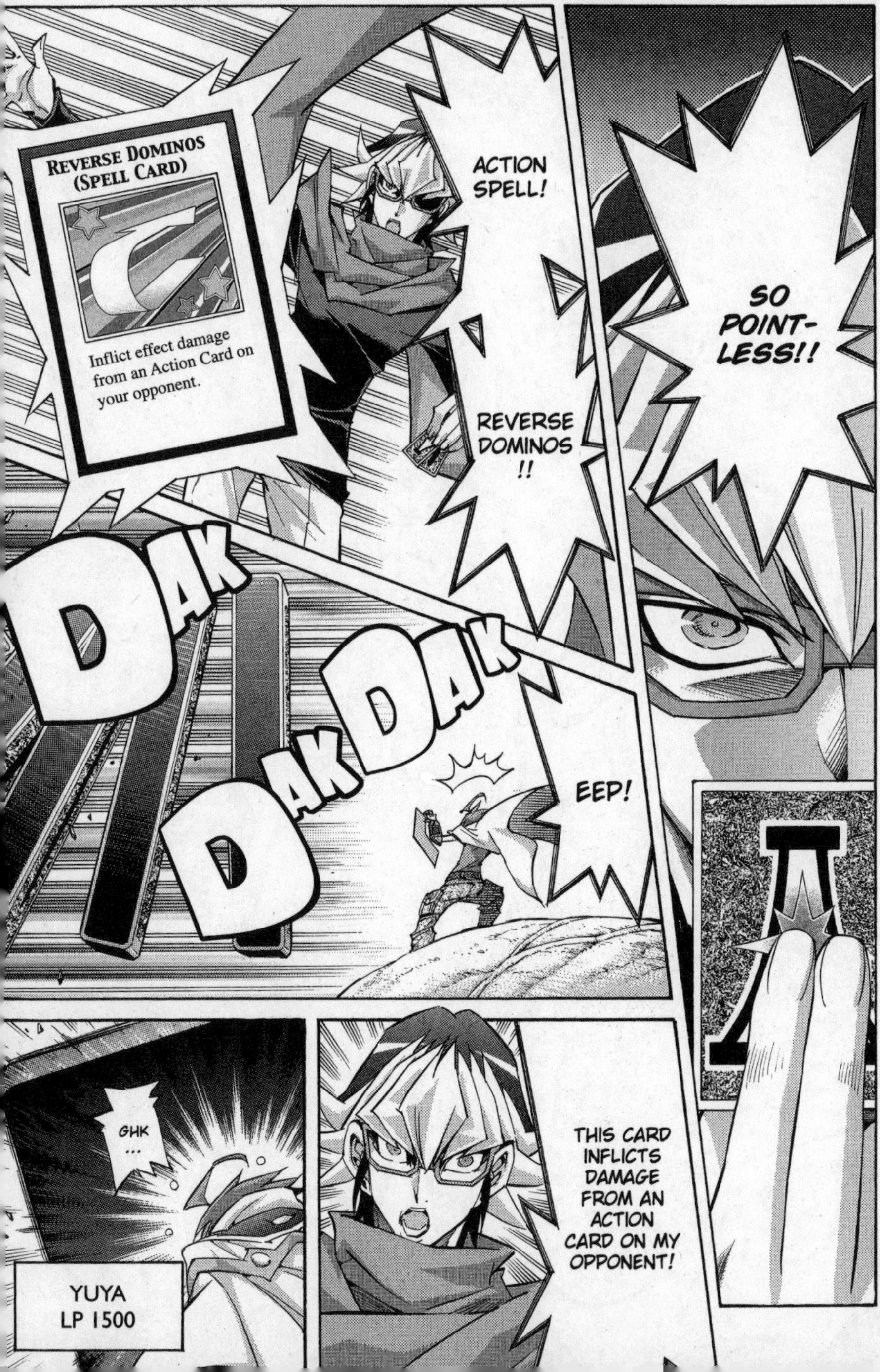
SO POINT-LESS!!
ACTION SPELL!
REVERSE DOMINOS!!
REVERSE DOMINOS (SPELL CARD)
Inflict effect damage from an Action Card on your opponent.
DAK DAK DAK
EEP!
THIS CARD INFLICTS DAMAGE FROM AN ACTION CARD ON MY OPPONENT!
GHK...
YUYA LP 1500

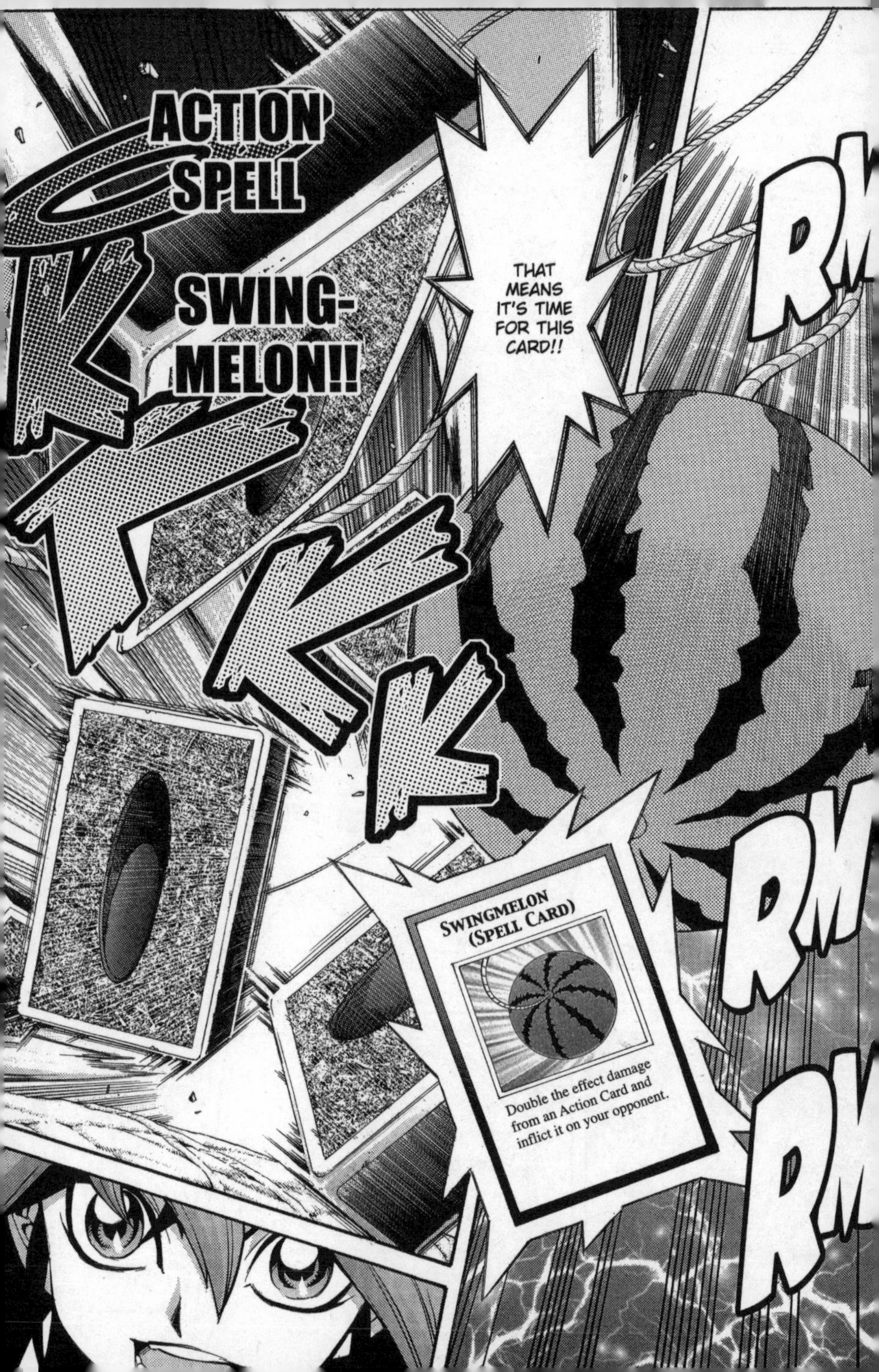
THAT MEANS IT'S TIME FOR THIS CARD!!
ACTION SPELL
SWING-MELON!!
SWINGMELON (SPELL CARD)
Double the effect damage from an Action Card and inflict it on your opponent.

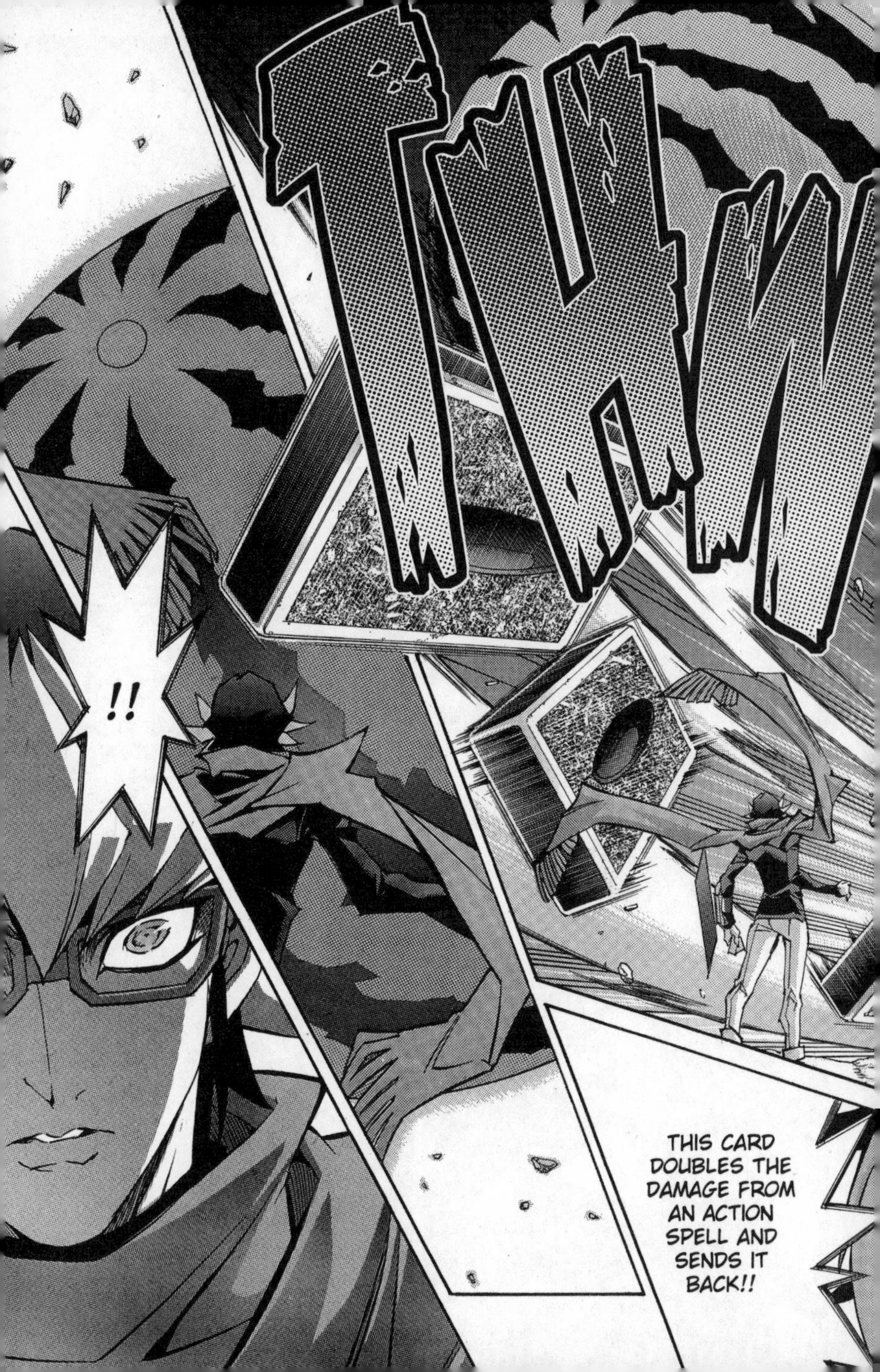

!!
THIS CARD DOUBLES THE DAMAGE FROM AN ACTION SPELL AND SENDS IT BACK!!

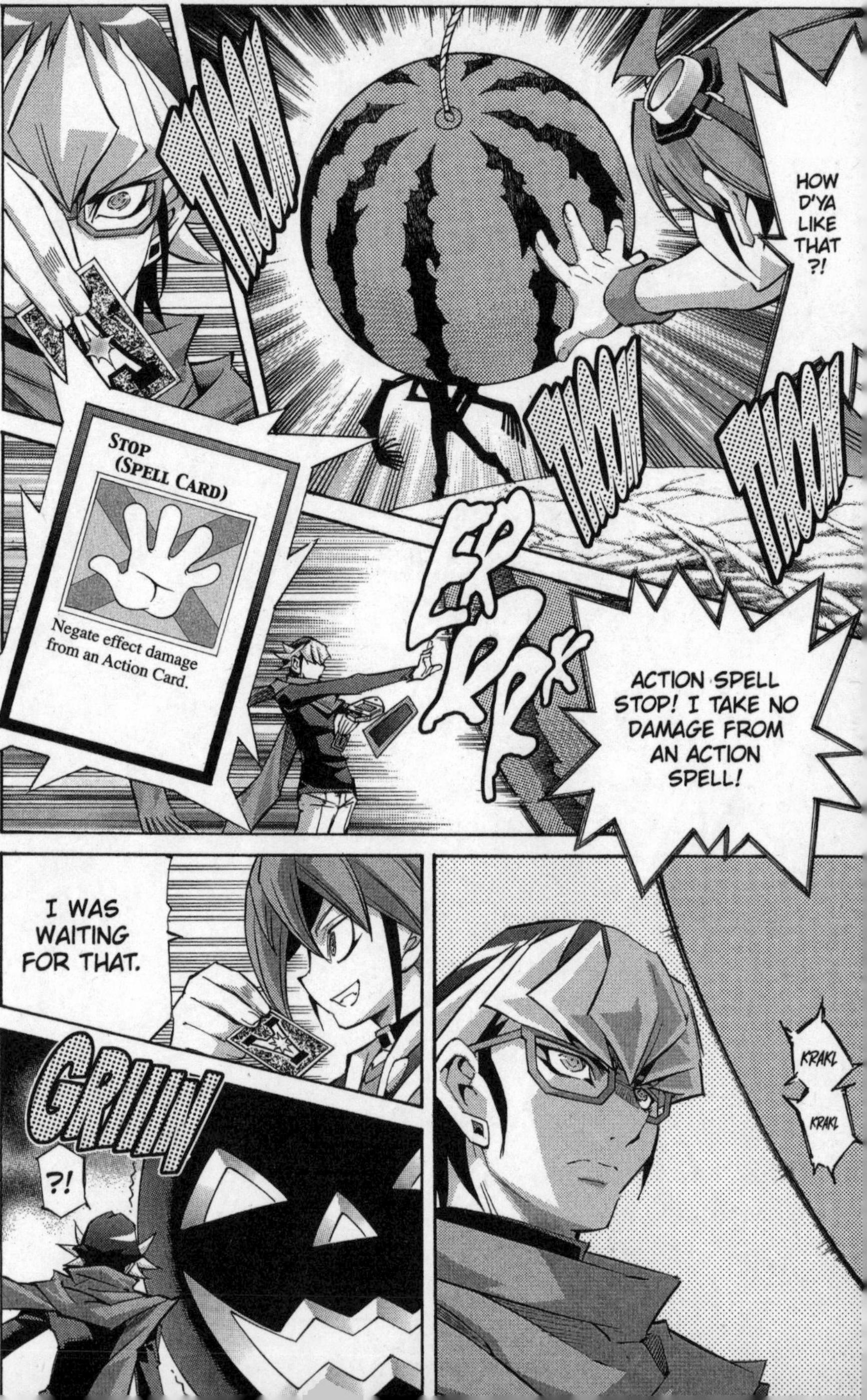
HOW D'YA LIKE THAT?!
STOP
(SPELL CARD)
Negate effect damage from an Action Card.
ACTION SPELL STOP! I TAKE NO DAMAGE FROM AN ACTION SPELL!
KRAKL
KRAKL
I WAS WAITING FOR THAT.
?!

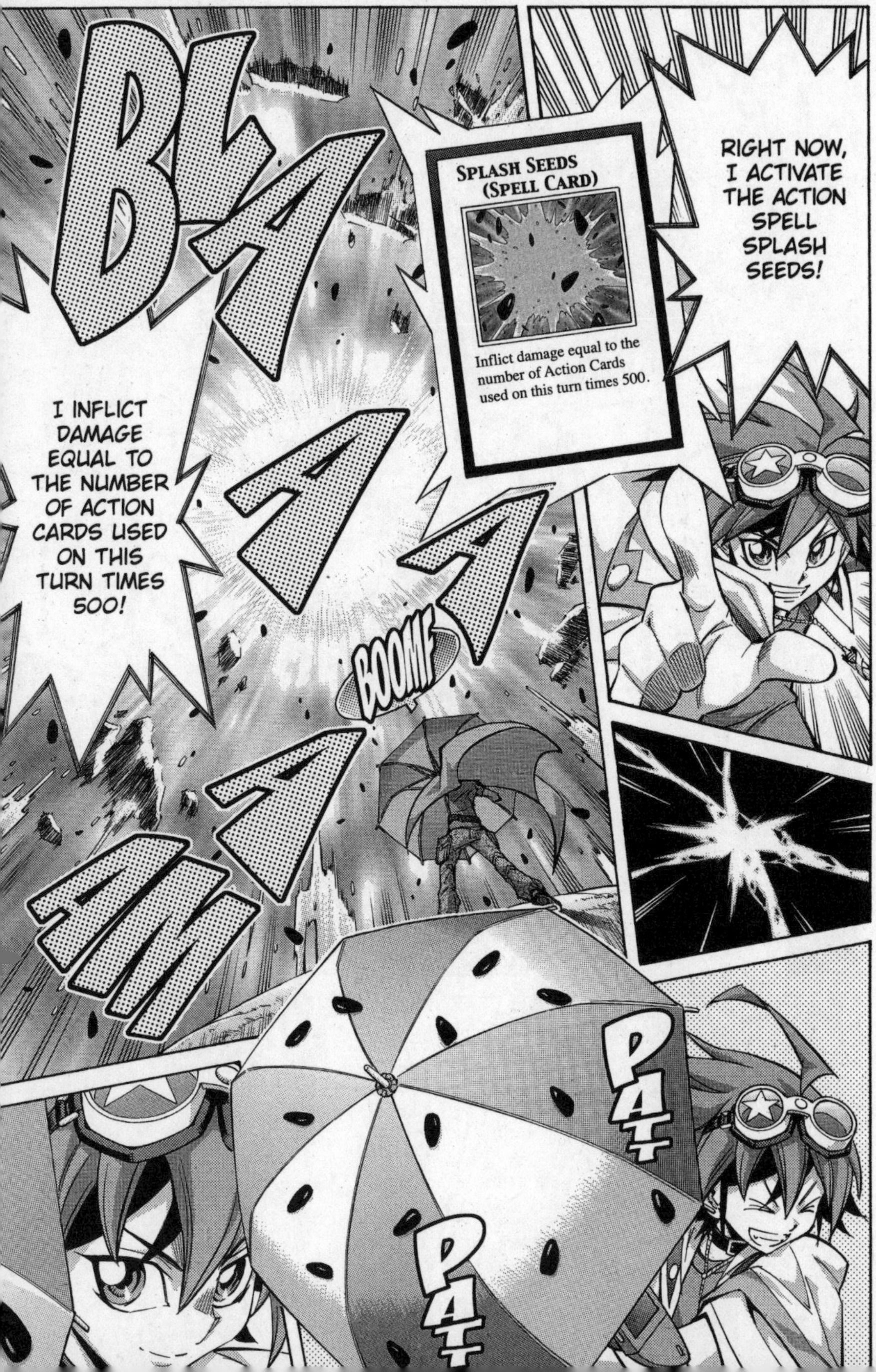
RIGHT NOW, I ACTIVATE THE ACTION SPELL SPLASH SEEDS!
SPLASH SEEDS (SPELL CARD)
Inflict damage equal to the number of Action Cards used on this turn times 500.
BLAAAAAM
I INFLICT DAMAGE EQUAL TO THE NUMBER OF ACTION CARDS USED ON THIS TURN TIMES 500!
BOOMF
PATT
PATT

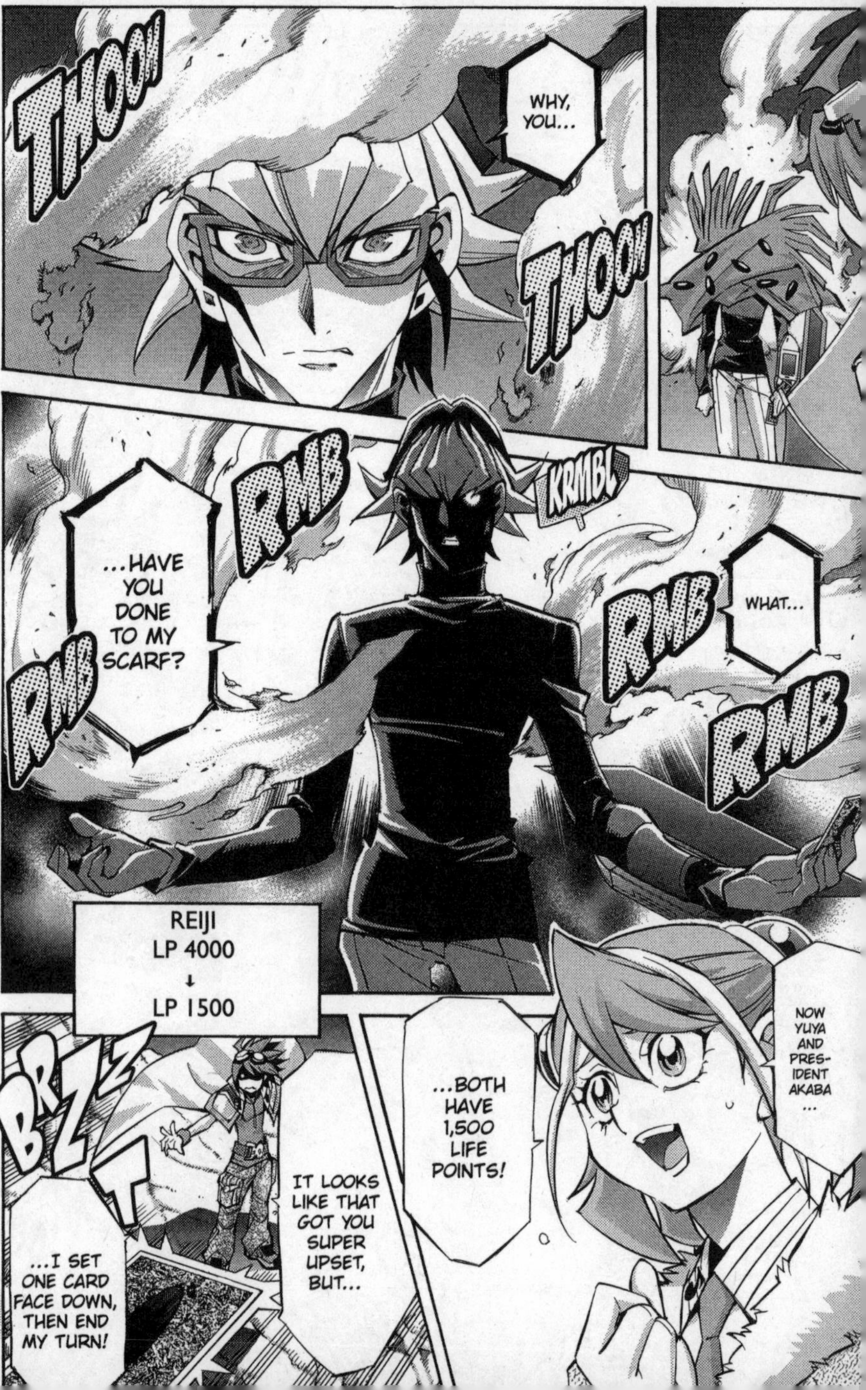
THOOM
WHY, YOU...
THOOM
KRMBL
WHAT...
RMB
RMB
RMB
...HAVE YOU DONE TO MY SCARF?
RMB
REIJI LP 4000 ↓ LP 1500
NOW YUYA AND PRES-IDENT AKABA...
...BOTH HAVE 1,500 LIFE POINTS!
BRZZT
IT LOOKS LIKE THAT GOT YOU SUPER UPSET, BUT...
...I SET ONE CARD FACE DOWN, THEN END MY TURN!

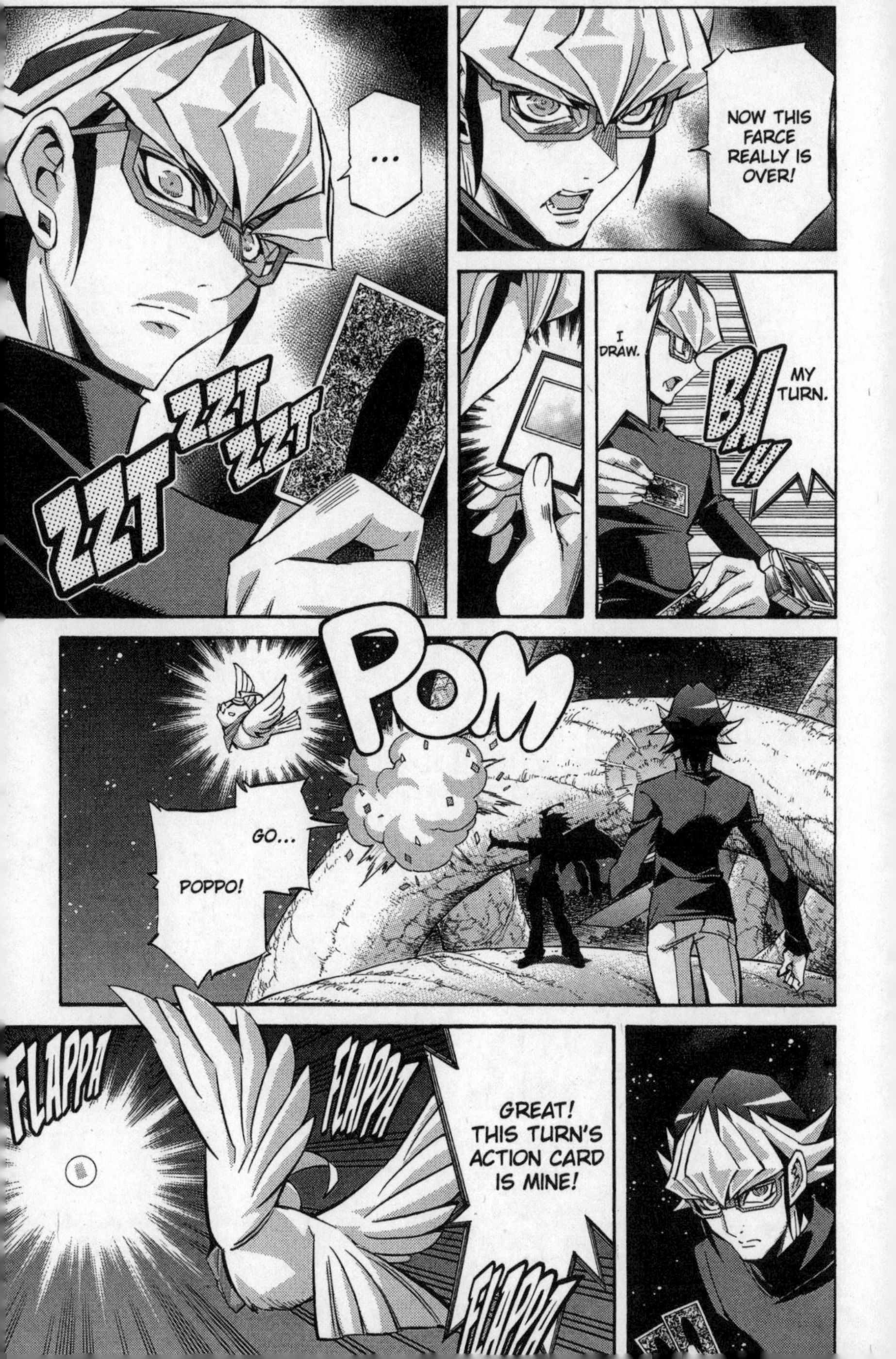
NOW THIS FARCE REALLY IS OVER!
MY TURN.
BA
I DRAW.
...
ZZT ZZT ZZT
POM
GO... POPPO!
GREAT! THIS TURN'S ACTION CARD IS MINE!
FLAPPA FLAPPA FLAPPA

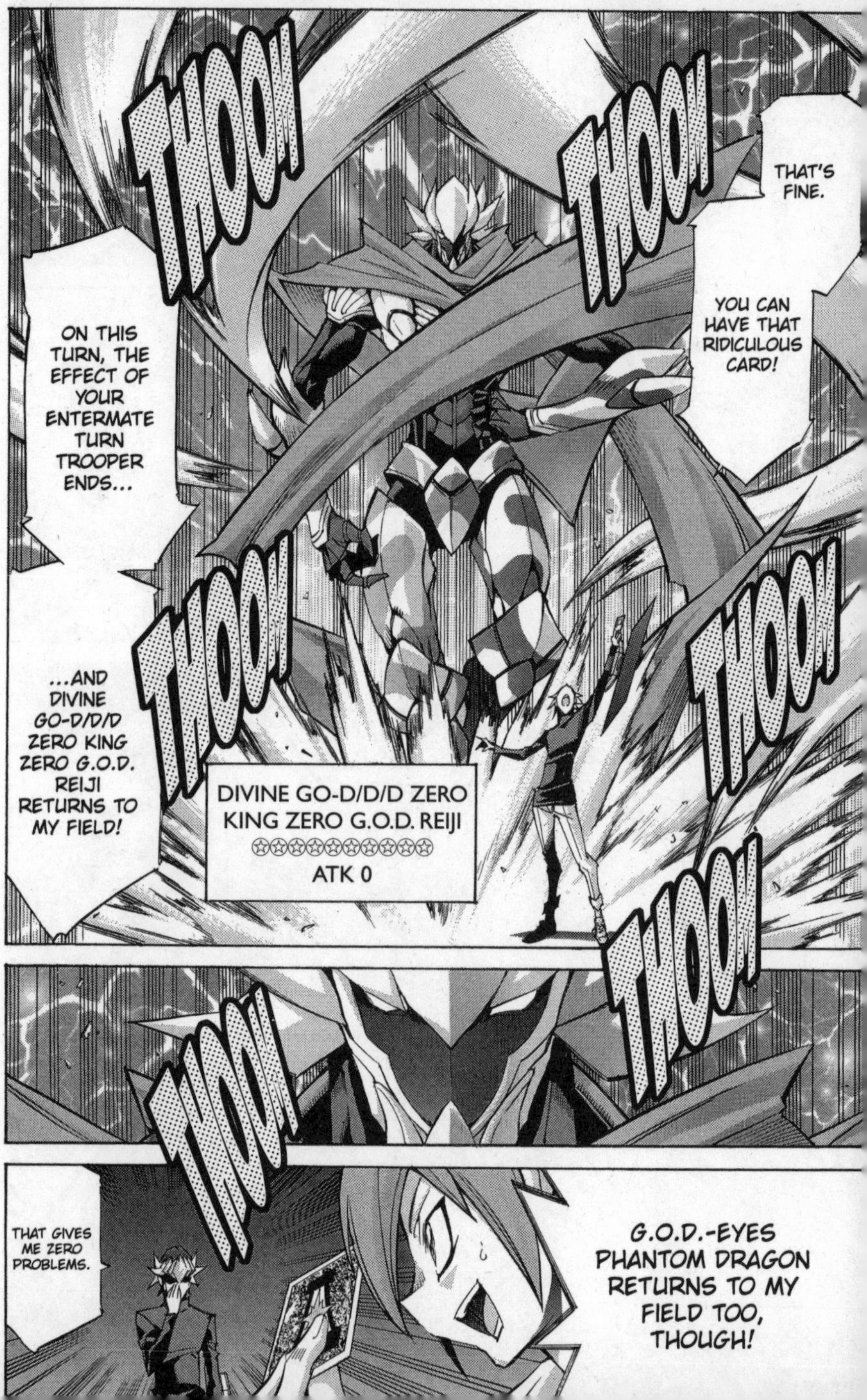
THOOM
THAT'S FINE.
YOU CAN HAVE THAT RIDICULOUS CARD!
THOOM
ON THIS TURN, THE EFFECT OF YOUR ENTERMATE TURN TROOPER ENDS...
THOOM
THOOM
...AND DIVINE GO-D/D/D ZERO KING ZERO G.O.D. REIJI RETURNS TO MY FIELD!
DIVINE GO-D/D/D ZERO KING ZERO G.O.D. REIJI
ATK 0
THOOM
THOOM
G.O.D.-EYES PHANTOM DRAGON RETURNS TO MY FIELD TOO, THOUGH!
THAT GIVES ME ZERO PROBLEMS.

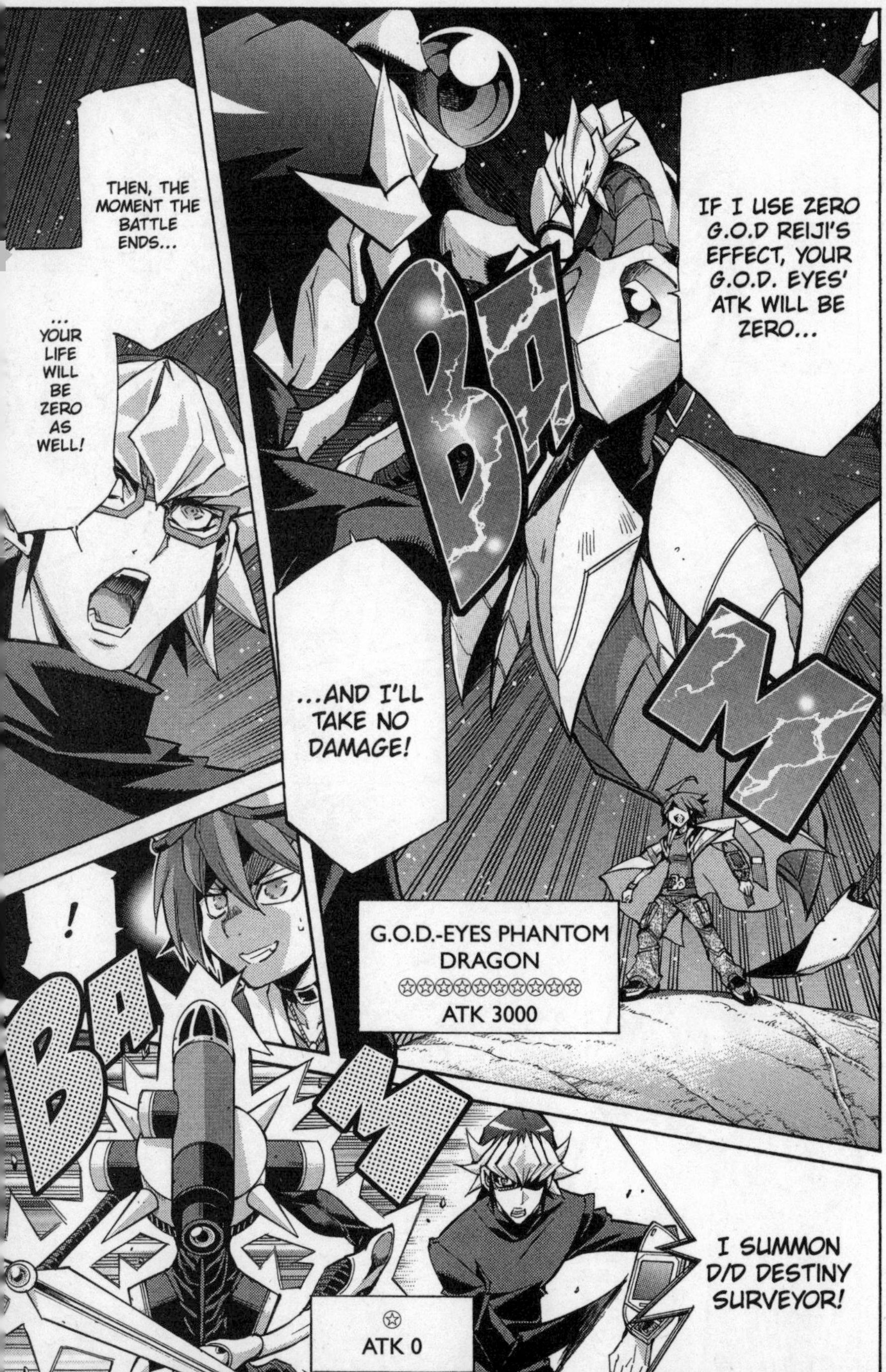
IF I USE ZERO G.O.D REIJI'S EFFECT, YOUR G.O.D. EYES' ATK WILL BE ZERO...
...AND I'LL TAKE NO DAMAGE!
THEN, THE MOMENT THE BATTLE ENDS...
...YOUR LIFE WILL BE ZERO AS WELL!
BAM
G.O.D.-EYES PHANTOM DRAGON
☆☆☆☆☆☆☆☆☆☆☆☆
ATK 3000
!
I SUMMON D/D DESTINY SURVEYOR!
BAM
☆
ATK 0

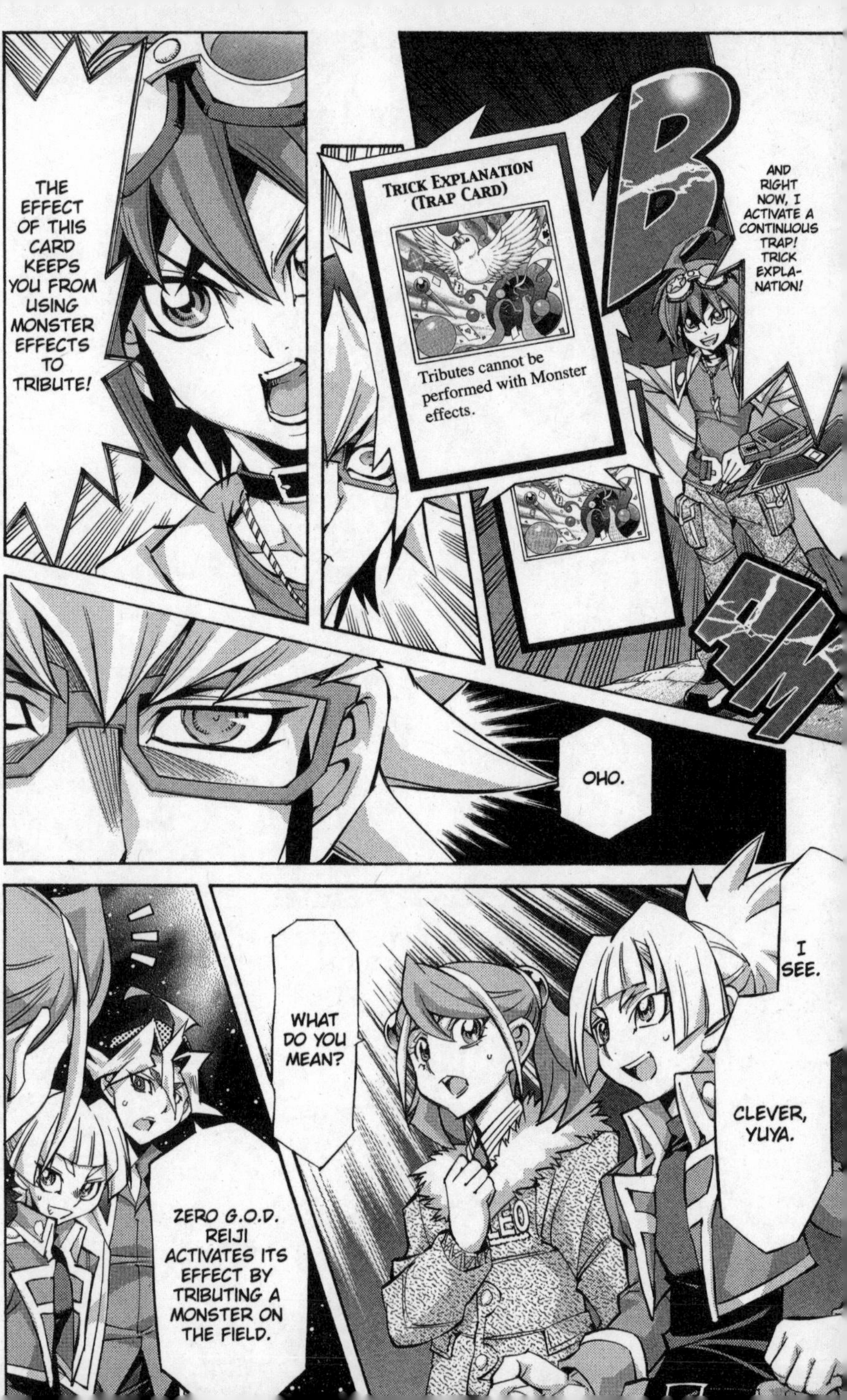
AND RIGHT NOW, I ACTIVATE A CONTINUOUS TRAP! TRICK EXPLA-NATION!
BAM
TRICK EXPLANATION (TRAP CARD)
Tributes cannot be performed with Monster effects.
THE EFFECT OF THIS CARD KEEPS YOU FROM USING MONSTER EFFECTS TO TRIBUTE!
OHO.
I SEE.
CLEVER, YUYA.
WHAT DO YOU MEAN?
ZERO G.O.D. REIJI ACTIVATES ITS EFFECT BY TRIBUTING A MONSTER ON THE FIELD.

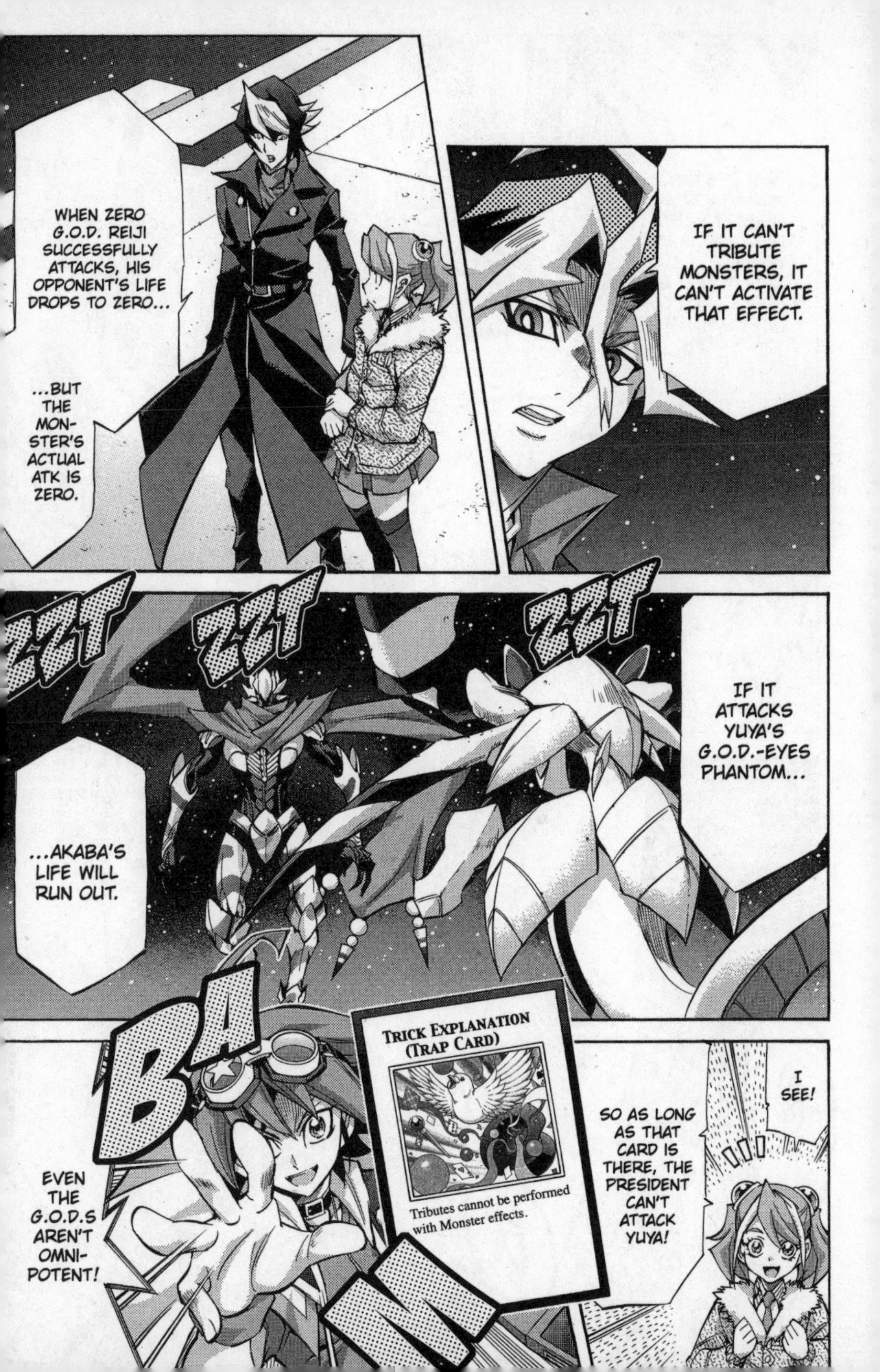
IF IT CAN'T TRIBUTE MONSTERS, IT CAN'T ACTIVATE THAT EFFECT.
WHEN ZERO G.O.D. REIJI SUCCESSFULLY ATTACKS, HIS OPPONENT'S LIFE DROPS TO ZERO...
...BUT THE MON-STER'S ACTUAL ATK IS ZERO.
ZZT
ZZT
ZZT
IF IT ATTACKS YUYA'S G.O.D.-EYES PHANTOM...
...AKABA'S LIFE WILL RUN OUT.
I SEE!
SO AS LONG AS THAT CARD IS THERE, THE PRESIDENT CAN'T ATTACK YUYA!
BAM
TRICK EXPLANATION (TRAP CARD)
Tributes cannot be performed with Monster effects.
EVEN THE G.O.D.S AREN'T OMNI-POTENT!

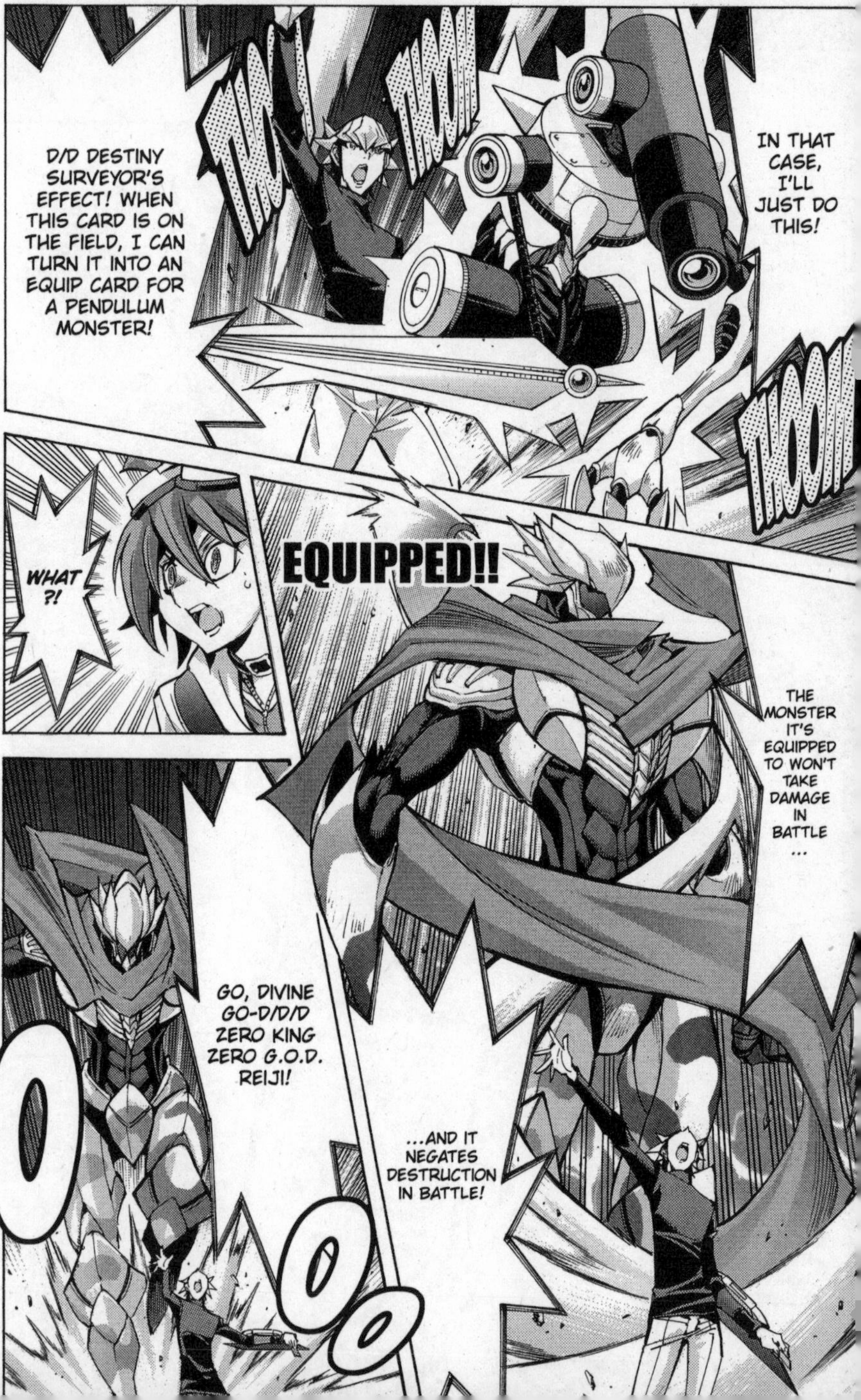
IN THAT CASE, I'LL JUST DO THIS!
THOOM
THOOM
D/D DESTINY SURVEYOR'S EFFECT! WHEN THIS CARD IS ON THE FIELD, I CAN TURN IT INTO AN EQUIP CARD FOR A PENDULUM MONSTER!
THOOM
EQUIPPED!!
THE MONSTER IT'S EQUIPPED TO WON'T TAKE DAMAGE IN BATTLE ...
...AND IT NEGATES DESTRUCTION IN BATTLE!
WHAT ?!
GO, DIVINE GO-D/D/D ZERO KING ZERO G.O.D. REIJI!
OOOO

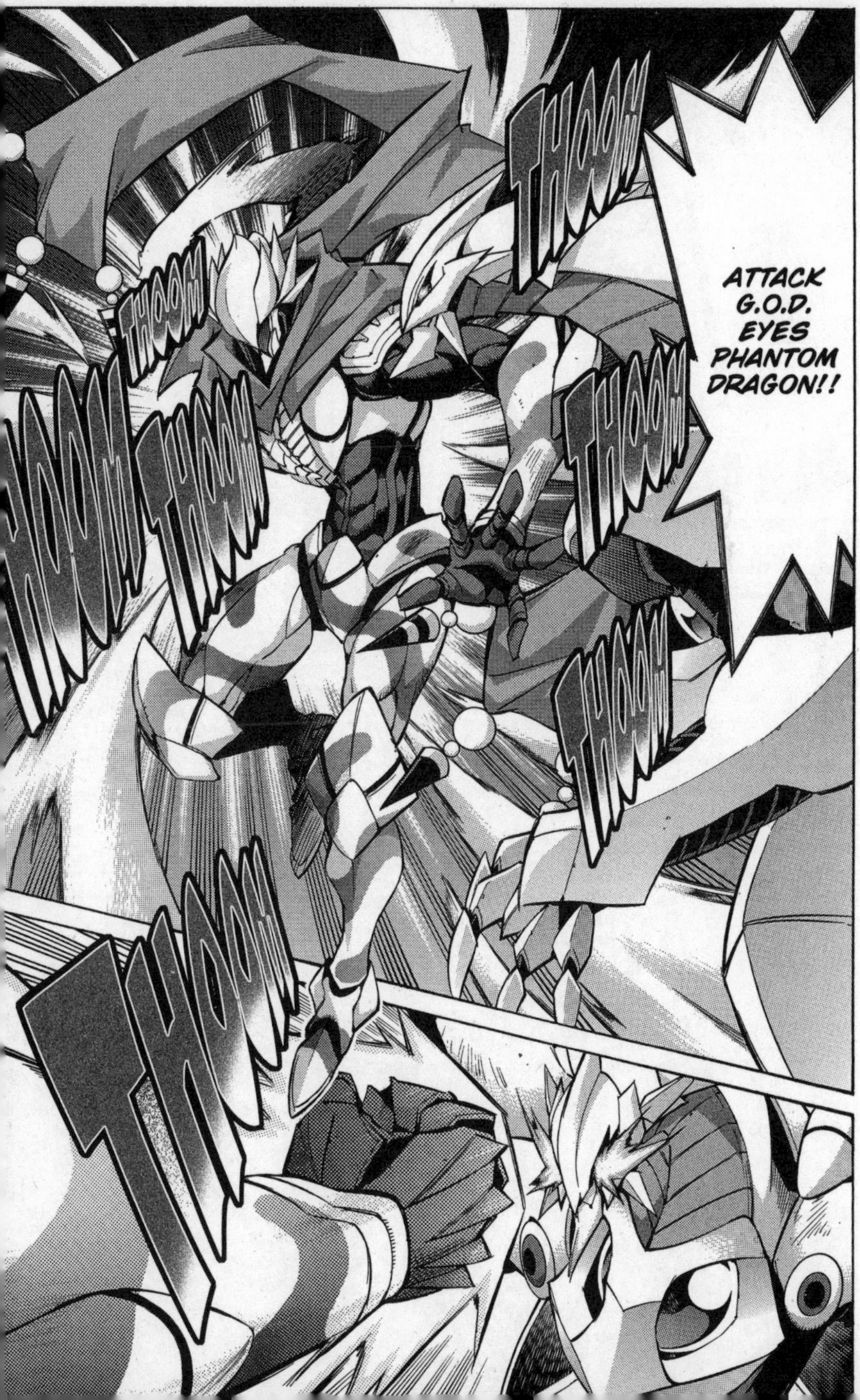
ATTACK G.O.D. EYES PHANTOM DRAGON!!
THOOM
THOOM
THOOM
THOOM
THOOM
THOOM
THOOM
THOOM

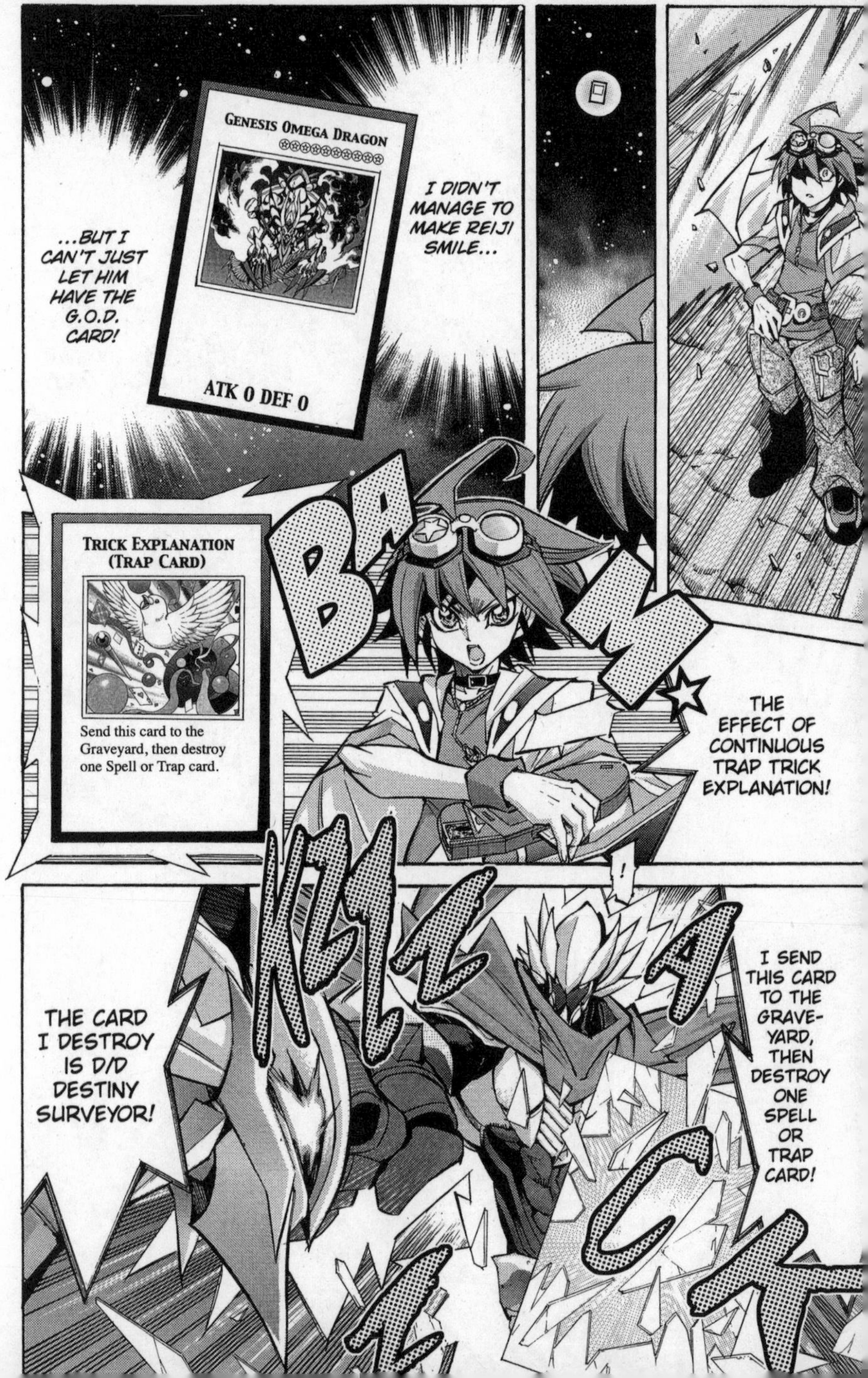
I DIDN'T MANAGE TO MAKE REIJI SMILE...
Genesis Omega Dragon
ATK 0 DEF 0
...BUT I CAN'T JUST LET HIM HAVE THE G.O.D. CARD!
BAM
THE EFFECT OF CONTINUOUS TRAP TRICK EXPLANATION!
Trick Explanation (Trap Card)
Send this card to the Graveyard, then destroy one Spell or Trap card.
!
I SEND THIS CARD TO THE GRAVEYARD, THEN DESTROY ONE SPELL OR TRAP CARD!
THE CARD I DESTROY IS D/D DESTINY SURVEYOR!

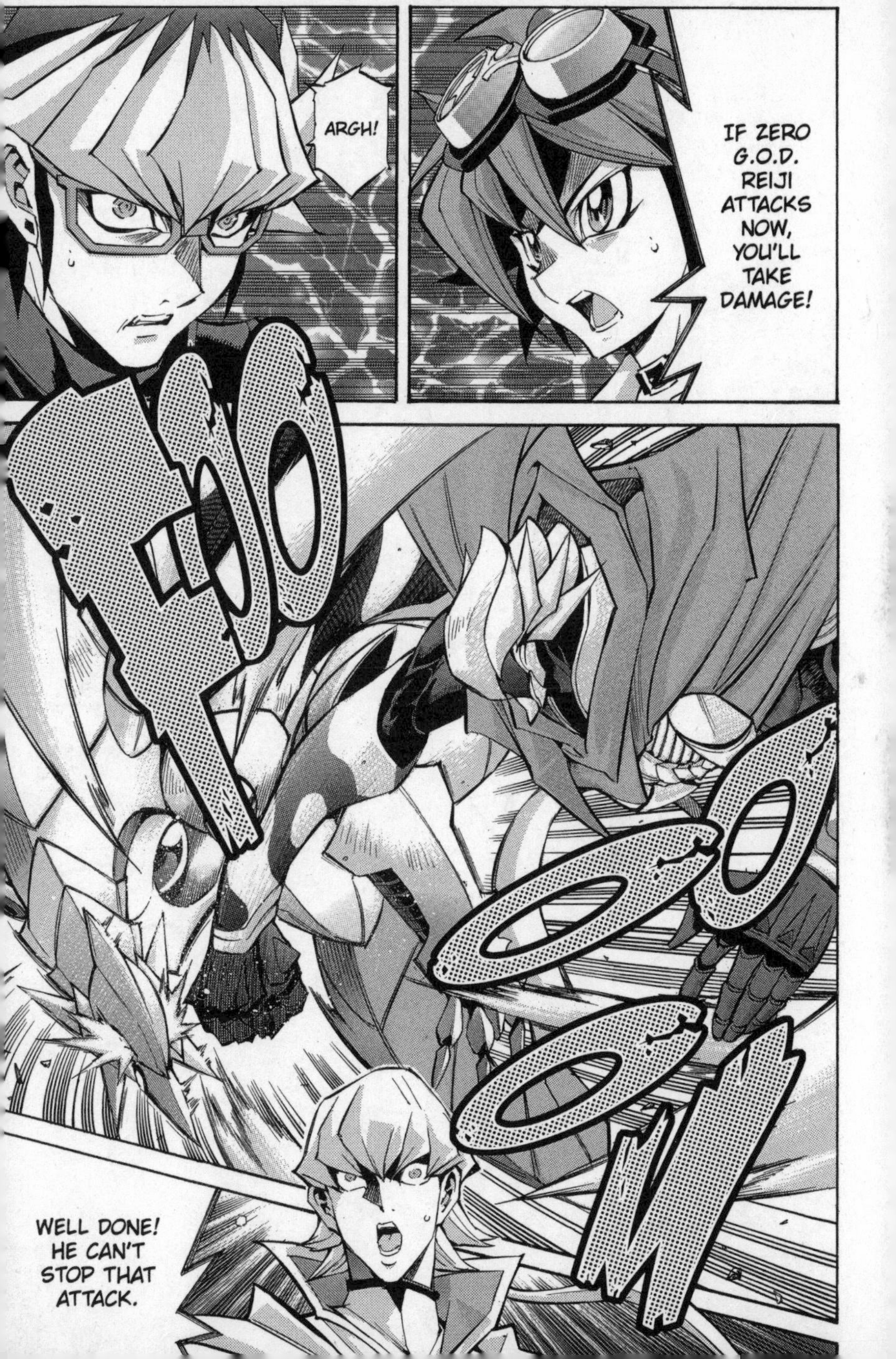
IF ZERO G.O.D. REIJI ATTACKS NOW, YOU'LL TAKE DAMAGE!
ARGH!
WELL DONE! HE CAN'T STOP THAT ATTACK.

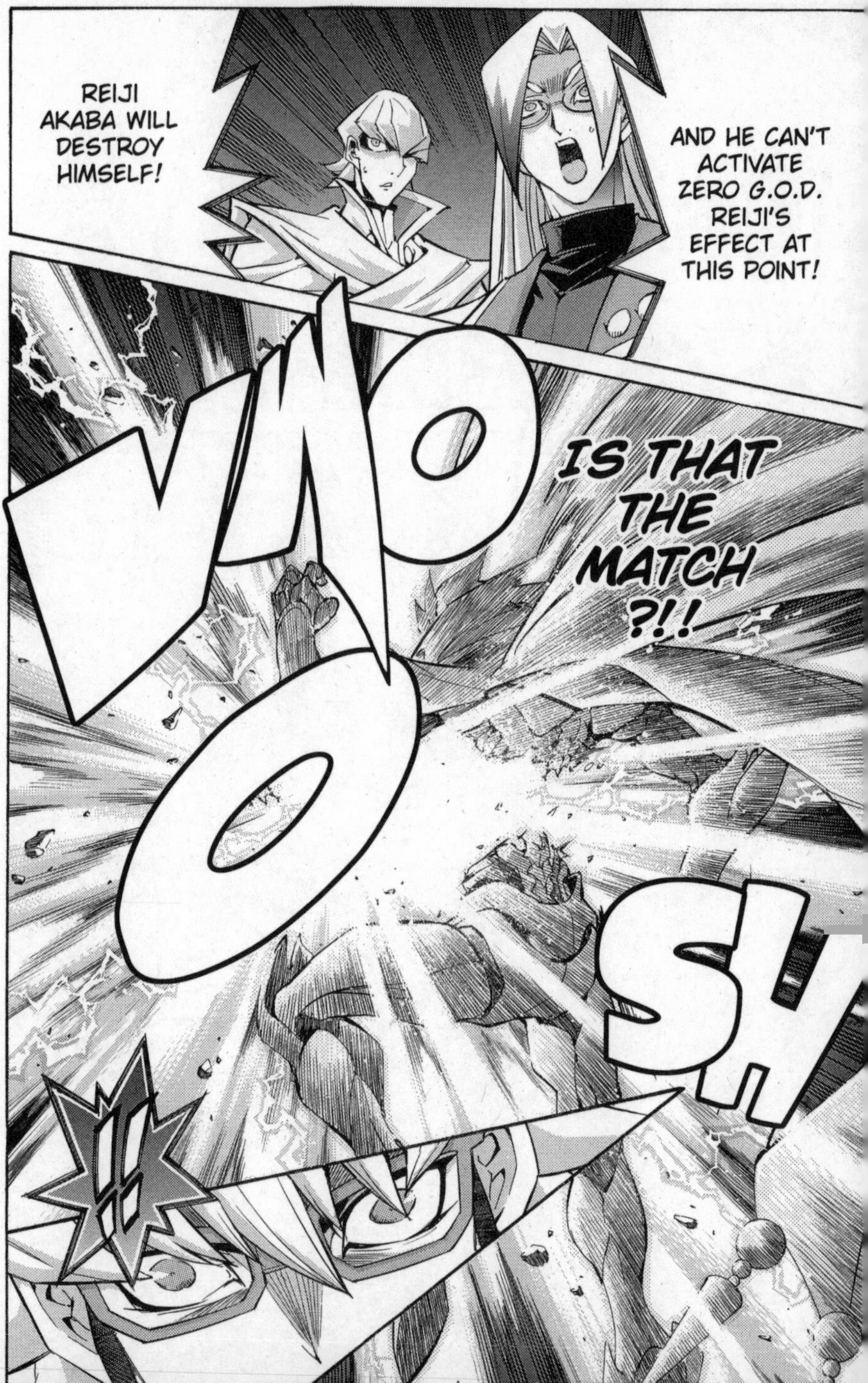
AND HE CAN'T ACTIVATE ZERO G.O.D. REIJI'S EFFECT AT THIS POINT!
REIJI AKABA WILL DESTROY HIMSELF!
IS THAT THE MATCH ?!!
VWOOSH
!!

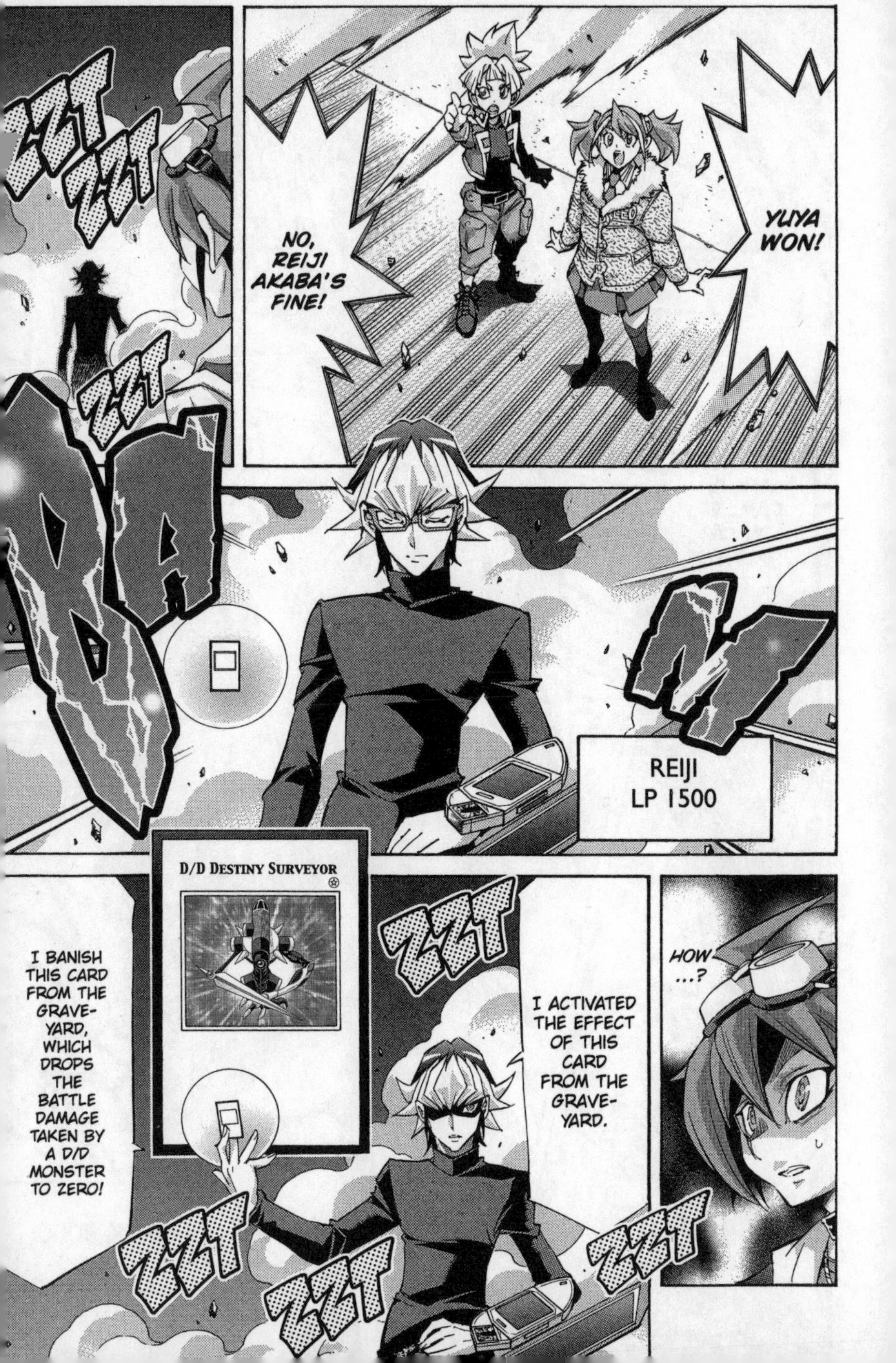
YUYA WON!
NO, REIJI AKABA'S FINE!
ZZT ZZT
ZZT
BAM
REIJI LP 1500
HOW ...?
ZZT
I ACTIVATED THE EFFECT OF THIS CARD FROM THE GRAVEYARD.
D/D DESTINY SURVEYOR
I BANISH THIS CARD FROM THE GRAVEYARD, WHICH DROPS THE BATTLE DAMAGE TAKEN BY A D/D MONSTER TO ZERO!
ZZT
ZZT
ZZT

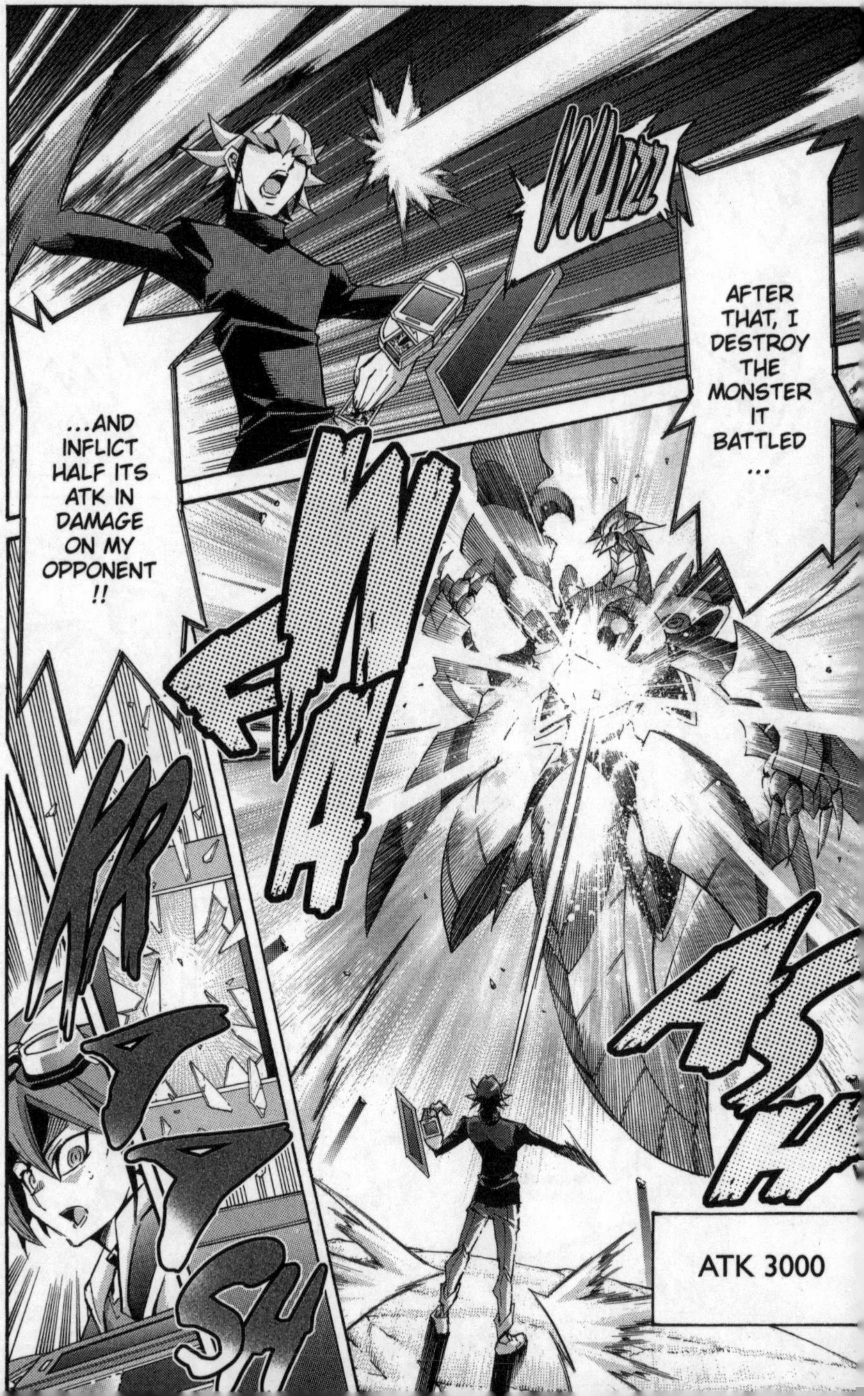
AFTER THAT, I DESTROY THE MONSTER IT BATTLED ...
...AND INFLICT HALF ITS ATK IN DAMAGE ON MY OPPONENT !!
ATK 3000

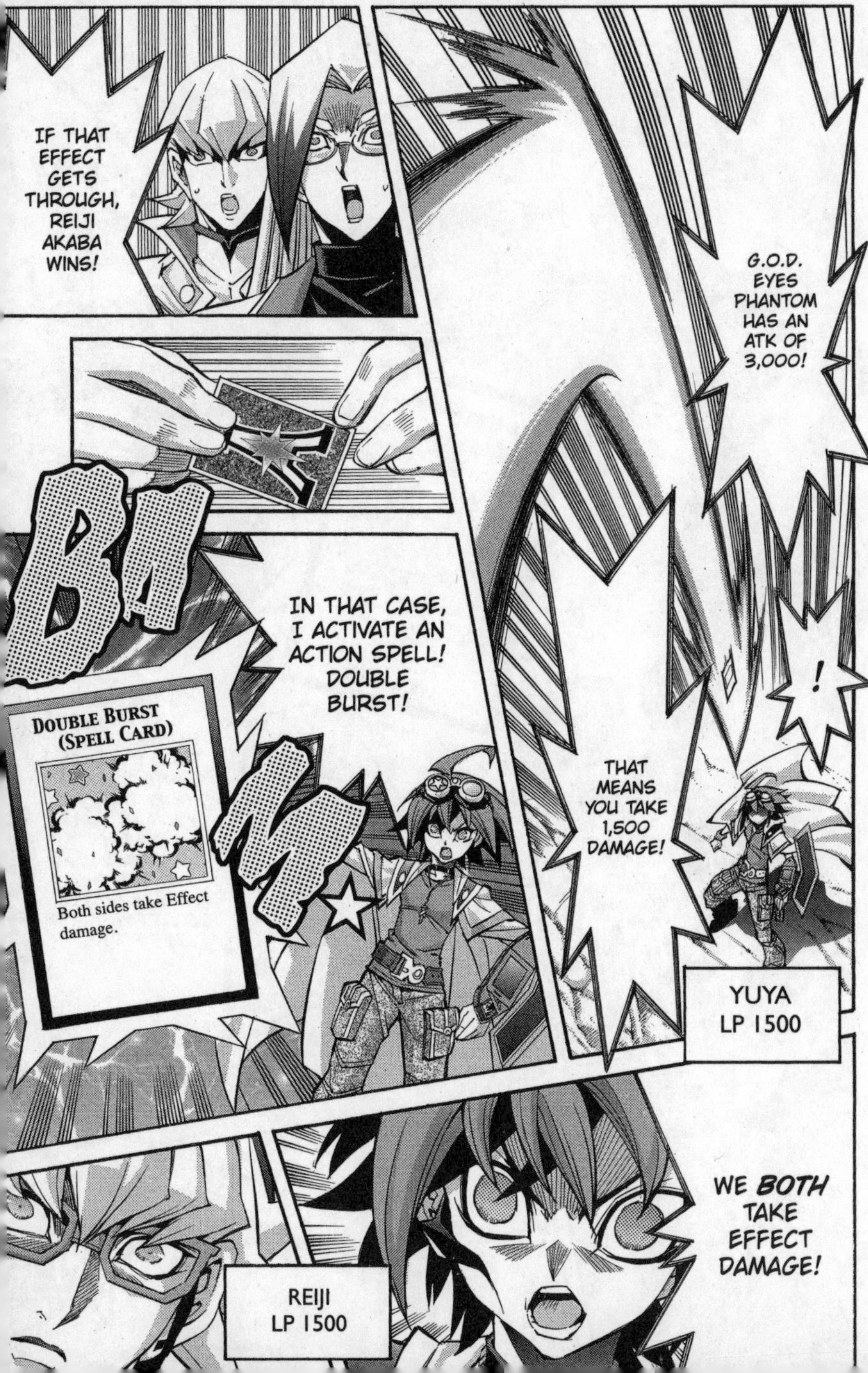
G.O.D. EYES PHANTOM HAS AN ATK OF 3,000!
!
THAT MEANS YOU TAKE 1,500 DAMAGE!
YUYA
LP 1500
IF THAT EFFECT GETS THROUGH, REIJI AKABA WINS!
BAM
IN THAT CASE, I ACTIVATE AN ACTION SPELL! DOUBLE BURST!
DOUBLE BURST (SPELL CARD)
Both sides take Effect damage.
WE BOTH TAKE EFFECT DAMAGE!
REIJI
LP 1500

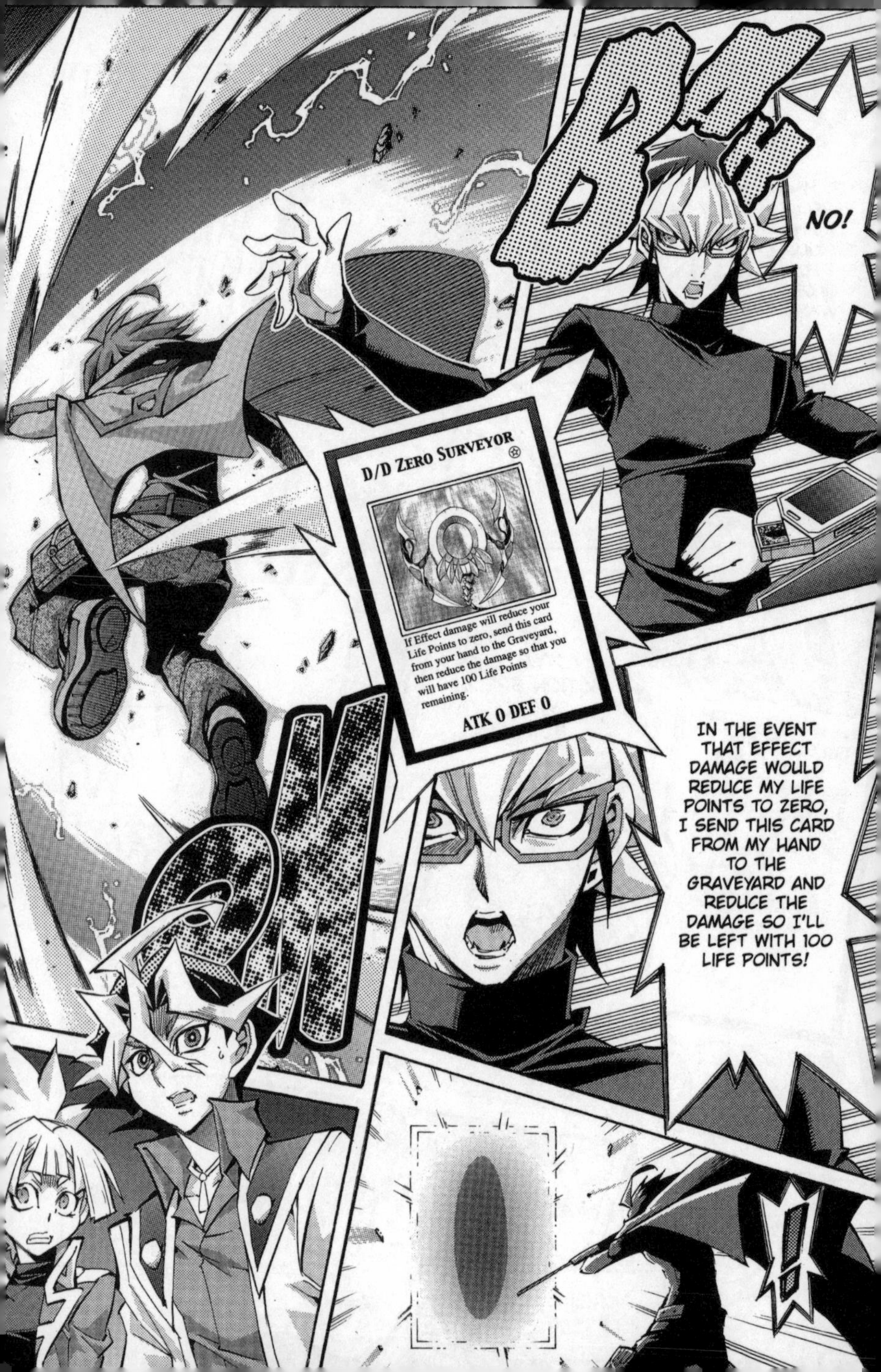
NO!
D/D Zero Surveyor
If Effect damage will reduce your Life Points to zero, send this card from your hand to the Graveyard, then reduce the damage so that you will have 100 Life Points remaining.
ATK 0 DEF 0
IN THE EVENT THAT EFFECT DAMAGE WOULD REDUCE MY LIFE POINTS TO ZERO, I SEND THIS CARD FROM MY HAND TO THE GRAVEYARD AND REDUCE THE DAMAGE SO I'LL BE LEFT WITH 100 LIFE POINTS!
!

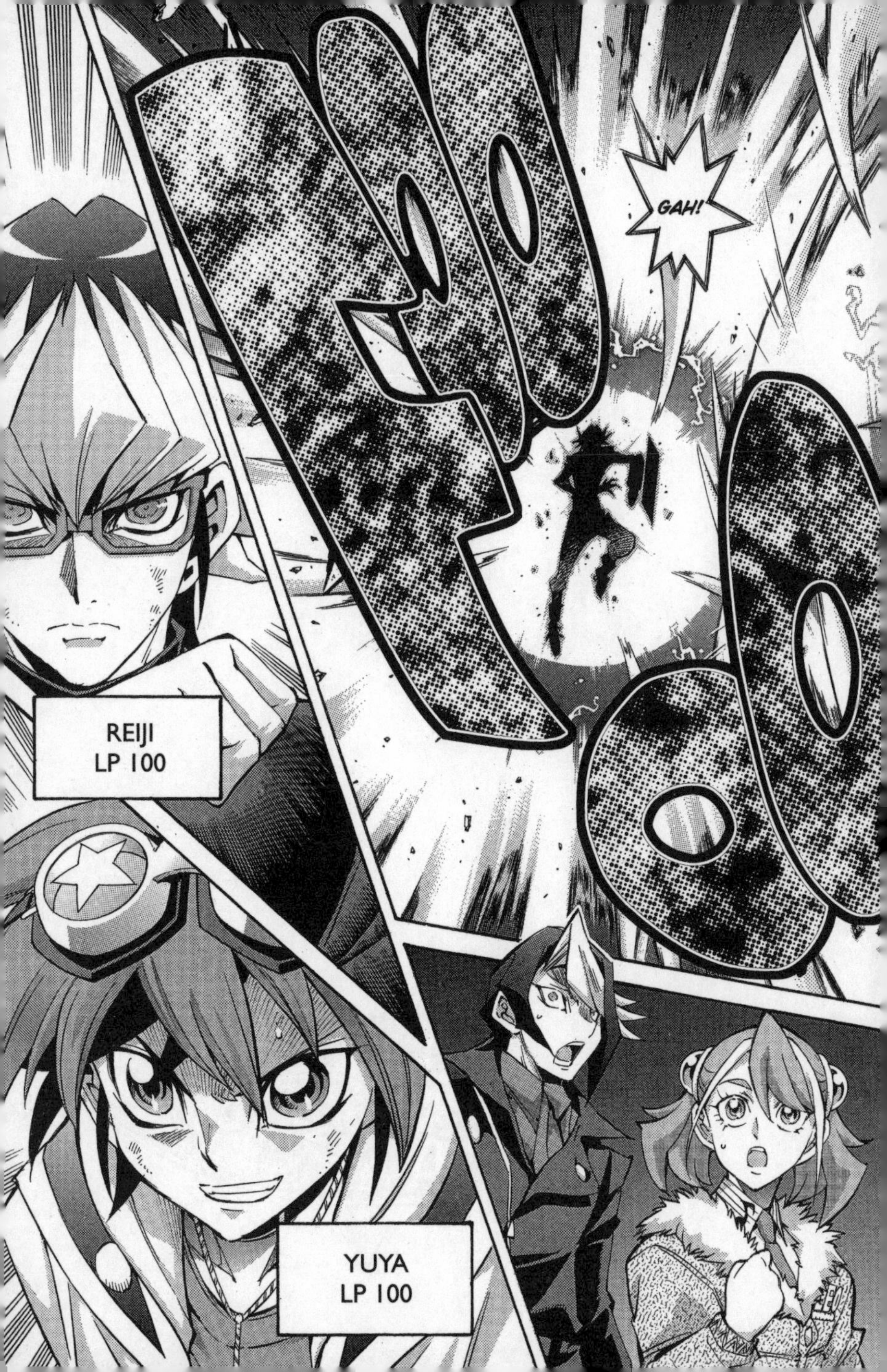
GAH!
REIJI
LP 100
YUYA
LP 100

Yu-Gi-Oh!
ARC-V

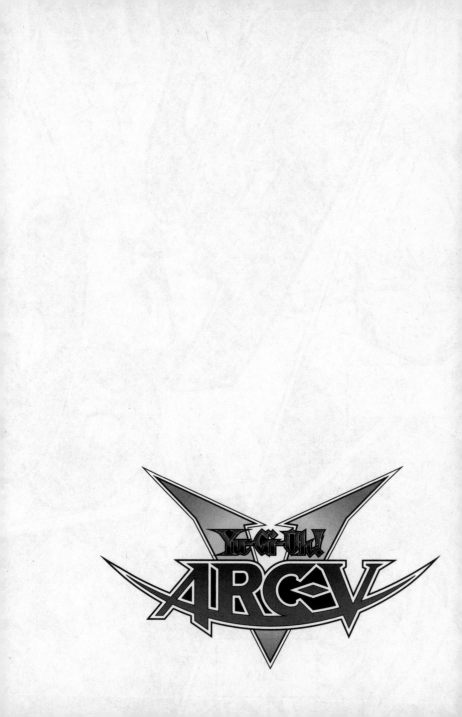

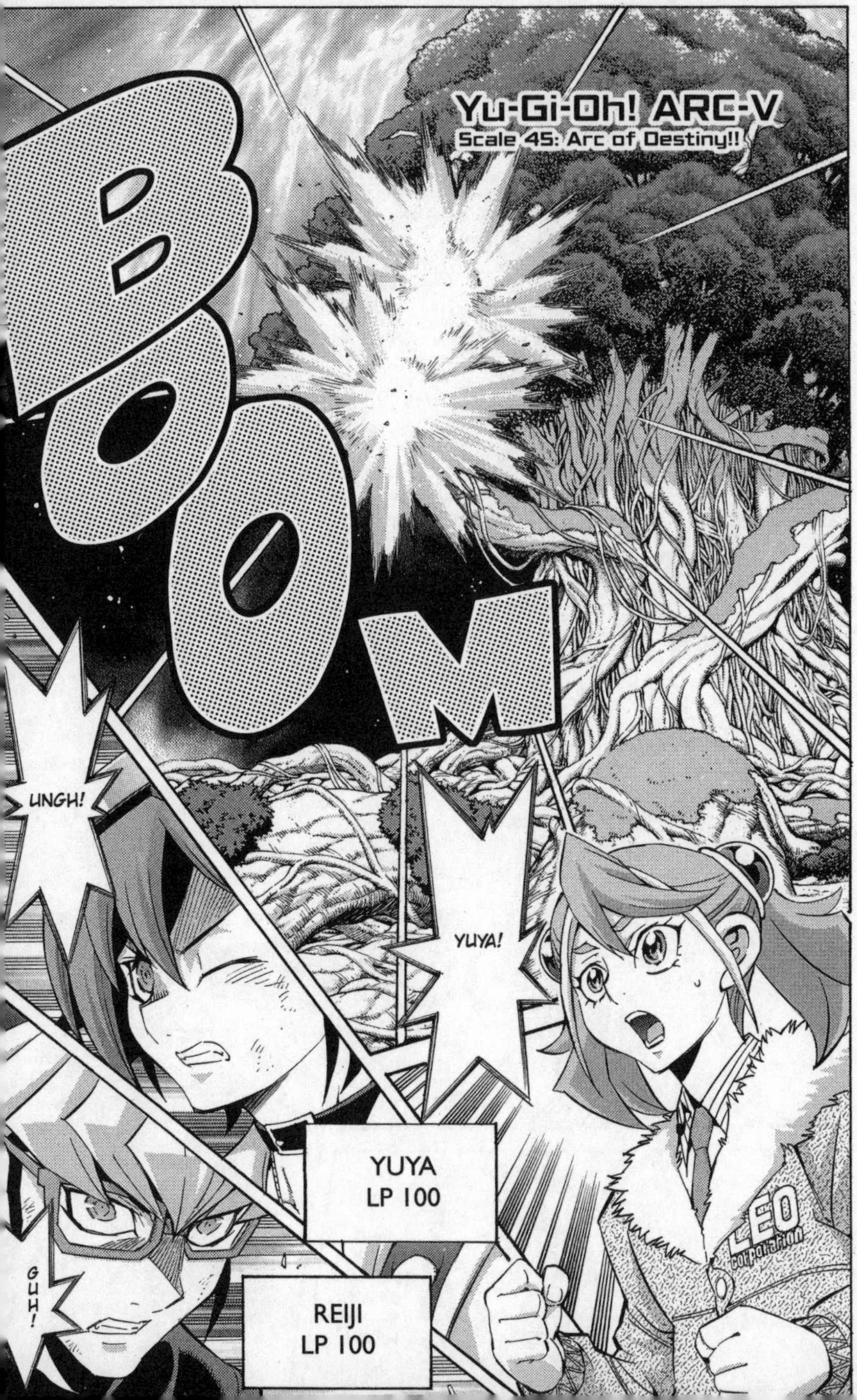
Yu-Gi-Oh! ARC-V
Scale 45: Arc of Destiny!!
BOOM
YUYA!
UNGH!
YUYA
LP 100
GUH!
REIJI
LP 100

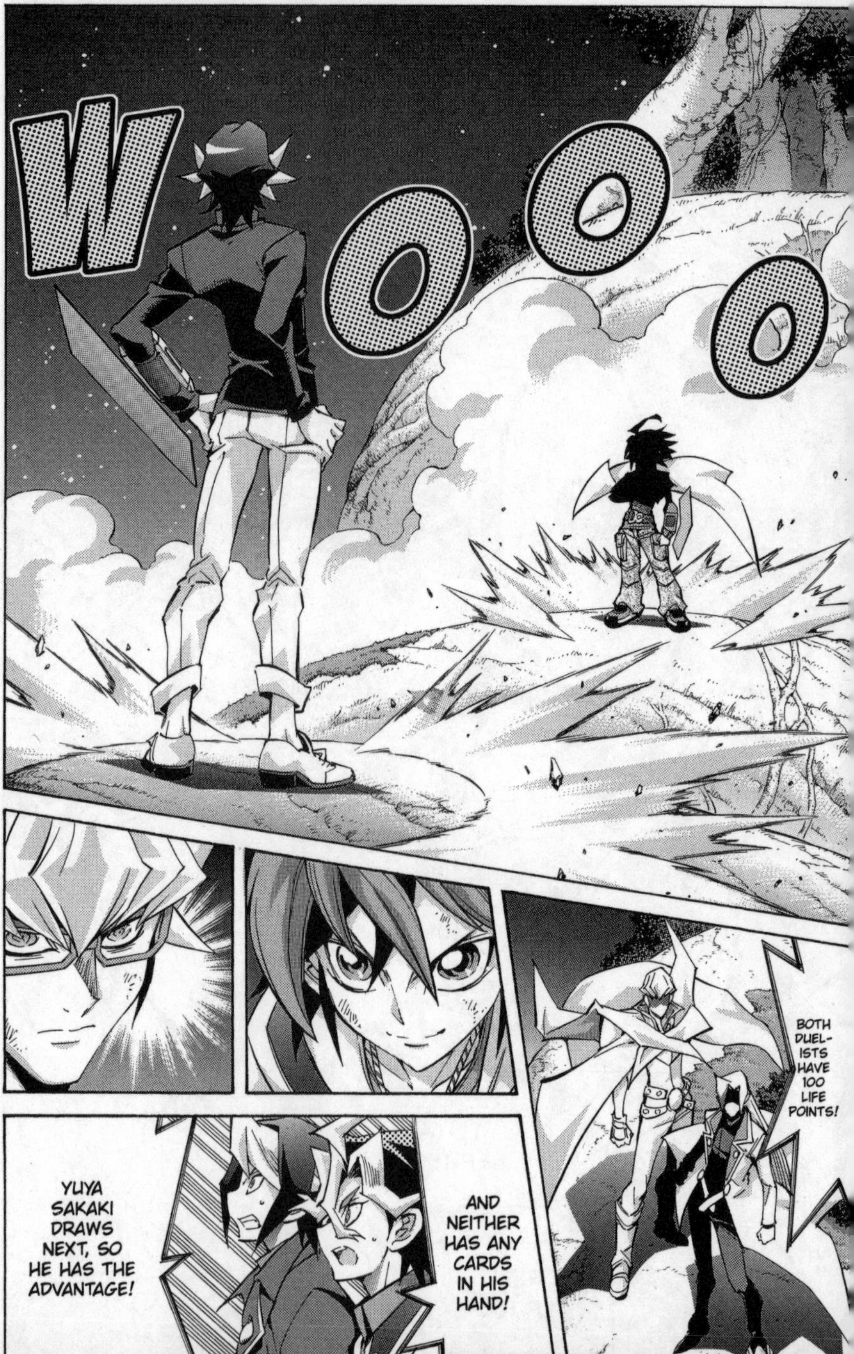
WOOOO
BOTH DUEL-ISTS HAVE 100 LIFE POINTS!
YUYA SAKAKI DRAWS NEXT, SO HE HAS THE ADVANTAGE!
AND NEITHER HAS ANY CARDS IN HIS HAND!

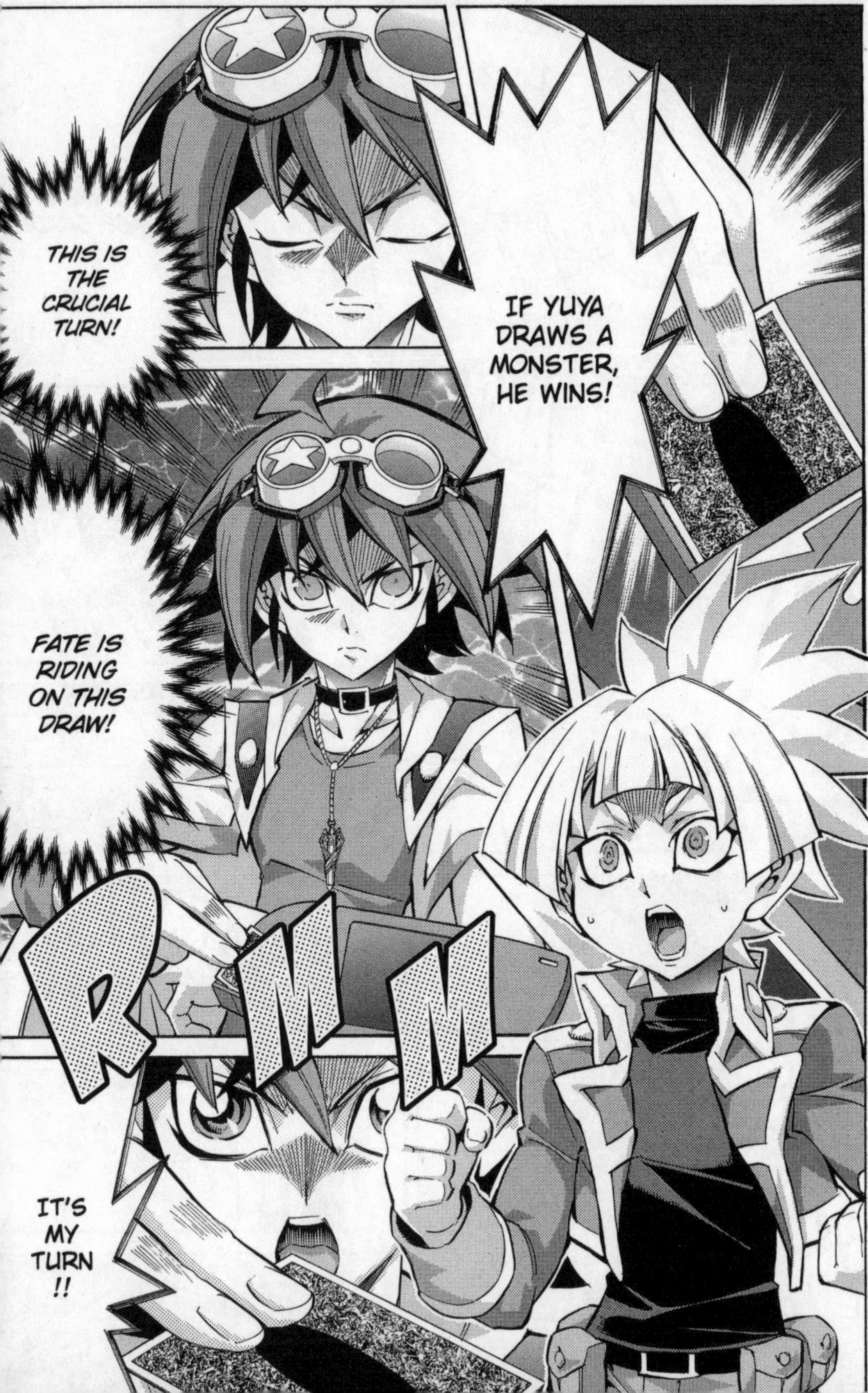
IF YUYA DRAWS A MONSTER, HE WINS!
THIS IS THE CRUCIAL TURN!
FATE IS RIDING ON THIS DRAW!
RMM
IT'S MY TURN !!

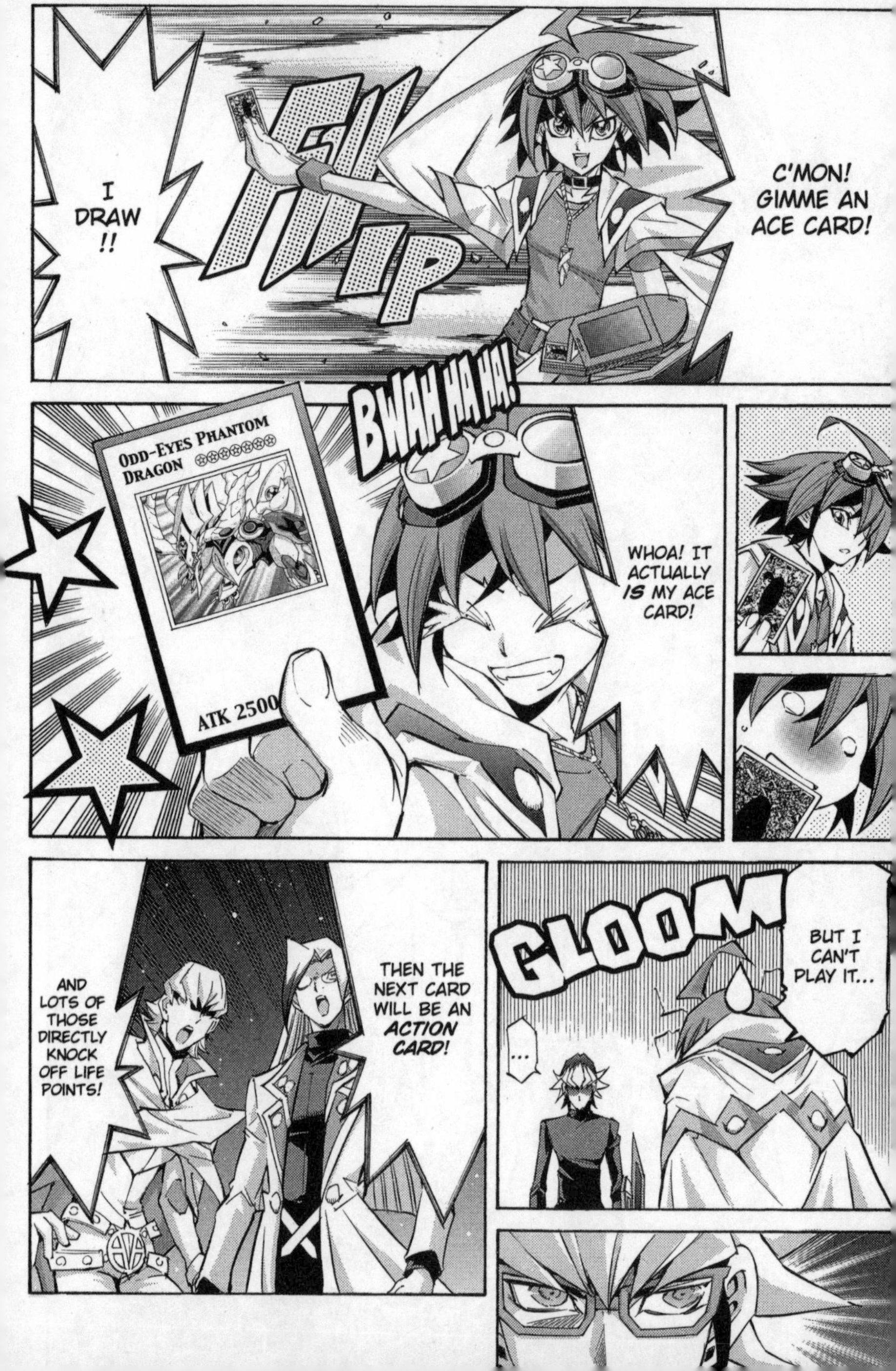
C'MON! GIMME AN ACE CARD!
FLIIP
I DRAW !!
BWAH HA HA!
WHOA! IT ACTUALLY IS MY ACE CARD!
ODD-EYES PHANTOM DRAGON
ATK 2500
GLOOM
BUT I CAN'T PLAY IT...
...
THEN THE NEXT CARD WILL BE AN ACTION CARD!
AND LOTS OF THOSE DIRECTLY KNOCK OFF LIFE POINTS!

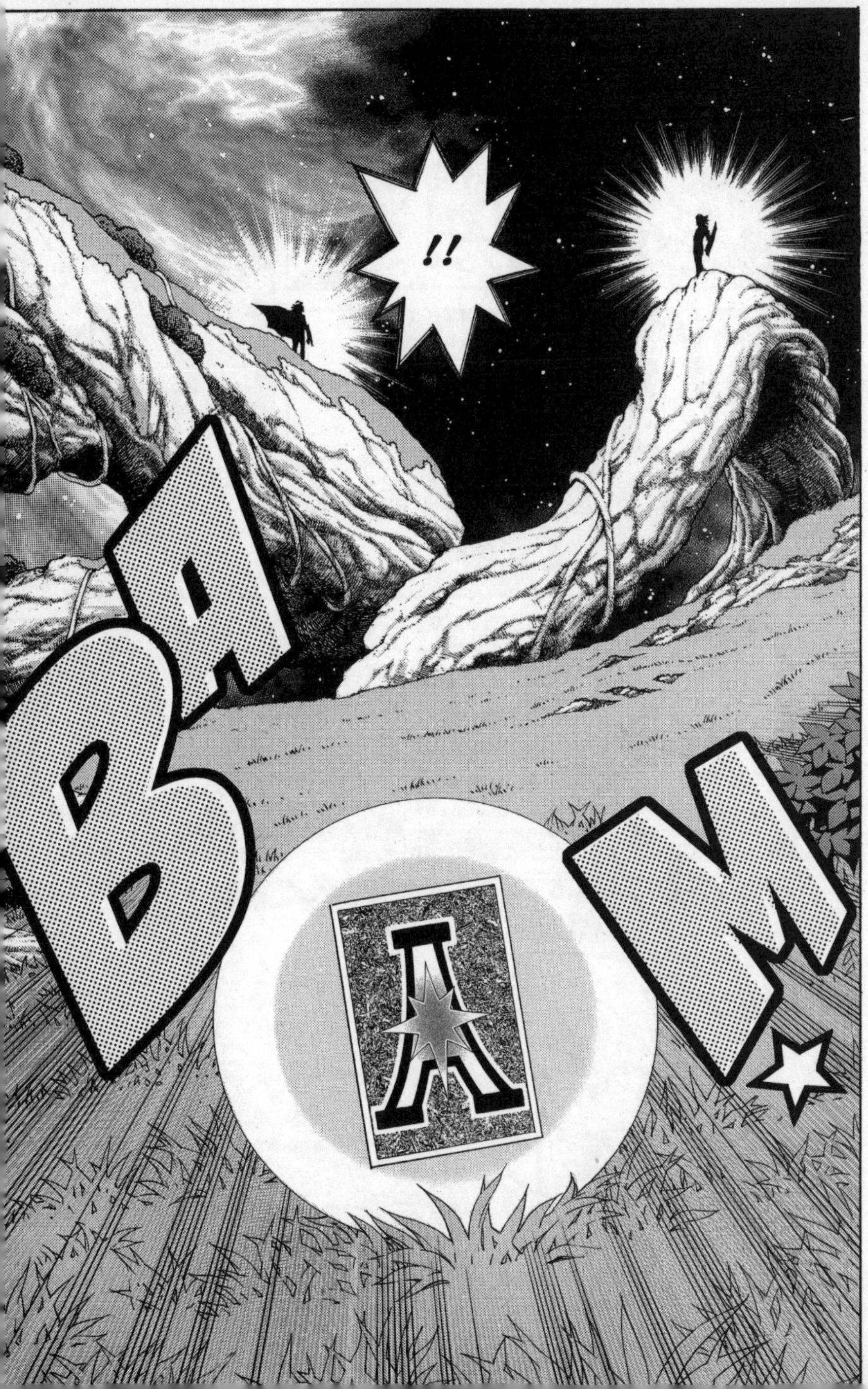
!!
BAM!

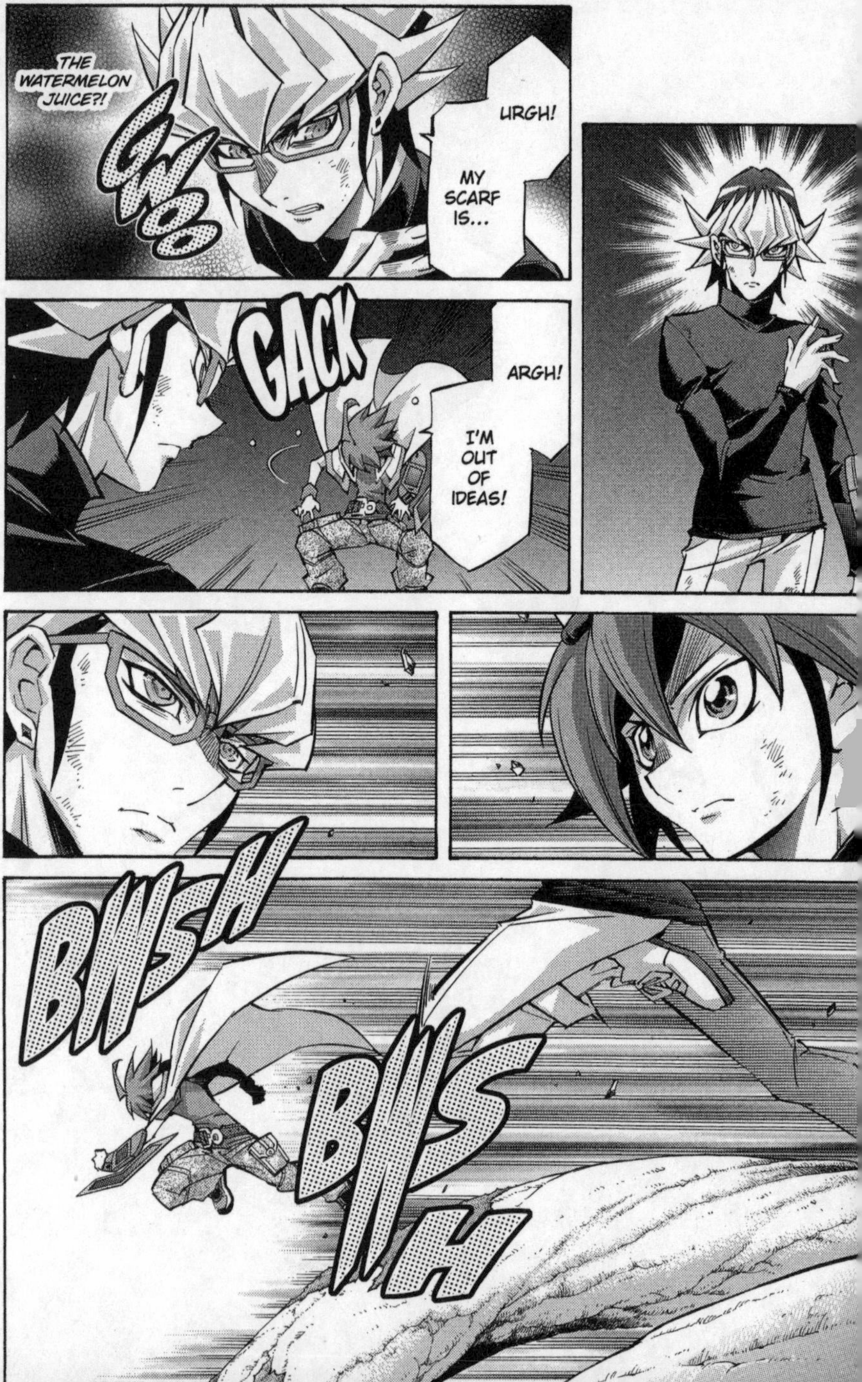
URGH!
MY SCARF IS...
THE WATERMELON JUICE?!
GWOO
ARGH!
I'M OUT OF IDEAS!
GACK
BWSH
BWSH

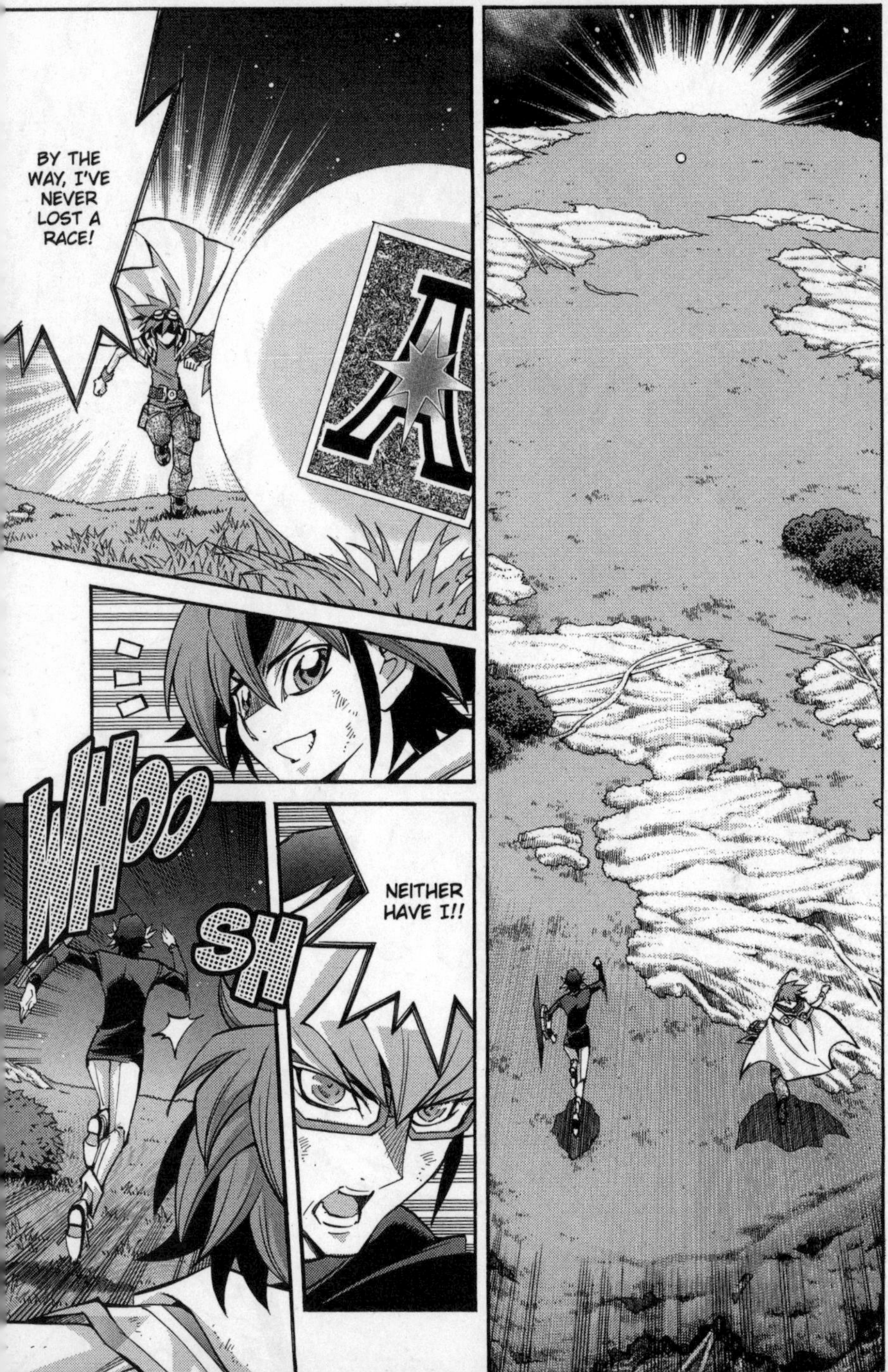
BY THE WAY, I'VE NEVER LOST A RACE!
WHOOSH
NEITHER HAVE I!!

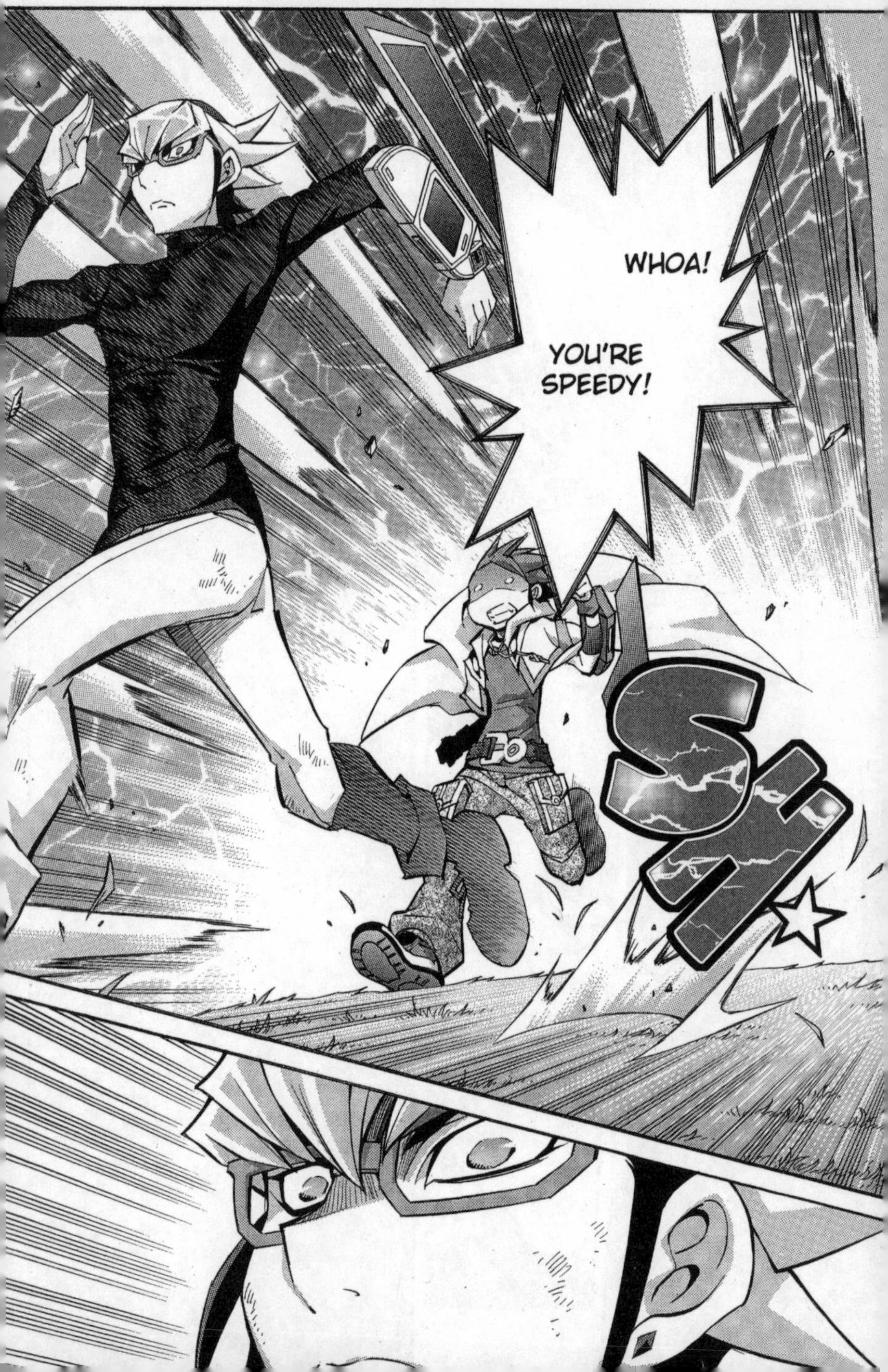
WHOA!
YOU'RE SPEEDY!

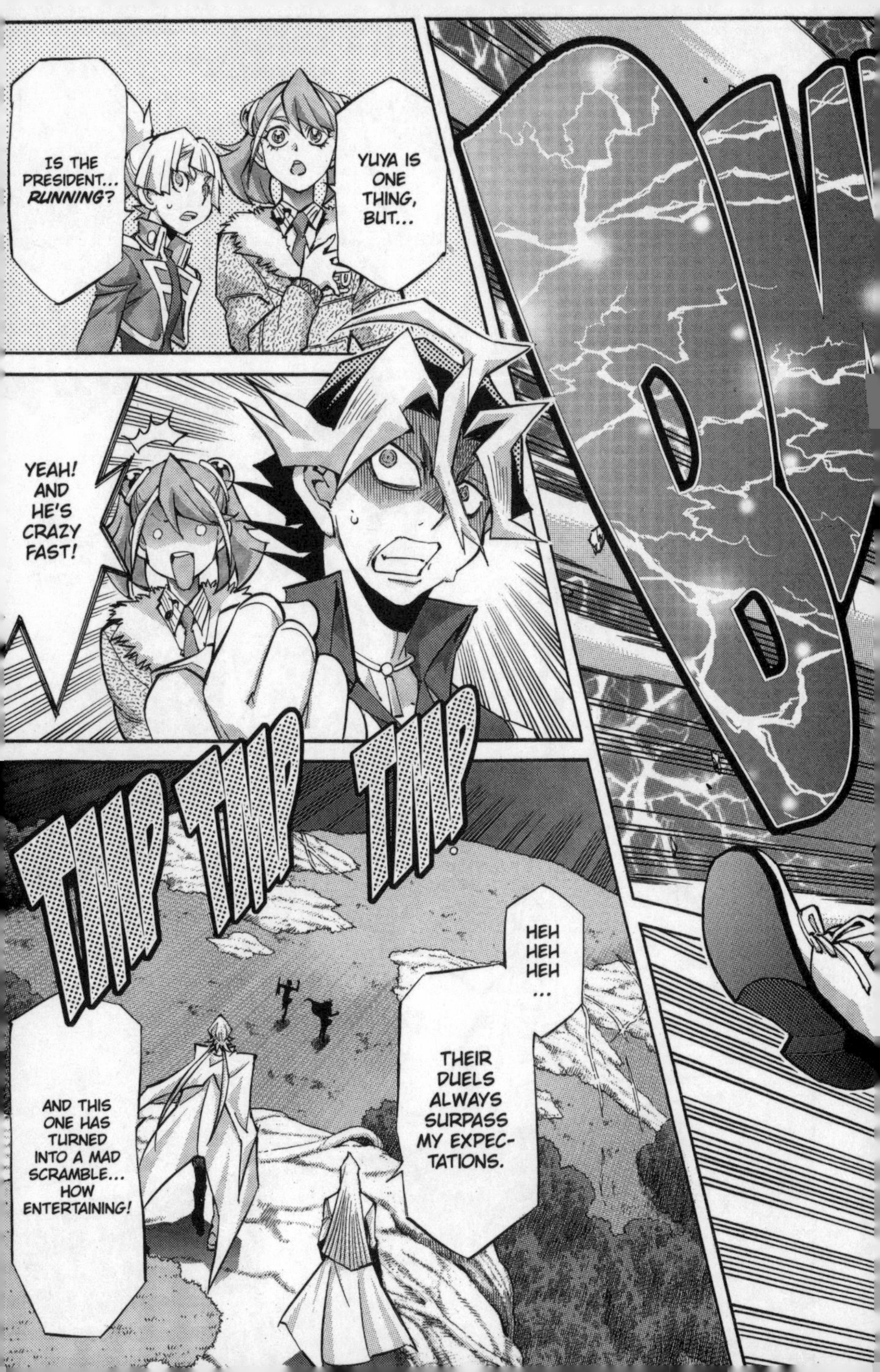
YUYA IS ONE THING, BUT...
IS THE PRESIDENT... *RUNNING*?
YEAH! AND HE'S CRAZY FAST!
TMP
TMP
TMP
HEH HEH HEH ...
THEIR DUELS ALWAYS SURPASS MY EXPECTATIONS.
AND THIS ONE HAS TURNED INTO A MAD SCRAMBLE... HOW ENTERTAINING!

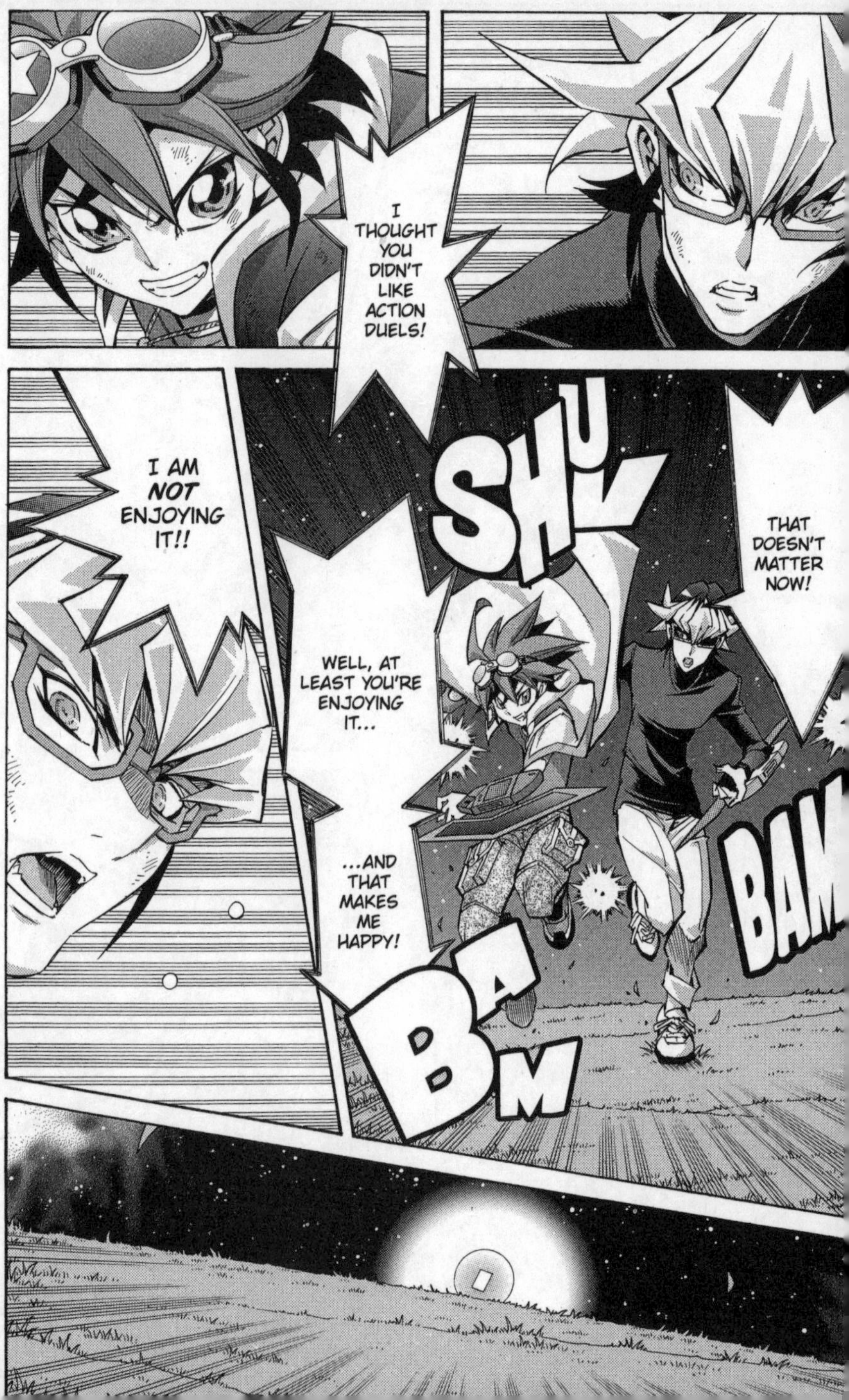
I THOUGHT YOU DIDN'T LIKE ACTION DUELS!
THAT DOESN'T MATTER NOW!
SHUV
BAM
WELL, AT LEAST YOU'RE ENJOYING IT...
...AND THAT MAKES ME HAPPY!
BAM
I AM *NOT* ENJOYING IT!!

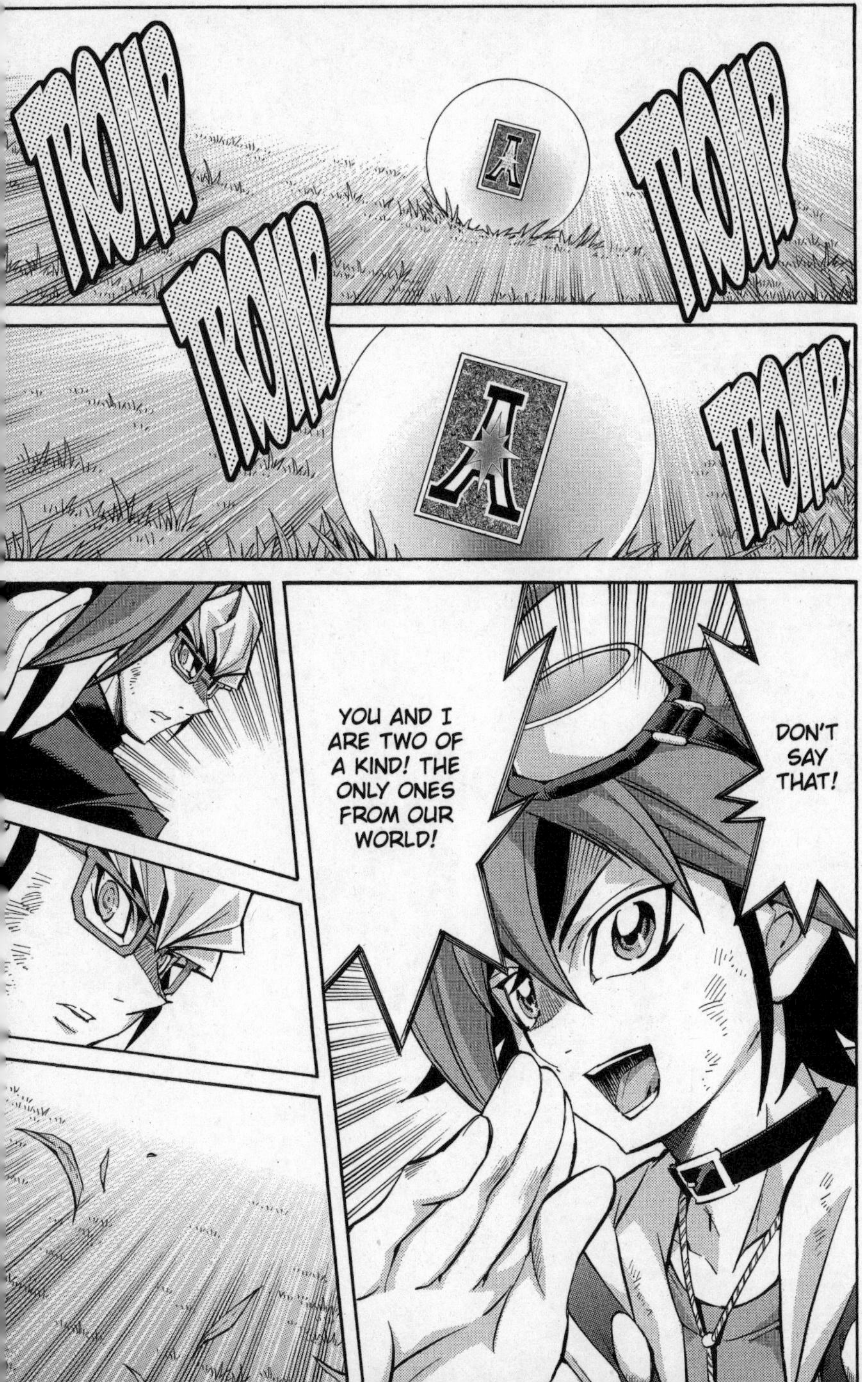
TROMP
TROMP
TROMP
TROMP
DON'T SAY THAT!
YOU AND I ARE TWO OF A KIND! THE ONLY ONES FROM OUR WORLD!

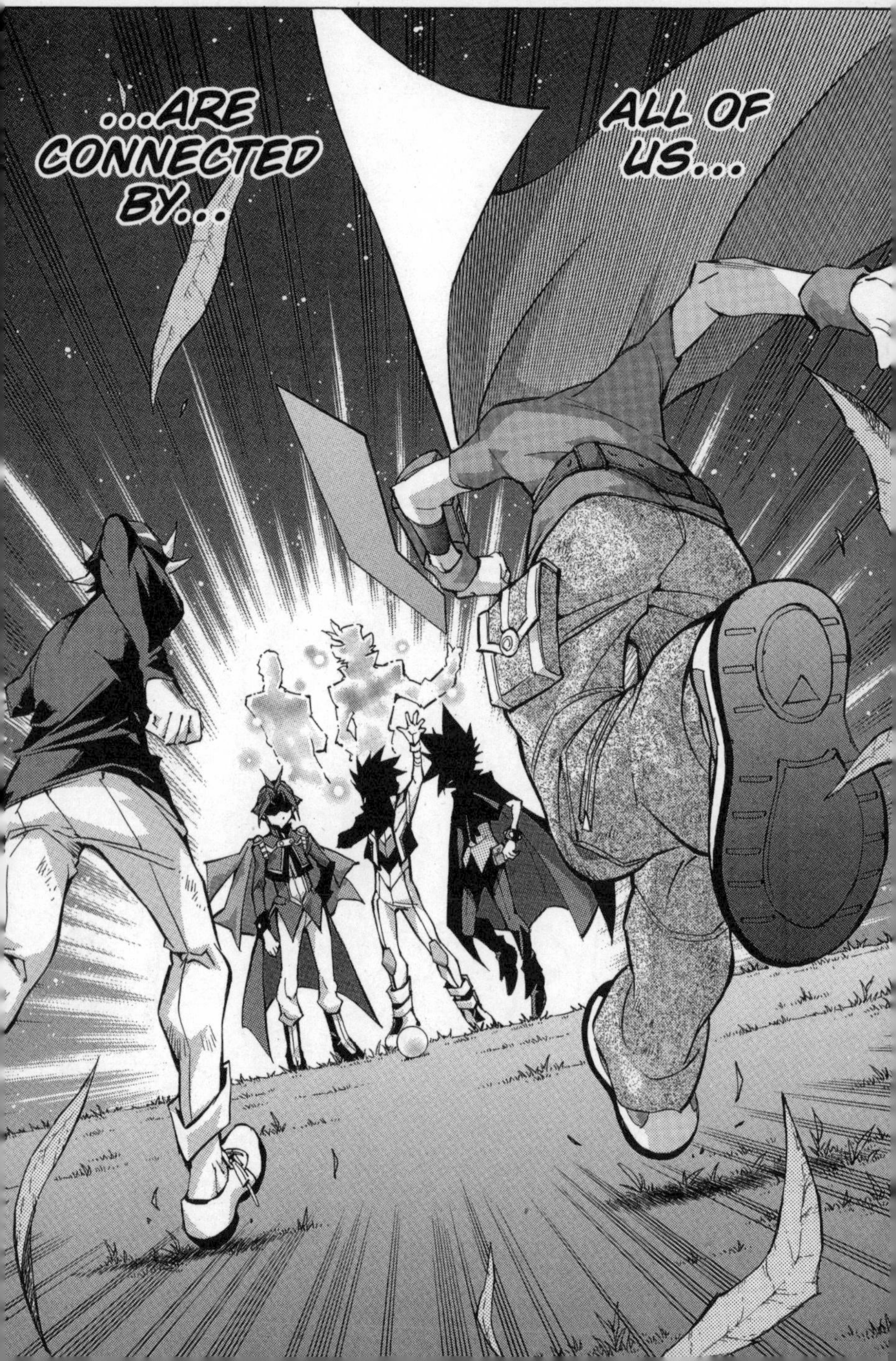
ALL OF US...
...ARE CONNECTED BY...

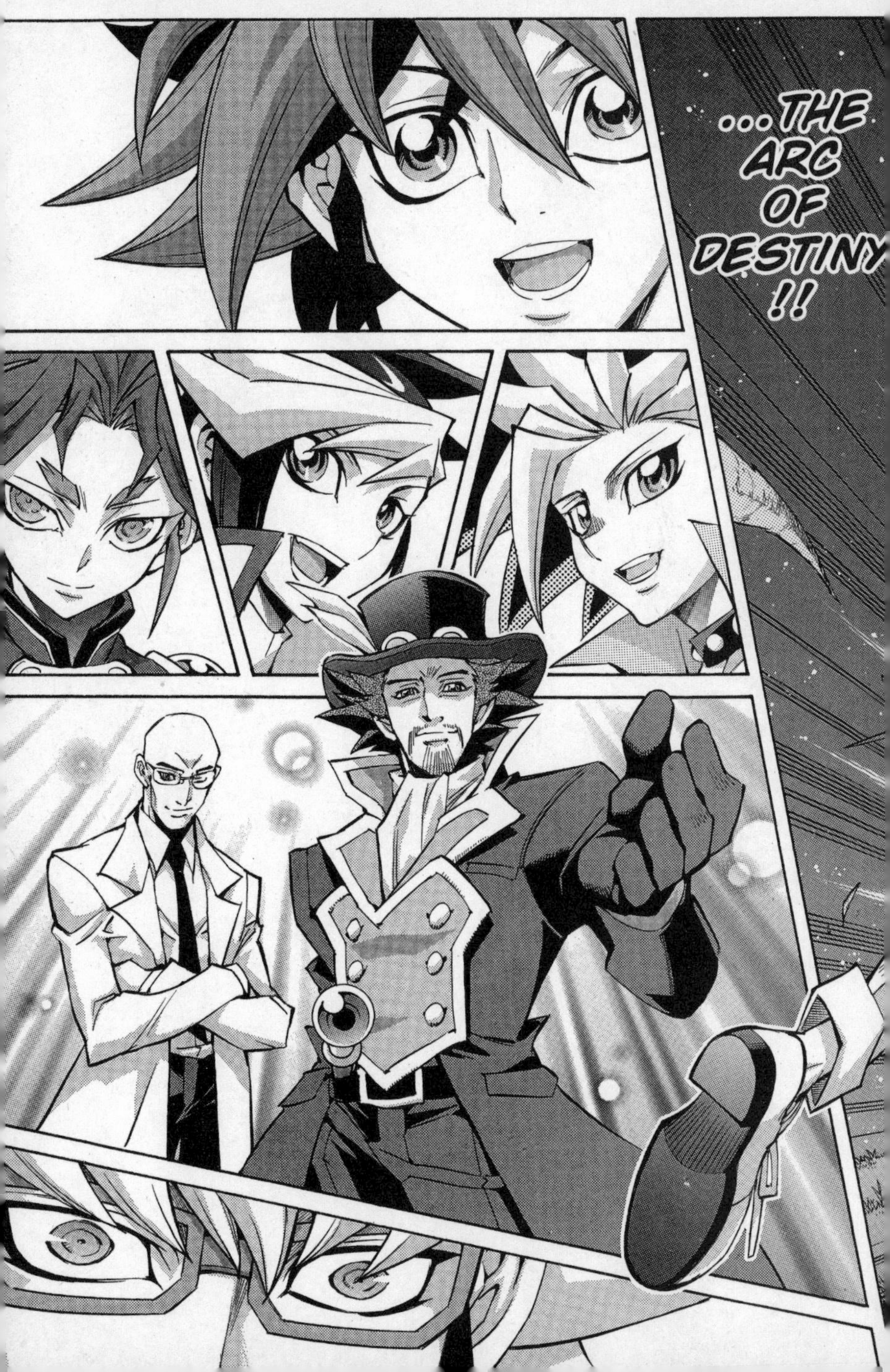
...THE ARC OF DESTINY !!

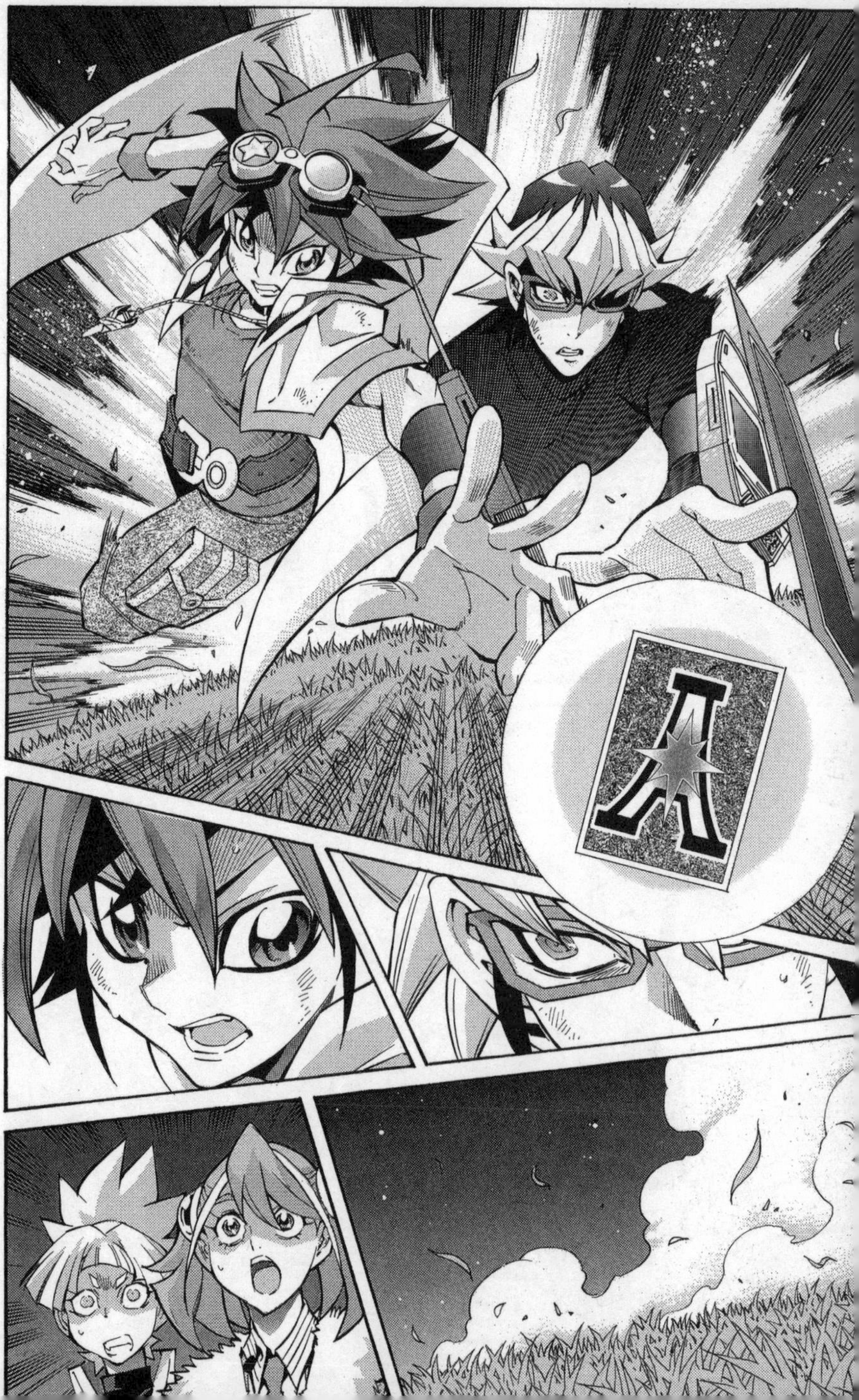

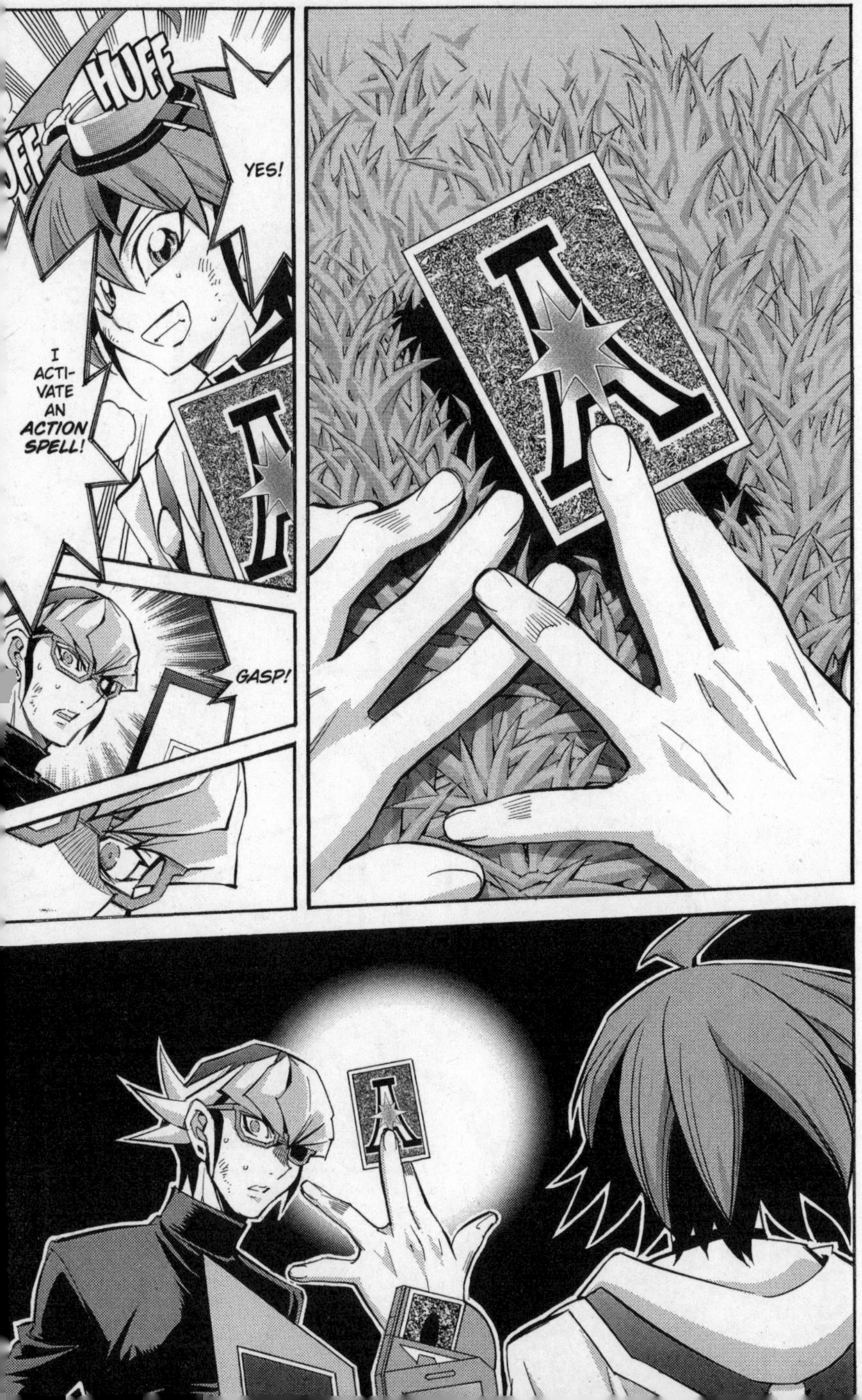
HUFF
HUFF
YES!
I ACTI-VATE AN ACTION SPELL!
GASP!

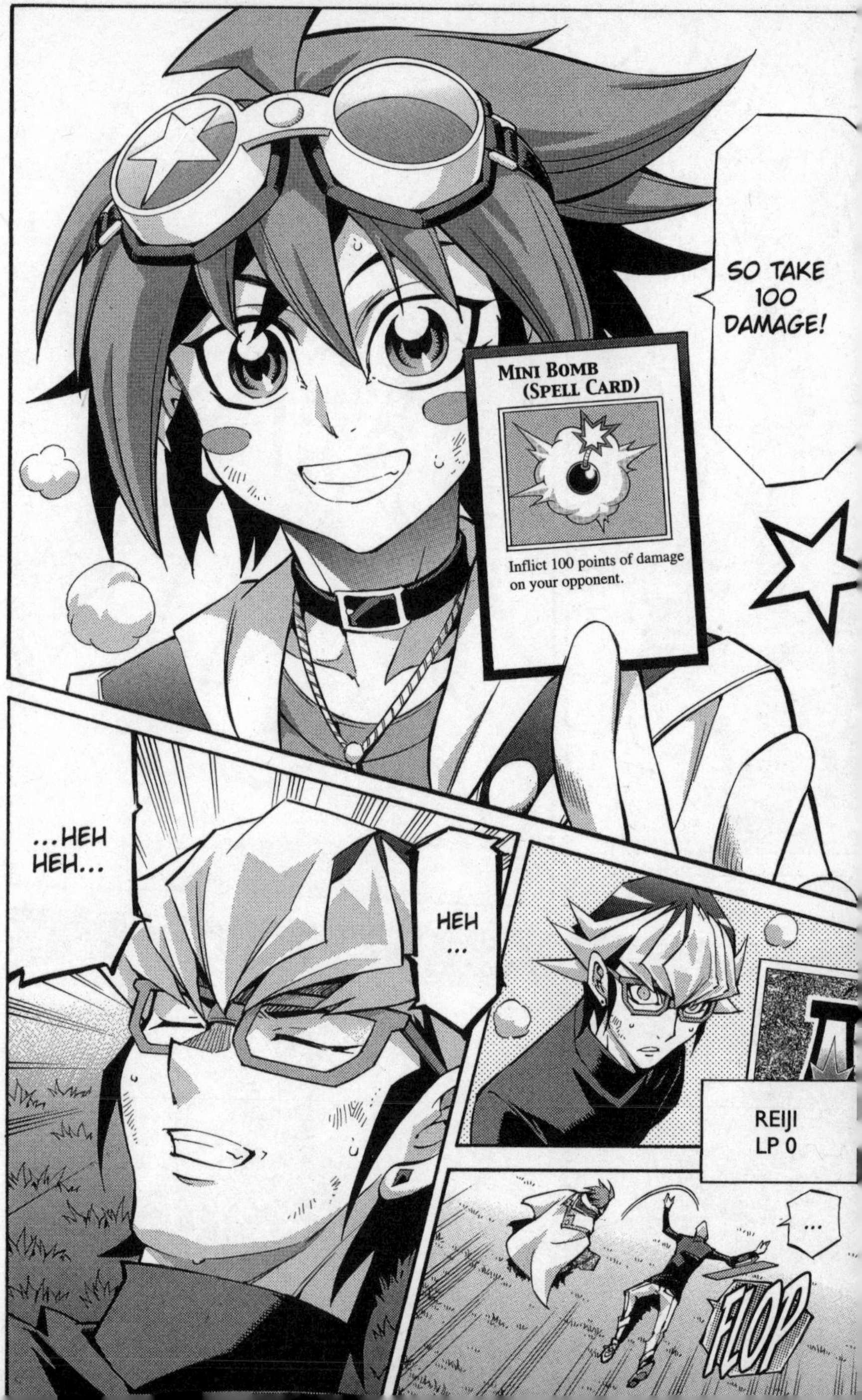
SO TAKE 100 DAMAGE!
MINI BOMB (SPELL CARD)
Inflict 100 points of damage on your opponent.
REIJI LP 0
...
FLOP
HEH ...
...HEH HEH...

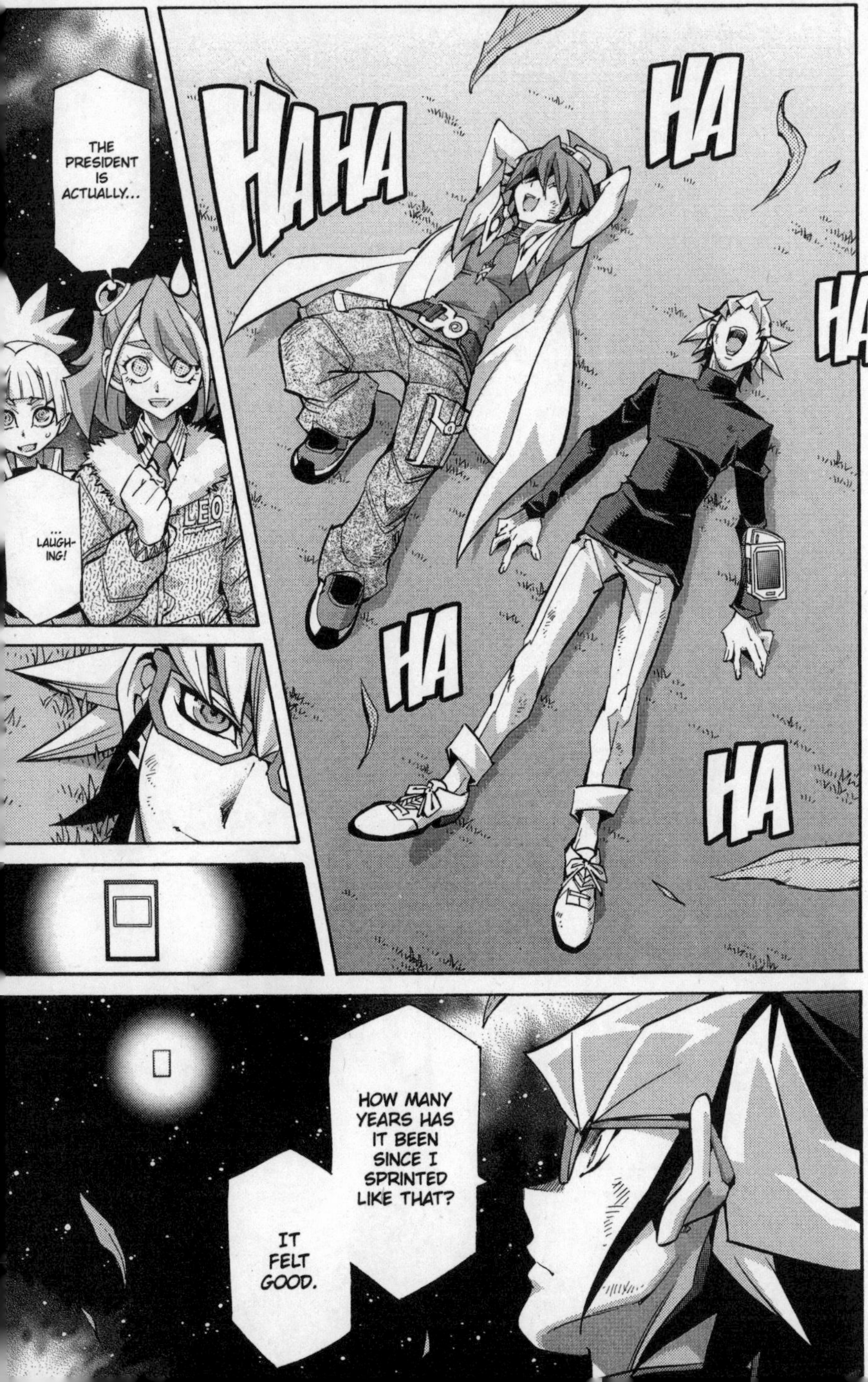
HA
HA
HAHA
HA
HA
THE PRESIDENT IS ACTUALLY...
...LAUGHING!
HOW MANY YEARS HAS IT BEEN SINCE I SPRINTED LIKE THAT?
IT FELT GOOD.

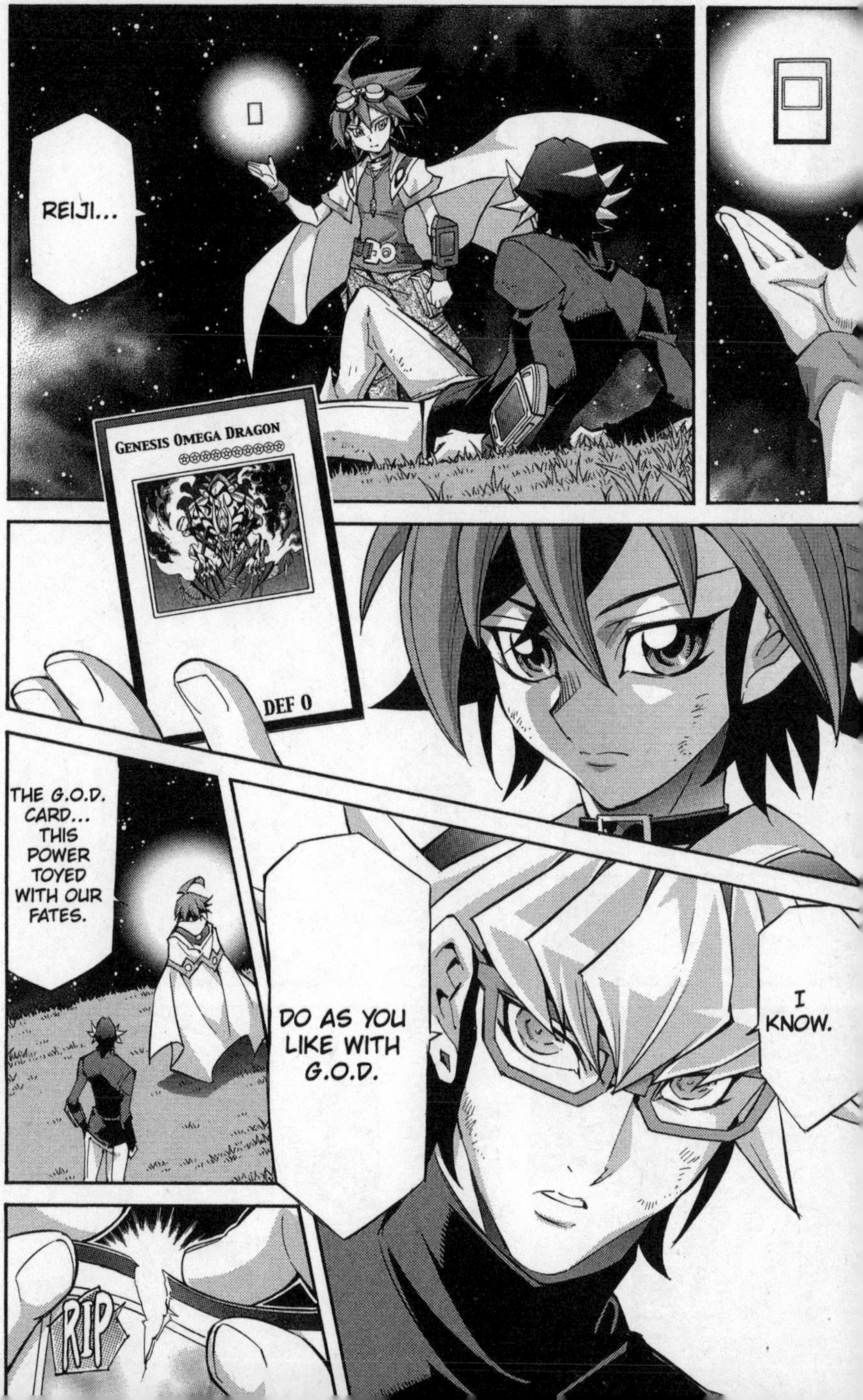
REIJI...
GENESIS OMEGA DRAGON
DEF 0
THE G.O.D. CARD... THIS POWER TOYED WITH OUR FATES.
DO AS YOU LIKE WITH G.O.D.
I KNOW.
RIP

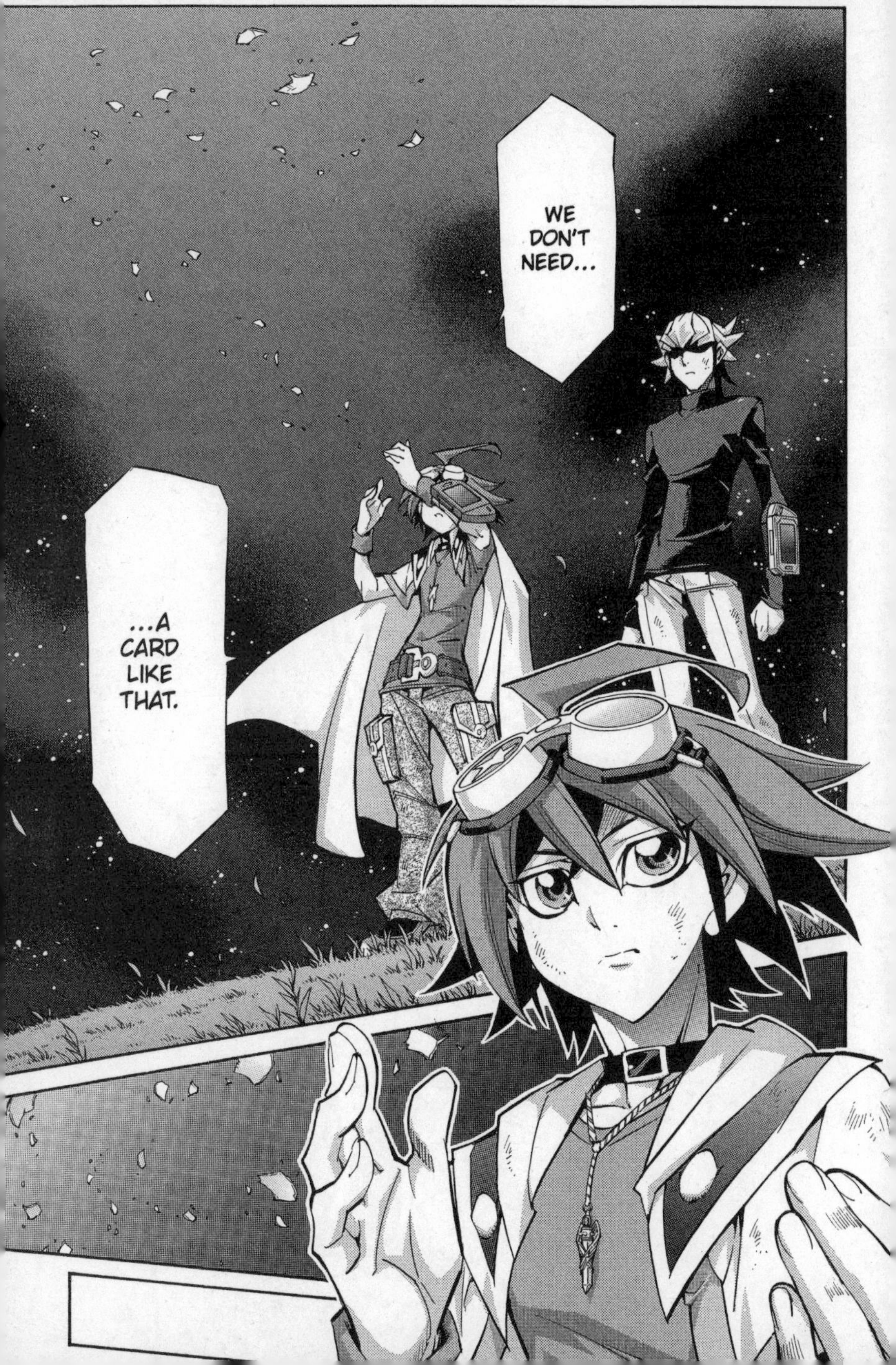
WE DON'T NEED...
...A CARD LIKE THAT.

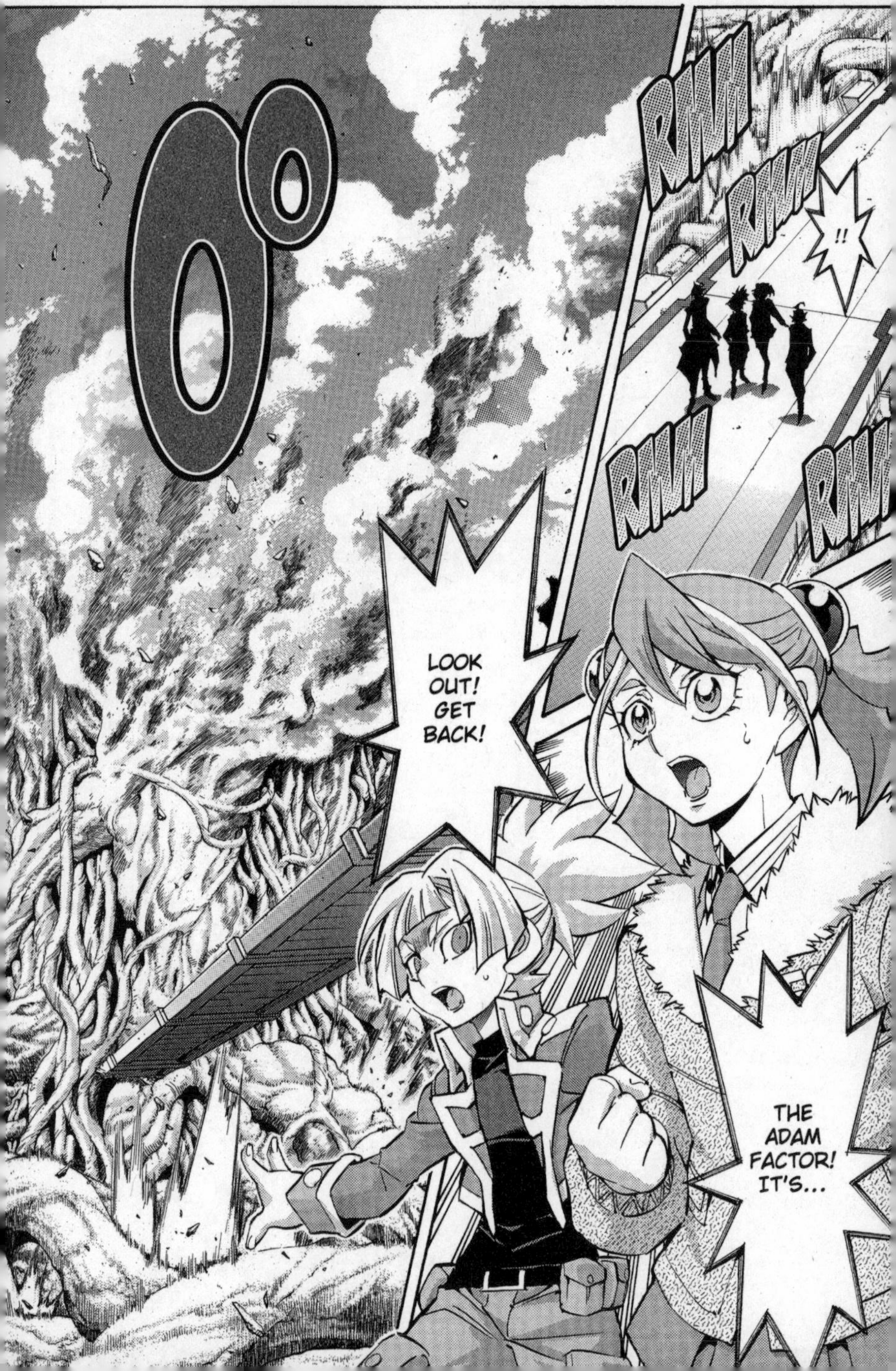
!!
THE ADAM FACTOR! IT'S...
LOOK OUT! GET BACK!

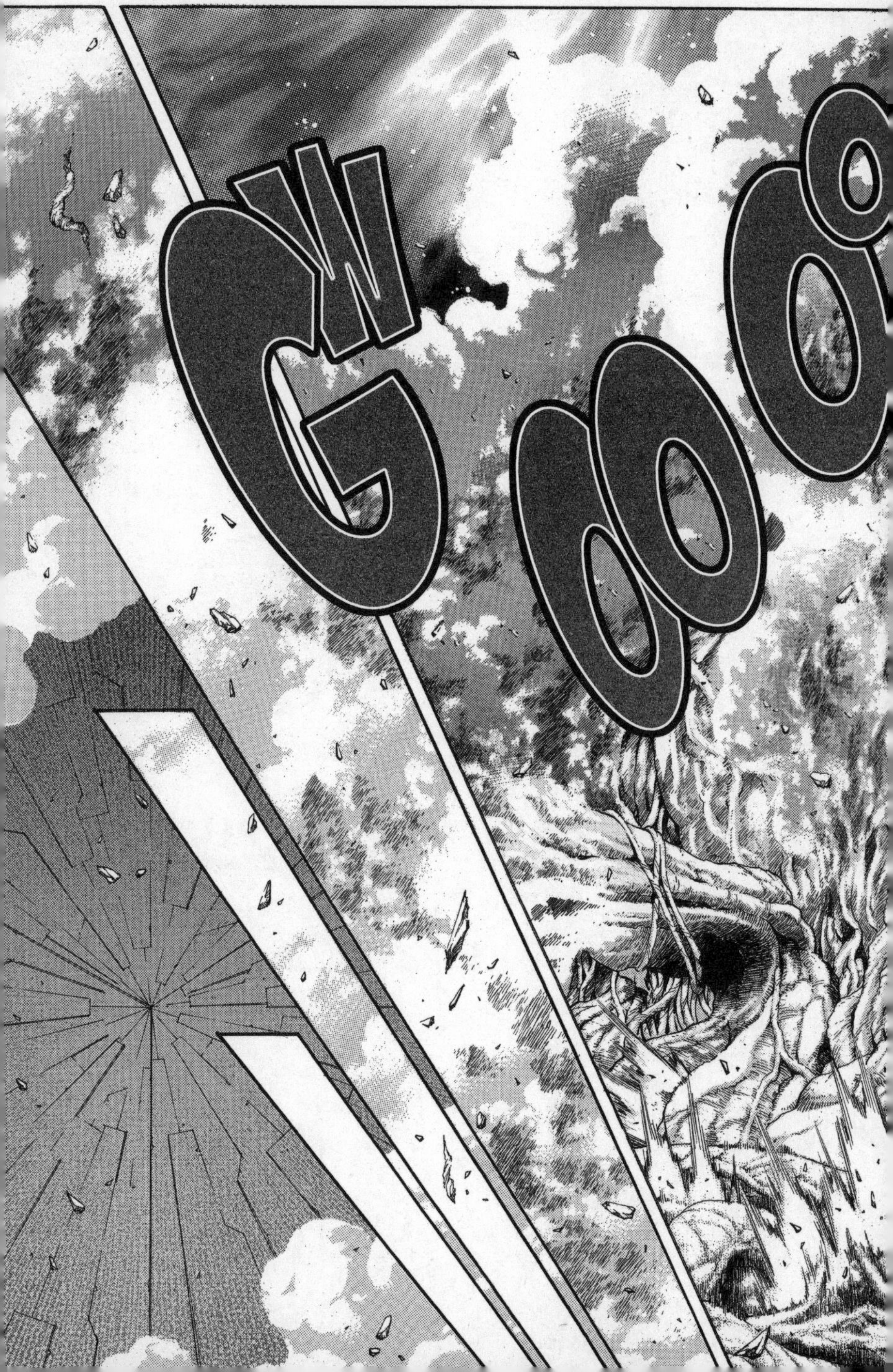
GWOOOO

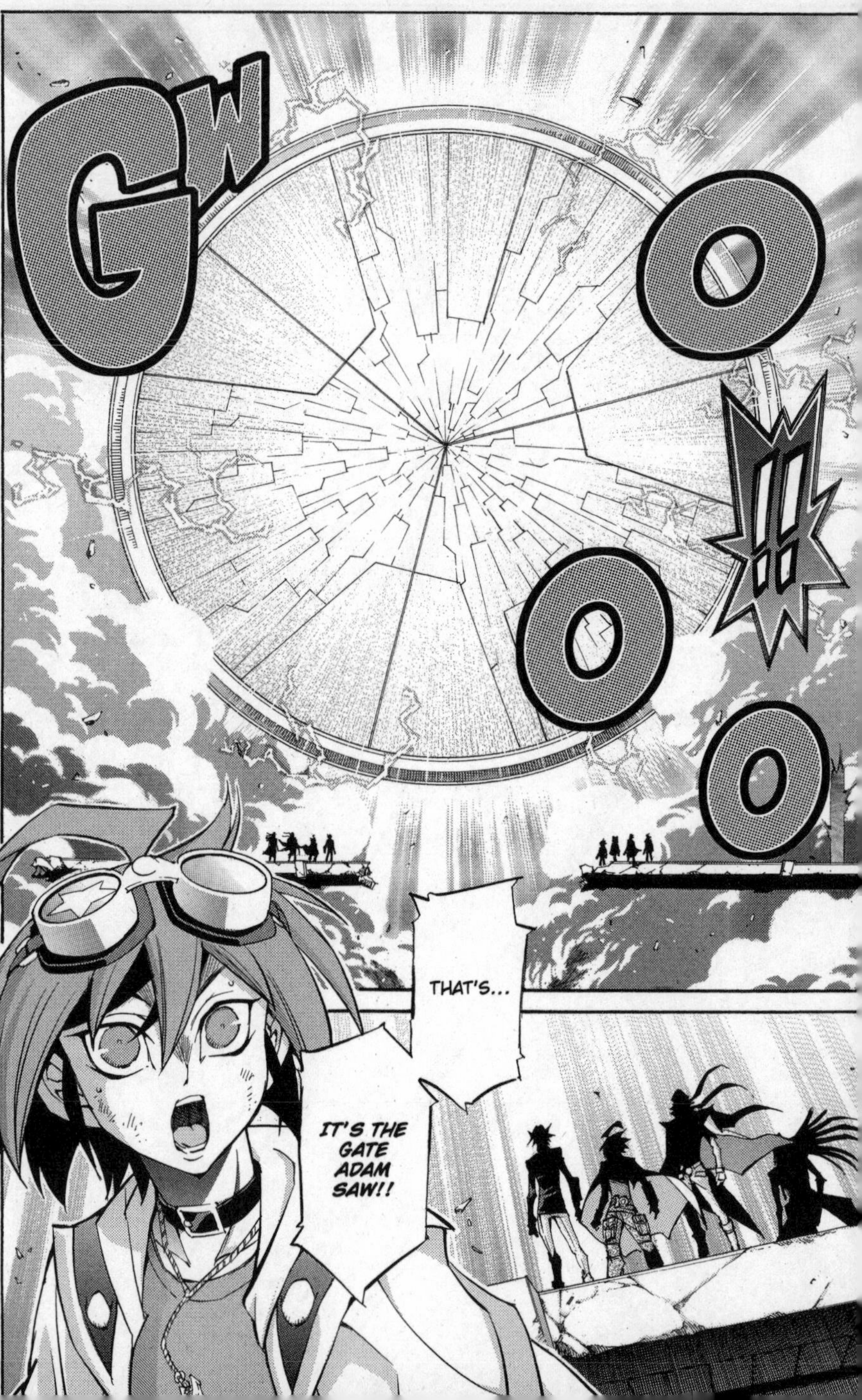
GWOOOO!!
THAT'S...
IT'S THE GATE ADAM SAW!!

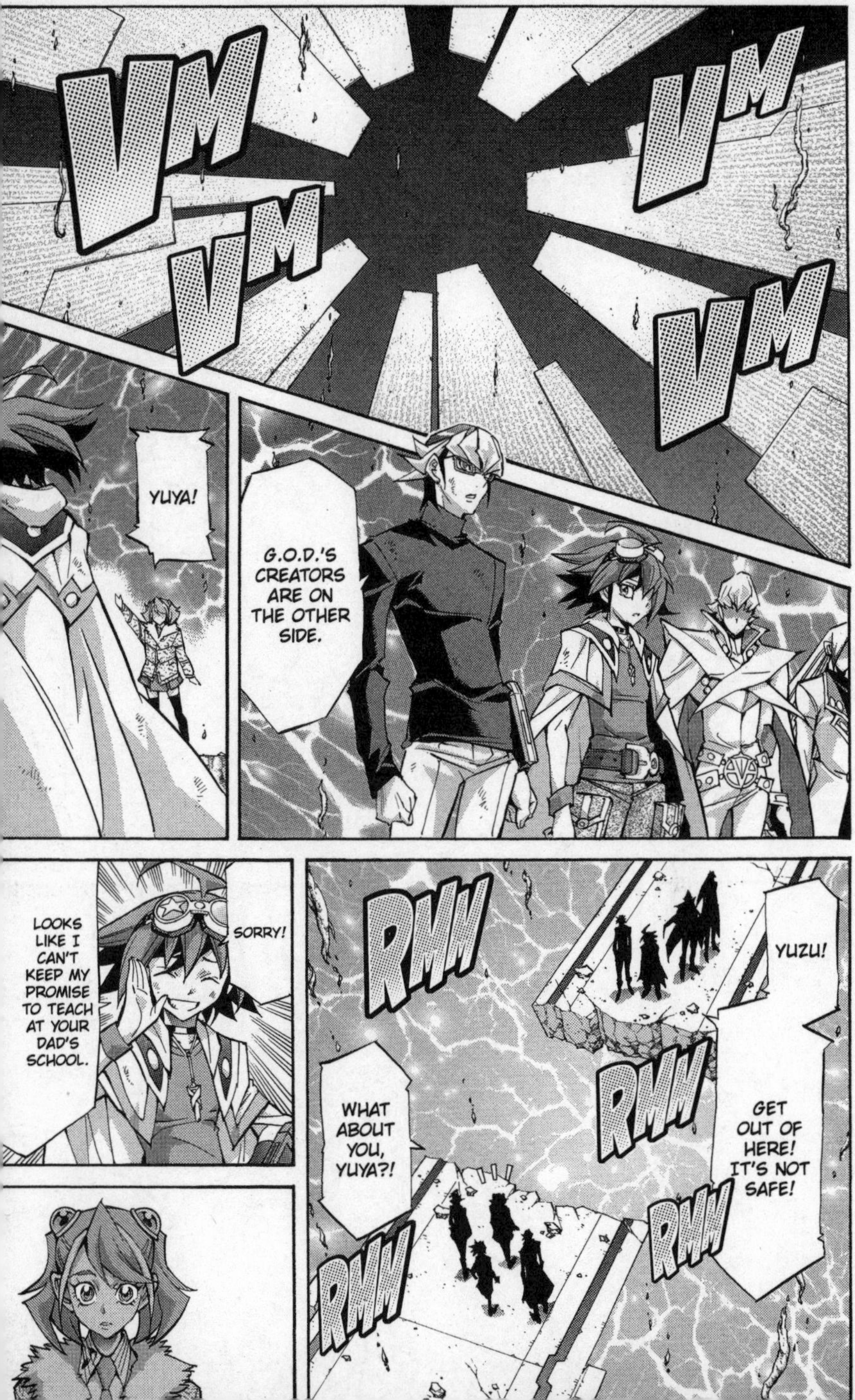
VM
VM
VM
VM
G.O.D.'S CREATORS ARE ON THE OTHER SIDE.
YUYA!
YUZU!
GET OUT OF HERE! IT'S NOT SAFE!
RMM
RMM
WHAT ABOUT YOU, YUYA?!
RMM
RMM
SORRY!
LOOKS LIKE I CAN'T KEEP MY PROMISE TO TEACH AT YOUR DAD'S SCHOOL.

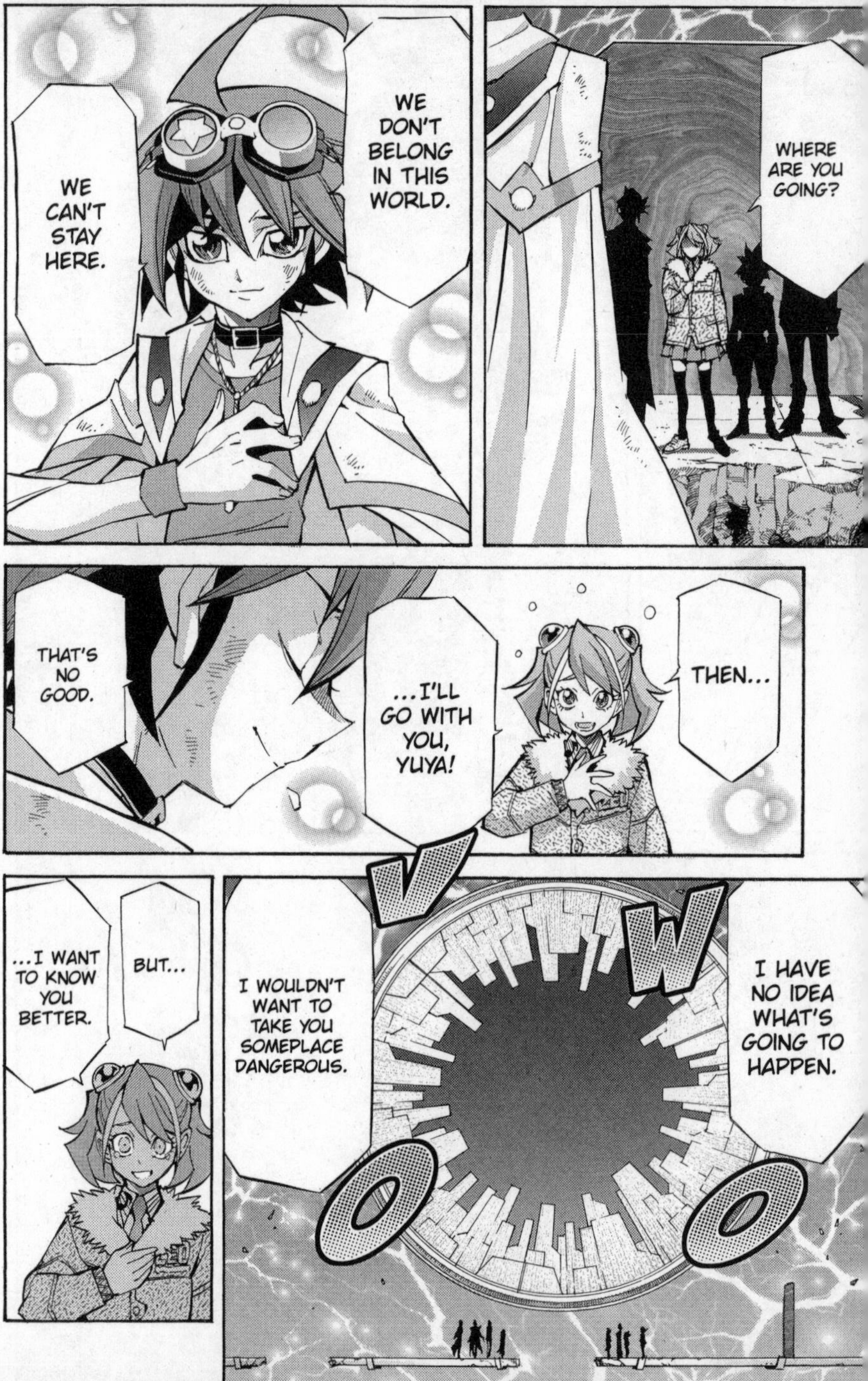
WHERE ARE YOU GOING?
WE DON'T BELONG IN THIS WORLD.
WE CAN'T STAY HERE.
THEN...
...I'LL GO WITH YOU, YUYA!
THAT'S NO GOOD.
I HAVE NO IDEA WHAT'S GOING TO HAPPEN.
VWOO
I WOULDN'T WANT TO TAKE YOU SOMEPLACE DANGEROUS.
O
BUT...
...I WANT TO KNOW YOU BETTER.

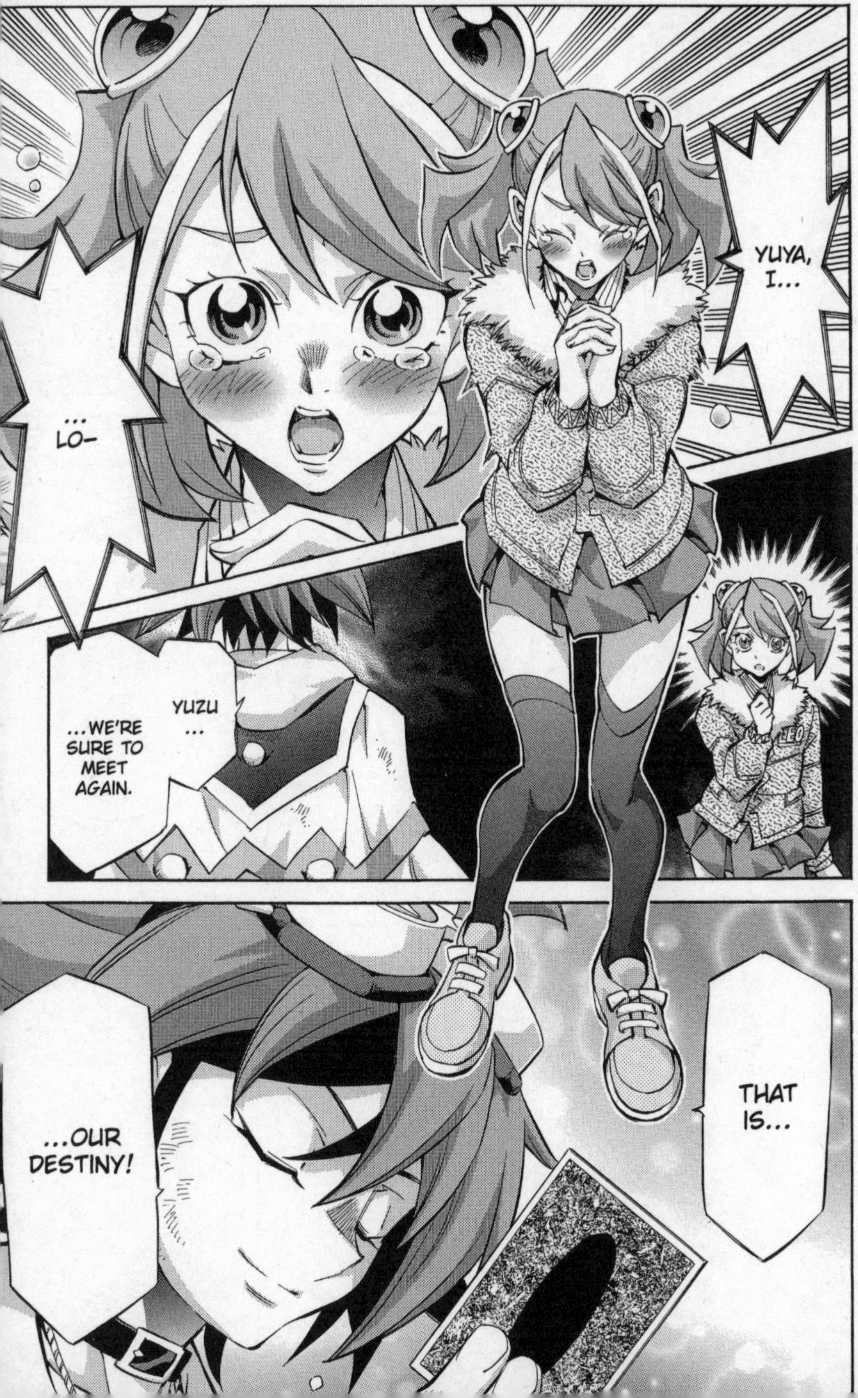
YUYA, I...
... LO-
YUZU ...
...WE'RE SURE TO MEET AGAIN.
THAT IS...
...OUR DESTINY!

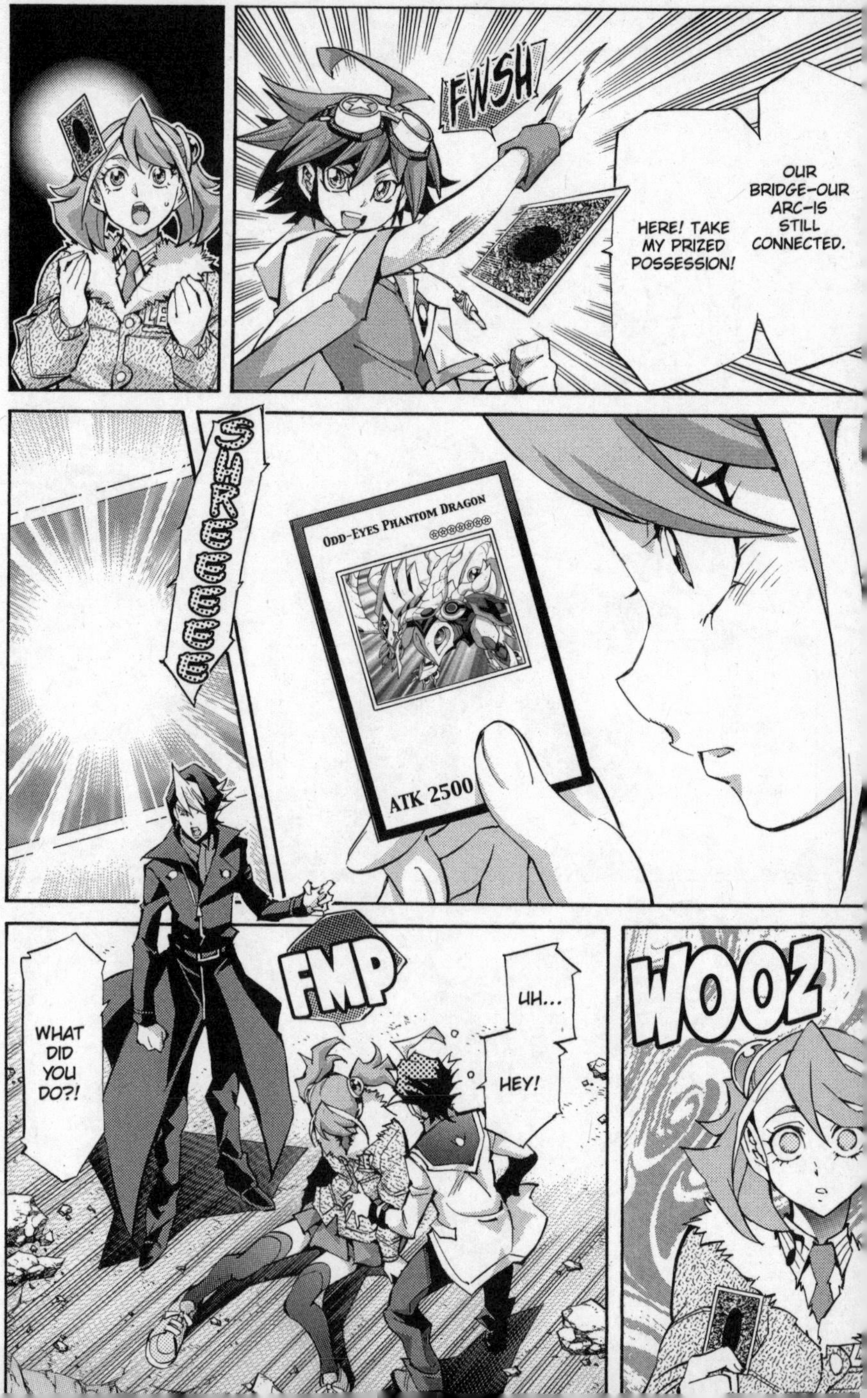

OUR BRIDGE—OUR ARC—IS STILL CONNECTED.
HERE! TAKE MY PRIZED POSSESSION!
FWSH
ODD-EYES PHANTOM DRAGON
ATK 2500
SHREEEEEEE
WOOZ
UH...
HEY!
FMP
WHAT DID YOU DO?!

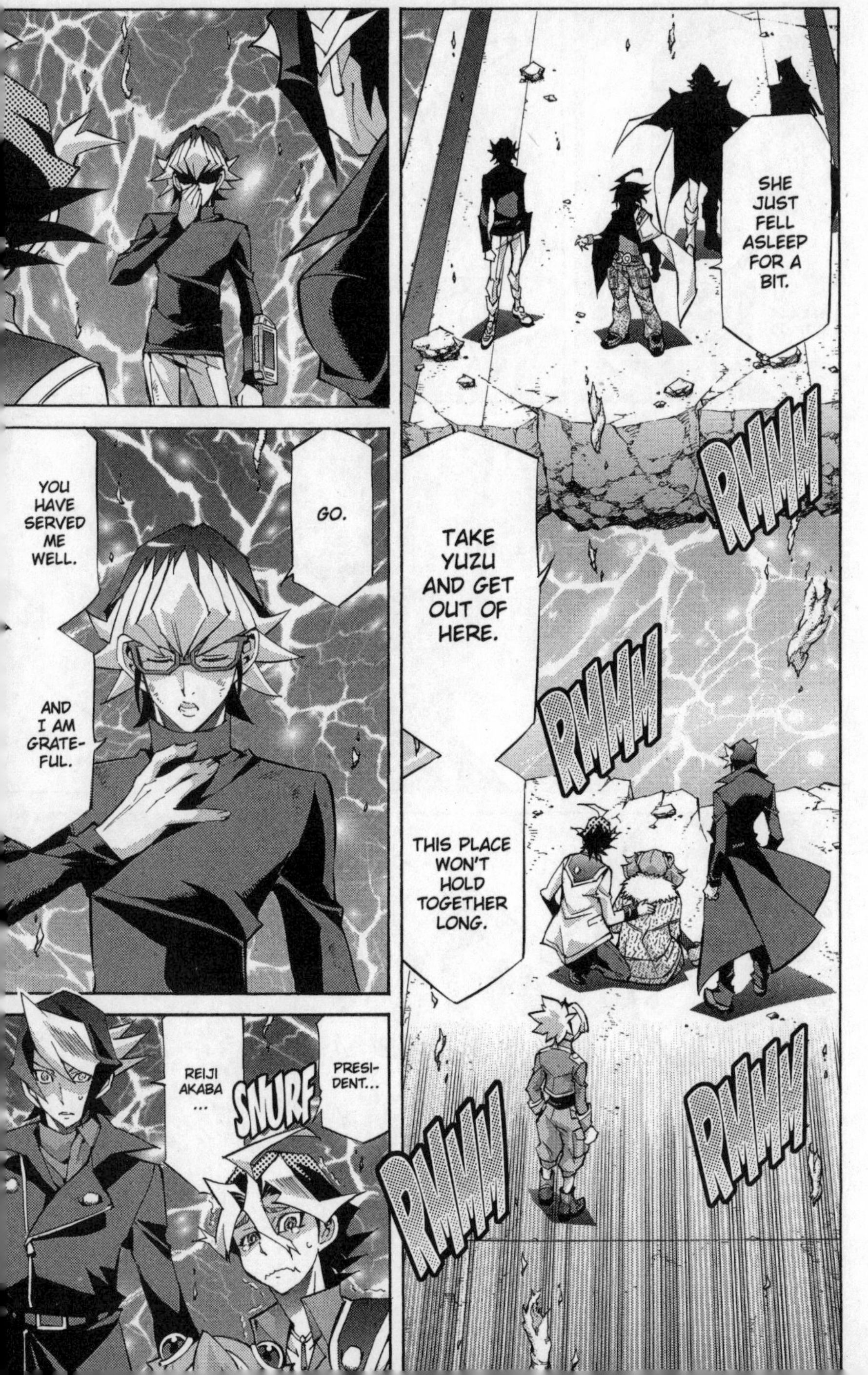
SHE JUST FELL ASLEEP FOR A BIT.
RMMM
TAKE YUZU AND GET OUT OF HERE.
RMMM
THIS PLACE WON'T HOLD TOGETHER LONG.
RMMM
RMMM
GO.
YOU HAVE SERVED ME WELL.
AND I AM GRATE-FUL.
PRESI-DENT...
SNURF
REIJI AKABA ...

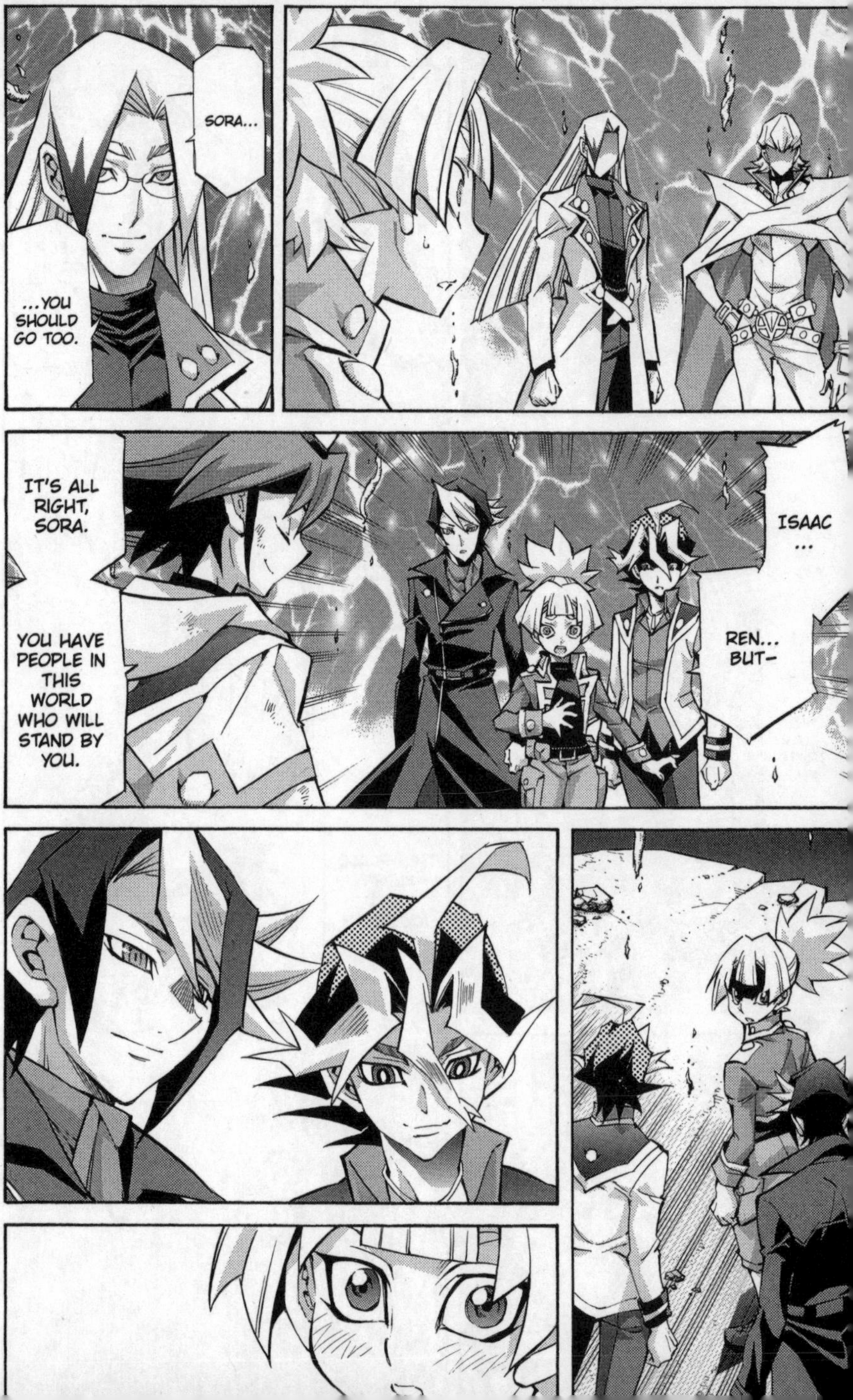
SORA...
...YOU SHOULD GO TOO.
IT'S ALL RIGHT, SORA.
YOU HAVE PEOPLE IN THIS WORLD WHO WILL STAND BY YOU.
ISAAC ...
REN... BUT-

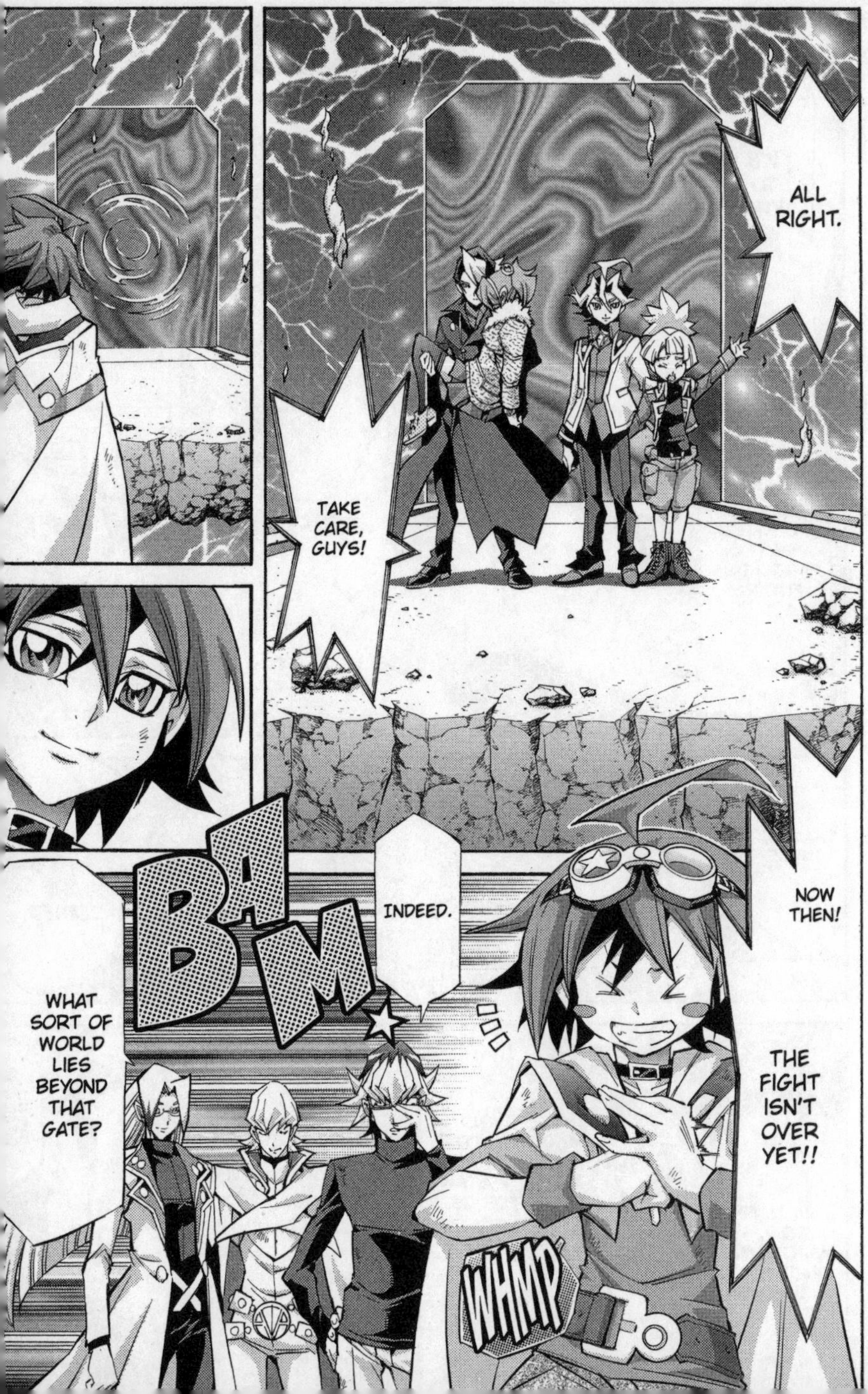
ALL RIGHT.
TAKE CARE, GUYS!
NOW THEN!
INDEED.
BAM
THE FIGHT ISN'T OVER YET!!
WHAT SORT OF WORLD LIES BEYOND THAT GATE?
WHMP

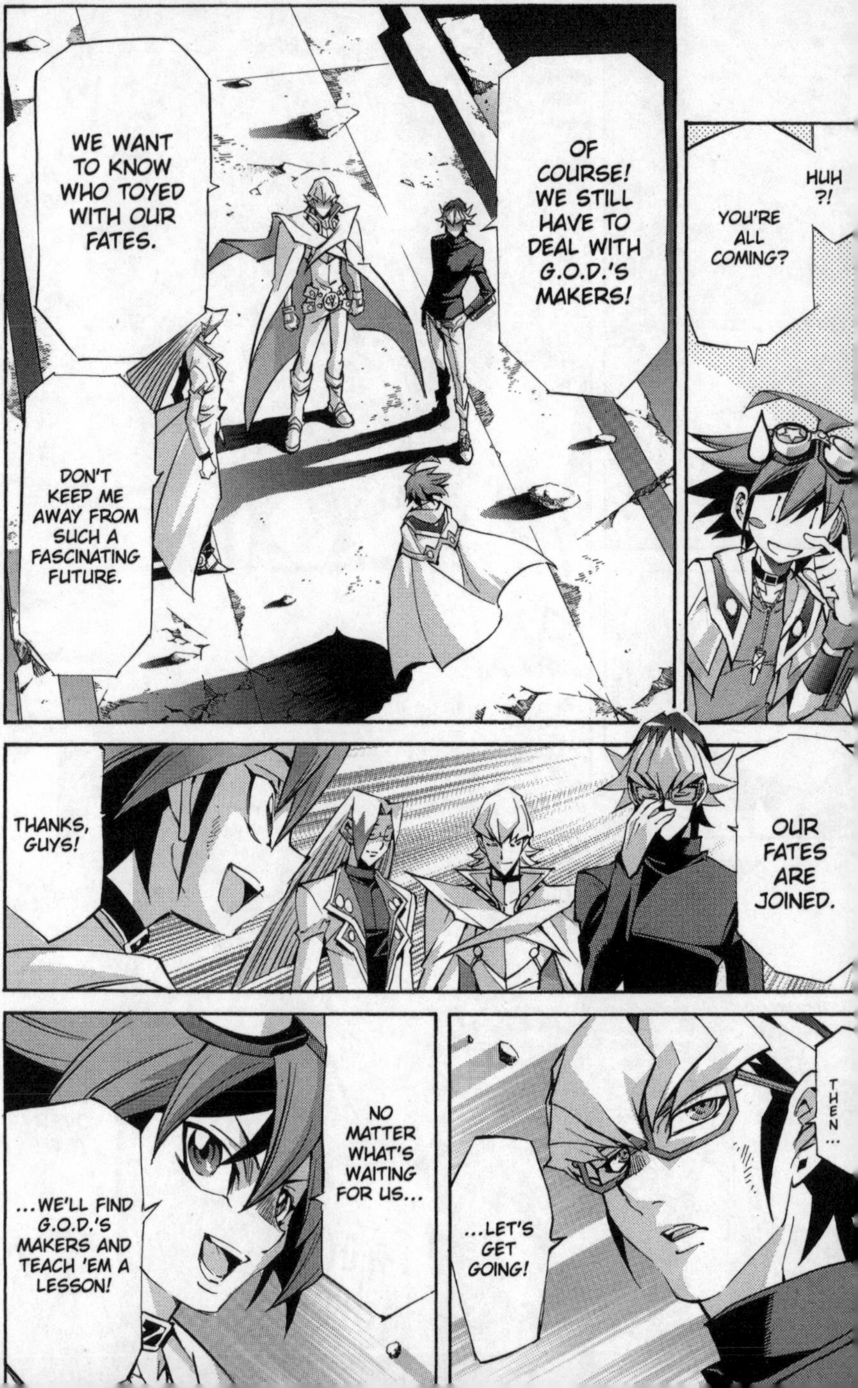
HUH ?!
YOU'RE ALL COMING?
OF COURSE! WE STILL HAVE TO DEAL WITH G.O.D.'S MAKERS!
WE WANT TO KNOW WHO TOYED WITH OUR FATES.
DON'T KEEP ME AWAY FROM SUCH A FASCINATING FUTURE.
OUR FATES ARE JOINED.
THANKS, GUYS!
THEN...
...LET'S GET GOING!
NO MATTER WHAT'S WAITING FOR US...
...WE'LL FIND G.O.D.'S MAKERS AND TEACH 'EM A LESSON!

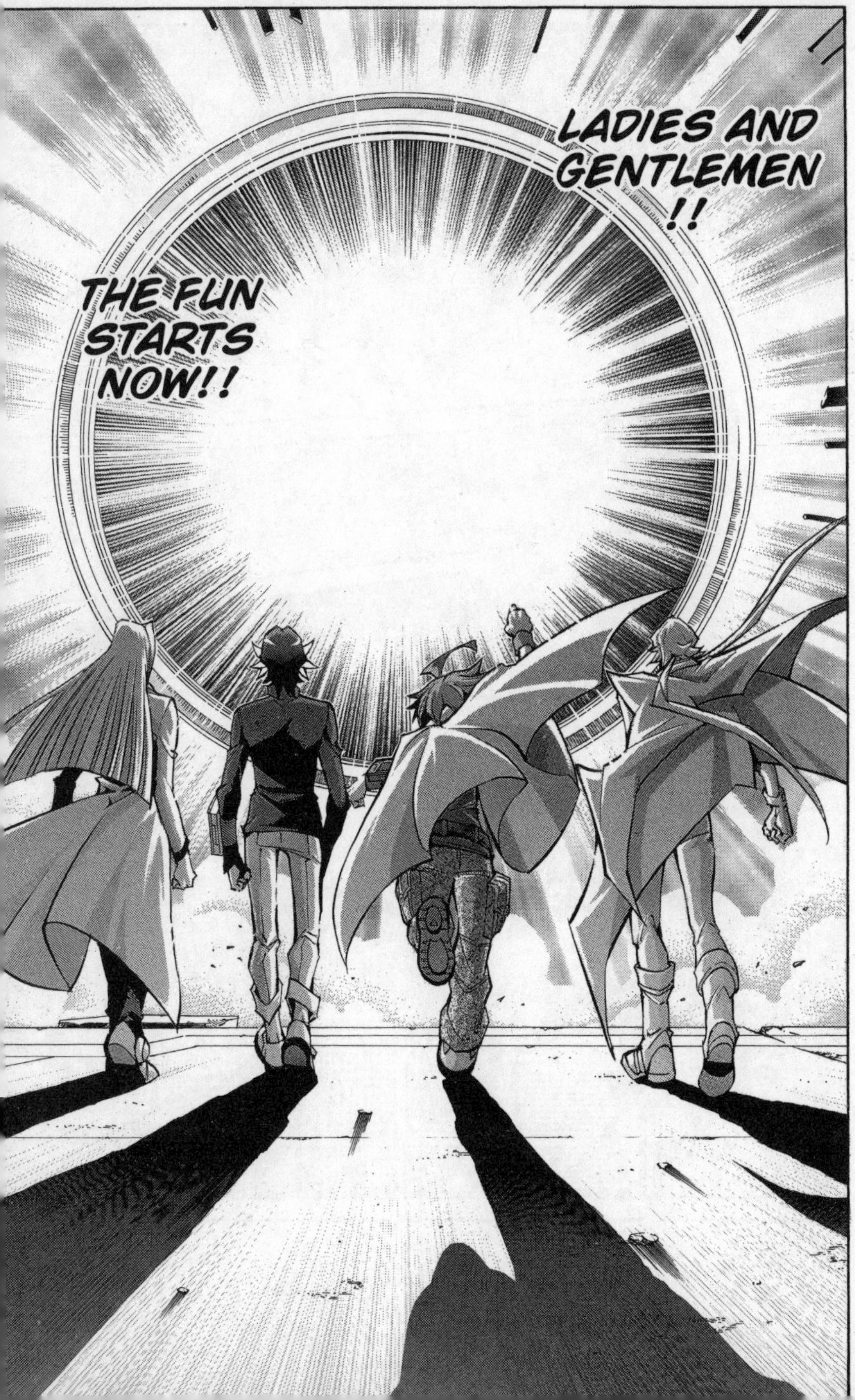
LADIES AND GENTLEMEN!!
THE FUN STARTS NOW!!

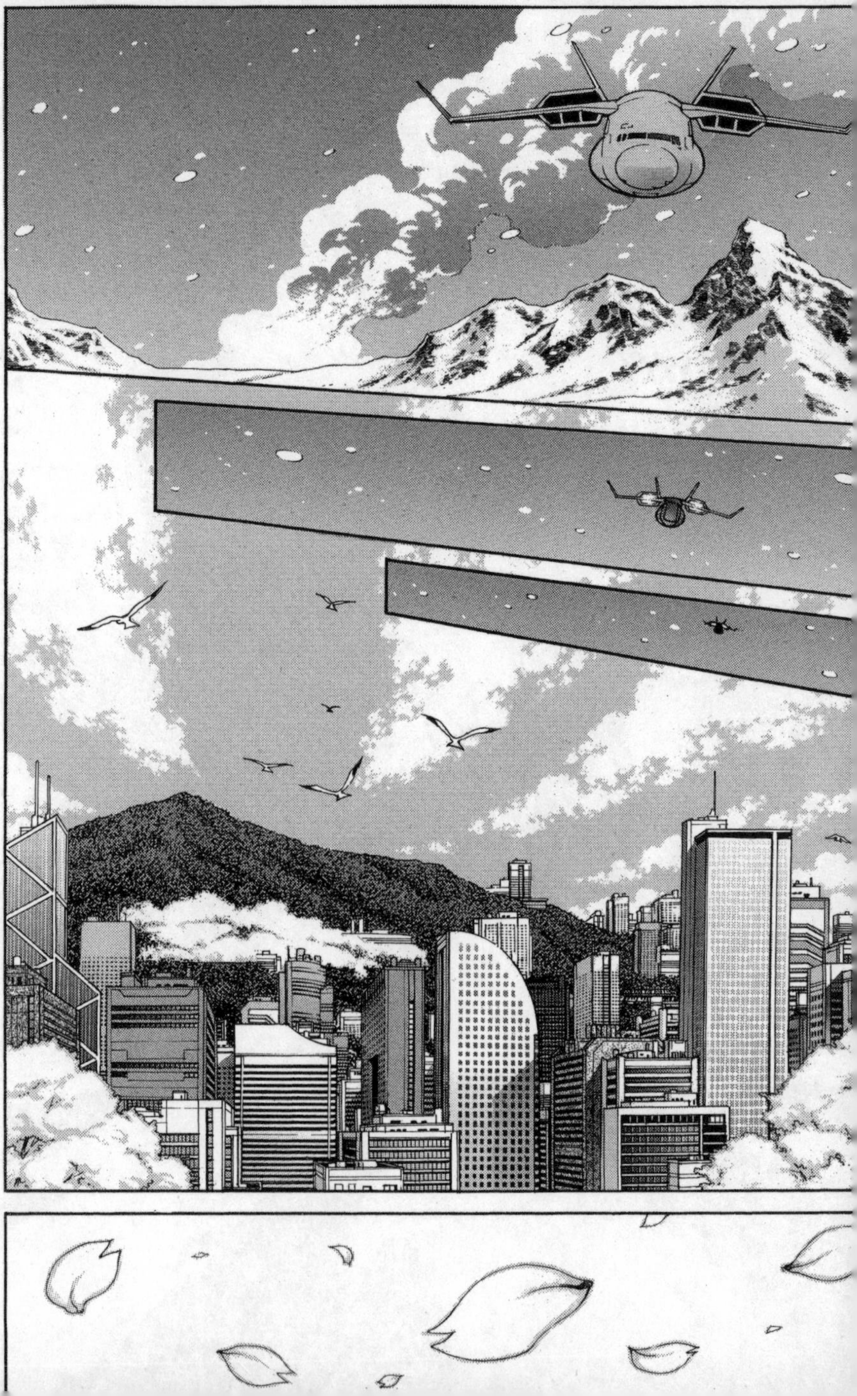

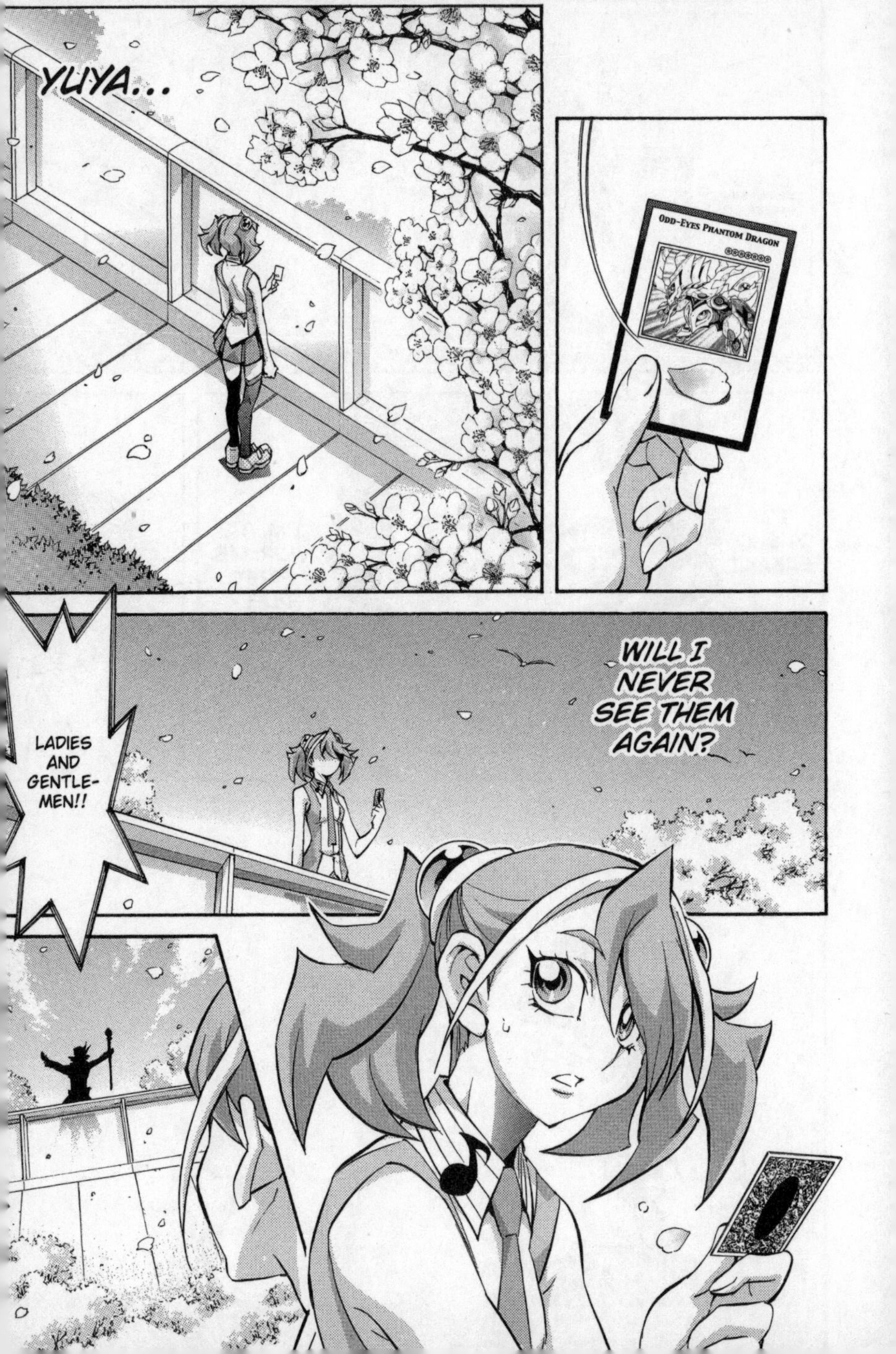
ODD-EYES PHANTOM DRAGON
YUYA...
WILL I NEVER SEE THEM AGAIN?
LADIES AND GENTLE-MEN!!

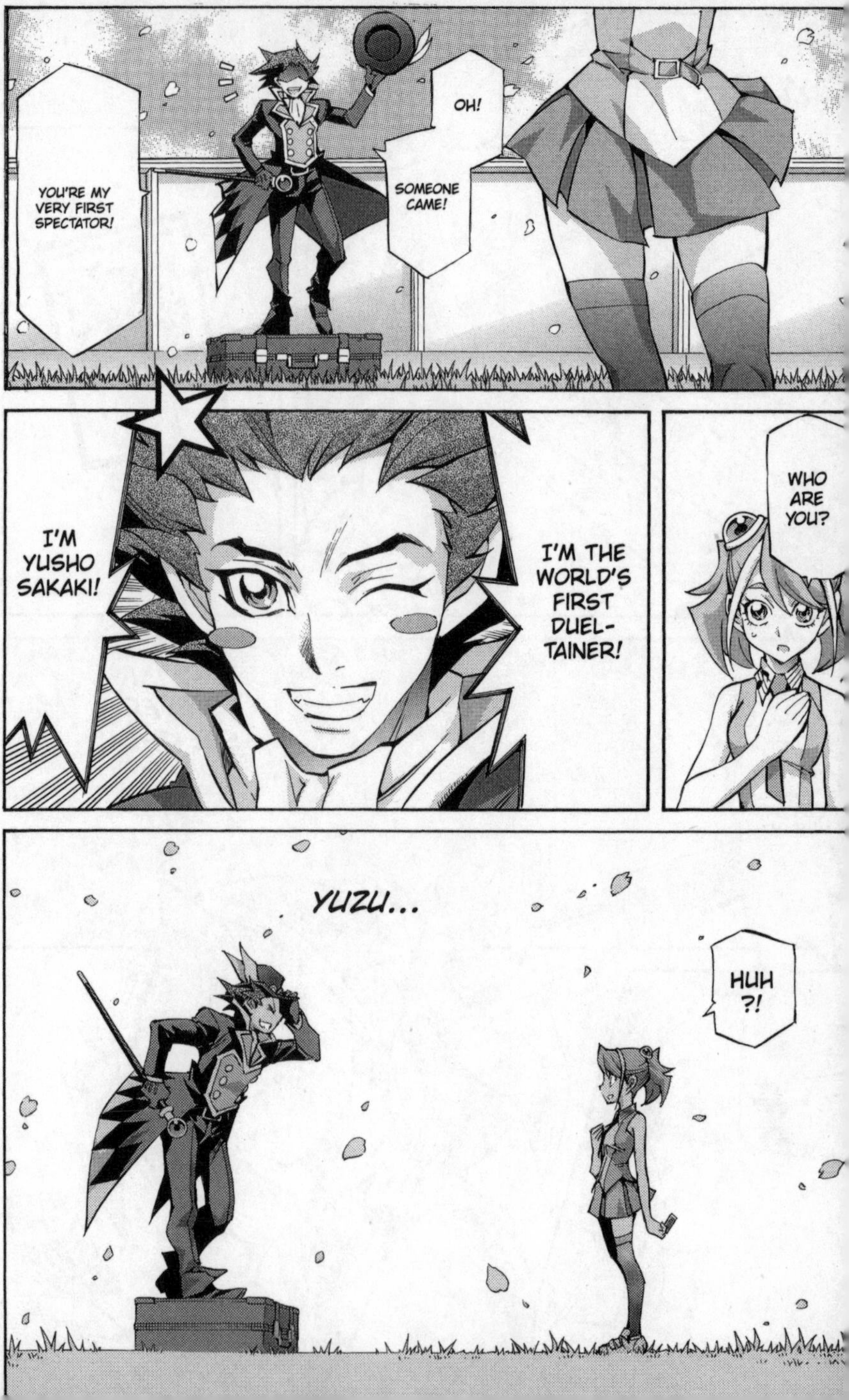
OH!
SOMEONE CAME!
YOU'RE MY VERY FIRST SPECTATOR!
WHO ARE YOU?
I'M THE WORLD'S FIRST DUEL-TAINER!
I'M YUSHO SAKAKI!
YUZU...
HUH ?!

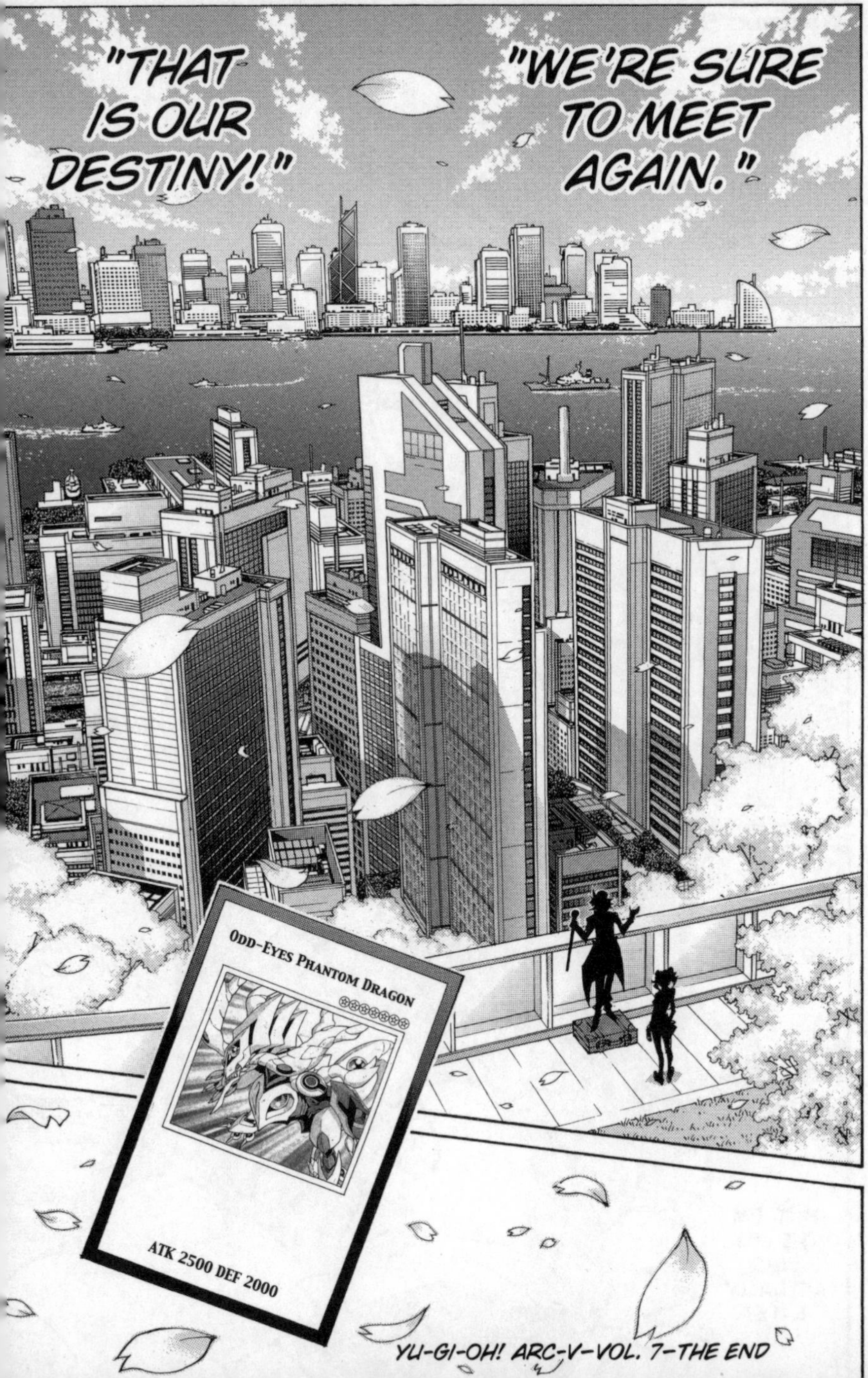
"WE'RE SURE TO MEET AGAIN."
"THAT IS OUR DESTINY!"
ODD-EYES PHANTOM DRAGON
ATK 2500 DEF 2000
YU-GI-OH! ARC-V-VOL. 7-THE END

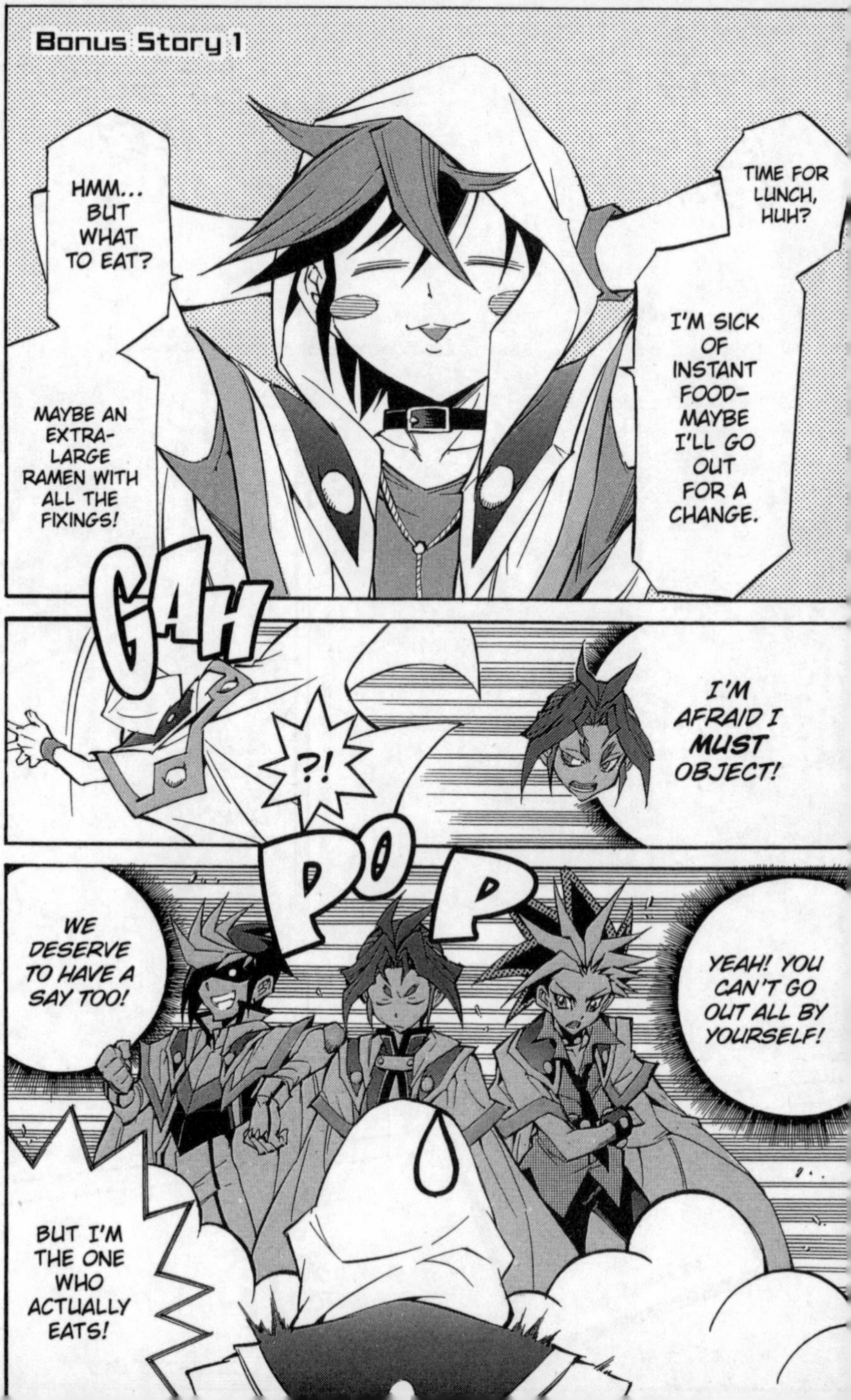
Bonus Story 1
TIME FOR LUNCH, HUH?
I'M SICK OF INSTANT FOOD- MAYBE I'LL GO OUT FOR A CHANGE.
HMM... BUT WHAT TO EAT?
MAYBE AN EXTRA-LARGE RAMEN WITH ALL THE FIXINGS!
GAH
I'M AFRAID I MUST OBJECT!
?!
POP
YEAH! YOU CAN'T GO OUT ALL BY YOURSELF!
WE DESERVE TO HAVE A SAY TOO!
BUT I'M THE ONE WHO ACTUALLY EATS!

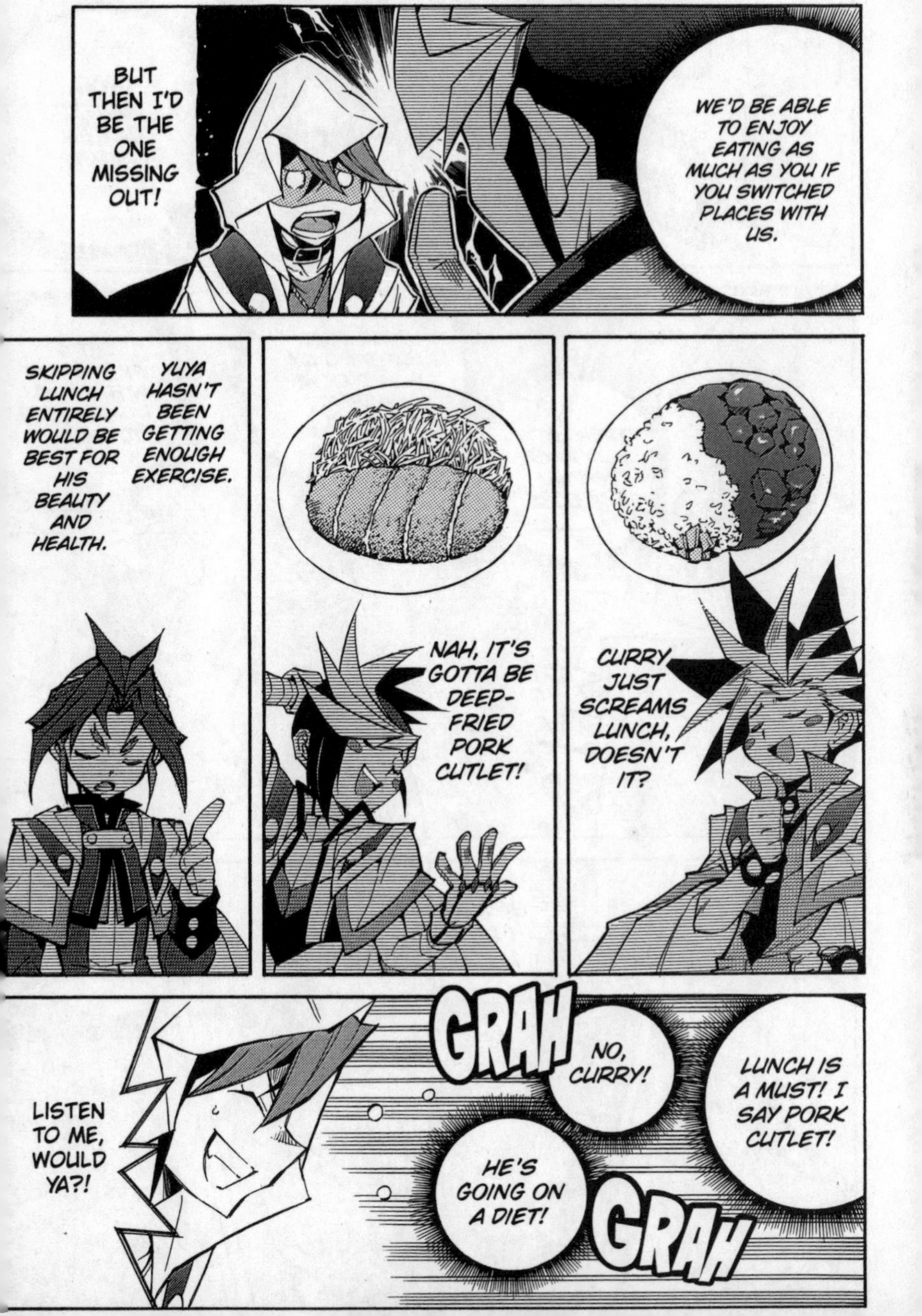
WE'D BE ABLE TO ENJOY EATING AS MUCH AS YOU IF YOU SWITCHED PLACES WITH US.
BUT THEN I'D BE THE ONE MISSING OUT!
CURRY JUST SCREAMS LUNCH, DOESN'T IT?
NAH, IT'S GOTTA BE DEEP-FRIED PORK CUTLET!
YUYA HASN'T BEEN GETTING ENOUGH EXERCISE.
SKIPPING LUNCH ENTIRELY WOULD BE BEST FOR HIS BEAUTY AND HEALTH.
LUNCH IS A MUST! I SAY PORK CUTLET!
GRAH
NO, CURRY!
HE'S GOING ON A DIET!
GRAH
LISTEN TO ME, WOULD YA?!

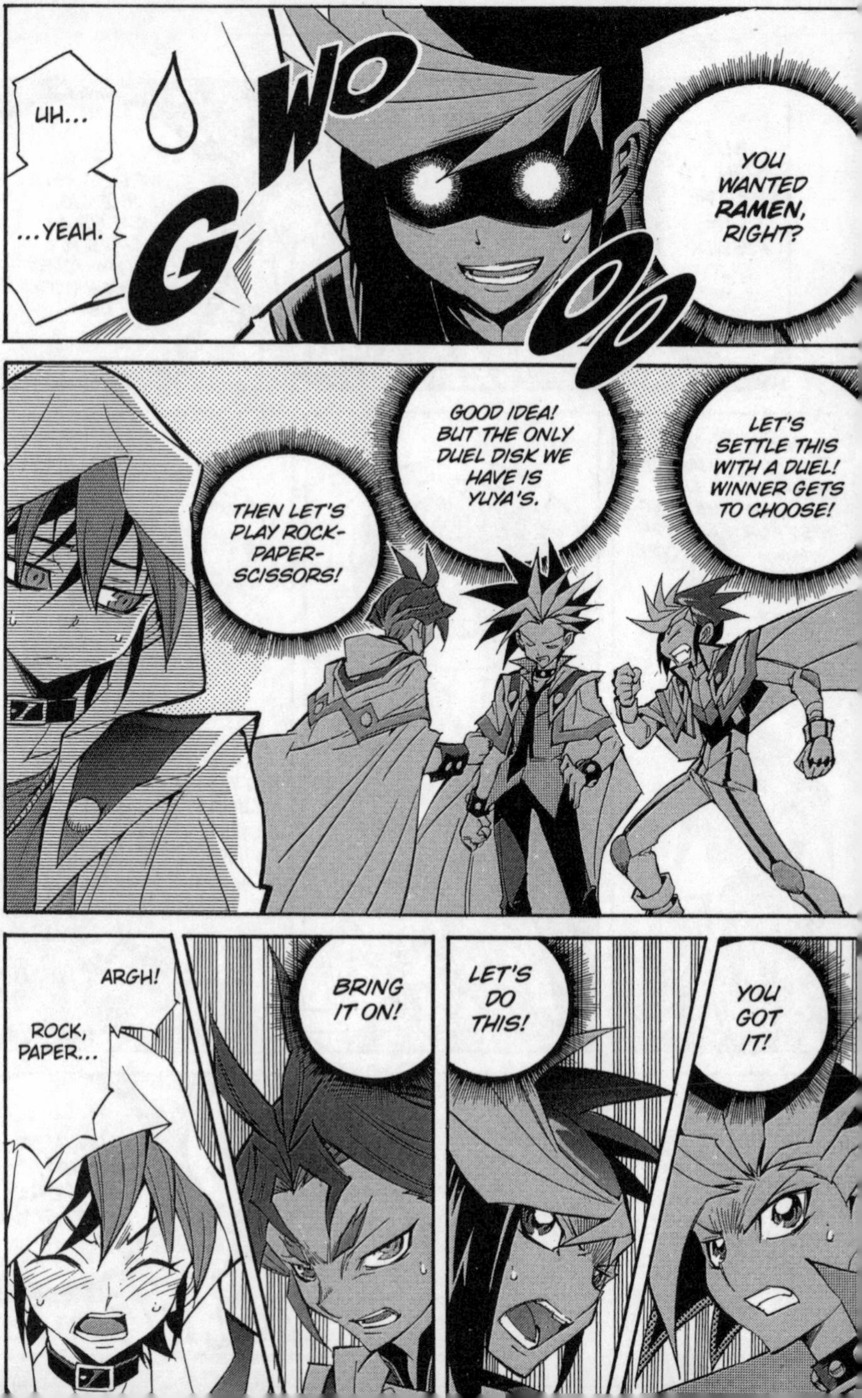
YOU WANTED RAMEN, RIGHT?
UH...
...YEAH.
LET'S SETTLE THIS WITH A DUEL! WINNER GETS TO CHOOSE!
GOOD IDEA! BUT THE ONLY DUEL DISK WE HAVE IS YUYA'S.
THEN LET'S PLAY ROCK-PAPER-SCISSORS!
YOU GOT IT!
LET'S DO THIS!
BRING IT ON!
ARGH!
ROCK, PAPER...

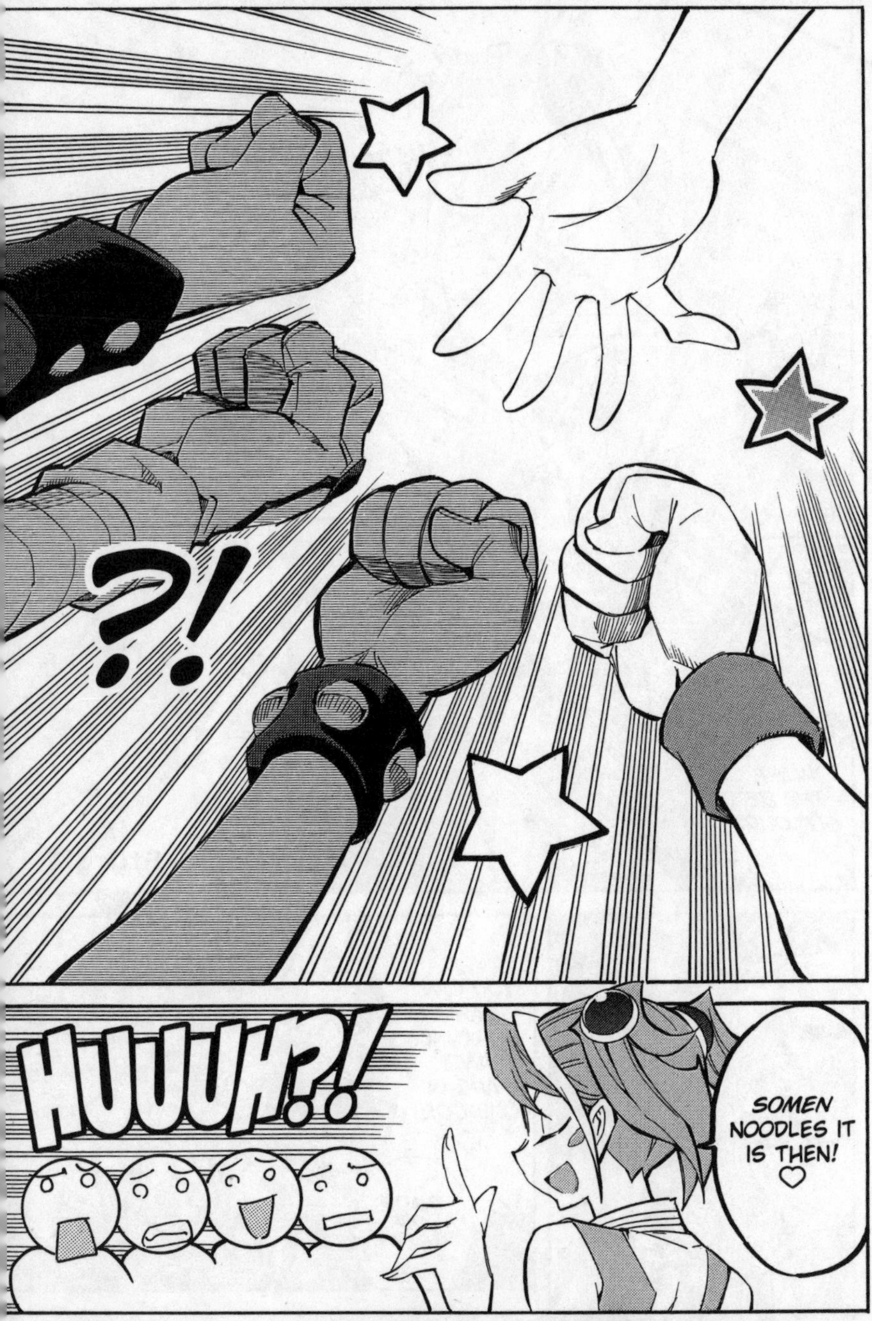
?!
SOMEN NOODLES IT IS THEN! ♡
HUUUH?!

(First published in the *Jump Victory Carnival 2016* official guidebook.)

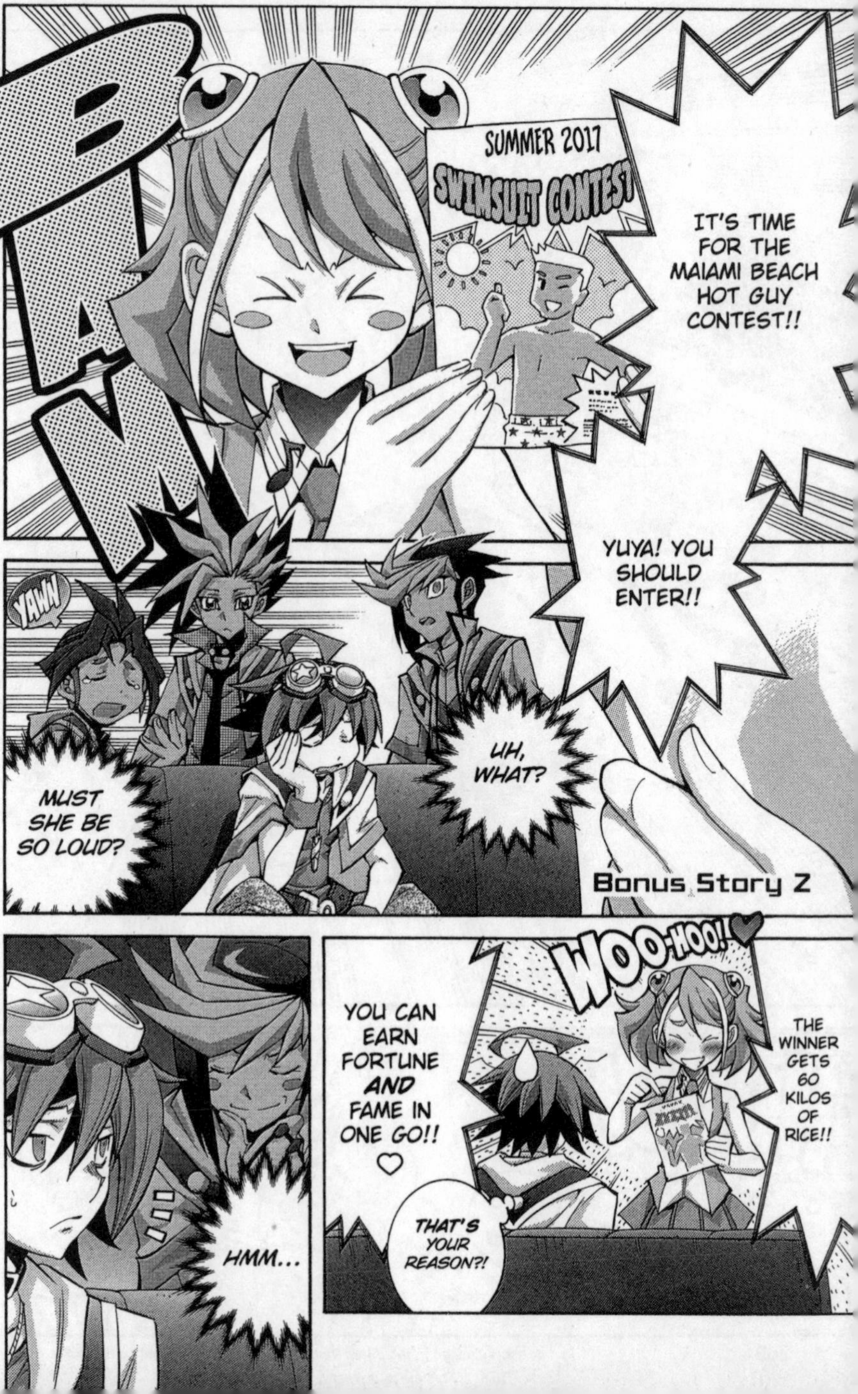
SUMMER 2017
SWIMSUIT CONTEST
IT'S TIME FOR THE MAIAMI BEACH HOT GUY CONTEST!!
BAM
YUYA! YOU SHOULD ENTER!!
UH, WHAT?
YAWN
MUST SHE BE SO LOUD?
Bonus Story 2
WOO-HOO! ♥
THE WINNER GETS 60 KILOS OF RICE!!
YOU CAN EARN FORTUNE AND FAME IN ONE GO!! ♡
THAT'S YOUR REASON?!
HMM...

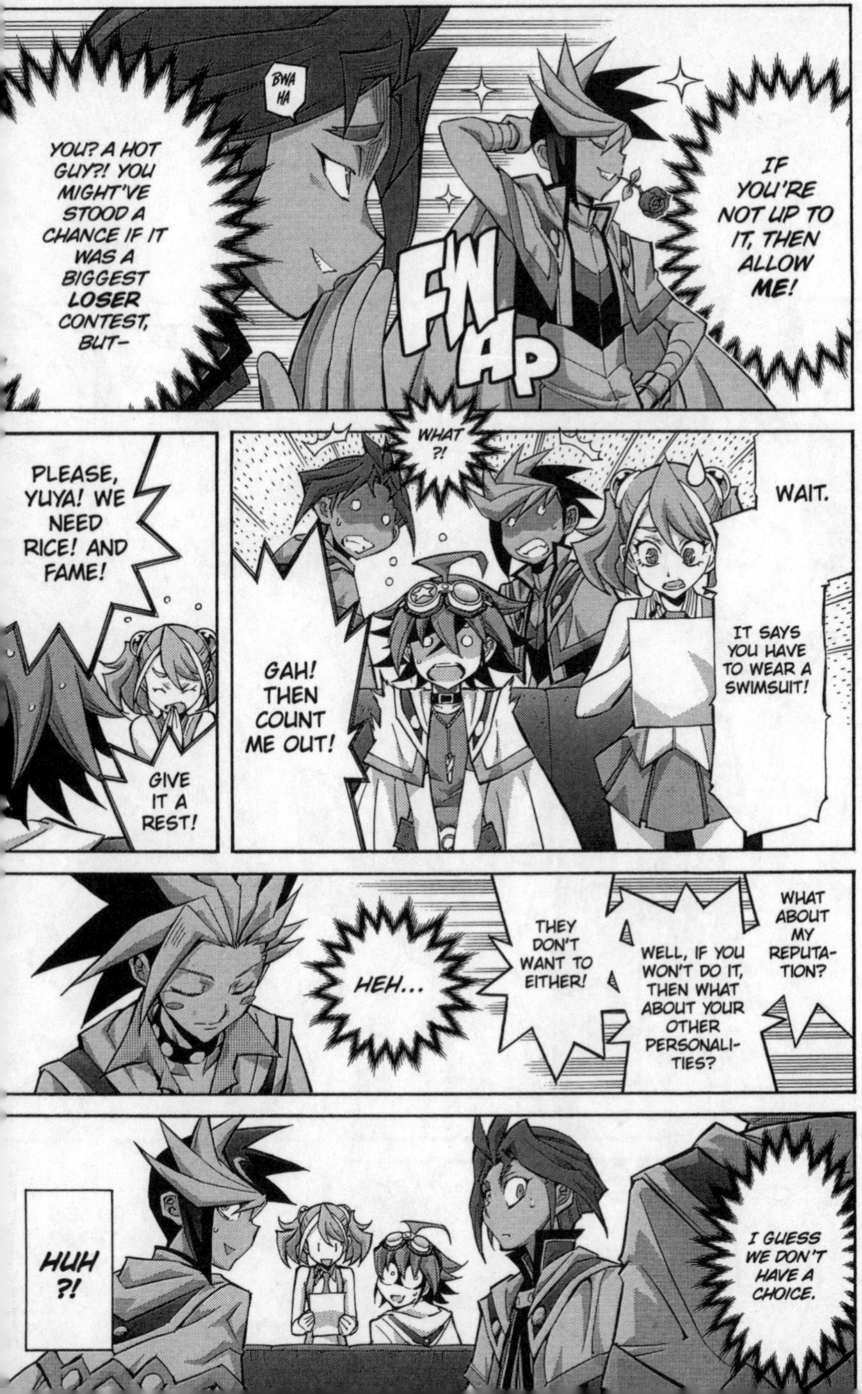
IF YOU'RE NOT UP TO IT, THEN ALLOW ME!
FWAP
BWA HA
YOU? A HOT GUY?! YOU MIGHT'VE STOOD A CHANCE IF IT WAS A BIGGEST LOSER CONTEST, BUT–
WAIT.
IT SAYS YOU HAVE TO WEAR A SWIMSUIT!
WHAT ?!
GAH! THEN COUNT ME OUT!
PLEASE, YUYA! WE NEED RICE! AND FAME!
GIVE IT A REST!
WHAT ABOUT MY REPUTATION?
WELL, IF YOU WON'T DO IT, THEN WHAT ABOUT YOUR OTHER PERSONALITIES?
THEY DON'T WANT TO EITHER!
HEH...
I GUESS WE DON'T HAVE A CHOICE.
HUH ?!

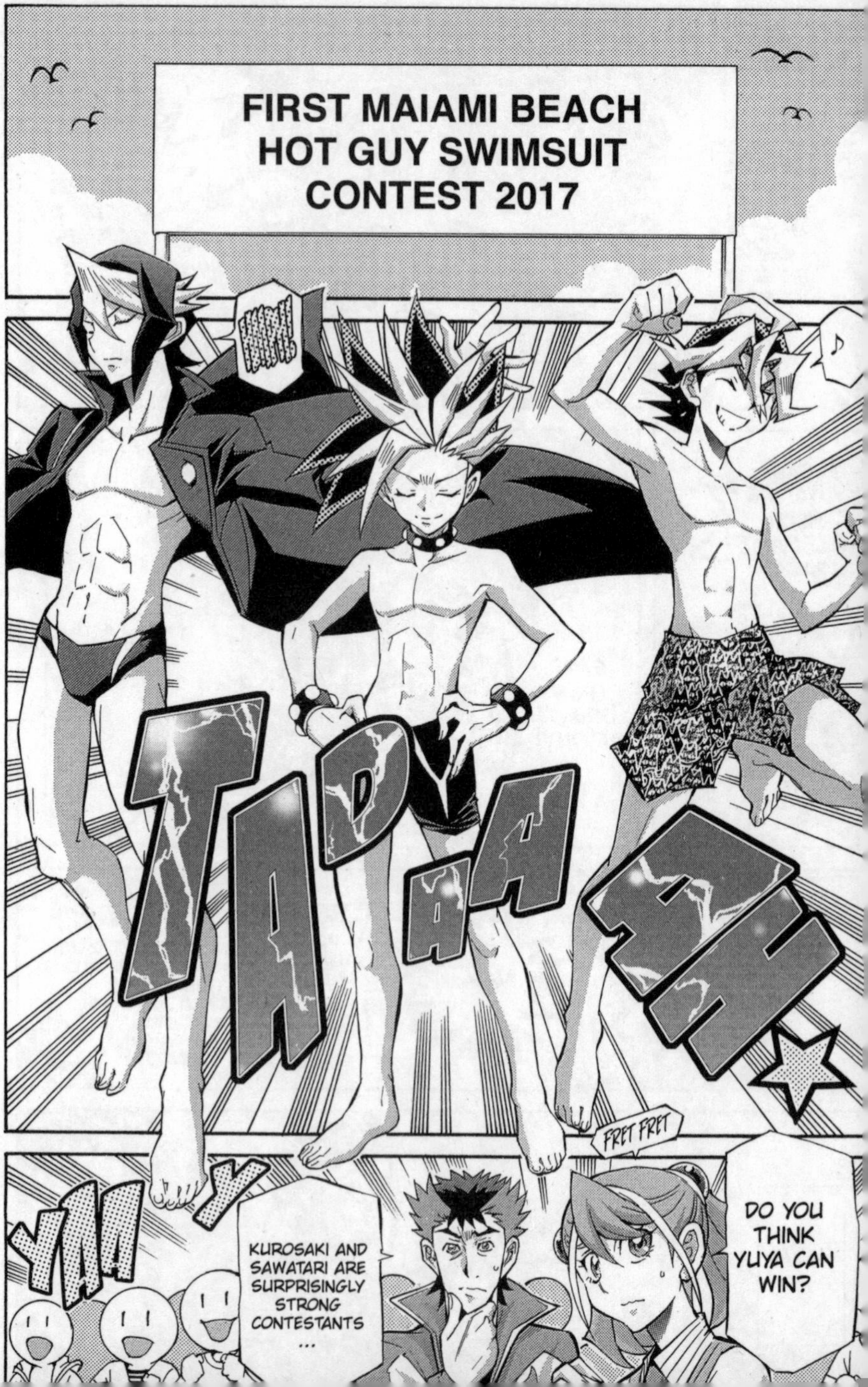
FIRST MAIAMI BEACH
HOT GUY SWIMSUIT
CONTEST 2017
TADAAAH
DO YOU THINK YUYA CAN WIN?
FRET FRET
KUROSAKI AND SAWATARI ARE SURPRISINGLY STRONG CONTESTANTS ...
YAAY

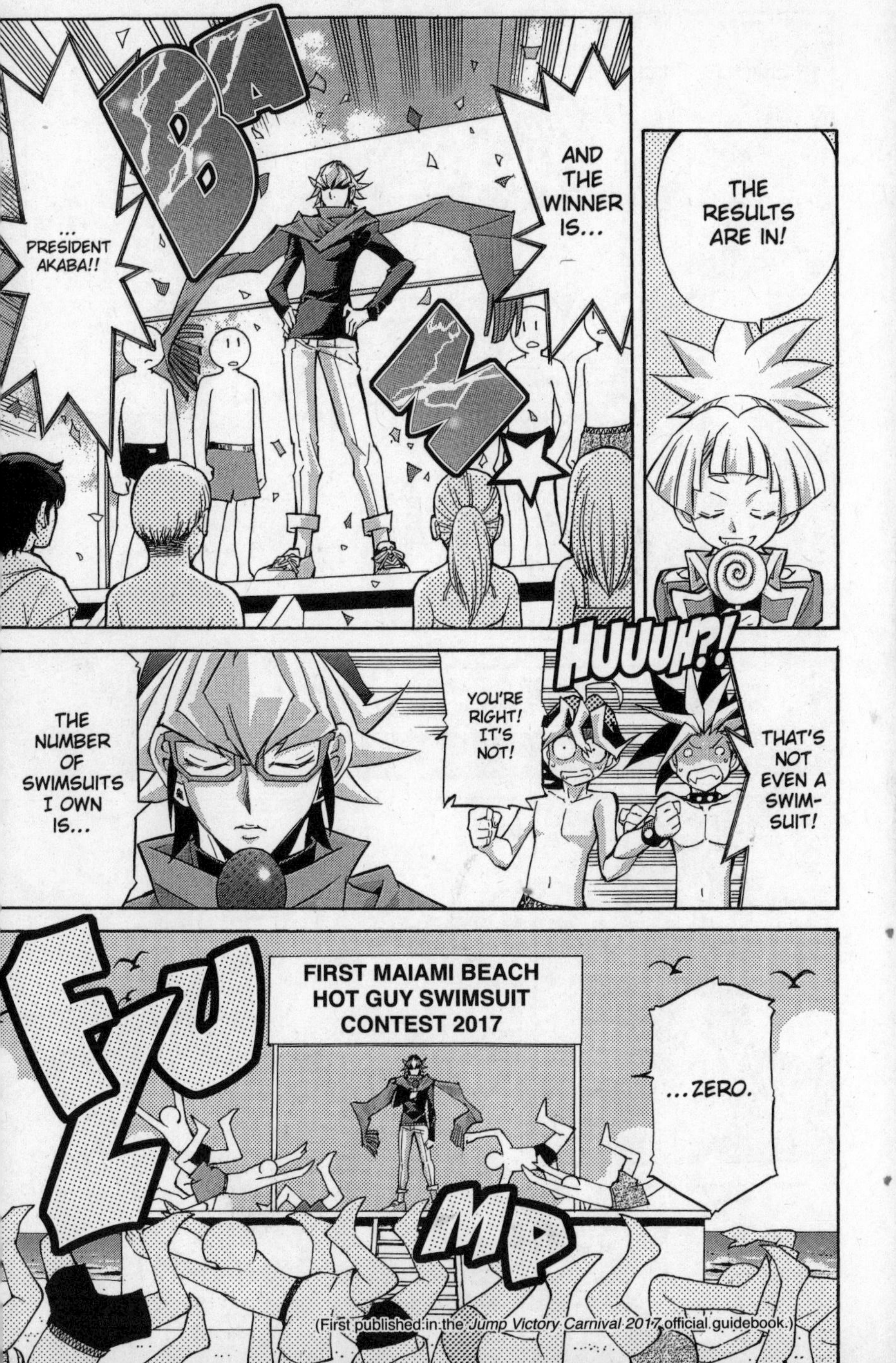
THE RESULTS ARE IN!
AND THE WINNER IS...
BAM
...PRESIDENT AKABA!!
HUUUH?!
THAT'S NOT EVEN A SWIM-SUIT!
YOU'RE RIGHT! IT'S NOT!
THE NUMBER OF SWIMSUITS I OWN IS...
...ZERO.
FIRST MAIAMI BEACH HOT GUY SWIMSUIT CONTEST 2017
FUMP

(First published in the *Jump Victory Carnival 2017* official guidebook.)

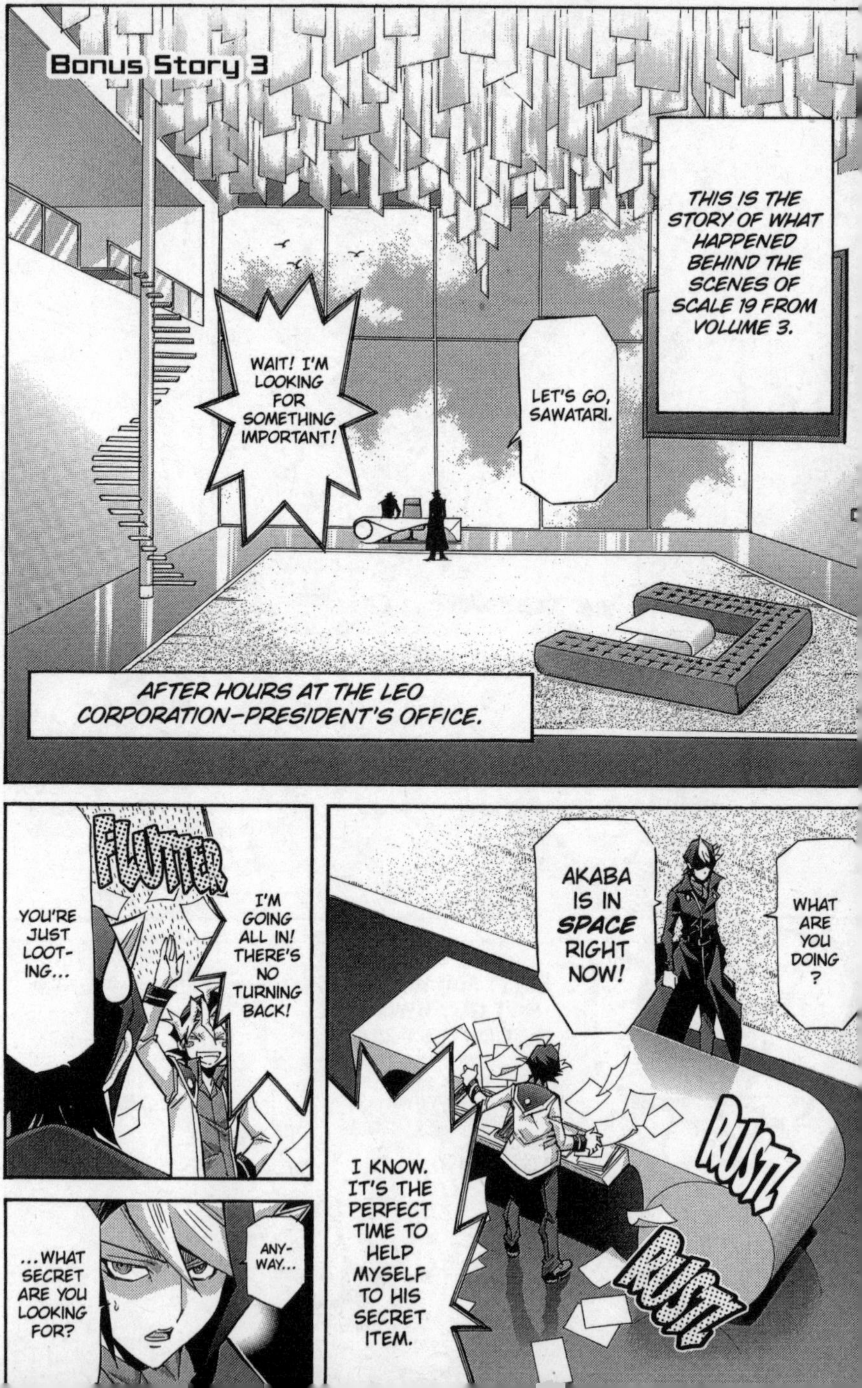
Bonus Story 3
THIS IS THE STORY OF WHAT HAPPENED BEHIND THE SCENES OF SCALE 19 FROM VOLUME 3.
LET'S GO, SAWATARI.
WAIT! I'M LOOKING FOR SOMETHING IMPORTANT!
AFTER HOURS AT THE LEO CORPORATION—PRESIDENT'S OFFICE.
WHAT ARE YOU DOING?
AKABA IS IN SPACE RIGHT NOW!
I KNOW. IT'S THE PERFECT TIME TO HELP MYSELF TO HIS SECRET ITEM.
RUSTLE
RUSTLE
FLUTTER
I'M GOING ALL IN! THERE'S NO TURNING BACK!
YOU'RE JUST LOOTING...
ANYWAY...
...WHAT SECRET ARE YOU LOOKING FOR?

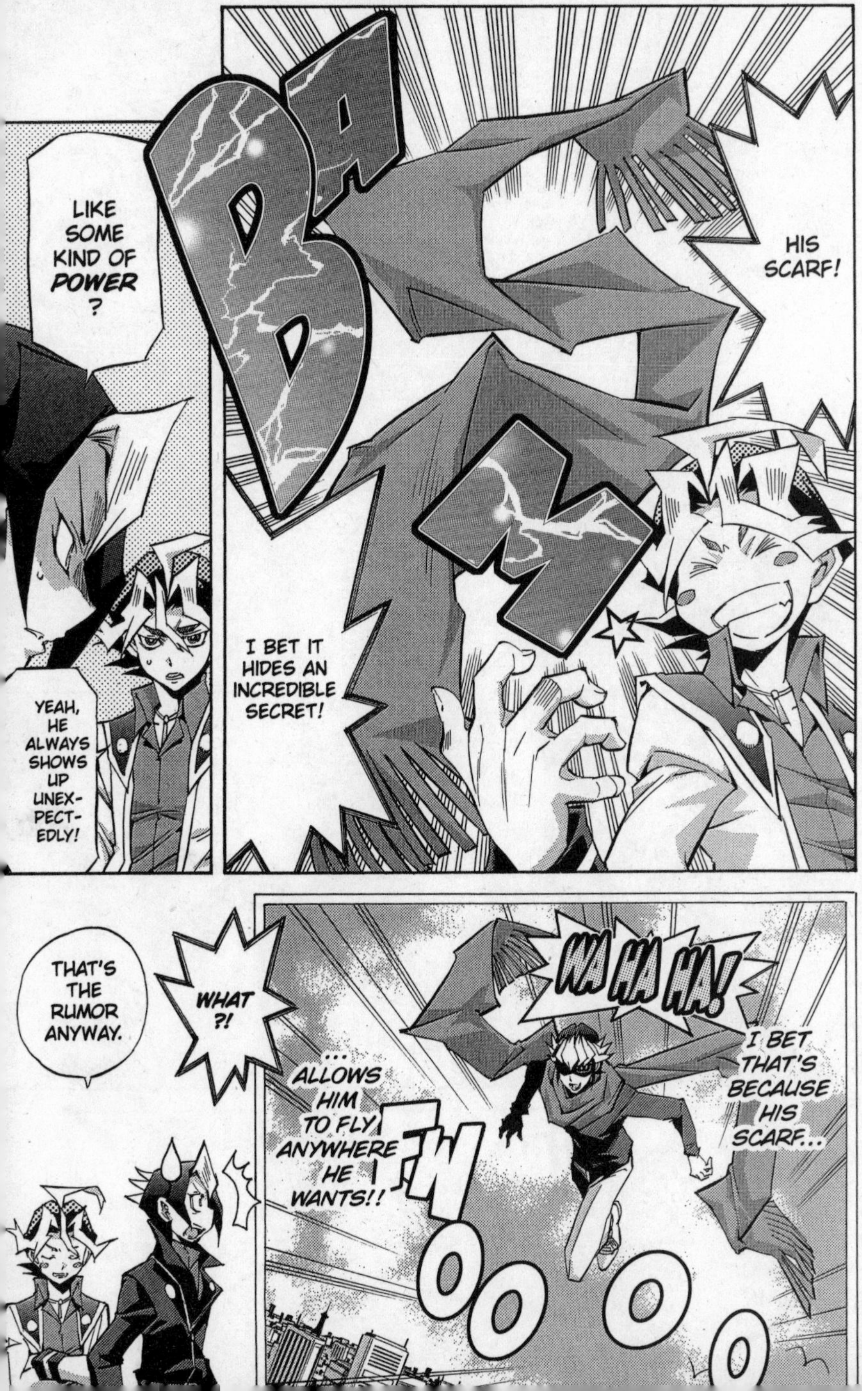
HIS SCARF!
BAM
I BET IT HIDES AN INCREDIBLE SECRET!
LIKE SOME KIND OF *POWER* ?
YEAH, HE ALWAYS SHOWS UP UNEXPECT-EDLY!
HA HA HA!
I BET THAT'S BECAUSE HIS SCARF...
... ALLOWS HIM TO FLY ANYWHERE HE WANTS!!
WOOOO
WHAT?!
THAT'S THE RUMOR ANYWAY.

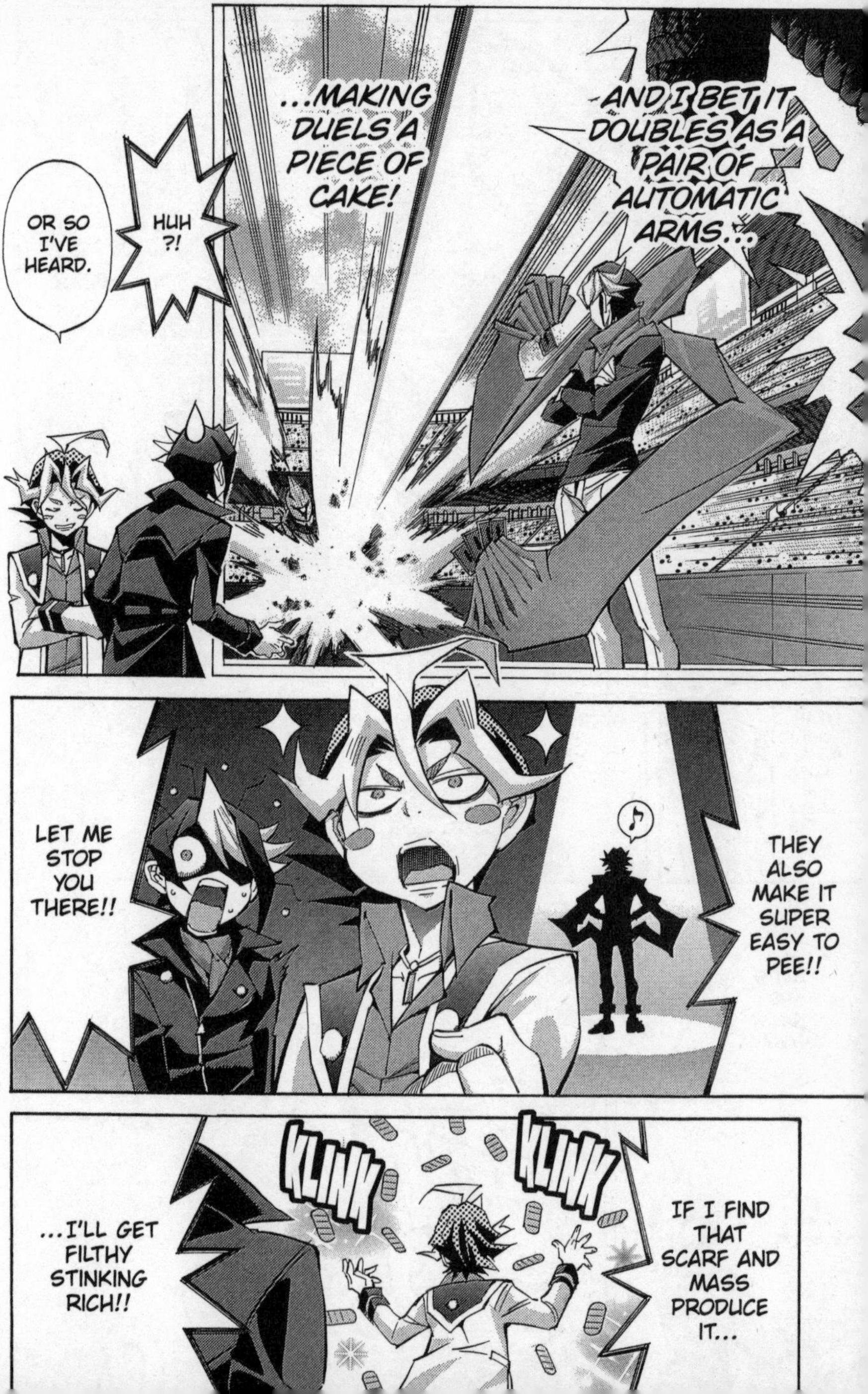
AND I BET IT DOUBLES AS A PAIR OF AUTOMATIC ARMS...
...MAKING DUELS A PIECE OF CAKE!
HUH ?!
OR SO I'VE HEARD.
THEY ALSO MAKE IT SUPER EASY TO PEE!!
LET ME STOP YOU THERE!!
IF I FIND THAT SCARF AND MASS PRODUCE IT...
KLINK
KLINK
...I'LL GET FILTHY STINKING RICH!!

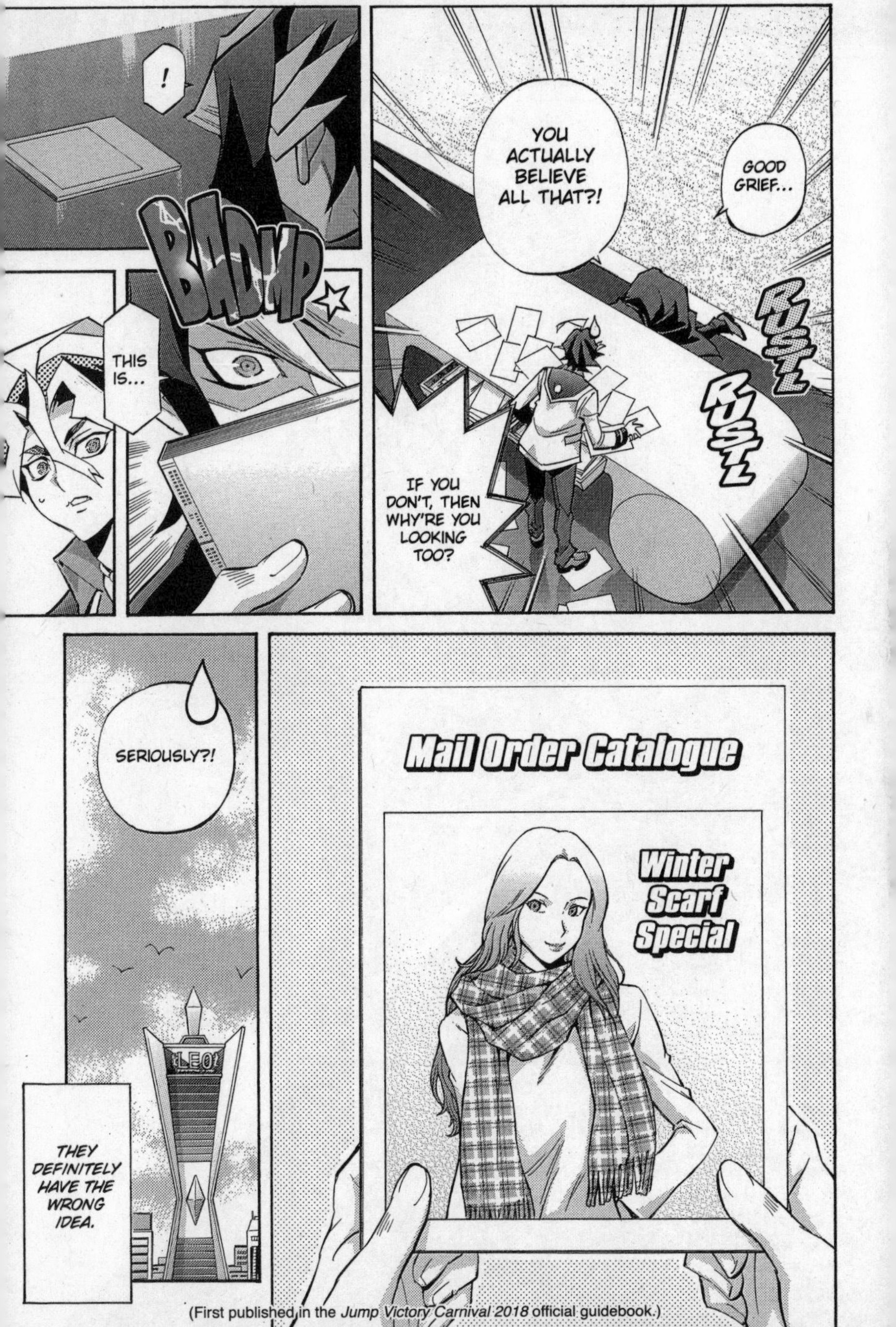
GOOD GRIEF...
YOU ACTUALLY BELIEVE ALL THAT?!
RUSTL
RUSTL
IF YOU DON'T, THEN WHY'RE YOU LOOKING TOO?
!
BADUMP
THIS IS...
Mail Order Catalogue
Winter Scarf Special
SERIOUSLY?!
THEY DEFINITELY HAVE THE WRONG IDEA.

(First published in the *Jump Victory Carnival 2018* official guidebook.)

AFTERWORD

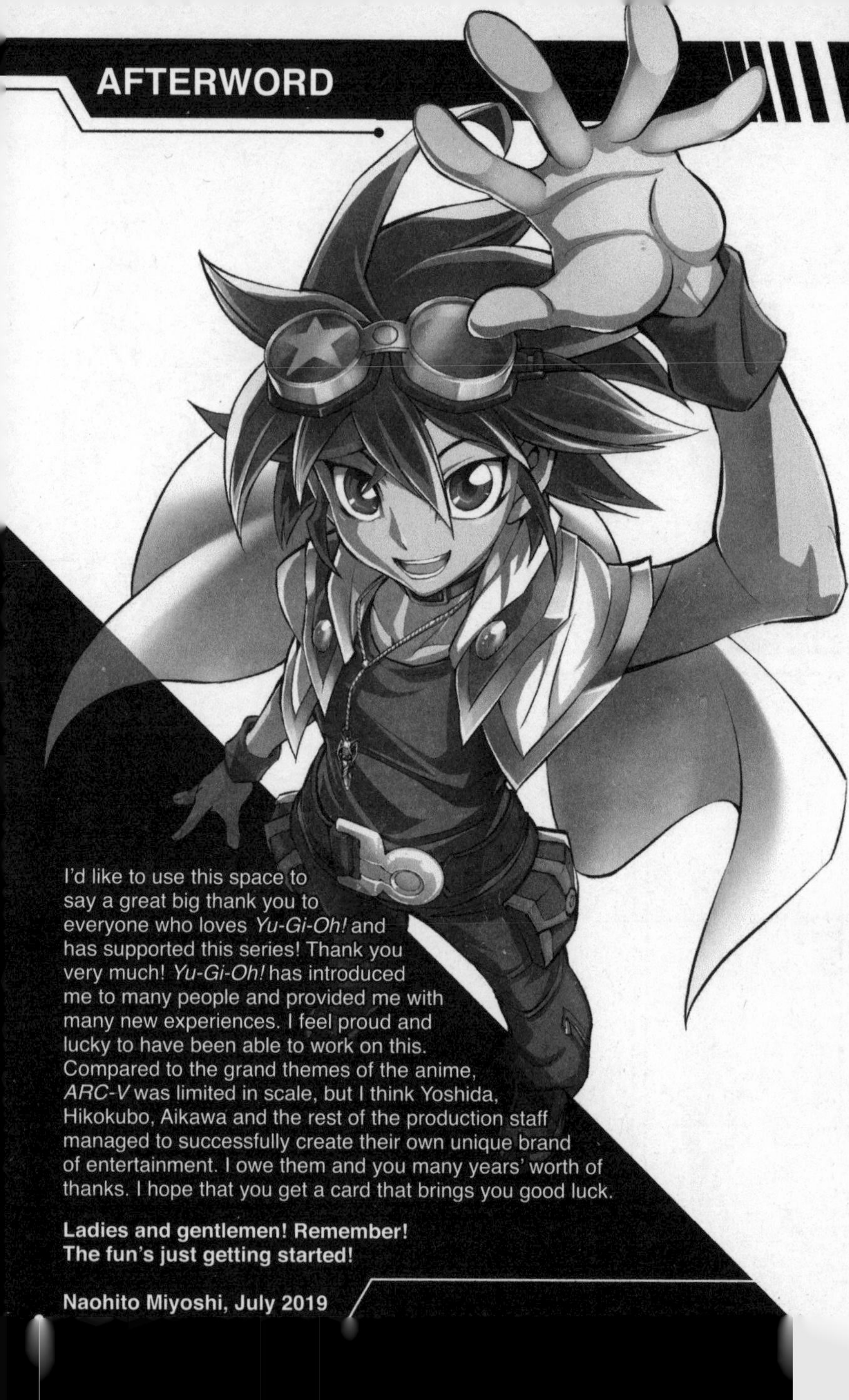

I'd like to use this space to say a great big thank you to everyone who loves *Yu-Gi-Oh!* and has supported this series! Thank you very much! *Yu-Gi-Oh!* has introduced me to many people and provided me with many new experiences. I feel proud and lucky to have been able to work on this. Compared to the grand themes of the anime, *ARC-V* was limited in scale, but I think Yoshida, Hikokubo, Aikawa and the rest of the production staff managed to successfully create their own unique brand of entertainment. I owe them and you many years' worth of thanks. I hope that you get a card that brings you good luck.

Ladies and gentlemen! Remember!
The fun's just getting started!

Naohito Miyoshi, July 2019

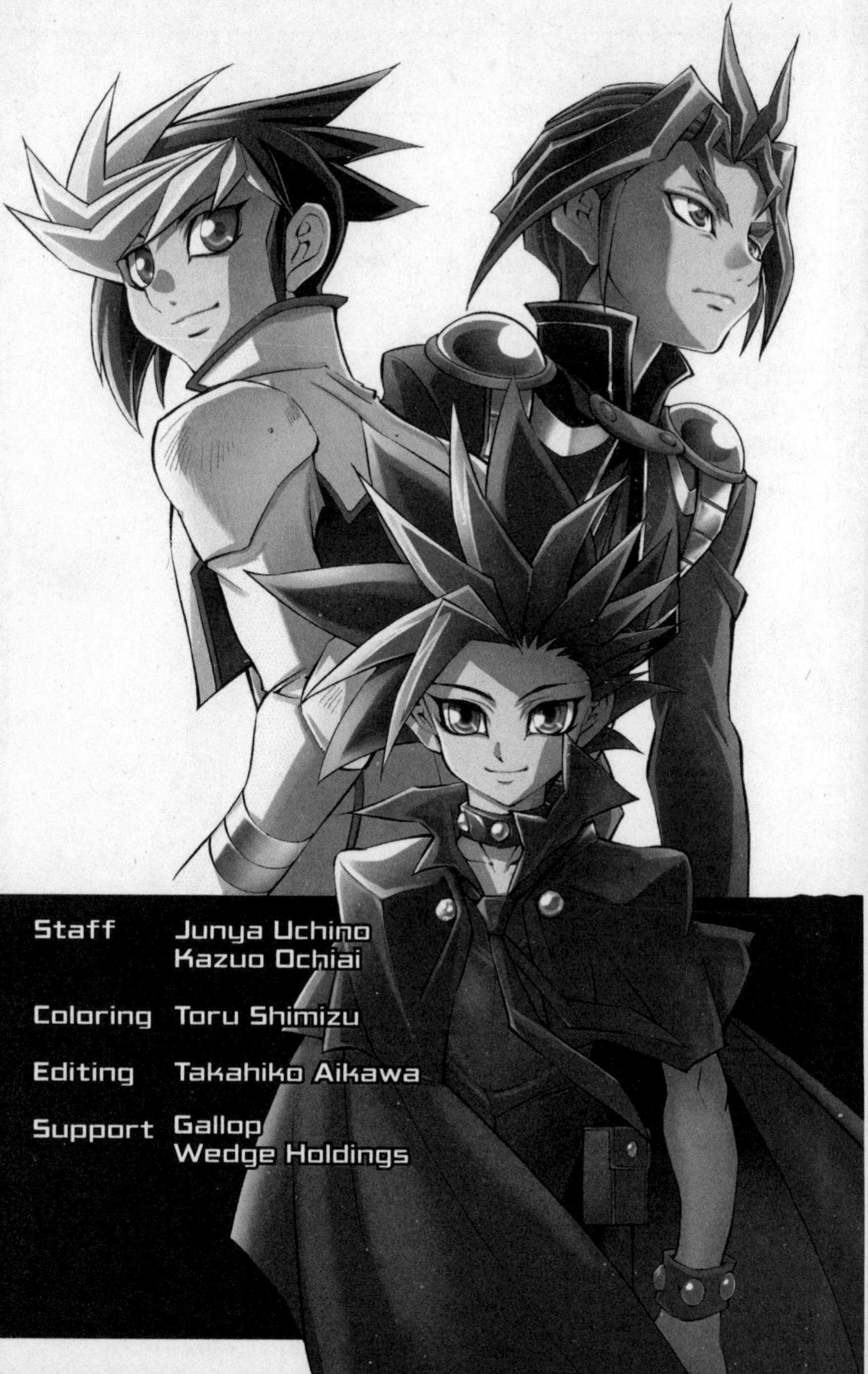

Staff Junya Uchino
Kazuo Ochiai

Coloring Toru Shimizu

Editing Takahiko Aikawa

Support Gallop
Wedge Holdings

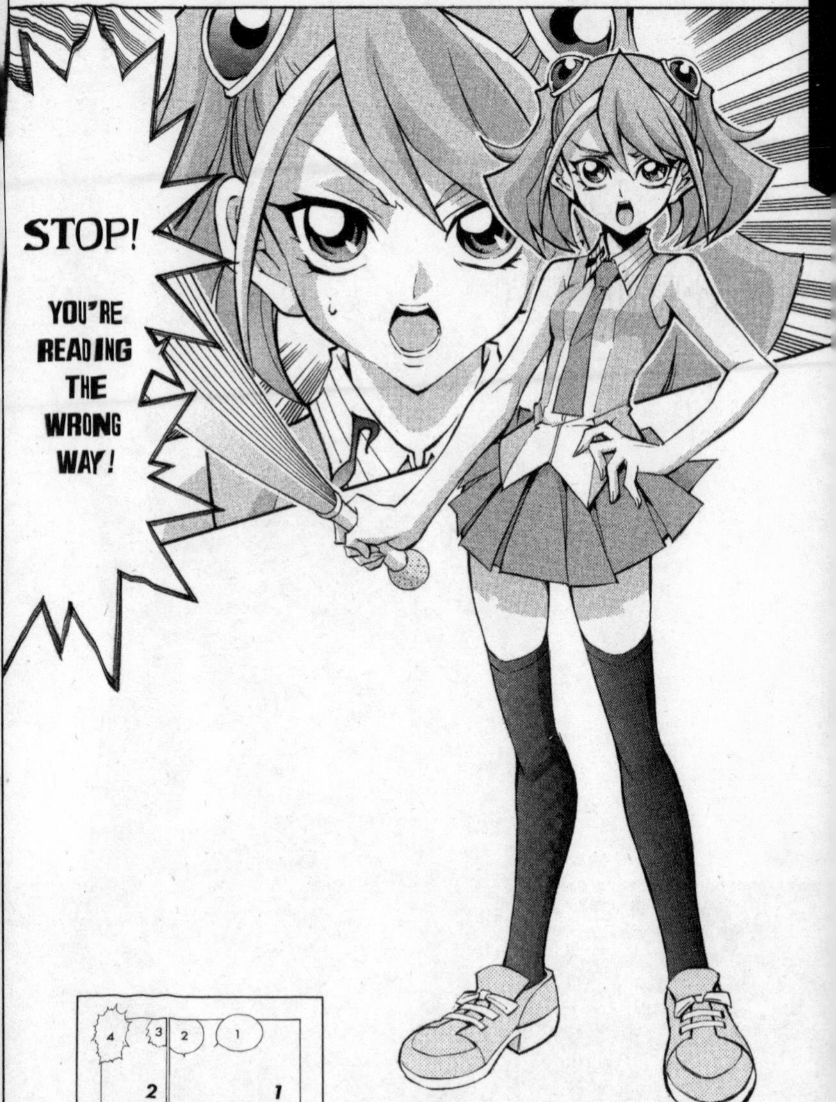
STOP!
YOU'RE READING THE WRONG WAY!

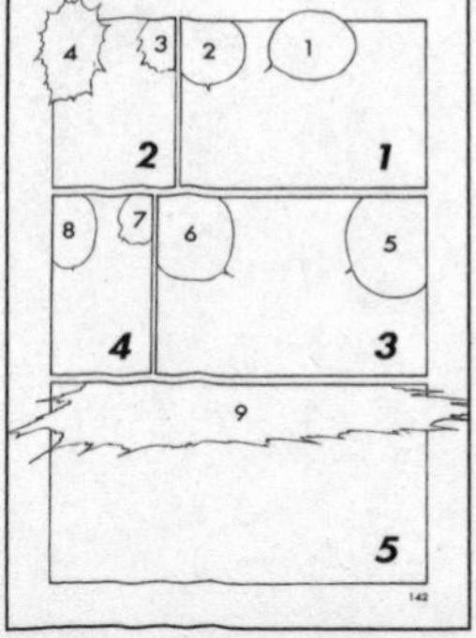

Yu-Gi-Oh! ARC-V

reads from right to left, starting in the upper-right corner. Japanese is read from right to left, meaning that action, sound effects and word-balloon order are completely reversed from English order.